Annette Kehnel

Clonmacnois – the Church and Lands of St. Ciarán

Change and Continuity in an Irish Monastic Foundation
(6th to 16th Century)

Vita regularis

Ordnungen und Deutungen religiosen Lebens im Mittelalter

herausgegeben von

Gert Melville

Band 8

LIT

Annette Kehnel

Clonmacnois – the Church and Lands of St. Ciarán

Change and Continuity in an Irish Monastic Foundation
(6th to 16th Century)

LIT

Die Deutsche Bibliothek – CIP-Einheitsaufnahme

Kehnel, Annette
Clonmacnois – the Church and Lands of St. Ciarán : Change and Continuity in an
Irish Monastic Foundation (6th to 16th Century) / Annette Kehnel . – Münster :
LIT, 1997
   (Vita regularis. Ordnungen und Deutungen religiosen Lebens im Mittelalter ; 8.)
   Zugl.: Dublin, Univ., Diss., 1995
   ISBN 3-8258-3442-5

NE: GT

© LIT VERLAG

   Dieckstr. 73   48145 Münster   Tel. 0251–23 50 91   Fax 0251–23 19 72

Distributed in North America by:

Transaction Publishers
Transaction Publishers   Rutgers – State University   Tel.: (908) 445–2280
New Brunswick, New Jersey U.S.A.   New Brunswick, N.J. 08903   Fax: (908) 445–3138

ACKNOWLEDGEMENTS

The present work was accepted as Ph.D Thesis at Trinity College Dublin in February 1995. TCD made my studies possible by awarding me an International Postgraduate Studentship. The Grace Lawless Lee Fund of Trinity College and the 'Stifterverband für die deutsche Wissenschaft' kindly provided means towards the publication of the thesis. For all this support I am most appreciative. I would also like to express my thanks to Katharine Simms for her patient supervision of the thesis. Greatly indebted I am to my friends and teachers at Trinity and elsewhere, amongst them Brian Blacker, Cormac Ó Cléirigh, Colmán Etchingham, Fiona FitzSimons, Tim Gorringe, Penny Iremonger, Ailbhe Mac Shamhráin, Linzi Simpson and Mario Sughi. I received most encouraging support towards the publication of the thesis from Seán Duffy. Michael Byrne, the president of the Offaly Historical & Archaeological Society, supplied me with helpful adresses. Liam Cox gave most instructive comments concerning the placenames. Gert Melville made the publication possible by kindly accepting the work in his series. I am very much obliged and most grateful to all of them! My husband Ludger Lieb and our children Paul, Klara and Friedrun I do thank for everything, hoping for many happy returns to Ireland.

Dresden, Saint Ciarán's day, the 9th of September 1997

TABLE OF CONTENTS

INTRODUCTION 1

1 SOURCES 4
  1.1 Annals 4
  1.2 Hagiography and saga material 14
    1.2.1 Dating of St. Ciarán's Lives 16
    1.2.2 Saga material 22
  1.3 Late medieval documents 24
    1.3.1 The 'Registry of Clonmacnoise' 24
    1.3.2 Papal Letters 25
    1.3.3 Books of Survey and Distribution 26

2 THE ORGANIZATION OF CLONMACNOIS PRIOR TO THE
CHURCH REFORM 28
  2.1 The organization of the monastic institution 29
    2.1.1 Abbots 29
    2.1.2 Bishops 34
    2.1.3 Vice-abbots 35
    2.1.4 Priests 38
    2.1.5 Scribes and Lectors 39
    2.1.6 Guestmaster (*airchinnech tige Oiged*) 41
    2.1.7 Head of the Little Church (*Airchinnech Eglaisi Bige*) 41
    2.1.8 Head of the Céili Dé and the poor (*cenn bocht*) 43
    2.1.9 The community of the Seniors 44
    2.1.10 Others 45
  2.2 Septs and families represented in offices in Clonmacnois 46
  2.3 Affiliations between Clonmacnois and other churches 51
    2.3.1 Armagh 53
    2.3.2 The Columban community in Scotland and Ireland 55
    2.3.3 Clonard 59
    2.3.4 Glendalough. 61
    2.3.5 Énda from Aran 65
    2.3.6 Senán of Inis Cathaig (Scattery Island) 67
    2.3.7 Íseal Chiaráin 68
    2.3.8 Inis Ainghin, or Hare Island on Lough Ree 71
    2.3.9 Inishmacsaint 72
    2.3.10 Ciarán of Saighir 72
    2.3.11 Birr 75
    2.3.12 Devenish 76

2.3.13 Inishkeen 77

2.3.14 Bangor 79

2.3.15 Roscrea 79

2.3.16 Fore 80

2.3.17 Killare 82

2.3.18 Terryglass 82

2.3.19 Drumlane and Rossinver 84

2.3.20 Lemanaghan (*Liathmancháin*) and Gallen 84

2.3.21 Kilmore (*Cell Mór Mag Enir*) 85

2.3.22 *Tamnuch, Cellola Toch* and *Dumech* 86

2.3.23 Ailech Mór. 87

2.3.24 Some unidentified churches in Mide 87

2.3.25 Kinneigh 88

3 CLONMACNOIS AND ITS NEIGHBOURS 90

3.1 Clonmacnois and its neighbours in Connacht (seventh to ninth centuries) 93

3.2 Clonmacnois and the kings of Tara of the Southern Uí Néill 106

3.3 The eleventh century 119

3.4 The Ua Conchobair kings as patrons of Clonmacnois (twelfth century) 126

3.5 Conclusions: patronage and politics 129

4 CHURCH REFORM AND ANGLO-NORMAN INVASION 133

4.1 Clonmacnois on the eve of the church reform 133

4.1.1 The Meic Cuinn na mBocht 133

4.1.1.1 Íseal Chiaráin - the dynasty's residence 136

4.1.1.2 Internal factions in Clonmacnois - opposition to the Meic Cuinn na mBocht 137

4.1.2 The ecclesiastical aristocracy of Clonmacnois 139

4.2 Clonmacnois and the reformers 145

4.2.1 Ireland and the continent 145

4.2.2 The successors of St. Ciarán in the twelfth century 149

4.2.3 Developments within the ecclesiastical estate 153

4.2.3.1 Reform orders in Clonmacnois? 154

4.2.3.2 The bishopric of Clonmacnois 155

4.2.3.3 Why had the reform so little effect on Clonmacnois? 158

4.3 The Anglo-Norman invasion 162

4.3.1 The immediate effects of the Anglo-Norman invasion 162

4.3.2 Clonmacnois and the restoration of Ua Conchobair power in Connacht 167

4.4 Summary 172

5 CLONMACNOIS IN THE LATER MIDDLE AGES............................. 173

5.1 The Extent of the diocese of Clonmacnois... 173

5.2 The bishopric of Clonmacnois 180
    5.2.1 The thirteenth century 180
    5.2.2 The fourteenth and fifteenth centuries. 185

5.3 The former ecclesiastical aristocracy in the later middle ages........ 194

6 THE 'REGISTRY OF CLONMACNOISE' 202

6.1 The Manuscript... 202

6.2 The content of the Registry 205

6.3 Dating of the document... 206
    6.3.1 The *Red booke* as a forerunner of the Registry 208
    6.3.2 The transmission of the document 209
        6.3.2.1 The early thirteenth-century redaction 210
        6.3.2.2 Rewriting of the Registry in the fourteenth century 211

7 THE LANDS OF ST. CIARÁN ACCORDING TO THE
REGISTRY 220

7.1 The Ua Ceallaigh donations 221

7.2 The grant of *Ceallach mac Finachta* 226

7.3 The Ua Máelsechlainn donations.. 227

7.4 The Ua Conchobair donations... 230

7.5 The Ua Ruairc donations 231

7.6 The Mac Diarmada donations 234

7.7 The Mac Carthaigh donations 236

7.8 The abbatial lands 237

7.9 An attempt to reconstruct the extent of the lands under the authority
    of St. Ciarán 238

8 SUMMARY 243

APPENDIX 1: CATALOGUE OF THE MEMBERS OF THE
COMMUNITY OF CLONMACNOIS, SIXTH TO THIRTEENTH
CENTURIES 246

Appendix 1.1 List of monastic officals 246
    Abbots (A) 246

Bishops (B) 268
Vice-Abbots, *equonimus, secnab, tánaisi* or *prior* (vA) 273
Priests (P) 277
Scribes, Lectors and Wise men (S) 280
Anchorites (An) 285
Head of the Céili Dé, *cenn Chéile Dhé* or *cenn bocht* (C) 287
Seniors and Wise men (Sen) 288
Head of the little church, *airchinnech Eglaisi Bige* (AE) 289
Guestmaster, *airchinnech tige oiged* (G) 290
Others (O) 292

Appendix 1.2: Tribes and families represented in offices in
Clonmacnois. 293
Ulster 293
Leinster 293
Connacht 293
Munster 294
Mide 295

Appendix 1.3: Churches from which ecclesiastical officials in Clon-
macnois came. 295

APPENDIX 2: THE LANDS OF CLONMACNOIS ACCORDING TO
THE REGISTRY. 297
The Ua Ceallaigh donations (nos. 1-40) 297
The Ua Máelsechlainn donations (nos. 41-60) 307
The Ua Conchobair donations (nos. 60-65) 314
The Ua Ruairc donations (nos. 66-72) 316
The Mac Diarmada donations (nos. 73-75) 317
The Mac Carthaigh donations (nos. 76-79) 318
Donations by the Geraldines from Desmond (nos. 80-87) 319
The livings of the abbot of Clonmacnois (nos. 88-93) 319
The livings of Ua Cillín (nos. 94-95) 321

BIBLIOGRAPHY 322
Manuscripts 322
Primary Works 322
Secondary Works 327

MAPS 339

INDEX 348

ABBREVIATIONS

AClon	*The Annals of Clonmacnoise*
AConn	*Annála Connacht: The Annals of Connacht*
ACott	*The Annals in Cotton*
AFM	*Annála rioghachta Éireann: annals of the kingdom of Ireland by the Four Masters*
AI	*The Annals of Inisfallen*
ALCé	*The Annals of Loch Cé*
Anal. Hib.	*Analecta Hibernica*
ant.	*antiquarian*
arch.	*archaeological*
AT	*The Annals of Tigernach*
AU	*The Annals of Ulster and Annála Uladh. The Annals of Ulster*
Cal. Doc. Irel.	*Calendar of documents relating to Ireland*
Cal. Pap. Let.	*Calendar of entries in the papal registers relating to Great Britain and Ireland: papal letters*
Corp. Gen. Hib.	*Corpus Genealogiarum Hiberniae*
CS	*Chronicon Scotorum*
Galway Arch. Hist. Soc. Jn.	*Journal of the Galway Archaeological and Historical Society*
hist.	*historical*
IER	*Irish Ecclesiastical Record*
IHS	*Irish Historical Studies*
Jn.	*Journal*
Jn. Kilk. SE. Irel. Arch. Soc.	*The Journal of the Kilkenny and South-East of Ireland Archaeological Society*
JRSAI	*Journal of the Royal Society of Antiquaries of Ireland*
n.	*note*
NHI	*A new History of Ireland*
PRIA	*Proceedings of the Royal Irish Academy. Section C*
Registry	*The Registry of Clonmacnoise*
Soc.	*Society*
ZCP	*Zeitschrift für celtische Philologie*

INTRODUCTION

Et veniens ad ipsum locum, dixit: 'Hic habitabo; multe enim anime in hoc loco exibunt ad regnum Dei; et in hoc loco mea resurreccio erit.' Deinde beatissimus Kiaranus cum suis habitauit, et cepit magnum monasterium ibi fundare; et multi vndique veniebant ad eum, et parrochia eius per circuitum multum dilatata est; et nomen sancti Kiarani per totam Hiberniam multum celebratur. Et clara ac sancta ciuitas in ipso loco in honore sancti Kiarani creuit, cuius nomen Cluain meic Nois vocatur.[1]

(And coming to the place, he said: 'Here will I live; for many souls shall leave this place to enter the kingdom of God, and this will be the place of my resurrection.' Thereafter the most holy Ciarán together with his disciples lived there and they started to found a great monastery; and many came to him from everywhere, his parish soon extended and the name of Saint Ciarán became famous in the whole of Ireland. A shinning and saintly city grew up in that place in honor of Saint Ciarán, and the name of the city was Clonmacnois.)

When the original of this brief account of the foundation of Clonmacnois was written down, probably sometime during the eighth century A.D., Clonmacnois was in fact a 'great monastery' with a flourishing religious community and it was also, as we are told, a 'shinning city', a large estate with extensive lands and a considerable number of church tenants, an ecclesiastical centre of power. It was a vital place for trading on the island, and of course it was one of the famous, perhaps the most famous center of learning in Ireland at the time, where poets lived and where many important Irish manuscripts were produced.

The nature of history, however, is that things change. Although time by its nature is a continuum, the perception of time functiones on the basis of change. This is how Marc Bloch once put into words the antithesis in which historical research is always caught. The historian works out periods of particular importance, standing out of the continuous series of time down the ages, but only continuance - durability - makes them different. Change and continuity thus appear as arbitrary terms enabling us to talk about the fundamentally human experience that even though the sun rises day after day it never shines upon the same world. They allow us to treat the object of historical investigation as an alleged entity, and to describe it in terms of development.

---

[1] C. PLUMMER (ed.), Vitae Sanctorum Hiberniae, Oxford 1910, vol. 1, p. 211.

In the present study an attempt is made to describe the development of Clonmacnois as an institution of ecclesiastical, religious, cultural and economic life in medieval Ireland and to trace the patterns of change and continuity which determined its story. The book will deal with the different ways in which authority was exercised within the institution, with the families who dominated the city of Ciarán, with the changing political constellations in its surroundings and with its various secular patrons. In the part most central to the book the question will be put how in the course of the twelfth and thirteenth centuries the once majestic city of St. Ciarán was transformed into the bishop's seat of one of the smallest and poorest dioceses in the Irish church, when under the influence of the church reform and the Anglo-Norman invasion structures of political and ecclesiastical organization in Ireland had changed fundamentally. Like most of the early monastic centres of learning in Ireland Clonmacnois lost its leading position within the Irish church. It survived as the see of the bishop of Clonmacnois down to early modern times until it was united with the diocese of Meath in the year 1568.

St. Ciarán's monastery did not survive the crisis of the twelfth century. There was a clear-cut rupture, and none of St. Ciarán's disciples would have recognized the place had he had the chance to revisit his former home, say in the late thirteenth century. However, the modern historian has ways and means stepping back, to look at the story in a long term perspective, as had the Irish historians at work in the fourteenth century. In a document known as the Registry of Clonmacnois they constructed what we might call, a projection of continuity: the function of St. Ciarán's graveyard as a burial ground for the Irish kings was invoked anew; in the name of St. Ciarán property rights were made valid by Irish dignitaries; learned families in Connacht confirmed their rights to certain positions and possessions in resurrecting ancient privileges, dating back to the heydays of Clonmacnois. Fictional continuity produced by a late medieval learned class, based on early medieval traditions, this facinating aspect of the late medieval history of St. Ciarán's lands will be the theme central to the final chapters of this book. The history of the Registry of Clonmacnois and the various stages of its transmission will be discussed, and a suggestion made as to a possible background against which it may have been re-worked in the course of the Gaelic revival. Finally, by taking the document at its word, an attempt will be made to use it as a potential source for the actual extension of the lands and churches once under the authority of St. Ciarán and his successors.

Historical explanations require methods of comparative investigation; the present study will hopefully add to future advances in this direction by supplying a body of material fit for comparison. The book will, it is hoped, have served a useful purpose if it contributes, in some small way, to an understanding of developments in the medieval Irish church as an integral part of European history.[2]

---

[2] No comprehensive work on Clonmacnois has been published. The most detailed work still remains the seventy pages of historical summary by Father John Ryan: J. RYAN, Clonmacnois. A historical summary, Dublin 1973; see also C. DOHERTY, Clonmacnois, in: Lexikon des Mittelalters 4 (1989), pp. 2166-2169; A. GWYNN / R. N. HADCOCK, Medieval religious houses. Ireland. With an Appendix to early sites, London 1970, reprint Dublin 1988, pp. 64f., 165; J. F. KENNEY, The sources for the early history of Ireland, vol. 1: Ecclesiastical, New York 1929, pp. 376-384; K. HUGHES, The distribution of Irish Scriptoria and centres of learning from 730 to 1111, in: K. HUGHES, Church and society in Ireland A.D. 400-1200, ed. D. DUMVILLE, London 1987, chap. XI; F. J. BYRNE, Irish kings and highkings, London 1973, pp. 171, 221f., 240f.; M. HERBERT, Iona, Kells, and Derry. The history and hagiography of the monastic familia of Columba, Oxford 1988, pp. 30, 32, 54, 66. Studies in the field of the history of art can be find in: T. J. WESTROPP, A description of the ancient buildings and crosses at Clonmacnois, King's county, in: JRSAI 37 (1907), pp. 277-306; H. S. CRAWFORD, Athlone excursion. Descriptive particulars of places visited, in: JRSAI 37 (1907), pp. 318-348, esp. 329; R. A. S. MACALISTER, The memorial slabs of Clonmacnois, Dublin 1909; B. MOLLOY, A guide to the ruins of Clonmacnois, Athlone 1957; F. HENRY, Studies in early Christian and medieval Irish art, vol. 3: Architecture and sculpture, London 1985; C. MANNING, Clonmacnoise, Dublin 1994. Historical geographers studied Clonmacnois with a special outlook on its function as an early monastic 'proto-town': C. DOHERTY, The monastic town in early medieval Ireland, in: A. SIMMS / H. B. CLARKE (eds.), The comparative history of urban origins in non-roman Europe, Oxford 1985, vol. 1, pp. 45-75, esp. 63-66. There is also a number of smaller monographic booklets on Clonmacnois: J. CORKERY, Cluan Chiaráin - The city of Ciarán, Longford 1979; D. DOYLE, The story of Clonmacnois, Dublin 1970; W. L. M. GIFF, The story of Clonmacnois, Athlone 1957; W. GAMBLE, Clonmacnois, its history and achievements, Dublin 1950.

1 SOURCES

1.1 Annals

Given the size and importance of Clonmacnois[1] as one of the main churches in Ireland prior to the twelfth century, comparatively little source material has come down to us. No foundation charters, no original church registers, no contemporary history of the church or biographies of its most outstanding abbots are preserved. Until such documents will be discovered we have to rely on the information scattered in the various sources. Some of them, such as the annals have, however, the great advantage of having partly been written in Clonmacnois itself.

The now extant annalistic compilations are generally divided into two main bodies, one represented by the Annals of Ulster, the other by the 'Clonmacnois group of annals' (including AT, CS, AClon, AI, ARoscrea), both named after their presumed places of origin. A comparison between the two reveals great agreement concerning the entries for the early period. It has been suggested that all of them go back to one ancestor text, a hypothetical common source, now lost, named by Professor K. Hughes the 'chronicle of Ireland'.[2] This chronicle was used as a common source down to the early tenth century, more precisely the year 911, when the Clonmacnois group of annals start to diverge considerably from the annals of Ulster,

---

[1] Note on the various spellings of Clonmacnois: Historical spellings including an -e in the end were to be found in a number of seventeenth-century sources, e.g. Clonmcnosse (1655-57), Clonemcnosse (1660, 1683) and also in some sources of the nineteenth-century Ordnance Survey Name Books for county Offaly, like Clonmacnose, Clonmacnoise (1801, 1826). This form was adopted by the Ordnance Survey in the first edition of the Ordnance Survey maps (I am much obliged to Dr Pádraig Ó Dálaigh, Placenames Branch in the Ordnance Survey Office, Phoenix Park, for his kind reply to my inquiries on the matter). For the purpose of the present study I chose the spelling without an -e in the end, the form consistent with the usage generally employed by medieval historians.

[2] K. Hughes, Early Christian Ireland: Introduction to the sources, London 1972, p. 101, also 117-119 for the incorporation of material from the hypothetical 'Iona Chronicle'; D. Dumville / K. Grabowski, Chronicles and annals of mediaeval Ireland and Wales. The Clonmacnoise-group Texts, Woodbridge 1984, pp. 53-56.

and apparently led an independent existence.[3] Using evidence from the Welsh chronicles David Dumville further suggested that a common ancestor text to the Clonmacnois group of annals, a hypothetical 'Clonmacnois chronicle', was written sometime between the year 911 and 954.[4] Unfortunately this original 'Clonmacnois Chronicle' - if it ever existed - like its hypothetical predecessor, was not preserved. It comes down to us in four rather incomplete recensions, all of which underwent later redactions.

First amongst them, and the most original one, are the so-called Annals of Tigernach (AT), misleadingly named after their presumed author Tigernach Ua Braoín.[5] They are fragmentarily preserved in two fourteenth century manuscripts Rawlinson B. 488 and Rawlinson B. 502.[6] Unfortunately entries are missing for over two centuries between the year 767 and 974. They continue recording for the following two hundred years and break off in the middle of an entry for the year 1178.[7] Secondly there is the Chronicon Scotorum (CS), preserved in a seventeenth century transcript only. It was made by Dubhaltach Mac Fhirbhisigh for James Ware, now Trinity College Dublin MS no. 1292 (formerly H. 1. 18). The chronicle ceases recording in the year 1150, with a brief hiatus for the years 1136 to 1139.[8] Then there are the so-called Annals of Clonmacnois (AClon), a seventeenth century trans-

---

[3] DUMVILLE / GRABOWSKI, Chronicles and annals, pp. 53-56; see also G. MAC NIOCAILL, The medieval Irish annals, Dublin 1975, pp. 22-23, 27; HUGHES, Early Christian Ireland, p. 107; J. V. KELLEHER, The Tain and the annals, in: Ériu 22 (1971), pp. 107-127, here 116.

[4] DUMVILLE / GRABOWSKI, Chronicles and annals, pp. 209-226.

[5] The supposed author was Tigernach Ua Braoín, abbot of Clonmacnois in the late eleventh century, who died in 1088 (see Appendix 1, A67). The theory of his authorship has been convincingly refuted by R. A. S. MACALISTER, The sources of the preface of the „Tigernach annals", in: IHS 4 (1944-50), pp. 38-57; P. WALSH, The annals attributed to Tigernach, in: P. WALSH (ed.), Irish men of learning, Dublin 1947, pp. 219-225.

[6] An other imperfect copy is preserved in Trinity College Dublin MS no. 1292 (formerly H. 1. 18), which also contains the Chronicon Scotorum. For the manuscripts of the principal Irish Annals see MAC NIOCAILL, The medieval Irish annals, pp. 40f.

[7] W. STOKES (ed.), The Annals of Tigernach, in: Revue Celtique 16 (1895), pp. 374-419; vol. 17 (1896), pp. 6-33, 119-263, 337-420; vol. 18 (1897), pp. 9-59, 150-197, 267-303, reprinted in 2 vols., Felinfach 1993. AT rarely uses the Christian era. Stokes therefore gave in brackets the corresponding years from the other annals. The dates of AT will therefore be cited in brackets (ibid., vol. 1, p. 79).

[8] W. M. HENNESSY (ed.), Chronicon Scotorum. A chronicle of Irish affairs, from the earliest times to A.D. 1135 (RS), London 1866.

lation of an Irish chronicle into English, made by Conell Mageoghagan. His autograph has not yet been discovered, and only copies of the translation exist, the most complete being that in the British Library, MS Add. 4817.[9] However the *olde Booke* which Mageoghagan translated was in bad repair and often defective, as apparent from his repeated complaints about the many pages missing, stolen or unreadable.[10] His source recorded events down to the year 1407. Finally there is the *Leabhar Cluana mic nóis*, a chronicle apparently now lost, but used as a source by the Four Masters, who state that it went down to the year 1227.[11]

The Annals of Tigernach are, together with the Annals of Ulster, generally regarded as the principal witness to the original Irish chronicle, be it the Iona chronicle or the chronicle of Ireland. The Chronicon has been classified as a faithful, though much abbreviated version of Tigernach's annals, or of the text from which they immediately derived.[12] Mageoghagan's annals for the early period have little material which is not contained elsewhere, and the same seems to apply for the Clonmacnois source used by the Four Masters. Only in the late eighth century do they start recording events not to be found in the other chronicles.[13]

In a sample study of the obituaries of the Clonmacnois clergy in the various sets of annals (compare Appendix 1), we will try to assess the value of the Chronicon Scotorum and the Clonmacnois source used by the Four Masters, as reliable representatives of the Clonmacnois annals. Part of the group of entries common to the Annals of Ulster and the Clonmacnois chronicles were obviously the obituaries of the abbots of Clonmacnois.

---

[9]   S. SANDERLIN, The manuscripts of the Annals of Clonmacnois, in: PRIA 82 (1982), pp. 111-123.

[10]   D. MURPHY (ed.), The Annals of Clonmacnoise being Annals of Ireland from the earliest period to A.D. 1408. Translated into English A.D. 1627 by Conell Mageoghagan, Dublin 1896, reprint Felinfach 1993; ibid., pp. 9, 215 (references to the annals are generally given by the year, to the Annals of Clonmacnois I refer by year and pagenumber).

[11]   J. O'DONOVAN (ed.), Annála rioghachta Éireann: annals of the kingdom of Ireland by the Four Masters, 7 vols., Dublin 1851, vol. 1, pp. Lxiv-Lxv.

[12]   HUGHES, Early Christian Ireland, pp. 106f.; MAC NIOCAILL, The medieval Irish annals, pp. 20, 23.

[13]   DUMVILLE / GRABOWSKI, Chronicles and annals, p. 177 n.76 for singular entries for Clonmacnois in AFM. See also below, p. 11 n.31.

Down to the year 766, when the Annals of Tigernach break off, the death notices in the Clonmacnois chronicles largely agree with those in the Annals of Ulster even in the choice of words and phraseology.[14] Sometimes additional information concerning the family background of the respective abbot is added in the Annals of Tigernach and the Chronicon, which appear to be later insertions, dating at least from the tenth century when the Clonmacnois chronicles were kept independently. Obviously the lacuna in the Annals of Tigernach, over two hundred years from the year 767 to 974, make a comparison for this period difficult. We have to rely on the Four Masters and the Chronicon; the latter, however, has no entries for the years 719 to 803. When it restarts continuous recording in the early ninth century the abbatial obituaries for Clonmacnois are still recorded in more or less the same way as in the Annals of Ulster.[15] Even the change in title, from the traditional

---

[14] Compare below in Appendix 1 (pp. 246-292):
A3:
AU 585.1 *Quies M. Nisse, abb Cluana Moccu Nois, .xuii. anno.*
AT (584) *Quies Maic (nisse) abadh Cluana maic nóis.*
CS 584 *Quies mic Nissi, dUlltoibh do, Ab Cluana muc Nois.*
A6:
AU 628.4 *Pausa Columbani filii Bairddaeni abbatis Clono.*
AT (627) *Pausatio Columbani filii Bardani do Dháil Baird Ulad, abbadh Cluana.*
CS 628 *Pausan Columbani filíí Baddani Abbad Cluana.*
A17:
AU 724.4 *Cuinnles, abbas Cluana M. Noois, obiit.*
AT (723) *Cuíndles abb Cluana maic Nois obit. Di Soghain Condacht dó.*
A23:
AU 762.3 *Quies Cormaicc abbatis Cluana Moccu Nois.*
AT (761) *Quies Cormaic ab Cluana maic Nois, + do Sil Cairpri do.*

[15] Compare below in Appendix 1:
A36:
AU 816.4. *Combustio Cluana M. Nois demedia ex maiore parte. 5. Mors Suibne m. Cuanach, abbatis Cluana M. Nois.*
CS 816 *Loscadh cluana muc Nois. Mors Cathail mic Oililla, Rí H. ffiacrach. Tibraide Ab Cluana ferta brenaind [quieuit]. Suibne mac Cuanach, do Ib briain [S]eola, Ab Cluana muc Nois, quieuit iar tricaid la ar loscad Cluana.*
A37:
AU 823.6 *Ronan, abbas Cluana M. Nois, reliquit principatum suum.*
CS 823 *Ronan, Ab Cluana muc Nois do [f]ágaibh a abdaine.*
A38:
AU 850.1 *Cetadhach abbas Cluana Moccu Nois + Tuathal m. Ferdadhaich abbas Rechrand + Dermaighe ... defuncti sunt.*
CS 850 *Cédadhach Ab Cluana muc Nois, de Ib Cormaic Maen Maighe, et Tuathal mac Feradhaigh, Ab Recrann et Dermaighe, quieuerunt.*

abb or *abbas* to *princeps* happens simultaneously in the later ninth century for abbot Ferdomnach.[16] Only with the tenth century, when the Clonmacnois chronicles began to be kept independently from the Annals of Ulster, do the obituaries differ considerably. The Annals of Ulster soon go over to the use of the title *comarba*, rather than *princeps*,[17] whereas the Chronicon adjusts to this convention only in the mid tenth century.[18] When the Annals of Tigernach restart recording with the year 974, the obituaries of Clonmacnois abbots are no longer included, whereas the Chronicon, down to its end in the mid twelfth century, together with the Clonmacnois source used by the Four Masters, represents the fullest account of the abbatial succession in Clonmacnois.[19]

---

[16] Compare below in Appendix 1:

A41:

AU 872.4 *Ferdomnach, princeps Cluana Moccu Nois, dormiuit.*

CS 872 *Feardomnach .i. do Mughdornaibh, Princeps Cluana muc Nois, quieuit.*

[17] Compare below in Appendix 1:

A50:

AU 931. 1 *Tipraiti m. Annseneb, comarba Ciarain, extenso dolore obiit. [b e2 add. subscript. H.]*

CS 930 *Tipraide mac Ainnsine de aíbh Briuin, Princeps Cluana muc Nois, quieuit.*

A51:

AU 948.3 *Anmere h. Adlai, comarba Ciarain m. int Sair.*

CS 947 *Ainmire .H. Catlain dUí mic Uais Midhe, Princeps Cluana muc Nois, quieuit.*

A52:

AU 952.1 *Ferdomnach comarba Ciarain.*

CS 951 *Ferdomnach .H. Maoinaigh, Abb Cluana muc Nois, quieuit .i. i nGlinn da loca mortuus .i. do Corco Moga.*

[18] Compare below in Appendix 1:

A53:

AU 954.6 *Ceilechair comarba Ciarain + Finnian.*

CS 953 *Celecair mac Robartaig do Ibh mic Uais Midhe, comorba Finnain ocus Ciarain.*

See also D. DUMVILLE, Latin and Irish in the Annals of Ulster, A.D. 431-1050, in: D. WHITELOCK / R. MCKITTERICK / D. DUMVILLE (eds.), Ireland in early medieval Europe. Studies in memory of Kathleen Hughes, Cambridge 1982, pp. 320-341, here 326f. for the changing titulation in AU.

[19] Apart from the abbots mentioned in AU the Chronicon has the following additional names: *Ua Beguláin* (deposed in 1002, CS 1000); *Macraith Ua Flaithéin, comarba Ciaráin ocus Cronáin Tuama gréine* (d.1098, CS 1096); *Cormac mac Cuinn na mbocht, do Mughdhornaibh Maigen, comarba Ciaráin Cluana muc Nois* (d.1103, CS 1099); *Flaithbertach Ua Loingsigh, comarba Ciaráin* (d.1109, CS 1105). Compare below in Appendix 1: A58, A69, A70, A71.

Hand in hand with the beginning of independent recording in Clonmacnois in the tenth century went a revision of the already extant annals. The
many notes concerning the origin of Clonmacnois abbots of the early period, exclusively contained in the Clonmacnois annals, seem to have been
added to the abbatial obituaries in the annals at this time. Obviously this
information must have been preserved in the monastery prior to the tenth
century, perhaps in a kind of necrology, or abbatial succession list, which
was then copied into the annals.

More detailed information on local affairs can be traced in the Clonmacnois chronicles from the tenth century onwards. The scribe sometimes adds
insider information about the political struggles in his ecclesiastical home,
such as for example the replacement of the sitting abbot Dedimus by one
Joseph in the year 901, or the deposition of abbot Ua Beguláin in the year
1002.[20] Or there is, in the Chronicon and in the Clonmacnois source used by
the Four Masters, the detailed account of the synod of Uisnech in the year
1111.[21] This event is unknown to the other annals, but was apparently a
highly important historic event in the eyes of the chronicler in Clonmacnois.

Other information on Clonmacnois affairs, of lesser political importance,
was sometimes also included, as for example a great flooding of Clonmacnois in the year 920, which according to the source used by the Four Masters reached the abbot's house as well as the causeway of the three
crosses.[22] On another occasion we are told by the writer of the Chronicon,
that the Crozier of St. Ciarán (*bachall Chiaráin*) got lost in Lough Gara in
the year 932.[23] The Clonmacnois source used by the Four Masters added
that it was the gold-surfaced staff, which was drowned in the accident
(*bachall Chiaráin .i. an óraineach*) indicating that a particularly well informed scribe was at work here.[24]

In the tenth century, when chronicles were first independently kept in
Clonmacnois, the most powerful secular friends of St. Ciarán's ecclesiasti-

---

[20]　CS 901; CS 1000.

[21]　CS 1107; AFM 1111. The only other annals which record this synod are ACott 1111.

[22]　AFM 918.

[23]　CS 930.

[24]　AFM 930.

cal settlement were the Clann Cholmáin kings of Mide. It seems plausible that their patronage also found reflection in the writing and rewriting of the chronicles. The portrayal of Flann Sinna, the then king of Mide for example, his friendship with Colmán, abbot of Clonmacnois at the time (904-926), their joint building activities, or the death of king Flann's daughters in Clonmacnois, seem to be the direct outcome of contemporary recording, reflecting the political alliances at the time.[25] It seems that in order to document the friendship between Clonmacnois and its Clann Cholmáin patrons the annals were revised to a certain degree in the tenth century. A note concerning the death of the mother of King Flann Sinna, and her interment in Clonmacnois, was inserted in an entry for the year 890.[26] Some additional information about the involvement of the royal dynasty of Mide in the foundation of Clonmacnois would also have found admission in the annals at that time.[27]

The latter half of the eleventh century can be identified as a further period of substantial revision of the annalistic records in Clonmacnois. A considerable number of entries dealing with one particular family in Clonmacnois, the Meic Cuinn na mBocht, are to be found in the Chronicon, in Mageoghagan's annals and in the *Book of Clonmacnois* used by the Four Masters.[28] Most of the entries in question here are obituaries or glosses to the obituaries of the ancestors of the Meic Cuinn na mBocht. In the Chronicon, for example, a death note of Gormán, the ultimate ancestor of the family who died in the year 758 according to the Annals of Tigernach seems to have been copied and added by mistake under the year 615. The entry reads *Gormán do Mughdhornaibh, a quo nati sunt Mic Cuinn.*[29] This kind of commentary concerning the pedigree and the relationship between the various members of the ancestors of the 'sons of Conn', the Meic Cuinn na

---

[25] CS 908; CS 925; AClon 901, p. 144; AClon 921, p. 148; AFM 904; AU 924. For king Flann's daughter CS 922; AClon 919, p. 147.

[26] AFM 886.

[27] Thus the foundation of Clonmacnois in the mid sixth century was associated with the accession of Diarmait mac Cerbaill (the ultimate ancestor of the Clann Cholmáin) to the kingship of Ireland, in the Clonmacnois annals. AT (548), CS 544, AClon 547, p. 81.

[28] DUMVILLE / GRABOWSKI, Chronicles and annals, pp. 176-180, where the respective entries are listed individually.

[29] CS 615.

mBocht, must date at least to the time after their eponymous family member, Conn na mBocht had died, which was in the year 1060. Together with a number of obituaries concerning various sons and grandsons of Conn, who never held an office in Clonmacnois, they testify to the involvement of the family in chronicle keeping at the time.[30] Their impact is traceable in the Chronicon, the Annals of Clonmacnois and the Clonmacnois source used by the Four Masters, but not in the Annals of Tigernach. They also left their traces in the hagiographical productions in Clonmacnois at the time.

To sum up we can make the following statements concerning the Clonmacnois chronicles: the Chronicon Scotorum, from the tenth down to its end in the mid-twelfth century includes a number of seemingly contemporary entries, giving details about internal affairs in Clonmacnois obviously relating insider knowledge. The source used by the Four Masters shows a similarly Clonmacnois-centered view. It apparently also included a large number of obituaries, most of them belonging to persons who held lesser offices in the ecclesiastical establishment, like scribes, seniors or guestmasters. Despite the unfortunate tendency of the Four Masters to adjust the terminology of the original entries according to their own ideas, these obituaries give an insight into the wide range of offices which existed in the medieval settlement of Clonmacnois.[31] In contrast the Annals of Tigernach, for the same

---

[30] See for example AFM 1056; AFM 1072; AClon 1069, p. 180; AFM 1085; AFM 1103; CS 1130.

[31] Obituaries of those who died in Clonmacnois only to be found in AFM:
AFM 763 - *Forgla, sruithe Cluana mic Nóis*, d.768.
AFM 768 - *Gallbran Ua Lingáin, scribhneoir*, d.773.
AFM 789 - *Colgu Ua Duineachda, ferleighind*, d.794.
AFM 814 - *Dubinse, sgribhneóir*, d.819.
AFM 855 - *Máel Oena son of Olbrand, fear leighinn*, d.857.
AFM 863 - *Luchairén, son of Eógan, scribhnid, + angcoire*, d.865.
AFM 865 - *Áedacán son of Finnsnecht, tanaisi abbadh Cluana*, d.867.
AFM 886 - *Flann, ben Máilsechlainn mic Maolruanaidh, mathair Fhloinn Sionna*, d.888.
AFM 893 - *Ecertach, airchinnech eccailsi bicce, athair Aenacáin + Dúnadhaigh*, d.898.
AFM 921 - *Fiachra of Eglais Beag, Fiachra eccailsi bicce*, d.923.
AFM 927 - *Máel Giricc, abb Tighe Sruithe*, d.929.
AFM 927 - *Máel Mucheirge, feirthighis*, d.929.
AFM 948 - *Oengus son of Bran, saccart, + sruith senoir*, d.950.
AFM 948 - *Donngal Ua Máelmídhe, fer leighinn*, d.950.
AFM 977 - *Cathasach, airchindeach Eaccailsi bicce*, d.978.
AFM 979 - Adga son of Dubcenn, *tigherna Teathbha*, (prince of Tethba) d.980.
AFM 986 - *Broen Ua hAedha, airchindech eccailsi bicce*, d.987.

period, show great concentration on the political history of the time, in par-

AFM 988 - *Loingsech son of Máel Pátraic, fearleighinn*, d.989.

AFM 994 - *Odrán Ua hEolais, scribhnidh*, d.995.

AFM 1005 - Dúnchad son of Dúnadach, *ferleighind Cluana mic Nóis*, + *a hangcoire iarsin, cend a riaghla*, + *a sencais*, d.1006

AFM 1011 - *Connmach Ua Tomrair, sacart*, + *toiseach ceiliabhartha*, d.1012.

AFM 1022 - *Catasach Ua Garbáin, ferleighinn*, d.1022.

AFM 1024 - *Dubsláine, prímh anmchara na nGaoidheal*, + *saccart Aird brecain*, d.1024.

AFM 1028 - *Cernach, aistire*, d.1028.

AFM 1031 - *Mac Finn, airchinnech tighe aoidhedh*, d.1031.

AFM 1032 - *Dubinse, liachtaire* (bellringer), d.1032.

AFM 1044 - Ailill son of Bresal, *saccart foir Cluana mic Nóis* (resident priest), d.1044.

AFM 1051 - *Mac Sluagadaig, uasal shagart*, d.1051.

AFM 1056 - *Daighre Ua Dubhatán, anmchara*, d.1056.

AFM 1056 - Máelfindén son of Conn na mBocht, *athair Chormaic, comharba Chiaráin*, d.1056.

AFM 1060 - *Ailill Ua Máelchiaráin, airchinneach Eccailsi bicce*, d.1060.

AFM 1061 - *Máelcoluim Ua Loingsigh, saoi* + *sagart Cluana mic Nóis Ciaráin, ferleighind Cenannsa*, d.1061.

AFM 1063 - *Ua Miadacháin, ferléighinn*, d.1063.

AFM 1063 - *Conaing Ua hEaghra, ferleighinn*, d.1063.

AFM 1073 - *Cormac Ua Máeldúin, aird fherleighinn* + *sruith senóir Ereann*, d.1073.

AFM 1077 - *Máel Martain son of Ua Certa, sruith senóir*, d.1077.

AFM 1081 - *Fothudh Ua hAille, ard anmchara Cluana mic Nóis*, + *Leithi Cuinn*, d.1081.

AFM 1085 - Gilla Chríst son of Conn na mBocht, *maic cleirigh as ferr baoi in Erinn ina reimher ordán* + *oirechus Cluana mic Nóis*, d.1085.

AFM 1089 - Concobar son of Fogartach Ua Máeldúin, *secnab*, d.1089.

AFM 1093 - *Aodh Ua Conghaile, airchinneach Taighe aidhedh*, d.1093.

AFM 1097 - *Máelán Ua Cuinn, airchinneach Eccailsi bicce*, d.1097.

AFM 1101 - *Máel Chiaráin Ua Donnghasa, sruith Shenóir*, d.1101.

AFM 1103 - *Máel Íosa, Mac Cuind na mBocht*, d.1103.

AFM 1105 - *Muirchertach Ua Catharnaigh, sruith tocchaidh do mhuintir Chluana mic Nóis*, d.1105.

AFM 1106 - *Muirchertach Ua Cearnaigh, airdfherleighind na nGaoidheal*, d.1106.

AFM 1106 - *Máelmuire, mac Mic Cuind na mBocht*, d.1106.

AFM 1116 - Congalach son of Gilla Chiaráin, *airchinneach Lis aeidheadh*, d.1116.

AFM 1128 - *Ceinnéittigh Ua Conghaile, airchinneach lis aoidheadh*, d.1128.

AFM 1134 - Máel Chiaráin son of Cormac (Meic Cuinn na mBocht) *uasal shaccart tuir crabhaidh*, + *eccnae uasal chend Cluana mic Nois*, d.1134.

AFM 1166 - *Céilechair Ua Conghaile, airchindeach tíghe aoidheadh*, d.1166.

AFM 1168 - Gallbrat son of Duaric Ua Tadgain, *sagart mor*, d.1168.

AFM 1180 - Máel Muire son of Conn na mBocht, *primhshenóir Erean*, d.1180.

AFM 1181 - *Máel Chiaráin Ua Fidabra, comarba Chiarain*, d.1181.

AFM 1187 - *Muirchertach Ua Máeluidir, espoc Cluana fearta*, + *cluana mic nois*, d.1187.

AFM 1200 - Uareirge son of Máel Mórda son of Uairergi Ua Nechtain, *ceann cele ndé cluana*, d.1200.

AFM 1205 - Tadg son of Cathal Crobderg, d.1205.

ticular that of Connacht, with an undisguised partiality for the Uí Chonchobair kings of Connacht, from the latter half of the eleventh century onwards.[32]

Maybe, instead of postulating a number of hypothetical 'original chronicles' and trying to restore their presumed original text by meticulous and
endless comparison of entries, one might simply accept that more than one
chronicle was kept in Clonmacnois at a time. The church had many affiliated houses, and the writing of history might not have been confined to the
scriptorium in Clonmacnois itself. Certainly books of history were kept in
the libraries of other monastic centres, copies wandered round, and information was exchanged between the various chroniclers at work. The Annals
of Tigernach with their narrow outlook on Connacht history in support of Uí
Chonchobair power might have been kept for some time in Roscommon.[33]
The Chronicon with its concentration on internal affairs in Clonmacnois and
the preferential treatment of political history in Mide,[34] might have been
kept in Clonmacnois itself, or one of the neighbouring centres of learning
such as, for example, Gallen or Íseal Chiaráin. A great proportion of the
'Book of Clonmacnois', as it is known through the Four Masters, apparently
consisted in obituaries of Clonmacnois clergy and we might assume that it
contained a kind of death register, where the names of those who died in
Clonmacnois, both clergy and laymen, were taken down. The Annals of
Mageoghagan finally have little exclusive material for the early period, and
might simply have been a copy of the Annals of Tigernach or their immediate predecessor. It seems possible that Mageoghagan, when translating his
original chronicle, added information from other Clonmacnois sources.
However, the two chronicles, that of Mageoghagan and Tigernach's annals,
share an overt Connacht bias in their political outlook, whereas the kings of

---

[32] J. RYAN, Toirdelbach O Conchubair (1088-1156), King of Connacht, King of Ireland co
fresabra, Dublin 1966, pp. 12-13; DUMVILLE / GRABOWSKI, Chronicles and annals, pp. 171-
176.

[33] MAC NIOCAILL, The medieval Irish annals, p. 28, suggests that the Annals of Tigernach in
the twelfth century were no longer of monastic origin, but written by secular historians, possibly the Uí Máelchonaire.

[34] MAC NIOCAILL, The medieval Irish annals, p. 27.

Mide are at times portrayed in a rather critical light.[35] In any case, the greatest value of Mageoghagan's annals seems to be the fact that they report on the history of Clonmacnois after the arrival of the Anglo-Normans. They are a most valuable source of information for affairs in Clonmacnois once the other original Clonmacnois chronicles had come to an end in the mid- and late twelfth century. Together with material on Clonmacnois supplied by the Four Masters they give witness that chronicles were kept in the monastic *scriptorium*, or somewhere nearby, down to the thirteenth century.

On the basis of the information supplied in the annals, a list of the ecclesiastical officials in Clonmacnois has been made available, and is added below in Appendix 1.

1.2 Hagiography and saga material

No primary text of an early Life of Ciarán of Clonmacnois has come down to us. The surviving Latin versions of the Life of St. Ciarán form part of the three major hagiographical collections relating to Irish saints.[36] The longest and most detailed one is that known as the 'Dublin Collection', sometimes also referred to as Codex Kilkenniensis, which has been edited by Charles Plummer.[37] It is preserved in two manuscripts, one in Archbishop Marsh's Library, Dublin, MS V. 3. 4., the other in the library of Trinity College Dublin MS no. 175 (formerly MS E. 3. 11). Sharpe has classified the collection as a thirteenth-century recension of earlier material on Irish saints. He gives as an approximate date of the redactors' work some time around 1220 and 1230.[38] The recension of St. Ciarán's Life contained here seems to

---

[35] See for example the criticism of king Máel Sechnaill Mór for his lack of support for Brian Bóruma, in the battle of Clontarf. According to Mageoghagan Máel Sechnaill was *content rather to lose the field then win it* (AClon, p. 167).

[36] R. SHARPE, Medieval Irish Saints' Lives. An introduction to Vitae Sanctorum Hiberniae, Oxford 1991; K. MCCONE, An introduction to early Irish Saints' Lives, in: The Maynooth Review. Reiviú Mhá Nuad 11 (1984), pp. 26-59, esp. 39ff.; C. PLUMMER, Miscellanea Hagiographica Hibernica (Subsidia Hagiographica 15), Brussels 1925, p. 239.

[37] SHARPE, Medieval Irish Saints' Lives, pp. 93-119; PLUMMER (ed.), Vitae Sanctorum Hiberniae, I, pp. 200-217.

[38] SHARPE, Medieval Irish Saints' Lives, pp. 347-367.

owe much to the hand of the thirteenth century redactor himself, since many of his most characteristic words and phrases reappear frequently.[39]

The second version is contained in two manuscripts in the Bodleian Library, Oxford (Rawl. B 485 and Rawl. B 505) in the so-called Codex Insulensis, otherwise known as the Oxford Collection.[40] The version of Ciarán's Life contained in this collection has been edited by Macalister in an appendix to his translations of St. Ciarán's Lives.[41] The Oxford Collection seems to be the work of one or several late thirteenth-century redactors, who much abbreviated the Lives, making them suitable for liturgical use. Many of the details, to be found in the Dublin Collection, especially those on geographical and local matters, are omitted by the redactors of the late thirteenth century.[42]

Thirdly, there is a fragment of a Latin Life of Ciarán preserved as part of the Codex Salmanticensis, a fourteenth century collection once preserved in Salamanca, now in the Royal Library at Brussels. This collection commands increasing attention because of its value as a relatively original and unrevised work, preserving many of the early elements of Irish hagiography.[43] The Life of Ciarán contained in the collection is however a mere fragment. The account starts with relatively detailed stories of Ciarán's childhood but ends abruptly after his time as a student under St. Finnian in Clonard.[44]

Finally, there is the Irish version of the Life of Ciarán which is preserved in the Book of Lismore, also known as the Book of Mac Carthaigh Reagh, a

---

[39] Some of his favourite adverbs and phrases, frequently reappearing in the *vita Ciaráni* are *prophetice, honorifice* or *accepta licentia et benedictione*; see SHARPE, Medieval Irish Saints' Lives, pp. 143n, 146n, 152n, 159n.

[40] See SHARPE, Medieval Irish Saints' Lives, pp. 247-273; C. PLUMMER, On two collections of Latin Lives of Irish Saints in the Bodleian Library, Rawl. B 485 and Rawl. B 505, in: ZCP 5 (1905), pp. 429-454, for a discussion of the MSS.

[41] R. A. S. MACALISTER (ed.), The Latin and Irish Lives of St. Ciarán, London 1921, Appendix 1, pp. 172-183; for a translation ibid., pp. 44-58.

[42] SHARPE, Medieval Irish Saints' Lives, p. 363.

[43] SHARPE, Medieval Irish Saints' Lives, pp. 227-246; W. W. HEIST (ed.), Vitae Sanctorum Hiberniae ex Codice olim Salmanticensi nunc Bruxellensi, Brussels 1965, Introduction, pp. xi-xiii.

[44] HEIST (ed.), Vitae Sanctorum, pp. 78-81; for a translation see MACALISTER, Latin and Irish Lives, pp. 59-65.

fifteenth century manuscript in Irish. Together with other saints' Lives from the same manuscript this version has been edited by Whitley Stokes. Another copy of the Irish Life, made by Micheal Ó Cleirigh in the friary of Athlone from the book of 'Aodh Óg Ua Dálacháin of Les Cluaine in Meath', is preserved in the Bibliothéque Royale at Brussels, vol. XI (4190-4200) fol. 149a.[45] Like the Latin Life of Ciarán contained in the Oxford collection the Irish version bears many homiletic characteristics, and seems to have been written and used as a sermon, preached on the saint's day, the ninth of September.[46]

Henceforth we will be talking about the Lismore version or the Irish Life of Ciaran, reference to the different Latin versions of St. Ciarán's Life will be made by the name of the collection in which they are contained, i.e. the Dublin version, the Oxford version, the Salamanca version.[47]

1.2.1 Dating of St. Ciarán's Lives

In their present form the various Latin Lives of Ciarán are the undoubted result of a thirteenth century redaction. As far as their original composition is concerned we know very little. It seems the Dublin and the Oxford versions derive from a common source whereas the Salamanca Life goes back to a different original.[48] However, like for „the great majority of Irish *vitae*, there are no named and datable authors and no early manuscripts which might provide some fixed point by which to date the texts."[49] Kenney assumed that all of the now extant Lives of Ciarán ultimately depend on a text

---

[45] W. STOKES (ed.), Lives of the Irish Saints from the Book of Lismore, Oxford 1890, pp. 117-134; see also PLUMMER, Miscellanea Hagiographica Hibernica, pp. 183f.

[46] STOKES (ed.), Lives of Saints, p. 118, ll. 3948f. MACALISTER, Latin and Irish Lives, p. 68, translates: „The date which the Faithful honour as the feast-day of this noble one is the fifth of the ides of September according to the day of the solar month and this day today according to the day of the week. Accordingly I shall relate a short memoir of the signs and wonders of that devout one, for a delight of soul to the Faithful."

[47] MACALISTER, Latin and Irish Lives, pp. 5-7, names these versions respectively LA, LB, LC. The Irish Life he denotes VG, i.e. Vita Goedelica. See ibid., p. 7 for the MS in Brussels.

[48] SHARPE, Medieval Irish Saints' Lives, pp. 291f.

[49] Ibid., p. 17.

or a collection of texts compiled sometime during the ninth century.[50] More
recently Sharpe has argued that most Latin Lives of Irish saints, preserved in
the thirteenth and fourteenth century manuscripts, might, in an original
form, prove to be datable to as early as the seventh or eighth centuries.
These were the heyday of Latin learning in Ireland, whereas Irish predominated from the ninth to the twelfth centuries as a literary medium. Sharpe
pointed out that „the dominance of the Irish language in this period makes it
seem unlikely that any Latin *vitae* were composed in Ireland at the least
between 850 and 1050, and perhaps over a longer period."[51] It is thus more
than likely that a Latin version of a biography of one of Irelands most famous saints at the time, should have been written sometime in the seventh
or eighth century at the latest. There is of course little chance to verify this
assumption on linguistic grounds, since the thirteenth century redactors
worked much towards a levelling of the text. But there is the possibility to
compare, as regards contextual and internal evidence, the Latin *vitae* of
Ciarán with those hagiographical sources which are securely datable to the
seventh or eighth centuries. Adomnán for example, writing some time between 688 and 704 mentions the visit of St. Colum Cille to Clonmacnois
during the abbacy of Ailither (585-599).[52] The Dublin version of Ciarán's
vita makes allusion to the same event, comparing the great party which was
given for the monks from Iona on the occasion with a feast, which took
place during Ciarán's life-time, where all the monks and the whole community of Clonmacnois was miraculously supplied with wine.[53] The story is
told in order to compare the splendid old days with the less splendid, and
more recent past. The party for the Iona monks is described without any
didactic overtone, as a very joyful occasion, on which a senior monk in
Clonmacnois talked about St. Ciarán's party as one of the most impressive

[50] KENNEY, The sources, pp. 376-384.

[51] SHARPE, Medieval Irish Saints' Lives, p. 22, see also pp. 15, 19-26, 320-324.

[52] A. O. ANDERSON / M. O. ANDERSON (eds.), Adomnán's Life of Columba, Oxford 1991, p. 24, §14a.; see ibid., p. xLii-xLiii for the dating; compare also Herbert, Iona Kells and Derry, p. 47-52.

[53] PLUMMER (ed.), Vitae Sanctorum Hiberniae, I, p. 214.

experiences in his youth.[54] The internal narrative structure of the text suggests that the visit of the monks from Iona, in the late sixth century, was not too far removed from living memory at the time when the episode was written down, maybe sometime in the mid-seventh century.

An original Irish Life would correspondingly need to be dated sometime between the ninth and eleventh century, when the vernacular predominated as the literary medium. Kim McCone pointed to the fact that the language of the Lismore version of Ciarán's Life preserved a substantial number of ancient forms, also supporting a date of composition in the Middle Irish period.[55] Internal evidence, and a reading of the saints'Life in the context of the political constellations in the surroundings of Clonmacnois possibly allows to narrow down its date of composition to the first half of the tenth century. As a whole, the Irish Life of Ciarán shows a greater fullness than the Latin *vitae* and contains a considerable amount of unique material.[56] Thus for example great emphasis is put on the fact that king Diarmait mac Cerbaill was personally involved in the foundation of Clonmacnois, and even appears as the co-founder of the church which Ciarán built there. On the occasion Ciarán promised to help him to the highkingship in Ireland.[57] King Diarmait was of course the ultimate ancestor of the Clann Cholmáin kings of Mide and we know from the annals, that in the early tenth century Flann Sinna, one of his descendants and successors to the kingship, was actively involved in the building of the main church in Clonmacnois. Also during Flann Sinna's reign the most famous 'cross of the scriptures' was erected and carved in Clonmacnois, which in analogy to the Irish Life of Ciarán shows king Diaramait together with the saint, jointly planting the foundation post of a church building. These analogies of course are no proof, but they do support the assumption, that an Irish Life of Ciarán was

---

[54] Ibid., p. 214: *Et cum illi venissent ad cenobium sancti Kiarani, suscepti sunt in magna hilaritate et diligentia; et illa cena refecti sunt largissime, et fama ipsius refectionis per totam ciuitatem et eius circuitum late diuulgabatur.*

[55] McCONE, An introduction, pp. 38f.; SHARPE, Medieval Irish Saints' Lives, pp. 21-24.

[56] MACALISTER, Latin and Irish Lives, pp. 11-14 for a synopsis of the stories contained in the respective Lives.

[57] STOKES (ed.), Lives of the Saints, p. 130.

composed in Clonmacnois sometime during the reign of Flann Sinna.[58] Also during his reign, Clonmacnois and Clonard were under the rule of one abbot, a fact which found expression in the Irish Life, where the friendship between Finnian and Ciarán is strongly emphasised.[59] In fact the Clonmacnois hagiographers put an almost suspicious stress on the equality of the two founder saints, which could be interpreted as the outcome of a kind of inferiority complex on their side, since the abbot of Clonard in effect annexed Clonmacnois, when he took over that church as well in the year 904.[60] Finally the Irish Life of Ciarán gives a very kind and friendly portrayal of St. Colum Cille from Iona, who was also the founder of Durrow. The hagiographer even points to him as the only saint who was never jealous of Ciarán. We know of course from other sources, that there were periods of outspoken hostility between the Columban community in Durrow and St. Ciarán's men in Clonmacnois. Only since the end of the ninth century, apparently under the impact of the consolidating church policy of the Clann Colmáin kings of Mide the relation between the two churches normalized. Friendship between their two founders would certainly not have been that much stressed in a composition prior to that date.[61]

So far we have outlined a number of arguments supporting the assumption, that a saints'Life of Ciarán, written in the Irish language was composed in the early tenth century, probably during the reign of Flann Sinna. Episodes from the already existing Latin biographies of Ciarán were certainly translated and included.

There is further evidence which points to a substantial redaction of the Irish Life of Ciarán some time around the turn of the eleventh and twelfth centuries. The composition in the form in which it came down to us, contains a singular episode according to which, shortly before his death, St. Ciarán prophesies great persecution for his community in Clonmacnois: *Adubart robudh mhor ingreim a cathrach o drochdhainib fri deredh ndo-*

---

[58] For the reign of Flann Sinna, and the discussion around the dating of the 'cross of the scriptures', see below, pp. 106-115.

[59] STOKES (ed.), Lives of Saints, pp. 122-127.

[60] See below, pp. 110f.

[61] STOKES (ed.), Lives of Saints, pp. 126f. For the relation between Durrow and Clonmacnois see below, pp. 56-58.

main.[62] The wording here is surprisingly similar to that used in an entry in the Chronicon Scotorum which records a raid on the monastic settlement in the year 1095: *Ingrem mor o droch dainibh for Clúain in hoc anno.*[63] The two phrases are indeed composed analogous to each other and use almost identical wording. They seem to stem from the same time and were perhaps even written by the same scribe. We do know that the writing of the annals in Clonmacnois in the late elventh century was dominated by members of the Meic Cuinn na mBocht family, who were also renowned for their learning and had a clearly attested influence on the literary productions in Clonmacnois.[64] It might therefore well be that the two passages were both written by a Meic Cuinn na mBocht scribe, who kept the annals of the time, but who also revised the then existing Irish Life of the founder saint. The continuation of the above passage from the saints' Life, about the great persecution in Clonmacnois could support this assumption. What follows is a fictional dialogue between Ciarán and his disciples, who ask the saint whether in the time of those evils it would be better to leave Clonmacnois and Ciarán's relics or to stay with them. Ciarán is made to say that it would be better to set off for a more peaceful place, and to leave behind his relics, which after all are nothing but dry bones.[65] In this context it is interesting to note that precisely the Meic Cuinn na mBocht family had left Clonmacnois and settled in the nearby church of Íseal Chiaráin, after the head of the family had bought this place in the year 1093.[66] The passage in the saints' Life supplies a reasonable justification for the family's emigration from Clonmacnois to Íseal Chiaráin, in pointing out that the founder saint himself had advised his disciples to do so.

---

[62] STOKES (ed.), Lives of Saints, p. 132.

[63] CS 1091 (recte 1095). Macalister earlier pointed to this congruence, but seems to use it as proof for a common belief in Ireland that the end of the world would come in the year 1096 (MACALISTER, Latin and Irish Lives, p. 5n).

[64] DUMVILLE / GRABOWSKI, Chronicles and annals, pp. 176-180; R. I. BEST / O. BERGIN (eds.), Lebor na hUidre, Dublin 1929, reprint 1992, Introduction, p. xiv; R. I. Best, Notes on the script of Lebor na Huidre, in: Ériu 6 (1912), pp. 161ff.

[65] STOKES (ed.), Lives of Saints, p. 132. This episode was probably translated into Latin by the redactor of the Dublin version (PLUMMER [ed.], Vitae Sanctorum Hiberniae, I, p. 215).

[66] See below, pp. 136-139.

What seems to be the literary outcome of the rival party to the Meic Cuinn na mBocht comes down to us in another hagiographical anecdote, also contained in the Lismore version of Ciarán's Life. In the context of a few descriptive anecdotes about St. Ciarán's time as a guestmaster in Íseal Chiaráin, we find a rather hostile remark in which the monks of Íseal are said to have evicted Ciarán from their house, because they could not bear his generosity to the poor.[67] Obviously such a statement implies the reproach of greed and could be read as a satirical comment on the Meic Cuinn na mBocht in Íseal Chiaráin who in the late eleventh century had occupied that place and who in fact were those in charge of the poor in Clonmacnois. Perhaps an anti-Meic Cuinn na mBocht bias could also be traced in the Annals of Tigernach, where Cormac, the first abbot of Clonmacnois supplied by the family is only acknowledged as *tániste abadh Cluana maic Nois*, whereas the Chronicon lists him as *comarba Chiaráin*.[68] In any case rival accounts dating from the late eleventh and early twelfth century found entrance in the Irish Life of St. Ciarán as it was preserved in the Lismore version. Different copies of an Irish Life, originally composed in the early tenth century, may have been circulating, they were later revised independently by different scribes belonging to different factions, one maybe seated in Clonmacnois, the other at home in Íseal Chiaráin.

To sum up: an original Irish version of St. Ciarán's Life might have been written in the early tenth century, and contains material which points to a substantial redaction in the late eleventh or early twelfth century. The now extant Latin *vitae* of Ciarán may date back to an original composed as early as the seventh century. In their present form all versions are the products of a thirteenth century revision. The most complete account is preserved in the Dublin version, which apparently goes back to the same original as the Oxford version. However its thirteenth century redactor apparently had an original copy of the Salamanca version, as well as a copy of the Irish Life of Ciarán at hand and thus supplied a kind of thirteenth century summary or survey of the then extant hagiographical writings about St. Ciarán.[69]

---

[67] STOKES (ed.), Lives of Saints, p. 129; PLUMMER (ed.), Vitae Sanctorum Hiberniae, I, pp. 209f.

[68] AT (1103); CS 1099; see also DUMVILLE / GRABOWSKI, Chronicles and annals, p. 179.

[69] SHARPE, Medieval Irish Saints' Lives, p. 391.

1.2.2 Saga material

Finally there is a large body of saga material, tales relating to St. Ciarán or his church, which often supply literary explanations for the respective political situations at the time of their composition. Some of these tales entered the annals but the majority are preserved amongst late medieval collections of religious and mythological tales.[70]

There are a great many stories about St. Ciarán which concern King Diarmait mac Cerbaill or his descendants, pointing to a date of composition when the Clann Cholmáin kings of Mide were closely associated with Clonmacnois. Mageoghagan's annals in particular contain several of these tales. It is of course possible that Mageoghagan, when he made his translation, had additional sources at hand, from which he copied these stories. One example is the anecdote about St. Ciarán's bell, which, so we are told, was the only adequate remedy for King Diarmait mac Cerbaill, when he suffered from deafness after having heard the news of St. Ciarán's death.[71] There is a similar tale, even more directly related to the reign of King Flann, about the apparition of the spirit of Flann's father to a bishop in Clonmacnois, who successfully laboured for the *post mortem* redemption of the dead king's soul. Details of the story are to be found in late medieval sources only.[72] It is, however, also mentioned in a gloss to the obituary of the bishop in the Chronicon.[73]

Often these tales have a strongly didactic overtone, and appear to be long-winded explanations of the fact that particular lands under particular circumstances came into the possession of Clonmacnois. An example here is the detailed account of the battle of Carn Conaill, to be found in all four versions of the Clonmacnois annals.[74] There the story is told how Diarmait, son of Áed Sláine, the ancestor of the Síl nÁedo Sláine, won the battle

---

[70] PLUMMER, Miscellanea Hagiographica Hibernica, pp. 206-208.

[71] AClon 547, pp. 82f.

[72] For the tradtition of the tale see below, p. 112 n.81.

[73] CS 904. Of course there is the possibility that Mac Fhirbhisigh, the transcriber of the Chronicon, who must have known the tale, added the gloss.

[74] AT 641 (recte 649); CS 646; AClon 642, p. 103f.; AFM 645; compare AU 649.2.

against his rival Guaire from Connacht, with the support and prayers of the community in Clonmacnois. In return and as a thanksgiving he made a large grant of lands to Clonmacnois. This story has the advantage of being quite clearly datable to the mid-tenth century, since that was the only period when the Síl nÁedo Sláine supplied a king of Tara.[75] The tale reads like a history lesson, especially designed for this king, admonishing him to remember that his dynasty owed much to the community in Clonmacnois.[76] A similarly didactic overtone is found in a tale linking Cairpre Crum, the ultimate ancestor of the kings of Uí Maine with the founder saint of Clonmacnois. We are told that Cairpre was once resuscitated from the dead by Ciarán himself, and in return granted a large amount of land to Clonmacnois.[77] What looks like a drastically abbreviated version of the same story, appears again in the Clonmacnois chronicles, this time applied to an early ninth century king of Uí Maine, but again promoting the same message, namely that a grand king made a grand donation to Clonmacnois.[78]

Of course there is always the question about the actual historical value of literary texts and about the proper way of reading the above introduced hagiographical works and mythological tales as historical sources. In the exposition of his examplary study of Clones Kim McCone outlined the problem, stating that „saints' Lives, like other branches of early Irish tradition such as sagas and genealogies, are first and foremost documents of their own time of composition, contemporary social and political propaganda that makes use of traditional materials in a kind of code. In the case of any given Life we are confronted with the end of a usually long process of adapting inherited traditions, sometimes drastically, to contemporary needs, and of more or less free invention of new traditions, so to speak, where occasion demanded."[79] The historian therefore is left with the task of decoding the text, to look for the contemporary aims of the composition, to decipher its message and to cleanse its alleged implications by comparision with other

---

[75] Congalach mac Máel Mithig, died as king of Tara in 956 (AU 956.3).

[76] Compare HERBERT, Iona, Kells, and Derry, p. 161f.

[77] For the tradition of the tale see below, p. 104 n.50.

[78] CS 823; AFM 834 (recte 835), see below, pp. 96-101.

[79] K. MCCONE, Clones and her neighbours in the early period: hints from some Airgialla Saints' Lives, in: Clogher Record 11 (1984), pp. 305-325, here p. 306.

sources. This has nothing to do with separating fiction from fact, not all all, but it is much more a question of coordination, the historian is asked to associate the various strata of these texts - regardless of their being fictional or historical - with the respective times of composition and with the political constellations they comment upon, and thus decipher the message they transport. For the purpose of the present study the texts will be read primarily as pieces of evidence for property claims brought forward in the name of St. Ciarán by those writing history, hagiography or saga tales in Clonmacnois.

1.3 Late medieval documents

1.3.1 The 'Registry of Clonmacnoise'

In a document dating from the early modern period, known as the 'Registry of Clonmacnoise', a detailed list of Clonmacnois' claims to lands and property came down to us.[80] The history of transmission of the document, which now exists in an early seventeenth century translation into English only, will be discussed below in chapter six, where I suggest that it ultimately depended on a pre-reform account of the lands and churches held, or at least claimed, by Clonmacnois. The land claims propagated in the medieval saints' Lives and saga tales can possibly provide a basis of comparision to test the reliability of the Registry. The seventeenth century document, probably for reasons of its transmission in the later middle ages, mainly concentrates on Connacht. Most of the lands and churches listed there can be identified with the aid of early modern administrative documents, such as the Books of Survey and Distribution. The history of individual parishes can often be traced on the basis of information contained in the Papal Letters, or epsicopal visitation reports and rental lists.[81] This existing source material

---

[80] J. O'DONOVAN (ed.), The Registry of Clonmacnoise. With notes and introductory remarks, in: Jn. Kilk. SE. Irel. Arch. Soc. 1 (1856/57), pp. 444-460 (in the following abreviated: Registry).

[81] K. W. NICHOLLS (ed.), The episcopal rentals of Clonfert and Kilmacduagh, in: Anal. Hib. 26 (1970), pp. 130-143; K. W. NICHOLLS (ed.), Visitations of the dioceses of Clonfert, Tuam and Kilmacduagh, c. 1565-67, in: Anal. Hib. 26 (1970), pp. 144-157; P. K. EGAN (ed.), The

seems to provide a basis for a policy of reconstructing the extent of the lands of Clonmacnois, by carefully reading the Registry alongside the early history of Clonmacnois, the geographical background of leading functionaries in the church, early hagiographical works, the medieval sagas and early modern administrative sources. In some cases place name studies and local traditions collected and preserved by nineteenth century antiquarians can provide additional help in tracing the places once associated with St. Ciarán and his church.[82] This strategy will be tested in chapter seven of the thesis, where I attempt to give a preliminary account of the lands associated with Clonmacnois. For reasons of perspicuity a list of the places named in the Registry, including references to them in sources and literature, will be added separately in Appendix 2.

1.3.2 Papal Letters

Papal letters, the outcome of papal administration in Ireland, have the great advantage of dealing with problems otherwise scarcely documented for the middle ages. Many of the cases concern the appointment of the ordinary parish clergy, who were often dominated by the local leading family. They therefore give insight into politics on a local level. Obviously complaints were brought before the pope when several candidates were competing for one and the same position. One way to fight a rival was to doubt his canonical right to the position, accuse him of fornication or defect of birth, and depose him on the authority of the pope.

Here, of course, the great disadvantage of the papal letters as a source for local politics is apparent. They are a very one-sided and fragmentary source. First of all the actual issues are known to us only through the letters of reply, sent from the *Curia* back to Ireland, copies of which were preserved in the Vatican archives. Although these letters often contain a detailed summary of the case in question, these are obviously very biased presentations of the actual situation. The counter-presentations from the rival position are occasionally preserved, when the other party also went to court in Rome. In

---

royal visitation of Clonfert and Kilmacduagh 1615, in: Galway Arch. Hist. Soc. Jn. 35 (1976), pp. 67-76.

[82] See for example the Ordnance Survey Letters, by John O'DONOVAN et al. (Dublin 1839, reproduced in typescript, Bray 1933, now in the Royal Irish Academy Dublin).

most cases, however, their position has to be reconstructed or remains unknown. Finally the editors of the papal letters relating to Ireland, especially
those of the early volumes, presented the student of history with a kind of a
'selected choice'. The material preserved in the Vatican archives is vast and
must wait for generations to come to explore its riches.

Nevertheless, bits and pieces of information are better than none at all,
and when taken together with the archiepiscopal records of Ireland and the
Irish annals, the papal letters present valuable details and allow insight into
the political landscape of Ireland on a very local level. They become even
more important with the beginning of the Gaelic revival in the course of the
fourteenth century, when large parts of Ireland, the Gaelic areas, were no
longer subject to Anglo-Norman administration.

1.3.3 Books of Survey and Distribution

The Books of Survey and Distribution, formerly in official use in the Quit
rent Office, are now lodged in the National Archives, in Dublin.[83] The series
consists of twenty folio volumes and includes all of the counties of Ireland.
They are the outcome of the Down survey (1654) and the Civil Survey (ca.
1652). The volumes for Galway, Mayo and Roscommon, most frequently
used in the present study, refer back to the Strafford Survey (ca. 1636). They
contain information about land ownership in 1641, the transfer of property
in that year and refer furthermore to the forfeitures in 1688 and the sales
thereof in 1701.[84] These administrative workbooks of the seventeenth century present us with detailed descriptions of landholding in Ireland, ultimately reporting on the state of affairs in the year 1641. They supply an
immense wealth of detailed information about the distribution of land in
post-Norman Ireland. While a number of plantations had taken place in the
sixteenth and early seventeenth centuries, continuity and development of
landholding can be demonstrated. This is especially true in the case of
churchlands, which can sometimes be traced from the early middle ages

---

[83] The following volumes are published: R. SIMINGTON (ed.), Books of Survey and Distribution, vol. I: Roscommon, Dublin 1949; vol. II: Mayo, Dublin 1956; vol. III: Galway, Dublin 1962; vol. IV: Clare, Dublin 1967; J. C. LYONS (ed.), Book of Survey and Distribution of
co. Westmeath, Ladiston 1852.

[84] SIMINGTON (ed.), Books of Survey, I, Introduction, pp. v-ix.

(according to early saints' Lives), through the Anglo-Norman invasion (in Anglo-Norman land grants and administrative documents), and the later middle ages (in papal letters) down to the early modern period (according to surveys of the seventeenth century).

2 THE ORGANIZATION OF CLONMACNOIS PRIOR TO THE
CHURCH REFORM

Saint Ciarán became famous as the founder of a monastery, as the first abbot of a community of monks who lived together under the same religious
rule. The purely monastic character of the Irish churches is however open to
question. In fact the Latin biographers of Ciarán, who may have been writing as early as the seventh or eighth century, use a very non-monastic terminology. Once it comes to the laying of the foundation stone of Clonmacnois
they simply talk of the first house (*domus*), which Ciarán founded in his city
of Clonmacnois (*in sua ciuitate Cluain meic Nois*).[1] It is also a well known
fact that by the time of the eighth century a large number of lay-people,
monastic clients, employed in work on the ecclesiastical estate, had come to
live nearby the Irish monasteries. Extensive lands were under the authority
of those who ruled the estate, and the originally monastic settlements were
gradually turned into urban-style communities, often referred to as monastic
cities, assuming the function of centres of trade and traffic.[2] Thus we are
talking about settlements and communities, which simply happen to be monastic in origin. However in the organization as well as in the political life
of these settlements monastic features persisted. The Latin titles for various
officials in the monastic hierarchy was preserved. In the settlements' foreign
policy, the founder saint played a most prominent part as the patron and
guardian of his community or *familia*. The true nature of the Irish churches
seems to lie somewhere between those poles. They were secular establish-
ments, where lay-people lived, worked and died, ruled over by great landowners, who played a decisive role in secular politics. At the same time the
spiritual dimension played an important part in the exercise of authority
over the people and lands belonging to the church. The monastic tradition
was cherished by those in power, in order to preserve one of their most essential means of legitimation. We might therefore talk of Clonmacnois as an
ecclesiastical settlement of monastic origin, which preserved essentially
monastic features in its structures of organization, in the titulation applied to

---

[1] PLUMMER (ed.), Vitae Sanctorum Hiberniae, I, p. 212, §28f.

[2] K. HUGHES, The church in early Irish society, London 1966, pp. 139-142; DOHERTY, The
monastic town, pp. 45-76.

those in leadership of the establishment and in particular in its selfunder-standing.

In the following the organization of Clonmacnois as an ecclesiastical institution will be discussed: the various offices and their function within the system, the leading families and - in the last part of this chapter - the ecclesiastical alliances, which existed between Clonmacnois and other churches.

2.1 The organization of the monastic institution

2.1.1 Abbots

Monasticism, as the most characteristic feature of the Irish church, has for a long time been an un-questioned paradigm.[3] The prominent role assigned to the abbot in the most accessible sources for the early Irish history led to the assumption that he was the actual head of the church, whereas the bishop was but a sort of employee, responsible for spiritual matters, in his service. Richard Sharpe was the first to suggest very convincingly that despite the seemingly monastic organization episcopal authority was of much greater importance in Ireland than generally imagined.[4] Moreover he pointed out that the conventional interpretation of the *paruchia*, as a non-territorial monastic federation, resulted from a premature generalization of the example of the Columban houses in Ireland and Scotland, as being typical of the whole of the Irish church. The Iona-type of monastic confederation was often confused with the *paruchia*, denoting the territorial sphere of jurisdictional authority of the head of a mother church over its dependencies.[5] It

---

[3] See for example J. RYAN, Irish monasticism. Origins and early development, London/New York 1931, pp. 167-190; HUGHES, The church in early Irish society, pp. 81-90; R. SHARPE, Some problems concerning the organization of the church in early medieval Ireland, in: Peritia 3 (1984), pp. 230-270, here 230-247 for a summary of the most current views on church organization in Ireland.

[4] SHARPE, Some problems; see also the more recent work of C. ETCHINGHAM, Aspects of early Irish ecclesiastical organization, 2 vols., Ph.D Thesis, Trinity College Dublin 1992.

[5] SHARPE, Some problems, pp. 243-247; C. ETCHINGHAM, The implications of paruchia, in: Ériu 44 (1993), pp. 139-162.

seems that the jurisdictional authority in a *paruchia* was essentially exercised by the bishop, even though historians long failed to appreciate his
position. The other most important person in ecclesiastical government,
variously entitled *abbas, princeps, airchinnech* or *comarba*, was basically
the lay ruler of the monastic estate, with the principal role of administrating
the temporalities of the church, as is apparent from the early eighth century
Irish canon law.[6] The over-emphasis on the monastic character of the Irish
church resulted, at least partly, from misleading linguistic conventions, the
fact that monastic vocabulary was applied to the temporal dimension of the
church. While the terms *princeps, airchinnech* and *comarba* express the
image of rulership quite unambiguously the title *abbas* still preserved the
monastic connotations, but was likewise used to designate the lay ecclesiastical ruler of the church.

The various titles seem to represent different facets of the abbot's position as the secular leader of an ecclesiastical settlement. There is his role as
a political figure, the head of a church with many dependencies, who had
control over a large number of people, which quite compares to the power of
a secular king over his clients. This power over people, depending ultimately on rights of property, is the power of the abbot as *princeps*, or
airchinnech (the Irish equivalent). The understanding of these rights of
property and jurisdiction as an inheritance, handed on by election, family
rights or political appointment, found expression in the use of the title *comarba*, as the heir of the patron saint in its widest sense.[7]

Strictly speaking we should, therefore, no longer use the title '*abbot*' for
the leader of the Irish churches, since its monastic connotations are entirely
inadequate. However, as with the traditional approach, where the monastic
character of the Irish church was much overstressed, the more recent view
tends to treat the unique position of the Irish abbots as lay rulers of an ecclesiastical estate, as the new 'be-all and end-all' of Irish ecclesiastical organization. Obviously the Benedictine definition of the abbot in its strict
sense as the spiritual father of a community of religious does not hold in the
whole of Christian Europe. It would be difficult to find a historical context
and time in which it could be applied to the abbot of a Christian monastery.

---

[6]   SHARPE, Some problems, pp. 236, 258, 263-265.

[7]   Ibid., pp. 259, 264.

Lay-abbots were a common feature in continental monasteries from the time of Charlemagne. None of the abbots of the great German *Reichsklöster* were simply the head of their monastic communities, but powerful lords over lands and people, with great political influence. Like the German *Reichsbischöfe*, who were primarily secular magnates, eventually even electing and crowning the German Emperors, they exercised secular power. The assumption of secular power did not reduce the ecclesiastical authority of these churchmen, in fact, quite the opposite was the case. However, nobody ever doubted the use of their traditional titles. Since the Irish sources use *abbas*, *princeps*, *airchinnech* and *comarba*, indistinguishably as the title assigned to an ecclesiastical ruler we will maintain the traditional title *abbot* in the present study.

Some eighty abbots of Clonmacnois are recorded in the annals from the time of its foundation by St. Ciarán in the mid-sixth century down to the late thirteenth century. This is a surprisingly high number, especially if we compare it with that for other Irish monasteries.[8] For the community of Clonard, for example, between the mid-sixth and the mid-twelfth century, forty-eight abbots are recorded in the annals, in Glendalough the names of only forty-two pre-Norman abbots are known to us. This striking divergence could be the result of a more accurate recording of events in Clonmacnois, due to the fact that chronicles were written in the *scriptorium* of Clonmacnois itself.[9] Ryan suggested that this large number of abbots was due to a frequent turnover in the abbot's chair in Clonmacnois. This, he thought, was a consequence of the fact that preference was given to older candidates in the abbatial elections in Clonmacnois.[10] It might also be, however, that political

---

[8]   P. BYRNE, The community of Clonard, sixth to twelfth centuries, in: Peritia 4 (1985), pp. 157-173; A. S. MAC SHAMHRÁIN, Prosopographica Glindelachensis. The monastic church of Glendalough and its community, sixth to thirteenth centuries, in: JRSAI 119 (1989), pp. 79-97.

[9]   In this case however the number of the pre-tenth century abbots of Clonard should come close to that of Clonmacnois, since prior to the time of abbot Colmán Conaillech (d.926) chronicles were apparently kept in St. Finnian's monastery. However Colmán, as head of both monastic houses, was the thirtieth abbot of Clonard, but the forty-seventh abbot of Clonmacnois. For chronicle keeping in Clonard in the early period see MAC NIOCAILL, The medieval Irish annals, pp. 21-23; also HUGHES, Early Christian Ireland, p. 107.

[10]   John Ryan suggested that the abbots' chair and other leading positions in the monastic community were filled from the group of seniors, who formed an integral part of the monastic community (RYAN, Irish monasticism, p. 271).

instability should be reckoned as an additional factor accounting for the quick succession of abbots in Clonmacnois. Occasionally the annalists give little hints, indicating disturbances which led to the end of an abbacy. There is for example the 'change of abbots in Clonmacnois' recorded in the Chronicon Scotorum in the early ninth century, in which abbot Rónán resigned, possibly due to political pressure from the king of Munster (see A37).[11] Disturbances preceded the abbacy of Colmán Conaillech in the early tenth century. A certain Dedimus resigned in the year 901 after five years as abbot. His successor, a Connachtman died only three years later and was followed by Colmán, head of the church in Clonard, who thus ruled the two major ecclesiastical centres in the kingdom of Mide at the time (see A47, A48, A49). Very similar circumstances preceded the abbacy of Flaithbertach son of Domnall, brother of King Máel Sechnaill Mór in the early eleventh century. Again, we have the deposition of an abbot from Tethba in the year 1002. His successor in office died in the course of a year, to be followed by the king's brother as holder of the abbacy in Clonmacnois and Clonard for the next ten years (A58, A59, A60). Due to the border position of Clonmacnois, changing political sympathies played an important part in its history. The interests of the three competing overkingdoms, those of Mide, Connacht and Munster, interfered with, and therefore determined, politics in the monastic settlement and might indeed have been partly responsible for the high turnover in its abbatial chair.

Down to the second half of the ninth century the annals generally refer to the head of the community in Clonmacnois as *abbas*. Ferdomnach, of the Mugdorna Maigen who died in the year 872 (A41), is the first abbot bearing the title *princeps Cluana*.[12] The traditional *abbas* is used for his immediate successors, then follows Blamac son of Tarcedach from Bregmaine (A46), again styled *princeps* in the annals.[13] Colmán Conaillech bears the title *princeps Cluana Iraird + Cluana M. Nois*. He was abbot for most of the first quarter of the tenth century.[14] It has been said above, that with the be-

---

[11] The figures in brackets refer to the 'Catalogue of members of the community of Clonmacnois', below in Appendix 1.

[12] AU 872.4; CS 872.

[13] AU 896.1; CS 896.

[14] AU 926.3; CS 925.

ginning of independent chronicle keeping in Clonmacnois in the tenth century, the titles assigned to the abbots in the Clonmacnois chronicles start to
vary slightly from those in the Annals of Ulster. Thus Colmán's successor
was *princeps* according to the Chronicon, but *comarba* according to the
Annals of Ulster.[15] From the time of abbot Céilechair in the mid-tenth century onwards, the title *comarba Ciaráin* is invariably used in all of the contemporary annals.

It seems the division between spiritual and temporal jurisdiction was
maintained in the church of Clonmacnois, despite the fact that the abbot's
power appears to be much more prominent. There is also some evidence
pointing to the suggestion that the abbot also assumed episcopal orders in
the tenth century. However, this problem might be one of scribal transmission. Two or three of the rulers of the monastic estate in the tenth century
might also have held episcopal orders.[16] Colmán is styled a bishop in the
Annals of Ulster only, but not in the Clonmacnois chronicles. *Episcopus* as
part of his title is preceded by one, or even two unreadable words in the
manuscript, which might possibly have been the name of a second person, a
bishop, commemorated in a joint obituary with abbot Colmán. The second
presumed bishop abbot was Cormac Ua Cillín, *comorba Ciaráin ocus
Comáin, ocus comarba Tuamagréne ... sapiens et senex, et Episcopus*, according to the Chronicon. The Four Masters, otherwise known for their pen-
chant to accumulate titles, simply style him *comharba Ciaráin*, suggesting
that this was the actual title assigned to Cormac by their Clonmacnois
source. His successor Tuathal finally appears as the only tenth century abbot
of Clonmacnois who was definitely a bishop according to the now existant
Clonmacnois chronicles. The annals of Ulster, however, simply name him
comarba Ciarain.

In any case, it seems clear that the abbot of Clonmacnois from the tenth
century onwards becomes increasingly prominent. He appears as the leader
of St. Ciarán's *familia*, i.e. the community of the people who lived in and
around the city of St. Ciarán. Maybe we should see him as a kind of mayor
of the settlement, who apart from administrating the income of the church of
Clonmacnois was also responsible for representation of his community in

---

[15]   AU 931.1; CS 930 (see A50).

[16]   Colmán son of Ailill (A49, d.926), Cormac Ua Cillín (A54, d.966), Tuathal (A55, d.971).

the outside world, as well as for public works. Thus he acted as the friend of kings, appears as the co-founder of churches in Clonmacnois or had the roads in the settlement rebuilt.[17]

2.1.2 Bishops

The spiritual counterpart to the abbot as the top manager of temporal affairs was the bishop, as the highest ecclesiastical dignitary in the Irish church. He was the spiritual head of his church and its dependencies, exercised pastoral jurisdiction, including the appointment and ordination of priests, the visitation of the dependent churches as well as the general responsibility for the maintenance of the church's ministry.[18]

St. Ciarán, in contrast to most Irish saints, is nowhere claimed to have been a bishop. The highest orders he received were priestly orders which he took on Aran island from St. Énda.[19] Only from the latter half of the ninth century do the obituaries of the bishops of the church of Clonmacnois and its dependencies start to be regularly recorded in the annals.[20] The obituaries of these late ninth and early tenth century bishops of Clonmacnois do not occur in the Annals of Ulster. It seems very likely that their names were included in the Clonmacnois chronicles subsequently, as the bishops who still survived in living memory in the early tenth century, when chronicles

---

[17] See Appendix 1, for example Colmán son of Ailill (A49), or Cormac grandson of Conn na mBocht (A70).

[18] SHARPE, Some problems, p. 263. The division of power between the bishop and the abbot, the role of the bishop in a monastic church and its paruchia has presented some problems to historians, see HUGHES, The church in early Irish society, pp. 83-88, where she discusses the example of Kildare, and RYAN, Irish monasticism, pp. 167-190. The Irish canon law, however, seems to make provision for the bishop in a very conservative sense, talking of him as the head of a territory and people under his ecclesiastical jurisdiction. See H. WASSERSCHLEBEN (ed.), Die Irische Kanonensammlung, Leipzig 1885, pp. xxxvii-xli; see also C. ETCHINGHAM, Bishops in the early Irish church: a re-assessment, in: Studia Hibernica 28 (forthcoming).

[19] PLUMMER (ed.), Vitae Sanctorum Hiberniae, I, p. 208: *Et ibi sanctus Kiaranus consecratus est sacerdos.*

[20] Tuadcar died in 889 (CS 889); Máel Odar, died in 890 (CS 890; AFM 886); Cairpre Cam, died in 904 (CS 904; AFM 899); Loingsech, died in 920 (CS 918; AFM 918). See Appendix 1, B2, B3, B4, B5.

started to be written in Clonmacnois itself. The writing of history was primarily a secular business, which might account for the fact that the spiritual heads of the Irish churches received so little attention from the contemporary chroniclers in the early period. It seems plausible, however, that the episcopal succession in Clonmacnois was listed separately from the annalistic records, which dealt with worldly affairs in the first place.

With the beginning of the tenth century the obituaries of the bishops of Clonmacnois were included in the annals. Generally they were recorded by their Christian name only. Dynastic affiliations are therefore difficult to trace. It appears, however, that several bishops in the tenth and eleventh century came of the Meic Cuinn na mBocht, the family which also led the community of the religious in the ecclesiastical settlement.[21] The two brothers, Dúnadach and Óenacán were successively bishops of Clonmacnois in the mid-tenth century.[22] Another two members of the family held episcopal orders in the eleventh century.[23] The organizational changes in the Irish church in the course of the twelfth century reform might account for the fact that after the death of Gilla Chríst Ua hEchtigern in the early twelfth century, uncertainty about the bishops of Clonmacnois prevails in the records. Only towards the end of the century can a regular succession of bishops of Clonmacnois, now bishops of the diocese, again be traced.[24]

2.1.3 Vice-abbots

The office of the vice-abbot, also known as *prior* or *praepositus*, was a traditional feature of Benedictine monasteries. In the *regula Benedicti*, the vice-abbot, or *praepositus* is admonished not to abuse his power and not to compete with the abbot for authority. The exact nature of his office and

---

[21] See below, pp. 41-43 under the Céili Dé.

[22] Óenacán son of Ecertach, died in 949 (CS 948; AFM 947); Dúnadach son of Ecertach, died in 955 (CS 954; AFM 953; AClon 950, p. 156). See Appendix 1, B9, B10.

[23] Conaing son of Óenacán, died in 1011 (CS 1008; AFM 1009); Céilechair Mugdornach died in 1067 (CS 1064; AFM 1067). See Appendix 1, B17, B20.

[24] Gilla Chríst Ua hEchtigern, died in 1104 (CS 1100; AT 1104; AFM 1104); Muirchertach Ua Máeluidir, died as bishop of Clonmacnois in the year 1187 (AFM 1187). See Appendix 1, B21, B24.

8888

status is not defined.[25] The title for the vice-abbot, generally used in the contemporary Irish annals was the Latin title *secundus abbas*, often contracted to *secnabb*. Since the later ninth century, when the vernacular became the main literary medium, *tanisi abbad* is most frequent. The Four Masters use the standard title *prioir*. Twice the term *equonimus*, is used by the scribe of the Annals of Ulster.[26]

Ryan assumes that the office of the vice-abbot in Irish monasteries developed from the position of the *equonimus*, the steward or administrator of the monastery's material resources. The importance of that office, he says, increased due to the growing land possessions of the church, so that eventually the actual power of the *equonimus* was nearly that of the abbot.[27] His position has therefore been characterized as the 'real power base in the monastery'.[28] Such a statement, however, remains historically unfounded as long as the actual tasks and the authority of the vice-abbots in the Irish churches cannot be clearly defined.

It seems in fact plausible that he had a kind of auxiliary position to the *abbas* in the government and administration of the ecclesiastical estate. He possibly functioned as the official of the abbot, once it came to the collection of the taxes. This idea is supported by the fact that he repeatedly attracted hostility. Thus vice-abbot Máel Achaid was killed by the people of Delbna. Another vice-abbot was drowned by the king of Uí Maine, a third one was expelled from office by the abbot himself.[29] It seems plausible that the *secnab* was a rather unpopular figure due to his function as tax collector.

Often the vice-abbacy in Clonmacnois was held by the abbot of one of its affiliated churches. Two, possibly four of them, between the early ninth and early tenth century, had links with Fore, the church of St. Fechin in Mide.[30]

---

[25] G. HOLZHERR (ed.), Die Benediktiner Regel, Zürich 1976, p. 306, chap. 65 *De Praeposito monasterii*.

[26] AU 797.2; AU 894.3.

[27] RYAN, Irish monasticism, pp. 273f.

[28] DOHERTY, The monastic town, p. 64.

[29] See Appendix 1, vA4, vA13, vA16.

[30] Cumuscach, *secnap Cluana M. Nois* died in the year 835 (AU). He was possibly the father of Cormac, abbot of Fore (d.868, AU); Máel Mide, son of Cumuscach, *secnap Cluana M. Nois* died in the year 871 (AU). Cormac, *princeps Fobair* + *tanisi abad Cluna M. Nois*,

Ruaidrí son of Donnchad was *secundus abbas* in Clonard and *tanaisi* of Clonmacnois in the first half of the ninth century.[31] Áedán his successor in office was abbot of Roscrea as well, according to the Clonmacnois source used by the Four Masters.[32] Máel Achaid, who was killed as *tanaisi* of Clonmacnois in the year 896, was also *princeps* of Devenish, St. Lasrén's church in Fermanagh.[33] Murchad son of Riata, *tanaisi Cluana muc Nois* in the second half of the tenth century was *princeps* of Roscommon as well.[34]

It seems possible that in the course of time, with the extension of the *paruchia* of Clonmacnois, a tendency towards regional jurisdiction of the vice-abbot resulted out of this practice. The abbot of a dependent house, in his function as vice-abbot of Clonmacnois, was in charge of the temporalities, the collection of tithes and rents, in one particular territory of the *paruchia* of Clonmacnois. The abbot from Fore would thus have been responsible for the churches and lands of Clonmacnois in what is now Westmeath. Devenish was the centre of ecclesiastical administration for St. Ciarán's churches in Fermanagh, whilst the vice-abbot from Roscommon would have had responsibility for the Clonmacnois churches in Connacht. By the time of the eleventh century the notion of territorial jurisdiction found expression in the vice-abbot's title as well. Cormac Ua Cillín, guestmaster in Clonmacnois and from a traditional Clonmacnois dynasty is styled *secnab Síl Muiredaig* by the author of the Chronicon. Probably this title should be rendered 'vice-abbot in Clonmacnois, responsible for St. Ciarán's churches and their congregations in the territory of the Síl Muiredaig' which would be the churches in the area to which Roscommon was central.[35] Cormac thus

---

died in the year 891 (AU). Flann Fobair, Flann from Fore was *tanaisi Cluana muc Nois*, for one year only in 923, according to the Chronicon. He retired to Fore where he died in 930 (CS 922; AU 930.2). See Appendix 1, vA5, vA9, vA11, vA16.

[31] Ruaidrí son of Donnchad, *secundus Abbas Cluana Iriaird, tanaisi Abb Cluana muc Nois* (CS 838). See Appendix 1, vA6.

[32] He is styled *abbas Rois Cre* in AU 839.2; *prióir Cluana mic Nóis, + abb Rosa Cré*, AFM 838. See Appendix 1, vA7.

[33] Máel Achaid, *tanusi Cluana M. Nois, + princeps Daminisi* (AU 896.8). See Appendix vA13.

[34] Murchad son of Riata, *ab Ruis Comain, et tanaisi Cluana muc Nois* (CS 978, recte 980). See Appendix 1, vA17.

[35] His full title, according to the Chronicon was *ard seacnab Síl Muiredaigh, ocus aricinnech tige aiged Cluana muc Nois.* (CS 1102). See Appendix 1, vA 24.

would have held the same position as Murchad son of Riata, who as abbot of Roscommon was *tanaisi Cluana muc Nois* in the second half of the tenth century.[36] Gilla na Coimdead might have been vice-abbot in Clonmacnois responsible for Ciarán's churches in Delbna in the early twelfth century.[37] Similarly Gilla Íosa Ua Braoín, *secnab Uí Maine*, might have been in charge of the churches belonging to Clonmacnois in the territory of the Uí Maine.[38] The vice-abbots in the church of Clonmacnois would thus have been officials, working in the service of the abbot, as his representative. It seems that in the late eleventh century, but possibly earlier, the title began to imply temporal authority in one particular geographical area of the *paruchia* of Clonmacnois.

Also in the eleventh century a tendency towards hereditary transmission of the vice-abacy in Clonmacnois can be observed. The Ua Máeldúin family who claimed common ancestry with the Clann Cholmáin kings of Mide, supplied vice-abbots of Clonmacnois over three generations.[39]

2.1.4 Priests

With the beginning of independent chronicle keeping in the early tenth century the obituaries of officials less central to the government of the church, such as priest, guestmaster or superintendant of individual churches

---

[36] See Appendix 1, vA17.

[37] The title assigned to him in his obituary in the Chronicon is not quite clear, possibly slightly distorted by the seventeenth century transcriber. It reads *Giolla an Coimdeadh mac Cuinn Dealbhnaigh, tanaisi Abbadh Cluana muc Nois, quieuit* (CS 1124). As the entry stands, the man's father was Conn Dealbhnach, 'Conn fostered in Dealbhna'. It seems however possible that Dealbnaig, as genitive plural referred to the men of Delbna, and in the original formed part of the title rather than belonging to the name of the man's father. See Appendix 1, vA25.

[38] Gilla Íosa Ua Braoín, *secnap ua maine*, died in the year 1187 (AFM 1187). Since he was of a traditional Clonmacnois dynasty it seems very likely that he was linked to Clonmacnois, even though this connection is not explicitly stated by the Four Masters. See Appendix 1, vA26.

[39] Longarg Ua Máeldúin, *secnab Cluana muc Nois*, died in 1021 (CS 1019); Concobar son of Fogartach Ua Máeldúin, *secnab Cluana muc Nois*, died in 1089 (AFM 1089); Muiredach Ua Máeldúin, *secnab Cluana muc Nois*, died in 1106 (AFM 1106). See Appendix 1, vA18, vA21, vA23.

in Clonmacnois, were also recorded in the annals. Most of the names were transmitted via the Clonmacnois source which the Four Masters had at their disposal.[40] Priests of the community are generally recorded as *sacart* or *uasal shacart*. The position of the priest within the ecclesiastical hierarchy has been studied by the late Cardinal Ó Fiaich, for the case of Armagh. He came to the conclusion that in general only one member of the community at a time would be in priestly orders.[41] This seems to have been the situation in Clonmacnois as well where a regular succession list of priests can be established from the early tenth century onwards. Several of the priests in Clonmacnois were linked through family ties with the respective abbot at the time, pointing to the important position they held in the community. The priest Rechtabra, son of Maonach was possibly related to Ferdomnach Ua Maonaigh, the abbot of Clonmacnois in the mid-tenth century.[42] Máel Pátraic Ua Beguláin, who died as priest in Clonmacnois in the year 1028, seem to have been abbot of Clonmacnois for a short term earlier in the century.[43] The priest Ailill, son of Bresal was most likely the son of abbot Bresal, who had died in 1030.[44] A striking predominance of family names from Tethba amongst the priests in Clonmacnois can also be observed.[45]

2.1.5 Scribes and Lectors

Prior to the tenth century the monastic scholars and scribes are generally recorded in the annals under the descriptive titles *scriba*, *sapiens*, *sui* or *doctor*. The title *fer léiginn*, literally a man of learning, applying to the head

---

[40] CS, and even more so AT contain little information about minor officials in Clonmacnois. See above, p. 11f. n. 31.

[41] T. Ó Fiaich, The church of Armagh under lay control, in: Seanchas Ardmhacha 5 (1969), pp. 75-127, here 103f.

[42] See Appendix 1, P4, A52.

[43] CS 1000 (recte 1002); AFM 1028. See Appendix 1, A58.

[44] AFM 1044. See Appendix 1, P10, A62.

[45] Guaire, son of Máel Acain, died in 922 (AU); Dubtach Ua Tadgáin, died in 996 (AU); Máel Pátraic Ua Beguláin, died in 1028 (AFM); Gallbrat son of Duaric Ua Tadgáin, died in 1168 (AFM); Ua Catharnaigh, died in 1196 (ALCé). See Appendix 1, P3, P6, P9, P14, P16. For family names from Tethba compare M. Dobbs, The territory and people of Tethba, in: JRSAI 68 (1938), pp. 241-259; vol. 71 (1941/42), pp. 101-110.

of a monastic school, was only introduced with the beginning of independent chronicle keeping in the early tenth century.[46] The names of some thirty-two learned members of the community in Clonmacnois are recorded between the early eighth and mid-twelfth century.[47] Kathleen Hughes suggested that with the tenth century the golden age of book illumination in the Irish *scriptoria* was over and the scribe lost much of his traditionally high prestige. Scribes were further employed in the *scriptoria* of the great churches like Armagh and Clonmacnois, but subject to the authority of the *fer léiginn* as the leader and administrator of the schools. His position in the ecclesiastical hierarchy was very high, and, as studies for the church of Armagh and Kells have shown, could even serve as the stepping-stone to the leadership of the whole church.[48] In this context it is significant that in the early tenth century Máel Tuile, son of Colmán, presumably the son of abbot Colmán Conaillech, was promoted to the leadership of the schools in Clonmacnois.[49] Another member of the family succeeded to the same position in the later tenth century.[50] It seems that in a kind of rotating system, the most influential of the ecclesiastical dynasties in Clonmacnois, who also dominated other leading positions in the church of Clonmacnois, supplied the *fer léiginn* henceforward.[51]

---

[46] HUGHES, The distribution of Irish scriptoria, pp. 243-269; MAC SHAMHRÁIN, Prosopographica Glindelachensis, p. 93.

[47] Compare Clonard where seventeen scribes, lectors or learned men are recorded in the sources (see BYRNE, The community of Clonard, pp. 171-173); or the monastic community in Glendalough, where we know the names of merely five lectors (see MAC SHAMHRÁIN, Prosopographica Glindelachensis, pp. 93f.).

[48] HUGHES, The distribution of Irish scriptoria, p. 248; HERBERT, Iona, Kells, and Derry, p. 102; B. NIC AONGUSA, The monastic hierarchy in twelfth century Ireland: the case of Kells, in: Ríocht na Midhe 8 (1990/1991), pp. 3-20, here 13f.

[49] He died in the year 923 (CS 922; AFM 921). See Appendix 1, S12.

[50] Diarmait, *fer leiginn*, died in 1000. He is called *Conaillech*, which was the family's surname (AFM 999). See Appendix 1, S17.

[51] There were two *fer léiginn* of the Meic Cuinn na mBocht (S18, S31); one from the Uí Máeldúin (S28); one, possibly two of the Uí Loingsig (S22, S24); one of the Uí Lachtnáin (S23).

2.1.6 Guestmaster (*airchinnech tige Oiged*)

From the eleventh century onwards the obituaries of the *airchinnech Lis Oiged*, or *tige Oiged*, the superintendant of the guesthouse in Clonmacnois are recorded in the annals. St. Ciarán himself, according to his eleventh century hagiographers, was master of the guests for a while in the monastery of his brother in Íseal Chiaráin, and is described as an extremely dedicated host.[52] It seems that as head of the guesthouse the *airchinnech* was responsible for organization and order in the coming and going of people in the ecclesiastical settlement. An episode is told in the *vita* of St. Columba of Terryglass in which the *castellum hospitum*, i.e the *Lis Oiged* of Clonmacnois is mentioned as the place where the monks of Terryglass took quarter for the night. A miracle happened, namely the hostel seemed to be in flames several times that night. But by the time the *fratres* had jumped out of their beds and reached the hostel no trace of a fire was seen. Eventually it turned out that the guests had with them the relics of St. Columba, the supernatural power of which caused the miracle.[53] Six masters of the guesthouse are recorded in the annals from the eleventh down to the second half of the twelfth century. Their names come down to us through the Clonmacnois source used by the Four Masters. Three, possibly four, of them belonged to Uí Chongaile from Tethba and it seems that the office in the twelfth century had become a hereditary family position.[54]

2.1.7 Head of the Little Church (*Airchinnech Eglaisi Bige*)

The *airchinnech Eglaisi bige*, the 'supervisor of the little church', is first mentioned in the annals in the late ninth century. Since the church had an independent head it has been suggested that it was a monastery somehow

---

[52] The episode about Ciarán in the church of Íseal Chiaráin formed an original part of the Irish Life of Ciarán, and seems to have been translated into the Latin and copied by the thirteenth century redactors (STOKES [ed.], Lives of Saints, pp. 128f.; PLUMMER [ed.], Vitae Sanctorum Hiberniae, I, pp. 209f., §§23-25; MACALISTER, Latin and Irish Lives, pp. 177f.).

[53] HEIST (ed.), Vitae Sanctorum, pp. 231-233, §§28f.

[54] See Appendix 1, G2, ?G4, G5, G6.

separate from Clonmacnois.[55] However in the Lismore version of Ciarán's Life the little church, *Eglais Beag* is mentioned as the building in which Ciarán died and was lying in state before his interment.[56] There is also an independent saga tradition, probably dating from the tenth century, according to which Diarmait mac Cerbaill reserved for himself the right to be buried in Clonmacnois and also ordered that his body should be guarded in the little church for one night.[57] This evidence points to the fact that *Eglais Beag* functioned as the mortuary chapel of Clonmacnois. The Latin *vita* simply talks of the house in which Ciarán died and where he conversed with St. Cóemgen before his soul ascended to heaven. Presumably Ciarán's monastic cell in Clonmacnois was turned into a chapel some time after his death and eventually functioned as a mortuary chapel for the prominent secular and monastic persons who died in Clonmacnois. We might also assume that the bed of Ciarán (*imleach Chiaráin*), mentioned by the Four Masters as the place where people died,[58] was another name for *Eglais Beag*, since it was the building in which Ciarán is said to have died, and therefore most likely would have sheltered his bed. It would also have been the place where the pillow of St. Ciarán, a stone on which the saint used to sleep, and which was venerated in Clonmacnois possibly as early as the eighth century.[59]

The introduction of a separate office for some one in charge of the dead in Clonmacnois testifies to a high burial rate in the monastery. The Irish version of St. Ciarán's Life, the original of which was compiled sometime during the tenth century, contains the promise of immediate ascent into heaven, to every soul that would die on the hide of St. Ciarán's cow.[60] Obviously such a story has particular relevance to those about to die. For the monastic city, however, it could be read as propaganda material for a burial

---

[55] GWYNN / HADCOCK, p. 32.

[56] STOKES (ed.), Lives of Saints, p. 133.

[57] See below, p. 115 n.95.

[58] AFM 997; AFM 1134.

[59] PLUMMER (ed.), Vitae Sanctorum Hiberniae, I, p. 215: *Ceruical lapideum sub capite semper habebat, quod vsque hodie in monasterio sancti Kiarani manet, et ab omnibus veneratur.*

[60] STOKES (ed.), Lives of Saints, p. 127.

in St. Ciarán's graveyard. The function of Clonmacnois as a burial place of many prominent nobles and kings of Ireland, was in fact much developed in the course of the tenth century.[61] It is therefore possible that an increasing demand for burials in Clonmacnois made the introduction of the office of the custodian of the mortuary chapel necessary. The first supervisors of *Eglais Beag*, in the late ninth and first half of the tenth century were of the Meic Cuinn na mBocht family.[62] They might have contributed considerably to the consolidation of the fame of the monastic graveyard as the place of rest for Irish dignitaries.

2.1.8 Head of the Céili Dé and the poor (*cenn bocht*)

The names of some fifteen anchorites of Clonmacnois are recorded in the annals, one in the eighth, six in the ninth, none in the tenth and nine in the eleventh century. Men from all over Ireland, Fingen from Munster or Fogartach from Ulster seemed to have lived and died as anchorites in Clonmacnois. Prominent scholars, such as Suibne son of Máel Umai in the late ninth, or Dúnchad a lector in the early tenth century, were anchorites in Clonmacnois.

Strictly speaking the abbot would have been the father of the group of religious men living together in the monastic community. Since, however, the title 'abbot' was often retained by the lay ruler of the monastic estate, new titles were created for the head of the group of religious who lived within the settlement.[63] It seems possible that those of the anchorites, who are mentioned in the annals were leading members, or possible the leaders of the religious community in Clonmacnois. Later on, from the eleventh century onwards the role seems to have been taken by the *cend Celedh ndhé*, the 'head of the Céili Dé', first assigned to Conn na mBocht, the eponym of the Meic Cuinn na mBocht family.[64] The son of Conn, Máel Chiaráin, is

---

[61] See below, pp. 117f.

[62] See Appendix 1, AE1, AE3.

[63] SHARPE, Some problems, p. 265.

[64] AFM 1031; AU 1060 talks simply of *Conn na mBocht*, i.e. 'Conn of the Poor'.

styled *cenn bocht Cluana M. Nois*, seemingly applying to the same offices held by his father.[65]

The fact that the Meic Cuinn na mBocht, apart from leading the religious community in Clonmacnois also took an active part in the chronicle writing from the latter part of the eleventh century, might account for the comparatively high figure of nine obituaries of anchorites recorded in the annals during the eleventh century. It seems the family scribes reported home affairs in the first place and had a special liking for members of their own group inside the ecclesiastical settlement.[66] From the eleventh century on there is also evidence, that the community of the Céili Dé were seated in Íseal Chiaráin, a church in the neighbourhood of Clonmacnois, which eventually became independent from its mother church and was privately held by the Meic Cuinn na mBocht from the end of the eleventh century.[67]

2.1.9 The community of the Seniors

According to Ryan the title *sruith* or *senóir* was assigned to senior members of the monastic community, from whose ranks offices of authority were often filled in Clonmacnois.[68] Already the Dublin version of the Life of St. Ciarán describes a separate community of seniors *qui habebant cellulam seorsum in monasterio sancti Kiarani*. They are mentioned in the account of the visit of St. Colum Cille to Clonmacnois, which seems to have formed

---

[65] AU 1079.1. The *bocht*, the 'Poor', were a feature of monastic life since the eleventh century, presumably a religious community largely identical or at least closely associated with the Céili Dé (B. Ó Cuív, Miscellanea 1. „Boicht" Chorcaige, in: Celtica 18 [1986], pp. 105-111). The office *cenn bocht* is also found in Armagh at the time (see AU 1074.4). See also below, pp. 135f.

[66] See Appendix 1. under Anchorites. Dúnchad is praised as lector as well as anchorite, his son Joseph was a bishop, and Conn his grandson is praised as head of the Céili Dé. The anchorite Dubsláine, a priest of Ardbraccan is styled *prím anmcara na nGaoideal* by the Four Masters. Fothud Ua hAille, is praised as *ard anmchara* of Leth Cuinn. Also the annals report a number of foreign anchorites, who died in Clonmacnois, Fingen from Munster, Fogartach from Ulster, Dubsláine from Ardbraccan. Daigre Ua Dubhatáin is mentioned as an *anchorite* based in Clonmacnois who died in Glendalough.

[67] The head of the Meic Cuinn na mBocht bought the church in the year 1093, see CS 1089; AClon 1087, p. 184; see below, pp. 136f.

[68] RYAN, Irish monasticism, p. 271.

part of the *vita* in its early seventh or eighth century version.[69] The annals attest to the community of the seniors as a constituent part of the monastic institution from the second half of the eighth century.[70] Obituaries of senior members are regularly included in the annals down to the twelfth century. They seem to have been closely associated with the community of religious in Clonmacnois, otherwise known as the community of the Céili Dé. The comparatively high number of seniors in Clonmacnois, recorded in the later eleventh and early twelfth century might again have been due to the fact that the Meic Cuinn na mBocht, who presided over the religious community were actively involved in chronicle keeping in Clonmacnois.

2.1.10 Others

In the eleventh century three rather unusual obituaries are included in the annals, all referring to those holding minor offices in the monastic community. There is Cernach styled *aistire*, a porter of Clonmacnois,[71] Connmach, *toiseach ceileabharta*, the chief singer, and the *liachtaire*, the bell-ringer of Clonmacnois. All of them lived in the first half of the eleventh century, and most likely obtained their obituaries in the annals through being friendly with or related to those who wrote the contemporary chronicles.

So far the various offices and groups within the church of Clonmacnois have been discussed. A wide variety of ecclesiastical officials, leaders of the monastic schools, priests, guestmasters, those in charge of individual churches in Clonmacnois, is recorded from the tenth century onwards, when due to the independent recording of history in Clonmacnois itself, the annalistic accounts become more detailed. It appears from these contemporary

---

[69] PLUMMER (ed.), Vitae Sanctorum Hiberniae, I, p. 214; see also STOKES (ed.), Lives of Saints, p. 131, where the *tich sruithi* is mentioned.

[70] The first abbot of the seniors, *abbas sruithe Cluana*, mentioned in the annals died in 768 (Sen2), his successor died in 811 (Sen3). The death of another holder of the office is recorded in the early tenth century (Sen4), after which follows a long gap.

[71] He seems to have been the equivalent to the *hostiarius* of a Benedictine monastery. The Regula Benedicti dedicates a whole chapter to this office, stating that it should be a *senes sapiens* of the community who sits at the door, responsible and mature enough not to be tempted to wander round. He lives near the main door of the monastery, so that every visitor always finds him there to give information (see HOLZHERR [ed.], Die Benediktiner Regel, p. 310).

records that most of the leading positions within the institution were dominated by several families, who had apparently settled in Clonmacnois. These
families will be discussed in the following section.

2.2   Septs and families represented in offices in Clonmacnois

Family background and local origin of the leading members of a monastic
community are often seen as one mechanism by which the interaction between the monastic and the secular world functioned, and are therefore examined as an indicator for the various political allies of the respective
church. Father John Ryan studied the abbatial succession in Clonmacnois
from the sixth to the eighth centuries primarily to demonstrate that, unlike
the case of Iona, clanship did not exist in the religious community of Clonmacnois.[72] Thus the kin of the founder St. Ciarán, the Latharna Molt, of Dál
nAraide in Ulster were in no way preferred in the choice of abbots in Clonmacnois. In fact no member of that people appears amongst the successors
of St. Ciarán.[73] Instead, the abbots of Clonmacnois came more or less from
all over Ireland in the early period. Preference was given to candidates from
the northern half of Ireland after the late seventh century. Furthermore,
Ryan observed that the monastery was primarily ruled by abbots of a non-
aristocratic background, which accounts for the fact that Clonmacnois never
became the appurtenance of any state, sept or family, and no secular power
ever succeeded in turning the monastery into its satellite. In a general as-
sessment of future developments he predicted no essential change in personnel or policy for the period between the Norse invasion and the late
twelfth century.[74]

---

[72]   J. RYAN, The abbatial succession at Clonmacnois, in: J. RYAN (ed.), Féil-scríbhinn Eóin
Mhic Néill. Essays and Studies presented to Professor Eoin MacNeill, Dublin 1940, pp. 490-
507, here 490. He contradicts Reeves, who in his edition of Adamnán's Vita Columbae points
out the connection between Iona and the Cenél Conaill, the branch of the founder saint. For a
more recent study of the abbatial succession in Iona, from the later sixth century see
HERBERT, Iona, Kells, and Derry, pp. 36-46.

[73]   In comparison nine of the eleven direct successors of St. Colum Cille in Iona, were of the
Cenél Conaill, the branch of the Uí Néill from which St. Colum Cille himself came.

[74]   RYAN, The abbatial succession, p. 507; compare BYRNE, Irish Kings, p. 171.

However, there are a few problems with these arguments, most decisive being the fact that the family background of St. Ciarán is rather controversial. According to one set of the Clonmacnois annals, as well as his hagiographers, he was of the Latharna,[75] a branch of the Dál nAraide in Ulster.[76] The Dublin Life of Ciarán, however, explains that Latharna was a region in Mide, in the middle of Ireland.[77] Mageoghagan, finally, transmitted a tradition according to which St. Ciarán's father was a Connacht man, who with his family lived in Mide for a while.[78]

Such disagreement in the sources seems indicative. The tribal origin of Ciarán with the Dál nAraide in Ulster, claimed in the Oxford Life, seems quite plausible. The fact that apparently later interpretations claim that the founder saint of Clonmacnois came from Mide, or Connacht respectively, appears to be a result of actual political constellations and alliances between the leading dynasties in Clonmacnois and their secular counterparts. Thus the claimed Mide origin must date to a period when the kings of Mide were the leading secular allies of Clonmacnois, namely in the tenth century. Connacht origin, accordingly, would be assigned to Ciarán at a time of predominant Connacht influence in the monastic settlement, which was the case in the early period, from the late seventh and throughout the eighth centuries, as well as from the latter half of the eleventh century onwards. Secular alliances found reflection in the various editions of the history of St. Ciarán's origin, and also influenced local politics within the ecclesiastical settlement. Thus under the impact of royal patronage from, for example, Connacht, ecclesiastical dynasties from that part of Ireland rose to power in Clonmacnois. The various traditions concerning Ciarán's origin would thus

---

[75] AT (548); CS 544. His descent from the Latharna is also mentioned in the Dublin version (PLUMMER [ed.], Vitae Sanctorum Hiberniae, I, p. 200), and in the Oxford version, which talks of the Dál nAraide and the northern regions of Ireland *Hic traxit originem de aquilonali parte Hibernie, Ardensium scilicet genere* (MACALISTER, Latin and Irish Lives, p. 172).

[76] J. BANNERMAN, Studies in the history of Dalriada, Edinburgh/London 1974, pp. 1-8; BYRNE, Irish Kings, pp. 109, 110, 217.

[77] PLUMMER (ed.), Vitae Sanctorum Hiberniae, I, p. 200: *Sanctus abbas Kyaranus de plebe Latronensium que est in regione Midhi, id est in medio Hybernie, ortus fuit.*

[78] AClon 547, p. 81. He says that Ciarán was brought up in *Templevickinloyhe* in *Kinaleagh*, which according to MACALISTER, Latin and Irish Lives, p. 111, was identical with *Temple Mac in tsair* in Ardnurcher parish in Mide, the home of St. Ciarán according to the Irish life of Ciarán (STOKES [ed.], Lives of Saints, p. 119).

represent the points of view of the various leading dynasties in Clonmacnois, which were in fact predominantly from the three alleged homes of St.
Ciarán, namely from the south-eastern parts of Ulster, from various
branches of the Southern Uí Néill in Mide, and from the kingdom of Connacht.

In the early period, from the seventh to the mid-ninth century, the leadership of Clonmacnois was clearly dominated by Connachtmen. Fifty per cent
of the abbots between the years 600 and 850 were from Connacht.[79] Possibly six of them were from Uí Maine, a sub-kingdom in Connacht, in the
immediate neighbourhood of Clonmacnois, west of the Shannon.[80] A high
proportion of churchmen in Clonmacnois, in this early period also came
from Ulster mainly from the area, represented by the kingdom of Airgialla,
in the counties Louth, Monaghan and Armagh. The Uí Méith and the Uí
Chremthainn, as well as the Mugdorna Maigen are represented in leading
positions in Clonmacnois.[81] Their neighbours, the Ciannachta Breg, a tribe
subject to the Southern Uí Néill kings, supplied two abbots of Clonmacnois
in the eighth century.[82] Only in the course of the ninth century did Mide-
men become prominent in leading offices. Ruaidrí son of Donnchad, most
likely a brother of Conchobar son of Donnchad, king of Tara of the Clann
Cholmáin, is said to have been *tanaisi* of Clonmacnois in the late thirties of
the ninth century.[83] Around the same time a family from Fore in the western

---

[79] Between the years 599 and 850, the names of thirty-four abbots of Clonmacnois are
recorded (see Appendix 1, A5-38). For four of them no family background is given (A13, 25,
28, 32), the descent of another six is unclear (A22, 24, 26, 30, 35, 37). Of the remaining
twenty-four, one was from Munster (A7), five were from Ulster (A6, Dál mBairdene; A14,
A18 from the territory of the Airgialla; A19, A33 from the Ciannachta Breg) and one from
Tethba (A15). The remaining seventeen abbots were all Connachtmen.

[80] See Appendix 1, A5, A21, A23, A26, A29, A38.

[81] See Appendix 1, A14 (d.694), A18 (d.832), A42 (d.877). See C1 (d.1060) for the Meic
Cuinn na mBocht who were of the Mugdorna Maigen.

[82] See Appendix 1, A19 (d.737), A33 (d.794).

[83] See Appendix 1, vA6 (d.838). He is only recorded in the Chronicon and is said to have
been vice-abbot of Clonard as well. The entry of his death seems to be a later insertion, added
in the annals some time in the reign of Flann Sinna. It seems however possible that in the first
half of the ninth century, under common pressure from the king of Munster, the leaders of
Clonmacnois and the kings of Mide joined their forces for the first time. A brother of the then
king of Mide as vice-abbot in Clonmacnois at the time seems therefore quite plausible.

parts of the kingdom of Mide first appears in the vice-abbacy of Clonmacnois.[84]

With the beginning of the tenth century, when history was first recorded
in Clonmacnois itself, more detailed information about the various office
holders in the monastic settlement is given in the annals. Family links between the various people can often be reconstructed, and hereditary dynasties holding offices in Clonmacnois over several generations can be traced
from then on.

One of the earliest examples are the 'Conaillech'-clan, surnamed after
their origin among the Conaille Muirthemne, a branch of the Ulaid, settled
in the territory of present county Louth, Dundalk Bay. The Clonmacnois
branch of the family was founded by Colmán son of Ailill, *princeps* of
Clonmacnois for over twenty years in the early tenth century. His son Máel
Tuile, was *fer léiginn*, the leader of the monastic schools. Another of
Colmán's descendants, held the same position in the later tenth century.
Bresal Conaillech became *comarba Ciaráin* in the year 1025 and his son
Ailill, was a priest of the church of Clonmacnois.[85] Another family also
originally from the same general area were the descendants of Gormán, an
eighth century abbot of Louth, who retired to and died in Clonmacnois.
They became later known as the Meic Cuinn na mBocht, named after an
eleventh century member of the dynasty. However, the family was settled in
Clonmacnois and provided many leading officials from at least the ninth
century.[86] Furthermore there was the Ua Maonaigh family whose surname
suggests that ecclesiastical functionaries were also recruited from the community of the ecclesiastical tenants (*manaig*) living nearby the church.[87]

In the eleventh century, due to even fuller annalistic accounts, many
more of the ecclesiastical dynasties in Clonmacnois become known by

---

[84] See Appendix 1, vA5 (d.835), vA9 (d.871); also from Fore was vice-abbot Cormac, vA11
(d.891).

[85] See Appendix 1, A49 (d.926), S12 (d.923), S17 (d.1000), A62 (d.1030), P10 (d.1044).

[86] KELLEHER, The Tain and the annals, pp. 107-127, here 125-127. For the family see also
below, pp. 133-139.

[87] For the *manaig* see C. ETCHINGHAM, The early Irish church: some observations on pastoral care and dues, in: Ériu 42 (1991), pp. 99-118, here 105-113; C. DOHERTY, Some aspects
of hagiography as a source for Irish economic history, in: Peritia 1 (1982), pp. 300-328, here
315-321.

name. The Uí Maélduín, who claimed common ancestry with the Clann Cholmáin kings of Mide, supplied several vice-abbots, as well as a head of the school in Clonmacnois in the course of the eleventh century.[88] Two of the eleventh century abbots were of the Uí Flaithéin, also a family from Mide.[89] Many of the Clonmacnois families during that period seem to have come from Tethba, a subkingdom in Mide. Uí Tadgáin, Uí Chongaile, Uí Chatharnaigh and Uí Lachtnáin were all Tethba family names. Other families who had a share in the government of Clonmacnois were from Connacht, like the Uí Braoín and the Uí Chillín, who provided several abbots and vice-abbots.[90] Several Uí Maine families, like the Uí Ruadáin, Uí Maonaigh or Uí Nechtain can be traced in various monastic offices. Finally the Uí Mháeleoin, most likely another family from Connacht appear in the leadership of the church of Clonmacnois at the beginning of the twelfth century.[91]

Thus we might agree with Ryan that clanship in terms of direct blood ties between one particular secular dynasty and those who ruled in Clonmacnois did not exist. However the appearance, for example, of Mide men in governmental offices in Clonmacnois from the tenth century onwards was certainly linked with the fact that the Clann Cholmáin kings from Mide cherished Clonmacnois as one of the main ecclesiastical centres in their kingdom. The predominance of Connacht abbots in Clonmacnois, throughout the seventh and eighth centuries, would correspondingly point to close alliances between the church and its secular neighbours to the west. This friendship seems to have seen a revival in the course of the eleventh century, when dynasties from Connacht again became more prominent amongst the ruling class in Clonmacnois.

A correlation between what we might call the secular patrons of Clonmacnois and its respective ecclesiastical rulers certainly existed. The evidence points further to the fact that the monastic establishment produced its own aristocratic ruling class. A policy of hereditary transmission of leading

---

[88] See Appendix 1, vA18, vA21, vA23, S28.

[89] See Appendix 1, A63, A69.

[90] See Appendix 1, Uí Braoín: ?P5 (d.948), A56 (d.989), A67 (d.1088), vA26 (d.1187); Uí Chillín: A54 (d.966), vA24 (d.1106).

[91] See A72.

offices was gradually adopted on different levels in the institutional hierarchy in Clonmacnois. This development can be traced in the annals from the
ninth century onwards.

2.3 Affiliations between Clonmacnois and other churches

One of the most valuable sources from which we learn about the interaction
between the individual churches and about the ecclesiastical hierarchy in
medieval Ireland are saints' Lives. Again hagiographical writings must be
read as sources for the history of the time when the saints' Life was composed, or, as is often the case, subsequently revised.[92] Thus if the Life of a
saint talks about friendship or union between two saints this should be read
as the outcome of an alliance which existed between their respective foundations at the time when the work was composed. For the chronological
context of such an alliance one must rely on the annals, where, apart from
the political history of the time, exchange of personnel between two
churches is frequently indicated in the obituaries, when office-holders are
commemorated for having held positions in two different churches at a time.

Those alliances are referred to by the hagiographers as *fraternitas*
(brotherhood), or the Irish *óentu* (unity) and appear in the first place as a
kind of confraternity of prayer.[93] There was, however, more than a merely
spiritual dimension to them. As a mutual agreement between two churches
they created an umbrella of peace which allowed for cooperation between
the two partners.[94] Other unions described in the saints' Lives clearly express less equal relations between the two partners involved. They seem to
have, in reality, functioned on a basis of dependency, including the obligations to pay tax and render services for the inferior of the two partners. The
image of spiritual friendships seems to have provided the theological super-
structure by which one church could claim authority over another, and from
which the right to exercise power was derived.

---

[92] KENNEY, The sources, p. 299; McCONE, An introduction, p. 56; C. DOHERTY, The Irish
hagiographer: resources, aims, results, in: T. DUNNE (ed.), The writer as witness: literature as
historical evidence, Cork 1987, pp. 10-22, here 11.

[93] RYAN, Irish monasticism, p. 326; DOHERTY, Some aspects of hagiography, pp. 325-327.

[94] Ibid., p. 326.

A considerable number of churches can be discovered as having been associated with Clonmacnois in the latter way. A church, placed by its founder patron under the authority of Ciarán, would thus be under the ecclesiastical jurisdiction of the bishop of Clonmacnois. It seems that he was responsible for the keeping of the ministry in the dependent church. The priest there might have been supplied by Clonmacnois, and the bishop would have the right of visitation, thus exercising control of affairs in the daughter church. In return the dependent house would render taxes and services to its ecclesiastical overlord, consisting of natural goods, or duties like providing food and lodging for members of the community of the mother house. A vivid picture of such a relation comes down to us in the so-called Registry of Clonmacnois, where the bishop of Clonmacnois is described as the head of a number of churches in what is now county Leitrim. As a kind of token he held certain lands in the respective churches, which were obliged to pay a yearly rent of two cows and one pig to the abbot, or *comarba* of Ciarán, who, as the one in charge of the temporalities, would come to collect the rent every St. Martin's day.[95] It seems this was primarily the nature of the relation between a mother church and the various dependencies, forming its *paruchia*.

Often such a friendship, even though it implies inferiority for the church dependent on Clonmacnois, is commented upon in detail in the Lives of the less powerful founder saint, but is not mentioned by St. Ciarán's hagiographers, implying that there must have been some advantage for the dependent church as well. It seems membership of the *paruchia* of a powerful church was, in fact, in high demand. This might have been partly the result of the fact that every church needed its priest, who in his turn, of course, needed episcopal authorization for the due performance of his ministry. Membership of a *paruchia* also constituted an element of security, since you had a powerful friend, who would, if needed, defend you against enemies, both secular and ecclesiastical. This aspect might be a reason for the fact that at times the friendship with St. Ciarán would be sought by churches relatively distant from Clonmacnois. Often those tendencies can be explained as the result of political pressure on the respective church by local secular or ec-

---

[95] Registry, p. 452. See below, pp. 202-219 for the transmission of the document.

clesiastical powers. Submission to the more distant church of Clonmacnois could provide helpful support in the local quarrels.[96]

In the following we will first look at the churches who seem to have been on equal terms with Clonmacnois, i.e other ecclesiastical centres who themselves had their own extended *paruchia*.

2.3.1 Armagh

The *vita* of St. Ciarán contains no direct comment on the relation between the founder of Clonmacnois and St. Patrick. In fact, the patron saint of the church of Armagh finds no direct mention at all. Only through comparison with the *vita* of St. Patrick can a link be discovered. A certain Diarmait, otherwise known as Justus, is mentioned as the one who baptised Ciarán.[97] Tírechán informs us that Justus was a deacon of St. Patrick's household, whom he installed in the church of Fuerty (Fidarta), one of the Patrician foundations in the territory of Uí Maine in Connacht. Deacon Justus, at the very end of his life, in his hundred and fortieth year baptized St. Ciarán, the son of the craftsman.[98] Such a statement, especially since it was apparently unknown to, or ignored by St. Ciarán's biographers, implied that Ciarán owed his faith, transmitted via baptism, to St. Patrick. This in any case seems to have been the opinion of St. Patrick's biographer in the later seventh century. At the same time Tírechán complains that the community of Clonmacnois had got hold of many of the Patrician churches in Connacht, mentioning the churches of *Cellola Toch, Tamnuch* and *Dumech* by name.[99] He accuses the *familia* of Clonmacnois for having taken advantage of the

---

[96] See McCone, Clones and her neighbours, p. 323, who named this mechanism 'Sletty syndrome', after the church for which he first observed it. In short it means that „if a powerful church nearby is threatening your independence, protect yourself by submission to a powerful church further away whose control is likely to be less pervasive and irksome" (ibid., p. 323).

[97] Plummer (ed.), Vitae Sanctorum Hiberniae, I, p. 201; Macalister, Latin and Irish Lives, p. 173, §3; Heist (ed.), Vitae Sanctorum, p. 78; Stokes (ed.), Lives of Saints, p. 120.

[98] L. Bieler (ed.), The Patrician texts in the Book of Armagh, Dublin 1979, p. 128, §7.2; pp. 146f., §28.1-3. The story is also contained in the Tripartite Life of Patrick (see W. Stokes [ed.], The Tripartite Life of Patrick, London 1887, pp. 104f.)

[99] For the identification of these churches see below, p. 86 n.224.

plague in the later seventh century.[100] We may conclude that Connacht was a particularly infested area, and many of the priests of the churches there died in the course of the plague. Tirechán's complaint seems to imply that Clonmacnois simply filled the vacant positions in the churches with its own priest - pointing to the fact that the foremost task of an ecclesiastical overlord was to provide a priest in its dependencies. Thus, whoever supplied the priest of a church could claim ecclesiastical overlordship, including tithes and ecclesiastical tax. Obviously competition for ecclesiastical authority in Connacht dominated the relations between the churches of Armagh and Clonmacnois in the late seventh century.

It seems Clonmacnois was, for the century to come, the more successful contestant and exercised ecclesiastical jurisdiction in Connacht for most of the eighth century. This was the time in which Connacht men dominated in the abbacy of Clonmacnois, and the *Lex Ciaráni*, with the support of the kings of the Uí Briúin, was four times promulgated in Connacht.[101] However, from the later eighth century onwards, Armagh regained authority in the area. The *Cáin Pátraic* was regularly promulgated in Connacht, often in association with a circuit of St. Patrick's relics.[102] Rivalries between Armagh and Clonmacnois for authority over churches seem to have been carried out down to the eleventh century. The complaints about churches rightly belonging to Armagh, but claimed by Clonmacnois, still form part of the middle Irish Tripartite Life of Patrick, and are extended to three churches in Mide.[103] This Life of Patrick also contains a polemical com-

---

[100] BIELER (ed.), The Patrician texts, pp. 142f., §25.2: *familia Clona per vim tenent locos Patricii multos post mortalitates novissimas.*

[101] AU 744.9; AI 775; AU 788; AU 814.

[102] AFM 779 (recte 783); AU 799; AU 811; AU 818; AU 825; AU 836; AU 845, 846. The fact that these circuits of the saint's relics were often performed by an abbot of Armagh expelled from his city (so in the year 811 and 845) only stresses the importance of Connacht as the loyal hinterland of St. Patrick's paruchia.

[103] STOKES (ed.), Tripartite Life, pp. lxiii, 76, 78, 80. Compare below, pp. 87f. The compilaton of stories belonging to St. Patrick, known as the Tripartite Life is preserved in MS Egerton 93, MS Rawl. B 512. e.a. On historical and linguistic grounds Stokes suggests that the Life was written before the middle of the tenth century and that its fashioning in homily form, dates from the eleventh (STOKES [ed.], Tripartite Life, p. lxiii). Confirmed by Prof. Kim McCone, in private correspondance. See also HERBERT, Iona, Kells, and Derry, p. 195. There is also the view that the Tripartite Life was compiled as late as the early twelfth century (D. Dumville, Saint Patrick A.D. 493-1993, Woodbridge 1993, pp. 255-258).

ment on the scarcity of relics in Clonmacnois, in which the superiority of Armagh over Clonmacnois as regards the possession of relics seems to have found expression.[104]

2.3.2 The Columban community in Scotland and Ireland

The earliest securely datable reference to links between Clonmacnois and the Columban community is contained in the *vita* of Colum Cille, written by Adamnán, abbot of Iona, in the late seventh century. It preserves the account of St. Colum Cille's visit to Clonmacnois during the time of abbot Ailither (585-599).[105] According to Adamnán Colum Cille was received by the monks like an angel of the Lord, they bowed before the saint and kissed him with all reverence. A kind of pyramid was built out of branches and carried over the head of the saint, to give shelter on his way to the church in Clonmacnois.[106] This story presents us with an ideal of harmony between the churches of Colum Cille and that of Ciarán, which seems to have existed in the late seventh century, when Adamnán wrote his biography.[107] The event is also told, though in a different context, in the Dublin Life of St. Ciarán.[108] According to an anecdote contained in the ninth century 'Rule of Tallaght' Adamnán once interferred in a conflict for the abbacy of Clonmacnois in the

---

[104] STOKES (ed.), Tripartite Life, p. 84. A second version of the same story is contained in a note to the Martyrology of Oengus in Rawlinson B 512, fol. 62, edited by STOKES (ed.), Tripartite Life, p. 556. The relevant passage in the manuscript contains the preface, part of the prologue and the epilogue to the Martyrology of Oengus, including some notes to it. See STOKES (ed.), Tripartite Life, p. xxiv, for a description of Rawl. 512.

[105] ANDERSON / ANDERSON (eds.), Adomnán's Life of Columba, pp. 24-27, Book I, 3. The visit allegedly took place when St. Colum Cille was in Ireland to found the church of Durrow. See Appendix 1, A4.

[106] ANDERSON / ANDERSON (eds.), Adomnán's Life of Columba, pp. 24-27, Book I, 3: *humiliatísque in terram uultibus eo uisco cum omni reuerentia exosculatus ab eis est; ymnís et laudibus resonantes honorifice ad eclesiam perducunt. Quandamque de lignís priramidem erga sanctum deambulantem constringentes a quatuor uirís eque ambulantibus subportari fecerunt, ne uidelicet santus senior Columba eiusdem fratrum multitudinis constipatione molestaretur.*

[107] Some time between 688 and 704 (ANDERSON / ANDERSON [eds.], Adomnán's Life of Columba, p. xlii; compare HERBERT, Iona, Kells, and Derry, p. 54).

[108] PLUMMER (ed.), Vitae Sanctorum Hiberniae, I, pp. 213f., §31; STOKES (ed.), Lives of Saints, p. 131.

late seventh and early eighth century and it has been suggested that the episode might reflect Iona claims to jurisdiction or supervisory authority over
Clonmacnois during the abbacy of Adamnán.[109]

In any case, harmony between Ciarán and Colum Cille did not survive
the political reality of the eighth century, in which the Clann Cholmáin rose
to power as the leading dynasty in Mide.[110] Those who seem to have profited most from the dynasty's initial success were the Columban churches in
Ireland. The *Lex Colum Cille* was twice proclaimed in Mide during the reign
of Domnall Midi (743-763), the founder of the dynasty.[111] When he died in
the year 763, he was buried in the Columban house of Durrow.[112] Domnall's church policy and his preferential treatment of the Columban community apparently provoked hostility from Clonmacnois, likewise striving
for the position of leading church in the kingdom. This kind of rivalry might
have been the background to the battle between the communities of Clonmacnois and Durrow in 764, one year after king Domnall's death.[113] Donnchad, son and successor to Domnall Midi, continued the policy of his father, the *Lex Colum Cille* was again promulgated in the year 778,[114] and the
king had the active military support of the forces of Durrow in his campaign
against the king of Munster.[115] However with his death in the year 797, the
Cenél nEógain of the Northern Uí Néill regained the over-kingship. The

---

[109] E. J. GWYNN / W. J. PURTON (eds.), The monastery of Tallaght, in: PRIA 29 (1911), pp.
115-179, here 162, §85; see ETCHINGHAM, The implications of paruchia, p. 155.

[110] F. J. BYRNE, The rise of Uí Néill and the high-kingsip of Ireland, Dublin 1969, p. 20;
HERBERT, Iona, Kells, and Derry, pp. 64-67.

[111] AU 753.4; AU 757.9.

[112] AFM 758. According to the Annals of Clonmacnois he was the *first K. of Ireland of
Clann Cholmáin or o'Melaghlynes & died quitly in his Deathbed the 12th of the kalends of
December* (AClon 759, p. 121).

[113] For the Battle of Argaman see AU 764.6; AT (764); AClon 759, p. 121. Diarmait son of
Domnall (possibly a son of king Domnall Midi) was killed in battle together with Diglach son
of Dubless. His opponent Bresal, son of Murchad (possibly nephew of Domnall Midi, the son
of his brother Murchad) was victorious on the side of Clonmacnois, he was killed later in the
same year (AU 764.11) (HERBERT, Iona, Kells, and Derry, p. 66).

[114] AU 778.4.

[115] AU 776.11.

Clann Cholmáin, if only temporarily, lost their leading position and the Columban houses in Mide lost a powerful secular patron.[116]

The dynasty's revival, their gradual ascent as the most powerful secular
rulers in the midlands in the course of the ninth century, went along with a
more balanced church policy. Whereas in the eighth century the Clann
Cholmáin patronage over the Columban churches was at the expense of
other ecclesiastical centres,[117] the ninth century saw the kings of the Clann
Cholmáin in peaceful alliance with several churches. Besides the traditional
links with Durrow, the kings maintained links with Clonard and Clonmacnois which during the reign of Flann Sinna (879-916) became the leading
churches in Mide, and were under joint government of a close friend of the
king.[118]

The period saw a comparatively peaceful consolidation of the relationship between the Columban churches in Ireland and Clonmacnois, since
both enjoyed Clann Cholmáin patronage. King Flann Sinna, the builder of
the main church in Clonmacnois, had the relics of Colum Cille enshrined in
Durrow.[119] Links between the two churches can be established on archeological grounds from the later ninth century.[120] It seems that a series of
tales, unique to the Irish Life of Ciarán, should be dated to this period. A
number of anecdotes from Clonard, where both founder saints, Colum Cille
and Ciarán are said to have studied, shed a particularly friendly light on the

---

[116] BYRNE, Irish Kings, p. 160; HERBERT, Iona, Kells, and Derry, p. 67.

[117] In the year 775 king Donchad had an armed encounter in Clonard with the community
(AU 775.6). In the year 789 he was accused of having dishonoured the staff of Jesus and the
relics of Patrick in an assembly at Ráith Airthir (AU 789.17). Compare BYRNE, Irish Kings,
p. 157.

[118] See below, pp. 106-114.

[119] LUCE e. a. (eds.), Evangeliorum Quattuor Codex Durmachensis, p. 55.

[120] A resemblance between the presentation of lions, found on a group of crosses, which
originated in Clonmacnois and the presentation of the lion symbolising the evangelist John in
the Book of Durrow has been described by C. Hicks. She assumes that there were close connections between the craftsmen of the two monasteries at least since 870, when the Book of
Durrow was first definitely in Durrow (C. HICKS, A Clonmacnois workshop in stone, in:
JRSAI 110 [1980], pp. 5-35, here 11).

founder of Durrow.[121] St. Finnian on one occasion was asked who would lead the prayers after his death. Finnian pointed out St. Ciarán, in consequence of which all the saints, with the notable exception of Colum Cille, were jealous of Ciarán, because of the pre-eminence given to him by St. Finnian. According to the second story St. Finnian once had a vision of two golden moons in the sky, one of which went to the north-east across the sea, the other over the middle of Ireland. The dream is interpreted as a vision about the future of Colum Cille and Ciarán. It portrays a harmonious coexistence of their ecclesiastical foundations and defines the respective spheres of interest, namely Ireland for Ciarán, and Scotland and the Scottish Isles for Colum Cille.[122]

Finally, friendship between Clonmacnois and the Columban foundation Kells can be traced in the annals for the latter half of the eleventh century, when two lectors from Kells had links with Clonmacnois as well. Máel Choluim Ua Loingsigh, *fer léiginn* in Kells, who died in the year 1061, seems to have come from an ecclesiastical dynasty of Clonmacnois, which was also the place where he died.[123] Donngal son of Gormán, another *fer léiginn* of Kells who died in the year 1070, was according to the Annals of Innisfallen lector in Clonmacnois as well.[124]

---

[121] STOKES (ed.), Lives of Saints, pp. 126f.; the anecdotes are also contained in the sixteenth century life of Colum Cille, compiled from various sources under the direction of Manus O'Donnell (A. O'KELLEHER / G. SHOEPPERLE [eds.], Betha Colaim Chille: Life of Columcille compiled by Manus O'Donnell in 1532, Urbana 1918, p. 128).

[122] Stokes (ed.), Lives of Saints, pp. 126f. The anecdotes are not contained in the Latin Lives of Ciarán.

[123] He was *saoi + sagart Cluana mic Nóis, Ciáráin, ferleighind Cenannsa*, according to the Four Masters died in the year 1061 (see P12). He was possibly the son of Flaithbertach son of Loingsech, *fer léiginn* of Clonmacnois a generation earlier, who died in 1038 (see B18). The Uí Loingsigh supplied an abbot of Clonmacnois in the early twelfth century (see A71).

[124] He was *tanaisi Abbadh Cluana muc Nois* according to the Chronicon (CS 1067); the Annals of Ulster say he was *fer léiginn* in Kells (AU 1070.10), the Annals of Innisfallen style him *fer legind Cluana M. Nois ocus Cenannsa* (AI 1070.7), and according to the Four Masters he was *áird ferleighinn Leithe Chuinn, + tánaissi abbaidh Cluana mic Nóis* (AFM 1070). See HERBERT, Iona, Kells, and Derry, p. 90 n.12; also below, Appendix 1, S27.

2.3.3   Clonard

Clonard, the foundation of St. Finnian, seems to have become the most important church in the kingdom of Mide, under the kings of the Clann Cholmáin in the course of the ninth century.[125] Together with many other famous Irish saints, like Colum Cille, Ciarán of Saighir, or Brendan of Clonfert, Ciarán is said, in all of the extant versions of his Life, to have been a disciple of Finnian, before founding his own church.[126] The teacher-pupil relationship obviously implies a superiority of some kind for the church of St. Finnian. There is an obvious tendency in the Lives of St. Ciarán, to stress the special position which Ciarán had amongst the twelve apostles of Ireland in Clonard. He is portrayed as having had a very special relationship with Finnian, his teacher. Thus according to the Salamanca version of his *vita* each of the apostles in Clonard had to grind corn with a quern (*molam manu sua*) on a given day. When it was Ciarán's turn, the angel of God in person used to grind for him.[127] According to another episode Finnian sent visitors to St. Ciarán. Thus a young girl who had decided to remain as a holy virgin under St. Finnian's charge is sent to study with Ciarán; similarly, twelve lepers once came to Clonard and were sent to Ciarán to be healed.[128] As we have seen earlier, St. Finnian himself is said to have given priority to Ciarán, when he appointed him as the one to lead the prayers, after his death.[129] At another occasion he gave a blessing to Ciarán, promising him that his name should be *Leath n-Eirinn*.[130]

---

[125] GWYNN / HADCOCK, p. 63; RYAN, Irish monasticism, pp. 115-118; HERBERT, Iona, Kells, and Derry, pp. 81, 90f.

[126] HEIST (ed.), Vitae Sanctorum, p. 101, §19; all the versions of St. Ciarán's Life comment on Ciarán's time as a student in Clonard (See PLUMMER [ed.], Vitae Sanctorum Hiberniae, I, pp. 205f., §§15-17; MACALISTER, Latin and Irish Lives, pp. 173f., §§4-6; HEIST [ed.], Vitae Sanctorum, pp. 80f., §§12f.; STOKES [ed.], Lives of Saints, pp. 122-127).

[127] HEIST (ed.), Vitae Sanctorum, p. 81, §13.

[128] STOKES (ed.), Lives of Saints, p. 123.

[129] STOKES (ed.), Lives of Saints, p. 126.

[130] STOKES (ed.), Lives of Saints, p. 124. It seems the episode was translated and incorporated by the thirteenth century redactor into the Dublin version (PLUMMER [ed.], Vitae Sanctorum Hiberniae, I, p. 206, §17).

St. Ciarán is occasionally brought in, in connection with St. Finnian's wealth. Again the Irish Life puts much emphasis on the fact that St. Ciarán's cow supplied not only the twelve disciples of Finnian with milk, but also fed the guests and the sick in Clonard, all in all three times fifty men a day.[131] Another time Ciarán was sent to grind corn at night in a mill, some miles away from Clonard. A petty king living nearby sent meat and drink to the holy man who used the food for the common good by throwing it into the mill and transforming it into flour. The king gave the mill to Ciarán, who passed the church, which was later built there, on to his master Finnian. This story is, in a short version, contained in the Oxford Life of St. Ciarán, and was possibly copied and translated from the Irish. There the episode is much embellished through the romantic involvement of the miller's daughter. Also the conclusion is drawn that Finnian owes his wealth to Ciarán. In return Ciarán receives from Finnian another blessing, promising fame, learning and wealth.[132]

The peak of St. Ciarán's ambitions for equality with his teacher is reached in the Lismore Life at the departure of Ciarán from Clonard. On that occasion, says the author, St. Finnian offered his church to his pupil, who politely refrained from taking the offer with the argument that none but God alone should receive such a gift. The two saints decide that instead unity (óentad) should exist between them, and that he who breaks the unity should have no share in earth or in heaven.[133]

These or comparable statements concerning the relationship between St. Ciarán and his teacher are not contained in St. Finnian's Lives. There, the only very vague indication of some kind of equality is the fact that the mothers of Ciarán and Finnian, together with that of Colum Cille, are said to have retired to the same cell.[134] A balance of power between the two churches is only suggested in the various versions of the Life of St. Ciarán, most outspoken in the Irish Life. They therefore probably express the rela-

---

[131] STOKES (ed.), Lives of Saints, p. 122.

[132] STOKES (ed.), Lives of Saints, pp. 124f.; for the Oxford version see MACALISTER, Latin and Irish Lives, p. 174, §6.

[133] STOKES (ed.), Lives of Saints, p. 127.

[134] HEIST (ed.), Vitae Sanctorum, p. 102, §21.

tion between the two churches as the Clonmacnois people would like to have had it rather than as it actually was.

Links between the two churches are first attested in the annals for the ninth century, when Ruaidrí son of Donnchad (d.838) held the vice-abbacy in both churches.[135] In the course of the tenth and early eleventh century Clonard and Clonmacnois were three times under the government of one and the same abbot, Colmán Conaillech (d.926), Céilechair son of Robartach (d.954) and Flaithbertach son of Domnall (d.1014). Two of the four men here were close relatives of the kings of the Clann Cholmáin, and a third, Colmán Conaillech appears to have been a very good friend of king Flann Sinna, his contemporary. Colmán had been abbot of Clonard for a considerable time already (his predecessor there had died in 888), when he was promoted to the abbot's chair in Clonmacnois in the year 904. This constellation, an old and trusted abbot of Clonard taking over the government in Clonmacnois, implies if not a mother-daughter relationship, at least a certain inferiority on the part of the latter. Moreover Clonard, situated right in the centre of Mide, established itself as the greatest of the churches in the kingdom ruled over by the kings of the Clann Cholmáin. This situation possibly provoked the insistence on equality and union between the two saints, most clearly expressed in the Irish Life of St. Ciarán.

2.3.4 Glendalough.

The *vita* of Cóemgen, as contained in the Dublin collection, includes a story about how the saint went to visit Clonmacnois, shortly after St. Ciarán's death.[136] He entered the mortuary chapel, and Ciarán was temporarily restored to life, so that the two men could engage in conversation. At St. Ciarán's request they exchanged their garments as a sign of eternal friendship, and the following morning the monks, when opening the chapel, found the two saints wearing each other's clothes. In the Dublin Life of Ciarán the episode is commented on very briefly. We are told that on the third night

---

[135] See Appendix 1, vA6; also below, pp. 109f.

[136] PLUMMER (ed.), Vitae Sanctorum Hiberniae, I, pp. 248f., §28. A very brief mention of the incident in just one sentence is to be found in Salamanca version of Cóemgen's Life (HEIST [ed.], Vitae Sanctorum, p. 364, §12). Compare KENNEY, The sources, pp. 403f.; GWYNN / HADCOCK, pp. 80-83.

after the death of Ciarán Cóemgen came from the province of Leinster for
the burial service (*exequias*) to Clonmacnois. Ciarán spoke to Cóemgen and
they exchanged their coats, and made a contract of brotherhood (*fraternitas*)
between themselves and their people for ever. The author ends the account
with a reference to the Life of Cóemgen, to the effect that further details of
the story may be there obtained.[137] The Irish Life of Ciarán contains a
slightly different version of the same story. Again Cóemgen arrived in
Clonmacnois three days after St. Ciarán's death. The monks, preoccupied
with mourning, failed to give proper attention to the saintly visitor, who
eventually pronounced upon them a prophecy of eternal sadness. The elders
in the community now woke up, obeyed St. Cóemgen and opened *Eglais
Beag*, where St. Ciarán lay in state, so that he could talk to his departed fellow saint, whose soul was still with the body. The two saints conversed with
each other, and Ciarán blessed Cóemgen. Cóemgen on his part blessed water and the two celebrated holy communion together. Ciarán then gave his
bell to Cóemgen as a sign of the covenant (*óentad*) between the two.[138]

Exchange of personnel between Clonmacnois and Glendalough is documented for the tenth and eleventh centuries. The abbot of Clonmacnois,
Ferdomnach Ua Maonaigh, is said to have died in the year 952, in Glendalough. The Four Masters credit him as abbot of Clonmacnois and Glendalough. One of his successors later in the century, who was also a bishop of
Clonmacnois, seems to come of the Uí Tuathail, a branch of the royal dynasty of Uí Muiredaig in Leinster. Finally, there was an anchorite of Clonmacnois who died in pilgrimage in Glendalough in the mid-eleventh century.[139] It has also been observed that the Annals of Tigernach contain a
substantial amount of Leinster material, after they restart recording in the
year 974, which again points to current exchange between Glendalough, as
the central church in Leinster, and Clonmacnois.[140]

Ailbhe Mac Shamhráin pointed to the political constellation in Leinster
in the ninth and tenth century as the most likely background to an alliance
between Glendalough and Clonmacnois. During this period the north Lein-

---

[137] PLUMMER (ed.), Vitae Sanctorum Hiberniae, I, p. 215, §32.

[138] STOKES (ed.), Lives of Saints, pp. 132f.

[139] See Appendix 1, A52 (d.952), A55 (d.971), B8 (d.941), An13 (d.1054).

[140] MAC NIOCAILL, The medieval Irish annals, p. 27.

ster kingdom of Uí Dúnlainge came under severe pressure, in the first place through the expanding power of Norse Dublin, but also through the impact of the Osraige from Munster, whose expansionist ambitions reached as far as the patrimonial Uí Muiredaig territory. The changing political balance of power found reflection in the ecclesiastical sphere, where Uí Dúnlainge dominance was reduced in the course of the tenth century. The abbatial succession in Glendalough clearly shows an Osraige bias, whereas names of the Uí Dúnlainge become rare amongst the officials in Glendalough. It has been said that ecclesiastical alliances were often sought by a monastery at times of political strain, as an attempt to strengthen its position through an affiliation with a bigger and more powerful monastery.[141] Mac Shamhráin suggested that the *óentad* between Glendalough and Clonmacnois was of such a nature. The political interests of the Osraige in Leinster were accompanied by efforts to establish themselves in Glendalough at the expense of the Uí Dúnlainge. The traditional Uí Dúnlainge party in Glendalough sought support through joining up with the great midland church of Clonmacnois.[142]

In the following an attempt is made to reconstruct the extent of the *paruchia* of Clonmacnois. We will no more ponder on the possible meanings and implications of the term. Ailbhe Mac Shamhráin pointed to the fact that in its basic sense it describes 'an ecclesiastical domain in charge of a clergyman', for the purpose of the present study we would thus be talking about units of ecclesiastical administration under the authority of the head of Clonmacnois.[143] Whether the churches belonging to the *paruchia* of Clonmacnois were located within the same province or whether they were widley scattery, whether or not the territorial delimination of the *tuath* was maintained, whether the bishop or the abbot of Clonmacnois had the ultimate

---

[141] HUGHES, The church in early Irish society, pp. 165f.; MCCONE, Clones and her neighbours, pp. 314, 323.

[142] A. S. MAC SHAMHRÁIN, The Unity of Cóemgen and Ciarán: a covenant between Glendalough and Clonmacnois in the 10th to 11th centuries, in: K. HANNIGAN / W. NOLAN (eds.), Wicklow: history and society, Dublin 1994, pp. 139-150. The author kindly allowed me to read the paper prior to publication. See also A. S. MAC SHAMHRÁIN, The Uí Muiredaig and the abbacy of Glendalough in the eleventh to thirteenth centuries, in: Cambridge Medieval Celtic Studies 25 (1993), pp. 55-75 and A. S. MAC SHAMHRÁIN, Church and Polity in Pre-Norman Ireland: The Case of Glendalough, Maynooth 1996, pp. 138-142.

[143] MAC SHAMHRÁIN, Church and Polity, p. 168.

authority within their *paruchia* will not be discussed here.[144] Instead we will, for a start, simply gather information to be found in the available medieval sources, about the relation between Clonmacnois and its associated churches. We will collect the tales commenting on the ecclesiastical network around Clonmacnois, which in general is contained in stories about the respective founder saints and their doings, their shared prayers, their joint journeys, their agreements or disagreements. Later these comments will be re-read in the light of the information on the land possessions of St. Ciarán, as it was preserved in the so-called 'Registry of Clonmacnoise' and possibly this comparison will serve to complete the evidence on the actual extent of the lands under the authority of Clonmacnois.[145]

There is one more observation regarding the nature of the evidence we deal with. In the reconstruction of the *paruchia* of Colum Cille, for example, we have a clear point to start from, since it consisted in the first place of all the churches founded by the saint. For Armagh we have detailed lists of churches belonging to - or more precisely claimed as established by - St. Patrick, compiled by Muirchú and Tirechán as early as the seventh century. Such lists of monastic possessesions, if they ever existed, did not survive in the case of Clonmacnois, at least not in an original early medieval version. St. Ciarán's hagiographers do agree on the fact that his sphere of influence was very large, that his *paruchia* was growing steadily, to the effect that his death was welcomed by all the other saints of Ireland as a blessing from God, since they feard that if Ciarán had lived longer, there would have been hardly a place in Ireland, that would not have been his.[146] However, the actual number of churches mentioned in connection with St. Ciarán in his Lives is comparatively small. The saint is said to have stayed in Clonard with St. Finnian, on the Aran islands with St. Énda, and on Inis Cathaig, at

---

[144] Ibid., pp. xvii-xx, 168-172 for a conclusive summary of this discussion. See also above, p. 28f. for a preliminary introduction of the main questions.

[145] See below, chap. 7, pp. 220-242.

[146] PLUMMER (ed.), Vitae Sanctorum Hiberniae, I, p. 211, §28: *et parrochia eius per circuitum multum dilatata est; et nomen sancti Kiarani per totam Hiberniam multum celebratur.* The term *paruchia* seems to be used here in a sense that includes distant subject foundations as well. Compare MAC SHAMHRÁIN, Church and polity in pre-norman Ireland, pp. 169, 214, n.1 for the use of the term in other saints' Lives. PLUMMER (ed.), Vitae Sanctorum Hiberniae, p. 215, §33; STOKES (ed.), Lives of Saints, p. 133.

the mouth of the Shannon in co. Clare, with St. Senán.[147] Apart from that there is Íseal Chiaráin, in co. Westmeath, a monastery where two brothers of Ciarán are said to have lived, with whom the saint stayed for a while.[148] Finally there is Inis Ainghin (Hare island on Lough Ree), where St. Ciarán was led by his stag, and which belonged to the envious presbyter Daniel. There and only there St. Ciarán is said to have founded a monastery which attracted many pious men to the island. The presbyter, jealous of Ciarán's success, intrigued to expel the saint from his island, but Ciarán reconciled him through a gift, Daniel repented and gave Inis Ainghin to Ciarán in return. Ciarán appointed Aenu (*Aengus filius Luigse*) as his successor to the abbacy in his monastery on the island,[149] and before his departure for Clonmacnois left the place to a fellow saint, namely a nephew of St. Senán.[150] Thus the one and only proper Ciaránian foundation besides Clonmacnois was donated to another saint by Ciarán himself, according to his own hagiographers.

2.3.5 Énda from Aran

Inishmore, the biggest of the Aran islands off the Galway coast, is said to have been granted to St. Énda in the early sixth century, by Aengus, king of Munster with the assistance of St. Ailbe.[151] We are told that Ciarán spent some time there after having left Clonard and before founding Clonmacnois. The island is commemorated by all the versions of Ciarán's Life as the place of what we might call the tree vision. In a dream Ciarán saw a large tree near a big river in the middle of Ireland, which was flowering and bearing fruit, the branches of which were covering all of Ireland. St. Énda was called upon to interpret the vision and he was quick to realize that the tree repre-

---

[147] PLUMMER (ed.), Vitae Sanctorum Hiberniae, I, pp. 205-208; STOKES (ed.), Lives of Saints, pp. 122-128; MACALISTER, Latin and Irish Lives, pp. 173-176.

[148] PLUMMER (ed.), Vitae Sanctorum Hiberniae, I, p. 209; STOKES (ed.), Lives of Saints, pp. 128f.; MACALISTER, Latin and Irish Lives, pp. 177f.

[149] Aena later became St. Ciarán's successor in Clonmacnois, see Appendix 1, A2.

[150] Thus the story goes according to the Irish Life and the Oxford version of Ciarán's Life. STOKES (ed.), Lives of Saints, pp. 129f.; MACALISTER, Latin and Irish Lives, pp. 179f.; compare also the annotations by Macalister (ibid., pp. 145-147).

[151] GWYNN / HADCOCK, p. 28; PLUMMER (ed.), Vitae Sanctorum Hiberniae, II, pp. 56, 66.

sented Ciarán himself, great before God and men, and that, just like the sheltering tree he would protect the whole of Ireland against demons and dangers.[152] The symbolic implications within this tree metaphor are indeed very down to earth, the idea to picture Ciarán as a tree near a river in the middle of Ireland appears as a very settled expression of the understanding of a saint as the embodiment of his foundation, i.e. Clonmacnois, at the shores of the river Shannon in the Irish midlands.

The Life of Énda comes to us in only one version, contained in the Oxford collection.[153] This *vita* sheds a slightly different light on the relationship between Ciarán and Énda, his former master. We learn first of all that Ciarán stayed for seven years in the service of Énda, and that he was the *triturator*, the thresher of the monastery. The tree vision of Ciarán is mentioned in almost the same words as in the Latin versions of Ciarán's Life. St. Énda's Life adds, however, that Ciarán left Aran at the order of Énda, that he put his *paruchia* under Énda's protection and that he suggested, that himself and his disciples should be Énda's monks for ever. Énda refused the humble offer and instead the two saints made an agreement of perpetual unity and fraternity between them.[154]

The account of another, very disturbing, vision is included in Énda's *vita*, in which the saint realized, that all the angels of Aran had left his island together with St. Ciarán. In great distress he started to fast until eventually an angel of the Lord appeared to whom Énda related all his trouble. The extraterrestial visitor assured Énda that St. Ciarán, being a very holy man, would send back all the angels to Aran and ordered Énda to stop fasting. Énda agreed on condition that God would grant him three wishes. The first that everybody who, repenting of his sins and seeking Énda's grave, should escape eternal fire, the second that whoever invokes Énda in fright-

---

[152] STOKES (ed.), Lives of Saints, p. 128; PLUMMER (ed.), Vitae Sanctorum Hiberniae, I, p. 208, §21; MACALISTER, Latin and Irish Lives, p. 177, §11. The Dublin version adds that it was on Inishmore, that Ciarán was ordained as a priest, and by order of St. Énda set out for the mainland with the prayer and blessing of all the saints on Aran.

[153] PLUMMER (ed.), Vitae Sanctorum Hiberniae, II, pp. 60-75; see SHARPE, Medieval Irish Saints' Lives, p. 393, who dates the Life in its present form to the thirteenth century.

[154] PLUMMER (ed.), Vitae Sanctorum Hiberniae, II, p. 72, §27; Ciarán performs another miracle on behalf of Énda, namely the expulsion of a beast from *Achad Draygnichi*, a place where one of Enda's disciples called Gigneus, a saint from overseas, lived as a hermit (PLUMMER [ed.], Vitae Sanctorum Hiberniae, II, p. 72, §28).

ening situations would be assisted by Jesus Christ, and the third that Énda himself would be allowed to sit at the right hand of God the father, together with the other saints. All three wishes were granted to him.[155]

A third anxiety vision of St. Énda follows, told by himself in a sermon to his monks. It happened when Ciarán was on Aran to take his monastic vows. On this occasion Énda again, saw a tree in the middle of his island, growing up high, stretching its branches to the sea. Then he saw many men climbing the tree, and the tree raised its roots and together with the men it lifted itself into the air and flew to the river Shannon, there it replanted itself. And Enda saw the same tree growing very high at its new location, so that its branches could reach the sea again. Saint Finnian happened to be on Aran at the same time, and he interpreted the vision as belonging to „our brother Ciarán, who will be the father of many congregations". And everybody was moved to tears by Énda's sermon including Ciarán himself, who then left Aran to fulfill his mission, and to found a monastery at the Shannon. This is of course a variation of the story of the tree vision as it is told earlier in the same Life and in the Lives of Ciarán.[156]

It is a small step to interpret Énda's hunger strike and anxiety as the expression of his inferiority complex towards his former pupil Ciarán. The competition for fame between St. Énda and his disciple, i.e between the church on Aran and Clonmacnois, figures prominently in St. Énda's *vita* only, whereas St. Ciarán's hagiographers have a comparatively brief and rather marginal comment on the founder of the church on Aran, as one of the former teachers of Ciarán. The saints' Lives here apparently comment on a period in which Aran had already lost its leading position in the Irish church, whereas Clonmacnois was at the height of its fame.

2.3.6 Senán of Inis Cathaig (Scattery Island)

Another incident common to all versions of St. Ciarán's Life is his visit to Inis Cathaig, or Scattery island, where the bright and holy city of St. Senán

---

[155] Ibid., p. 74, §32.

[156] PLUMMER (ed.), Vitae Sanctorum Hiberniae, II, pp. 73f., §§30-32.

was situated.[157] On his way to the island Ciarán met a poor man to whom he gave his cloak. St. Senán, who foresaw Ciarán's arrival and his nakedness, hid a cloak under his armpit and went to meet Ciarán, scolding him by saying that it was not decent for a priest to wander round without clothes. St. Ciarán on his part, foreseeing that Senán had a cloak for him, laughingly replied that his nakedness would see consolation very shortly through Senán himself. The two saints stayed together, shared communion, and made a contract of fraternity (*societas et fraternitas*) between them. The Lismore Life adds that after founding Clonmacnois St. Ciarán sent back a cloak to St. Senán on the waterway. He ordered his monks to throw it into the Shannon and the cloth arrived dry on the shores of Scattery island.

In the Dublin Life the island is described as situated at the mouth of the river Shannon, to the west in the channel of Limerick, between the regions of the Ciarraige of north Kerry and the Corco Baiscind of west Clare. It has been suggested that these two tribes formed a maritime federation controlling the Shannon estuary, and thus the access provided by the river to the midlands and Connacht.[158] Good relations with the monastic house situated at such an important strategic point were certainly essential for the economy of Clonmacnois, especially since the Shannon was a very important waterway for foreign trade in Ireland.

2.3.7 Íseal Chiaráin

A further station on the pilgrimage of St. Ciarán before he found the place of his resurrection in Clonmacnois, was Íseal Chiaráin, which the saint visited after he had left Scattery island.[159] The Irish Life mentions that the place was given to Ciarán by Cobthach son of Breccan, the grandson of

---

[157] STOKES (ed.), Lives of Saints, p. 128; PLUMMER (ed.), Vitae Sanctorum Hiberniae, I, pp. 208f.; MACALISTER, Latin and Irish Lives, p. 177, §12. The most detailed account is that in the Dublin version (PLUMMER). See also GWYNN / HADCOCK, pp. 96f.; D. F. GLEESON / A. GWYNN, A history of the diocese of Killaloe, Dublin 1961, pp. 15-23; B. Ó CÍOBHÁIN, Logainmneacha ó bharúntacht Mhaigh Fhearta. co. An Chlair - V. Inis Cathaigh, in: Dinnse-anchas 4 (1970), pp. 113-125.

[158] BYRNE, Irish Kings, p. 170.

[159] PLUMMER (ed.), Vitae Sanctorum Hiberniae, I, pp. 209f., §§23-25; STOKES (ed.), Lives of Saints, pp. 128f.; MACALISTER, Latin and Irish Lives, pp. 177f.

Maine, son of Niall Noígiallach. Moreover it was the place where Lúchran and Odran the two brothers of Ciarán are said to have lived and were buried.[160] We are told that Ciarán stayed with them as the almoner and guestmaster for a time.[161]

An incident is recorded, which happened once when Ciarán, totally absorbed by his task of welcoming newly arriving guests, accidentally left his gospel book outside in the grass. The book miraculously survived a whole night's rain, without one wet spot. The other noteworthy event in Íseal Chiaráin concerned the neighbours of the church who lived on an island in the nearby lake. With their loud and noisy behaviour they constantly disturbed the monks in their prayers. St. Ciarán solved the problem by removing the lake, the island and the people altogether, through the power of prayer. Thirdly the saint's departure from the place receives special mention by the hagiographer and differs very much from the farewell scenes with St. Énda or St. Senán. We are told that the brothers of Ciarán literally ordered him to leave because they could not bear his generosity towards the poor.[162]

Íseal Chiaráin translated as the *hospitall of st. Queran* by Mageoghagan was sometimes thought to be identical with the guesthouse in Clonmacnois.[163] However the evidence of the saints' Lives clearly shows that it was

---

[160] Stokes (ed.), Lives of Saints, p. 119, l. 3998; P. Walsh (ed.), Genealogiae Regum et Sanctorum Hiberniae, Dublin 1918, p. 109. The episodes in Íseal Chiaráin seem to have been translated and copied from the Irish Life by the thirteenth century redactor in the Dublin version (Plummer [ed.], Vitae Sanctorum Hiberniae, I, pp. 209f.).

[161] See the geneaologies in the Book of Ballymote, where Breccan is also mentioned as the one who gave Íseal Chiaráin to God and Clonmacnois (M. C. Dobbs [ed.], The genealogies of the Southern Uí Néill, in: ZCP 20 [1936], pp. 1-30, here 5).

[162] Stokes (ed.), Lives of Saints, p. 129, ll. 4327-4343; Plummer (ed.), Vitae Sanctorum Hiberniae, I, p. 210.

[163] AClon 1087, p. 184: *Isill Kieran or the hospitall of S. Queran.* O'Donovan translates Íseal Chiaráin as „St. Ciarán's lowland" and explains it, to be the name of one of the churches in Clonmacnois (O'Donovan [ed.], AFM II, p. 824 note r). In the Ordnance Survey Letters he expresses a different opinion: „I always thought and do still think, that Isil Chiarain was a tract of low-lying (Iseal) country, belonging to Clonmacnois. What could be the meaning of an Abbot of Clonmacnois purchasing the Hospital of Clonmacnois from the King of Meath? If the Book of Lecan be right, Isil Chiarain was mort-main to the Abbey since the time of ? great grandson of Maine (600); how then could the King of Meath have any claim on it? ...I do suspect that it is a blunder of Archdall's or Mageoghagan's to make Isil Chiarain the same as the Hospital house of Clonmacnois. Perhaps Mageoghagan wrote or intended to have

a separate church situated some distance from Clonmacnois. Liam Cox identified Íseal Chiaráin as Twyford, a townland in the Western parts of the parish of Ballyloughloe.[164] Ruins there as well as local tradition, testifiy to a connection between this part of Ballyloughloe parish and St. Ciarán. Moreover a sculptured cross in Twyford townland, known as Bealin cross can clearly be recognized as the work of a Clonmacnois sculptor, dating from sometime around the year 800 according to recent studies in art history.[165] It is possible that Íseal Chiaráin at one stage functioned as the guesthouse of Clonmacnois, which could well have been situated in some distance to the monastery. Also the hagiographers portrayal of St. Ciarán as the guestmaster in Íseal would make sense in such a context.[166] However, the Life also implies that the monks there were related to St. Ciarán, but no longer on extremely friendly terms with him. This episode might have found entrance in the saints' Life at the time when the church had come into possession of the Meic Cuinn na mBocht family some time during the eleventh century, which is also the time in which the Four Masters simply refer to Íseal as the church of Conn na mBocht, and Mageoghagan talks of the *family of Moylekyeran mcCon ne mboght in Isillkyeran*.[167] It has been suggested

---

written Isill Cieran or the Hospital lands of Clonmacnois? I am wearied with conjectures" (O'DONOVAN, Ordnance Survey Letters, King's county I, p. 178). A glance at the saints Lives of Ciarán could certainly have relieved O'Donovan's mind in this respect. Compare O'DONOVAN, Ordnance Survey Letters, co. Westmeath I, pp. 25-35, Letter dated 4. 9. 1837, where he describes Ballyloughloe parish as the site of Lough Luatha, the lake which dried out according to St. Ciarán's Life.

[164] L. COX, Íseal Chiaráin, the low place of St. Ciarán, where was it situated?, in: Jn. of the Old Athlone Soc. 1 (1969), pp. 6-14. Traces of the monastery are still to be found on the nineteenth century Ordnance survey map, where the site of an abbey is indicated a little north-west of the Catholic chapel near Mount Temple (Ordnance Survey, 6 inch maps, co. Westmeath, sheet 30, Dublin 1838, which I had the pleasure to consult in the Royal Irish Academy, Dawson Street, Dublin).

[165] HICKS, A Clonmacnois workshop, pp. 5-35; N. EDWARDS, The South Cross Clonmacnois, in: J. HIGGITT (ed.), Early medieval sculpture in Britain and Ireland, Oxford 1986, pp. 23-48, here 23; N. EDWARDS, The archaeology of early medieval Ireland, Philadelphia 1990, p. 64. See also H. S. CRAWFORD, Bealin Cross, Twyford, county Westmeath, in: JRSAI 37 (1907), pp. 320-322. The cross finds special mention for its unusual zoomorphic design. Its situation in the graveyard at 'Twyford House' is still given on the Ordnance Survey 6 inch Maps, co. Westmeath, sheet 29, Dublin 1838, in the Royal Irish Academy.

[166] For the guesthouse in Clonmacnois see above, p. 41.

[167] AFM 1031, AClon 1069, p. 180, on the occasion of the over-taxation of the church by the son of the king of Mide in 1072.

above, that the hostility towards St. Ciarán's brothers in Íseal Chiaráin, most apparent in the Irish Life of the saint, should be understood as a direct comment on internal politics, and to the ever increasing power of the Meic Cuinn na mBocht in Clonmacnois in the course of the eleventh century.[168]

2.3.8 Inis Ainghin, or Hare Island on Lough Ree

Finally there is Inis Ainghin in Lough Ree, the last station on Ciarán's pilgrimage before the foundation of Clonmacnois. It has been mentioned earlier as the only proper monastic foundation by St. Ciarán, apart from Clonmacnois itself.[169] At his departure from the island Ciarán is said to have given it away to Donan, a nephew of St. Senán of the Corco Baiscind. This construction of a link between Inis Ainghin on Lough Ree and Scattery island at the estuary of the Shannon possibly reflects the importance of both places as two crucial points for foreign trade in Ireland which went via Clonmacnois. Trading ships from France and Spain arriving at the west coast of Ireland, possibly stopped at Scattery island before sailing up the Shannon. The next station would have been Lough Ree, where the island Inis Ainghin might have had auxiliary functions as a harbour of Clonmacnois.

As associated churches Clonmacnois and Inis Ainghin repeatedly attracted the hostility of common enemies and were attacked simultaneously.[170] Perhaps the island also functioned as a kind of ecclesiastical conference centre for Clonmacnois, suggested by the fact that a synod under the lead of Cairpre, bishop of Clonmacnois was held there in the year 899.[171]

---

[168] See above, pp. 20f., and below, pp. 136-139.

[169] See above, p. 65. For the identification of Hare island as Inis Ainghin see O'DONOVAN, Ordnance Survey Letters, co. Westmeath I, pp. 4-25, Letters from Athlone, dated 1.9.1837. O'Donovan eventually could identify the island, but went through great trouble in doing so: „I considered these islands until I got sick of them - I dreamed of them - I gave them up...". For the islands of Lough Ree compare O'DONOVAN, Ordnance Survey Letters, co. Roscommon II, pp. 217-226, Letter dated 9.7.1839.

[170] In the year 899 the bishop of Clonmacnois was attacked by the Connachtmen on Inis Ainghin (CS 899, AFM 894; see also AU 922, CS 921; AT [1089], AFM 1089).

[171] CS 899; AFM 894.

2.3.9 Inishmacsaint

S. Ninned's church in Inismacsaint (Inis-Maige-Samh on Lough Erne, north of Devenish in county Fermanagh) appears as another ally of Clonmacnois.[172] Very little is known about the founder saint. Ninned appears, however, in a very favourable light in the Irish Life of Ciarán, as a fellow student in Clonard. We are told that Ciarán was the only one amongst St. Finnian's students willing to give his book of studies to St. Ninned, after he had arrived in Clonard.[173] Such an anecdote obviously implies that St. Ninned at one stage had profited from St. Ciarán's generosity, thus being always indebted to him. The friendship between the two saints is further elaborated in that Ciarán trusted his most precious earthly possession, his cow, to St. Ninned.[174] The message of this anecdote heavily relies on the importance of the hide of St. Ciarán's cow as a relic which guarantees direct ascent into heaven for the soul of every one who would die on it. This myth was the ground on which the salvation-bringing function of St. Ciarán's graveyard was developed from the tenth century onwards.[175] The friendship between Ciarán and Ninned therefore seems to reflect good relations between the churches of Clonmacnois and Inishmacsaint around the time of the tenth century. Links between the two churches might have been maintained via the common friend Devenish, situated a little south of Inishmacsaint, also on Lough Erne.

2.3.10 Ciarán of Saighir

Once Clonmacnois was founded the Lives of St. Ciarán are already nearing their end, since the saint is said to have survived his greatest achievement by only seven months. The only ecclesiastical foundation which was visited by Ciarán after the foundation was, according to his hagiographers, Saighir in

---

[172] RYAN, Irish monasticism, pp. 118, 124; GWYNN / HADCOCK, p. 38.

[173] STOKES (ed.), Lives of Saints, p. 123.

[174] Ibid., p. 127.

[175] See below, pp. 117f.

Ossory, the foundation of his namesake Ciarán, the Elder.[176] The story goes that Crithir, a boy of the family of Clonmacnois, fled from Ciarán to the city of Saighir, where he stayed for some time with Ciarán the Elder. Although a good boy he was bad tempered and poured the drink of the monks of Saighir over the fire and extinguished it. This was not only a holy fire, but also the only fire which existed in Saighir, and Crithir fled from the anger of Ciarán the Elder into the woods, where he was killed by the wolves. Ciarán of Clonmacnois hearing about the death of one of his men went to Saighir and asked his fellow saint to restore his disciple to life and give him back. Ciarán of Saighir responded that first of all the feet of Ciarán needed to be washed, which, however, could not be done because there was no fire to heat the water in the whole monastic city. Once Ciarán of Clonmacnois heard of the evil deed which his man had commited in Saighir he restored the holy fire by a miracle through prayer. In return Crithir was restored to life by Ciarán the Elder. Afterwards the two saints made an alliance of unity and fraternity between themselves and their successors. Ciarán the Younger blessed the foundation of Ciarán the Elder, foretelling that honour and abundant wealth would always remain in Saighir. In return Ciarán the Elder promised that power and wisdom would be perpetual properties of Clonmacnois. Ciarán then returned to Clonmacnois, together with Crithir, the boy.[177]

---

[176] The Life of Ciarán of Saighir survived in the Dublin collection, the Codex Salmanticensis and two Irish versions in the O'Clery manuscript in Brussels. Kenney assumes that although the four versions differ considerably, they go back to a common original of great antiquity, composed by a monk of Saighir himself. Local details and bias indicate a date of compilation, when Saighir was still a flourishing monastic community (KENNEY, The sources, pp. 316f.; see also J. HOGAN, St. Ciarán, Patron of Ossory, Kilkenny 1887; W. CARRIGAN, The history and antiquities of the diocese of Ossory, 4 vols., Dublin 1905, here vol. 2, pp. 12f.; GWYNN / HADCOCK, pp. 194f.).

[177] Contained in the Dublin versions of both the saint's Lives: PLUMMER (ed.), Vitae Sanctorum Hiberniae, I, pp. 212f., §30 (Ciarán of Clonmacnois); ibid., pp. 230f., §32 (Ciarán of Saighir). Likewise in the Lismore version of the Life of Ciarán of Clonmacnois (STOKES [ed.], Lives of Saints, pp. 131f.) and in the O'Clery MS Life of Ciarán of Saighir (C. PLUMMER [ed.], Bethada Náem nÉrenn: Lives of Irish Saints, 2 vols., Oxford 1922, reprint 1968, here I, pp. 110f.; II, pp. 106f.). Here the main 'hero', instead of Crithir is a certain Trichem, a rich man of Clonmacnois (*fer saidhbhir*). The version retold above is that in the Dublin version of the Life of Ciarán of Clonmacnois (PLUMMER [ed.], Vitae Sanctorum Hiberniae, I, pp. 212f.).

This story is contained in the Lives of both saints, and clearly implies mutual friendship between Saighir and Clonmacnois. The obvious need to stress the harmony and equality of the two saints might in actual fact attest to tension between the two churches. The annals, however, do not comment on links between the communities.[178] The fact, however, that the founder saint of Saighir receives such detailed attention already by the Latin hagiographers in Clonmacnois, appears to confirm the postulated early date of an original *vita* of St. Ciarán, since Saighir, portrayed as a flourishing, large and important ecclesiastical settlement seems to have lost its leading position in the Irish church at a comparatively early stage.

The Life of Ciarán of Saighir has an additional tale, in which Ciarán the Younger is rescued from serious trouble by the patron of Saighir. A certain regional king Furbicius had entrusted his treasures to Ciarán of Clonmacnois, who, as befitted a saint, distributed the riches amongst the poor. When the king saw this he got angry and made the bad treasurer his prisoner, promising freedom only on condition that Ciarán would supply him with 'seven cows without horns, and red bodies and white heads'. Ciarán got leave to find what the king desired and ran straight off to the church of his namesake in Saighir to seek assistance. It happened that at the time the two Brendans, from Birr and Clonfert, were visiting Saighir as well, and the four saints, after a miracle performed over dinner, made a fraternity pact between them. All of a sudden the seven cows came out of nowhere and Ciarán from Clonmacnois could take them to the tyrant and regain his freedom.[179] It seems the story wants to convey that the founder of Clonmacnois should be much obliged to the patron saint of Saighir. It seems to belong to the time when Saighir was about to lose its position and authority in the ecclesiastical world. The fact that Birr is explicitly mentioned as partner in the fraternity pact might point to a date as late as the eleventh century, when Saighir and Birr were united under the rule of one abbot.[180]

---

[178] CS 842, where a raid by the gentiles on the churches of Birr and Saighir is recorded, appears to be the only reference to Saighir in the Clonmacnois annals.

[179] HEIST (ed.), Vitae Sanctorum, pp. 352f., §§16-18; PLUMMER (ed.), Vitae Sanctorum Hiberniae, I, pp. 229f., §§30f.; PLUMMER (ed.), Bethada Náem nÉrenn I, p. 106; II, p. 110.

[180] AFM 1079.

2.3.11 Birr

The appearance of Brendan of Birr in this tale, as one of the partners in the fraternity pact between the holy quartet, is certainly an anomaly in the light of the St. Ciarán's Life. There, the very same saint figures as a jealous fellow disciple of Ciarán during his apprenticeship under St. Finnian of Clonard. We mentioned earlier the story about St. Finnian appointing Ciarán as the one to lead the prayers after his death, which aroused the anger and envy of all the saints present, but in particular that of St. Brendan, who became the object of a prophecy by St. Finnian, foretelling that both Brendan and Ciarán would found two churches at two streams, the size of the rivers indicating the size of the respective foundations.[181] Obviously Camcor river and the Little Brosna (sidebranches of the Shannon) at the meeting of which Birr is situated can hardly compare in size with the Shannon, the largest river in Ireland. This sounds like a polite version, to express a certain lack of sympathy between the two communities. However the annals are less polite and reveal unconcealed hostility between the two houses in the late eighth century. A battle between the community of Clonmacnois and that of Birr is mentioned in the annals under the year 770.[182]

So far the churches mentioned in the hagiographical works of St. Ciarán have been discussed. They were all situated in the extended neighbourhood of Clonmacnois. With the exception of Íseal Chiaráin and Birr, Ciarán had good relations with all of them, *fraternitas* and *óentad* forming a steady part of each of the stories. A further number of churches were associated with Clonmacnois, which will be dealt with in the final part of the chapter. Links between them and Clonmacnois are, however, only documented in the hagiographical literature concerning the other church. It seems the position of a church in the ecclesiastical hierarchy at the time determined the selection of fellow saints mentioned by its hagiographers. The Life of Ciarán itself shows a tendency to deal with the churches founded by saints somehow superior to Ciarán. It primarily defines St. Ciarán's relations with the ce-

---

[181] STOKES (ed.), Lives of Saints, p. 127.

[182] Called the battle of Máin Choise Blae (i.e. the Bog at the foot of the river Blai) AU 760, AT (759); GWYNN / HADCOCK, p. 30.

lebrities of the Irish church, such as Finnian, Ciarán of Saighir or Cóemgen of Glendalough. Obviously the need to specify the relation with inferior saints, was not as urgent - the same mechanisms might have functioned for the churches who sought St. Ciarán's friendship more than he theirs.

2.3.12 Devenish

Friendship between Devenish and Clonmacnois is claimed in the Life of St. Lasrén, alias Molaisse, the founder of Devenish. His *vita* contains a vision, in which the hagiographers in Devenish express their opinion about the position of their church, by styling their founder saint very close friend of Ciarán.[183] The story is told how Colum Cille together with some of his monks once visited Devenish. Baithene, the nephew and successor of Colum Cille had a vision there, seeing three chairs, one made of gold the other of silver and the third one made of glass. Colum Cille, 'who was like another Daniel in the interpretation of dreams', explained that the golden chair was that of Ciarán, the son of the carpenter, because of his charity which outshines all other colours. The silver chair, he said, belonged to Lasrén, who is more eloquent and learned than all the others. The glass chair, finally, was that of Colum Cille because it best compares to his fragile nature.

This story is obviously the expression of a very subjective perception of Devenish itself. The total exclusion of other prominent saints such as St. Finnian or St. Brigit and in particular the striking omission of St. Patrick point to the context of this vision within a particular ecclesiastical federation, seemingly the *paruchia* of Clonmacnois. Only as a very close associate of Ciarán, could Lasrén, i.e Devenish claim such a high position.

According to the Irish Life of Lasrén, a late medieval work, compiled from earlier sources, Devenish held lands in Connacht, in the immediate neighbourhood of Clonmacnois.[184] We are told that a certain king Áed, once gave a feast in Moycarnan. When the messenger of St. Lasrén came there, he was refused ale and meat by the royal steward. The messenger caused food and drink to vanish on the spot, so that the banquet was ruined. The

---

[183] PLUMMER (ed.), Vitae Sanctorum Hiberniae, II, p. 139, §32.

[184] Contained in a sixteenth century MS Additional 18205 in the British Library. Edited by S. H. O'GRADY, Silva Gadelica, London 1892, pp. 17-37.

king, to make up for the bad behaviour of his steward offered the lands of Moycarnan to Lasrén.[185] Since the lands in Moycarnan, now represented by the parish of Moore, west of the Shannon, opposite Clonmacnois, apparently belonged to Clonmacnois, the claims of Devenish seem again rather far-fetched.[186]

The annals attest to links between Devenish and Clonmacnois during the ninth century, for the first time around the year 869, when the abbot of Clonmacnois was also leader of the church in Devenish. Later in the century an abbot of Devenish also functioned as *tanaisi* of Clonmacnois. He was murdered in very unlucky circumstances, possibly in his function as vice-abbot, who was charged with responsibility for levying service and taxes.[187]

2.3.13 Inishkeen

Another church which at some stage was closely linked with Clonmacnois was Inishkeen, the church of St. Daig mac Cairill, situated at the border between Louth and Monaghan, some four miles north west of the church of Louth. Previously Kenney and more recently McCone have pointed to Inishkeen as a church which acknowledged the authority of Clonmacnois, at least in the early period, at the time of the composition of the *vita* of Daig.[188]

The Codex Salmanticensis contains three unique stories, linking Daig mac Cairill with Ciarán of Clonmacnois.[189] Daig is said to have spent his

---

[185] Ibid., p. 28.

[186] For St. Ciarán's lands west of the Shannon, see below, pp. 175-179.

[187] See Appendix 1, A40 (d.869); vA 14 (d.896). Máel Achaid was accused for having killed the son of the king of Delbna, and was murdered by the Delbna in revenge.

[188] KENNEY, The sources, pp. 383f.; more recently McCONE, Clones and her neighbours, p. 325; I wish to thank Dr Colmán ETCHINGHAM, who allowed me to read the section on Inishkeen, from his unpublished work on the paruchia of Armagh, on which my presentation largely relies.

[189] HEIST (ed.), Vitae Sanctorum, p. 390, §4, Mochta of Louth prophesies that Daig's foundation would be subject to Ciarán of Clonmacnois and not to him. See also pp. 390f., §§7f., when Daig went to Clonmacnois he is welcomed by Ciarán, prostrates himself on the ground, and willingly undertakes subjection and humility before Ciarán. See also pp. 392f., §16, for the incident with the nuns.

youth in Louth, the foundation of St. Mochta, who at some stage prophesied
that the boy would found a beautiful church not far north from Louth.
Moreover Mochta had the vision of how Daig was given by God into the
hand of a yet unborn saint, namely Ciarán of Clonmacnois, and therefore
would not be under his own overlordship, which is to say subject to the
authority of Louth. The prophecy is fulfilled when Daig later in his life went
to Clonmacnois where he was welcomed by Ciarán and formally acknow-
leged the authority of Ciarán over him by a kind of ceremonial subjection.[190] After some time and at the order of Ciarán, Daig returned to his
home territory to found Inishkeen. The fame of Daig's sanctity spread all
over Ireland, so that many came to live under his rule. Amongst them were
three virgins, Cunnea, Lassara (Daig's sister) and Dulvina. When the abbot
of Clonmacnois learned this news he sent messengers to Inishkeen, forbid-
ding Daig to accept women in his community. The messengers from Clonmacnois, however, when they arrived in Inishkeen were convinced of the
rightness of Daig's conduct through the humility and deeds of the three virgins themselves.[191] It has been suggested by Colmán Etchingham that this
incident might reflect actual control, exercised from Clonmacnois over the
community in Inishkeen.[192] Neither the Life of Ciarán, nor the annals, indicate connections between the two houses. However the appearance of two
men from the Ciannachta Breg, who also supplied officials in Inishkeen, in
the abbacy of Clonmacnois in the eighth century might have been a result of
the alliance between the two churches.[193] It seems possible that other families, as for example the 'Conaillech' clan, surnamed after their origin with
the Conaille Muirthemne, also migrated to Clonmacnois at a time when its
relations with Inishkeen, also situated in the territory of the Conaille
Muirthemne, were very close.[194] Moreover it has been suggested that the
stress on Daig's submission to Clonmacnois, was in the first place an ex-

---

[190] HEIST (ed.), Vitae Sanctorum, p. 391, §7.

[191] Ibid., p. 392, §16.

[192] See above, n. 188.

[193] See Appendix 1, A19 (d.737), A33 (d.794).

[194] By the tenth century Inishkeen was clearly perceived as a church associated with the
Conaille Muirthemne. Matudán mac Áeda, king of the Ulaid, attacked Inishkeen on a campaign against the Conaille (AFM 949). The 'Conaillech' family appears for the first time in
leading office in Clonmacnois in the early tenth century (see A49).

pression of the struggle for exemption from the authority of the nearby monasteries of Louth and Armagh.[195]

2.3.14 Bangor

In the Life of Daig mac Cairill, Comgall, founder of Bangor, is acknowledged as the superior of St. Daig, before his submission to St. Ciarán's authority.[196] The Dublin version of the Life of Comgall claims a genealogical link between Ciarán of Clonmacnois and Comgall.[197] Again later in Comgall's Life he is said to have been in Clonmacnois, and was ordained there as a deacon by a certain bishop Lugidus.[198]

2.3.15 Roscrea

Both extant versions of the Life of St. Cronán of Roscrea contain evidence for links with Clonmacnois.[199] Cronán is said to have stayed in the community of Clonmacnois for a time. A blessing by the abbot of Clonmacnois foretelling that riches and charity would rule in the future foundation of Cronán is part of an episode which took place in Clonmacnois.[200] Another

---

[195] McCone, Clones and her neighbours, p. 325.

[196] Heist (ed.), Vitae Sanctorum, p. 391, §7. Before his time in Clonmacnois Daig was in Bangor with St. Comgall and from there set out to meet Ciarán in Clonmacnois. The story goes, that on his way from Bangor to Clonmacnois Daig did not take any food or drink, because according to his reasoning he could not see 'How without a head the body could consume any food?' Comgall founded Bangor in 555 or 559, and is said to have died in 602.

[197] Plummer (ed.), Vitae Sanctorum Hiberniae, II, p. 3, §1. One of the manuscripts gives an extensive version of Comgall's pedigree, going back to a certain Rudraige, adding in a note that it is here where Brendan, Ciarán and Comgall (i.e. their pedigree) meet.

[198] Plummer (ed.), Vitae Sanctorum Hiberniae, II, p. 6, §11 Lugidus could be Ciarán's brother Lúchran, named Luccenus in the Dublin version of Ciarán's Life (Plummer [ed.], Vitae Sanctorum Hiberniae, I, p. 200, §1).

[199] One version is preserved in the Dublin collection, the other in the Codex Salmanticensis. Kenney assumes that the original was written at Roscrea sometime in the eleventh or first half of the twelfth century (Kenney, The sources, pp. 460f.; see also Sharpe, Medieval Irish Saints' Lives, p. 393).

[200] Heist (ed.), Vitae Sanctorum, p. 275, §4; Plummer (ed.), Vitae Sanctorum Hiberniae, II, p. 23, §5. Cronán together with an otherwise unknown St. Molan stayed in the community of

story is told about how a leper came to Cronán to be cured, whilst he was in Clonmacnois. Since the saint was deeply involved in prayer the leper did not want to disturb him, and instead washed himself with the rain water which ran from the roof of the house in which Cronán was praying. The leper was cured by the power of Cronán, transmitted through the water.[201]

Roscrea, in north-eastern Tipperary was the principal church of Elé. Cronán its founder is, however, nowhere mentioned in the annals. Colgan in a note to his 'Acta Sanctorum Hiberniae' reckons that he lived some time between the year 571 and 636.[202] As in the case of Devenish, links between the two ecclesiastical settlements, claimed in the hagiographical works, are confirmed by evidence from the annals. Áedán, an abbot of Roscrea, according to the Four Masters, was also *prióir* in Clonmacnois in the first half of the ninth century.[203]

2.3.16 Fore

Even though the *vita* of the founder of the church of Fore in Westmeath does not comment on a relation between Fechin and Ciarán, links between the two foundations are testified to in the annals.[204] A steady tradition of officials from Fore was kept in Clonmacnois during the ninth century, in which four of the ten vice-abbots of Clonmacnois had links with Fore.[205]

Ciarán near Clonmacnois. St. Cronán carried with him the remains of his lunch (*reliquias sui prandii*) and gave them to the poor; whereas St. Molan left his in the community. The abbot, seeing this is made saying, „this will be the difference between the two places of the two saints: at the place of St. Cronán riches and charity will be superfluous, whereas at the other place the rule will always be kept."

[201] HEIST (ed.), Vitae Sanctorum, pp. 275f., §5; PLUMMER (ed.), Vitae Sanctorum Hiberniae, II, p. 24, §6.

[202] Colgan, Acta Sanctorvm, p. 304 n. 11 and 18. Colgan deduces the dates for Cronán's floruit based on references to him in Mo-Chuda's Life and the dates for Mo-Chuda given by the Four Masters. Many thanks to Dr K. Simms, who pointed this reference out to me. See also GWYNN / HADCOCK, pp. 43, 95f.

[203] See Appendix 1, vA7.

[204] PLUMMER (ed.), Vitae Sanctorum Hiberniae, II, pp. 76-86; also STOKES (ed.), Betha Féchin Fabair. The Life of Féchin of Fore, in: Revue Celtique 12 (1891), pp. 318-353.

[205] Possibly they came from one family. Vice-abbot Cumuscach son of Aengus, died in 835; a certain Máel Mide, son of Cumuscach died as holder of the same office in 871. His next but

According to a tale contained in Mageoghagan's translation of the Annals of Clonmacnois a certain *Lowna*, or *Loway* was parish priest in Clonmacnois during the abbacy of Aenu, Ciarán's direct successor. He was actively involved in curing King Diarmait mac Cerbaill from deafness, with the help of St. Ciarán's bell. After his time in Clonmacnois Lowna went on to the church of Fore where he stayed, and with him went the bell of St. Ciarán, which henceforward was kept in Fore.[206] This tradition of friendly relations between the two churches apparently came to an end in the early tenth century when vice-abbot Flann Fobair was forced to resign his office in Clonmacnois, and returned to Fore in the year 923.[207] Fore was situated in the territory of the Caílle Follamain, a royal branch of the Southern Uí Néill. They were however excluded from the kingship of Mide from the second half of the eighth century onwards.[208] The community of St. Fechin, aware of the loss of power of their secular patrons, probably saw one means by which to maintain their position in a rapprochement with Clonmacnois. By the time of the tenth century Clonmacnois had however become, together with Clonard, the central church in Mide, subject to the kings of the Clann Cholmáin. It is possible that the break with Fore followed out of the growing links with Clonard. Colmán Conaillech, the abbot at the time when Flann Fobair resigned, originally came from Clonard. The changing ecclesiastical alliance was one result of the changes in the secular power balance in Mide. The Clann Cholmáin as the leading dynasty in Mide from the tenth century onwards actively promoted a brotherly union between the successors of St. Finnian and St. Ciarán, whereas St. Fechin's church in the territory of the Caílle Follamain was outside their sphere of interest.

one successor in office was Cormac, who was princeps of Fore at the same time. He died in 891, and was succeeded as vice-abbot in Clonmacnois by Fergus son of Máel Michil (d.894). See Appendix 1, vA5, vA9, vA11, vA16.

[206] AClon, pp. 82f.

[207] Flann died happily as a bishop and anchorite in Fore (AU 930). See Appendix 1, vA16. There is one more bishop of Clonmacnois who was abbot of Fore as well in the late tenth century (B16).

[208] See BYRNE, Irish Kings, pp. 90, 116.

2.3.17 Killare

An unnamed nunnery is mentioned as a cell under the cure of Ciarán in the
vita of Áed mac Bricc of Killare in Westmeath.[209] Here Áed mac Bricc figures as an antagonist to Ciarán's authority over the church of the nuns. According to the Salamanca version of his *vita*, he once came to the *hospitum*
of the virgins who were friends with Ciarán. The nuns fed Áed a meal which
was originally prepared for Ciarán, who turned up as soon as Áed had finished with the little refreshment. Áed, seeing the virgins in great fear of
Ciarán, rescued the situation by a miracle and transformed the bones and
leftovers from his tea back into a delicious and complete meal ready to be
eaten by the approaching Ciarán.[210]

Killare, the church of St. Áed, was situated in what is now county Westmeath. The tale here seems to be a rather humorous and critical comment on
the relationship between Clonmacnois and the churches under its authority.
Ciarán's right to a proper meal at his arrival in the convent, reflects on food
and drink, possibly feasting (*cáe, coinnem*), as part of a dependency's obligation towards its ecclesiastical overlord.

2.3.18 Terryglass

Another subversive comment on Clonmacnois' claims to authority over
other churches is preserved in the *vita* of St. Columban, the founder of Terryglass.[211] He is said to have died and been buried in Cluain Hi, a now un-

---

[209] HEIST (ed.), Vitae Sanctorum, p. 174, §20: *que erant amice sancto Kerano artificis filio*;
PLUMMER (ed.), Vitae Sanctorum Hiberniae, I, pp. 34f., §15: *que erant sub cura sancti
Cyarani abbatis.*

[210] For Killare see GWYNN / HADCOCK, p. 392; Kenney dates the Life of Áed mac Bricc fairly
late, around the twelfth century (KENNEY, The sources, p. 393). A similar episode is contained in the C and S version of the Irish Life of Colum Cille, when the saint allowed one of
his workmen, a former warrior, to eat as much as he was used to when still a fighting man,
which was no less than the whole of the ox just in preparation. In order to feed the rest of his
workmen, Colum Cille had the ox-bones reassembled and through his blessing restored their
flesh and thus mde them fit to give another meal (HERBERT, Iona, Kells, and Derry, p. 239,
who dates the Life into the twelfth century [pp. 188-193]).

[211] HEIST (ed.), Vitae Sanctorum, pp. 231-233, §§28f.

known location somewhere near Clonard. Nadcuimius (Nathcheime) his
successor, wanted to transfer the relics of the founder saint to Terryglass,
where Columban wished the place of his resurrection to be. But the Uí Néill
of Mide were eager to retain the relics for themselves. Nathcheime therefore
took them secretly, hiding them in one of twelve wagons loaded with corn.
Six of the wagons returned to Terryglass via Leinster, the other six including the relics returned through the territory of the Uí Néill. They stayed
overnight in the guesthouse (*castellum hospitum*, i.e. the *Lis oiged* in the
annals) of Clonmacnois. During the night flames were seen at the guesthouse, the brothers jumped out of their beds to extinguish the fire, but when
they arrived everything was calm, quiet and dark. This happened three times
in a row. Finally Aengus (i.e Aenu, St. Ciarán's direct successor) the abbot
of the city, called Nadcuimius to account, who knowing that the abbot of
Clonmacnois was a man filled with the fear of God revealed his secret.
Aenu sank to the ground, lifted his arms and thanked God, for having
brought such a treasure to his monastery. Nadcuimius had a hard time per-
suading the abbot of Clonmacnois not to insist on keeping the relics. Only
after he had promised that the name of Aenu's master Ciarán would come
before the name of his own master Columba in the Book of offerings
(*librum offerendi*) did Aenu allow him to take the relics with him.

The incident is said to have happened in the late sixth century.[212] The
compilation took place at a time when someone afraid of the Southern Uí
Néill could find shelter and a bed for a night in Clonmacnois. It should
therefore possibly be regarded as an early composition, predating the ninth
century, when Clonmacnois gradually became close friend to the Clann
Cholmáin kings of Mide.[213] The text apart from demonstrating the immense
value of relics, also criticises a certain greed for spiritual treasures in Clon-

---

[212] Nathcheime, alias Nadcuimius died as abbot of Terryglass in 584. Oengus the abbot of
Clonmacnois was Ciarán's immediate successor Aenu moccu Loígse who died in 570 (AU);
see Appendix 1, A2.

[213] Kenney recognizes an element of antiquity in the Life of Colmán, but dates the produc-
tion as a whole 'rather late' (KENNEY, The sources, pp. 385f.). SHARPE regards the text as an
original compilation, belonging to the eighth century (SHARPE, Medieval Irish Saints' Lives,
pp. 311ff., 392). For Terryglass see GWYNN / HADCOCK, p. 45; GLEESON / GWYNN, A history
of the diocese of Killaloe, pp. 36-40.

macnois, which would compare to the polemic tale about the lack of relics in Clonmacnois contained in the Tripartite Life of Patrick.[214]

Columban, a disciple of Colmán Cúle of Clonkeen and of Finnian of Clonard, founded several churches, the most important being Clonenagh, Iniscaltra and Terryglass. Terryglass, with Tallaght and Finglas was one of the leading centres of the Céili Dé movement.[215] Links between the churches might have resulted out of the contact maintained amongst the Céili Dé communities in the various foundations. Connmach, abbot of Clonmacnois in the late ninth century is said to have come from the 'Cenél Eachach Gall', which should perhaps be read as the 'familia of Echar Gabul', referring to a church of this name in Leinster which is said to have been founded by St. Columban of Terryglass.[216]

2.3.19 Drumlane and Rossinver

Links between the two main churches in the territory of Bréifne existed according to the hagiographers of St. Maedóc, the founder saint of Drumlane and Rossinver. In the Dublin version of his Life we are told that at some stage St. Maedóc went to Clonmacnois to bind his alliance and covenant with Ciarán.[217] The passage might preserve a genuine tradition concerning an early affiliation of St. Maedóc's churches in Bréifne with Clonmacnois.

2.3.20 Lemanaghan (*Liathmancháin*) and Gallen

There are two more churches in the immediate neighbourhood of Clonmacnois which also belonged to St. Ciarán's sphere of influence. One is Liathmancháin, the founder of which is sometimes claimed to have been a

---

[214] See above, p. 54f.

[215] Máel Dithruib, a monk of Terryglass, and prominent disciple of Máel Ruanaid of Tallaght, died in the year 840 (AFM).

[216] HEIST (ed.), Vitae Sanctorum, p. 228, §12. The location of Echar Gabul, or Etar Gabul has not been identified. See Appendix 1, A39 (d.868).

[217] PLUMMER (ed.), Bethada Náem nÉrenn, I, p. 251.

Welshman, or, alternatively a brother of Ciarán.[218] The lands of Liathmancháin were according to a gloss in the Clonmacnois annals given to
Clonmacnois by the ultimate ancestor of the Síl nÁedo Sláine, a branch of
the Southern Uí Néill.[219] The dynasty was excluded from the kingship from
the late seventh century onwards, but again provided a king of Tara in the
mid-tenth century, which seems to be a very suitable time for the insertion
of the gloss in the Clonmacnois annals.

Links between Clonmacnois and Gallen, the church neighbouring Liathmancháin to the south-west, seem to have existed in the early ninth century,
when Gallen was attacked, seemingly as an ally of Clonmacnois, by the king
of Munster.[220] Its patron saint Cólman Brit, otherwise known as Mo Chonnóc was at some stage venerated at Glendalough.[221] The church which is
also referred to as *Galinne na mBretan*, has a tradition as a Welsh foundation. A number of entries, relating affairs from Wales, were inserted in the
Clonmacnois chronicles between the years 911 and 950. The information
might have reached Clonmacnois via its ally Gallen.[222]

2.3.21 Kilmore (*Cell Mór Mag Enir*)

Another of the dependencies of Clonmacnois was a church called Kilmore.
We do know that the church was under the secular authority of the king of
Mide, therefore situated somewhere in his kingdom. In the early twelfth
century Kilmore became a bone of contention between the king of Mide and
the community in Clonmacnois, who eventually fasted against the king, in

---

[218] AFM 664, AClon 661, p. 107. O'DONOVAN, Ordnance Survey Letters, Kings county I, p.
221.

[219] Namely after their victory in the battle of Carn Conaill (CS 646; AT [649]; AClon 642, p.
104; AFM 645; AU 649).

[220] AU 823.9; CS 823. For the political background of these attacks see below, pp. 97f.,
especially 96, n.33. GWYNN / HADCOCK, p. 176; J. WARE, De Hibernia et Antiquitatibus ejus,
London 1654, p. 161.

[221] BYRNE, Irish Kings, p. 221. A. Mac Shamhráin pointed out that Mo Chonnóc (clearly
identical with Colmán Brit of Gallen), appears as one of the saints associated with Cóemgen
of Glendalough in the litany of Irish saints. He doubts however the historicity of this association (MAC SHAMHRÁIN, Church and Polity, pp. 124, 174f.)

[222] DUMVILLE / GRABOWSKI, Chronicles and annals, pp. 209-226.

order to obtain immunity, i.e. freedom from secular taxation (*saoire*) for their dependency Kilmore.[223]

2.3.22 *Tamnuch, Cellola Toch* and *Dumech*

These were three churches in Connacht, belonging to the paruchia of Clonmacnois as early as the late seventh century, according to the witness of Tirechán.[224] *Tamnuch* in the territory of the Uí Ailella is the modern Tawnagh in county Sligo, north of Lough Arrow, near Riverstown.[225] *Dumech* also in the territory of the Uí Ailello seems to be Shankill in the former barony of Tirerrill, county Sligo.[226] *Cellola Toch* near the well of Slán, in the territory of the Corcu Teimne was probably situated in Aglish parish, some three miles south-west of Turlough, in county Mayo.[227] Tirechán states that these churches originally belonged to Armagh, but more recently had come under the authority of Clonmacnois. He also seems to suggest that the ecclesiastical overlordship of Armagh was much more agreeable with these churches, in stating that the people of the church of *Cellola Toch* suffered hardship under Clonmacnois government.[228] Links between Clonmacnois and the northern parts of Connacht are also attested in the artistic field.

---

[223] AT (1108) where the name of the church is given as *Cilli Moire i Muig in fhir*, i.e. 'Cell mor in the plain of the man'. See also CS 1104 (recte 1108). Probably the same as *Ceall Mor Muighi Ainir, Kell Mór of Mag Enir*, mentioned elsewhere in AU 874.5.

[224] BIELER (ed.), The Patrician texts, pp. 142f., §25.2 for *Tamnuch* and the *familia Dumiche* or *Dumech*; pp. 154f., §39.8 and pp. 160f., §47.4 for *Cellola Toch*.

[225] K. W. NICHOLLS, Some Patrician sites of eastern Connacht, in: Dinnseanchas 5 (1972), pp. 114-118, here 114 n.5.

[226] See also BIELER (ed.), The Patrician texts, pp. 140f., §23.

[227] See ibid., pp. 152f., §39, and p. 254 n.2, for *Corcu Temne*, and *Findmag* within it. *Slán Findmag* has been identified by K. W. NICHOLLS with a ruined church in Ballynew townland in Aglish parish, former barony Carra, in county Mayo (K. W. NICHOLLS, Tobar Finnmhuighe - Slán Pádraig, in: Dinnseanchas 2 (1966/67), pp. 97f. *Cellola Toch* is described by Tirchán as being situated in the territory of the Corcu Theimne, *Temenrige in Cerae ... prope fontem Slán*, and must thus have been somewhere near Ballynew in Aglish parish. Many thanks to Dr Colmán Etchingham who kindly drew my attention to this reference for the identification of the placename.

[228] BIELER (ed.), The Patrician texts, pp. 160f., §47.4: *et est locus eorum cum familia Clono et ingemescunt uiri loci illius*.

A cruxifiction plaque, found in county Mayo, in the previous century, has a close resemblance, both in style and craftsmenship, to a cruxifiction plaque found in Clonmacnois.[229]

2.3.23 Ailech Mór.

Also in the Tripartite Life a tale is contained according to which one Cormac, the son of Énda in Carn Fiachach was offered to Ciarán by his father. He was reared in the territory of *Enda Artech*, that is to say (in the church of?) bishop Domnall in Ailech Mór, which the community of Clonmacnois is said to have taken away from the authority of Armagh (*furóxail muintir Cluana macc Noiss*).[230] This was also a church in Connacht, possibly north county Roscommon, somewhere in the plain of Artech, south of Lough Gara, where a number of officials in Clonmacnois came from in the early period.

2.3.24 Some unidentified churches in Mide

Further churches in Mide belonged under the ecclesiastical authority of Clonmacnois according to the witness of the Tripartite Life of Patrick, possibly testifying to the situation in the tenth century.[231]

First of all there is *Caill hUallech*, the church of Lonan son of Senach, and of Rígell, his mother. It was possibly situated somewhere near Donnaghmore, in Navan, south-east of Kells, where Patrick is said to have stayed before coming to Senán's church.[232] The church, originally under Patrick's authority, was obtained by Clonmacnois, who later exchanged it

---

[229] P. HARBISON, A lost cruxifixion plaque of Clonmacnoise type found in county Mayo, in: H. MURTAGH (ed.), Irish Midland Studies. Essays in commemoration of N. W. English, Athlone 1980, pp. 24-38.

[230] STOKES (ed.), Tripartite Life, p. 80; GWYNN / HADCOCK, p. 372.

[231] For the dating of the Tripartite Life compare above, p. 54 n.103.

[232] Perhaps somewhere near the church of Fennor (a little north-east of Donnaghmore), the airchinnech of which in the early eleventh century was a priest from Clonmacnois (see Appendix 1, P8).

with the community of Clonard for Cell Lothair in Brega (*Cill Lothair i mBregaib*) and Cluain Alad Deirg in the west (*Cluain Alad Deirg tiar*).[233]

Also there is the church *Imliuch Sescainn*, described as situated near *Tech Laisrén* on the shores of Lough Aininne. There, we are told, lived Molue, a pilgrim of the Britons, one of Patrick's household (*do muintir Pátraic*). Again we are told that the community of Clonmacnois obtained authority over the church (*fordosrola muintir Clúana ma Nóis*).[234] A church named *Imbliuch Sescinn* is mentioned as a Patrician foundation in the *notulae*, a kind of incomplete index to the Patrician works, probably written sometime in the first half of the ninth century.[235] It has been identified as Imlech, or Emlagh, near Lough Ennel, county Westmeath.[236]

2.3.25 Kinneigh

This seems to have been a church in Mide. King Flann Sinna died somewhere near the hill of Tara according to the Four Masters. The Chronicon names Kinneigh as the place where this king died and we are also informed, that the church in which Flann Sinna died belonged to the family of Clonmacnois (*Cind eich muintire Cluana)*. We might conclude that the church of Kinneigh was situated somewhere near the hill of Tara.).[237] There is of course a very symbolic meaning, contained in the royal choice concerning the place of death. Kinneigh was associated with Clonmacnois, the burial ground of the Christian kings of Ireland, it was however also situated close to the ancient Tara, where the mythological Irish kings and heroes used to be buried.

---

[233] STOKES (ed.), Tripartite Life, p. 76.

[234] Ibid., p. 78; Tech Laisrén in the south is the place were Patrick baptised the men of Mide. There is also a well and he left two virgins, named Bice and Lugaid.

[235] BIELER, The Patrician texts, p. 180, §19; see ibid., pp. 49-52 for the nature and dating of the *notulae*.

[236] According to HOGAN, St. Ciarán, Patron of Ossory, p. 260, *Imliuch* could possibly be related to, or somewhere near *Imlech-forderach*, where an abbot of Clonmacnois in the early eleventh century is said to have come from (A61).

[237] CS 915; AFM 914; AU 916. A battle fought in Kinneigh in the sixth century is recorded in the annals (CS 528, AT [532], AU 533.3).

Since the churches belonging to the ecclesiastical authority of Clonmacnois, are known to us by more or less incidental references, scattered in
different sources, we must assume there are more of them still to be discovered. However, the above-listed communities give an impression of the extent of St. Ciarán's sphere of influence. It was not confined to lands and
churches in the neighbourhood of Clonmacnois, but included territories
situated as far east as county Louth. The two churches in county Fermangh
probably constituted the northern extremities of the *paruchia*, which also
extended to the north-western parts of Connacht in county Sligo. Scattery
Island and Roscrea appear as the most southern foundations for which
claims to authority were made by Clonmacnois.

So far we looked at the internal organization of the church of Clonmacnois. It appears to have been an ecclesiastical estate, under the authority of a
bishop, but governed and administered by the abbot, and various other officials, in charge of individual tasks. We have seen that rulership was exercised by several families, ecclesiastical dynasties who lived in Clonmacnois,
as their home town so to speak. They provided leading officials in the ecclesiastical settlement over generations. Finally the churches affiliated to
Clonmacnois were looked at. Unlike other churches who claimed authority
over their dependencies by right of a common founder, Clonmacnois could
not make recourse to St. Ciarán's activities as a founder of many churches.
Instead St. Ciarán had friends all over Ireland, in Connacht, Leinster, the
northern parts of Munster, in Mide and Bréifne, as well as in Ulster, especially in the area of what is now county Louth.

In the following chapter the political history of the church of Clonmacnois will be discussed, including the relationship with the neighbouring
kingdoms and tribes, and the interaction between Clonmacnois as an ecclesiastical power and its secular counterparts.

To talk about church and polity obviously presupposes a straightforward division between ecclesiastical and secular power. It has been argued above that the supposed monastery of Clonmacnois was in fact a large ecclesiastical estate, under the headship of a bishop, ruled over by the abbot, also called *princeps* or *comarba*. This functionary would often have been a layman, who governed the settlement and its lands. The temporal or secular dimension, its function as a landholding unit, exercising authority over lands and people seems to outweigh the merely spiritual aspects of the church. The question therefore is, whether the distinction between the secular and the ecclesiastical or spiritual is a valid concept underlying an analysis of political history in medieval Ireland. A strong argument in favour of the division is that the contemporary medieval writers had no problems with these categories. Their notion of St. Ciarán's power and rights, his property and his community, is quite distinct from that of the power of any secular lord. Even though a secular ruler might occasionally do what is pleasing to God or even act on behalf of God or a saint, St. Ciarán himself, and therefore his community and his successors, enjoy constant and direct divine support. In making the distinction between the divine ecclesiastical world and that of profane politics we are therefore only being true to the understanding of affairs by the contemporary historians and hagiographers. In fact it seems that spiritual power, exclusively held by the church, was made an implement, used as a powerful weapon in the church's participation in secular politics. The king who raided the territory of his secular neighbour would have to reckon with a military counter-attack; the one who raided the estate of Clonmacnois would meet with St. Ciarán's forces, which not only existed in, say the army of St. Ciarán's friend, but could also mean things like immediate death, illness or loss of eternal life. The fact that Clonmacnois participated in secular politics, and of course constituted a significant secular power factor, did not impair its position as a saintly foundation, invested with spiritual authority. On the contrary, spiritual authority was the means by which secular power was claimed and in fact held.

Et clara ac sancta ciuitatis in ipso loco in honore sancti Ciaráni creuit, cuius nomen Cluain meic Nois vocatur; que est in occidentali plaga regionis Nepotum Neill super ripam orientalem fluminis Synna, contra provinchiam Connactorum; in qua siue reges siue duces nepotum Neill et Connactorum apud sanctum Kiaranum sepeliuntur.

Flumen enim Synna, quod est fructiferum ualde in diuersis piscibus, regiones Neill, id
est Midhi, et provinchiam Connactorum diuidit.[1]

Vital for its political role was the geographical situation of Clonmacnois.
The Dublin version of St. Ciarán's Life here gives a description of the localities, pointing out three features essential for Clonmacnois' history and
development: Clonmacnois was situated at the western extremities of the
territory of the Southern Uí Néill, it was on the border between the kingdom
of Mide and the province of Connacht, and finally it lay on the river Shannon, which, as explicitly stated by the author, was very rich in fish. The first
aspect concerns the political affiliation with the kingdom of Mide. Clonmacnois was founded in Delbna Ethra, a territory at the western fringe of
the kingdom of Mide, ruled by the Cenél Fiachach, a branch of the Southern
Uí Néill.[2] St. Ciarán's foundation therefore belonged to the territory under
the secular authority of the Southern Uí Néill kings of Tara. The hagiographer also points out the immediate neighbourhood of the province of Connacht. The function of Clonmacnois as a burial ground for kings and lords
from both regions is explained as an outcome of this border position between the two kingdoms. Clonmacnois was not, like Clonard for example,
central to any medieval Irish kingdom. This seems to have been the main
reason for the fact that, as Ryan observed, Clonmacnois never became a
direct satellite of one particular secular dynasty or power.[3] Instead, all the
neighbouring states and dynasties, the various branches of the Southern Uí
Néill as well as the kings and subkings of Connacht, like the Uí Briúin, the
Uí Fiachrach, the Uí Maine and later the lords of Bréifne as well as the
kings of Munster, took an interest in and sought the alliance with St. Ciarán,
as soon as their political ambitions demanded that they should. A final observation of the hagiographer concerned the economic foundations of St.
Ciarán's settlement. He points to the river Shannon as a rich fishing ground,
indicating its important role as a natural source of food supply for the monastery. Moreover, the river was one of the preconditions for trading, both
home- and foreign trade, thus guaranteeing a certain degree of economic
independence for the settlement. Apart from that, the river provided a link
of communication with those churches and people situated up and down the

---

1   PLUMMER (ed.), Vitae Sanctorum Hiberniae, I, p. 211, §28.

2   RYAN, The abbatial succession, p. 492.

3   RYAN, The abbatial succession, p. 507.

Shannon. Furthermore Clonmacnois was situated at one of the main roads in Medieval Ireland, the great Road, an tSlighe Mhór, leading from Dublin to the west coast, right through central Ireland.[4] Sufficient means of transport together with nearby natural resources of food supply were essential for the maintainance of the community, and for its relative economic independence.

Apart from the annals, the most important source of information for links between Clonmacnois and its secular neighbours is the hagiographical saga-tradition which developed around St. Ciarán over the centuries. As we have said earlier friendly relations between one particular secular dynasty and the church of St. Ciarán found expression in hagiographical tales. Alleged past links are claimed, such as for example cordial friendship between one of the ancestors of the dynasty and the founder saint of Clonmacnois. In general such a friendship relies on a miracle performed by Ciarán for the benefit of the ancestor of the dynasty, who in return offers great gifts to Ciarán and, even more important, his successors. These stories reflect on periods of secular patronage and clearly have a function as means of propaganda. Some of these tales are preserved in the Lives of St. Ciarán, either as consistent stories, like that of the foundation of Clonmacnois with the assistance of the king of Mide, or as more hidden hints, such as the marginal mention of over-taxation in the kingdom of Mide, which caused Ciarán's parents to leave the country. Those stories and remarks need to be coordinated with (and often serve to identify) the various strata of the hagiographical texts and their dates of composition or redaction.[5] Ideally they can be recognized or interpreted as a reflection of a particular political constellation, prevailing at a particular period. A further source of information are the Clonmacnois chronicles. The Chronicon Scotorum in particular has a number of additional remarks, which, although fragmentary in character, give some background information about the relation between secular powers and Clonmacnois not contained elsewhere.[6] A substantial body of tales is preserved

---

[4] C. Ó Lochlainn, Roadways in ancient Ireland, in: J. Ryan (ed.), Féil-scríbhinn Eóin Mhic Néill. Essays and Studies presented to Professor Eoin MacNeill, Dublin 1940, pp. 465-474, here 471.

[5] See above, pp. 17-22 for an attempt to date the various versions of Ciarán's Life. Compare Macalister, Latin and Irish Lives, pp. 1-14, and annotations on pp. 98-171; also Sharpe, Medieval Irish Saints' Lives, pp. 291f., 391.

[6] E.g. CS 904 (recte 900) the apparition of the spirit of Máel Sechnaill, son of Máel Ruanaid; CS 827 the installation of an external vice-abbot from Munster.

in late medieval collections of hagiographical saga tales, scattered in various manuscripts.[7] The Book of Uí Maine preserved the memory of the friendship between Cairpre, the ultimate ancestor of the Uí Maine and St. Ciarán.[8] Further material seems to have been incorporated by Mageoghagan,[9] and by the Four Masters in their seventeenth century compilations from earlier annals.[10] No original documents, such as foundation charters or grants by secular lords have come down to us. In the reconstruction of the political history of Clonmacnois we have therefore to rely on these traditions, which, accumulative in character, are preserved in highly stratified textual sources.

3.1 Clonmacnois and its neighbours in Connacht (seventh to ninth centuries)

The first securely datable historical evidence indicating expansion of Clonmacnois' ecclesiastical sphere of influence into Connacht, dates from the late seventh century. It is contained in Tírechán's collections for a Life of St. Patrick, in which he inserted complaints about the expansionist policy of Clonmacnois in Connacht.[11] Apparently many of the churches there, which at one time belonged to Armagh, sought affiliation with Clonmacnois in the later seventh century. Tirechán's complaints clearly imply that Clonmacnois had dependent houses in Connacht at the time. This statement is confirmed by annalistic evidence for the eighth century, during which the promulgation of the *lex Ciaráni* in Connacht is mentioned repeatedly. On the other hand, influence from the western regions of Ireland is traceable in Clonmacnois, as we can see from the fact that abbots from Connacht clearly predominated

---

[7]   See for example BL MS. Egerton 92; Royal Library Brussels, O'Clery MSS 5057-5059.

[8]   R. A. S. MACALISTER (ed.), The Book of Uí Maine otherwise called „The Book of the O'Kelly's", facsimile edition, Dublin 1942, fol. 126c.

[9]   AClon, p. 10. In his preface Mageoghagan mentions amongst *the authors wch I have taken for this booke* two members of the community of Clonmacnois, *Gillernew Mac Conn ne mboght, archpriest of Clonuickenos, Keilachar Mac Con als Gorman.* See SANDERLIN, The manuscripts of the Annals of Clonmacnois, for a discussion of the manuscript tradition of Mageoghagan's translation.

[10]   AFM, vol. 1, pp. lxivf.

[11]   See above, p. 86 n.224. BIELER (ed.), The Patrician texts, pp. 142f., 154f., 160f.

amongst St. Ciarán's successors from the second half of the seventh to the early years of the ninth century.[12]

There is evidence which suggests that St. Ciarán's authority in Connacht grew together with the power of the Uí Briúin, the up and coming dynasty in the west. During the reign of King Indrechtach mac Muiredaig (707 -723) their position as the dominant dynasty in Connacht was established.[13] He was the first king of the dynasty mentioned in the annals as having died in Clonmacnois.[14] Forgus, son of Cellach, one of his successors to the kingship of Connacht, and also of the Uí Briúin, enacted the *lex Ciaráni et lex Brendain* in Connacht for the first time in the year 744.[15] As K. Hughes pointed out the enactment of a saint's law, often associated with the carrying round of his relics, was an act by which ecclesiastical jurisdiction was exercised. It went hand in hand with the collection of the ecclesiastical fees and tithes.[16] The Uí Briuin king thus actively supported the consolidation of Clonmacnois' ecclesiastical authority in Connacht. The *lex Ciaráni* was again proclaimed in Connacht in the years 775 and 788, and for the last time promulgated at Ráth Cruachan in 814 under King Muirgius, son of Tomaltach.[17] It seems that during this early period the greater part of the churches and lands subject to St. Ciarán's ecclesiastical jurisdiction was situated in the western regions; only there is Ciarán's law said to have been promoted.

Apart from the Uí Briúin, the people of Uí Maine, the territory adjacent to the western bank of the river Shannon, played a dominant part in the history of Clonmacnois during the early period. Already during the seventh, and increasingly from the middle of the eighth century, several Uí Maine men appear in the abbacy of Clonmacnois. This tradition was continued

---

[12] See above, p. 48.

[13] BYRNE, Irish Kings, pp. 248-253; 300 for their genealogy.

[14] AT (722).

[15] AU 744.9.

[16] K. HUGHES, The church and the world in early Christian Ireland, in: K. HUGHES, Church and society in Ireland A.D. 400-1200, ed. D. DUMVILLE, London 1987, chap. VIII, pp. 99-116, here 103. See also HUGHES, The church in early Irish society, pp. 167-169.

[17] AI 775; AU 788.9; AU 814.

until the end of the ninth century.[18] With at least six, but possibly nine, candidates they supplied more abbots of Clonmacnois during this period than the Uí Fiachrach and the Uí Briúin, the two leading Connacht dynasties, taken together.[19]

The Uí Maine are traceable in Connacht from the middle of the sixth century as one of the subject tribes to the Uí Fiachrach Aidne.[20] By the time of the late seventh century their territory, situated west of the river Suck reached out to county Mayo, if we give credit to Tiréchan's *collectanea*, who at one occasion describes Findmag, in the former barony of Carra, as being part of the territory of Uí Maine.[21] In the middle of the eighth century the Uí Maine under the leadership of the Clann Cremthainn conquered the neighbouring territory to the east, the land between the river Suck and the Shannon, from the tribe of the Delbna Nuadat in the battle of Belach Cró (756).[22] Herewith they became immediate neighbours of St. Ciarán, separated from his church only by the river Shannon.

During the latter part of the eighth century and in the early ninth century repeated victories by the up and coming Uí Briúin dynasty of Connacht over the Uí Maine are recorded in the annals especially during the reign of Muirgius, son of Tomaltach, indicating significant resistance to Uí Briúin overlordship amongst the Uí Maine.[23] It seems their traditional alliance with the Uí Fiachrach Aidne resulted not only in hostility towards the Uí Briúin

---

[18]   See Appendix 1, A5(d.614), A10 (d.665), A17 (d.724), ?A21 (d.747),?A23 (d.762), ?A26 (d.770), A29 (d.784), A38 (d.850), A44 (d.885).

[19]   For the Uí Fiachrach abbot see A31 (d.789) plus one scribe S5 (d.789); for Uí Briúin abbots see A27 (d.771), A34 (d.799), A36 (d.816).

[20]   J. V. KELLEHER, The Uí Maine in the annals and Genealogies to 1225, in: Celtica 9 (1971), pp. 61-112, here 65-67; as an appurtenance of Connacht they played a decisive role in the succession struggles for the kingship of Connacht. Kelleher suggested that the domination of Uí Maine in the eighth and ninth century was necessary to any claimant for the kingship of Connacht. Compare BYRNE, Irish Kings, pp. 92f., 237, 250-252.

[21]   BIELER (ed.), The Patrician texts, pp. 154f., §41. For Slán Findmag see ibid., pp. 152f., §39.2, and above, p. 86 n.227. *Tirechán* also mentiones 'Fidarta', i.e. Fuerty in county Roscommon, as one of the churches in Uí Maine (ibid., pp. 146f., §28.1-2).

[22]   AT (755); AFM 751; KELLEHER, The Uí Maine in the annals, pp. 70f.; BYRNE, Irish Kings, p. 237.

[23]   AU 775.8 battle of Athleague. See also AU 778.10, 802.8, 814.6, 818.9.

kings but possibly also in a temporary opposition to Clonmacnois, which
was the main ecclesiastical ally of the Uí Briúin at the time. One of the battles fought by Muirgius, son of Tomaltach against the Uí Maine, namely
that in the year 814, was supported by a certain Fairceallach. The only person named Fairceallach appearing in the annals at the time was the abbot of
Clonmacnois, and it has been suggested that he was supporting the Uí
Briúin king in battle against the Uí Maine.[24]

The king of Uí Maine at the time was Cathal, son of Murchad, of the
Clann Cremthainn; he was defeated and killed by Diarmait, son of Tomaltach (the brother of Muirgius and his successor to the kingship of Connacht)
in the year 818. His successor Cathal, son of Ailill (818-846) was of the
Cénel Cairpre Cruim. Under him the Uí Maine, gave up their traditional
alliance with the Uí Fiachrach Aidne and joined the up and coming Connacht dynasty of the Uí Briúin Aí. In the year 822 the Uí Maine supported
Diarmait, son of Tomaltach in the battle of Tarbga, in gaining supremacy
over the whole of Connacht.[25]

With the succession of Cathal, son of Ailill to the kingship the Cenél
Cairpre Cruim had replaced the Clann Chremthainn as the dominant force in
Uí Maine. King Cathal became famous as the one who violated St. Ciarán's
sanctity by not only attacking the church of Clonmacnois, but also killing
the vice-abbot of Clonmacnois at the time.[26] The early ninth century, the
period of his reign, has therefore been characterized as a period of apparent
hostility between the Uí Maine and Clonmacnois.[27] The traditionally good
relations between Clonmacnois and the Uí Maine, as well as the political

---

[24] AU 814.6; KELLEHER, The Uí Maine in the annals, p. 74, suggested the campaign was
performed in revenge for (a speculative) raid on the termon of Clonmacnois by the Uí Maine;
Byrne assumes a different connection. The bishop and airchinnech of the church of Aughrim
(*Echdruim*) in Uí Maine was killed earlier in the year 814 (AU). Byrne speculates, that it was
a dependent church of Clonmacnois, that the Uí Maine had killed the airchinnech there, and
that the secular and the ecclesiastical overlords together undertook a revenge campaign
(BYRNE, Irish Kings, p. 252).

[25] AU 822.6.

[26] CS 823; AFM 834 (recte 835).

[27] See for example BYRNE, Irish Kings, p. 222; RYAN, Clonmacnois, p. 43; P. HARBISON,
The inscription on the Cross of the Scriptures at Clonmacnois, county Offaly', in: PRIA 79
(1979), pp. 177-188; HOLLO, MA Thesis, University College Cork, pp. 180f.; KELLEHER, The
Uí Maine in the annals, pp. 76f.

constellation in the early ninth century suggest, however, a different interpretation of the evidence. The relevant entry in the Chronicon under the year
823 reads as follows:[28]

> Ronan, Ab Cluana muc Nois do fágaibh a abdaine. Saruccadh Cluana muc Nois do
> Cathal mac Aililla, Rí H. Maine, for secnabad Muman .i. Flann mac Flaithbertaigh,
> do Uib Forga, contard isin Sinainn contorcair. Dligedh .vii. cell ind. Maidm ria Ca-
> thal mac Oililla for Fedlimid mac Crimthain a Maig Hí ubi multi cediderunt.

> Ronan, Abbot of Cluain-muc-Nois, left his abbacy. The profanation of Cluain-mic-
> Nois by Cathal son of Ailill, king of Uí Maine, against the Munster vice-Abbot, viz.
> Flann, son of Flaithbertach of the Uí Forga, whom he threw into the Shannon, so
> that he was drowned. Seven churches were adjudged in atonement. A victory was
> gained by Cathal, son of Ailill over Feidhlimidh, son of Crimthann in Magh Aí, in
> which many fell.

The dishonouring of Ciarán's church by the king of Uí Maine is only reported in the Chronicon. The Annals of Tigernach are not preserved for the
period, and Mageoghagan's annals do not comment on the matter. The
problem is that the installation of the vice-abbot from Munster according to
the same source, i.e. the Chronicon, took place in the year 827, four years
after his supposed death! Clearly there must have been a later glossator at
work. Due to the uncertain nature of this evidence one might doubt the
whole story. Thus Kelleher suggested the entry to be a late insertion by the
Clonmacnois chroniclers with the intention of showing the danger of the
cost of violating churches.[29]

However, there is evidence to support a historical core to the tale, which
had its background in the hostilities which existed between the leading
forces in Connacht, the Uí Briúin Aí, their allies the Uí Maine and the king
of Munster, Feidlimid mac Crimthainn.[30] The contemporary annals agree
that the king of Munster plundered the Cenél Cairpre Cruim (i.e. the dynasty
of Cathal, son of Ailill) in the year 837. The deed was immediately re-
venged by the Uí Briúin Aí, who plundered the men of Munster in the very
same year.[31] Feidlimid must have counted as their enemy at least from the
year 830 when he had invaded the southern parts of the Uí Briúin king-

---

28 CS 823.

29 KELLEHER, The Uí Maine in the annals, p. 77.

30 For Feidlimid see BYRNE, Irish Kings, pp. 220-229.

31 AU 837.7+8.

dom.[32] Clonmacnois likewise appears as the target of Munster aggression in the region, during the period.[33] Finally the aforesaid Munster vice-abbot Flann came from a branch of the Muscraige Tire, who were settled in the northern parts of Munster right in the neighbourhood of Birr, a church, which - as we know - was not on very friendly terms with Clonmacnois (vA4). According to the principle that my enemy's enemy is my friend one might deduce, that the king of Connacht, the royal family of the Uí Maine and the monastic centre of Clonmacnois joined their forces against their common foe, the king of Munster.

Feidlimid, king of Munster, was renowned for his close association with the church. Earlier in his reign he had made friends with St. Patrick.[34] Presumably St. Ciarán's monastic settlement at the Shannon originally appeared to him as another potential ally. However Clonmacnois' allegiance at the time was with Connacht. Moreover St. Ciarán's successors were competing for ecclesiastical supremacy with St. Patrick, who with the support of Feidlimid had extended his authority over Munster. In this context it was more or less impossible for the king of Munster to win the support of Clonmacnois. Nevertheless Feidlimid somehow managed to impose his man Flann as vice-abbot in Clonmacnois, presumably sometime around 830 after he had successfully damaged the forces of the southern Uí Briúin in Connacht. Flann was able to hold his position for some time but had to deal with constant resistence from inside the community. Feidlimid's repeated military actions against Clonmacnois in the years 832 and 833, in the course of which even people were killed, might have been interventions in support of his man Flann. When Diarmait, son of Tomaltach, king of Connacht of the Uí Briúin Aí died in the year 833 the church of St. Ciarán lost its most pow-

---

[32] AU 830.6.

[33] In 823 he burnt Gallen (CS 823), three years later he plundered the territory of Delbna Ethra (CS 823). In 830 the annals report that he burnt *Faire* in Mide, possibly the monastery Fore, which at the time had close relations with Clonmacnois (The place is called *Faire* in CS, *Foire* in AU, and has been doubted as bein identical with Fore by BYRNE, Irish Kings, p. 221). Delbna Ethra was again devastated three times in a row in 832. The termon of Ciarán, the land immediately subject to the abbot of Clonmacnois, was burned on that occasion (CS 832). The following year we read of the *jugulatio* of the family of Clonmacnois by the king of Munster, in which the termon of Ciarán was again burned right to the very church doors, and members of the community of Clonmacnois were put to death (CS 833, AU 833.7).

[34] AU 823.5.

erful secular patron. It was in this particular political constellation, that Cathal, son of Ailill, king of Uí Maine, took it on himself to defend St. Ciarán
against Munster infiltration. He interfered on behalf of the opposition party
in Clonmacnois and in a skirmish inside the monastic city he drowned the
vice-abbot from Munster. The attack on the Cenél Cairpre Cruim, the royal
dynasty of Uí Maine, by the king of Munster appears as a revenge campaign
for the affair in Clonmacnois.

Still there remains the problem of chronology. Clearly the killing of the
vice-abbot from Munster must have happened prior to 837, when Feidlimid
took revenge on Cathal. Also, needless to say, his installation must have
preceded his being killed. If the violent attacks on Clonmacnois by the king
of Munster in the years 832 and 833 were in fact the response to increasing
opposition to the vice-abbot from Munster, the interference of the king of Uí
Maine must have happened sometime afterwards, between the years 833 and
837. Possibly the Clonmacnois source used by the Four Masters was
chronologically more correct. They inserted the episode in an entry for the
year 835.[35]

The assumption that the king of Uí Maine acted in agreement with the
community of St. Ciarán, but against the interests of their common enemy,
the king of Munster, is confirmed by the fact that the Clonmacnois chronicles are extremely hostile to Feidlimid. According to the Chronicon he, who
was otherwise known as a pious anchorite, and sometime abbot of Cork,
died in consequence of a mortal stroke by St. Ciarán after he had again
plundered Ciarán's church in the year 846.[36] The report on King Cathal's
murder of the Clonmacnois vice-abbot in comparison reads almost like a
panegyric, expressing unconcealed sympathy for the offender, who after all
was generous.[37] The claim that Cathal gave seven churches to Ciarán might

---

[35] AFM 834 (recte 835). Ryan argues for 823 as the correct date of the attack, which he
assumes was followed by the (possibly forced) resignation of abbot Rónán (RYAN, Clonmacnois, p. 47); see also HARBISON, The inscription on the Cross, who offers a similar interpretation and dating.

[36] CS 846. The story is told in charming detail by Mageoghagan under the year 844. According to AU 847 Feidlimid died as a *scribe and anchorite, and the best of the Irish*. Compare AFM 845, where a laudatory poem for Feidlimid is included, stating that *slaughter
spread through sacred Ireland from the hour that Feidhlimidh died.*

[37] CS 823.

therefore very well rely on an actual donation resulting out of the friendship which existed between Clonmacnois and its neighbours across the Shannon during the later eighth and early ninth centuries.

The entry reporting on the affair in the Chronicon, in its present form, appears as the work of an eleventh-century glossator. He probably had the information about the affair from the now lost Clonmacnois chronicle. He gave a slightly different twist to the incident, by interpreting the data according to the needs of his own times, when the Uí Maine were one of Ciarán's foremost enemies.[38] The same seems to apply to a story known from the Book of Lecan, where Diarmait, son of Tomaltach is said to have rewarded the king of Uí Maine for his support in battle, with the abbot's chair in Clonmacnois.[39] Again the king of Uí Maine appears as the villain, who forced the expulsion of the sitting abbot in Clonmacnois. But the tale might have been less hostile to the Uí Maine in an earlier version. The historical background to the original version of the tale was possibly the succession of a Uí Maine man to the abbacy of Clonmacnois after the death of Rónán in the year 844.[40]

The saga material, as well as the hagiographical tradition, confirm the importance of the Uí Maine as allies of St. Ciarán in the early period. They figure as the most prominent of the Connacht tribes in Clonmacnois. Ac-

---

[38] Compare below, pp. 122f. n.130.

[39] The story is cited by RYAN, The abbatial succession, p. 506. Diarmait, son of Tomaltach of the Uí Briúin Aí, the brother of Muirgius and his successor to the kingship, was about to engage the men of Bréifne in battle and came to the king of Uí Maine to seek help. The latter agreed, on condition that his half-brother would be given the abbot's chair in Clonmacnois in the event of victory. Accordingly after their combined forces had defeated the men of Bréifne, Ailgile, the sitting abbot of Clonmacnois, was expelled from his office, to vacate the position for the Uí Maine candidate. In return Ailgile cursed Diarmait and prophesied that none of his descendants would succeed to the kingship. Ryan suggested that this story reflected the circumstances of the resignation of abbot Ronan, recorded in the Chronicon Scotorum under the year 823. The version of the story, as it is now preserved, must be the result of a later rewriting of the tale, from the time when the Meic Dhiarmada were rivals to the Uí Chonchobair for the kingship of Connacht. The descendants of Diarmait were the O'Concannons and the O'Fallons, lords of Meic Dhiarmada since the eleventh century. The men of Bréifne would then have replaced what in the original story might have been the men of Munster. See The Book of Lecan. Leabhar Mór Mhic Fhir Bhisigh Leacain. Facsimile edition (Dublin 1937) fol. 67ᵛc.d., 68ʳa.

[40] Appendix 1, A37, A38.

cording to Mageoghagan St. Ciarán, like his father, was a Connachtman.[41] The Lives of Ciarán, which agree that the saint was from the Latharna, maintain, however, that he was conceived and born in Connacht.[42] The story goes that Beoit and Darcea, the parents of Ciarán, originally lived in the kingdom of Mide until Ainmire, the king of Tara at the time, imposed a heavy tribute on his subjects. Like Joseph, the earthly father of Christ, Beoit took his family and fled from the country to the province of Connacht, where a more benevolent king reigned. Thus it came about that Ciarán was born and brought up in Connacht, namely in the plain of Mag nAi, i.e. the plain of Roscommon, near a place called Ráth Crimthainn.[43] A certain Deacon Justus is named as Ciarán's baptizer and teacher during his youth. He is said to have lived in the church of Fuerty, in the north of the plain of Mag nAi. This place is named amongst the churches in Uí Maine by Tirechán.[44] This information taken together clearly implies that Ciarán was brought up in Uí Maine, since their territory at the time when Tirechán wrote expanded as far north as Fuerty, and therefore must have included the whole of the plain of Mag nAi, where St. Ciarán is said to have spent his youth.

The name of the king of Connacht at the time when Ciarán was born, according to his Irish hagiographer was Crimthann, son of Lugaid, son of Dallan.[45] He is anachronistically called *ri Érenn* by the author. We might

---

[41] AClon, p. 81.

[42] PLUMMER (ed.), Vitae Sanctorum Hiberniae, I, p. 200: *Cum autem ipse Beonedus artifex tributis Ainmereach, regis Temorie, ualde premeretur, devitans grauitatem tribute, exiit a regione sua, id est a finibus Midhi in regionibus Conacthorum; habituitque ibi in Campo Aei apud Crimthanum regem*; HEIST (ed.), Vitae Sanctorum, p. 78: *Post hec, cum pater eius sub tributis regis Anmerei, id est Ainmirech, premeretur, relinquens patriam suam, abiit in regionem Conacteorum, ibique in campo Ay genuit fillium ...*; STOKES (ed.), Lives of Saints, p. 119: *Bai, tra, rí ecraibhdech intansin i Crich hua-Neill .i. Ainmiri mac Colgan a ainm-sidhe. Noordaighedh-sidhe na tuatha ocus na cenela fo chíss rotrom. Luidh didiu Beoid for teiched in righ-sin i crich Connacht cu Cremthann mac Lugdach meic Dallain .i. ri Eirenn, co Raith Cremthainn a Muigh Ai.*

[43] *Ráth Crimthainn* is placed in Mag nAi here, and might possibly be identical with Ráth Cruachain (MACALISTER, Latin and Irish Lives, p. 110).

[44] PLUMMER (ed.), Vitae Sanctorum Hiberniae, I, p. 201, §4; BIELER (ed.), The Patrician texts, p. 128, §7.2, and 146f., §28.1-3, the church is named 'Fidarta'.

[45] PLUMMER (ed.), Vitae Sanctorum Hiberniae, I, p. 200: *habitauit ibi in Campo Aei apud Crimthanum regem; ibique genuit sanctum Kyranum, cuius est hec vita*; STOKES (ed.), Lives of Saints, p. 119, ll. 4001-4005: *Cremhthann mac Ludhdach meic Dallain .i. ri Eirenn.*

doubt his aspirations to the kingship of Ireland. But the Latin version already acknowledges him as the ruler of the territory to which Ciarán's parents migrated. No king of Connacht bearing this name is known. There is however one Crimthann, son of Lugaid listed in the genealogies of the Uí Maine as the eponymous ancestor of the Clann Cremthainn. These were a branch of the Uí Maine, who provided kings of Uí Maine during the eighth and again in the early tenth century.[46] Possibly the hagiographers had this king in mind, when writing the story of St. Ciarán's youth in Connacht. If so, the fact that they claim a local king of the people in their neighbourhood, to have been king of Connacht, might be interpreted as a reflection of the high status held by the Uí Maine at the time of the original composition of the saints' Life. Most likely it has to be dated sometime in the mid-eighth century when the Clann Cremthainn were at their height. During this period they conquered the territory of Delbna Nuadat, between the river Suck and the Shannon, thus becoming direct neighbours of St. Ciarán. In the ninth century Clann Cremthainn power was overthrown by the forces of an expansive Uí Briúin.[47]

The links between Clonmacnois and the Uí Maine are reflected in another literary product of the period. There is a tale belonging to the Ulster cycle, known as 'The Feast of Bricriu and the exile of the sons of Dóel Dermait' (*Fled Bricrenn ocus Loinges mac nDúil Dermait*). A certain Eochu Rond, king of Uí Maine, figures as an antagonist to Cú Chulainn in the text, preserved in a copy extant in the the Yellow Book of Lecan.[48] The text contains not only a magnificent description of the king, Eochu Rond, as a splendid warrior, but also what could be read as a rather ludicrous account of the way he is defeated by Cú Chulainn. Dr Kaarina Hollo, who has been working on the text, interprets this passage as a rather negative portrayal of

---

[46] J. O'DONOVAN (ed.), The tribes and customs of Hy-Many, commonly called O'Kelly's Country, Dublin 1843, p. 14; KELLEHER, The Uí Maine in the annals, p. 109. Thanks to Dr Colmán Etchingham who drew my attention to this.

[47] In the battle of Forad in 818 (CS, AClon, p. 130, AU, AFM). Three more kings of this branch of the Uí Maine are mentioned for the late ninth and early tenth century, when their genealogies come to an end. The very last king of Uí Maine from among the Clann Cremthainn died in 938 (KELLEHER, The Uí Maine in the annals, pp. 77-79).

[48] An edition of the text is in preparation by Dr Kaarina Hollo, who kindly supplied me with the relevant passages of the text. It has been edited once before by Ernst Windisch in: W. STOKES / E. WINDISCH, Irische Texte, zweite Serie, I. Heft, Leipzig 1884, pp. 164-216.

the king of Uí Maine. Moreover she deduces hostility between the Uí Maine and the place of composition of this version of the tale, for which a *scriptorium* in Clonmacnois appears to her as the most favourable candidate. On linguistic grounds the text has been dated to the ninth century. On grounds of historical evidence Hollo suggests the early decades of the ninth century as a more precise date of composition. She follows Ryan, Byrne and Kelleher in identifiying this period as a time of apparent hostility between Clonmacnois and the Uí Maine.

The reading of the text as an expression of apparent hostility towards the Uí Maine is ambiguous. There are merely two textual indications supporting the assumption of hostility. One is the contrast between the glamourous description of Eochu Rond as a warrior and his subsequent defeat by Cú Chulainn, while the second is the mere fact that the king of Uí Maine figures as an antagonist of the hero of the tale. It seems to me that it is much more significant that we find mention of the Uí Maine, who do not otherwise figure in the Ulster cycle, in this tale. They are portrayed as a warriorlike and grand people, whose approach towards the camp of Cú Chulainn can be heard from afar and compares to a great thunder from the sky. Also the daughter of the king has enough good taste to fall in love with Cú Chulainn. The implications are that these people, in the eyes of the compiler of the text, were powerful enough to meet Cú Chulainn and his men, to defend the honour of their women and to compete in fame and rank with the other peoples figuring in the Ulster cycle. Their inclusion in the story does not so much express hostility as reflect the position and importance the Uí Maine had in local politics in the surrounding world of the place of composition of the tale.

I would be inclined to maintain the characterisation of the time from the later seventh through most of the ninth century as a period of close relations and friendship between Clonmacnois and the neighbouring Uí Maine. Only in the later ninth century, when the kings of Mide gradually gained the leading position as patrons of St. Ciarán's settlement on the Shannon, was the former friendship neglected, eventually giving way to open hostility, apparent from the annals for the tenth and eleventh centuries.

Another hagiographical remnant from this period is the story of the donation of seven churches to St. Ciarán by the king of Uí Maine. It is briefly mentioned in the eleventh century gloss in the Chronicon, which reports about the events said to have happened in Clonmacnois in the year 823. An extended version of the donation survived in the seventeenth century Registry of Clonmacnois.[49] It found an even more spectacular elaboration in the later period, preserved in a fragment of the Book of Uí Maine and the Book of Lismore, where Cairpre Crum, the acclaimed fore-father of the Cenél Cairpre Cruim is portrayed as a contemporary and close friend of St. Ciarán himself.[50] The story is told how Cairpre, well known as a notorious evil doer, was attacked and killed at night, after another act of plundering. His head was cut off from his body on this occasion. However, just before his death Cairpre had made submission to St. Ciarán, and so the saint and his monks, hearing about the killing, came towards Cluain Burren, where the body lay, and rang their bells and walked with them around the dead man's body. Afterwards he was brought to Clonmacnois where the head was rejoined to the body and, at the word of Ciarán, Cairpre was resuscitated from the dead. Unfortunately there was a twist in his neck from the stone pillow where his head was placed, which gave Cairpre his surname, the Crooked. Thus restored to life, Cairpre granted seventeen townlands to the monastery of his benefactor. The story bears all the characteristics of later medieval propaganda literature, which has little to do with historical reality, but even propaganda needs some material to draw on. It seems likely that this material was the genuine literary outcome of the eighth or early parts of the ninth century, possibly as an extended version of an actual donation made by king Cathal, sometime during his reign.

Another Connacht tribe connected by saga tradition with Clonmacnois are the Uí Fiachrach Aidne. The most famous king of Connacht of this dynasty was Guaire Aidne, who according to tradition died and was buried in Clonmacnois in the year 663.[51] Tradition styles him the incarnation of un

---

[49] See below, pp. 221-226.

[50] The story is printed from British Library MS Egerton 92, fol. 29ᵛ, col.2 (a fragment of the Book of Fermoy - not of the Book of Uí Maine as O'Donovan says) by J. O'Donovan in Registry, pp. 453f. n.2. An edition from the version in the Book of Uí Maine, fol. 126ᵛ, was made by K. MEYER (ed.), Wunderbare Geschichten von Corpre Cromm mac Feradaig, in: Archiv für Celtische Lexikographie 3 (1907), pp. 224-226. A third version of the story is contained in the Book of Lismore (STOKES [ed.], Lives of Saints, pp. xvi - xviii).

[51] CS 659, AFM 662. His death in Clonmacnois is mentioned in other sources, such as the anonymous poem on the kings and chieftains buried in Clonmacnois, edited by M. Stokes (G. PETRIE, Christian inscriptions in the Irish language, ed. M. STOKES, 2 vols., Dublin 1872, I, pp. 76-78). See also the list of the kings of Connacht transcribed by an Dubhaltach Mac Fhirbhisigh in 1664 (J. O'DONOVAN [ed.], The genealogies, tribes and customs of Hy-

bounded hospitality and munificence, the Lebor na hUidre preserved the memory of his generosity in a tale, according to which the king many years after his death and burial in Clonmacnois, turned sand into gold.[52] Even though later tradition seems to have interfered with Guaire's fame and greatness,[53] close links existed between this dynasty and Clonmacnois also around the eighth century, prior to the rise of the Uí Briúin. At that time an apparently very prominent member of Guaire's offspring, Connmach son of Muirmid, *nepos Guaire Oidni*, was active as a scribe in Clonmacnois.[54] It also seems that the fame of the ultimate king of the Uí Fiachrach was much fostered in Clonmacnois under the impact of Uí Maine historiographers and hagiographers, since he was their most powerful ally prior to the allegiance with the Uí Briúin Aí in the early ninth century.

Finally there are the Uí Briúin who receive surprisingly little attention from St. Ciarán's hagiographers, at least during this early period. Presumably their status as patrons of Clonmacnois was too soon outshone by the kings of Tara of the Southern Uí Néill, who seem to have monopolized the patronage of St. Ciarán's church from the later parts of the ninth century onwards.

Fiachrach, Dublin 1844, pp. 312f.); for the saga tradtion around this king see BYRNE, Irish Kings, pp. 239-246, 316.

[52] STOKES (ed.), Lives of Saints, p. 358, mentions the story according to the Lebor na hUidre, fol. 117b, 13-18.

[53] His 'arch-fiend' Áed Sláine, king of Tara, happened to be the ancestor of the Síl nÁedo Sláine branch of the southern Uí Néill, who likewise claimed St. Ciarán's friendship, most likely some time in the tenth century. The Clonmacnois chronicles unanimously preserved the memory of how Guaire was defeated by Áed Sláine in the battle of Carn Conaill in the year 649, with the support and prayers of the abbot, prelates and clergy at Clonmacnois. CS 646, the record of the battle is preserved as a gloss in the original hand here, AT (648), AClon 642, pp. 103f.

[54] See Appendix 1, S5 (d.798).

3.2 Clonmacnois and the kings of Tara of the Southern Uí Néill

Clonmacnois was founded in the territory subject to the kings of Mide.[55] Whereas the Latin Lives of Ciarán simply report about the construction of a building at the place which St. Ciarán had recognized as the place of his resurrection,[56] the Irish Life adds to the tale by introducing Diarmait mac Cerbaill, the ultimate ancestor of the royal dynasties of the Southern Uí Néill, as co-founder of St. Ciarán's church:[57]

> *Then Ciarán set up the first post in Cluain and Diarmait mac Cerbeil along with him. Said Ciarán to Diarmait when they were planting the post, 'Warrior, suffer my hand to be over thy hand and thou shalt be over the men of Ireland in the high-kingship (ard-ri Erenn).' 'I permit it', said Diarmait, 'only give me a token thereof.' 'I will' said Ciarán, 'though thou art solitary to-day, thou shalt be king of Ireland this time tomorrow.' That was verified, for Tuathal Moel-Garb, King of Ireland was slain that night and Diarmait took the kingship of Ireland on the morrow, and he bestowed a hundred churches on Ciarán.*

The same story, with a slightly more dramatic emphasis is retold by Mageoghagan in his translation of the Annals of Clonmacnois.[58] Finally the story is also contained in the Tripartite Life of Patrick, and apparently was

---

[55] BYRNE, Irish Kings, pp. 87-90; P. WALSH, Meath in the Book of Rights, in: J. RYAN (ed.), Féil-scríbhinn Eóin Mhic Néill. Essays and Studies presented to Professor Eoin MacNeill, Dublin 1940, pp. 508-521.

[56] PLUMMER (ed.), Vitae Sanctorum Hiberniae, I, pp. 211f., §28; MACALISTER, Latin and Irish Lives, p. 180, §17; the Salamanca version ends after St. Ciarán's time of studies in Clonard.

[57] STOKES (ed.), Lives of Saints, pp. 130f., ll. 4379-4398. See MACALISTER, Latin and Irish Lives, p. 91, for the translation.

[58] *King Twahal hauing proclaimed throughout the whole K.dom the banishment of Dermot mc Kervel (as before is specified) with a great Reward to him yt would bring him his hart, the said Dermot for feare of his life lived in the desert of Cluonvicknose (then called Ardtibra) and meeting with the abbot S. Cieran in the place where the Church of Clonvickenose now standes, who was but newly come thither to live or dwell from Inis Angin & having noe house or place to Reside & dwell in, the said Dermot Gave him his assistance to make a house there, & in thrusting down in the earth one of the peeces of the timber or wattles of the house, the sd Dermot took S. Queran's hand & and did put it ouer his one head or hand in sign of Reverence to the St., whereupon the saint Humbly besaught God of his great Gookness that by that time tomorrow ensuing that the hands of Dermot might have superiority over all Ireland, which fell out as the S. Requested* (AClon, pp. 79f.). The same story is preserved as a part of the lost 'Book of Sligo', known from the fifteenth century manuscript Egerton 1782 (see O'GRADY [ed.], Silva Gadelica, I, pp. 72f.; see also introduction vol. II, pp. viiif.).

so popular that it even found its way in non-Ciaránian hagiography.[59] The tale gives the impression that the fortunes of Clonmacnois were closely linked to the royalty of the Southern Uí Néill from its very foundation. The tale bears two implications. First of all Diarmait became king of Tara with the help of St. Ciarán; the killing of the former king, Tuathal Máelgarb, is interpreted as an immediate result of the saint's blessing.[60] The second implication is that Diarmait mac Cerbaill supported St. Ciarán and his church from the very start. Moreover he acknowledged Ciarán's ecclesiastical supremacy in his kingdom.[61]

King Diarmait reigned according to the Annals of Ulster as king of Tara from 544 to 565. The Clonmacnois chronicles give his obit and add that after his death his head was brought to Clonmacnois and buried there.[62] He was the father of Colmán Mór, Áed Sláine and Colmán Becc, thus the ultimate ancestor of the Clann Cholmáin, the Síl nÁedo Sláine and the Caílle Follamain.[63] The Síl nÁedo Sláine were the kings of Brega, the eastern kingdom in Mide, the Clann Cholmáin dominated the western parts of the province. The two branches were rivals for the kingship of Tara. From the second half of the eighth century the Clann Cholmáin successfully domi-

---

[59] STOKES (ed.), Tripartite Life, p. 88.

[60] According to the Annals of Ulster Diarmait became king in 544, and Clonmacnois was only founded in 548. The Clonmacnois annals, possibly as a result of the tenth century revision, agree that the foundation of Clonmacnois, the death of St. Ciarán and the beginning of the reign of Diarmait as king of Tara happened in one year (AT [548], CS 544). For the chronology see J. J. MCNAMEE, The chronology of the Life of St. Ciarán of Clonmacnois, in: Ardagh and Clonmacnois Ant. Soc. Jn. 2, no. 10 (1945), pp. 3-16; see also Appendix 1, A1.

[61] The *Aided Dhiarmada*, the death tale of King Diarmait, enforces the same claim. There, a story is included of how Ciarán, whilst present with King Diarmait at the royal assembly at Uisnech, performed a miracle to bring on rain over the country after a long period of drought. It is stated that. Here aswell the king *made obeisance to Kieran, and settled on him his own service and his children's forever.* (O'GRADY [ed.], Silva Gadelica, I, p. 74, translation cited from vol. II, p. 78). See below, pp. 121f.

[62] AClon 569, pp. 88f.; CS 565; AT (564); AFM 558; BYRNE, Irish Kings, pp. 94-105, for the saga material about Diarmait mac Cerbaill.

[63] M. A. O'BRIEN (ed.), Corpus Genealogiarum Hiberniae, Dublin 1962, revised by J. V. KELLEHER, 1976, p. 159 (143 bc 53); Genealogies of the Clann Cholmáin according to Rawlinson B 502, p. 425 (335 d 46); Genealogies of the kings of Mide according to the Book of Leinster (S. PENDER [ed.], The O'Clery Book of genealogies, in: Anal. Hib. 18 [1951], pp. 1-194, here 57f., §§763f.); BYRNE, Irish Kings, pp. 87, 90.

nated the title, with the exception of a brief period in the tenth century when the Síl nÁedo Sláine supplied the king of Tara during the years 944 to 956. The Caílle Follamain finally ruled a territory corresponding to the former barony of Fore. They were excluded from the kingship of Tara from the early period.

The Clann Cholmáin took the leading part in Mide politics from the eighth century onwards. During the early part of their career the kings of the Clann Cholmáin clearly favoured the Columban community as their most important ecclesiastical allies.[64] The battle of Argaman, in the year 764, between the communities of Clonmacnois and Durrow has been interpreted as the outcome of rivalries between the two churches for the position as leading church in Mide.[65] It seems indeed plausible that inter-ecclesiastical tensions, eventually resulted in open hostility and an armed conflict.[66] However the battle might also point to the fact that the two churches were actively involved in the succession struggles for the kingship of Tara, after the death of Domnall Midi.[67] Diarmait Dub, son of Domnall fought and died alongside the men of Durrow. The army of Clonmacnois on the other hand won the battle with the support of Bresal son of Murchad. Diarmat Dub might have been a son of the former king, and Bresal his grandson (Murchad was the name of one of King Domnall's sons).[68] Both would thus have been potential contenders for the vacant kingship, mobilising ecclesiastical forces, and taking advantage of the hostilities resulting from the ecclesiastical policy of the deceased king. However, despite the support of the saints and their armies neither of the two parties won the kingship. Niall Frossach, the candidate provided by the Northern Uí Néill became king of Tara for the following years.

The battle of Argaman testifies to the involvement of Clonmacnois in the political career of the Clann Cholmáin kings of Mide as early as the later

---

[64] See above, pp. 56-58.

[65] AU 763.6, AT (763).

[66] HERBERT, Iona, Kells, and Derry, p. 66.

[67] He died in 763 (AU).

[68] AU 765.5 Murchad fell in the battle of Fiachach against his brother Domnall (Bresal might also have been a brother of Domnall Mide, whose father was also named Murchad [AU 763]).

eighth century. Further evidence can be found in the Clonmacnois annals, in an entry for the year 838, where the death of Ruaidrí son of Donnchad, as *secundus Abbas Cluana Iraird, tanaisi Abb Cluana muc Nois* is commemorated. He seems to have been a brother of Conchobar son of Donnchad, king of Mide of the Clann Cholmáin at the time. His obituary is not mentioned in the Annals of Ulster, who otherwise record most of the vice-abbots from Clonmacnois. Ruaidrí as the brother of King Conchobar would have been an uncle of King Flann Sinna, who ruled from 887-916.[69] It is possible that his obituary was a subsequent insertion made by the Clonmacnois chroniclers in the early tenth century, during the reign of King Flann.[70] The claim that a brother of King Conchobar was involved in the government of Clonmacnois and Clonard seems nevertheless plausible. The king actively supported Artrí, who may have been a son of his, in his claims to the abbacy of Armagh, and there is no reason why he should not put his brother in a leading position in the churches of his own kingdom.[71]

By the time of the early tenth century the position of Clonmacnois, together with Clonard as the most important ecclesiastical allies of the kings of Mide seems to have been firmly established. During the reign of King Flann Sinna members of the community in Clonmacnois interfered in politics on behalf of their secular overlord. In the year 899 Cathal, son of Conchobar, the king of Connacht, submitted to King Flann Sinna. The Clonmacnois annals report that the king of Connacht came into the house of Flann (i.e. made submission to him) under the protection of the clergy of Ciarán, implying that the clergy of Ciarán took a leading part in the talks which led to the peace treaty.[72]

In the year 904, Clonmacnois and Clonard came under the joint rule of one abbot, Colmán Conaillech, who although not a member of the royal dynasty appears to have been a close friend of the king. In Clonard a grand-

---

[69] BYRNE, Irish Kings, p. 282.

[70] See Appendix 1, vA6.

[71] King Conchobar died in 833 (AU); HERBERT, Iona, Kells, and Derry, p. 72; BYRNE, Irish Kings, pp. 124f., 282; BYRNE, The community of Clonard, pp. 170f.

[72] AFM 896, CS 899. Earlier in the same year the men of Connacht had been plundering Inis Ainghin, and the shrine of St. Ciarán there. Possibly the obligation to submit to the king of Mide was part of the compensation demanded by the community of Ciarán.

son of King Flann held the position as vice-abbot for a time.[73] In Clonmacnois royal patronage manifested itself in a huge stone church built according
to the Chronicon by Flann Sinna and Colmán Conaillech in the year 909.[74]
This church was and still is the largest amongst the buildings in Clonmacnois; the annals refer to it as the great stone church (*damhliag mór*). Later it
is often called the cathedral of Clonmacnois, and from the later middle ages
it became known as 'Temple Mc Dermot'.[75] On the west side of the church,
opposite the main entrance a beautiful high cross was erected, which became known as the 'Cross of the Scriptures'. One of the carvings on it
shows two men planting a pole, which is generally interpreted as represent-
ing Ciarán and king Diarmait mac Cerbaill, or possibly their tenth century
successors, jointly founding Clonmacnois. It also bears an inscription asking
a prayer for King Flann, son of Máel Sechnaill and abbot Colmán.[76] The
two monuments witness to the close ties which existed between the secular
lord of Mide and the powerful abbot of Clonard and Clonmacnois as the
leading ecclesiastical figure in his kingdom. The king's generosity towards
Clonmacnois might have been an act of thanks-giving for the victory over

---

[73] He died in 923 (CS 923); BYRNE, The community of Clonard, p. 171.

[74] CS 908 (recte 909); AFM 904, 924; AClon 901, p. 144.

[75] Manning suggested that the name 'Temple McDermot' derived from the Meic Dhiarmada
of Magh Luirg, who probably restored the church in the later middle ages (private conversation). See WESTROPP, A description of the ancient buildings, pp. 282-285; C. MANNING, The
earliest plans of Clonmacnoise, in: Archaeology Ireland 8, no. 1 (1994), pp. 18-20; MANNING,
Clonmacnoise, pp. 23f.

[76] The cross is referred to as the highcross in 957 (AFM) and as the Cross of the Scriptures
in 1060 (AFM). According to the latest rubbings taken of the cross the inscription on the
West face reads: *OR DO RIG FL. IND M MA...N...ROIT DO RIG HERENN OR...* („Pray for
king Flaind son of Ma[elseachlainn]...pray for the king of Ireland") and on the East face: *DO
COLMAN DORRO AN CROSSA AR RIG FL.ND* („For Colmán who made the cross ... on
king Flann"). See D. Ó MURCHADA, Rubbings taken of the inscriptions on the Cross of the
Scriptures, Clonmacnois, in: JRSAI 110 (1980), p. 50; compare PETRIE, Christian inscriptions, I, pp. 42-44, fig. 86-88; Peter Harbison questioned the traditional dating of the cross
and suggested that the inscriptions refer to the early ninth century abbot Rónán and his alleged friend Flann, the vice-abbot (HARBISON, The inscription on the Cross, compare A37).
The theory has been refuted by F. HENRY, Around an inscription: the Cross of the Scriptures
at Clonmacnois, in: JRSAI 110 (1980), pp. 36-46; more recently Harbison revised this opinion, returning to the traditional reading of the inscription (HARBISON, The High Crosses of
Ireland, I, p. 357). See also MANNING, Clonmacnoise, pp. 36-39, for illustration and photographs; EDWARDS, The archaeology of early medieval Ireland, p. 167 and fig. 36.

the forces of Munster in the battle of Belach Mugna, won in the year 908.[77]
The donation emphasized royal greatness both to his defeated enemy and to
his subjects. The fact that Clonmacnois and not Clonard this time benefited
from the king's generosity might possibly be linked with its geographical
location. Clonmacnois was situated at the border of the kingdom of Mide.
The position at the Shannon made it an obvious target for the Munster army
on its way for campaigns and raids into Mide. A huge stone building in a
place so much exposed to hostilities from neighbouring peoples might also
have had military and strategic relevance. Since churches repeatedly functioned as shelter for the ecclesiastical communities in case of military attacks, King Flann's generosity also went towards the fortification of his
befriended ecclesiastical settlement (possibly in consideration of its potential function as a supportive stronghold in case of another attack by a king of
Munster).

Furthermore, as the founder of a church in Clonmacnois King Flann
Sinna secured his influence and a say in the ecclesiastical affairs of Clonmacnois. Traditional church law acknowledged and in fact guaranteed certain rights to the builder of a church regardless of whether he was a layman
or in ecclesiastical orders.[78] The *edificator* would have the right to give
advice in ecclesiastical matters, a say in the choice of the priests, or, in case
the church was presided over by a bishop, in the episcopal elections, and he
was entitled to a share of the income of his church.[79] Those rights were hereditary, so that with the foundation of a church in Clonmacnois Flann Sinna
laid the ground for himself and his successors to rights which would safeguard a share in ecclesiastical government as well as in the income of one of
the main churches in his kingdom.

Changing ecclesiastical alliances in the kingdom of Mide, during the
reign of Flann Sinna, are reflected in the hagiographical writings of St. Ciarán. It has been suggested above, that the Irish Life of Ciarán was origi-

---

[77] Flann made expeditions into Munster in 905 and 906, and was defeated by the king of
Munster in the battle of Mag Léna the following year. AU 905, 906, CS 906 (recte 907). For
the battle of Belach Mugna see CS 907 (recte 908); D. Ó CORRÁIN, Ireland before the Normans, Dublin 1972, p. 116.

[78] See below, pp. 145-147; P. LANDAU, Ius Patronatus (Forschungen zur kirchlichen Rechtsgeschichte und zum Kirchenrecht 12), Cologne 1975.

[79] Ibid., p. 4.

nally composed in the early tenth century during the reign of Flann Sinna.[80] Another literary product of the time appears in the form of a saga tale dealing with Máel Sechnaill, son of Máel Ruanaid, the father of Flann. Anticipating Shakespeare, the author tells us that the spirit of the king's father appeared at night to a member of the community in Clonmacnois, namely to bishop Cairpre. He had to suffer pains in hell, since during his life time Máel Sechnaill had failed to have an *anmchara*, a spiritual confessor. The purpose of his visit was to ask the bishop and his priests to pray for the redemption of his tormented soul. Bishop Cairpre took pity, and set out to pray, to the end that the soul of Máel Sechnaill might be relieved. Eventually after reciting prayers for over a year the work of redemption was completed. The king thanked his benefactors by pointing out a place where he once hid some treasures, gained on a raid against the Vikings. The story comes to us as a religious tale, contained at the earliest in a fifteenth century manuscript.[81] It might be dismissed as a late medieval ghost story. There is, however, a note in the Chronicon Scotorum, inserted under the year 904, in the obituary of bishop Cairpre, stating that it was this bishop, to whom the spirit of Máel Sechnaill, son of Máel Ruanaid appeared.[82] Of course the note might have been inserted in the text by Mac Fhirbhisigh, who probably knew about the tale, when transcribing the annals. However, further evidence points to an early date of composition of the tale. First of all the tale supplies an explanation for the fact that Máel Sechnaill, and his descendants, were much obliged to the church in Clonmacnois, which of course neatly fits into the political context of the reign of Flann Sinna. The insistence on the *anmchara*, the confessor as an absolute 'prerequisite' for every Christian king, clearly promotes the interests of the Céili Dé movement, pointing to a time of composition when they were very influential in the

---

[80] See above, pp. 18f.

[81] The story is preserved amongst the religious tales in the fifteenth century MS Egerton 92, fol. 28b, now in the British Library. Other copies are known from the Lebor Brecc, p. 259, col. 2; and from Brussels MS 5100-5104, fol. 76b. See FLOWER, Catalogue of Irish manuscripts, II, pp. 514f., article 52. In the Martyrologium of Donegal bishop Cairpre is wrongly given the pedigree of Cairpre Crum, mythological king of Uí Maine, an alleged friend of St. Ciarán. The tale about the spirit of Máel Sechnaill is told here in an abreviated version (TODD / REEVES [eds.], Martyrology of Donegal, pp. 66f.). A Latin version of the tale is contained by Colgan, Acta Sanctorvm, 508-[599]509).

[82] CS 904. The Annals of Tigernach are lost for the period (A.D. 768 to 973).

Irish church.[83] In the ninth century, when the rule of the monastery of Tallaght was composed, they propagated that one should see a confessor at least once a year.[84] It seems therefore very plausible that such a story circulated and eventually was written down in Clonmacnois - possibly within the community of the Céili Dé - some time during the reign of Flann Sinna.

The successors to Flann Sinna in the kingship of Tara were, at first his rival and son-in-law, Niall Glúndub of the Northern Uí Néill (916-919),[85] followed by Donnchad Donn, a son of Flann (919-944). In his ecclesiastical policy Donnchad seems to have given priority to the Columban churches in his kingdom. He appears to have enjoyed the special frienship of Kells, where in his youth he once found sanctuary, when rebelling against his father Flann Sinna.[86] This situation was to change under Donnchad's successor, Congalach mac Máel Mithig (950-956). He was of the Síl nÁedo Sláine of Brega, a dynasty which had been excluded from the kingship of Tara for more than two centuries.[87] It seems the king made great efforts to guarantee for himself the support of Clonard and Clonmacnois, at the same time neglecting the Columban houses, under the headship of Kells.[88] Like during the reign of Flann Sinna, Clonard and Clonmacnois were again under the rule of one abbot Céilechair son of Robartach (d.954). In the year 951 King Congalach granted freedom from taxation (*soere*) to the community of

---

[83] GWYNN / PURTON (eds.), The monastery of Tallaght, §§2, 23, 44, 54, 78, 79; see also HUGHES, Sanctity and secularity in the early Irish church, in: K. HUGHES, Church and society in Ireland A.D. 400-1200, ed. D. DUMVILLE, London 1987, chap. IX, pp. 22f.

[84] GWYNN / PURTON (eds.), The monastery of Tallaght, §86. This source contains an anecdote bearing a very similar character to Colgan's tale; there a layman, who lived under the spiritual guidance of Eocha Ua Tuathail from Louth, was murdered by his enemies. The confessor, as well as the layman's wife and son were ordered by abbot Dublitir to pray and fast for seven years. They obeyed the order and eventually the spirit of the layman appeared to them to thank them for his redemption from hell.

[85] Niall's wife Gormlaith is said to have been the daughter of Flann (AClon 905 [recte 916], p. 145).

[86] AU 904.2.

[87] BYRNE, Irish Kings, p. 87; here pp. 281f. for the pedigree of the two dynasties. For the genealogy of the Síl nÁedo Sláine see O'BRIEN (ed.), Corpus Genealogiarum Hiberniae, p. 161 (144 b 44).

[88] M. HERBERT / P. Ó RIAIN (eds.), Betha Adamnáin, London 1988, pp. 8-20, where the compilation of the Betha Adamnáin, as an outcome of Congalach's hostility towards Kells, is discussed.

Clonard.[89] The Irish Life of Adamnán, written during the period, seems to suggest that other churches, such as Armagh and Clonmacnois, likewise benefited from the privilege. Kells, however, up to then unique in enjoying freedom from secular impositions, was not mentioned at all. Instead it had been plundered by the king's army in the preceding year.[90] Clonmacnois and its allies were also clearly perceived as a church on the side of Congalach mac Máel Mithig, by the king's enemies. In the year 950 Congalach went on a raid into Munster, seemingly in revenge, Clonmacnois and its neighbouring ally Gallen being plundered in the following years.[91]

The Life of Adamnán, written between the years 956 and 964, with unconcealed antipathy for the king, appears as the Kells comment to Congalach's biased church policy. His short reign and his violent death are interpreted as the immediate result of him having violated the rights of the church, i.e the rights of Kells.[92] A kind of counter statement, the state of affairs according to the view of those who profited from royal power during Congalach's reign, comes to us in a number of tales, apparently written in Clonmacnois around this time. First of all there is the acccount of the battle of Carn Conaill, as preserved in the Clonmacnois annals. The battle, in which the king of Mide defeated Guaire Aidne, the king of Connacht, took place in the year 649.[93] The king of Mide in question here was Diarmait, son of Áed Sláine, the ancestor of the Síl nÁedo Sláine, which was the dynasty of Congalach mac Máel Mithig. The Annals of Tigernach seem to have originally reported on the event in Latin. In a gloss, written in Irish, we are further told that

„...Guaire fled and Diarmait, son of Áed Sláine, was victor. Now Diarmait had marched to that battle through Clonmacnois. The community of Clonmacnois made supplication to God that he might come back safe by virtue of their guarantee. So after the return of the king he offered Tuaim n-eirc - Erc's Mound - with its subdivision of land - Liath Mancháin is its name to day - as a 'sod on altar' to God and to saint

89 CS 950, AFM 949; see HERBERT, Iona, Kells, and Derry, pp. 158, 170.

90 HERBERT / Ó RIAIN (eds.), Betha Adamnáin, pp. 13-16, 43. compare HERBERT, Iona, Kells, and Derry, pp. 177f.

91 Gallen and Delbna Ethra were plundered in 952 (AFM 949), Clonmacnois in the year 953 (AFM 951).

92 HERBERT / Ó RIAIN (eds.), Betha Adamnáin, p. 8.

93 AU 649.2, AFM 645.

Ciarán. And he bestowed three curses on the king of Meath if any of his people
should consume even a draught of water therein. Wherefore Diarmait demanded to be
buried in Clonmacnois".[94]

The probability that this gloss was added in the annals sometime in the reign
of King Congalach is very high indeed. The story, claiming that an ancestor
of Congalach, who lived in the seventh century, granted lands and freedom
from taxation to the church of Clonmacnois, appears as a projection into the
past of contemporary politics in the mid-tenth century.

A second tale, possibly also commenting on ecclesiastical affairs in Mide
under King Congalach is a tale about the reciprocal relations between Diarmait mac Cerbaill, St. Ciarán and St. Colum Cille. We are told that King
Diarmait mac Cerbaill, hearing the news of St. Ciarán's death lost his hearing out of grief so that none of the physicians in Ireland could heal him. He
went to Colum Cille to seek recovery. The saint, unable to heal the king,
sent him to Clonmacnois instead. He advises that earth from St. Ciarán's
grave be put onto the king's ears as the medicine most likely to cure his
disease. Diarmait obeyed the saintly order and found release and the recovery of his health in Clonmacnois. The tale comes to us in a seventeenth-
century manuscript.[95] It was translated and included by Mageoghagan in his
version of the Annals of Clonmacnois.[96] The message seems straightforward: Colum Cille is unable to help the king, who therefore relies on the one
who is more powerful, i.e, Clonmacnois. Clearly such a tale, with unconcealed traces of gloating, could only have been written in Clonmacnois at a

---

[94] *Cath Cairn Conaill in die Pentecostes, ubi da Cuan ceciderunt .i. Cuan mac Amalgaid
maic Enda, rí Muman, + Cuan mac Conaill, rí Hua Fi[d]gheinte, + Folamnach rí hua Lia-
thain, + Guaire fu[g]it, + Diarmaid mac Aeda Slane uictor erat. Is edh doluidh Diarmuit
don cath sin .i. tria Cluain maic Noiss. Doríndsead sámadh Cíarain étla fri Dia fair co tis-
sadh slan dia n-inchaib a coraigecht[a] som. Iar sódh in rig iarom roidbair Toim n-E[i]rc
cona fodlaib feraind .i. Líath Mancháin indíu a ainm [amail] fód fo[r]altoir do Dia + do
Chiaran, + dobert teora trisste for righ Midhi dia caithedh neach dia mundtir cidh digh n-
uisci and, conidh desin dorogart Diarmuid a adnacol a Cluain maic Nóis* (AT [649]); the
same version is preserved in CS 646, and AClon 642, p. 104.

[95] O'Clery Manuscripts in the Royal Library in Brussels, MS 5057-5059, fol. 37^r-37^v. Edited and translated by P. GROSJEAN (ed.), Notes d'hagiographie Celtique, No. 17: Aní día fil
manchine Chloinde Colmáin ocus Sil Aodha Sláine do Chlúain. Un miracle posthume de St.
Ciarán de Clúain en faveur du roi Diarmait mac Cerrbéoil: in: Analecta Bollandiana 69
(1951), pp. 96-102, here 98.

[96] AClon, pp. 82f.

time when there was no need to conceal existing rivalries, since the king at the time was entirely on one's side.

Furthermore the ecclesiastical dynasties who apparently rose to power in Clonmacnois in the course of the tenth century, under the patronage of the kings of Mide, were linked to their secular patrons by hagiographical saga tales. Thus the 'Conaillech'-family, for example, appears in a decisive role in the Clonmacnois version of the foundation story of Clonmacnois. St. Ciarán according to tradition was the one who, through his blessing, helped Diarmait mac Cerbaill to the kingship of Tara. Another helper, a certain Máelmor finds mention in the same story, who as Diarmait's half-brother killed Tuathal Máelgarb, the reigning king of Tara. He was, according to the Clonmacnois annals, of the Conaille Muirthemne.[97] It seems likely that this tradition had its origin in Clonmacnois itself, where two *fer léiginn* were supplied by the 'Conaillech' family in the tenth century.[98]

Similarly the Uí Máeldúin, prominent as hereditary vice-abbots in Clonmacnois during the eleventh century, were linked to the kings of the Southern Uí Néill by genealogical ties.[99] They were of Mide origin and are mentioned as a Clonmacnois dynasty in the genealogies contained in the Book of Lecan.[100] According to a tradition preserved in the O'Clery genealogies they claimed direct links with the secular rulers, by postulating that Diarmait mac Cerbaill, besides his otherwise attested offspring, namely Colmán Mór, Colmán Becc and Áed Sláine had a fourth son called Máeldúin. He was, so we are told, the ancestor of the Uí Máeldúin from Clonmacnois.[101] Since this fourth son of Diarmait mac Cerbaill is otherwise unknown, he

---

[97] AT (548), CS 544. The version contained in the Aided Dhiarmada preserved Máelmor's origin of the Conaille Muirthemne, see O'GRADY (ed.), Silva Gadelica, I, p. 73, and II, p. 554 for note and translation; see L. P. MURRAY, The Pictish kingdom of Conaille-Muirthemhne, in: J. RYAN (ed.), Féil-scríbhinn Eóin Mhic Néill. Essays and studies presented to Professor Eoin MacNeill, Dublin 1940, pp. 445-453.

[98] For the ecclesiastical dynasty, see Appendix 1, A49.

[99] See Appendix 1, vA18, vA21, vA23.

[100] The Book of Lecan, fol. 178ᵛ, the family is mentioned as *Uí Máeldúin chluana m. Nois*.

[101] PENDER (ed.), The O'Clery Book of genealogies, p. 58, §764: *ocus Maelduin (o fuilit muinter Maileduin a ccluain mac Nois)*. Compare O'BRIEN (ed.), Corpus Genealogiarum Hiberniae, p. 159 (143 bc 53).

must have been either a very late, or only a locally known discovery, made by the genealogists at work in Clonmacnois.

Finally it seems that in the course of the tenth century, under the patronage of the kings of Tara of the Clann Cholmáin and of the Síl nÁedo Sláine the salvation-bringing function of the graveyard of Clonmacnois, its establishment as an attractive place of burial for Irish dignitaries was much developed. The Irish Life of Ciarán contains what we might call the foundation story of this tradition, which is based in the first place on the extraordinary characteristics of a cow. Against the will of his mother Ciarán is said to have taken a cow and her calf with him, when he left his home to join St. Finnian's school in Clonard. There the brave animal supplied the whole community and even the guests with her milk. When Ciarán departed from Finnian, he left the cow to St. Ninned, but made sure that eventually her hide would come back to him, and he prophecised that even though many had lived on her milk, even more should be succoured by her hide, because every soul that would part from its body on the hide of the cow would not be tormented in hell (*Cech ainim raghus asa churp do sheichid na hUidhre nocha pianfaider a n-ithfrenn*).[102] The hagiographers twice insist on the fact that the hide, at the time they were writing, was kept in Clonmacnois, and thus made sure that thoses who wanted to avoid torments in hell should come to Clonmacnois to dy and to be buried there.

It seems more than right that the kings of the Southern Uí Néill, the grand patrons of Clonmacnois at the time, should be the first to profit from this miracle. In logical conclusion their ancestors, in an act of *post mortem* redemption, were declared to have been buried in Clonmacnois, in what appear to be subsequent insertions in the Clonmacnois annals. Thus the head of Diarmait mac Cerbaill, is said to have been brought to Clonmacnois after his death;[103] king Diarmait, son of Áed Sláine, is said to have ensured the right to be buried in Clonmacnois, for himself and his descendants, after his victory in the battle of Carn Conaill.[104] Máel Sechnaill, the father of king

---

[102] STOKES (ed.), Lives of Saints, pp. 122f., 127.

[103] AT (565), CS 565, AClon 547, pp. 79f.

[104] CS 646, AT (648).

Flann, was also declared to have died in Clonmacnois by later tradition.[105]
Flann Sinna himself did apparently not profit from the blessing, but died and
was buried in Kinneigh (*Cind eich muintire Cluana*), a church near Tara,
which was however a dependency of Clonmacnois.[106] Two of his daughters
are listed amongst those who found their rest in Clonmacnois. Muirgal died
as an 'old and rich woman' in Clonmacnois and Ligach was also buried
there.[107]

Down to the early eleventh century, during the whole of the reign of
Máel Sechnaill Mór (980 -1022) friendly realtions between the king of Mide
and the successors of St. Ciarán prevailed. Like under king Flann Sinna, and
under king Congalach mac Máel Mithig, Clonmacnois and Clonard were
under the joint rule of one abbot, Flaithbertach, son of Domnall, most likely
the brother of Máel Sechnaill Mór. He ruled in Clonmacnois since the year
1003, and assumed the headship of the church in Clonard in the year 1008.
He died in 1014, and was succeeded in Clonard by one of Máel Sechnaill's
sons.[108] King Máel Sechnaill made a spectacular donation to the church of
Clonmacnois in the year 1007:

> „The Eneclar of the great altar of Cluain muc Nois was purchased by Maelsechlainn,
> son of Domnall and a hide (was given) from each fort in Midhe on account
> thereof."[109]

The nature of the object is not quite clear. It is elsewhere mentioned as *cair-
recan* of Solomon's temple, sometimes interpreted as a model of the temple.[110] It seems to have been a very precious object, made of wood or metal.
The king commissioned the object to be made, and paid for it with a tax

---

[105] He died in 862 (AU). He was buried in Clonmacnois according to the 'Poem on the chiefs
and kings buried in Clonmacnois', edited by M. Stokes (PETRIE, Christian inscriptions, I, pp.
76-78, verses 15f.).

[106] CS 915; AFM 914, give Tara as the place of death.

[107] For Muirgal: CS 927; AClon 923, p. 148. For Ligach: CS 922; AClon 919, p. 147. She
was the wife of Máelmithigh, Lord of Brega, and mother of Congalach, of the Síl nÁedo
Sláine, who was to reign as king of Tara from 944-956.

[108] See Appendix 1, A60.

[109] *Eneclar altoire moire Cluana muc Nois do cennac la Maolseclainn mac Domnail,l ocus
seche cech Lis a Midhe da cinn* (CS 1005 [recte 1007], the respective folio in AT is missing).

[110] AT (1129); CS 1125; AFM 1129 when the object was stolen from the altar in Clonmacnois.

especially levied on that occasion from his subjects. The donation fell in the same year in which Máel Sechnaill revived the celebrations of the fair of Tailtiu.[111] It has been suggested, that the kings church policy, e.g. the demonstration of royal greatness through donations, or the attempt to get control of the churches by filling leading positions with members of his dynasty, was an attempt to immitate the strategies by which Brian Bóruma, the Munster king of the Dál Cais, facilitate his meteroic rise as claimant to the kingship of Ireland.[112]

3.3 The eleventh century

With the slow but steady decline of central royal power in Mide and the shrinking of the territory traditionally ruled over by the kings of Tara in the course of the eleventh century, the nature of the relation between Clonmacnois and the kings of Mide of the Southern Uí Néill was bound to change.[113] After the death of Máel Sechnaill Mór in the year 1022, violent succession struggles for the kingship followed out of which Conchobar, son of Domnall, a grandson of Máel Sechnaill Mór emerged as the victor. He held the kingship in Mide for more than forty years from 1030 to 1073.

Conchobar was closely linked to the main ecclesiastical centres in his kingdom by family ties. His great uncle Flaithbertach had been abbot of Clonard as well as Clonmacnois for the years 1008 to 1014. His father Domnall was coarb of Clonard from 1014 to 1019.[114] Flann, a brother of Conchobar, whom he blinded in the course of the rivalries to the kingship of Tara, [115] had married into the Clonmacnois aristocracy. His wife Cantigern was the daughter of Guaire Ua Lachtnáin, a scribe in Clonmacnois. Their

---

[111] AU 1007.10; CS 1005.

[112] HERBERT, Iona, Kells, and Derry, p. 86.

[113] F. J. BYRNE, The trembling Sod: Ireland in 1169, in: NHI II, pp. 1-42, here 19-21, for the borders and tribes of Mide in the eleventh century; P. WALSH, The Ua Máelsechlainn kings of Meath, in: IER 57 (1941), pp. 165-183, here 169-171.

[114] BYRNE, The community of Clonard, pp. 165f.

[115] AFM 1037.

two sons, Domnall and Murchad were both future kings of Mide.[116] Murchad later became the murderer of his uncle and succeeded to the kingship
in the year 1073.[117] Despite his ecclesiastical family background Conchobar
was not particularly friendly with the churches in his kingdom. In 1039 he
plundered Clonard, the main ecclesiastical ally of his predecessors, which at
the beginning of the century had been ruled by his own father.[118] Clonmacnois apparently was not involved in the conflict and when Conchobar was
killed in 1073, he was buried in Clonmacnois, indicating that some kind of
alliance, if only the keeping of the tradition of his forefathers, existed. He
appears once as the benefactor of Clonmacnois, namely as soon as he was
dead. According to a saga preserved by Mageoghagan the dead king's head
was stolen by the king of Munster shortly after the burial. A sickness befell
the thief so that he brought the head back only three days later. As a little
gift he added two rings of gold to reconcile the community of Clonmacnois,
who thus ultimately had made a profit from the head of the dead king.[119]

Conchobar's son Máel Sechnaill appears as the active military defender
of St. Ciarán's church. In 1080 he plundered the men of Tethba, which according to Mageoghagan was God's revenge on them for having plundered
Clonmacnois earlier in the year.[120] Again in the following year, when Máel
Sechnaill killed the lord of Calraige, the annalist interprets the event as a
punishment by God and Ciarán on him, he having earlier robbed the goods
of the church in Clonmacnois.[121] However Máel Sechnaill was killed by the
men of Tethba in 1087.[122] Domnall, another son of Flann, became king of
Mide after his cousin. He was slain by his own subjects, the men of Luigne,
in the year 1094.[123] Mide was divided between two rival candidates and

---

[116] Guaire, *ferleigind* of Clonmacnois died in 1054 (AI), for his daughter Cantigern see: M.
C. DOBBS (ed.), The ban-Shenchus, in: Revue Celtique 48 (1931), pp. 163-234, here 190.

[117] AFM 1073; CS 1070; AClon 1070, p. 180-181; AT (1073); Murchad himself was killed
in Kells by the lord of Gailenga three years later, see AT (1076).

[118] AT (1038).

[119] CS 1070; AClon 1070 (recte 1073), pp. 180f.

[120] AT (1080); AFM 1080; AClon 1078, p. 182.

[121] AClon 1079, p. 182; AFM 1081.

[122] AFM 1087; AClon 1084, p. 183.

[123] CS 1083 (recte 1087); and CS 1090 (recte 1094).

none of the successors to the kingship was able to restore the power once held by their ancestors in the tenth and early eleventh century.

The changing fortunes of the Ua Máelsechlainn dynasty in Mide found reflection in the way in which their ancestor Diarmait mac Cerbaill was reviewed in the saga tradition of the eleventh century, as preserved in the *Aided Dhiarmada*, the death tale of king Diarmait mac Cerbaill, a text written in Middle Irish which has been dated roughly to the eleventh century.[124] In these stories, he, who was otherwise known as the first Christian ruler, the friend of St. Colum Cille, the co-founder of Clonmacnois, is portrayed as the last pagan high king of Ireland. Diarmait's ongoing conflicts with many saints - who in their turn cursed his royal seat in Tara - eventually led to the decline of his power and brought about his most violent but classically pagan threefold death.[125] Even his relation with St. Ciarán, otherwise known as his intimate friend and promoter to the kingship, becomes ambiguous. At one occasion we are told how the king once gave a piece of land to St. Ciarán. Since his enemy lived on the land Diarmait promptly burned him within his house. Ciarán in consequence refused the gift and prophesied his threefold death (Of course, this prophecy had it been fulfilled, would have undermined the otherwise attested Clonmacnois tradition, that the head of King Diarmait was buried in Clonmacnois).[126]

An anti-Ua Máelsechlainn bias is also apparent in the Annals of Mageoghagan. Not only do we find no mention of the apparition of the spirit of Máel Sechnaill son of Máel Ruanaid, but neither is there any mention of the great gift which Máel Sechnaill Mór made to Clonmacnois in the year 1007. Whereas the Chronicon Scotorum portrays the battle of Clontarf as a fight of the foreigners against the combined forces of Brian and Máel

---

[124] K. JACKSON, The Motive of the threefold death, in: J. RYAN (ed.), Féil-scríbhinn Eóin Mhic Néill. Essays and Studies presented to Professor Eoin MacNeill, Dublin 1940, pp. 535-550, here 535 n.1. The story comes to us from the lost book of Sligo in a fifteenth century manuscript in the British Library, MS Egerton 1782, see O'GRADY (ed.), Silva Gadelica, II, pp. viiif.

[125] See BYRNE, Irish Kings, pp. 95-100; O'GRADY (ed.), Silva Gadelica, I, p. 78; JACKSON, The motive of the threefold death, pp. 535f.; J. N. RADNER, The significance of the threefold death in Celtic tradition, in: P. K. FORD (ed.), Celtic folklore and christianity. Studies in memory of William W. Heist, Los Angeles 1983, pp. 180-199.

[126] O'GRADY (ed.), Silva Gadelica, I, pp. 73f.; CS 565 for the burial of king Diarmait's head in Clonmacnois.

Sechnaill, the Annals of Clonmacnois have but a critical comment on Máel Sechnaill's unchivalrous behaviour. It is stated that Máel Sechnaill not only refused to fight on Brian's side, but also that 'he was content rather to lose the field then win it.'[127] There is the obvious problem of dating any of Mageoghagan's stories. The critical attitude towards Diarmait, king of Ireland expressed in them is however very close to that found in the *Aided Dhiarmada*. It can also be said that the stories must have been compiled at a time when Clonmacnois' sympathy for the kings of Mide was fading.

Mageoghagan maintains that after the death of Máel Sechnaill Mór, Ireland was governed as a *free state, & not like a monarchy* by the two leading poets of Ireland.[128] We may doubt his romantic seventeenth century perception of an idyllic medieval Irish poet-state. It seems instead that with the decline of a central power the smaller kingdoms, formerly vassals of the kings of Tara gained increasing importance, under local lords who were able to establish their authority to a considerable degree.[129] Those of them situated in the neighbourhood of Clonmacnois became involved in the politics of that church. The annals report on these developments mainly in terms of an increasing number of plunderings and raids of their church, by its various neighbours. Those raids however appear as an integral part of the struggles for power in the region, in which Clonmacnois seems to have been directly involved and often took sides.[130] The peoples foremost concerned, and most

---

[127] AClon, p. 167.

[128] AClon, p. 173.

[129] BYRNE, Irish Kings, pp. 268-271.

[130] Between the years 1015 and 1115 a total of thirty of these supposed raids on the settlement in Clonmacnois are recorded in the annals.
1. 1016 (AU, CS 1014) Burning by unnamed people.
2. 1019 (AClon, AFM) Domnall, son of Tadg Ua Ceallaigh plundered the shrine of Ciarán.
3. 1020 (AU, ALCé, AFM) Burning by unnamed people, together with Clonard and Swords.
4. 1021 (AFM) The *reachtaire* (chief lawgiver) of Máel Sechnaill Mor, together with Branacán Ua Máeluidir, plundered St. Ciarán's shrine.
5. 1023 (AT 1023, AFM) Plundering by Gadra Ua Dúnadaigh.
6. 1034 (AT (1034), CS 1032) A fight in Clonmacnois between the men of Munster and the men of Tethba.
7. 1038 (AU, ALCé, AT (1038), CS 1036) Battle between the Delbna and the Uí Maine.
8. 1044 (AT (1044), CS 1042, AClon 1044) Plundering by the Conmaicne.
9. 1044 (AFM, AClon) Plundering by the men of Munster.

often mentioned for having violated the church of Clonmacnois were the Delbna, the Uí Maine, the men of Tethba, the Conmaicne, the Calraige as well as tribes from North Munster such as the Uí Fógartaig.

In connection with Clonmacnois the annals most frequently mention families from Tethba, a subkingdom of the southern Uí Néill, covering the

---

10. 1050 (AU, AT (1050), CS 1048) Clonmacnois was thrice plundered in the same quarter of the year, once by the Síl Anmdacha and twice by the Calraige under Ua Catharnaigh.
11. 1050 (CS 1048) Plundering by the Conmaicne.
12. 1060 (AT (1060), CS 1058, AClon 1060) Plundering by those from Éli and by Ua Fógartaig.
13. 1065 (AT (1065), CS 1062) Plundering by the Conmaicne and the Uí Maine.
14. 1077 (AT (1077), CS 1074) Burning by unnamed people.
15. 1080 (AT (1080), AFM) Plundering by the men of Tethba.
16. 1081 (AFM) Plundering by the Calraige.
17. 1082 (AFM) The cemetery of the nuns in Clonmacnois was burned.
18. 1089 (AT (1089), AFM) Attempted plundering by an army from Munster.
19. 1092 (AT (1092), CS 1088, AFM) A fleet of the men of Munster plundered Clonmacnois.
20. 1094 (AClon 1094) Plundering by an army from Bregmaine (represented by the former barony Brawny, county Westmeath).
21. 1094 (CS 1090) Plundering by the Delbna.
22. 1095 (AT 1095), CS 1091) Plundering by the Conmaicne.
23. 1095 (CS 1091) Great persecution from evil men.
24. 1098 (AFM) Burning of the oratory by the *muintir Tlamain* (from Tethba) under Cucaille, son of Áed.
25. 1101 (AT (1101), CS 1097) Encounter between the Muinter Tadgáin and the Muintir Cinaeith.
26. 1106 (AFM) Plundering by unnamed people.
27. 1111 (CS 1107) Forcible refection by Áed, son of Domnall Ua Ruairc.
28. 1111 (CS 1107) Plundering by the Dál Cais.
29. 1115 (CS 1111) Plundering by the men of Munster.
30. 1115 (AT (1114)) Desecration of the bell of Ciarán through Ua Loingsigh, king of Dál nAraide.
Compare the tenth century, where some nine raids are recorded
1. 922 (AU, CS 921, AFM 920) The foreigners of Limerick.
2. 936 (AU 936, CS 935) The foreigners of Dublin.
3. 936 (CS 935) The men of Munster.
4. 942 (AU, CS 941) The heathens of Dublin.
5. 946 (AU, AFM 944) The foreigners of Dublin.
6. 953 (AU, CS 952, AFM 951) The men of Munster with the Foreigners of Limerick in their company.
7. 959 (AU 959, CS 958, AFM 957) The men of Munster.
8. 962 (AFM 960) The men of Ossory.
9. 986 (CS 984, AFM 985) Burning by unnamed people.

area from Durrow to Lough Ree and the river Inny.[131] Since the later tenth
century Tethban activities in Clonmacnois can be traced. Agda, the son of
the lord of Tethba died after a good life in Clonmacnois in the year 980;[132]
another prince of Tethba was killed in Clonmacnois in the year 999.[133] The
men of Tethba seem to have had their own habitations within the settlement,
which were raided in the year 1034.[134] It is therefore not surprising to find
an increasing number of Tethban families active in the government of
Clonmacnois.

The Uí Lachtnáin, named after Lachtnan, lord of Tethba who died in the
late ninth century, supplied a prominent *fer léiginn* in the eleventh century.[135] The Uí Tadgáin cherished a tradition as priests and artists in the
settlement since the later tenth century.[136] Ua Catharnaig, a branch of the
Muinter Tadgáin who became famous under their nickname 'na Sionnaig',
the Foxes, became the leading force in Tethban politics in the eleventh century. One branch was settled in Clonmacnois, their most outstanding member being Muirchertach the cleric, a nephew of Muiredach mac Catharnaig,
king of Tethba. He died in the year 1105 as a learned senior in Clonmacnois,
and left three sons behind.[137] Obviously close links, even blood ties existed
between the Clonmacnois aristocracy and the leading dynasty in Tethba. In
this context it can be understood that in the late eleventh century, the abbot
of Clonmacnois retired to Mag Eli (Moyelly), which were the mensal lands

---

[131] L. Cox, Historic Moyelly - Home of Colonel Richard Grace, in: Jn. of the Old Athlone
Society 1, no. 4 (1974/75), pp. 238-241, here 238; M. C. Dobbs, The territory and people of
Tethba, in: JRSAI 68 (1938), pp. 241-259; vol. 71 (1941/42), pp. 101-110.

[132] AFM 979. He is said to have died in *imdhaidh Chiaráin*, the bed of Ciarán, which was
probably located in Eglais Beag, the church where Ciarán himself is said to have died. See
above, pp. 41f.

[133] CS 997.

[134] CS 1032.

[135] AFM 889; see Guaire Ua Lachtnáin (S23, d.1054 AI, AFM).

[136] See Appendix 1, P6 (d.996); P14 (d.1168); Dúnchad Ua Tadgain of the family was the
artist who made the shrine of the Stowe Missal in the mid eleventh century (G. F. Warner,
The Stowe Missal, London 1906, vol. 2, Introduction, p. xlvi).

[137] AFM 1105; Dobbs, The Genealogies of the Southern Uí Néill, pp. 9, 11. See Appendix 1,
Sen9.

of Uí Chatharnaigh co-extensive with the parish of Kilmanaghan.[138] Another branch of the Uí Tadgáin were the Ua Conghaile, who became hereditary guestmasters in Clonmacnois in the latter half of the eleventh century.[139] Finally a member of the Tethba family, Ua Muirecán, was amongst the first diocesan bishops of Clonmacnois in the early thirteenth century.[140]

The predominance of Tethban families in Clonmacnois seems to be contemporary with the rise of the former petty kingdom to a significant power in Mide. It apparently led to the direct involvement of Clonmacnois in the political rivalries within the kingdom. Thus the settlement of Clonmacnois was often plundered by the various parties involved in Tethban politics, and the Uí Chatharnaigh plundered St. Ciarán's foundation just as well as their neighbouring enemies the Calraige of Western Mide.[141] The Tethban army fought their enemies from Munster within the ecclesiastical settlement.[142] At the turn of the eleventh to the twelfth century the two leading Tethban dynasties had an armed conflict in Clonmacnois itself.[143] The close association between the rulers of Tethba and the church of Clonmacnois found reflection in a little contemporary poem citing a scholar, coming from Clonmacnois, who, when asked how things were in his monastic school, replies, that it was all invaded by Foxes:

Canastic mac leghind, ticim o chluain chelbind
iar leghadh mo leghind, teghim sis co sord.
indis scela cluana, indisfet nacuala
Sinnaigh imahuadha, etait bruana bolg.
(Whence are you, learning's son? From Clonmacnois I come.
My course of study done, I'm off to Swords again.

---

[138] Abbot Ua Flaithéin retired to Magh Eli, and was plundered by the *Muintir Tlamain* a local Tethba branch, subject to Ua Catharnaigh in the following year (1098). Possibly in consequence he moved further east to Aghadboe, where he died in the year 1100. CS 1096; CS 1092; AFM 1100; AFM 1098. Compare Appendix 1, A69.

[139] AFM 1093; AFM 1116; AFM 1166. See Appendix 1, G2, ?G4, G5, G6.

[140] See Appendix 1, B26.

[141] AU 1050.7; AT (1050); CS 1048.

[142] AT (1034); CS 1032.

[143] AT (1101); CS 1097.

'How are things keeping there?' Oh things are shaping fair,
Foxes round the churchyards bare, gnawing the guts of men).[144]

3.4 The Ua Conchobair kings as patrons of Clonmacnois (twelfth century)

In the final part of this chapter the rise of the Ua Conchobair kings of Connacht to the position as the most powerful secular allies of Clonmacnois
shall be discussed. Throughout the eleventh century Connacht was dominated by the rivalries between Ua Ruairc and Ua Conchobair. Tadg an eich
gil (Tadg of the White Steed) Ua Conchobair killed his rival Áed Ua Ruairc
in 1015.[145] Tadg was murdered in 1030,[146] and succeeded by Art Uallach
Ua Ruairc.[147] Áed Ua Conchobar, surnamed Áed an-ga-bearnaigh, i.e. Áed
of the gapped Spear, successfully established his power in Connacht after
Art's death in 1046. But, like his predecessors he was killed eventually by
his arch rival, Áed Ua Ruairc in 1066. According to the Annals of Tigernach
Áed Ua Ruairc took the kingship of Connacht in that year.[148] However
Ruaidrí, the son of Tadg (surnamed Ruaidrí na Soige Buide, Ruaidrí of the
Yellow Bitch), was the more successful candidate for the kingship and
eventually killed Áed Ua Ruairc in a battle in the year 1087.[149] Despite the
fact that Ruaidrí Ua Conchobair was blinded some five years later[150] and

---

[144] R. THURNEYSEN, Mittelirische Verslehren, in: W. STOKES / E. WINDISCH (eds.), Irische
Texte mit Übersetzung und Wörterbuch, Leipzig 1891, pp. 93f., §142. Translated by F.
O'CONOR, Kings, Lords and Commons, London 1961, p. 46. See also C. NÍ MAOL-CHRÓIN,
Macalla as Cluain-mhac-Nóis A.d. 1050, in: Galvia 1 (1954), pp. 15-17, who dates the poem
to the mid-eleventh century, as a direct comment on three raids of Clonmacnois performed by
the Foxes in the year 1050 (AI,AU). Thanks to Dr Katharine Simms who helped me to trace
the poem and pointed out to me the article by C. Ní Maol-Chróin.

[145] AU 1015 probably in revenge for the murder of his brother Domnall the year before (AU
1014).

[146] AT (1030); AU 1030.12.

[147] AT (1046) Art was killed by the Cenél Conaill.

[148] AT (1066); CS 1064; AFM 1066.

[149] AT (1087); CS 1083; AU 1087.

[150] He was blinded by two of his sub-chiefs, Ua Fógartaig and Ua Flaithbertaig (AT [1092];
CS 1088). Áed Ua Flaithbertaig king of the west of Connacht had been killed by Ruaidrí

therefore lost the capacity to be king, the kingship in Connacht was monopolised by the Uí Chonchobair dynasty from his time onwards throughout the twelfth century. Domnall, one of the sons of the blinded Ruaidrí, gained the kingship after his father. According to the Clonmacnois chronicles he was dethroned in 1106 and his eighteen-year-old brother Toirdelbach was elected and inaugurated instead.[151] Under this king (1106-1156) the power in Connacht was finally consolidated as a property of the Ua Conchobair dynasty which brought the internecine rivalries of the eleventh century to an end. The Uí Ruairc consolidated their power as lords of Bréifne and Conmaicne.

Both the Ua Conchobair kings as well as the Ua Ruairc dynasty become increasingly prominent in the Clonmacnois chronicles from the latter half of the eleventh century onwards. Whereas the Ua Ruairc lords of Conmaicne figure as one of the most persistent enemies of Ciarán, their rivals receive a very sympathetic review. Clonmacnois' alliance with the Ua Conchobair dynasty is first apparent in the battle of Corann (A.D. 1087) in which Ruaidrí Ua Conchobair won the decisive victory over the Conmaicne under Áed Ua Ruairc. According to the Chronicon Scotorum the victory was brought about with the active military support of St. Ciarán. We are told that Cormac Ua Cillín, an offical in Clonmacnois stood in front of the Connacht army during the battle with the staff of Ciarán in his hands.[152] As *aird secnab Síl Muiredaig*, he seems to have been vice-abbot in Clonmacnois with special jurisdiction for the Síl Muiredaig territory in Connacht. In any case he functioned as mascot-bearer in battle and made use of St. Ciarán's relics in support of the Uí Chonchobair king of Connacht. When king Ruaidrí, five years after his military success was blinded by one of his vassals, he seems to have retired to Clonmacnois where he died as chief senior, noble and repentant in the year 1118.[153]

---

more than ten years before (AT [1079]). His avenger was blinded himself by the Síl Muiredaig in 1097 (AT [1097, 1098]).

[151] AT (1106); CS 1102. AU 1088.6, gives as the year of birth for Toirdelbach.

[152] CS 1083; ALCé 1087; AT (1087) does not mention the involvement of Ua Cillín from Clonmacnois.

[153] AT (1118); CS 1114; ACott 1118. He was blinded in the year 1092 according to AT (1092).

His son Toirdelbach continued the tradition of his father, and cherished the alliance with St. Ciarán. In the year 1115 he made a huge donation of precious golden altar implements to Clonmacnois.[154] The donation was made right after a victory over Murchad Ua Maelsechlainn, king of Mide, the former overlords and patrons of Clonmacnois. Toirdelbach was also involved in the building of a *cloictheach*, a belfry in Clonmacnois in the year 1124.[155] Like his father he died in Clonmacnois and was buried there. In his obituary in the Annals of Tigernach he is praised as the 'Augustus of the West of Europe, the splendour and glory of Ireland and a benefactor of the churches and monasteries'. The author also adds that he was buried under the altar of Ciarán, and that he gave 160 ounces of gold and 60 marks of refined silver, and all his treasures except for his sword, drinking horn, shield and weapon to the churches.[156]

Ruaidrí, the son of Toirdelbach, famous as the last 'High-king of Ireland' was certainly less effective than his father in promoting his authority over Connacht. Nevertheless he appears as the one who defended Clonmacnois against the army of Hugh de Lacy, when they plundered the settlement in the year 1178.[157] Ruaidrí died in the abbey of Cong in 1198. The annals explicitly state that his body was transferred to Clonmacnois to be buried there.[158]

Donations, building activities in the monastery, as well as military support, had been the characteristic features of Ua Máelsechlainn patronage over Clonmacnois during the tenth and early eleventh century. All three domains were taken over by the Ua Conchobair kings of Connacht. Moreover they made Clonmacnois the exclusive burial ground of the Connacht nobility. All of the twelfth-century kings of Connacht died and were buried

---

[154] AT (1115); CS 1111: *He offered three jewels to Saint Ciarán in Clonmacnois, to wit a drinking horn inlaid with gold (corn co n-ór), a goblet inlaid with gold (bledhe co n-ór) and a paten of copper inlaid with gold (mullóc uma co n-ór).*

[155] CS 1120 (recte 1124). This was probably the same tower which later became known as O'Rourkes tower in Clonmacnois, see MACALISTER, Memorial slabs of Clonmacnois, pp. 141ff.

[156] AT (1156); see also AClon 1153, p. 200, where Clonmacnois as his burial place is not mentioned.

[157] AT, AFM.

[158] AFM 1198; Ruaidrí had resigned his kingship and retired to Cong in 1183 (ALCé).

in St. Ciarán's graveyard. Other noble Connacht families made Clonmacnois their preferential place of burial, as apparent from an entry in the Annals of Loch Cé, when they record that in the year 1181 some twenty Connacht nobles who were killed in the battle of Mag-Dingba were 'conveyed
after their deaths, to Cluain-mic-Nois, and interred in the sepulchre of the
nobles of their ancestors'.[159] Finally Ua Conchobair patronage in Clonmacnois gave support the rise of several Connacht families in leading offices in
Clonmacnois. The Ua Maeleoin family, presumably linked with the royal
dynasty, could secure itsself a position as the almost exclusive holders of
the abbacy in Clonmacnois during the twelfth century. Members of the Ua
Neachtain family from Uí Maine took over the leadership of the Céili Dé
community and the Ua Dubhtaigh, a traditional ecclesiastical dynasty in
Connacht apparently got a share in government in Clonmacnois.[160]

3.5   Conclusions: patronage and politics

The teaching of the church concerning the relation between secular and ecclesiastical power, relies in the first place on St. Augustine, who primarily
defined secular power as the institution which was to defend the church
against its enemies, i.e the enemies of God. The prime task of a Christian
ruler therefore was to protect, with his military forces, the churches and
monasteries in his realm, members of which were by definition not allowed
to bear arms. Obviously this theory no longer holds ground, once the church
disposes of its own army. The nature of what is generally referred to as
secular patronage, therefore, needs to be re-defined. From the example of
Clonmacnois we might deduce some essential features of the interaction
between secular power and an ecclesiastical estate. An important aspect,
still, was that of military protection, provided by the secular lord for his
church. This seems to have been the view underlying the promulgation of
St. Ciarán's law in Connacht with the support of the king, as it happened in
the late eighth and early ninth centuries. Ecclesiastical authority was exercised and expanded in agreement and with the support of the secular rulers
at the time. However, the concept of the church as a neutral entity, a help-

---

[159] ALCé 1181.

[160] See below, pp. 152f.

less protégé of a powerful king is totally inadequate, since we know that right at the same time the ecclesiastical army participated in battles and got involved in the succession struggles to the kingship of Tara, after the death of Domnall Midi.[161] More often, it seems, the ecclesiastical protégé got involved in battles as the guarantor of supernatural support. This notion seems to underlie the tenth century account of the battle of Carn Conaill, which is said to have been won by the king of Mide through the prayers of St. Ciarán's community.[162] Similarly, in the later eleventh century, the king of Connacht gained the decisive military victory over the Conmaicne due to the assistance of St. Ciarán's deputy, who functioned as a kind of mascot-bearer in battle, by carrying the staff of Ciarán before the Connacht army.[163] However, direct military support for a secular patron seems to have remained the exception. There were other more peaceful means of interference in secular politics. The leading churchmen of Clonmacnois, for example, apparently functioned as mediators between their royal patron and his potential vassal, the king of Connacht, when they brought about the latter's submission to the overlordship of the king of Mide.[164] Such direct involvement of the church with secular politics seems to have functioned on the basis that secular lords had their allies, or even close family members placed in leading positions in the churches concerned. The abbot of Clonmacnois would thus often have been a member of a loyal branch of the leading secular dynasty. When in the course of the eighth century the Uí Briúin rose to power in Connacht, this would lead to the appearance of Uí Briúin churchman in the abbacy of Clonmacnois.[165] Likewise the Uí Maine, who supported the community in Clonmacnois in their opposition to the king of Munster in the early ninth century, supplied two of the abbots of Clonmacnois thereafter. Contemporary with the rise of King Flann Sinna as the most prominent of St. Ciarán's secular friends, was the rise of a family from the Conaille Muirthemne, allies of the Clann Cholmáin kings of Mide, in lead

---

[161] AU 765.5.

[162] AT (649); CS 646; AClon 642, pp. 103f.

[163] CS 1083 (recte 1087).

[164] CS 899; AFM 896.

[165] Forbasach (d.771), Anaile (d.799), and Suibne (d.816) were abbots from the Uí Briúin. See Appendix 1, A27, A34, A36.

of Clonmacnois.[166] The king on the other hand might have often recruited his ministers from the monastic schools within the churches, which probably functioned as training colleges for royal officials. Thus the *aird-rechtaire* (chief-lawgiver, or steward) of Máel Sechnaill Mór came most likely from Clonmacnois, as a member of the leading dynasty of the settlement, closely allied with their secular patrons from Mide.[167]

This close interaction on a personal level meant that the king could directly interfere in ecclesiastical politics. The lay ecclesiastical rulers of the church, on the other hand, as the friends and advisors of the king would have a decisive vote in secular affairs. It seems in fact that the rights of the church to interfere with secular politics were also promoted with spiritual means. Thus the Céili Dé movement seems to have made loud propaganda for the *anmchara*, the confessor, as an absolute requirement of every Christian king in the ninth and tenth centuries. Obviously the spiritual well-being of the king was the foremost concern of his confessor. However, in his position as the closest spiritual friend of a king, the *anmchara* might have functioned as the centre of coordination between secular and ecclesiastical power. Furthermore, as a man of the church, invested with spiritual authority by God, the salvation of the king's soul stood and fell with the confessor's benevolence. This of course was a very effective means by which to control royal decisions, i.e. secular politics.

Finally there is, what is usually the most prominent aspect of patronage, namely that of donations and gifts to the church made by a secular ruler to his protege. These deeds find most attention in the chronicles, and were apparently perceived as most spectacular events by contemporaries. Thus it made headlines in the annals when King Flann Sinna paid for the building of a great stone church in Clonmacnois. It seems that, comparable to the meaning of sacraments for a believer, those donations were perceived as visible signs of the grace of one particular patron. They were, however, at the same time, one of the main sources from which a patron could draw his right of interference within ecclesiastical affairs, since his spiritual friends would always be greatly obliged to their powerful and generous benefactor.

---

[166] See above, p. 116.

[167] AFM 1021.

Secular patronage over churches and monasteries, always symbolizing the understanding of the relation between the spiritual and the wordly powers within society, obviously functioned on the basis of personal bonds between the respective magnates within a particular territory. In a closely knit network of interaction the secular patron and his ecclesiastical protégé cooperated towards their common good or, to put it otherwise, towards mutual stability. The mechanisms to enable such cooperation, the ways in which it found expression as well as potential factors of disturbances, as they could be worked out for the case of Clonmacnois, appear to be in agreement with the general patterns, according to which power was exercised in the European middleages, indicating that politics in medieval Ireland worked in the same way as in the rest of Europe.[168]

---

[168] Compare for example the German realm, where the king exercised and expanded his power by relying on either close relatives or members of loyal dynasties: Bruno, a brother of Otto I, was archbishop of Cologne and one of his strongest and most reliable supporters. Otto's natural son William became archbishop of Mainz, after the previous rebellious archbishop Friederich, had died in 954. William was followed by Otto's nephew Hatto. Otto's niece Gerberga, was abbess of the important abbey of Gandersheim (B. H. HILL, Medieval monarchy in action, London 1972, pp. 27f., 32, 40).

4 CHURCH REFORM AND ANGLO-NORMAN INVASION

The moral conduct of its clergy and monks had always been an important issue for the church. With the Gregorian Reform in the eleventh century the idea of celibacy as a requirement for every man of the church was promoted and eventually became obligatory church law. Inside the Irish Church reformers with the same concern had been active as early as the eighth century. They were known as the Céilí Dé movement, and strictly objected to the ever-increasing number of lay-abbots in Irish monasteries.[1] However, laymen continued to dominate in leading positions in the Irish church. Their children also assumed ecclesiastical offices or succeeded to their fathers' position. Thus families established themselves in the churches, who over generations held various offices and are generally referred to as lay ecclesiastical dynasties. The traditional concept of the monastic *familia* assumed increasing reality in a literal sense. Thus by the eleventh century the main ecclesiastical centres in Ireland were dominated by families, the Clann Sínaich ruled in Armagh, Uí Fallomain in Clonard, Uí Chathail in Glendalough, Uí Uchtáin and Uí Robartaig in Kells.[2]

4.1 Clonmacnois on the eve of the church reform

4.1.1 The Meic Cuinn na mBocht

In Clonmacnois the most prominent lay ecclesiastical dynasty was known as the Meic Cuinn na mBocht, the sons of Conn na mBocht. The annals provide a detailed pedigree of the family documenting their presence in Clonmacnois as early as the mid-eighth century. According to the Annals of Tigernach, Gormán, their ultimate ancestor, a scribe and abbot of Louth came to live for a year as an anchorite on the waters of Fingén's well in

---

1 P. O'DWYER, Céli Dé - Spiritual reform in Ireland 750-900, Dublin 1981, p. 192.

2 T. Ó FIAICH, The church of Armagh, pp. 75-127; BYRNE, The community of Clonard, pp. 166f., nos. 41, 43, 45, 47; MAC SHAMHRÁIN, Prosopographica Glindelachensis, pp. 85f.; HERBERT, Iona, Kells, and Derry, pp. 89f., 98f.

Clonmacnois where he died in the year 758.[3] His son Torbach was abbot of Armagh, his grandson Áedacán, another abbot of Louth, also died on pilgrimage in Clonmacnois in the early ninth century. This tradition of the anchorites was cherished in the family for the following three generations;[4] along with the connection with Armagh, it links the family with the monastic reform movement of the Céili Dé, active in the Irish church since the eighth century. From the latter half of the ninth century onwards the descendants of Gormán are found in various other positions in their monastic home. They provided lectors, guardians of the mortuary chapel, bishops and seniors as well as leaders of the Céilí Dé community in Clonmacnois.[5]

As far as their tribal origin is concerned two alternative versions are preserved in the annals. Repeatedly kinship with the Uí Cheallaigh of Brega is claimed,[6] at other occasions they are said to belong to the Airgiallan tribe of the Mugdorna Maigen.[7] Since the latter were situated in the immediate neighbourhood of Louth (the monastery whence the family originally came and which one would not forge a link since they were rather insignificant), it seems the more plausible version.[8] The Uí Cheallaigh instead were a branch of the Síl nÁedo Sláine of the Southern Uí Néill, in the eastern parts of

---

[3]   AT (757). For a summary of the family history see KELLEHER, The Tain and the annals, pp. 125f. He assumes that the Conaillech clan also belonged to the Meic Cuinn na mBocht, since the Conaille Muirthemne were neighbours of the Mugdorna Maigen. There is however a lack of evidence to support this suggestion. For the family background in Louth and their connection with Armagh see C. DOHERTY, The cult of St. Patrick and the politics of Armagh in the seventh century, in: J.-M. PICARD (ed.), Ireland and Northern France A.D. 600-850, Dublin 1991, pp. 53-94, esp. 56f.

[4]   For the anchorites of Clonmacnois provided by the family see Appendix 1. An2 (d.758), An3 (d.835), An4 (d.847), An5 (d.865), An8 (d.1006), An11 (d.1022), An14 (d.1060).

[5]   See Appendix 1. Offices holders provided by the family:
Lectors: S9 (d.865), S18 (d.1006), S31 (d.1106).
Airchinnech of Eglais Beag: AE1 (d.898), AE3 (d.949), AE9 (d.1097).
Bishops: B9 (d.949), B10 (d.954), B17 (d.1011), B19 (d.1060), B20 (d.1067).
Seniors: Sen10 (d.1134), Sen11 (d.1180).
Head of the Céili Dé: C1 (d.1060), C2 (d.1079).

[6]   Claimed for Torbach (AFM 807), Áedacán (AClon 832, p. 136), Dúnadach (AClon 950, p. 156) and Céilechair (AFM 1067).

[7]   Óenacán (AFM 947), Conaing (CS 1011), Céilechair (AFM 1067, where he is called Céilechair Mugdornach of the Uí Cheallaigh of Brega) and Cormac (CS 1099).

[8]   KELLEHER, The Tain and the annals, p. 126.

Mide, who produced several kings of Mide during the ninth, and one in the mid-tenth centuries. Most likely the claim to be related to the Uí Cheallaigh of Brega was the later version of the Meic Cuinn na mbocht pedigree, which had its origin in the attempt to establish a genealogical link with the Southern Uí Néill kings (maybe dating from the mid-tenth century when Congalach mac Máel Mithig of the Síl nÁedo Sláine was king of Tara).

The family is occasionally referred to as Muintir Gormán or Cinél Torbaig, after the seventh-century founders of the dynasty.[9] However, the name Meic Cuinn na mBocht derives from an eleventh-century personality. Conn, the eponymous family member, died in the year 1060. Five of his sons are commemorated in the annals: Céilechair, who died as bishop in 1067 and was the father of Máel Muire the famous scribe of Lebor na hUidre;[10] Máel Chiaráin, whom the Four Masters style *comarba Chiaráin*; also Máel Finnén, Gilla Chríst and Máel Íosa, mentioned in the annals without any special title but simply as the sons of Conn.[11]

Conn na mBocht himself according to the Four Masters was head of the Céili Dé in Clonmacnois, and anchorite.[12] The Clonmacnois annals simply call him Conn na n.Bocht, Conn of the poor.[13] Brian Ó Cuív suggested that the Irish *boicht*, i.e. the poor, stood for a group of monastic dwellers who were either identical or closely associated with the Céili Dé, the two groups together formed the actual community of the religious within the settlement. The term appears first in a monastic context in the eleventh century.[14] He proposes that Conn was head of the poor and the Céili Dé community of Clonmacnois.[15] He passed the office on to his son who held it up to the year

---

9   AClon 832, p. 136; AFM 807.

10   AT, AFM 1067, CS 1064. See BEST / BERGIN (eds.), Lebor na hUidre, p. xiv.

11   For the sons of Conn see Appendix 1:?B20 (d.1067), A66 (d.1079), O4(d.1056), O6 (d.1085), O7 (d.1103).

12   AFM 1031.

13   CS 1057; Conn's obituary is not preserved in AT and AClon.

14   See Ó Cuív, Miscellanea 1, using evidence from the Aislinge Meic Con Glinne, an eleventh century text.

15   Ibid., p. 107. He translates the title given to Conn by the four Masters: *cend Celedh ndhé, + ancoiri Cluana mic Nóis*, as 'the person responsible for the Culdees and anchorites of Clonmacnois'; see above, pp. 43f.

1079.[16] The fact that the head of the Meic Cuinn na mBocht family in the eleventh century assumed the office as head of the poor, *cenn bocht*, appears therefore as the continuation of the family's tradition as anchorites and members of the Céili Dé.

4.1.1.1 Íseal Chiaráin - the dynasty's residence

'Conn na mBocht, the person responsible for the Culdees and anchorites in Clonmacnoise, was the first to assemble a herd for the poor of Clonmacnoise at Íseal Chiaráin'.[17] It has been said above that Conn na mBocht, the poor and the community of the Céili Dé had something to do with Íseal Chiaráin. In fact there is evidence which suggests that this church gradually became family property of the Meic Cuinn na mBocht. It was according to tradition the location of Ciarán's first settlement in the area.[18] A verse couplet in praise of Conn na mBocht, inserted by the Four Masters under the year 1031, seems to have Íseal Chiaráin in mind when it refers to *do chill*, (your church) again implying that this place was regarded as intimately associated with Conn.[19] However, as a member of the *paruchia* of Clonmacnois the church was liable to pay services and taxes to the successor of Ciarán. Moreover, the king of Mide as the secular overlord had a share in Íseal Chiaráin. The royal rights were strenuously resisted by the monastic familia, when in the year 1076 the king's son tried to exact certain services from his church. In the course of the monastic resistance the overseer of the poor in Íseal Chiaráin was killed.[20] Again the notion of the church as family property is implied in the account of these events by Mageoghagan who talks of the inhabitants of Íseal Chiaráin as the *family of Moylekyeran mc Con ne mboght in Isellkyeran*. Eventually in the year 1093 Cormac, a grandson of

---

[16] Ibid.; AU 1074.4; AU 1077.6.

[17] AFM 1031; see Ó Cuív, Miscellanea 1, p. 109, who suggested this translation. O'Donovan translated 'the first that invited a party of the poor'.

[18] AFM 1031. For Íseal Chiaráin see above, pp. 68-71.

[19] AFM 1031: *A Chuinn Chluana, atclos tú a hErind i nAlban,* | *A chind ordain, nochan usa do chill dargain* ('O Conn of Cluain! thou wert heard from Ireland in Alba; | o head of dignity, it will not be easy to plunder thy church'). Thanks to Dr Seán Duffy who pointed out to me some important details on Conn na mbocht.

[20] AClon 1069, p. 180; AFM 1072.

Conn, bought the church from the king of Mide and from the abbot of Clonmacnois.[21] This purchase meant exemption from secular and ecclesiastical authority and taxation for the *familia* in Íseal Chiaráin, a term which in this context should probably be understood in the literal sense. Moreover this was the final step to the transformation of Íseal Chiaráin, once in the possession of St. Ciarán, into an independent church run by a lay ecclesiastical dynasty. Despite the fact that the Meic Cuinn na mBocht themselves came from Clonmacnois, the purchase came up tp the alienation of Íseal Chiaráin from the authority of the abbot of Clonmacnois. At the same time the influence of the family in Clonmacnois itself persisted. When three years after the purchase abbot Ua Flaithéin went on pilgrimage, Cormac, a grandson of Conn na mBocht succeeded him in the abbacy of Clonmacnois.[22]

4.1.1.2 Internal factions in Clonmacnois - opposition to the Meic Cuinn na mBocht

Such an accumulation of power and wealth in the hands of one family was bound to attract opposition. Evidence for hostility towards the Meic Cuinn na mBocht can be traced in the hagiographical works dealing with St. Ciarán. The Irish Life, in what appears to be an eleventh century redaction, comments rather critically on the relation between Clonmacnois and the community in Íseal Chiaráin.[23] The story goes that the brethren there asked Ciarán to leave since they could not endure his generosity towards the poor. Ciarán abided by their wish and left the place with a blessing, more precisely a curse:

> „Although lowly, it were high,
> Had not censure come me nigh;

---

[21] CS 1089; AClon 1087, p. 184; AFM 1089.

[22] Ua Flaithéin died in 1100, but went on pilgrimage to Aghaboe four years before he died. It seems plausible that Cormac took the abbacy during his absence . Thus he was abbot from 1096 to 1103, when he died (CS 1092, CS 1099). See Appendix 1. A69, A70.

[23] STOKES (ed.), Lives of Saints, pp. 128f.; the story is also contained in the Dublin version of the Life of Ciarán (PLUMMER [ed.], Vitae Sanctorum Hiberniae, I, pp. 209f., §§23-25); see above, pp. 19-21.

Had I not been censured so,
It were high though it be low."[24]

This story expresses first of all the opinion of the writer (presumably at Clonmacnois), that the brethren in Íseal Chiaráin were greedy. Moreover the name of the church, Íseal Chiaráin, 'the low place of Ciarán', is used to make a pun and thus turned into a curse, prophesying lack of fame and honour to the place. It certainly was not composed by someone who lived in Íseal Chiaráin and is indeed very hostile to the *familia* there. The anecdote could be interpreted as the literary outcome of what we might call the 'anti-Meic Cuinn na mBocht faction' in Clonmacnois. The brothers in Íseal Chiaráin, i.e. the descendants of Conn na mBocht, were not only accused of lack of generosity but also blamed for the expulsion of Ciarán from their monastery, which is one way to complain about the alienation of Íseal Chiaráin from the authority of the abbot of Clonmacnois. The position of the Meic Cuinn na mBocht in Clonmacnois in the late eleventh century, when Íseal Chiaráin became their private domain, seems a very plausible background for the composition of such a tale. The fact that linguistic evidence also points to the late eleventh century as the time of a further redaction of the Irish Life of Ciarán, makes this suggestion even more likely.[25] In this case we owe the traditon of the anecdote in the Latin Life of St. Ciarán to the thirteenth century redactor of the Dublin collection, who seems to have added a translation of the story to his compilation.[26]

So far we have established evidence for the suggestion that the tale discussed above was the work of someone writing in favour of the 'anti-Meic Cuinn na mBocht' faction in Clonmacnois. On the other hand, it is well known that the family themselves had a big share in the literary productions of the time; several members of the family were known to have held the office of the *fer léiginn*, i.e. they were in lead of the monastic school. Máel Muire, son of Céilechair Mac Cuinn na mBocht, who was killed by raiders in Clonmacnois in the early twelfth century, was the chief scribe of Lebor

---

[24] *Ciarsa isiul robadh ard | mina thísedh in fodhard: | in fodhard mina thisedh | robadh ard gersa ísel* (STOKES [ed.], Lives of Saints, p. 129). I cite here Macalister's translation (MACALISTER, Latin and Irish Lives, p. 88).

[25] See above, p. 21.

[26] See SHARPE, Medieval Irish Saints' Lives, p. 391, for the thirteenth century redactor's contribution to the Dublin version of Ciarán's Life.

na hUidre.[27] The family's impact on the annalistic compilation can be traced especially for the eleventh century, when cases of death in the family are recorded even if the person concerned had never held an office in the church. Possibly this was also the period in which the detailed genealogy of the family was copied into the Clonmacnois chronicle from some kind of family album. It might well be that their acknowledged influence on contemporary literature and chronicle keeping in the monastery, was the main source for the family's fame amongst later historians. They were probably but one of several families who combined monastic life with wealth, learning and power.

4.1.2 The ecclesiastical aristocracy of Clonmacnois

Marc Bloch defined the aristocratic class in medieval society in terms of two main characteristics, one being an independent legal status, the second being the hereditary right by which the status was transmitted over the generations.[28] The hereditary nature of the position of the Meic Cuinnn na mBocht in Clonmacnois is obvious. Their legal status they derived from a tradition as anchorites, associated with the Céili Dé. They had established their power in an ecclesiastical context, over an estate which happened to be monastic in its origin. Therefore we can talk of the family as an ecclesiastical dynasty, a member of the ruling elite in Clonmacnois, alongside other families who also participated in the government of the estate. None of them is as well documented as the family of Conn. Usually these people are only known by their obituaries. Sometimes the same surname reappears, often with a whole century's intermission, but these entries highlight the presence of a particular family in Clonmacnois over generations. We already discussed the 'Conaillech' family, who supplied abbots, scribes and priests from the early tenth, and the Ua Máelduin who were hereditary vice-abbots of Clonmacnois throughout the eleventh century. The Ua Flaithéin from the Cuircne in Western Mide held the abbacy in Clonmancois twice during the eleventh century. The Ua Ruadáin from Uí Maine supplied an abbot and a

---

[27] See Appendix 1, S31 (d.1106). It has been suggested that a prototype of the Lebor na hUidre belonged to the family and was brought by them from Louth in the early ninth century (see KELLEHER, The Tain and the annals, p. 126).

[28] M. BLOCH, Feudal society, transl. L. A. MANYON, Padstow 1961, reprint 1989, p. 283.

vice-abbot. Members of the Ua Cillín and the Ua Braoín are found repeatedly amongst the abbots and vice-abbots of Clonmacnois. Like the Meic
Cuinn na mBocht who had a second base in Íseal Chiaráin, these ecclesiastical dynasties often had links with other churches. The Conaillech family in
the tenth century had connections with Clonard.[29] The Uí Flaithéin and the
Uí Chillín had a share in the government of Roscommon and Tuamgraney.[30]
The Uí Braoín had another family base in Roscommon, which became their
main residence in the twelfth century.[31] Apparently the government of Irish
churches in the eleventh century was held by a group of families in possession of wealth and power in at least one but often two or three different ecclesiastical centres. They transmitted ecclesiastical offices by hereditary
right to their offspring, and claimed authority in right of their traditional
status as men of the church in the service of St. Ciarán, since time out of
mind, best documented in the case of the Meic Cuinn na mBocht. It seems
therefore appropriate to talk of an ecclesiastical aristocracy, in the leadership of the church of Clonmacnois in the eleventh century.

A further question relates to the economic sources of the ecclesiastical
elite. Their wealth is fragmentarily documented in the annals. Thus Conn na
mBocht had sufficient means to provide for the poor with twenty cows. His
son could afford to have a new causeway built in Clonmacnois, his grandson
had enough wealth to pay for a church, a ransom which was certainly a
handsome amount of money.[32] An accumulation of wealth, natural goods
and cattle as well as precious relics in the settlement can also be deduced
from the annals at the time. Clonmacnois' wealth was certainly one of the
causes for the increasing number of raids on its church recorded in the annals for the eleventh century. Cows are regularly mentioned as the prey of
the raiders. According to the Annals of Tigernach many hundred cows were

---

[29] Colmán Conaillech (A49, d.926).

[30] See Appendix 1, Cormac Ua Cillín (A54, d.966); Conall Ua Cillín died as comarba
Crónáin in 1026 (AI); Loingsech Ua Flaithéin (A63, d.1042); Macrait Ua Flaithéin (A69,
d.1100).

[31] See Appendix 1, Dúnchad Ua Braoín (A56, d.989) was *comarba Chiaráin*, Tigernach Ua
Braoín (A67, d.1088) was *comarba Chiaráin & Comáin*; for the twelfth century members of
the family who were abbots of Roscommon see AFM 1187, 1232, 1231, 1234.

[32] AFM 1031; AFM 1070, CS 1089 (recte 1093).

carried off in the year 1023.[33] Even the church with the shrine of St. Ciarán attracted the attention of plunderers. One can see why when reading a description of St. Ciarán's riches hidden under the main altar in the church, which included gold and silver goblets, several drinking horns, chalices and a silver cup, as well as the precious model of Solomon's temple.[34]

The source of these riches were first of all donations, gifts from secular rulers, like the above-mentioned altar vessels. There were also donations from the ordinary folk and of course their payments for spiritual services such as baptism, marriage and burial. Moreover it seems that Clonmacnois had an additional source of income through selling the ground in its graveyard to those who wanted to avoid the torments of hell.[35]

Finally *manchine*, a term denoting the equivalent of vassalage in the ecclesiastical context added to the monastic economy. *Manchine* included all kinds of services, from farm labour to military service, performed by the ecclesiastical tenants living in the monastic surroundings. Through offering *manchine* to a saint one assumed the status of a monastic vassal.[36] The Irish version of the Life of Ciarán contains reference to the services due to Clonmacnois. There is for example a childless couple who offered their *manchine* to St. Ciarán.[37] The arrangement implies that the church of Clonmacnois cared for the couple in old age, and in return became their lawful heir. At another occasion Ciarán ordered Cluain, a farm labourer living in the neighbourhood of Clonmacnois, to come and help in the harvest on the monastic fields. Cluain promised to come, but, waking up the following morning, did not feel like labouring all day. He stayed in bed pretending to be sick, when St. Ciarán's messengers came to look for him. The saint, hearing this story, of course saw through the game and caused the malingerer to die on the spot. Cluain's family, after discovering the unexpected death, started to weep and went to Ciarán promising their labour and services to the saint for ever, if only he would resurrect the boy. Ciarán took pity on them and

---

[33] AT (1023).

[34] The shrine was plundered in 1021 (AFM) and again in 1129 (AT; CS 1125), at which occassion the description is given.

[35] See above, pp. 117f.

[36] DOHERTY, Some aspects of hagiography, pp. 313-321.

[37] STOKES (ed.), Lives of Saints, p. 144.

caused Cluain to rise from the dead, who without delay went to Ciarán and promised obedience as well as his *manchine* for ever to the saint.[38] This story is clearly designed as a warning to the ecclesiastical tenants never to neglect their duties or refuse their services to the monastery. A very similar message is transmitted in a tale contained in the *Aided Dhiarmada*, which has also been classified as an eleventh century compilation.[39] *Manchine* as a form of ecclesiastical punishment became increasingly popular in the eleventh century. In the year 1044 the Conmaicne performed a raid on Clonmacnois. The compensation paid by them to St. Ciarán included amongst other things the *manchine* of the son of their chief and the sons of twelve other Conmaicne nobles.[40] Clearly the labour performed by these people formed a solid base for the economy of the monastic estate. The stress on *manchine* in particular in eleventh-century sources points not only to the increasing importance of manual labour in the service of an ecclesiastical landlord, but also to a growing tendency to refuse it, which made exhortations necessary.

Interaction between the monastic and the secular aristocracy is another important aspect of ecclesiastical government in the eleventh century. It happened on different levels, one being that of intermarriage. Thus Cantigern, a daughter of the scribe Guaire Ua Lachtnáin, married Flann Ua Máelsechlainn, the brother of the king of Mide.[41] Her two sons both succeeded their uncle in the kingship. Domnall the younger was king of Mide at the time when Cormac Mac Cuinn na mBocht bought Íseal Chiaráin in the year 1093. The purchase was thus a transfer between two nobles, who were both associated by family links with the ecclesiastical settlement of Clonmacnois. Moreover Ua Flaithéin, the abbot of Clonmacnois at the time, came from the Cuircne in Western Mide, who were allies of the Ua Máelsechlainn dynasty. There are also apparent inter-dynastic relations between the Clonmacnois aristocracy and the rulers of Connacht. The victory gained in the battle of Corann by Ruaidrí Ua Conchobair over the Conmaicne in the year 1087, was brought about with the assistance of Cormac Ua Cillín from

---

[38] STOKES (ed.), Lives of Saints, p. 126.

[39] O'GRADY (ed.), Silva Gadelica, I, p. 74; see II, p. 78 for translation. See above, pp. 121f.

[40] AFM 1044.

[41] DOBBS (ed.), The ban-Shenchus, p. 190.

Clonmacnois.[42] The Uí Chillín were a Connacht family, allied with the Uí Chonchobair, and later became leading officials of Roscommon, which was the family church of the royal dynasty. Tigernach Ua Braoín, abbot of Clonmacnois at the time, was himself of the Uí Briúin Aí, which gives him common ancestry with the ruling Uí Chonchobair dynasts. The battle of Corann, therefore, appears as the joint victory of the Connacht nobility, regardless of whether it was secular or ecclesiastical in origin, over their opponents in their north-eastern neighbourhood.

In the context of smooth and constant interaction between secular and ecclesiastical politics, the increasing use of relics in battles, in the course of the eleventh century, can be understood. Saintly implements were carried in front of the army assuming the function of mascots. According to the eleventh century hagiographers of St. Finchú, for example, the crozier of this saint is said to have brought about a victory over the Vikings in the battle of Ventry.[43] The contemporary annals testify to a similar use of St. Ciarán's relics. The *Bernán Ciaráin*, the bell of Ciarán, for example was used as a powerful weapon against the lord of Tethba who in consequence was killed soon afterwards.[44] In the year 1052 a victory was won by the Conmaicne over the Calraige *per uirtutem scrine Ciaran*, through the virtue of St. Ciarán's shrine, which presumably was carried in the battle.[45] In 1087, in the above-mentioned battle of Corann, it was the crozier of St. Ciarán, *mada Chiaráin* which was carried before the Connacht army and brought about the victory.[46] Even St. Ciarán himself is said to have turned up to make use of his relics in order to defend his property. In the year 1129 he prevented a ship in Limerick from leaving the harbour with his staff, since a man who had stolen the altar vessels of Clonmacnois was on board.[47] Relics were here understood as tools to be employed in the service of the saint, or rather in the service of his friends. Of course a victory won in this way, would be seen as the outcome of cooperation between the military forces of the secu-

---

[42] AT (1087), CS 1083; see above, p. 127.

[43] STOKES (ed.), Lives of Saints, p. 95; see HUGHES, Early Christian Ireland, pp. 243f.

[44] AT(1043); CS 1041.

[45] AT(1052); CS 1050.

[46] CS 1083.

[47] CS 1126 (recte 1130); AClon 1130, p. 190-191; AT (1130).

lar lord and the spiritual power of the ecclesiastical leaders, demonstrating a further aspect of interaction between the secular and the ecclesiastical aristocracy.

A final noteworthy characteristic becomes apparent in a number of entries reporting on attempts to do away with secular taxation of the churches belonging to Clonmacnois during the eleventh century. In the year 1044 an army from Munster raided the settlement. In return the community demanded perpetual freedom from taxation by the king of Munster. Similarly the eleventh century gloss reporting on the king of Uí Maine as the murderer of a vice-abbot in Clonmacnois makes allusions to the freedom of seven churches as well *manchine*, which was imposed on the king as punishment.[48] Towards the end of the century Íseal Chiaráin, one of the churches of St. Ciarán's *paruchia*, was successfully ransomed from Domnall Ua Máelsechlainn, and gained perpetual freedom from secular taxation. Some fifteen years later the monks of Ciarán undertook a similar request, and fasted against the king of Mide, with the aim of gaining freedom for the church of Kilmore in Mag Enir.[49] In the *Aided Dhiarmada* Clonmacnois' aspirations for freedom from their secular overlord found expression when Diarmait mac Cerbaill is said to have given one hundred churches to Ciarán as a little acknowledgement to the saint who had helped him to the kingship of Tara.[50] The story of Íseal Chiaráin is the best known case of these efforts to gain freedom from secular domination. It shows most clearly, that these struggles for freedom from secular taxation were not simply fights for the sake of ecclesiastical liberty, but also the outcome of the strife for economic independence amongst the more and more powerful lay-ecclesiastical dynasties.

---

[48] CS 823; AFM 834 (recte 835). Compare above, pp. 96-98.

[49] AT (1108). See above, p. 86 n.223.

[50] O'GRADY, Silva Gadelica, I, p. 74.

4.2 Clonmacnois and the reformers

4.2.1 Ireland and the continent

This was the condition of the Irish church on the eve of the church reform. It was dominated by laymen, who lived with their concubines and ruled by a lay aristocracy who transmitted ecclesiastical honours to their children by hereditary right. However, the immoral condition of its clergy was only one of many evils. There was the influence of secular rulers, who were not only entitled to certain services and taxes from the churches in their kingdoms, but also frequently put their own candidates into leading ecclesiastical positions, thus impeding the principle of the free election of abbots and bishops. Another problem was the absence of a diocesan structure in the Irish church, indicative of its supposed lack of episcopal authority. This was not because there were no bishops, who of course formed a steady part of the monastic equipment since the early days of Irish Christianity. The problem was that those bishops seemed to rule without clearly confined diocesan boundaries over a number of churches and subjects who might be scattered in different parts of the country.[51] Since the diocese, as an administrative unit under the authority of the bishop, was the core of the centralized system of papal power promoted in the eleventh century reform on the continent, the Irish church in the eyes of a continental reformer must have appeared as a comparatively federal and decentralized system. The rise of lay ecclesiastical dynasties as rulers of the churches in the course of the tenth century, meant a further degree of decentralization. In short, the Irish church seemed to lack the kind of hierarchical structures which would enable its absorption into the ecclesiastical concept of omnipotent papal authority, so popular amongst the reformers of the Roman church since the eleventh century.

Of course Ireland was in no way singular as regards the condition of its church. In the Frankish realm under the Carolingian rulers churches were held as quasi private property by laymen, mostly by the owner of the land

---

[51] Compare above, pp. 28f.

on which the church was founded.[52] With the restriction that he was not to divert the church from its religious purpose the lay owner had full civil rights over his church. He could sell or exchange it, he could pass it on by hereditary right to his heirs, also he had the right to appoint the priest. Obviously such a system totally undermined episcopal authority. The diocese of Chur, now in Switzerland, in the early ninth century is a well documented example. There the bishop possessed thirty-one, the king and other laymen more than two hundred of the total number of churches in the bishopric.[53] Contemporary reform efforts show that the system was perceived as a threat to episcopal power; however, the Emperor and the secular magnates were themselves the largest lay owners of churches. Carolingian legislation therefore was designed to maintain and defend the concept of the proprietary church. The problem of subversion of episcopal authority was solved by assimilating the bishops as private churchowners within the system, in their authority as secular magnates.

Lay abbots were another constant feature of the Frankish realm.[54] Einhard, the biographer of Charlemagne as abbot of St. Peter in Ghent, is the earliest example attested in the sources. In contrast to lay ownership of churches, the appointment of a layman to an abbacy was apparently not perceived as an abuse. The discussion about reform in contemporary synods does not even mention the problem.

Lay authority over churches and monasteries far outlived the Carolingian empire. A case study for Lucca in Northern Italy shows that still in the tenth and down to the twelfth century the rural parishes, including the parish churches, were completely absorbed in the North- Italian feudal system, i.e.

---

[52] U. STUTZ, Die Eigenkirche als Element des mittelalterlich- germanischen Kirchenrechts, Inauguralvorlesung, Basel 1894, translated by G. BARRACLOUGH, The proprietary church as an element of medieval Germanic ecclesiastical law, in: G. BARRACLOUGH (ed.), Medieval Germany 911-1250. Essays by German Historians, Oxford 1967, vol. 2, pp. 35-70. For a general survey of the development of the diocesan organization on the continent see: H. JEDIN (ed.), Handbuch der Kirchengeschichte, Freiburg 1969, vol. 3: Die mittelalterliche Kirche; K. SCHÄFERDIEK, Das Heilige in Laienhand, in: H. SCHRÖER / G. MÜLLER (eds.), Vom Amt des Laien in Kirche und Theologie. Festschrift für Gerhard Krause, Berlin 1982, pp. 122-140.

[53] STUTZ, The proprietary church, p. 46.

[54] F. J. FELTEN, Äbte und Laienäbte im Frankenreich, Stuttgart 1980, esp. pp. 47-52, 280-304.

they were held by the local landlords.[55] Likewise lay domination over monasteries survived the pressure of the reformers. Despite the fact that royal authority over the monasteries was restricted in the course of the eleventh century, local dynasts could maintain power over 'their' monasteries. They safeguarded their influence by associating themselves with the monastic reformers, who were likewise in opposition to the king. They also supported the establishment of the *Vogt*, an advocate or administrator, as a permanent institution in the reformed monastery, a position which was regularly filled by a member of the local dynastic family.[56]

Even after the fundamental changes in the continental church, brought about in the eleventh century reform, lay authority over churches and monasteries survived. The twelfth century canonical collections still make provision for the rights of a patron over his church.[57] The Decretum Gratiani, compiled around 1130-40, rejects secular jurisdiction over churches in general, but makes special provision for the founder of a church. The *fundator* or *edificator* of a church or a monastery has a say in internal church affairs (*ius providendi et consulendi*) and the right of presentation, which means that he was allowed to present the candidate for the office to the local bishop (*ius inveniendi sacerdotem*). Moreover he is entitled to a share of the revenues of the church in case of emergency, known as the right of alimentation.[58] Of course these regulations apply equally to ecclesiastical and

---

[55] K. E. BOYD, Tithes and parishes in medieval Italy, Ithaca/New York 1952, pp. 87-102.

[56] H. HIRSCH, Die Verfassung der Reformklöster des Investiturstreits, in: H. HIRSCH (ed.), Untersuchungen zur Verfassungsgeschichte des deutschen Reiches und der deutschen Kirche, Weimar 1913, pp. 26-65 [transl. by BARRACLOUGH, Medieval Germany, II, pp. 131-173]. The Zähringer in the Black Forest were one of the earliest examples for a dynasty who established their position against the emperor by such a close association with the reformed monasteries, namely that of St. Blasien and St. Georgen. For studies in other regions see for example J. WOLLASCH, Reform und Adel in Burgund, and K. SCHMID, Adel und Reform in Schwaben, both essays are contained in J. FLECKENSTEIN (ed.), Investiturstreit und Reichsverfassung, Sigmaringen 1973, pp. 277-294 and 295-320.

[57] LANDAU, Ius Patronatus.

[58] For Gratian see ibid., pp. 3-7: *Hic autem distinguendum est, quid iuris fundatores ecclesiarum in eis habeant, vel quid non? Habent ius providendi, et consulendi, et sacerdotem inveniendi, sed non habent ius vendendi, vel donandi, vel utendi tamquam propriis.*

secular patrons. For the latter, even the hereditary nature of patronage was acknowledged by the twelfth century canonists.[59]

On the continent in the course of the eleventh century the various issues of the reformers were eventually superseded by the spectacular conflict between Pope Gregory VII and Emperor Henry IV, known as the Investiture Contest.[60] The problem of the relation between secular and ecclesiastical authority was more or less absorbed by the rather technical question of royal participation in the filling of higher ecclesiastical offices in the German realm. In Ireland royal rights as regards the investiture of bishops were not at stake. Instead, the eleventh century saw the advent of Norman claims to authority over the Irish church, in the person of Lanfranc, archbishop of Canterbury, who made the Norse towns in Ireland his suffragan sees.[61] Secular interference in ecclesiastical affairs was not perceived as a problem, as long as the kings interfered on behalf of the papal ideas of reform. Thus one of the main forces behind the Irish church reform were the Uí Briain kings of Munster, most prominent amongst them Muirchertach Ua Briain (1086-1116), under whose supervision the first two reform synods in the twelfth century were held. The main impetus of the Irish reformers went towards:

1. The abolition of lay domination over churches and monasteries - which meant a struggle against the lay ecclesiastical dynasties.

2. The establishment of a hierarchical diocesan church structure in accordance with that of the continental Roman catholic church.

3. The assimilation of the Irish church into the hierarchical system of the papal church.

---

[59] Ibid., p. 52.

[60] A. FLICHE, La réforme grégorienne, 3 vols., Louvain/Paris 1924, 1926, 1937, reprint Geneva 1978; J. LAUDAGE, Gregorianische Reform und Investiturstreit, Darmstadt 1993.

[61] For Lanfranc, archbishop of Canterbury and his claims to supremacy over the bishoprics of Dublin, Waterford and Limerick, see J. A. WATT, The church and the two nations in medieval Ireland, Cambridge 1970, pp. 5-9; M. T. FLANAGAN, Irish society, Anglo-Norman settlers, Angevin kingship. Interactions in Ireland in the late twelfth century, Oxford 1989, pp. 12-55; A. GWYNN, Lanfranc and the Irish Church, in: A. GWYNN, The Irish church in the eleventh and twelfth centuries, ed. G. O'BRIEN, Dublin 1992, pp. 68-83.

4.2.2 The successors of St. Ciarán in the twelfth century

War was declared against the lay ecclesiastical dynasties in leading positions in the Irish church at the first reforming synod in Cashel in the year
1101. There it was decreed that no layman should be abbot and no abbot
should be married.[62] A decree is generally a declaration of intent, and might
or might not be implemented. It appears that the hereditary principle not
only persisted in the Irish Church, but was even adopted by some of the
newly invented diocesan bishops. The Uí Dhubthaigh, as bishops of Connacht are one example of an ecclesiastical dynasty, members of which were
present at many a reforming synod, whilst at the same time episcopal honours were passed on in the family from father to son. Muiredach Ua Dubthaigh died as bishop of Connacht in 1150.[63] He was the son of Domnall,
bishop and also *comarba* of Clonmacnois, and father of Bishop Cadla, who
died in the year 1200.[64]

As far as the Meic Cuinn na mBocht in Clonmacnois are concerned, the
family lost its prominent position with the advent of the reforming century.
Cormac Mac Cuinn na mBocht died as *comarba Chiaráin* in 1103. Members of his family can be traced in the annals down to the end of the twelfth
century; the family supplied a priest and two seniors of Clonmacnois, but
does not appear again in leading offices. They even lost their status as leader
of the Céili Dé community in Clonmacnois.[65]

The successor of Cormac to the abbacy was Flaithbertach Ua Loingsigh,
also a member of a traditional Clonmacnois dynasty. It seems that with his

---

[62] Eight decrees of the Synod of Cashel are preserved in the genealogies of the Uí Briain
family; see A. GWYNN, The first synod of Cashel, in: IER 66 (1945), pp. 81-92, and a revised
version of the article in GWYNN, The Irish church, pp. 155-179, here 158ff. The third and
fifth decree state that no layman should become *airchinnech* of a church, and that no *airchinnech* should be married.

[63] AT.

[64] AFM 1136, AFM 1200. That Cadla was a son of Muiredach is evident from a letter by
Innocent III, see: A. GWYNN, Tomaltach Ua Conchobhair coarb of St. Patrick, in: Seanchas
Ardmhacha 8 (1977), pp. 231-274, here 235.

[65] See Appendix 1. Máel Íosa son of Conn na mBocht (d.1103); Máel Muire son of Céilechair son of Conn (d.1106); Máel Chiaráin son of Cormac (d.1134); Céilechair (d.1134);
Máel Muire (d.1180). See Appendix 1, O7, S31, P13, Sen10, Sen11.

death in the year 1109 the principles of abbatial succession in Clonmacnois changed. Before, especially since the tenth century, the abbacy appears as an office, in the hands of an aristocratic ruling class, filled according to a more or less rotating system by candidates from the various families. In the twelfth century this policy was to change drastically. The names of the leading Clonmacnois families, familiar from the tenth and eleventh century, disappear from the records. They were replaced by newcomers to the governmental scene in Clonmacnois, most dominant amongst them the Uí Mháeleoin.

Gilla Chríst Ua Máeleoin, abbot of Clonmacnois from 1109 to 1127, ruled over Clonmacnois during the reforming synods in Ráth Bresail and Uisnech in the year 1111. The Annals of Ulster praise him as *comarba Ciarain Cluana M. Nois sonus + sobarthu airchinnech chell nErenn*, 'successor of Ciarán of Clonmacnois, happiness and prosperity of the superiors of the churches of Ireland'.[66] In the Chronicon Scotorum he is commemorated as the builder of the bell tower in Clonmacnois.[67] Then there was Áed Ua Máeleoin, who died in the year 1153, and was followed in the abbacy by Tigernach, his kinsman.[68] Abbot Tigernach as well as his son, Gilla Chríst died in the year 1172.[69] For the following nine years the abbacy went to the Ua Fidabra family, who might have been related to the Ua Máelsechlainn dynasty and possible came from Louth.[70] However the next abbot of Clonmacnois mentioned in the annals was again an Ua Máeleoin, namely Máel Muire, the 'great and worthy house keeper' who died in the year 1230. He was succeeded by Máel Chiaráin Ua Máeleoin, who held the abbacy until his death in 1263 and is the last abbot of Clonmacnois mentioned in the annals.[71] In the thirteenth century members of the Ua Máeleoin family also assumed episcopal honours: bishop Cathal Ua Máeleoin died in the

---

[66] AU 1127.9.

[67] CS 1120 (recte 1124).

[68] AFM 1153; AU, missing for these years gives 1098 as his date of birth.

[69] AT(1172); AU 1172.

[70] In the early thirteenth century the family supplied an abbot of Louth, see below, p. 166 n.140.

[71] AU 1230; ALCé 1263.

year 1208, bishop Áed Ua Máeleoin drowned in 1220, and his namesake retired to Kilbeggan in the year 1236.[72]

The Ua Máeleoin family first appears on the records in the early days of the twelfth century, in the course of which they assumed almost exclusive rights to the abbacy of Clonmacnois. As an ecclesiastical dynasty they not only survived the church reform, but also the Anglo-Norman invasion for nearly a century. Some notes concerning the tribal background of the family are contained in an eighteenth century manuscript, now in the Royal Irish Academy.[73] The author claims that the family was a branch of the Uí Chonchobair of Connacht, who settled in Bregmaine in the western parts of Mide and were first active as private benefactors of the neighbouring monastery of Clonmacnois, which they eventually took over and ruled as abbots and bishops for over a century. The document appears to be a late eighteenth-century compilation of an anonymous author, possibly an Ua Máeleoin himself. His notes continue with the history of some noble gentlemen of that family down to the eighteenth century. Where he got his information from is obscure, but the alleged Connacht origin of the Uí Mháeleoin, as well as their being related to the Uí Chonchobair dynasty of Connacht, seem highly plausible, since the family came to power when Clonmacnois enjoyed the patronage of the kings of Connacht. In addition some of the Christian names of members of the family, like Áed or Cathal, bear strong Connacht connotations and were common amongst the Ua Conchobair dynasty at the time.[74]

Since Gilla Chríst Ua Máeleoin, in the early twelfth century, did not come from one of the traditional ecclesiastical dynasties of Clonmacnois it is possible that he was initially appointed to the abbacy as the candidate of the reform party. Still under the impact of the first reform synod of Cashel, the hereditary principle in regard to the abbatial succession was broken. Gilla Chríst Ua Máeleoin might have been elected as an external candidate, with no connections to the traditional Clonmacnois aristocracy. Also the handiwork of Toirdelbach Ua Conchobair, king of Connacht, might be rec-

---

[72] AClon 1206, p. 221; AConn 1220; AConn 1236.

[73] Royal Irish Academy MS 14. B4, which contains as the last but one of the MSS transcribed in the volume: *Notes relative to the O Malone family of Westmeath.*

[74] Most prominent bearer of the name was Cathal Crobderg (d.1224), who had a brother and a son named Áed (d.1228).

ognized in the abbatial appointment in 1109. In 1106 Toirdelbach assumed the kingship of Connacht (1106-1156). His father Ruaidrí had enjoyed the active support of the Clonmacnois clergy in the battle of Corann.[75] Toirdelbach himself had a belltower built in Clonmacnois, after his death was buried under the main altar of the great church and we also know of his generous donation of silver cups and gold and other riches; he thus clearly appears as the most prominent patron of St. Ciarán's church at the time.[76] It is therefore highly plausible that he took an active part in the abbatial election in Clonmacnois and that he forwarded his own interests by promoting a Connacht candidate to the office. In the course of his church policy the Meic Cuinn na mBocht might have lost their traditional status as leaders of the anchorites and the Céili Dé in Clonmacnois. The position was instead filled with Uareirge Ua Nechtain, a man of the Uí Maine in Connacht, who were allies of King Toirdelbach. Under the patronage of a common secular lord, the Ua Máeleoin abbot as well as the Ua Nechtain head of the Céili Dé were both successful in reserving their offices for their descendants.[77]

Another family prominent in Clonmacnois in the twelfth century was Ua Dubthaigh from Connacht. In the context of the synod in Brí maic Taidg in the year 1158 the annals of Tigernach talk of the bishop of Clonmacnois and the bishop of Connacht as two successors of Ciarán, *dá comurba Ciarain*. Mageoghagan's translation of the annals of Clonmacnois also makes mention of *2 of the cowarbs of St. Queran*, whereas the Four Masters simply omit the relevant part of the entry.[78] The bishop of Clonmacnois at the time was Muirchertach Ua Máeluidir, who was present at the synod of Kells, and died in 1187.[79] The most likely candidate for the bishop of Connacht in question here appears to be Flanucan Ua Dubthaigh, who died a bishop and sage in Cong, in the year 1168.[80] The family dominated the episcopate in

---

[75] CS 1083 (recte 1087).

[76] AT (1156).

[77] For the Uí Nechtain see CS 1128 (recte 1132); AT (1170); AFM 1200. Appendix 1, C3, C4, C5. See also KELLEHER, The Uí Maine in the annals, pp. 94f.

[78] AT (1158); AClon 1158, p. 204; AFM 1158.

[79] AFM.

[80] AT (1168); AU 1168; MS B and C style him *epscop na tuath*, the explanatory *Síl Muiredaig* is added im MS A. *Coblach Síl Muiredhaigh + na Tuath*, the fleet of the Síl Muiredaig and the Tuatha is mentioned in AT (1145).

Connacht. They generally held the title 'bishop of Síl Muiredaig', which corresponds to the bishopric of Roscommon, and later that of Elphin.[81] However, most likely the title should be understood in the not yet strictly diocesan-organized church of Connacht as 'bishop of the territory and people under the authority of the Uí Chonchobair'. After 1152, when four archbishoprics were erected at the synod of Kells, the family also supplied the archbishop of Tuam. The entry in the annals of Tigernach suggests that the leading ecclesiastical dynasty of the Connacht church was also involved in Clonmacnois affairs. Earlier in the twelfth century Domnall Ua Dubthaigh was bishop of Elphin and *comarba Chiaráin*. Muirchertach, also a bishop of the same family had a share in the church yard of Clonmacnois.[82] It seems plausible that Flanucan, like his relatives and predecessors had connections with Clonmacnois and that he was the bishop of Connacht, referred to here in the annals of Tigernach as the second *comarba Chiaráin*.[83] Clearly members of the Ua Dubthaigh dynasty, who monopolized episcopal offices in Connacht, had a power base in the monastery of Clonmacnois, which apart from Roscommon was the main monastic ally of the Ua Conchobair dynasty. Finally the Uí Fidabra, a third family, until then unknown, appears in the abbacy of Clonmacnois, in the years after the arrival of the Anglo-Normans.[84]

4.2.3 Developments within the ecclesiastical estate

Various possibilities are conceivable for the development of an unreformed ecclesiastical establishment with monastic traditions, under the impact of the reformers. It could be a) reformed and brought under the authority of the local bishop, as for example Derry; b) dissolved; c) there was the possibility that it would be transformed into a bishopric, which was the case for Lismore, and temporarily for Clonard and Kells; finally, d) it could continue to exist as a subdivision within the diocese, as for example Kells, which be-

---

[81]   GWYNN, The Irish church, pp. 230f.

[82]   AClon 1135, p. 194.

[83]   GWYNN, The Irish church, pp. 231f. for Ua Dubthaigh.

[84]   See below, pp. 166f.

came an archdeaconry of the diocese of Meath in the early thirteenth century.[85]

4.2.3.1 Reform orders in Clonmacnois?

It is generally assumed that Augustinian Canons were introduced into Clonmacnois under the auspices of Toirdelbach Ua Conchobair sometime around 1144.[86] Apart from very general grounds like the fact that Toirdelbach is known to have supported the Augustinians, this assumption relies on Archdall who in his turn cites Ware as his source. However, Archdall in an introductory account to the Monasticon Hibernicum explains his understanding of 'Augustinian Canons' as a merely linguistic result of the church reform in Ireland.[87] Ware, the stated source of Archdall's knowledge, in his account of the monastic orders in Ireland, does not list Clonmacnois amongst the Augustinians.[88] Only Walter Harris, the editor of Ware's works in the eighteenth century, maintains that Clonmacnois was a monastery of

---

[85] See WATT, The church and the two nations, pp. 60-65, 81-82. Compare also the traditional monastic foundations of Bury St. Edmunds (dio. Norwich) or Glastonbury (dio. Bath) in England, which survived the English church reform as archdeaconries (J. SAYER, Monastic Archdeacons, in: C. N. L. BROOKE [ed.], Church and government in the middle ages, Cambridge 1976, pp. 177-204); other examples are Westminster and St. Alban's (D. A. WATKIN [ed.], The great Chartulary of Glastonbury, London 1947-52, 3 vols; V. H. GALBRAITH, The East Anglian See and the Abbey of Bury St. Edmunds, in: English Historical Review 40 [1925], pp. 222-228).

[86] GWYNN / HADCOCK, p. 165; M. ARCHDALL, Monasticon Hibernicum, Dublin/London 1786, pp. 390f.

[87] ARCHDALL, Monasticon, Introduction, pp. xvii-xciii. He declares, that the „Irish clergy had for many centuries preserved an independant hierarchy, and resisted every attempt of the Roman Pontiff to subject them to the Papal See; but in the late 12th century the Popery had broke in on the liberties of the Church; her legates were received, and her various orders found protection and support. It was natural therefore to expect, that our ancient orders, from a change of times, now esteemed heretical, should no longer be called by their old titles, but by new and fashionable names. And hence it is, that of the numerous monasteries founded by Columba, not more than the names of three or four are handed down to us, the rest were ranked as Augustinians, and continued to be recorded, as such by succeeding writers."

[88] WARE, De Hibernia, pp. 160-162, for the Augustinian foundations in county Offaly (King's county).

regular Canons of the Order of St. Augustine. According to Harris, the same applied to the Nunnery in Clonmacnois.[89]

There is contemporary evidence to support the suggestion that the nuns in Clonmacnois were reformed according to the Arrouaisian rule. In the year 1144 the church of the nuns in Clonmacnois was granted by Murchad Ua Máelsechlainn to the Arrouaisian nuns in Clonard.[90] Later in the century Dearbhforgaill had the church of the nuns in Clonmacnois rebuilt.[91] She was the daughter of Murchad Ua Máelsechlainn and the sister of Agnes, abbess of the nuns in Clonard, and with her deeds supported reform interests as well as family policy.

4.2.3.2 The bishopric of Clonmacnois

However, even if the religious community in Clonmacnois adopted a new monastic rules, it never assumed particular fame as a reformed community. The more lasting status, in which Clonmacnois survived the reorganization of the Irish church, was as that of a bishopric. The evidence as regards the diocese of Clonmacnois in the course of the twelfth century is rather ambiguous.[92] The decrees issued at the synod of Ráth Bresail in 1111 do not make provision for a diocese of Clonmacnois. Two episcopal sees were established in Mide, Clonard becoming the centre of a diocese comprising the western parts of Mide and Duleek being chosen as the bishop's seat in

---

[89] W. HARRIS (ed.), The whole works of Sir James Ware concerning Ireland II, part I: The antiquities of Ireland, Dublin 1745, pp. 263, 269.

[90] *Ecclesiam S. Maria de Cluaynmacnois, ad orientem cum villa de Kellogainechan, cum suis perinentiis*; the papal confirmation of the grant from 1195 also mentions a church west of Clonmacnois: *Ecclesiam S. Maria ad occidentem cum villa Drumalgach, cum suis pertinentiis*, which might have belonged to Clonmacnois as well. (W. DUGDALE, Monasticon Anglicanum, ed. J. CALEY / H. ELLIS, London 1830, vol. VI, part II, 1144-1145). Compare GWYNN / HADCOCK, p. 316 and 413 for the Arrouaisian nuns in Clonard. See also M. T. FLANAGAN, St. Mary's Abbey, Louth, and the introduction of the Arrouaisian observance into Ireland, in: Clogher Record 10 (1979-81), pp. 223-234. The nun's church in Clonmacnois became later an appurtenance of Kilcreevanty (H. T. KNOX, Notes on the early history of the dioceses of Tuam, Killala and Achonry, Dublin 1904, pp. 280-285).

[91] AFM 1167.

[92] Compare P. L. Ó MAOLEACHLAINN, Clonmacnois and the XII century Synods, in: Teathba 1 (1973), pp. 195-201, which to the best of my knowledge is the only comparatively detailed discussion of Clonmacnois and the twelfth century reform synods.

the east.[93] At the synod of Uisnech, which took place later in the year, the arrangements of Ráth Bresail were again revised. According to the Clonmacnois chroniclers their church was promoted to the seat of the bishop of West Mide, who's territory might have reached as far as Castlekieran, in county Meath near Kells, Clonard became the centre of the diocese of East Mide. Duleek lost its status as a bishopric.[94] Forty years later at the synod of Kells, two more archbishoprics, Tuam and Dublin as well as some further suffragan dioceses were established.[95] A bishop of Clonmacnois, namely Muirchertach Ua Máeluidir, was at the synod according to Keating's list of those present.[96] The bishopric of Clonmacnois is however not mentioned in the most authentic source about the arrangements made in 1152, namely the list of the bishoprics created at the synod of Kells which survived in a Cistercian manuscript found in Montpellier.[97] Eventually, another twenty two years later, in 1174, the author of the Annals of Tigernach reports that in

---

[93] J. MAC ERLEAN (ed.), The synod of Ráith Breasail. Boundaries of the dioceses of Ireland [A.D. 1110 or 1118], in: Archivium Hibernicum 3 (1914), pp. 1-33. The decrees of the synod were preserved in the annals of Clonenagh which are now lost. Keating copied this passage in his History of Ireland in 1635 (G. KEATING, Foras feasa ar Éirinn: The history of Ireland, ed. D. COMYN / P. S. DINEEN, 4 vols., London 1902-14, here vol. 3, pp. 298-307).

[94] MAC ERLEAN, The synod of Ráith Breasail, p. 26. The Cottonian Annals under the year 1111 have an entry reporting *Senad Usnig ac clerib Érend* (ACott 1111). In the Chronicon the entry reads: *The great synod of Uisnech was held in the same year and it was at this synod, that the diocese of Fer-Midhe was divided into two parts, between the bishop of Cluain-Muc Nois and the bishop of Cluain-Iraird viz from Clochan-an-imrim west to the bishop of Cluain-Muc-Nois and from the same Clochan eastwards to the bishop of Cluain-Iraird, by Murchadh Ua Maoil Seachlainn and by Eochaidh Ua Ceallaigh, and the congregation of Ciarán with Gillachrist Ua Maoileoin, abbot of Cluain* (CS 1107). However two bishops of Duleek are mentioned in the annals, one died in 1117, the other in 1160 (AFM).

[95] For a discussion of the exact place and date of the synod as well as the sources see A. GWYNN, The Synod of Kells, 1152, in: A. GWYNN, The Irish church, pp. 218-234.

[96] KEATING, Foras feasa an Éirinn, III, pp. 314-316.

[97] Edited by D. LAWLOR, A fresh authority on the Synod of Kells, in: PRIA 36 (1921), pp. 16-22; see GWYNN, The Irish church, pp. 223, 246-249. The list is full of errors as regards the spelling of placenames. Two of the suffragan bishops of the archbishop of Tuam are listed as *episcopum de aicbal* and *episcopum de conairi. Aicbal* appears as a corrupted form of Achad, here standing for Achonry. Ware assumed that the second, Conairi stood for Cluanensis. The assumption was dismissed by Lawlor as a bold impossibility. Since *Achad Conairi* (Conaire) is the Irish spelling for Achonry, it seems that the scribe (or someone else) made two bishoprics out of one. Gwynn suggested that through the fact that the bishopric of Achonry filled two lines in the manuscript there was simply no space left for Clonmacnois, which is therefore missing in the list.

this year the diocese of West Mide was annexed to the city of Clonmacnois, which of course according to the Chronicon Scotorum had happened long before in the year 1111.[98]

Likewise the evidence for the bishops of the supposed see of Clonmacnois is ambiguous. Bishop Ua hEchtigern died in 1104.[99] He was bishop of Clonmacnois as well as *airchinnech* of Ardagh, but certainly not a diocesan bishop in the eyes of the reformers.[100] As the first bishop mentioned in the annals in connection with Clonmacnois after the synod of Ráth Bresail there is Domnall Ua Dubthaigh, who died in the year 1136.[101] In the Annals of Tigernach he is called *in t-espoc .i. comurba Ciarain*, the bishop, a *comarba* of Ciarán. As we have seen earlier, in his family a tradition as bishops of Connacht, combined with the headship of Roscommon, was cherished. Domnall died in Clonfert and it seems that in his authority as bishop of Connacht he had a share in the government of Clonmacnois, which was after all one of the most prominent churches under Toirdelbach Ua Conchobair's patronage. Domnall was clearly not bishop of the diocese of Clonmacnois. The first man who held that position appears rather late in the century. It is Muirchertach Ua Máeluidir mentioned amongst those present at the synod of Kells in 1152. He died in 1187 as bishop of Clonfert and Clonmacnois.[102] Obviously there is a huge gap between the death of bishop Ua Echtigern in 1104, and the time of activity of Ua Máeluidir, as the first diocesan bishop of Clonmacnois. Nevertheless the Chronicon Scotorum makes explicit mention of the bishop of Clonmacnois as early as the year 1111, when the creation of the diocese of Clonmacnois was decided at the synod of Uisnech.[103] Since we know of no bishop of Clonmacnois during the reign of Gilla Chríst Ua Máeleoin (1109 - 1127), one might conclude

---

[98] Compare above n.94.

[99] AT (1104); CS 1000; AFM 1104.

[100] There is also Muiredach Ua Máeldúin styled *bushop of Clonvickenos* by Mageoghagan. However the Four Masters give him the probably more correct title *secnab*, which was the hereditary office held by his family (see AClon 1105, p. 189; AFM 1106).

[101] AT (1136); AFM; AClon 1136, p. 194.

[102] AFM 1187; KEATING, Foras feasa ar Éirinn, III, pp. 314-316. Gwynn doubts the statement of the Four Masters that Muirchertach was bishop of Clonfert as well (GWYNN, The Irish church, pp. 249f.).

[103] CS 1107 (recte 1111).

that the abbot himself had or at least claimed episcopal authority over the territory outlined as the diocese of Clonmacnois in Uisnech. In this context the concept of the diocese, namely as the territory in Mide under the authority of the head of Clonmacnois might have been understood as a slightly transformed version of the traditional *paruchia* of St. Ciarán in Mide.

The diocese of Clonmacnois in its 'modern' sense and in the shape it existed down to the sixteenth century, when it was united with the diocese of Meath, was first established in the latter half of the twelfth century, even after the synod of Kells. Possibly 1174, the year in which the diocese of Western Mide was annexed to the city of Clonmacnois demarcates the date in which it was established. From now on episcopal succession at Clonmacnois can be traced in the sources.[104] An episcopal residence in Clonmacnois is first attested in the annals around that time.[105]

4.2.3.3 Why had the reform so little effect on Clonmacnois?

The importance of Clonmacnois as an ecclesiastical centre in Ireland prior to the twelfth century is entirely at variance with the insignificant role it played in the course of the church reform, of which its being omitted as a bishopric in the synod at Ráth Bresail is indicative. Why did Clonmacnois remain at the periphery of the new developments, and why was it originally ignored by the diocesan reorganization of the Irish church? It has been suggested that the ecclesiastical division of Mide between Duleek and Clonard resulted from the fact that both houses enjoyed the patronage of Murchad Ua Máelsechlainn, whereas Clonmacnois as a larger church was politically more independent.[106] Aubrey Gwynn seems to suggest that Clonmacnois, as the bastion of the 'stout defenders of the Old Irish tradition', was in opposi-

---

[104] AFM 1187; AU 1214; AU 1220; AClon 1236, p. 235; AFM 1253; compare W. H. G. FLOOD, The episcopal succession in Clonmacnois, in: IER 32 (1912), pp. 76-82.

[105] The house of the bishop of Clonmacnois is mentioned by the Four Masters, as having been spared by Hugh de Lacy when he plundered the monastery (AFM 1178).

[106] K. SIMMS, The origins of the diocese of Clogher, in: Clogher Record 10 (1980), pp. 180-198; see AFM 1123 and 1131.

tion to the modern diocesan arrangements and therefore excluded as a bishopric at Ráth Bresail.[107]

The lack of adequate secular patronage as well as a certain element of conservatism seem indeed two decisive factors concerning Clonmacnois' position in the Irish church during the reform in the twelfth century. The most powerful secular forces in support of the Irish reform movement in the twelfth century were the Uí Briain and the Meic Carthaig kings in Munster, the Meic Lochlainn kings of Cenél nEógain, together with Diarmait Mac Murchada of Leinster and Murchad Ua Máelsechlainn of Mide. The ecclesiastical leaders were the Columban community under Ua Brolcháin, the reformers from Armagh, the Cistercians and the Arrouaisian order. None of these, neither the secular nor the ecclesiastical patrons of the reform, were amongst the allies of Clonmacnois. In the foundation of bishoprics, rural deaneries and parishes in Ireland in the twelfth century the boundaries of pre-Norman kingdoms and lordships were in many cases maintained.[108] Clonmacnois, lacking adequate secular patronage, was bound to be left over, since, at the time it could not claim ecclesiastical authority over the territory of one particular king or lord, but over parts of various medieval Irish kingdoms, such as Uí Maine and Bréifne in Connacht, and Tethba and Delbna in Mide.

A comparison with Derry as another traditional Irish church might be helpful.[109] There reform ideas were first promoted by its secular patron, Domnall Mac Lochlainn (1083-1121). Rivalries with Muirchertach Ua Briain, paragon of the reformers in Munster, seems to have inspired reform efforts on the part of the Cenél nEógain king. He chose Derry as his ecclesiastical power base near Cenél Conaill, and it has been suggested that Derry's aspirations to the headship of the Cenél Conaill diocese at the synod

---

[107] Gwynn, The Irish church, pp. 188f.

[108] See for example the diocese of Kildare encompassing the territory of Uí Fáeláin and Uí Failge (M. T. Flanagan, Henry II and the kingdom of Uí Fáeláin, in: J. Bradley [ed.], Settlement and society in medieval Ireland. Studies presented to F. X. Martin, Kilkenny 1988, pp. 229-239, here 234f.); or the bishopric of Cenél nEógain (Simms, The origins of the diocese of Clogher).

[109] Herbert, Iona, Kells, and Derry, pp. 109-123. Compare also Killaloe, for example, which was turned into a bishopric under the patronage of the Dál Cais, see D. Ó Corráin, Dál Cais - church and dynasty, in: Ériu 24 (1973), pp. 52-63.

of Ráth Bresail, was part of Mac Lochlainn's strategy to dominate that territory.[110] Links between Derry and Armagh, the leading ecclesiastical reform
force, were intensified after the death of the reform abbot Cellach in 1129.
Malachy succeeded, but resigned in 1137 and nominated Gilla Mac Liag,
previously abbot of Derry, to the headship of the church of Armagh. In
1150, when the abbacy of Derry fell vacant, the association between the two
churches was further enforced, when Flaithbertach Ua Brolcháin, who came
from an ecclesiastical family in Armagh, possibly the son of a former
bishop of Armagh, became head of the Columban *familia* in Derry.[111] These
close personal links with Armagh together with the political fortunes of the
Cenél nEógain in the twelfth century were decisive. The ascendancy of the
Meic Lochlainn kings since the end of the eleventh century, their double
role as promoters of the reform as well as political supporters of Derry was
an essential pre-condition for the development of Derry throughout the
church reform. Derry's neat assimilation into the Irish reform movement
culminated in the creation of a singular position for Ua Brolcháin, the abbot
of Derry, who as head of all the Columban churches in Ireland was given
the same status as a diocesan bishop at the synod of Brí maic Taidg in
1158.[112] Eventually, in the late twelfth century, the monastic settlement
became the episcopal seat of the diocese of Cenél nEógain.[113]

Clonmacnois in comparison was, to put it bluntly, situated in the wrong
place. Central secular power in Mide had been gradually declining since the
mid eleventh century. The role of the Uí Mháelsechlainn kings as the traditional patrons of Clonmacnois became ambiguous in the light of the ever
growing Uí Chonchobair influence. Obviously Murchad Ua Máelsechlainn
actively promoted reform in his kingdom. This, however, resulted in support
of the reform order in Clonard, rather than Clonmacnois. In fact his patronage over the churches of Clonard was at the expense of Clonmacnois, when,

---

[110] HERBERT, Iona, Kells, and Derry, p. 110; SIMMS, The origins of the diocese of Clogher,
pp. 187f.

[111] HERBERT, Iona, Kells, and Derry, p. 115.

[112] AU 1158; HERBERT, Iona, Kells, and Derry, p. 116.

[113] GWYNN / HADCOCK, p. 68.

for example, he he granted the nuns' church in Clonmacnois to the Arrouaisian canonesses under his daughter Agnes in Clonard.[114]

On the other side of the Shannon, in Connacht, political power was centralized in the hands of Toirdelbach Ua Conchobair. Even though he was known as a pious supporter of the churches, even of the new monastic orders and in particular of the Augustinians, the west of Ireland lagged behind in the developments taking place in the Irish church. Still in 1179 church assemblies were held to take action against married clergy, where seven bishops were deposed because they were laymen.[115] Due to Ua Conchobair patronage and influence Clonmacnois was assimilated into the Connacht church system. This role was difficult to combine with its aspirations to the position as a bishopric for Mide. The first diocesan bishop of Clonmacnois, Muirchertach Ua Máeluidir, was a Mide man.[116] Possibly the attempt to erect a bishopric in Clonmacnois were primarily the work of what we might call the Mide faction in the settlement. At the synod of Uisnech they had the support of the Ua Máelsechlainn king of Mide as well as that of the newly installed Ua Máeleoin abbot, whose election in 1109 was originally a success of the reform party. It was decided to make Clonmacnois the seat of the bishop of the West of Mide, but the decision had little effect, since the abbot interpreted the new diocesan arrangements according to the traditional concept of the *paruchia*. It is possible that he himself was claiming episcopal authority over the alleged diocese of Clonmacnois. Moreover his family, with the support of their royal patron from Connacht, turned the abbacy of Clonmacnois into a family property, sought assimilation into the Connacht church system, and eventually left the problems of bishops and dioceses to the reformers. Since secular support on the Mide side of the Shannon was weak, the bishopric as well as the bishop of Clonmacnois was little more than a formality. Power was in the hands of the Ua Máeleoin abbots. Only towards the end of the twelfth century were the two functions successfully combined. The Ua Máeleoin family adapted to the changes in the national ecclesiastical landscape and became bishops of Clonmacnois. One Cathal

---

[114] See above, p. 154f.

[115] This was the synod of Clonfert recorded in AClon under the year 1170, pp. 213f. For the dating of the synod see GWYNN, The Irish church, p. 306.

[116] The Uí Máeluidir were lords of a subkingdom in Mide and supplied royal officials in the eleventh century (see AU 1021; CS 1019).

died as the first Ua Máeleoin bishop in Clonmacnois in the year 1208. He was 'arch Bushop with the O'Neales and Connaught men', according to Mageoghagan, a title which probably should be read as 'eminent bishop of the Southern Uí Néill and of Connacht'. Cathal could claim to be bishop of the Southern Uí Néill since the diocese of Clonmacnois was a Mide bishopric. His aspirations to episcopal authority in Connacht resulted from the family's tradition as abbots of a Connacht monastery. The former lands of Clonmacnois in Connacht, probably considered to be family property, were claimed as a part of the diocese of Clonmacnois, so that they would not be lost to the Ua Máeleoin family. Still the title with its claim to archieopiscopal honours is rather pretentious. It might express the wishful thinking of an ecclesiastical dynasty who had failed to join in with the reformers, whereas the latter eventually turned out to be those in power in the Irish church.

4.3   The Anglo-Norman invasion

4.3.1 The immediate effects of the Anglo-Norman invasion

The final formation of the diocese of Clonmacnois seems to have happened only in end of the twelfth century. In the year 1169 the first Anglo-Normans arrived in Ireland. One of the formal reasons given by Henry II's in coming to Ireland was his concern for the Irish church, which to his mind was still in need of reform. It seems indeed that the Anglo-Norman invasion gave a new impulse to the Irish reform movement, in particular in the western parts of the country. In the year 1179 a synod was held in Clonfert, opposing layman in offices in the church of Connacht, and reinforcing episcopal authority instead. The decree may also be interpreted as having decided on the reformation of the Connacht cathedral chapters, since until then canonries and prebends were apparently often detained by married churchmen.[117] It seems highly plausible that Clonmacnois, as one of the Connacht

---

[117] AClon 1170, pp. 213f.: *it was laid down by them by a Constitution that noe layman should have the rule of any Church or Church matters from thence forth, that noe portion Canons should be sought of women theire husbands liveing, that Holy Orders should not be given to bushopp nor Priests sonns, and for example of these their Constitutions, they tooke the livings of seven bushopps that had Bushopricks and were laymen.*

churches, was one of the main targets of the reformers, who had gained new strength. Earlier in the decade between 1170 and 1180 the Ua Máeleoin family, if only temporarily, was deposed as hereditary abbots of Clonmacnois. The bishop on the other hand seems to have gained additional authority, when in 1174, lands in Westmeath were definitely attached to his bishopric.[118] We might deduce that Anglo-Norman pressure eventually settled matters concerning the final formation of the diocese of Clonmacnois. This suggestion is supported by the fact that the episcopal residence was spared by the Anglo-Normans when they raided the settlement of Clonmacnois in 1178.[119] When in the early thirteenth century an Anglo-Norman castle was built, the rights of the bishop of Clonmacnois at the time were apparently respected.[120]

Clonmacnois, as an ecclesiastical settlement with monastic features continued to exist even after the dramatic changes which took place in the twelfth century. This is best documented through the fact that chronicle-keeping in Clonmacnois continued down to the thirteenth century. The Annals of Tigernach reflect on the arrival of the Anglo-Normans in Ireland in a laconic entry under the year 1169, stating that 'a large body of knights came oversea to Mac Murchada'. News of the military campaigns by the foreigners in the following years rapidly reached Clonmacnois and was carefully recorded in the Annals of Tigernach. Plundered territories, especially the churches and monasteries therein, are frequently mentioned.[121] Clonmacnois, however, lay outside the areas afflicted through Anglo-Norman warfare. Eventually in the year 1178 'The Foreigners of Dublin, including Hugo went on a raid against the Fir chell, and Hugo de Lacy came with a great and strong battalion to plunder Clonmacnois'. According to the annalist the

---

[118] AT.

[119] AFM 1178.

[120] See below, p. 165.

[121] Ossory and its churches in 1169, Mide with Clonard and Kells in 1170, the monastery of Fore in 1172, Clonard, Durrow and the whole of Mide from Athlone to Drogheda in the year 1175, Glendalough in 1176, Downpatrick in 1177, the churches of the plain of Munster in the year 1177.

foreigners soon took to flight out of fear of the men of Ruaidrí Ua Conchobair.[122]

In the very year of the first Anglo-Norman attack on Clonmacnois the
Annals of Tigernach break off in the middle of an entry. The Chronicon
Scotorum had finished long before, with the year 1150.[123] Mageoghagan in
his translation of the Annals of Clonmacnois has a brief lacuna beginning
with the year 1173.[124] It might seem as if chronicle keeping came to an end
in Clonmacnois at the latest in the year 1178. However, the Annals of the
Four Masters for the time between 1172 and 1200 supply some additional
information on Clonmacnois.[125] They state that the 'Booke of Cluain' which
they used as a source was carried to the year 1227.[126] Moreover, Mageoghagan's annals of Clonmacnois do continue after a few years' intermission. A
summary of events for the years 1170 to 1190 is given, at the end of which
the translator complains about the *many leaves lost or stolen out of the ould
Irish book which I Translate, that I doe not know how to handle it.*[127] His
source was obviously in a poor state by the time he made the translation and
it seems the lack of entries after the year 1172 results out of his defective
copy rather than the end of the chronicle he used. Mageoghagan takes up
continuous chronological recording with the year 1200.[128]

The writer of the copy he translated shows familiarity with the localities
around Clonmacnois. He mentions placenames such as *snamh da en*, a place
a little north from Clonmacnois, up the Shannon,[129] or *Liseanabbey*, the

---

[122] AT (1178); the raid is also recorded in ACott 1178, and AFM 1178.

[123] There exists a possible continuation for the years 1141 to 1153, see CS, Introduction, p.
xli.

[124] He states that *King Henry hearing of the good success the said englishmen had in Ireland, the kings majesty in his owen person came over, who made a final end of an entire
conquest in Ireland in the year of our Lord God 1173. - Finis-* (AClon, p. 208).

[125] AFM 1179, AFM 1200.

[126] AFM I, Introduction, p. lxv.

[127] AClon, p. 215.

[128] AClon 1199 (recte 1200), p. 215.

[129] AClon 1201 (recte 1203), p. 218. The place is also mentioned in AT(1159). This was also
the place where St. Patrick crossed the Shannon to proceed from Mide into Connacht according to Tirechán, where it is mentioned as *Vadum Duorum Auium* (see BIELER [ed.], The Pa-

abbot's fort, as the exact location of a fire in Clonmacnois.[130] The whole town of Clonmacnois, except the churches and the bishop's house, are said to have been plundered in 1178.[131] Twice a precise number of buildings burnt down is given: one hundred and five houses in the year 1179 and forty five houses in 1206.[132] The writer often gives very precise datings for events happening in Clonmacnois. An attack in the year 1203 is said to have happened on the 'feast day of St. Gregory', and the raiders are said to have come back the 'next Friday'.[133] The death of bishop Cathal Ua Máeleoin is dated to the precise day, the 8th of the Ides of February, in the year 1206 (recte 1208). Uareirge Ua Nechtain, head of the community of the Céili Dé, died on the 10th of March in the year 1200, according to the copy the Four Masters used. Several of his descriptions of raids on the monastic settlement are so detailed and vivid that we must take them as eyewitness accounts.[134] Clearly the nature of the surviving annalistic accounts strongly suggests that contemporary history in Clonmacnois was still recorded even after the Anglo-Norman invasion, perhaps down to the year 1227, as the Four Masters state, or at least somewhere around then.[135]

---

trician texts, p. 138, §19.1). See also the Tripartite Life of Patrick: STOKES (ed.), Tripartite Life, p. 92. Compare the treatise about the history of the place and its name in the Dindsenchas: E. GWYNN (ed. and transl.), The Metrical Dindshenchas (Todd Lecture Series), Dublin 1903-1935, reprint in 5 vols., Dublin 1991, here vol. IV, pp. 350-367.

[130] AClon 1205, p. 221. The abbot's fort is mentioned earlier in AFM 918 and AClon 1135, p. 194.

[131] AFM.

[132] AFM 1169; AClon 1206, p. 221.

[133] AClon 1202 (recte 1203), p. 219.

[134] See for example the account of de Burgh's plundering of Clonmacnois in 1203, AClon, pp. 218f.

[135] Possibly the end of chronicle keeping was connected with a raid on the settlement in the year 1223, where Clonmacnois and two of its churches were burned and many jewels (and books?) taken away (ALCé 1223, p. 266). Dumville and Grabowski concentrate on the early period in their study of the Clonmacnois chronicles. They did however find out that annalistic recording continued in Clonmacnois even after the break off of the Chronicon in the year 1150! (DUMVILLE / GRABOWSKI, Chronicles and annals, p. 175n). Mac Niocaill comments briefly on the close relation between AClon, CS and AT in the twelfth century. He also points to the possibility to reconstruct the incomplete text of Mageoghagan's annals with the aid of the material transmitted by the Four Masters (MAC NIOCAILL, The medieval Irish annals, pp. 28f.). It seems that such completion confirms the suggestion that these two Clonmacnois sources contained entries as far down as the early thirteenth century.

Apart from the *scriptorium* in Clonmacnois, which apparently remained intact, other traditional ecclesiastical institutions need to be looked at. The abbacy of Clonmacnois had been held by members of the Ua Máeleoin family for most of the twelfth century, disregarding the reform efforts and the various decrees opposing lay abbots. Only towards the end of the twelfth century, did the family lose its status as hereditary successors of St. Ciarán. When in the year 1172 abbot Tigernach Ua Máeleoin died one Máel Mocht Ua Fidabra was made his successor.[136] We might assume, that his promotion to the headship over the community of Clonmacnois was made possible, through the fact that the son of abbot Tigernach, as his expected successor in office, had died the same year as his father.[137] Máel Mochta Ua Fidabra survived his promotion to the abbacy for only one year. In his obituary in the annals of Tigernach he is styled *ardab Cluana maic Nois*.[138] Another member of the family, Máel Chiaráin Ua Fidabra, held the abbacy of Clonmacnois from the year 1173 to 1181. The Uí Fidabra appear as a Mide family and were possibly a branch of the Uí Máelsechlainn, which is given as their alternative surname in the Annals of Ulster and by the Four Masters.[139] They were active in the reform during the twelfth century, and remained successful in the Irish church even after the reform was completed.[140] The appearance of this family in the headship of Clonmacnois might be interpreted as an active step towards reform within St. Ciarán's community. However after the death of Máel Chiaráin Ua Fidabra the Uí Mháeleoin reclaimed their traditional position. They retained the abbacy of Clonmacnois down to the second half of the thirteenth century, even though the precise nature of the community they presided over remains unclear. The community of the Céili Dé in Clonmacnois disappears from the records

---

[136] AT 1172.

[137] AU 1172.

[138] AT (1173).

[139] AU 1173; AFM 1173.

[140] The most successful member of the family, Donatus Ua Fidabra, was abbot of Louth, bishop of Clogher and subsequently archbishop of Armagh from the year 1227 to 1237. B. SMITH, The Armagh-Clogher dispute and the 'Mellifont conspiracy': diocesan politics and monastic reform in early thirteenth century Ireland, in: Seanchas Ardmhacha 14 (1991), pp. 26-38, here 32-34.

with the beginning of the thirteenth century.[141] The guesthouse of Clonmacnois, as another traditional institution of the settlement, was still in existance
around the year 1200.[142] The Ua Máeleoin abbots of the thirteenth century
appear therefore as the rulers of an ecclesiastical estate which was drastically reduced in size as well as in power. There is evidence to suggest that
the family survived on the former abbatial lands west of the Shannon, which
they turned into family property. We know from Archdall that in the late
thirteenth century the bishop of Clonmacnois claimed these lands for himself, and declared the abbot deposed, that is, he deprived the abbatial family
of their hereditary portion of churchland.[143]

4.3.2 Clonmacnois and the restoration of Ua Conchobair power in

  Connacht

A most striking feature of Mageoghagan's annals, when they restart recording in the year 1200, is an unmistakable Connacht bias. The succession
struggles for the kingship of Connacht, after the death of Ruaidrí Ua Conchobair in 1198, are mainly reflected in terms of raids which in the process
were inflicted on the settlement of Clonmacnois. The annalist also reveals
an undisguised sympathy for Cathal Crobderg, whereas his rival, Cathal
Carrach and his allies, appear as St. Ciarán's enemies who repeatedly raided
Clonmacnois.[144] Cathal Carrach's death in the year 1202, is interpreted as a
miracle performed by Ciarán himself.[145] His ally De Burgh is made respon-

---

[141] AFM 1200.

[142] See AClon 1199 (recte 1200), p. 215, where for the last time in the annals a guestmaster
of Clonmacnois is mentioned.

[143] ARCHDALL, Monasticon, 390. Compare further down, pp. 177f.

[144] Cathal Carrach together with William de Burgh expelled Cathal Crobderg out of Connacht. Together they took hostages in their territory and raided the guesthouse in Clonmacnois in the year 1200 (AClon 1199, recte 1200, p. 216). The following year Clonmacnois
served as a meeting place for Cathal Carrach and Meiler fitz Henry, the king's justiciar, and
the settlement was plundered on this occasion (AClon 1200, recte 1201, pp. 216f.). The Four
Masters refer to the meeting as a battle between Meiler and Cathal Carrach; but the latter was
the king's candidate at that time, so the Four masters probably slightly mistranslated here
(AFM 1200). Compare F. X. MARTIN, John, lord of Ireland, 1185-1216, in: NHI II, p. 131.

[145] AClon 1201 (recte 1202), pp. 217f.

sible for the violation of all the churches of Connacht in the year 1203, Clonmacnois being the most severely affected one.[146] We are told that God himself together with all the Connacht saints, including St. Ciarán, caused him to die in consequence of a horrible disease in the following year. The Four Masters thought the illness 'too shameful to be described' whereas Mageoghagan, less prudish here, describes in detail an illness which especially affected the victims *privie place*.[147]

In contrast to his deceased opponents, Cathal Crobderg is portrayed as the grand king of Connacht, who never seems to have raided or spoiled one single church.[148] Obviously such a flattering portrayal points to cordial friendship between the king and a Clonmacnois-based writer of the history of Connacht. This friendship became most apparent when in the year 1208, after the final consolidation of Cathal's power the body of King Ruaidrí Ua Conchobair, the king's predecessor and brother was elevated and enshrined in a stone shrine in Clonmacnois.[149] The elevation of the remains of a former king in medieval times was not only an act of veneration for one's ancestor, but also an expression of the present king's political ambitions. A

---

[146] AClon 1202 (recte 1203), pp. 218f. The passage reads like an eyewitness account: *The Englishmen of Milick and Sile Anmchye accompanied with the 2 families of Moyntyr Kenay, and Moyntyr Milchon came to Clonvicknose upon the feast day of Saint Gregory, preyed and spoyled the church, Sanctuary, and towne of Clonvicknose; the next friday the said company came to Clonvicknose and tooke the like spoyles from thence, and though the first spoyles were much, yett the second were farr greater. Some of Delvin were at the taking of the said spoyles, they took from out of the church the holy vestments, books, chalices, cloth, Linnen, and corn, and all other things they could finger soe that they left the croftes, gardens, and houses of the town wast and voyde, like an empty chaos without any manner of thing but their empty and foot-troden grounds. After doing of which William Burke returned again to Milick, and from thence marched to Limerick and left a good company to guard the castle of Meelick.* The men of Delbna apparently fought in de Burgh's army (compare ALCé 1203, p. 228).

[147] AFM 1204; AClon 1204, p. 220.

[148] When in 1190 on one occasion Clonmacnois served as a gathering place for his army, this incident is nowhere in the sources related to the plundering of the monastery, which certainly would be the most natural thing to do in such a case; compare AClon 1200, p. 216; AFM 1190; ALCé 1190.

[149] AFM 1207 (recte 1208). Probably Ruaidrí, who had died in 1198 in the abbey of Cong, but was buried in Clonmacnois (AFM 1198). There is, however, also the early twelfth century king of Connacht, Ruaidrí who won the battle of Corann (1118). He as well was said to have died and been buried in Clonmacnois.

comparable event was the elevation of the remains of Charlemagne in Aachen under Frederick Barbarossa the 29th of December 1165. The purpose was to demonstrate a political intention, namely to restore the power of their imperial predecessor.[150] Similarly the political programme of Cathal Crobderg was to restore the former glory of his dynasty as well as that of his kingdom. Clonmacnois in its function as a burial ground played a central part in this antiquarian revival.

A number of literary works in praise of Uí Chonchobair power in Connacht, composed at the time have come down to us.[151] The Ua Máelchonaire family was prominent amongst the men of learning in support of Cathal's policy. Their best known contribution towards royal propaganda is the prose tract on the inauguration of the kings of Connacht, together with a poem of praise on the same topic.[152] It seems highly plausible that Conaing Buide Ua Máelchonaire on this occasion composed the poem which celebrates Clonmacnois as the cemetery of the heroes from Connacht.[153] The work is basically an enumeration of the kings of Connacht buried in Clonmacnois. Guaire Aidne, of the Uí Fiachrach Aidne as well as his rival Ragallach mac Uatach, of the Uí Briúin, are mentioned.[154] There follows Fergus (d.654),

---

[150] Compare B. GEBHARDT, Handbuch der deutschen Geschichte, ed. H. GRUNDMANN, Stuttgart ⁹1973, vol. 1, p. 399.

[151] See for example two poems, preserved in the Book of Uí Maine, edited by B. Ó CUÍV, Tairnic in sel-sa ac Síl Néill, in: Ériu 34 (1985), pp. 157-174.; also B. Ó CUÍV, A poem of prophecy on Ua Conchobair kings of Connacht, in: Celtica 19 (1987), pp. 31-54.

[152] Edited by. M. DILLON (ed.), The inauguration of O'Conor, in: J. A. WATT / J. B. MORRALL / F. X. MARTIN (eds.), Medieval studies presented to Aubrey Gwynn, Dublin 1961, pp. 186-202. Dillon dates the tract to the year 1310. This date has been corrected by K. SIMMS, „Gabh umad a Fheidhlimidh" - a fifteenth-century inauguration ode?, in: Ériu 31 (1980), pp. 132-145. She suggests an archetype of the prose tract may have dated to the early thirteenth century, whereas the poem is addressed to Feidhlim Ó Conchobair Ruad (d.1490).

[153] M. STOKES (ed.), A reigleag laoch leithe cuinn, in: PETRIE, Christian inscriptions, I, pp. 79-81; MS preserved in Trinity College Dublin (MS H.1.17); there in another edition by R. I. BEST (ed.), The Graves of the Kings at Clonmacnois, in: Ériu 2 (1905), pp. 161-171, from MS Rawl. B 512 in which four additional stanza are preserved.

[154] CS 642, AFM 645 (recte 649); CS 662, AFM 662 for Guaire's death. Compare O'DONOVAN (ed.), The genealogies, tribes and customs of Hy-Fiachrach, pp. 312f., for a list of kings of Connacht transcribed by Dubhaltach Mac Fhirbhisigh in 1664, which mentions Clonmacnois as Guaire's burial place after thirteen years in government. See BYRNE, Irish Kings, pp. 248-253, for the Uí Briúin.

Muiredach Muillethan (d.702), Indrechtach (d.723), Tomaltach (d.774) and Muirgius (d.815) all being of the Uí Briúin Aí, and each king being the son of his predecessor. Other kings of Connacht, such as Cellach (d.705), from who the Síl Ceallaigh claim descent, or Cathal (d.735) the ancestor of the Síl Cathail, find no mention at all. The poem obviously tries to suggest that the kingship of Connacht was a property of the Uí Briúin Aí, as early as the seventh century. This of course was the Connacht branch from which the Uí Chonchobair dynasty came.

The composition seems to have been modelled on earlier examples of this species. Thus a very similar poem, attributed to Torna Éices, the mythical fosterfather of Niall of the Nine Hostages, exists which gives an account of the pre-historic Connacht aristocracy who found their rest at Ráth Cruachan, the ancient inauguration site of the kings of Connacht.[155] The poem forms part of the Clonmacnois manuscript, Lebor na hUidre, and seems to represent a very popular tradition of adding to the fame of a place by stressing its function as the burial place of Irish celebrities.[156] Similar lists of the graves of pre-historical heroes exist for Tara, as well as for New Grange, alias Brug na Bóinde. The latter of the two for example is praised for having covered 'many a true prince of the race of every king that has possessed thee'.[157] Clonmacnois in this context seems to function as the successor institution of these early pagan ritual sites. Under the patronage of Cathal Crobderg, it assumed a decisive role in the programme of restoration of royal power in Connacht. As such the ecclesiastical settlement in its traditional sense survived the early years of the Anglo-Norman invasion, still outside the immediate sphere of influence of the foreigners.

With the visit of King John to Ireland in 1210 the Anglo-Norman advance into Connacht began.[158] By now the effects of the Anglo-Norman

---

[155] H. D'ARBOIS DE JUBAINVILLE (ed.), Le poème de Torna-Éices sur le cimetière de Croghan, in: Revue Celtique 17 (1896), pp. 280-285.

[156] I wish to thank Dr K. Simms, who examined the poem, and reported that on linguistic grounds there is no need to date the work much earlier than its earliest MS source Lebor na hUidre, c. 1100 A.D.

[157] E. GWYNN (ed.), The Metrical Dindshenchas, I, pp. 14-27 for Tara; II, pp. 10-17, here 11 for New Grange.

[158] For the conquest of Connacht see H. WALTON, The English in Connacht, Ph.D Thesis, Trinity College Dublin 1980.

presence were much in evidence in Clonmacnois at the borders between Mide and Connacht. Land in Connacht was granted to Anglo-Norman nobles by the king already in the early years of the thirteenth century.[159] The building of the castle of Athlone was commenced in 1210 and caused a major emergency by falling down the following year.[160] In Clonmacnois a royal castle, a little south of the walls of the settlement, was built in the year 1214.[161] Thus the settlement assumed some importance as a royal stronghold. The castle presumably functioned to guard the bridge over the Shannon near Clonmacnois.[162] Also it had some importance in the fight against Ua Máelsechlainn power in Mide. Cormac Ua Máelsechlainn was eventually killed by the Foreigners in Clonmacnois together with his wife, fosterfather and steward whilst he *lay at a certaine house at Clonvicknose.*[163]

The building of the castle in Clonmacnois was carried out with some respect for ecclesiastical property in the area. In a royal letter dating from 1216 the king commands the justiciar to compensate the bishop of Clonmacnois 'for his land occupied in fortifying the castle of Clonmacnois, for his fruit trees cut down, his cows, horses, oxen and household utensils taken away.'[164] It is significant that the abbot of Clonmacnois is not mentioned at all here, whereas episcopal rights and property are listed in detail, and compensated for. We may conclude, that the bishop's position was strengthened in Clonmacnois under Anglo-Norman impact, whereas the former leaders of the church, the Ua Máeleoin abbots lost their influence. There is evidence pointing to the fact that by the later half of the thirteenth century the bishop

---

[159] The cantred of Tír Maine, between Athlone and Roscommon, was granted to Geoffrey de Costentin in 1201. Dunglave, land around Galway, was given to Richard Tyrel (Cal. Doc. Irel. I, p. 25 no. 153); six cantreds in Connacht adjoining Mide were granted to Hugh de Lacy in 1203 (Cal. Doc. Irel. I, p. 37 no. 241); Gilbert Mac Costello (alias Nangle) was granted the cantred of Maenmagh, in Connacht in 1207 (Cal. Doc. Irel. I, p. 46, no. 311; compare WALTON, The English in Connacht, pp. 34f.).

[160] ALCé 1210, 1211. See G. H. ORPEN, Athlone Castle: its early history, with notes on some neighbouring castles, in: JRSAI 37 (1907), pp. 257-276.

[161] ALCé 1214.

[162] For the bridge called Cuirr Cluana see AT (1158), AClon 1158, p. 204.

[163] AClon 1226, pp. 231f.; see also ALCé 1214 for Cormac, son of Art Ua Máelsechlainn who with his people *carried off a prey of cows from the castle of Cluain and defeated the Foreigners of the castle.*

[164] Cal. Doc. Irel. I, p. 107, no. 694 (30. May 1216).

of Clonmacnois in his authority as head of a royal bishopric made infringements of the former abbatial rights, to the end that the abbot lost both his
position as well as his possessions, to the bishop of the diocese of Clonmacnois.[165]

4.4 Summary

With the beginning of the church reform the traditional ecclesiastical dynasties in Clonmacnois lost their governmental functions. The abbacy of
Clonmacnois became the property of the Ua Máeleoin family, who came to
power under the secular patronage of Toirdelbach Ua Conchobair, possibly
with the support of a reform party in Clonmacnois itself. Throughout the
twelfth century Connacht influence is evident in Clonmacnois at both secular and ecclesiastical levels. Toirdelbach Ua Conchobair as well as his son
Ruaidrí were most prominent as secular patrons of the church of St. Ciarán,
at the same time the Ua Dubthaigh family, as a most powerful ecclesiastical
dynasty in Connacht, gained a share in government. In the early thirteenth
century Clonmacnois played an important part in the political revival of Ua
Conchobair power under Cathal Crobderg, when its traditional function as
royal burial ground was revived. Only towards the end of the thirteenth
century, with the death of the last abbot, does Clonmacnois, in its shape as a
traditional ecclesiastical settlement, disappear from the records.

The formation of the diocese of Clonmacnois was a gradual process
which came to completion only towards the end of the century, apparently
in consequence of the Anglo-Norman impact on Irish church affairs. It
seems that the lack of secular support in Mide caused the delays and the
ignoring of the bishopric of Clonmacnois at various reforming synods. In
the early thirteenth century the bishopric assumed, if only temporarily, a
supportive function for Anglo-Norman control in the area, when a castle
was built in Clonmacnois in the year 1210.

---

[165] See below, pp. 177f.

Most of the great Irish churches which had become bishoprics in the twelfth century reform lost their episcopal status in the course of the reorganization of the arrangements under Anglo-Norman impact in the early thirteenth century. Clonard ceased to be the diocesan centre of Meath, when the see was transferred to Trim during the episcopate of Simon Rocheford. Likewise Kells, which held diocesan status for some time after 1152, became one of the two archdeaconries in the diocese of Meath. The see of Glendalough was united with Dublin in 1216. Inis Cathaig, or Scattery Island lost its episcopal authority to the bishops of Killaloe already in the late twelfth century. Lismore, however, survived the often violent infringements from Waterford in the first decades of the thirteenth century as an independent bishopric, down to the year 1363, when the two dioceses were eventually united.[1] The history of the reluctant origin and rise of the bishopric of Clonmacnois in the course of the twelfth century has been discussed in the preceding chapter. Here things seem to have happened the other way round. It was supressed as a bishopric by the reformers, and it was only as a result of the Anglo-Norman impact on Irish church affairs in the latter parts of the twelfth century that it was eventually acknowledged as a bishopric.

5.1 The Extent of the diocese of Clonmacnois

Little is known about the diocesan boundries in the late twelfth century, the only information being the fact that the lands of West Meath, what ever their exact extension might have been, were under the authority of the bishop of Clonmacnois from 1174.[2] There were also the lands of Athlone on the east side of the river Shannon. According to the Four Masters the Franciscan Friary of Athlone, which they claim was founded by Cathal Crobderg

---

[1] WATT, The church and the two nations, pp. 60-65, 81f. For Inis Cathaig see GWYNN, The Irish church, pp. 239f.

[2] AT (1174); compare J. D. DALTON, Ancient boundaries of Ardagh and Clonmacnoise dioceses, in: Ardagh and Clonmacnois Ant. Soc. Jn. 1 (1926), pp. 9-70; vol. 2 (1929), pp. 1-73; J. MONAHAN, Records relating to the diocese of Ardagh and Clonmacnoise, Dublin 1886; J. J. McNAMEE, Clonmacnois as a diocese, in: Ardagh and Clonmacnois Ant. Soc. Jn. 2, no.10 (1945), pp. 27-36.

in the year 1224, was situated in the diocese of Clonmacnois.[3] The precise
number and the names of the churches belonging to the bishopric of Clonmacnois is clear only from the royal taxation list of the churches in Ireland,
drawn up in the early fourteenth century. Apart from the parish church of
Clonmacnois itself, the document mentions the rectory of *Loghloch*, i.e.
Ballyloughloe, comprising the vicarages of Ballyloughloe, Athlone and
Kilcleagh. Furthermore there was the priory of *Galyn*, now Gallen, the
community of nuns de Kelbyguneth, the vicarage of *Tethsaran*, now Tisaran
or Ferbane alias Wheery parish, and the vicarage of *Lieth*, now represented
by Lemanaghan parish.[4] Ballyloughloe with its three vicarages, forms part
of county Westmeath and it seems plausible that this was the territory united
to the diocese of Clonmacnois in 1174. Already prior to the formation of the
diocese of Clonmacnois the lands in question here had links with the monastic predecessor institution of the bishopric. Ballyloughloe parish itself
was the site of the church of Íseal Chiaráin, which, as the seat of the Céili
Dé community and later that of the Meic Cuinn na mBocht.[5] Lands in Athlone parish were held by St. Ciarán's successors according to the writer of
Mageoghagan's chronicle.[6] Lemanaghan, says the eleventh century com-
mentator of the Clonmacnois chronicle, was in possession of St. Ciarán
from the seventh century when it was donated to the saint by the king of the
Síl nÁedo Sláine.[7] The church of Gallen appears as the ally of Clonmacnois
since the early ninth century, when it first attracted the hostility of the king
of Munster, the arch-enemy of St. Ciarán at the time.[8] Obviously the area in
the immediate neighbourhood of St. Ciarán was bound to be under the jurisdiction of the nearby ecclesiastical overlord. The diocese of Clonmacnois

---

[3]   AFM 1224. GWYNN / HADCOCK, p. 243, strongly question the early date of foundation,
preferring a year or two before the consecration of the friary's church in 1241 (AFM). The
fact that the friary was situated in the diocese of Clonmacnois would however not be effected
by the alternative dating.

[4]   Cal. Doc. Irel. V, p. 216. The parish church of Ballyloughloe was divided into the three
vicarages in 1451 (Cal. Pap. Let. X, pp. 541f. [15. Jan. 1451-1452]).

[5]   Compare above, pp. 68-71, 136-139.

[6]   AClon 1210, p. 224.

[7]   Compare above, pp. 85f.

[8]   CS 823; compare above, pp. 85f., 98 n.33.

could thus be described as the successor institution of the - albeit drastically diminished - *paruchia* of St. Ciarán.

The diocese of Clonmacnois existed down to the mid-sixteenth century, when it was united with Meath. *A Certificate of the State and Revennewes of the Bishoppricke of Meath and Clonemackenosh*, taken in 1622, was preserved amongst the works of James Ussher, bishop of Meath at the time. There the above mentioned parishes are still listed as the lands of the former diocese of Clonmacnois.[9] However the Certificate also mentions *lands in the Countie of Roscommon belonging to the said B^{prick}*, also *two quarters of land lying neere vnto Galloway* and *Fower quarters of land in the Countie of Mayo called Killshamy*. The writer refers to a then lost church register for details concerning Clonmacnois' lands in Connacht.[10] We are told that all the lands in Roscommon belonging to the bishopric of Clonmacnois were held in fee farm by Anthony Brabazon from 1592. This man died in 1597, and fortunately a *post mortem* inquisition of his possessions, taken by the exchequer at Roscommon in the year 1604 has come down to us. The deceased was seised of

> the ruined Castle of Tuam Srower and of the quarter of the same name upon which the said castle is built, and also of a 1/2 villata of land called the half Towne of Clonburryn, and of 1 quarter called Coylagh, and of 1 other quarter called Kylbeglagh, and of 1 quarter called Ardneglogg, and of 2 quarters called Kylcashel and Kyly, and of a quarter called Tullagh and Skehernagh, and a 1/2 quarter called Tyrnedarrowe and of 1 cartron called Dyrry McChy. He held the aforesaid 9 quarters with 3 cartrons ... and the moiety of all the tithes from the Lord Bishop of M[eath] and Clonmacnois in fee farm by an annual rent.[11]

Here we have the details about the bishop's possession in Connacht. All of the lands mentioned can be identified through a comparison with the documentation of the lands in Connacht according to the report of the Survey commissioners from around 1641.

Tuam Srower is Tuaimsruthra, otherwise known as Ashford townland in Creagh parish, county Roscommon. In 1641 it was still held by the Braba-

---

9   A Certificate of the State and Revennewes of the Bishoppricke of Meath and Clonemackenosh, ed. C.R. ELRINGTON, The whole works of the Most Rev. James Ussher, vol. 1, London 1864, Appendix V, pp. liii -cxxv, here cxxii-cxxiv.

10   Ibid., pp. lviiif.

11   Edited in an Appendix by P. K. EGAN, The parish of Ballinasloe, Dublin/London 1960, p. 304.

zon family.[12] *Clonburryn* i.e. Clonburren was situated on the west side of the Shannon right opposite Clonmacnois, and also included three islands on the river. It belonged to Moore parish, bordering Creagh to the North East. In the early fourteenth century *Clouyn in Bernan*, possibly standing for Clonburren was part of the diocese of Elphin.[13] In the seventeenth century, according to the Survey report from 1641, the lands of Clonburren were in joined possession of the bishop of Clonfert and Clonmacnois. One quarter of Clonburren was held by the bishop of Clonfert, the other by the bishop of Meath, *having no certaine Mear betwixt them*.[14] In 1407, prior to the union of the diocese of Clonmacnois with that of Meath, the bishop of Clonmacnois is said to have held half of the lands in Clonburren.[15] *Coylagh* seems to be Culliagh townland, also in Moore parish. *Kylbeglagh* is Kilbegley, also in Moore parish and also in possession of the bishop of Meath in 1641.[16] *Ardneglogg* alias Ardnaglog was part of Creagh parish, again in possession of the bishop of Meath in 1641.[17] *Kylcashel* appears to be Kilcashell in Moore parish.[18] *Kyly* could be the anglicised version of Cuillen, in the north- eastern parts of Creagh parish, also known as Culleenmulroney, which in 1641 was in possession of the dean of Clonmacnois.[19] *Tullagh and Skehernagh* seems to be Tullaghanmore and Skeagh in Moore parish.[20] *Tyrnedarrowe* is Tirnedarne.[21] and finally *Dyrry McChy* appears as Derrymackie.[22] Again these lands were all situated in Moore parish.

---

[12] SIMINGTON (ed.), Books of Survey, I, p. 60.

[13] Cal. Doc. Irel. V, p. 223.

[14] SIMINGTON (ed.), Books of Survey, III, p. 64.

[15] Namely the part of it called Raghra, according to the rental list of the bishop of Clonfert, dating from 1407, see NICHOLLS (ed.), The episcopal rentals, p. 139.

[16] SIMINGTON (ed.), Books of Survey, I, p. 62.

[17] Ibid., p. 60; EGAN, The parish of Ballinasloe, p. 14.

[18] SIMINGTON (ed.), Books of Survey, I, p. 62.

[19] Ibid., p. 60.

[20] Ibid., p. 62.

[21] Ibid., p. 63.

[22] Ibid., p. 62.

The greater proportion of the lands in Roscommon, claimed as belonging to the bishopric of Clonmacnois, were situated in the parishes of Moore and in the northern parts of Creagh. These parishes covered land west of the Shannon, opposite Clonmacnois, expanding southwards. The parish of Moore appears as the rectory of Moycarn or Moycarnan in late medieval papal documents. Together with the vicarages of Clonburren and Drumalgach it formed an enclave of the diocese of Tuam, within the borders between the dioceses of Clonfert and Elphin.[23]

It is somehow surprising to find the bishop of Clonmacnois holding land in the diocese of Tuam. However, it is even more surprising to find lands adjacent to the river Shannon, far removed from Tuam, and totally isolated from the actual diocese, belonging to the ecclesiastical jurisdiction of the bishop of Tuam. Reasons for such peculiar diocesan boundaries must be sought in the history of their development: According to a royal letter dating from the year 1255, the bishop of Clonmacnois was in dispute with the archbishop of Tuam over certain lands in Connacht.[24] The bishop of Clonmacnois at the time was the Franciscan Friar Tomás Ua Cuinn (1251-1279), notorious for his claims to authority in Connacht, beyond the boundaries of his diocese.[25] The lands in question here are nowhere specified, but the case becomes clearer in the context of another quarrel settled during the episcopate of Tomás. According to Archdall the bishop was also fighting with the abbot of Clonmacnois (amongst others) over the possession of former ecclesiastical lands. Archdall gives an enumeration of the lands concerned. He lists

five carucates and a half, and forty acres of land in Nagylt, Clonbonnyn, Clonfada, Kulletha, Kilbegalla, Arnaglog, and Tesaya; he also sued Phillip Mc YWard for a carucate and a half in Bothkeran; William de Pendergast for a carucate in Coathyn, John Dolfyn for a carucate in Glonmolydun, and Gilbert...for a carucate and a half in Killesobotha; and Donethud O'Donechada for a carucate in Karthyn.[26]

---

[23] GWYNN / HADCOCK, Map of monastic Ireland; WATT, The church and the two nations, p. 53. See also for the rectory of Moycaranan: Cal. Pap. Let. VII, p. 228; X, 410-11; XI, 206-207; for the vicarage of Clonburren Cal. Pap. Let. VIII, p. 564.

[24] Cal. Doc. Irel. II, p. 73, no. 456.

[25] See below, pp. 181f.

[26] ARCHDALL, Monasticon, p. 390.

Most of the placenames listed here appear as holdings on the Connacht side of the river Shannon. A number of them sound very familiar indeed. There is *Clonbonnyn* standing for Clonburren; *Clonfada* is a townland in Moore parish.[27] *Kudetha* seems to be Culliagh in Moore parish.[28] *Kilbegalla*, is Kilbegley, alias Killvegley, also in Moore parish. *Arnaglog* is the townland Ardneglog in Creagh parish.[29] These holdings are identical with the lands in Connacht belonging to the bishopric of Clonmacnois, according to early seventeenth-century evidence.[30] Apparently, in the thirteenth century, the Clonmacnois lands in Connacht were in possession of the abbot of Clonmacnois, who was then accused by the bishop of unlawfully detaining them.

This problem was a very common one in the churches of Connacht. Former ecclesiastical lands were claimed as private possession by the traditional coarbial families, i.e. the descendants of the pre-reformed ecclesiastical dynasties. They were alienated from the bishop's authority, and held back from integration into the diocesan system. Earlier in the century, in the year 1210 a synod, especially concerned with the conflicting interests between abbatial claims to authority and episcopal rights, was held before the archbishop of Tuam. A number of coarbial families were dispossessed and their lands assigned to the respective bishopric.[31] The *cowarb of St. Queran* was present, and it seems plausible that on this occasion the lands of St. Ciarán west of the Shannon, represented by the rectory of Moycarnan and the vicarages of Clonburren and Drumalgach, were assigned to the bishopric of Tuam. Possibly the Ua Máeleoin family who claimed the lands as their property preferred affiliation to the distant bishopric of Tuam, rather than to come under the authority of the nearby bishop of Clonmacnois.

Moycarnan, Clonburren and Drumalgach remained part of the diocese of Tuam throughout the middle ages. However, it seems the bishop of Clonmacnois regained authority as the largest land owner in the area. The Ua Máeleoin family on the other hand, who lost their lands in terms of property

---

27 SIMINGTON (ed.), Books of Survey, I, p. 63.

28 Ibid., p. 62

29 Ibid., p. 60.

30 See above, p. 175.

31 AClon 1210, p 224.

rights to the bishop of Clonmacnois, reappear in ecclesiastical offices in the parishes and dominated the rectory of Moycarnan.[32]

The case of Moore parish appears as a very well documented example of the claims to authority by the bishop of Clonmacnois over land outside his diocese. There is evidence that other lands in Connacht were also associated with the bishopric of Clonmacnois. There is for example a vicarage in the diocese of Clonfert, which bears the name 'Killespucmalone'. It seems to date from the early thirteenth century, when the Ua Máeleoin family temporarily held the bishopric of Clonmacnois, and presumably claimed these parts of the former ecclesiastical estate as part of the episcopal lands. The tradition of churchland was preserved when the former cell of the bishop Ua Máeleoin became part of the diocese of Clonfert and was transformed into a prebend of that church.[33] The lands in Galway, referred to in the Certificate, might have been identical with the Clonmacnois property situated in Killerean parish, in the former barony of Dunmore, in county Galway. According to the Compossicion Booke of Connought four quarters there were in possession of the Bishop of Clonmacnois in 1585.[34]

It seems those claims to land outside the diocesan boundaries derived from former ecclesiastical rights in the areas concerned. Thus the lands in Moore parish, the best documented case, apparently represented the former abbatial lands within the church of Clonmacnois.

---

[32] See below, pp. 194-196.

[33] EGAN (ed.), The royal visitation, pp. 68f.; NICHOLLS (ed.), The episcopal rentals, p. 138.

[34] A. M. FREEMAN (ed.), Compossicion Booke of Connought 1585, Dublin 1936, pp. 80f. The land is specified as *the third of Walter Bermingham scept consisting of 70 qrs whereof belongeth to the Bishop of Clon mc Dnosy 4 qrs*. The 4 qrs are not mentioned by name. However in the survey report from 1641 we find the townland *Caronkilleene* in Dunmore parish and barony, which was then in possession of *Ld Birmingham* (SIMINGTON [ed.], Books of Survey, III, p. 294).

5.2 The bishopric of Clonmacnois

5.2.1 The thirteenth century

The Anglo-Norman castle, built in Clonmacnois in the year 1214, might be interpreted as a visible sign of royal control over the settlement, as well as over the bishopric of Clonmacnois.[35] However, little is heard about the castle once the initial building phase was over. In 1221 the castle was given into the custody of Geoffrey de Marisco.[36] Three years later, in 1224, it was taken over by Richard Tuite,[37] who in the following year received more land in the neighbourhood.[38] The last mention of the castle in Anglo-Norman administrative documents is that in the year 1233, when Richard de Burgh was ordered by the king to deliver the castles of Connacht, amongst them Athlone and Clonmacnois, to the justiciar Maurice fitz Gerald.[39] It seems the castle soon lost its importance as a military stronghold.

The bishops of Clonmacnois in the early years of the thirteenth century were supplied by the Ua Máeleoin family. Bishop Áed Ua Máeleoin drowned in the year 1220.[40] His namesake and successor in office resigned in the year 1235, and retired to the Cistercian house of Kilbeggan, where he died the following year.[41] It seems that here members of the former ecclesiastical dynasty attempted to continue their tradition as successors of St. Ciarán by assuming episcopal honours. The attempt failed. According to a papal letter, indicating the resignation of Áed to the archbishop of Armagh, the last Ua Máeleoin bishop of Clonmacnois resigned because his church was placed 'in the midst of a perverse nation'.[42] It seems possible that racial

---

[35] Compare above, p. 171f.

[36] Cal. Pat. Rolls Henry III 1216-25, p. 316.

[37] Cal. Pat. Rolls Henry III 1216-25, p. 433.

[38] This was land near Athlone Cal. Doc. Irel. I, p. 191, no. 1261 (21. April 1225).

[39] Cal. Pat. Rolls Henry III 1232-47, p. 9.

[40] AU.

[41] AClon 1236, p. 235.

[42] Cal. Pap. Let. I, p. 145 (5. Kal May 1235)

conflicts in the church of Clonmacnois were the backround to the resignation of the Irish bishop. Tomás, the successor of Áed was the first bishop of Clonmacnois, elected with royal consent and invested with the temporalities of the see by the king's justitiar.[43] We also know that later in his episcopate he travelled to England, under the protection and at the expense of the king.[44] This might suggest Anglo-Norman affinities of bishop Tomás, and one might infere that the resignation of his predecessor Áed was a consequence of Anglo-Norman interference.

Bishop Tomás must have died in 1253 or sometime before. In that year the Franciscan Tomás Ua Cuinn was appointed to the see of Clonmacnois, whilst in Rome. He held the bishopric until his death in 1278.[45] His appointment to Clonmacnois happened with the consent of the king.[46] Before his career as a bishop, he was Guardian of the Franciscan custody of Drogheda. This was the most Anglo-Norman amongst the five Franciscan custodies in Ireland and the appointment of an Irishman to the position is quite remarkable.[47] He was, however, likewise familiar with the Irish parts of the church, and we know of his sermons against superstition, preached to a congreation in Connacht, which are preserved in a Franciscan preacher's book of the time.[48] He was a man of the church active on both sides, in Anglo-Norman domains as well as in the church of the Irish.

His episcopate in Clonmacnois saw a series of latent conflicts with the Irish archbishops of Tuam, mostly concerning episcopal authority about lands in Connacht, formerly in possession of the church of Clonmacnois.[49] Also around this time the archdeacon of Clonmacnois, one *Milo Corr*, i.e. Máel Sechnaill Ua Conchobair, was promoted to the see of Elphin, which he

---

[43] Cal. Doc. Irel. I, p. 344, no. 234 (8. April 1236); Cal. Doc. Irel. I, p. 344, no. 2318 + 2319 (18. April 1236).

[44] Cal. Doc. Irel. I, p. 470, no. 3166 + 3167 (8. July 1252).

[45] ALCé 1253, 1278; AConn 1253.11, 1278.7; AFM 1253, 1278. See WATT, The church and the two nations, p. 180.

[46] Cal. Doc. Irel. II, p. 23, no. 151 (20 Feb. 1252-53).

[47] Cal. Pap. Let. I, p. 281 (6 Kal Dec. 1252).

[48] J. A. WATT, The church in medieval Ireland, Dublin 1972, pp. 76f.; A. G. LITTLE (ed.), Liber exemplorum ad usum praedicantium, London 1966, pp. 85f., §142 'De fide'.

[49] See above, pp. 178f.

held against the will of the archbishop of Tuam, who refused consecration for over two years, between 1260 and 1262,.[50] Instead the archbishop of Armagh, only recently confirmed in his claims to primatial authority over the whole of the Irish church, confirmed Milo in the year 1260.[51] Both the dispute over lands in Connacht, as well as the claims of a Clonmacnois clergyman to the see of Elphin, point to the fact that Tomás Ua Cuinn as bishop of Clonmacnois claimed ecclesiastical authority beyond his diocesan boundaries, in particular in Connacht. The Clonmacnois clerk in his claims to the see of Elphin probably operated not only with the backing of the archbishop of Armagh, but also with support from Anglo-Norman side, since he had close links with the de Geneville.[52] William de Geneville, the brother of the justiciar Geoffrey, was the vicar of Ardnurcher church. He together with the want to be bishop of Elphin was involved in trade with London, which testifies to peaceful interaction between Irish and Anglo-Norman nobles in the region at the time.[53]

Finally, evidence points to an ongoing conflict between the bishop and the descendants of a former ecclesiastical dynasty of Clonmacnois, during the episcopate of Tomás. The Ua Máeleoin had settled on former monastic lands, west of the Shannon, which apparently they regarded as their possession. However, the bishop of Clonmacnois claimed jurisdiction over these lands, possibly attempting to integrate them into his diocese. In the course of the conflict he simply declared the abbot deposed.[54] Nothing more is heard of an abbot henceforward; we lose sight of the few remainders from the former community in Clonmacnois which had outlived the twelfth century.

---

[50] According to the letter of royal assent *this grace was granted to the elect on the prayer of the Archdeacon of Besancon, brother of G. de Geneville* (Cal. Pat. Rolls Henry III 1258-66, p. 116 [30. Jan. 1260]; Cal. Doc. Irel. III, p. 105, no. 647).

[51] Cal. Pat. Rolls Henry III 1258-66, p. 125 (8. Nov. 1260). The *ius primatie* of archbishop of Armagh was confirmed by the pope in 1255 (see WATT, The church and the two nations, pp. 113f.).

[52] Cal. Doc. Irel. III, p. 105, no. 647; Cal. Pat. Rolls Henry III 1258-66, p. 116 (30. Jan. 1260); Cal. Doc. Irel. III, p. 105, no. 648; Cal. Pat. Rolls Henry III 1258-66, p. 120 (3. Feb. 1260).

[53] Cal. Doc. Irel. II, p. 105, no. 645 (Hilary 1259-60).

[54] ARCHDALL, Monasticon, p. 390.

Tomás died in 1278. The chapter of Clonmacnois elected one Gilbert as his successor, up to then dean of Clonmacnois. The failure to get royal licence for the election prior to its taking place, was explained by the chapter two years later by the fact that the messenger sent to the king had died on his way to England. Royal assent to the election was therefore only given in 1280.[55] However, the royal purse profited from these kinds of delays, since during vacancy the king had the custody of the see and received the temporalities.[56] Bishop Gilbert resigned his office in 1288.[57] As is apparent from a royal letter to the archbishop of Armagh he was blinded by *some sons of perdition*.[58]

His successor, William Ua Dubthaigh, again a Franciscan, was invested by the king's justiciar two years later in 1290.[59] The temporalities for the time between 1288 and 1290 went again to the king.[60] Bishop William is said to have died of a fall from his horse in the year 1298.[61]

---

[55] Cal. Doc. Irel. II, p. 351, no. 713 (20. July 1280); Cal. Doc. Irel. II, p. 397, no. 1849 (27. July 1281).

[56] Account of the escheator, Pipe Roll X. Ed. I., in: Appendix to the 36th report of the deputy keeper, Dublin 1904, p. 61: *Account of John de Sandford, escheator of the issues of certain bishoprics in the hands of the king and in John's custody. Clonmacnoys bishopric: He accounts for the period from Friday after the feast of St. Martin a.r. VII after the death of Tomás Ocyn or Ocuyn, the late bishop, to the 18. Feb. a.r. X when the temporalities were delivered to Gilbert formerly dean of Clonmacnois, provided to the said church by J. archbishop of Armagh.*

[57] Cal. Doc. Irel. III, p. 177, no. 401 (17. June 1288). Cal. Doc. Irel. III, p. 182, no. 414 (12. July 1288).

[58] Cal. Pap. Let. I, p. 501 (13 Sept. 1289).

[59] Cal. Doc. Irel. III, p. 343, no. 726 (15. July 1290); Cal. Doc. Irel. III, p. 433, no. 735 (18. July 1290).

[60] Account of the escheator. Pipe Roll a.r. XVIII, Ed. I, in: Appendix to the 37th report of the Deputy keeper, Dublin 1905, p. 40.

[61] ALCé 1297; AConn 1297.5; AU 1297. In a ninteenth century description Thomas Cooke, describes a cross found in Banagher, county Offaly, formerly known as Kill-Regnaighe, now Reynagh, in the diocese of Clonmacnois. This cross shows a deer, hunted after by dogs. According to Cooke this was bishop Ua Dubthaigh's cross (see T. L. COOKE, The ancient Cross of Banagher, King's county, in: Transactions of the Kilkenny Arch. Soc. 2 [1853], pp. 277-280). The cross, now known as the Banagher cross is infact closely related with the Bealin Cross (found in Twyford, Ballyloughloe) and the North Cross in Clonmacnois. One seems to agree that it should be dated to the early period, rather than to the late thirteenth

William Ua Finnáin, the Cistercian abbot of Kilbeggan, succeeded Ua Dubhthaigh in the year 1298.[62] The Annals of Ulster state that he took the bishopric of Clonmancois in the year 1294, four years prior to the death of his predecessor. This irregularity in the sources might be read as an indication that Ua Dubhthaigh's fall from a horse was not merely an accident.[63] In the year 1302 another Franciscan, Domnall Ua Bruyn (O Beirne?) was elected by the chapter of Clonmacnois. This time licence from the king was given beforehand.[64] Domnall was guardian of the Franciscans of Killeigh, in county Offaly. Apparently the archbishop of Armagh was reluctant to consecrate, since a royal order advises him to perform his duty immediately in the year 1303.[65] The see of Clonmacnois was again vacant in 1324. In that year a royal pardon was granted to the chapter of Clonmacnois for electing without the king's licence.[66] This is the last documented sign of royal interference with ecclesiastical affairs in the bishopric of Clonmacnois.

At the beginning of the fourteenth century the see of Clonmacnois fell outside the sphere of the Anglo-Irish administration, which is indicative of the decline of Anglo-Irish influence in the area. Up to then adminstrative formalities, such as the king's licence to elect a new bishop, his assent to the elected candidate and the investiture with the temporalities of the see by the royal justiciar, were generally respected as a necessary requirement for a new episcopal appointment, although the chapter of Clonmacnois persistently failed to fulfil this obligation. The see of Clonmacnois during the period figures in the accounts of the excheator, indicating that the temporalities during vacancy went regularly to the king. However, already towards the end of the thirteenth century, in 1289 according to the account of Walter

---

century (see P. HARBISON, The High Crosses of Ireland, 2 vols., Bonn 1992; HICKS, A Clonmacnois workshop, pp. 5-35; EDWARDS, Medieval archeology of Ireland, p. 64).

[62] ALCé 1298, 1302; AConn 1298.8, 1302.10; AU 1294 (recte 1298?); AClon 1302, p. 259; Cal. Doc. Irel. IV, p. 204, no. 429 + 430 (5. Aug. 1297); for Kilbeggan see AClon 1236, p. 235.

[63] AU 1294, p. 393.

[64] Cal. Doc. Irel. V, p. 50, no. 121 (27. Aug. 1302); Cal. Doc. Irel. V, p. 53, no. 130 + 131 (12. Oct. 1302); Cal. Doc. Irel. V, p. 67, no. 171 (14. Jan. 1303).

[65] Cal. Doc. Irel. V, p. 72, no. 193-196 (14. April 1303).

[66] Cal. Pat. Rolls, Edward II 1324-27, pp. 45f. (11. Nov. 1324).

de la Haye, the escheator of Ireland, the royal demesne in Clonmacnois could no longer be taxed *because they lay uncultivated among the Irish*.[67]

In the second half of the thirteenth century the number of Franciscans amongst the episcopal candidates increased. The first Friar appointed to the see was Tomás Ua Cuinn (1253-1268), then William Ua Dubthaigh (1290-1297) and Domnall Ua Bruyn (Beirne) (1302-1324). By the end of the thirteenth century the Franciscans were already perceived as a political risk by the Dublin government, and repeatedly accused of racism.[68] Their repeated success in securing appointment to the see of Clonmacnois indicates its gradual alienation from royal authority.

5.2.2 The fourteenth and fifteenth centuries.

Due to the meagre documentation of the Gaelic areas in royal administrative documents, and comparatively fragmented communication with the papal curia, little information concerning the small diocese of Clonmacnois is preserved for the fourteenth century. Lugaid Ua Dálaigh died as bishop of Clonmacnois in 1337.[69] One Henry, a Dominican Friar, is named as late bishop of Clonmacnois in a papal letter from the year 1349.[70] Simon, a Friar preacher of Roscommon, sought appointment to the see of Clonmacnois from the pope in this very year.[71] He got the see, but was later in the same year transferred to Derry, since the death of bishop Henry in Clonmacnois turned out to have been only a rumour.[72] One Hugh is named as bishop of Clonmacnois in the year 1383, when together with the bishop of Killala he

---

[67] Account of the escheator. Pipe Roll a.r. XVIII, Ed. I, in: Appendix to the 37th report of the Deputy keeper 40. Account of Walter de la Haye, escheator of Ireland of bishoprics in the kings land: *Clonm'noys bishopric: He accounts for 25L issues of temporalities in the kings land from the feast of nativity of St. John baptist a.r. XVI to 6 Oct. a.r. XVIII, when the temporalities were delivered to brother William Oduschy, clerk there. Sum: 25 L. No extent could be made of the demesnes because they lay uncultivated among the Irish.* Thanks to Dr Katharine Simms who pointed this reference out to me.

[68] WATT, The church and the two nations, pp. 181-183.

[69] ALCé 1337; AConn 1337.13; AClon 1337, pp. 235f.; AFM 1337.

[70] Cal. Pap. Let. III, p. 290 (5. Id May 1349).

[71] Ibid.

[72] Cal. Pap. Let. III, p. 339 (15. Kal Jan. 1349-50).

was accused by the papal curia in Avignon of supporting the Roman pope
Urban VI.[73]

In the year 1388 the Friar Minor *Milo Corr* (Máel Sechnaill Ua Conchobair) was appointed to the see of Clonmacnois by Pope Urban IV.[74] Henceforward complaints about the poverty of the see of Clonmacnois become
very frequent. The diocese of Clonmancois was exempt from communal tax
in 1391, since it was gravely impoverished.[75] After the death of Milo in the
year 1397,[76] Philip Nangle, who had been abbot of the Cistercians in Abbeylara, alias Granard for fourteen years, was elected to the see of Clonmacnois. According to the papal confirmation of his appointment the value of
the see at the time was but 20 marks. Philip therefore got papal dispensation
to hold certain lands belonging to his former monastery of St. Mary's in
Granard as well as a rectory in the diocese of Ardagh, besides his episcopal
lands *to the end that he may not on account of the slender revenues of his
see be compelled to beg, to the shame of the pontifical dignity.*[77] Nevertheless, towards the end of the episcopate of Philip, in the year 1410, the monks
of Granard did their best to further reduce the already slender revenues of
the see of Clonmacnois. In a petition to the pope they claimed the lands of
the diocese of Clonmacnois as their property, in the name of their thirteenth
century founder Richard Tuite.[78] Around the same time the Ua Fergail fam-

---

[73] Cal. Pap. Let. IV, p. 245 (16. Kal Feb. 1383).

[74] Cal. Pap. Let. IV, p. 336 (9. Nov. 1389).

[75] M. A. COSTELLO (ed.), De Annatis Hiberniae. A calendar of the first fruits' fees levied on
papal appointments to benefices in Ireland A.D. 1400 to 1535, Dundalk 1909, I, p. 153 (20.
Dec. 1391).

[76] Misc. Irish Ann. 1397.7, p. 159. The editor corrected the printed *Gallchorr*, which should
be read *Corr* (ibid., Corrigenda, p. 221).

[77] Cal. Pap. Let. V, pp. 154f. (16. Kal Dec. 1397).

[78] In a petition to the pope dating from the year 1410 they claimed a number of lands including *the parish churches of Lochlocha, Lyach, Faygri, Galingy, Thechsaran or their
rectories with all their chapels and appurtenances...* (Cal. Pap. Let. VI, pp. 234f. [1410]). See
also Cal. Pap. Let. IX, pp. 29-31 (17. Kal Sept. 1438), for the papal confirmation of the char-
ter. According to the letter the Cistercians of Abbeylara had the patronage of these churches,
which included the right of presentation of the parish clergy, as well as the moiety of the
tithes, from the early thirteenth century on. A. Otway-Ruthven suggested that the parishes
held or claimed by Anglo-Norman abbeys could provide a valuable index of the extent of
Anglo-Norman domination and of the possessions of particular grantors. It seems plausible,
therefore, that the whole group of parishes claimed by the monks of Abbeylara in the diocese

ily intruded into the abbacy of Granard. The sitting abbot William was deposed in the year 1411 and Richard Ua Fergail assumed the headship over the monks. Richard himself was accused of *notorious fornication* and abuse of the fruits of his office in the year 1422. He temporarily lost his job in Granard only to be promoted to the see of Ardagh instead. As bishop he was again appointed to the abbacy *in commendam* in the year 1435. Until shortly before his death in the year 1444 he was bishop of Ardagh as well as abbot of Granard.[79] During his abbacy, in the year 1438, the lands of the diocese of Clonmacnois were again confirmed by the pope as the possession of the monks of Granard. It seems that the expansionist claims of the Cistercian house went back mainly to the initiative of the political ambitions of the Uí Fhergail, who built up their power in the area from the early fifteenth century on, when they built a castle in Granard.[80] Their antagonists, at least in the ecclesiastical sphere, appear to have been a family variously named *O Mael*, *O Moyl*, *Omaild* or *O Mayl*, perhaps standing for Ua Máelmuaid, lords of the neighbouring Fera Cell. One *Philip Ó Mael* was provided with the see of Clonmacnois in 1411 and held it until his death in 1422.[81] *John Omayl*, dispensed as the son of a Cistercian monk and priest, was promoted to a canonry of Clonmacnois in 1414.[82] Later he was admitted as a monk to Granard, and it was he on whose initative the Ua Fergail abbot was removed from the abbacy in the year 1422. In 1434 John himself was accused of the same abuses which he had brought against his opponent in 1422. This time John lost his position.[83] Also there is 'Gregory Omayl', the son of bishop Philip, who was a clerk of the diocese of Clonmacnois as well as a monk in Granard. The vicarage of Wheery (i.e Ferbane, alias Tisaran), in the diocese

---

of Clonmacnois represents an original grant by Richard Tuite to his Cistercian protégés in Abbeylara (A.J. OTWAY-RUTHVEN, A history of medieval Ireland. With an introduction by Kathleen Hughes, London 1968, p. 121).

[79] AConn 1444.7.

[80] Misc. Irish Ann. 1405.5, p. 175.

[81] J. WARE, De Praesulibus Hiberniae, London 1665, p. 173. He is mentioned as late bishop of Clonmacnois in a papal letter from 1422 (Cal. Pap. Let. VII, p. 243f. [8. Id Nov. 1422]).

[82] Cal. Pap. Let. VI, p. 456 (12. Kal Jan. 1414).

[83] Cal. Pap. Let. VII, pp. 233f. (4. Kal Nov. 1422). Cal. Pap. Let. VIII, p. 506 (4. Kal Dec. 1434). See P. KEARNEY, The Cistercian Abbey at Abbeylara A.D. 1205-1540, in: Teathbha 1 (1969-1973), pp. 202-205.

of Clonmacnois, was assigned to him in 1426.[84] His successor to the vicarage was *Niger Omaild*, again a Cistercian monk from Granard.[85] Finally there is 'James Yamyl' who claimed the vicarages of Wheery later in the century.[86] It seems that during the first half of the fifteenth century the political rivalries in the area dominated the fortunes of the bishopric of Clonmacnois. Granard eventually came under the domination of the Ua Fergail family, whereas Clonmacnois bishopric became largely absorbed into the political fortunes of the Meic Cochláin.

For a brief period after the death of *Philip O'Mael* in 1422 the bishopric of Clonmacnois was held by David Pendergast. Since he was again a Cistercian we might assume he also came from Granard.[87] His successor was Cormac Mac Cochláin, provided with the see of Clonmacnois by the pope in 1426. Dispensed as the son of a priest he had held the deanery of Clonmacnois since the year 1421.[88] Ware styled him a *Man of Liberality, and a Patron to the learned.*[89] The bishop was killed in battle in the year 1444. With the episcopate of Cormac members of the Mac Cochláin family appear in diocesan offices in Clonmacnois. James, the son of bishop Cormac, was provided with the archdeaconry of Clonmacnois some time after the year 1426.[90] James was succeeded as archdeacon by Troleus *Mechoclan*, another member of the family.[91] Likewise the deanery of Clonmacnois for some time after 1475 was held by a Mac Cochláin, namely *Eugenius Macholayn*.[92] A grandson of bishop Cormac, also named Cormac, was a member of the cathedral chapter of Clonmacnois towards the end of the century.[93] In

---

[84] Cal. Pap. Let. VII, p. 455 (11. Kal June 1426).

[85] Cal. Pap. Let. IX, p. 403 (14. Kal Nov. 1443).

[86] Cal. Pap. Let. XIII, p. 49 (9. Feb. 1475-76).

[87] WARE, De Praesulibus Hiberniae, p. 173, lists him as *David Brendog*.

[88] Cal. Pap. Let. VII, p. 440 (8. Id July 1426); Cal. Pap. Let. VII, p. 164 (3. Id March 1421).

[89] WARE, De Praesulibus Hiberniae, p. 173.

[90] Cal. Pap. Let. IX, pp. 430f. (6. Id. Oct. 1444)

[91] He resigned in 1463, Cal. Pap. Let. XI, pp. 480f. (21. May 1463).

[92] Cal. Pap. Let. XIII, p. 521 (24. Feb. 1475-76).

[93] That he was the grandson of bishop Cormac is apparent from his obit in the annals of Ulster, AU 1498 (vol. 3, p. 430).

1486 he was in Rome, seeking provision of the see of Clonmacnois as well as that of the priory of St. Mary's Gallen.[94] He died in the year 1498. Finally there was Cahir Mac Cochláin who died as erenagh of Clonmacnois in the year 1539.[95]

It seems that bishop Cormac governed spiritual affairs in his diocese much to the liking of the secular dynasts, who were of course of his own clan. During his episcopate he sanctioned the divorce between Donat, alias Donnchad Mac Cochláin and his wife *Una Ó Melaghlin*, Most likely this was Donnchad, later lord of Delbna Ethra.[96] It appears, however, that after the death of Toirdelbach, lord of Delbna the bishop himself showed aspirations to secular power, which led him into opposition to his former ally.[97] Donnchad now appeared as the expected successor to the lordship. He had the support of David and Felim, two sons of Toirdelbach. His claims to the overlordship were contested by the bishop and his people. In a decisive battle in the year 1444 bishop Cormac, his son James the archdeacon and many others were defeated and killed. Donnchad was victorious and succeeded to the lordship.[98] Cormac's family maintained their ecclesiastical career. It seems a branch of the descendants of Felim, who were discarded from the

---

[94] Cal. Pap. Let. XIV, p. 168 (27. March 1486-87).

[95] AFM 1539.

[96] As apparent from the later revision of the case under his successor John Dálaig (see W. G. H. QUIGLEY / E. F. D. ROBERTS [eds.], Registrum Johannis Mey, Belfast 1972, pp. 128, 213f.).

[97] AConn 1444.4.

[98] J. O'DONOVAN (ed.), Annals of Ireland by Dudley Firbisse 1443-1468 (Irish Archeological Society Miscellanea), Dublin 1846, pp. 198-302, here 204, AD 1444: *Great war stirred up in Dealbna Eathra, the sonns of Dauid Mag Cochlan and Felim Mag Cochlan on the one partie, and the Bishop Mag-Cochlan, with the sept of Connor Mag-Cochlan on the other partie, soe that each partie gathered their several friends, to wit Mag Eochagan and his son and the sons of Daniel O-Bryan and the sons of Daniel O-Kelly his son, on Mag Cochlans side; and Breasel fitz Brian fitz Eogan O-Kelly with the Bishop...the bishop and his men were defeated...(and killed). James (the Bishop's son) Archdeacon of Clonmacnoise was killed.* For the presumed family ties amongst the participants in battle see K. W. NICHOLLS, The Mac-Coghlans, in: The Irish Genealogist 4, no. 4 (1983), pp. 445-460, here 449.

lordship of Delbna later in the century, established themselves in the monastery of Gallen.[99]

After Cormac's death in 1444 John Ua Dálaigh, was provided with the see of Clonmacnois.[100] The top ecclesiastical office in Delbna Ethra was no longer in the hands of the leading secular dynasty. The divorce between Donat, alias Donnchad Mac Cochláin, since 1444 captain of his nation, and *Una Ó Melaghlin*, was now declared illegal by bishop John. At the instigation of Una, bishop John revised the former verdict and simply interdicted Mac Cochláin and his people, ignoring the fact that the latter had already appealed to the pope to obtain a revision of John's action.[101] Instead, bishop John pursued his own family interests in the diocese. His son Eugene was provided with the vicarage of Gallen, in the diocese of Clonmacnois, against the will of the prior of the Augustinian house there.[102] Also during John's episcopate, in the year 1451, the parish church of Ballyloughloe in Clonmacnois diocese was divided into three independent vicarages.[103] When in 1459 a Collegiate church was established in Clonmacnois the church of Ballyloughloe was united with Clonmacnois and turned into the living of the four resident priest canons who formed the College.[104] This plan met with opposition from the monks of Granard, i.e Abbeylara, who still claimed the rectory of Ballyloughloe as their property. In 1460 they complained to the archbishop of Armagh about the diocesan policy of bishop John and his archdeacon Odo Ua Máeleoin. The two were ordered by the archbishop to appear at the provincial synod at Drogheda.[105] Since John did not appear

---

[99] James, the grandson of Felim became prior of Gallen, and was killed in 1519 (AFM); James Og the son of the prior, was beheaded by Ceadach Ua Máelsechlainn in the castle of Feddan, his very own stronghold in 1540 (AFM).

[100] Cal. Pap. Let. IX, p. 432 (14. Kal Oct. 1444).

[101] QUIGLEY / ROBERTS (eds.), Registrum Johannis Mey, p. 128, no. 130 (24. Oct. 1450); also pp. 213f., no. 215 (20. Dec. 1451).

[102] Ibid.

[103] Cal. Pap. Let. X, pp. 541f. (15. Jan. 1451-52).

[104] Cal. Pap. Let. XII, pp. 51f. (12. April 1459).

[105] A. LYNCH (ed.), A calendar of the reassembled register of John Bole, Archbishop of Armagh, 1457-1471, in: Seanchas Ardmhacha 15 (1992), pp. 113-185, here 150 (Octavian Register no. 27, see also no. 43, 44). See also National Library MS No. 2691, Canon Leslie Collection: Typescriptcopy of Bishop W. M. Reeves calendar of Primate Octavian, with an

and did not even respond to the letters sent to him concerning the case, he was suspended from office and fined.[106] The abbot and monks of Granard won the case and were admitted as true rectors of Ballyloughloe in the year 1460.[107] John remained in office and acted again as bishop in the year 1463. He is again referred to as the late bishop of Clonmacnois, who died outside the Roman curia, in a papal letter written in 1487.[108]

During the episcopate of John Ua Dálaigh several other bishops of Clonmacnois are mentioned in the papal documents. It seems they were not exactly rival bishops but perhaps absentees, who were provided with the see but never took possession of it. There is bishop Thomas, who in 1449 complained in a letter to the pope that the fruits of his episcopal mensa, were so diminished due to wars and other calamities, and had been so neglected (presumably by those supposed to collect it for him) that he could not live from it. The letter states also that there is no place belonging to the episcopal mensa where the bishop could go and stay; this clearly points to the fact that he was an absentee. Tomás prayed the pope to be presented to an additional benefice during his time as bishop of Clonmacnois.[109] A certain Robert is mentioned as 'late bishop of Clonmacnois' in the year 1458.[110] The problems of these absentee bishops are best documented by the case of his successor William, prior of Brinkburn, an Augustinian house in the diocese of Durham in England. Papal provision of the see of Clonmacnois was made to him in July 1458.[111] Two or three months later he sent a letter to the pope stating that he was not able to obtain possession of the see nor to receive any

---

index by Rev. J. B. Leslie, c.1935, no. 27; Bishop Reeves' transcript of Primate Octavianus Register Trinity College Dublin MS 557/9, 73-77. To the *rectory of Ballylagh alias Lura* is added in margin *de Luetha Mór*.

[106] LYNCH (ed.), A calendar of the reassembled register of John Bole, p. 153 (Octavian, no. 42).

[107] Ibid., pp. 153f. (Octavian, no. 44). The document is undated and incomplete, beginning is missing. (probably June 1460).

[108] Cal. Pap. Let. XI, pp. 480f. (21. May 1463), when the archdeacon resigned his office to bishop John; Cal. Pap. Let. XV, p. 88, no. 190 (26. March 1487) mentions John as late bishop of Clonmacnois. Ware doubts the identity of the two: *I do not suppose that he was the same John, with the former John Oldais* (WARE, De Praesulibus Hiberniae, p. 173).

[109] Cal. Pap. Let. X, p. 53 (27. Oct. 1449).

[110] Cal. Pap. Let. XI, p. 359 (21. July 1458).

[111] Ibid.

of its fruits, in fact he thinks it very unlikely that he would ever be able to do so. He therefore asked papal permission to continue to hold his priory, despite his promotion to the see in Ireland.[112] Apparently William never got possession of the see of Clonmacnois, and remained active as a suffragan bishop in Durham until he died in 1484.[113]

A final attempt to restore Mac Cochláin power in Clonmacnois was made after the death of John Ua Dálaigh. In 1486 Cormac Mac Cochláin, a grandson of bishop Cormac reclaimed the bishopric of Clonmacnois. The pope did not provide him with the see but instead with the priorship of Gallen.[114] One Walter Blake received the bishopric of Clonmacnois.[115] He died in the year 1508.[116] The Mac Cochláin family was still present in the diocese. They did not have possession of the see, but nevertheless seem to have dominated church affairs, reviving the position of the early medieval *airchinnech*. Cahir Mac Cochláin died as 'erenagh' of Clonmacnois in the year 1539.[117]

The following sixteenth-century bishops of Clonmacnois are mentioned by Ware: Thomas O'Mullally, Conal O'Higgin, Richard O'Hogan, Florence Kirwan, Peter Wall.[118] However, during this period 'Roderic Ó Malone', the bishop of Ardagh, acted as representative of the bishop of Clonmacnois and we might assume that the actual bishops of Clonmacnois were no longer resident in their bishopric.[119] The final destruction of the settlement happened in the course of the reformation, when in the year 1552

„Clonmacnoise was plundered and devastated by the English of Athlone, and the large bells were taken from the bell tower. There was not left, moreover, a bell, small

---

[112] Ibid., pp. 371f. (7. Oct. 1458).

[113] FLOOD, The episcopal succession, p. 81.

[114] Cal. Pap. Let. XIV, p. 168 (27. March 1486-87).

[115] Cal. Pap. Let. XV, p. 88, no. 190 (26. March 1486-87).

[116] Walter died in the year 1508 (AConn 1508.5; AFM 1508). J. HARDIMAN (ed.), A chorographical description of West or H-Iar Connaught written A.D. 1684 by Roderic O'Flaherty, Dublin 1846, pp. 224f., ibid. 213, for the pedigree of the Blake family, William was the brother of Geoffrey Blake.

[117] AFM 1539.

[118] WARE, De Praesulibus Hiberniae, p. 174.

[119] AFM 1540.

or large, an image, or an altar, or a book, or a gem, or even glass in the window, from the wall of the church out, which was not carried off. Lamentable was this deed, the plundering of the city of Kieran, the holy patron."[120]

In the aftermath of the reformation, after the death of Bishop Peter Wall in 1568, the diocese of Clonmacnois was united to the bishopric of Meath.[121]

To sum up: Clonmacnois diocese might be interpreted as the successor institution of St. Ciarán's church in so far as its diocesan boundaries included a significant part of the former church lands. Parts of the early pre-reformed ecclesiastical estate, which were not assigned to the bishopric, were at least temporarily, in the thirteenth century, claimed as part of the diocese by the bishop of Clonmacnois. These were lands on the west side of the river Shannon. Possibly their annexation to the diocese of Tuam, as an isolated enclave, in between Elphin and Clonfert dioceses, might have been a result of the fact that the Ua Máeleoin family, as the hereditary abbots of Clonmacnois, claimed the lands in question as their private property by right of succession to St. Ciarán, and in the course of the formation of the diocese tried to withhold them from episcopal authority.

The fortunes of the bishopric of Clonmacnois in the later middle ages were determined by the respective political constellations at the time. Thus, in the course of the expansionist policy of the Uí Fhergail in Angaile (co. Longford) for example, land in the diocese of Clonmacnois was claimed as the property of the Cistercians in Granard, which at the time had assumed the status of being the Uí Fhergail home monastery. Later on the Meic Chochláin dominated the see, down to the first half of the sixteenth century. Throughout this period several bishops of Clonmacnois, who were appointed but seemingly never took possession of the see, appear in the papal letters. In one case we know for certain that the supposed bishop of Clonmacnois was an English prior from Durham. It seems these bishops were absentees, who received the bishopric of Clonmacnois as an additional, though financially not very attractive ecclesiastical benefice in Ireland.

---

[120] AFM 1552.

[121] WARE, De Praesulibus Hiberniae, p. 174. In the seventeenth century the arrangements were again changed and Clonmacnois diocese was annexed to the bishopric of Ardagh, as it is still today (compare P. F. MORAN, The see of Clonmacnois in the 16th century, in: IER 1 [1865], pp. 153-159).

5.3 The former ecclesiastical aristocracy in the later middle ages

The gradual dissolution of Clonmacnois as a traditional ecclesiastical estate, from the end of the twelfth century onwards, must have caused grave changes in the population structure in the area. In modern terms we would talk of a surplus of labour set free by increasing unemployment, caused through the breakdown of a major employer in an area. What did those, who had traditionally ruled the settlement, or the people who lived in its surroundings as farm labourers do? Obviously there is very little we can know about the latter category, since those people tend not to appear in contemporary records. However, a number of the ecclesiastical dynasties which were active in higher governmental positions can be traced beyond the dissolution of St. Ciarán's church, down to the later middle ages. In general it seems that some of them remained active in ecclesiastical offices in the area around Clonmacnois, in some cases these were churches which used to be part of St. Ciarán's *paruchia* in the old days. Other families can be traced as priests or priors in churches formerly associated with the settlement of Ciarán by bonds of fraternity. Again others seem to have moved away from the Clonmacnois area altogether but held on to a tradition as hereditary church officials.

We already mentioned the fortunes of the Ua Máeleoin family, who as hereditary abbots lost their job in Clonmacnois with its decline in the course of the thirteenth century. They withdrew to church lands west of the Shannon, which they held in their capacity as abbots of Clonmacnois down to the end of the thirteenth century, when their estate was claimed by the bishop of Clonmacnois. Nevertheless they remained active in the churches of the area. The best documented period for ecclesiastical affairs in Gaelic areas is the fifteenth century, when a vivid correspondence between the papal curia and the parish churches was maintained, and a high proportion of conflicts and rival claims to ecclesiastical offices were brought before the pope. During that period the Ua Máeleoin family appears in various ecclesiastical positions in the diocese of Clonmacnois and its near surroundings. There were several canons of Clonmacnois supplied by the family.[122] In the latter half of the fifteenth century the family was in possession of the vicarage of Kil-

---

[122] Marianus: Cal. Pap. Let. V, p. 180; Eugenius: Cal. Pap. Let. X, p. 542; XII, p. 40; XIII, p. 49; Christinus: Cal. Pap. Let. XIV, pp. 146, 236f.; XV, no. 687; XVI, no. 733.

cleagh in Clonmacnois diocese.[123] The alternative names of Kilcleagh parish *Killeomilenyn*, alias *Kyllomyleon* seem to derive from an original *Cell Ua Máeleoin*, the church of Ua Máeleoin.[124] Their memory is also preserved in the name of a townland in the parish called *Boggaghmalone*.[125] The family held major parts of the land in the parish in the later middle ages. Still at the time of the surveys in the early seventeenth century *Edmond and Richard Malone*, and *Katherine Malone alias Pettit*, appear as the largest land owners in Kilcleagh parish.[126] One *Gilatius Ó Malone* was vicar of Kilkerrin and rector of Corco Moga, in the diocese of Tuam during the first half of the fifteenth century.[127] Most enduring was Uí Mháeleoin domination in the rectory of Moycarnan, which represented parts the former abbatial lands of Clonmacnois. One *Marianus Ó Malone* was rector of Moycarnan in the early years of the fifteenth century. His successor in 1422 was John Ua Máeleoin, the son of a priest and himself priest of the diocese of Tuam.[128] John, the rector, was famous enough to deserve an obituary in the Annals of Connacht.[129] After his death in 1439 the rectory was held for some time by another Marianus Ua Máeleoin, also from Clonmacnois diocese. He was accused of detaining the rectory and removed from it in 1448. The rectory was then assigned to *Dermot Odonelean*, clerk of the diocese of Clonfert.[130] When he died in 1455 the rectory was again assigned to Marianus Ua Máeleoin, who seems to have held it down to the end of the century.[131] Members of the family were also prominent in high positions in

---

[123] Cal. Pap. Let. X, pp. 541-552 (15. Jan. 1451-52); XIII, p. 66; XIV, pp. 146f. (13. March 1486-87).

[124] Cal. Pap. Let. X, pp. 541f. (15. Jan. 1451-52). J. J. MCNAMEE, Identification of certain placenames, in: Ardagh and Clonmacnois Ant. Soc. Jn. 2, no. 8 (1942), pp. 3-27, here 15f.

[125] One-Inch Ordnance Survey Map of Ireland (Phoenix Maps, Dublin), sheet 108.

[126] LYONS (ed.), Book of Survey, co. Westmeath, pp. 121-125.

[127] Cal. Pap. Let. VI, p. 427 (5 Kal Jan. 1413). He died in 1449 at Viterbo on his way to Rome. Cal. Pap. Let. X, p. 377 (3. Dec. 1449).

[128] Cal. Pap. Let. VII, p. 228 (Id Oct. 1422).

[129] AConn 1439.4.

[130] Cal. Pap. Let. X, pp. 410f. (5. Sept. 1448).

[131] Cal. Pap. Let. XI, pp. 206f. (20. Aug. 1455). Only in the year 1507 the rectory was again disputed over. *Bernard O Celaig* is mentioned as late rector, his successor was *Donald*

the church of Clonmacnois itself. Odo Ua Máeleoin was dean of Clonmacnois during the episcopate of John Ua Dálaigh.[132] He acted as vicar general
of the bishop during absence.[133] At the same time he held the rectory of the
church of Ballyloughloe, which he vigorously defended against claims of
the monks from Granard.[134] In the course of this conflict he, together with
bishop John, was suspended from his office by John Bole, archbishop of
Armagh, and accused of being the 'self-styled' dean of Clonmacnois.[135]
This happened in the year 1460. In the following year dean Odo died. According to the Four Masters he was 'the most learned man in all Ireland'.[136]
The power held by this man in the church of Clonmacnois is also apparent
from the impressive northern doorway of the cathedral, built during his time
in office and still to be seen today. It shows St. Francis, St. Patrick and St.
Dominic, and in an inscription Odo himself is commemorated as the builder
of the monument.[137] In the early half of the sixteenth century there was
Ruairí Ua Máeleoin who became bishop of Ardagh. His function as vicar
general, or representative of the bishop of Clonmacnois, certainly resulted
from his family's background in the church of St. Ciarán.[138]

A branch of the Ua Braoín, a Connacht family related with the Uí Chonchobair dynasts, active in Clonmacnois from the late eleventh century onwards, had traditional links with Roscommon, which became their main
ecclesiastical seat in the course of the twelfth century. The family tradition
as an ecclesiastical dynasty was continued throughout the period of the
church reform, and the tradition of monastic learning, extended to secular

---

Ocynyd, again a cleric of the diocese of Clonmacnois (Cal. Pap. Let. XVIII, no. 678 [29. Jan.
1507]).

[132] Cal. Pap. Let. XI, p. 501; XIII, p. 521; Odo died in 1461 (AFM, AConn).

[133] QUIGLEY / ROBERTS (eds.), Registrum Johannis Mey, pp. 213f., no. 215 (20. Dec. 1451).

[134] LYNCH (ed.), A calendar of the reassembled register of John Bole, pp. 153f. (Octavian,
no. 44), undated and incomplete, beginning is missing (probably June 1460).

[135] Ibid., p. 150 (Octavian, no. 27): Mandate of Archbishop John Bole, from the provincial
synod at Drogheda, dated 14. June 1460; compare ibid., p. 153 (Octavian, no. 43), undated
(probably 9.-14. June 1460).

[136] AConn 1461.16; AFM 1461.

[137] WESTROPP, A description of the ancient buildings, pp. 285f.

[138] AFM 1540.

knowlege, was further cherished in the family.[139] Another branch of the family was settled in Brawny in county Westmeath, i.e. Bregmaine, a territory now represented by St. Mary's parish Athlone. The Ua Braoín dominated the area from the mid-twelfth century down to the later middle ages. It seems the area formed part of the diocese of Clonmacnois from the year 1174, when it was united to the bishopric as one of the parishes of Westmeath. According to the Clonmacnois chronicler it used to form part of St. Ciarán's lands.[140] It therefore seems plausible that we have here an example of an ecclesiastical dynasty which made parts of the former *paruchia* of St. Ciarán their patrimonial lands and held them down to the later middle ages.[141]

The fortunes of the Uí Chillín are more difficult to trace in the surviving material. In the Registry of Clonmacnois Ua Cillín is mentioned as the water clerk of the church, who held a portion of land in Clonmacnois. The family might have kept up the tradition to supply the local handyman in Clonmacnois down to the seventeenth century.[142] It seems one branch of the family settled on the monastic lands in county Galway. Still in the late sixteenth century there were lands in Killerean parish near Dunmore, in county Galway, in possession of the bishop of Clonmacnois.[143] They are named in the survey report from 1641 as *Caronkilleene* then in possession of Walter Birmingham, who also held the surrounding lands.[144] Caronkilleene, i.e. carton of Killin possibly took its name from the Ua Cillín family, who presumably settled on the land, holding it from the bishop of Clonmacnois

---

[139] Gilla Íosa, son of Ailill Ua Braoín, *secnap Uí Mhaine*, a historian, scribe and poet died in 1187 (AFM 1187); Tiobraide Ua Braoín, *comarba Commain* is praised for his knowledge in theology, history and law (AFM 1232); Gilla na Naemh, son of Art Ua Braoín, *erenagh* of Roscommon died in 1234 (AFM 1234). Bran Ua Braoín died as tympanist in the year 1364 (AU 1364).

[140] According to the Clonmacnois chronicler the castle of Athlone was built on St. Ciarán's land, which might have been part of what later became St. Mary's parish (AClon 1210, p. 224).

[141] See J. PINKMAN, Placenames of St. Mary's Parish, Athlone, in: Ardagh and Clonmacnois Ant. Soc. Jn. 2, no. 10 (1945), pp. 37-47, here 37f.

[142] See below, p. 320 (Appendix 2, nos. 94-95).

[143] FREEMAN (ed.), Compossicion Booke, pp. 80f.

[144] SIMINGTON (ed.), Books of Survey, III, p. 294.

down to the late sixteenth century. The family name also appears in Moore parish, and we know of Granina, the daughter of Ua Cillín who was married to one *Dermit Domnallan*, most likely the same person who in 1448 claimed the rectory of Moycarnan against the Ua Máeleoin candidate.[145] Finally another branch of the family settled on Inis Ainghin, an island in Lough Ree, where a daughter house of Clonmacnois used to exist in the old days. The 'Killen' family still lived on the island in the nineteenth century when O'Donovan investigated the localities in the area.[146]

The Ua Loingsigh, prominent in Clonmacnois since the latter parts of the tenth century, apparently withdrew to the western extremities of the former *paruchia* of Clonmacnois. They were active in the diocese of Killaloe and reappear in the early fifteenth century as priors and vicars in the church of St. Senán, in Inis Cathaig, Scattery island, which is said to have been associated with St. Ciarán's church by a contract of fraternity.[147]

There is also the Ua Lachtnáin family who continued the ecclesiastical tradition seemingly without any interruption throughout the twelfth century. They adapted to the requirements in the changing ecclesiastical landscape. Already in the mid-thirteenth century Máel Muire Ua Lachtnáin had obtained a degree in canon law, and became archbishop of Tuam in 1237. He held the archbishopric as *airchinnech* of Tuam, according to the annals of Connacht, pointing to the unproblematic way in which old-style family traditions were applied to the only recently reformed church.[148] Other members of the family held various episcopal sees in Connacht in the fourteenth

---

[145] In the year 1430 the two got dispensed for fornication by marriage in the double third degree Cal. Pap. Let. VIII, p. 162; for *Dermit*, the rector of Moycarnan see Cal. Pap. Let. X, pp. 410f.; compare above, p. 195.

[146] For Inis Ainghin see above, p. 71; O'DONOVAN, Ordnance Survey Letters, co. Westmeath I, p. 12. In a letter from Athlone written the 1.9. 1837 O'Donovan mentions one Rose Killen, whom he interviewed about the antiquities of Inis Ainghin, alias Hare Island. According to this lady's statement „herself and her father and his family before lived on the island".

[147] See above, p. 71; Cal. Pap. Let. VI, p. 313 (2. Kal. Dec. 1411); VIII, pp. 571f. (3. Non. July 1427).

[148] AConn 1249.14.

century.[149] The family name also frequently appears in lesser ecclesiastical offices in the dioceses of Tuam and Clonfert.[150]

A branch of the Ua Neachtain family from Uí Maine, who held the headship over the Céili Dé community in Clonmacnois continued to cherish an ecclesiastical career. They reappear as churchmen in lesser ecclesiastical offices in the diocese of Clonfert.[151]

The Ua Cearnaigh family in Clonmacnois were of the Luigne of Connacht, in Sligo and parts of Mayo. Perhaps the family returned to their original territory, and assumed ecclesiastical offices in their home church. This would explain the frequent appearance of the name Ua Cearnaigh, alias Ó Cearnaid or Okearnaig in the diocese of Achonry, largely identical with the former territory of Luigne. There is a particularly high proportion of Uí Chearnaig amongst the vicars of Kilmacteige parish, in the diocese, which as a prebend was united to a canonry of that church.[152] The family name is also very frequent amongst the clergy in the neighbouring archdiocese of Tuam.[153]

Ua Cuinn, possibly the late medieval version of the family name Meic Cuinn na mBocht, turns up frequently in the diocese of Clonmacnois itself. There was Tomás Ua Cuinn, bishop of Clonmacnois in the middle of the thirteenth century. One *Cornelius Ó Quinn* was canon of Tuam and of Clonmacnois, who held the prebend of Drumalgach, together with the vicarage of Moycarnan in the mid-fifteenth century.[154] The name Ua Tomaltaigh

---

[149] AConn 1307.3; AConn 1326.4; AConn 1354.10.

[150] Cal. Pap. Let. IX, p. 556, for Nigel, vicar of Killeluane and Addergoole; ibid. IX, p. 395, for William, vicar of Inisrobe; ibid. X, pp. 408, 639f., for Nicholas, vicar of Kilmoylan; ibid. XI, p. 491, for William priest of Tuam; ibid. XII, pp. 71, 72, 385, 431, for Nicholas canon of Tuam and vicar of Clonburren, dio. Tuam, later Kilosolan, dio. Clonfert; ibid. XIII, pp. 461, 497, for William, canon of Tuam; ibid. X, p. 409, for William, vicar of Killeenadeema, dio. Clonfert.

[151] Cal. Pap. Let. IV, p. 420, for John Oneachtayn; ibid. XIII, p. 86, for Cornelius, prior of Athlone; NICHOLLS (ed.), Visitations of the dioceses, p. 148, where *Cornelius O Nectayn* appears as vicar in the diocese of Clonfert.

[152] Cal. Pap. Let. IX, p. 393; X, pp. 427f.; X, p. 395; XI, p. 587.

[153] See for example Cal. Pap. Let. V, p. 169; VI, pp. 422, 425, 426, 436, 477; VII, pp. 226, 143; IX, pp. 149, 150, 190; XI, p. 454.

[154] Cal. Pap. Let. XVI, pp. 698, 741.

might possibly represent the descendants of this bishop, repeatedly it appears amongst church officials the area around Clonmacnois.[155]

Amongst the families who left the gerneral neighbourhood of Clonmacnois but continued an ecclesiastical career in other churches were the Ua Fidabra. They appear as a family closely related with the reform party in the Irish church, and came possibly from the area around Armagh, where they reappear in the early thirteenth century.[156] It seems possibly that the Uá Máelchiaráin family, who was likewise active in the area around Armagh at the time,[157] were also originally from Clonmacnois.[158]

Others who had lived in St. Ciarán's church might have sought spiritual guidance and life under a monastic rule. They found admission into other communities, mostly those of the newly established orders. It seems that the Cistercians in particular appealed to the religious of Clonmacnois. A drift towards Cistercian houses can be observed from the second half of the twelfth century. Máel Íosa Ua Máelchiaráin, seemingly the offspring of an ecclesiastical dynasty in Clonmacnois, became abbot of Mellifont in 1177. The Cistercian house Kilbeggan in Meath, founded in the mid-twelfth century by a Mac Cochláin, seems to have functioned as a kind of retreat centre for retiring or frustrated Clonmacnois clergy from the late twelfth century. In the year 1196 Ua Catharnaigh, a priest of Clonmacnois, died as a novice in Kilbeggan.[159] Áed Ua Máeleoin, ex-bishop of Clonmacnois, member of the traditional abbot's family, withdrew to Kilbeggan after his resignation in 1235, and died there the following year. Possibly these links provided the

---

[155] William Ua Tomaltaigh, a Cluniac monk, became prior of the only Cluniac foundation in Athlone, on the west side of the Shannon, in the diocese of Elphin, Cal. Pap. Let. V, p. 572; VI, pp. 202, 394. See GWYNN / HADCOCK, pp. 110f.; Reginald Ua Tomaltaigh was vicar of Tuachmna (possibly Tawnagh, in county Sligo) also in Elphin diocese, Cal. Pap. Let. VII, pp. 47f.

[156] See above, pp. 166f. Donatus Ua Fidabra was bishop of Clogher and subsequently archbishop of Armagh (AConn 1237.3).

[157] Máel Íosa Ua Máelchiaráin was Cistercian abbot of Mellifont and, after 1193 bishop of Airgialla. He died in 1197 (see C. CONWAY, The story of Mellifont, Dublin 1958; SMITH, The Armagh-Clogher dispute, p. 29).

[158] One Ailill Ua Máelchiaráin was master of the mortuary chapel in Clonmacnois, Congalach mac Gilla Chiaráin, possibly his son was guest master in Clonmacnois (Appendix 1, AE7, G4).

[159] ALCé 1196.

background for the appointment of the abbot of Kilbeggan to the bishopric
of Clonmacnois at the end of the thirteenth century. Links with the Cistercian house in Knockmoy, founded by Cathal Crobderg in the early thirteenth
century,[160] are also attested in the sources. The dean of Clonmacnois appears regularly as witness in the late medieval charters of Knockmoy abbey.[161]

---

[160] ALCé 1224. KNOX, Notes on the early history, pp. 265-292, for Knockmoy, Ballintobber
and Kilcreevanty, all monasteries which are said to have been founded by Cathal Crobderg.

[161] A medieval abstract of charters of the abbey of Knockmoy survived fragmentarily
(between the years 1235 and 1326): M. BLAKE, Knockmoy Abbey. The monastery of the „hill
of victory". Notes on its history and some ancient charters relating to it, in: Galway Arch.
Hist. Soc. Jn. 1 (1901), pp. 65-84. It mentiones C. Dean of Clonmacnois in Chart. no. 3, 4,
11. D. Dean of Clonmacnois Chart. no. 7; Philip Dean of Clonmacnois Chart. no. 6.

6 THE 'REGISTRY OF CLONMACNOISE'

Little is known about the possessions of St. Ciarán from contemporary records. Obviously the various powerful friends of his church appear as benefactors, making donations, including those of land, to their ecclesiastical ally. However, details about the names or locations of these donations are rarely given. We owe our knowledge about the lands of St. Ciarán primarily to scattered hints contained in medieval hagiographical works and saga tales, which can be completed by information from the annals. Despite the fact that in the eleventh century references to lands of Clonmacnois become slightly more frequent, it is very surprising to find so little about the lands under the authority of St. Ciarán in the respective hagiographical works. There is but one single church claimed as a Ciaránian foundation by his hagiographers. This fact might justify the assumption that separate books, let us say instruments of ecclesiastical accountancy, were kept in Clonmacnois, as an inventory of its lands, which would have been periodically updated by new acquisitions. However, there is no contemporary medieval evidence, or surviving fragments of such a list. The only hint dates from the early seventeenth century, when in the course of the union of the diocese of Clonmacnois with that of Meath, the lands of the church were registered anew. In the report of the visitation, taken under the supervision of James Ussher, then bishop of Meath, the surveyors state that there existed a register of the lands belonging to the church of Clonmacnois, *but the originall booke hath lately beene convayed away by the practize of a leude fellow whoe hath thereyppon fled the Countrey.*[1] From around the same period, amongst the papers of James Ware, a curious account of churches and lands in possession of St. Ciarán is preserved.

6.1 The Manuscript

The document known as the *Registry of Clonmacnoise* is basically an enumeration of lands which were granted to Clonmacnois by various Irish kings and lords in return for the right to be buried in St. Ciarán's churchyard. The list, translated into seventeenth century English, is now preserved in the

---

[1] A Certificate of the State and Revennewes, p. lix.

British Library (BL Add. MS 4796, 36r-43v). It was published by O'Donovan in the year 1857.[2]

The MS volume BL Add. 4796 forms part of the Milles collection, 49 manuscript volumes presented to the British Library by the Rev. Jeremiah Milles, Dean of Exeter, in May 1766. It is one of the sixteen volumes in the collection which were formerly in the possession of James Ware.[3] The small quarto volume, consisting of 144 folios, written on seventeenth century paper, contains material both in English and Latin chiefly relating to Ireland.[4] The so-called 'Registry of Clonmacnoise', not known as such in the manuscript, covers sixteen pages of the volume. The rather short document bears no heading in the original. It seems as if it was written very quickly and rather carelessly, though the hand is easy to read. Since O'Donovan's edition of the document it has gone unquestioned that it was An Dubhaltach Mac Fhirbhisigh who made the transcript for Ware. Nollaig Ó Muraíle has however shown that this idea is totally unfounded and probably originated in the fact that O'Donovan himself never saw the original manuscript, or at least never examined it in any detail, but published it from a transcript made for him by Daniel Mac Carthy. In any case the hand which appears in the original manuscript is simply not that of Mac Fhirbhisigh.[5]

---

2   J. O'DONOVAN (ed.), The Registry of Clonmacnoise. With notes and introductory remarks, in: Jn. Kilk. SE. Irel. Arch. Soc. 1 (1856/57), pp. 444-460 (abbreviated: Registry).

3   For Milles' collection (BL Add. 4755-4802) see British Library Catalogue of Additions to the Manuscripts 1756-1782, Additional Manuscripts 4101-5017 (British Museum Publications), London 1977, pp. 201-220. The MSS formerly in Ware's collection are those numbered as Add. 4783-4801 in the BL; Milles was also known as the executor of Richard Pococke, bishop of Meath (d.1765), whose MSS collection (sixteen vols, two of which were formerly in the collection of James Ware) he also transmitted to the British Library in 1767 (see ibid., pp. 222-230).

4   S. H. O'GRADY, Catalogue of Irish manuscripts in the British Museum, vol. I, London 1928, p. 63.

5   Many thanks Dr Nollaig Ó Muraíle, Queens College Belfast, who very kindly sent me the relevant parts of his doctoral dissertation: N. Ó MURAÍLE, The background, life and writings of Dubhaltach Mac Fhirbhisigh, 2 vols., Ph.D Thesis, National University Ireland, Dublin 1991, vol. 1, part II, chap. 11, pp. 269f. and part III, chap. 12, p. 458, where he discussed the presumed authorship in detail. O'DONOVAN himself states that his edition is printed from „copies of Mac Firbis's translation, recently made from Mac Firbis's autograph in the British Museum by Daniel Mac Carthy, Esq., and William John O'Donnavan, Esq., of the Inner Temple London, who has carefully compared it in proof" (Registry, p. 448). The handwriting

Apart from Ware, who must have known about the document in his possession, Thomas Crofton Croker in the early nineteenth century is the first who comments on the Registry. In his 'Researches in the South of Ireland' published in 1824 he mentions the Registry as 'a very curious account of the ancient celebrity of Cloyne as a place of sepulchre...'.[6] He could not, however, identify the 'Cloyne' in question here. Petrie's work on the Round Towers of Ireland (1845) contains the first relatively detailed account of the Registry.[7] As Ó Muraíle pointed out, the passage is almost identical with the introductory remarks on the first page of O'Donovan's edition of the Registry and there can be little doubt that he supplied Petrie with the relevant information.[8] O'Donovan again quotes the Registry in his edition of 'Tribes and Customs of the Hy-Many' in the year 1843,[9] and eventually edited the text in the years 1856-57.[10] John Ryan mentions the existence of a church registry of Clonmacnois in his historical summary.[11]

---

of the scribe of the Registry appears again in a commentary to a plan of Clonmacnois in another of Ware's manuscripts in the British Library (British Library, MS Additional 4784, fol. 20).

[6] T. C. CROKER, Researches in the South of Ireland, London 1824, pp. 242n and 246n.

[7] G. PETRIE, The ecclesiastical architecture of Ireland. An essay on the origin and uses of the Round Towers in Ireland, Dublin 1845, reprint Shannon 1970, pp. 265f.

[8] Ó MURAÍLE, The background, life and writings, I, pp. 269f.

[9] O'DONOVAN (ed.), The tribes and customs of Hy-Many, pp. 15, 80, 98, 188.

[10] He worked from a copy of the manuscript in the British Library, made for him by Daniel Mac Carthy; only a few minor corrections are necessary. (Minor mistakes like punctuation or those like the spelling of bishop as bushop are not considered here; the numbers in [ ] refer to the pagenumbers of O'Donovan's edition of the text): fol. 38ᵛ for *Kilchronagh* [450] read *Killchaeragh*? (smeared ink); fol. 38ᵛ for *Bella Athanurchoir* [450] read *Bellathanurchoir*; fol. 39ʳ for *three Dunta, wch signifieth 3 houses, or els three places of building...* [453] read *three Dunta, wch signifieth 3 houses, or els three stillocks or steep places of building*; fol. 39ᵛ for *Kill Coirill* [455] read *Killgoiril*; fol. 40ʳ *Disiort* is corrected to *Dysyort* [455] by a second (Ware's?) hand; fol. 40ʳ for *Creagha* [455] read *Creagga*; fol. 42? for *Coill Belacha* [457] read *Coill Belatha*.

[11] RYAN, Clonmacnois, p. 69.

6.2 The content of the Registry

The document opens with a kind of prologue where the origin of St. Ci-arán's riches and land-holdings is explained as the result of the salvation-bringing function of his graveyard. The fact that whoever was buried under the earth of Clonmacnois would not see damnation at the day of judgement caused the Irish nobility to divide the graveyard amongst them, each paying for the right of burial with a land donation to the saint. Then follows an ac-count of the various noble families who gained the right of burial in Clon-macnois. Their respective donations are listed individually.

First amongst them are the Uí Mháelsechlainn of the Southern Uí Néill. Máel Sechnaill himself, probably their ninth-century eponymous ancestor, is said to have made over to St. Ciarán thirteen holdings in his kingdom of Mide, which are listed by name. Two obviously late-medieval episodes fol-low. The first of them explains that the *O Molmoy*, probably Ua Máelmuaid had failed to pay for their right of burial in Clonmacnois. One *Cosney Duff* presumably head of the family, made up for it by donating lands to and building a church for Clonmacnois. The second story concerns an otherwise unknown *sonn of Senimnyn McColmain* who, we are told, entered the church and gave his hereditary portion of the family possessions, seven in-dividual grants, to the church of Clonmacnois.

The succeeding paragraph deals with the lands of Clonmacnois in Con-nacht. First of all there are six donations, which, according to the claims in the Registry, were given to Clonmacnois by king Cathal, presumably the early thirteenth century King Cathal Crobderg Ua Conchobair. Ua Ruairc is said to have bought the burial right by granting to Clonmacnois seven churches in Bréifne. Again a brief anecdote follows explaining how St. Ci-arán came to possess a large amount of lands in county Leitrim. The story goes that Mac Ragnaill and Mac Shamhradháin, when building the church in the service of Ua Ruairc in Clonmacnois, suddenly stopped working and refused to take up work again until they also got the right of burial in Clon-macnois. Their wish was granted and Mac Ragnaill gave parts of his land in Kiltoghert to Clonmacnois in return. The obligations of Ua Ruairc towards the church of Clonmacnois are further specified, namely to maintain the chapels and to re- build the road leading from west to east via Clonmacnois. Three donations of the Meic Dhiarmada, also a Connacht dynasty, are listed, followed by a very extensive grant to St. Ciarán made by the early medieval ancestors of the Uí Cheallaigh. Here a passage about the rights of the Uí Dhubhagáin, who are said to have been employed to preserve the memory of the possessions of the church of Clonmacnois, is inserted. One Siacus Mór, another member of the Ua Ceallaigh family, is mentioned as having slain a child and by way of repentence making a donation to Clonmacnois. Finally there is Lochlainn Ua Ceallaigh, who received from the bishop a portion of the church lands, which are again individually named. The list of the noble dynasties buried in Clonmacnois comes to an end with the Mac Carthaigh family, who are said to have donated nine churches to Clonmacnois. A dispute over the burial rights between the Meic Charthaigh and the Geraldines is mentioned which was settled through a compromise, allowing the Geraldine family to participate in the Mac Carthaigh's share of the graveyard.

A third part of the document is concerned with the ecclesiastical income. The rent due to Clonmacnois from an otherwise unknown church of St. Grellan in Leinster is defined, followed by an enumeration of the lands belonging to the abbot of Clonmacnois and those in possession of the nuns of Clonmacnois. Finally the rights of *O Kyllin, the chiefe water cleark*, i.e. Ua Cillín are set down. These include a living from the churchlands as well as the tenth of the total of the tithes.

Perhaps the original document came to an end here, since a concluding, though severely distorted, passage indicates to the reader that the possessions bestowed to the church of Clonmacnois mentioned in the document are also engraved, allegedly in Hebrew, on a stone monument in the graveyard.

In an additional section several late medieval families, the Ó Cobthy, Ó Floinn, Ó Hidersgoil ... Ó Tressey, Ó Cynnydhe and Ó Cuaghan are commemorated for having donated various altar utensils to Clonmacnois. In the epilogue finally the *auncient life of St Kyran* and an otherwise unknown *Red booke* are mentioned as the sources from which the translation was made.

6.3 Dating of the document

The epilogue of the Registry also talks about the time of compilation, stating that *it was the Bushop Muirchertagh O'Muridhe that caused this to be written ... when the yeare of the Lord was 20, three hundred and a thousand yeares.* We are also told that Muirchertach was *Bp of Clone, Head of all Meth*, and that his fosterbrother Slanan had a gravestone in Clonmacnois erected for him and engraved with this title.[12]

Obviously there are a number of inconsistencies here. Ware, the owner of the document, himself pointed out that the year 1320 is impossible as the date of the final composition on internal evidence.[13] First of all the document mentions the friary in Kilconnell, which was only founded in the late fourteenth century,[14] and also there was no bishop Muirchertach in Clonmacnois in the early fourteenth century. Another problem concerns the person of the bishop himself. The claim that the bishop of Clonmacnois was head of all the churches in Meath is rather pretentious. The only time such a title would be justified would be after the year 1568 when Clonmacnois was united to the bishopric of Meath. There are, however, two earlier bishops of Clonmacnois whose names come close to the corrupt anglicised form of the Irish name given in the Registry. One is Muirchertach Ua Máeluidir, bishop of Clonfert and Clonmacnois, who died in the year 1187, the other is Ua Muirecán, his successor, who died as bishop of Clonmacnois in the year 1214. Ware, who apparently had the Registry at hand when compiling his work on the Irish episcopate, thought that the latter was the bishop in question here.[15]

---

[12] British Library, MS Additional 4796, fol. 43ᵛ; Registry, p. 460.

[13] British Library, MS Additional 4796, fol. 44ʳ; see Registry, p. 460 n.1.

[14] See below, p. 213 n.33; also B. JENNINGS, The abbey of Kilconnell, in: Galway Arch. Hist. Soc. Jn. 21 (1944/45), pp. 184-189; F. J. BIGGER, The fanciscan friary of Kilconnell, co. Galway, in: Galway Arch. Hist. Soc. Jn. 1 (1901), pp. 145-167; vol. 2 (1902), pp. 3-20; vol. 3 (1903), pp. 11-15.

[15] He mentiones Ua Muirecán as *Mureachus O-Murrechan vir doctus, vitam cum morte commutavit anno 1213. Hic videtur idem cum eo, quem alii Muriertacum O-Murry vocant, & sepultum asserunt Clonmacnoisae, sub monumento, quod illius memoriae erexerat Slamanus collactaneus ejus* (WARE, De Praesulibus Hiberniae, p. 97). The same is said about O'Muridhe, the bishop of the Registry in the epilogue (Registry, p. 460).

6.3.1 The *Red booke* as a forerunner of the Registry

The Registry is said to have been compiled at the instigation of the bishop of Clonmacnois. The *successor of Kyran* is mentioned as the one who was supposed to preserve the records about the land possessions. As the *comharb or corbe* he appears to have been in charge of the exaction of taxes from the churches belonging to the bishop. The extent of his lands, the abbatial lands in Clonmacnois, is also outlined in detail in the final section of the Registry.[16]

The underlying pattern of jurisdiction seems very close to the way in which the Irish churches in the earlier middle ages were organized. The bishop functioned as the authority by which the lands were held; the abbot was the administrator of the temporalities of the church. As the one in charge of the collection of the ecclesiastical rents, he was also responsible for the keeping of the books of accountancy in the estate. It seems therefore very plausible indeed, that the *Red booke*, mentioned as one of the sources of the Registry, represented a book of ecclesiastical accountancy, and was a genuine outcome of the administration of the church of Clonmacnois prior to the church reform.[17] Such a *Red booke* might have been the original copy, which would then have been revised subsequently in various redactions, when material of later date was also included. The result, a document consisting of several different strata, reflecting the various stages of redaction, comes down to us in an English seventeenth-century translation. The latest revision of the original Irish copy must date at least to the later parts of the fourteenth century, some time after the foundation of Kilconnell.

There is one more argument in favour of the authenticity of the *Red booke* as a genuine document dating from the pre-reform period. It is mentioned as one of two sources by the seventeenth-century scribe of the Registry. The other source was the *auncient life of St. Kyran*. In the prologue of the Registry the origin of the miraculous powers of St. Ciarán's graveyard are explained. We are told that St. Ciarán was such a holy bishop, *that what soules harboured in the bodies buried under that dust may neuer be adi-*

---

[16] Registry, pp. 460, 459, 452, 458.

[17] Compare the early monastic 'rental' books discussed by DOHERTY, Some aspects of hagiography, pp. 321-326.

udged to damnation. This appears as an almost literal translation of a passage in the Irish Life of Ciarán, where the hide of the Dun Cow is mentioned in the same context: *Cech ainim raghus asa churp do sheichid na hUidhre nocha pianfaider a n-ithfrenn.*[18] It has been said earlier that the Irish Life of Ciarán probably dates in its original to the tenth century, and was again revised in the late eleventh century, and it could well have been used here for the compilation of the Registry. We therefore might well trust the bibliography of the sources, added in the document, and rely on the fact that the *Red booke* was not simply an invention of the seventeenth-century transcriber.

6.3.2 The transmission of the document

At first we will look at the possible date and authorship of the seventeenth-century English translation of the Registry. It is one of various medieval documents relating to church possessions preserved in copies made for Ware.[19] The handwriting of the scribe of the Registry, who could not be identified, appears again on a sketch plan of Clonmacnois, also amongst the Ware manuscripts in the British Library (BL MS 4784, f 20).[20] This plan seems to be a copy of another plan of Clonmacnois (BL MS 4787, f. 276), which, since it bears the date 1621, might have been drawn up on the occasion of the visitation of the ancient diocese of Clonmacnois by the surveyers of bishop Ussher in 1621-22.[21] It seems this sketch plan of Clonmacnois, was copied and commented on by the same person who copied and perhaps translated the church registry, which originally was thought missing by Ussher. Possibly Ussher later got to know the Registry himself, since it seems to be annotated by him as well as by Ware.[22] It seems therefore

---

[18] STOKES (ed.), Lives of Saints, p. 127.

[19] Like for example the rentals of Clonfert and Kilmacduagh, preserved amongst the Ware manuscripts: British Library, MS Additional 4787; NICHOLLS (ed.), The episcopal rentals.

[20] The passage in question is almost identical to the epilogue of the Registry, giving an account of the sources and purpose of the document. Compare Registry, pp. 459-460.

[21] Certificate of the State and Revennewes, pp. liii -cxxv.

[22] I wish to thank Mr. William O'Sullivan, formerly keeper of Manuscripts in Trinity College Dublin, who kindly looked at a copy of the original manuscript. He pointed out to me a reference in the handwriting of Ussher, towards the identification of 'Killmanachan' as being situated in Westmeath (British Library, MS Additional 4796, fol. 39^r). He confirmed the idea

plausible that the document was re-discovered, and translated in the 1620's, in the course of the stock-taking of the churchlands in Clonmacnois.

6.3.2.1 The early thirteenth-century redaction

The earliest feasible historical period for a revision of the church registries appears to be the early thirteenth century, when the ancient ecclesiastical records on land-holding were re-written according to the needs of the newly established episcopal church. In the early phase of the diocese of Clonmacnois, from the late twelfth century down to the year 1236, when episcopal elections in the church came under Anglo-Norman control, the affairs of the new bishopric were closely knit into the pattern of its early medieval predecessor church. Ua Máeleoin, the hereditary abbatial family, dominated the church of Clonmacnois including the bishopric down to the thirteenth century.[23] The boundaries of the diocese were not yet definitely set up, and were still in dispute in the late thirteenth century.[24] It seems plausible that the extent of the former church lands was outlined in detail in a document extracted from the *Red booke*, with a view to justify an expansion of the territory under the bishop's authority.

The first two decades of the thirteenth century seem a very suitable time for the writing of such a document, when the Uí Chonchobair dynasts of Connacht became prominent once more as patrons of Clonmacnois. In the year 1208 the remains of king Ruaidrí Ua Conchobair were elevated and enshrined in Clonmacnois at the instigation of King Cathal Crobderg.[25] With such a ceremony the function of St. Ciarán's graveyard as the burial place of the Connacht nobility was publicly revived. The possibility that the poem on the chiefs and kings buried in Clonmacnois, by Conaing Buidhe Ua Máelchonaire, was composed on this occasion has been considered earlier.[26]

---

that the document was written or translated around 1622, in the course of the preparations for the survey of the property of the bishopric of Meath and Clonmacnois.

[23] They supplied the bishops of Clonmacnois between the years 1214 and 1236. See above, pp. 166f., 178f.

[24] See above, pp. 173-179.

[25] AFM 1207 (recte 1208).

[26] See above, p. 169f.

The celebrations in the year 1208, as a revival of the former glory, might also have appeared as a suitable opportunity to compile a document which outlines in detail the boundaries of the church lands of Clonmacnois. As in the Ua Máelchonaire poem, the right to be buried in the graveyard of Clonmacnois is central to the Registry, it was the motivation for the noble families to make donations to Clonmacnois. The presumed instigator of the Registry, *bishop O'Muiride* would thus be Ua Muirecán, bishop of Clonmacnois at the time.[27] Apart from him, as ecclesiastical authority, the secular patron Cathal Crobderg Ua Conchobair had a share in the compilation of the document. This would explain why a high proportion of the nobles listed as benefactors of Clonmacnois were from Connacht. Five of a total of seven were close allies of Ua Conchobair: Ua Ceallaigh, Ua Ruairc, Mac Diarmada and Mac Ragnaill had actively taken part in Toirdelbach Ua Conchobair's expansionist policy during the twelfth century. During Cathal's fights for the kingship of Connacht, Fingen Mac Carthaigh with his men was fighting in the army of Cathal Crobderg.[28]

All in all it seems plausible that in the early thirteenth century the ancient ecclesiastical records concerning landholdings were revised in order to document the extension of the churchlands of Clonmacnois. The compilation might have been inspired by the intent to document the extent of the land which should be under the authority of the bishop of Clonmacnois.

6.3.2.2 Rewriting of the Registry in the fourteenth century

A most striking element in the Registry is the disproportionate extent of the land donations made to St. Ciarán by the alleged ancestors of the Uí Cheallaigh from Uí Maine. First there is *Cairpre Crum*, who is said to have granted seventeen townlands to St. Ciarán, which in the actual text is extended to thirty-three individual donations. Another seven donations are ascribed to *Kellagh Mc Finachta Mc Oillille*, so that the total of the Uí Cheallaigh endowments to Clonmacnois amounts to the respectable number of forty separate donations.

---

[27] He died in 1214 (AFM).

[28] ALCé 1202.

The second benefactor, Ceallach, son of Finacht, son of Ailill, is the eponymous ancestor of the Uí Cheallaigh. He is said to have given seven churches to St. Ciarán. The same claim is made in the Chronicon Scotorum in regard to Cathal, son of Ailill, king of Uí Maine in the early ninth century, who supported the community in Clonmacnois in defending it against the king of Munster.[29] The memory of him seems to have got lost in the later middle ages. He does not appear on the list of the lords of Uí Maine, in a poem addressed to Eogan Ó Madden, composed in the fourteenth century.[30] Instead Ceallach, son of Finacht appears as king of Uí Maine during the mid-ninth century. Cathal, as the son of Ailill, would have been the uncle of Ceallach, the grandson of Ailill. It seems likely that by the fourteenth century the memory of king Cathal had merged with that of king Ceallach, the alleged eponym of the Uí Cheallaigh dynasty. It is therefore plausible that a gift of seven churches to St. Ciarán by the Uí Maine dates back to an original ninth century grant, when friendly relations between St. Ciarán and his neighbours to the west prevailed.

The other Ua Ceallaigh benefactor is Cairpre Crum. As the eponymous ancestor of the Cenél Cairpre Cruim, he lived several hundred years before Cathal, alias Ceallach. However, little is known about him as a historical figure. The annals do not mention him at all, and St. Ciarán's hagiographers are silent about this alleged friend of the saint. Only in a fragment of the Book of Uí Maine, compiled in the late fourteenth century under the aegis of archbishop Muirchertach Ua Ceallaigh, are the adventures of Cairpre Crum and the background to his friendship with St. Ciarán recorded.[31] The story of how he was once rescucitated from the dead would supply a very valid reason for the large donation he made to St. Ciarán's church. It seems possible that the elaboration of the donation, its extension to thirty-two individual grants, was fabricated in the same school and together with the Uí Maine version of the tale of Cairpre Crum's resurrection.

Other hints in the Ua Ceallaigh section of the Registry also point to the late fourteenth century as the date of a revised edition of the document. A

---

[29] See above, pp. 96f.

[30] O'DONOVAN (ed.), The tribes and customs of Hy-Many, pp. 14-16.

[31] See above, p. 104 n.50.

whole paragraph deals with the rights of the Ua Dubhagáin family, as chroniclers of the Uí Cheallaigh:

> *they did bestowe the land of Baile an ruan to O Dugain for makeing knowen unto them the true chronikles and antiquities that did belong unto them to knowe in that behalf, and for the keeping and due recollection of the life and right of St. Kieran in all partes of Irelande wheresoeuer it were, and it was inioyned to O'Dubhagain uppon euery Good Fryday to repayre to Cluain, and to make recorde of anie thing bestowed to that church in that peregrination or time of pilgrimadg, and it was for such causes O'Dubhagain had his land.[32]*

As witness to this contract between Ua Dubhagáin and Tadg Ua Ceallaigh, one Ua Breslean of Dunbeg is mentioned. Both families, as hereditary poets and historians, became prominent in the fourteenth century. The Uí Cheallaigh part of the Registry also contains the passage about the friars in Kilconnell, who are said to have received *ten days out of the churchland belonging to the bishop of Clonmacnois*. The Franciscan house in Kilconnell was a late medieval foundation, built alternatively either in 1353 or 1414.[33]

The postulated fourteenth century revision of the text seems to combine the interests of the Ua Dubhagáin family, and those of the Uí Cheallaigh, with the alleged territorial possessions of the bishop of Clonmacnois. Furthermore the Sliocht Lochlainn, a particular branch of the Uí Cheallaigh who apparently lived on former church land near Clonmacnois, finds special mention. If we look for a time when the fortunes of these families were particularly linked we are led to the late fourteenth century, when the Book of Uí Maine was compiled. Its main contributors were members of the Ua Dubhagáin family. The one who instigated its composition was Muirchertach Ua Ceallaigh, as archbishop of Tuam (1392-1407).[34] In his

---

[32] Registry, p. 456.

[33] The exact date of the foundation of the friary is unclear. It might be 1353 as the Four Masters say, or 1414 according to Ware (see Bodleian, Rawl. B 484, fol. 29). The date 1414 is also given in the list of Franciscan houses in British Library, MS Additional 4814, fol. 6, where Uilliam Ua Ceallaigh is mentioned as the founder (see GWYNN / HADCOCK, p. 251).

[34] W. O'SULLIVAN, The Book of Uí Maine formerly the Book of Ó Dubhagáin: Scripts & structure, in: Éigse 23 (1989), pp. 151-166, here 151. Muirchertach was archbishop already when the genealogies of his family were drawn up in the Book of Uí Maine, since the title ardeaspac appears as an integral part of the text. See MULCHRONE, Book of Hy Many, p. 3316. For the Book of Uí Maine see MACALISTER (ed.), The Book of Uí Maine; R. A. BREATNACH, The Book of Uí Mhaine, in: L. DE PAOR (ed.), Great Books of Ireland, Dublin 1967, pp. 77-89; N. Ó MURAÍLE, Leabhar Ua Maine alias Leabhar Uí Dhuibhagáin, in: Éigse

service one John Ua Ceallaigh, of the Sliocht Lochlainn was employed as archdeacon of Tuam.[35]

From the mid fourteenth century on the Uí Dhubhagáin were attached as hereditary historians and poets to the Uí Cheallaigh. Seán Mór Ua Dubhagáin, a poet and historian who died in the year 1372, worked under the patronage of Uilliam Buidhe Ua Ceallaigh.[36] One *Richard O'Dowagan, chronicler by profession* died, according to the Annals of Clonmacnois, in the year 1379.[37] Cam Cluana Ua Dubhagáin, again a historian and poet, was kept prisoner and killed by the English in the year 1394, when Richard II was in Ireland.[38] The latter's sobriquette, Cam Cluana, i.e. the Crooked of Cluain, indicates a physical handicap, but it also points to the fact that he came from Cluain. The Registry seems to support the assumption that the Cluain in question here was Clonmacnois, since Ua Dubhagáin as the keeper of the records of the church of Clonmacnois is talked about as a matter of fact here. Links between the family and the church of St. Ciarán might have existed earlier. Although the Uí Dhubhagáin do not appear as an ecclesiastical dynasty in Clonmacnois in the old days, they were apparently attached to the church of St. Énda on the Aran islands, which according to St. Ciarán's hagiography was a member of the *paruchia* of Clonmacnois.[39] Giollagori Ua Dubhagáin died as coarb of Énda in the year 1167.[40] It is possible that the late medieval connection between the Uí Dhubhagáin and Clonmacnois were the continuation of earlier links which existed between the family settled on Aran islands and Clonmacnois as their ecclesiastical overlord. In any

---

23 (1989), pp. 167-195; K. MEYER, Das Buch der Húi Maine (Stowe Collection, R. I. A.), in: K. MEYER, Neue Mitteilungen aus irischen Handschriften, in: Archiv für Celtische Lexikographie 2 (1904), pp. 136-146, here 138-146.

35 O'DONOVAN (ed.), The tribes and customs of Hy-Many, p. 128.

36 AConn 1372.3. He is otherwise known as the author of the topographical poem *Triallam timcheall na Fódla*, written under the patronage of Uilliam Ua Ceallaigh, lord of Uí Maine (1334-1375), who was a great-uncle of archbishop Muirchertach. For the poems see: J. CARNEY (ed.), Topographical poems by Seaán Mór Ó Dubhagáin and Giolla-na-Naomh Ó hUidhrín, Dublin 1943.

37 AConn 1372.3; AClon 1379, p. 306.

38 Misc. Irish Ann., 1394.31, p. 153. His title reads *ollamh of history, eloquence, and poetry*.

39 See above, pp. 65-67.

40 AFM.

case the family appears in various ecclesiastical positions in the territory west of Clonmacnois, in the diocese of Clonfert and Elphin, in the later middle ages. One David Ua Dubhagáin became archdeacon of Clonfert in the year 1405.[41] The family occupied the vicarage of Killosolan in the diocese of Elphin for most of the fifteenth century. Malachy Ua Dubhagáin was vicar around the year 1430.[42] His successor was Dermot Ua Dubhagáin, who held the vicarage down to the year 1460.[43] The rectory of Cam, also in the diocese of Elphin and bordering Killasolan, was held by Marianus Ua Dubhagáin in the early fifteenth century.[44] Members of the family also appear in the vicarage of Clonburren, the territory west of Clonmacnois across the Shannon, which belonged to the diocese of Tuam.[45] One John Ua Dubhagáin was a monk in Athlone, claiming the rectory of Killaan, a parish west of Kilconnell in county Galway, belonging to the diocese of Clonfert.[46]

It seems plausible that the keeper of the church records in Clonmacnois came from this branch of the Uí Dhubhagáin, who were more or less neighbours of Clonmacnois and called themselves the Ua Dubhagáin of Cluain, i.e. Clonmacnois. The assumption is confirmed by the fact that although Killosolan and Killian (as the parish churches held by the Uí Dhubhagáin) belonged to the diocese of Elphin, they were, according to the Registry itself, part of the lands under the authority of the bishop of Clonmacnois.[47] The Registry also states that Ua Dubhagáin received a piece of land called *Baile an ruan, alias Baile Ua Dubhagáin* in reward for his service to the church of Cluain and to Ua Ceallaigh. O'Donovan identified the place as a townland a little west of the river Suck, in the parish of Ahascragh.[48] The

---

41 Cal. Pap. Let. VI, p. 46 (7. Kal. April 1405).

42 Cal. Pap. Let. VIII, pp. 201f. (19. Kal Jan. 1430); VIII, p. 557 (3 Id July 1435).

43 Cal. Pap. Let. XII, p. 72 (Non Jan. 1459-60).

44 Cal. Pap. Let. VI, pp. 255, 310.

45 Cal. Pap. Let. VIII, p. 564 (5. Id. July 1435).

46 Cal. Pap. Let. XV, p. 831. See B. MITCHELL, A new genealogical atlas of Ireland, Baltimore 1986, p. 56.

47 Registry, p. 455, states that *the town and lands of Killithain, the towne and lands of Killosaigelean* were in posession of Clonmacnois since the days of Cairpre Crum.

48 Registry, p. 456n. K. Grabowski attempted to identify the place with Ballinruane in par. Ardrahan, bar. Loughrea, since the Uí Dhubhagáin are usually associated with that area.

identification seems highly plausible since it is in the area where the Uí Dhubhagáin held ecclesiastical positions in various parish churches. When the surveys were made in the seventeenth century the townland was adjoined to the parish of Fohinah, bordering Ahascragh. It appears as 'Ballydoogane' in the surveyor's report from the year 1641 and was then in possession of 'Teige o Doogane'.[49]

So far we might conclude that the Ua Dubhagáin who appears in the Registry as keeper of the records of the church of Clonmacnois was a member of the branch of the family which had settled in the area west of Clonmacnois, in the eastern parts of county Galway, where they dominated various parish churches. This was presumably also the Uí Dhubhagáin branch to which Cam Cluana belonged.

Parallel with the rights of the Uí Dhubhagáin the rights of the *Sliocht Lochlainn*, a branch of the Uí Cheallaigh, are documented in the Registry. They claimed descent from Lochlainn, a son of Domnall Mór Ua Ceallaigh (d.1224).[50] The story is told how Lochlainn, the eponymous ancestor, once found a lost Life of Ciarán, giving account of the possession of the church of Clonmacnois. He brought his discovery to the bishop who rewarded him with six quarters of his lands. The lands in question are individually named and the rent due for them to be paid by Lochlainn's descendants to the bishop is set down in detail. The passage points to the involvement of a member of the Sliocht Lochlainn in the re-writing of the document. The most likely candidate here is of course Seán Ua Ceallaigh of the Sliocht Lochlainn, the archdeacon of Tuam at the time when Muirchertach Ua Ceallaigh was archbishop.[51] Possibly this episode reflects the circumstances in which the ancient document, from which the fourteenth-century revision was drawn up, came to light. The suggestion that the archdeacon of Tuam

---

However the purpose of the passage in the Registry here seems to be to justify the fact that a branch of the family held land not traditionally in possession of the Uí Dhubhagáin, which therefore might well be outside the hereditary family domain. Moreover the Uí Dhubhagáin of Cluain seem to have been a separate branch from those in Loughrea (see K. GRABOWSKI, The interaction of politics, settlement and church in medieval Ireland: Uí Mhaine as a case study, D.Phil. Thesis, Cambridge 1988, p. 415).

[49] SIMINGTON (ed.), Books of Survey, III, p. 134.

[50] O'DONOVAN (ed.), The tribes and customs of Hy-Many, pp. 102, 128.

[51] Ibid., p. 128.

discovered the document is possible, and might indicate that a copy of the early version of the Registry was kept in Tuam. Possibly it came into the possession of the church of Tuam in the course of the quarrels about the lands west of Clonmacnois between the bishop of Clonmacnois and the archbishop of Tuam in the thirteenth century.[52]

The Registry itself gives the details about the purpose of its re-edition in the later middle ages, when it tells us the story how Tadg Ua Ceallaigh once had an argument with the bishop of Clonmacnois concerning the property of Ciarán in Uí Maine. To the mind of Ua Ceallaigh the bishop demanded more rent than he was entitled to. In mutual agreement the two contestants decided to employ an Ua Dubhagáin to keep the books of the church of Cluain, and once a year, on Good Friday, Ua Dubagáin had to come and report on everything bestowed to the church.[53] The Registry was thus the record of the possessions of the church of Clonmacnois, kept by the Ua Dubhagáin in the service of an Ua Ceallaigh lord. A member of the Ua Dubhagáin family, perhaps Cam Cluana himself, was at work here, re-writing an earlier document, ensuring his own rights on the occasion, by making sure that his pay was also set down in the document itself. 'Baile Ua Dubhagáin', alias 'Baile an ruan', the land given to Ua Dubhagáin for his service, is nowhere mentioned as belonging to St. Ciarán. Apparently Ua Ceallaigh paid for the deal, and we might conclude that it was primarily his concern to protect his lands against the claims by the bishop of Clonmac-nois.

This points to the possibility that the Ua Ceallaigh in question here was an ecclesiastical lord in the neighbourhood of Clonmacnois, rather than a secular magnate. In fact Muirchertach Ua Ceallaigh, the archbishop, had been bishop of Clonfert, prior to his promotion to Tuam (1377-1393). He was succeeded by his son Tomás in the year 1405, who despite several ir-regularities seems to have remained bishop of Clonfert until his death in 1441.[54] The archbishop's family had a firm grip on the bishopric of Clon-fert, as is apparent from the fate of the two direct successors of Muirchertach. One, William Ua Cormacáin, was simply removed after five

---

[52] See above, pp. 177f.

[53] Registry, p. 456.

[54] W. O'SULLIVAN, The Book of Uí Maine, p. 152.

years in office, the other, Enrí Ua Conmhaigh, was translated to Kil-macduagh, to make way for Tomás in the year 1405. From the time of bishop Muirchertach, the family also held former churchland of the diocese of Clonfert in private possession.[55] It seems possible therefore that the Uí Cheallaigh of the Registry refer to the family of bishop Muirchertach Ua Ceallaigh, who dominated the bishopric of Clonfert from the latter part of the fourteenth down to the middle of the fifteenth century.

If we take the Registry by its word, the lands given to Ua Dubhagáin in reward for his service, should therefore have been formerly in possession of the bishop of Clonfert. A place called *Lisdhubghain* is listed amongst the possessions of the bishop of Clonfert in the rental list from 1407. It is stated that the bishop used to get one mark from his lands in Lisdhubhagain, but more recently he has let it for nothing, simply by his grace.[56] This would perfectly suit the transfer of property described in the Registry, where we are told that Ua Dubhagan received some land from Ua Ceallaigh, i.e. the Ua Ceallaigh bishop of Clonfert. The memory that the bishop used to get rent for the piece of land in question was still alive in 1407, but clearly even though it still counted as bishop's land it had fallen into other hands, namely into the possession of the Uí Dhubhagáin, from whom it took the name. *Lisdubhagain* in the diocese of Clonfert would therefore be identical, or lie somewhere in the vicinity of *Baile Ua Dubhagáin*, in Ahascragh, mentioned in the Registry as the payment to Ua Dubhagáin.

The Registry of Clonmacnois in its late medieval redaction therefore seems to be a piece of work commissioned by the Ua Ceallaigh bishop of Clonfert, carried out by a member of the Uí Dhubhagáin of Cluain. He transformed the document into an Ua Ceallaigh eulogy, by stressing the generosity of the ancestors of his lord and at the same time ensuring his own rights to certain lands in Uí Maine. It is possible that the document, as an Ua Dubhagáin compilation, was intended to form part of the Book of Uí Maine. In the manuscript the story of Cairpre Crum and his resurrection by St. Ci-

---

[55] NICHOLLS (ed.), The episcopal rentals, p. 134n.

[56] NICHOLLS (ed.), The episcopal rentals, p. 138: *Lisdhubghain olim una marca sed modo in gratia Ep scopi.*

arán is followed by blank space and three cancelled leaves.[57] This seems to support the assumption that the Registry of Clonmacnois was supposed to be copied here, as an extended commentary on the preceding saints' legend.

---

[57] The story appears on fol. 126ᵛ, running from the last quarter of col. 1 to the first third of col. 2, as part of a passage filled in by a hand, different from that of scribe C (Adam Cuisin), who wrote the preceding pages. Then follows a blank space with a note by the eighteenth century owner of the book: *This book Belongs to Laughlin Kelly of Tonelig. Left him by his Father Edmond Kelly Deceased in 1754.* The folio is part of quaternion no. 13, now incomplete since its last three leaves were cancelled (O'SULLIVAN, The Book of Uí Maine, pp. 159, 164).

7 THE LANDS OF ST. CIARÁN ACCORDING TO THE REGISTRY

In the preceding chapter, the Registry of Clonmacnois as a potential source for the reconstruction of the former ecclesiastical lands belonging to Clonmacnois has been discussed. We came to the conclusion that the document, which in its present form dates from the seventeenth century, probably goes back to a genuine account of St. Ciarán's lands, as they existed prior to the church reform. This account, which might have been identical with the *Red booke*, would have been kept in the church of Clonmacnois as an instrument of accountancy for the ecclesiastical estate.

The majority of the lands mentioned in the Registry, can be traced in the seventeenth century surveys.[1] Most of them have a tradition as churchlands. The presence of ecclesiastical ruins for example, or the existence of an ancient burial ground might attest to an ecclesiastical past. In addition these sites are often connected by local tradition with one particular saint. In other cases references in administrative documents point to an ecclesiastical tradition of a piece of land. A method of working for the identification of former churchland was first introduced by bishop Dawson in the seventeenth century. He undertook the same task as we do in the present study by trying to identify the former possessions of his church (he of course did so to restore them to his see of Clonfert). The bishop gave three criteria towards the identification of churchlands: first of all he goes through the *ancient rentall*, the still extant records of the churchlands; secondly he identifies churchlands according to the *generall knowne marke, that where the Deane or any of the Chapter have the tythes there the land did bellonge to the Bishopp*; finally he says that the lands which paid rent to the bishop or were supposed to do so, were churchlands.[2] I will basically rely on this method in the following analysis of the lands claimed for Clonmacnois.

---

[1] SIMINGTON (ed.), Books of Survey; LYONS (ed.), Book of Survey, co. Westmeath.

[2] NICHOLLS (ed.), The episcopal rentals, p. 132.

7.1 The Ua Ceallaigh donations

The first section to look at will be the Ua Ceallaigh part of the Registry, which seems to form the late medieval appendix to the document, fabricated in the service of the bishop of Clonfert. The lands listed can all be located in county Roscommon and Galway. With the exception of Tuamgraney, in the very southern extremity of county Galway, at the southern end of Lough Derg the lands comprise a self contained area, roughly reaching from Clonfert in the south, to Roscommon in the north, and from Tuam in the west to the Shannon in the east.

For most of the lands a tradition as churchland can be established.[3] Examples here are *Tomcattry* in Clontuskert parish (6), where a burial ground is situated; in Kilcloony parish (8) St. Griollan, the patron saint of the Uí Maine, is said to have built his church; *Tuaimsruthra* (23) has been identified as the church of St. Raoillin, now in Creagh parish, county Roscommon; Tuamgraney (26) has been the site of a church since the sixth century; Fuerty (30) is the place where Deacon Justus, who baptized St. Ciarán, used to dwell; the townland Kilkenny (35) in Taghmaconnel houses a church and burial ground; *Bellaneany* (36) also in Taghmaconnel parish was the site of a Franciscan Abbey; *Cuillen*, in Creagh parish (37) finally, used to house a convent of nuns.

In some cases there is unmistakable evidence that the lands were still in possession of the church of Clonmacnois in the seventeenth century. The diocese was then united with the bishopric of Meath, so that the bishop of Meath and Clonmacnois appears as the proprietor of these lands in the records. The holdings of Clonmacnois west of the Shannon, in Roscommon, represented by the medieval rectory of Moycarnan were discussed earlier. According to the survey of the former diocese, taken in 1622 they were leased to Anthony Brabazon by the bishop. The details about Brabazon's holdings in Roscommon can be found in the Exchequer inquisition taken after his death in the year 1604.[4] Most of the lands which he held from the

---

3   The numbers in brackets refer to Appendix 2 (pp. 297-321).

4   Anthony Brabazon died in 1597, the inquisition was taken seven years after his death only (see: Exechequer inquisition post mortem taken at Roscommon, 23 October, 1604 be-

bishop of Clonmacnois, appear in the Registry as Clonmacnois' possession. There is *Dun Beglaitt* (2), Kilbegley a townland in Moore parish which appears as *Kylbeglagh* in the inquisition and was still in possession of the bishop of Meath and Clonmacnois in 1641.[5] *Coillin Molruany* (37) is Culleenmulrony, or Cuillen in Creagh parish, referred to as *Kyly* in the inquisition. In 1641 the lands in Cuillen were still in possession of the dean of Clonmacnois, who had leased it to Edward Brabazon.[6] Also there is *Tuaimsruthra* (23), alias Ashford townland in Creagh parish, which appears as *Tuam Srower* in the the Exchequer inquisition. *Tuaim-taghar* (38) finally has been identified by Egan as the townland Ardnaglog in Moore parish. It was formerly in Creagh parish and was also held by Anthony Brabazon from the bishop of Meath and Clonmacnois.[7] It seems possible that Kilkenny alias *Kill Killchuynne* (35) in Taghmaconnel parish was also still in possession of the church of Clonmacnois in the seventeenth century, since it was also held by Edward Brabazon when the surveys were made. It is not stated from whom he held it: it is possible, that like in the case of the neighbouring Cuillen, the proprietor was the dean of Clonmacnois.[8] Apart from the church lands right opposite Clonmacnois across the Shannon there is also *Killiarainn* (32), possibly a townland in Killererin parish, bordering Dunmore in county Galway. It seems to have formed part of Dunmore parish in the sixteenth and seventeenth century. Four quarters of land there still belonged to the bishop of Clonmacnois in 1585.[9] *Killmeas* (34), finally, is Kilmass in Rahara parish, county Roscommon. Part of Rahara belonged to the bishop of Clonmacnois according to an early fifteenth century rental.[10]

So far, in the case of these six, maybe seven donations, the Registry seems to be confirmed by other independent sources, as a reliable account of the property of the church of Clonmacnois. However, it appears from further

---

fore John Crofton, edited by EGAN, The parish of Ballinasloe, p. 304). Compare above, pp. 175f.

[5] SIMINGTON (ed.), Books of Survey, I, p. 62.

[6] Ibid., p. 60.

[7] EGAN, The parish of Ballinasloe, pp. 14, 304.

[8] SIMINGTON (ed.), Books of Survey, I, p. 104.

[9] FREEMAN (ed.), Compossicion Booke, pp. 80f.

[10] NICHOLLS (ed.), The episcopal rentals, p. 139.

material that the bishop of Clonfert was the proprietor of many of the presumed Clonmacnois possessions. This evidence is preserved in the episcopal rental list of Clonfert, which dates from around the same period as the posited late fourteenth century revision of the Registry of Clonmacnois. The rental list, like the Registry, was copied for Ware in the early seventeenth century, and bears the date 1407.[11] It lists in detail the lands paying rent to the bishop of Clonfert, amongst them many of the supposed Clonmacnois possessions:

There is *Gortacharn* (5) which as a townland in Clontuskert parish, is possibly *Gort an chuill* and according to the rental list ought to be in the hand of the bishop of Clonfert.[12] *Kill Tormoir* (10), a townland in Kiltormer parish, paid one mark rent to the bishop of Clonfert. *Killorain* (11) paid half a mark a year to the bishop.[13] *Killmolonog* (12) is Kilmalinoge townland in the parish of the same name and paid forty pence rent to the bishop.[14] *Killchuirin* (21) is Kilkerrin, a townland and parish in county Galway, also known as *Kyllcaryn, alias Corkomaga* in the papal documents. This might be *Corramore* which was bought with his own money by archbishop Muirchertach Ua Ceallaigh.[15] All these lands are situated in county Galway. Furthermore there is *Dundomnaill in Maghfinn* (22), Dundonnell townland in Taghmaconnell parish in county Roscommon. In 1407 one part of *Taghmcconayle* was belonging to the church of Clonfert, paying one mark rent to the bishop.[16] Finally there is *Tuaimsruthra* (23), or Ashford, a townland in Creagh parish, county Roscommon. According to the rental list the bishop of Clonfert received *ex terris de Tuaymsrura duae marcae*.[17]

Other lands listed as appurtenances of Clonmacnois in the Registry were also in possession of the bishop of Clonfert according to later sources. There is *Dunanoght* (1), i.e. the small parish of Donanaghta near Clonfert, which was a benefice belonging to the church of Clonfert according to a visitation

---

[11] Ibid., pp. 130-143.

[12] Ibid., p. 137.

[13] Ibid., p. 136.

[14] Ibid., p. 138.

[15] Ibid., p. 139. Cal. Pap. Let. IV, p. 426.

[16] Ibid., p. 139.

[17] Ibid.

report from 1565.[18] *Dunmeadhain* (3) seems to be *Kilmeadain* alias Kyllcomeddan, which was held by Anthony Brabazon from the bishop of Clonfert in the late sixteenth century.[19] *Tuaim Catrighe* (6) is Tomcattry in
Clontuskert parish. According to the Headford set of the Books of Survey
and Distribution, it was held in the seventeenth century by the son of the
dean of Clonfert.[20] *Grainsy* (8) is Grainseach or Grange, in Kilclooney parish. Parts of it were held by the dean of Clonfert in the seventeenth century.[21] *Kill Coirill* (13) is Kilgerrill, a townland and parish in county Galway. The surveyors in 1640 state about Kilgerrill townland that *this qur
payes 4 li p Annu. to ye Bpp of Clonfert*.[22] *Killuir Beg* (15) in Kilgerrill parish was held by Anthony Brabazon from the bishop of Clonfert in the late
sixteenth century.[23] The same might have applied to *Killuir Mor* (14), also
held by Anthony Brabazon, even though it is not explicitly stated that he
held it from the bishop of Clonfert.[24] Finally *Killithain* (17), is Killane or
Killian townland and parish; the tithes of the vicarage belonged to the community of the church of Clonfert according to a papal letter from 1448.[25]

Clearly we have here an apparent contradiction in the sources: Two
documents apparently dating from around the same period, and the same
region, make entirely opposite statements concerning the ownership of land
in the area. A brief recapitulation of the history of the origin of the fourteenth century re-edition of the Registry might supply a possible explanation. It has been suggested that the bishop of Clonfert, possibly
Muirchertach Ua Ceallaigh or Tomás, his son and successor to the see, instigated the re-writing of the Registry of Clonmacnois in the late fourteenth
or early fifteenth century. The purpose of the document was to avoid the
situation whereby the *Bushop* [i.e. the bishop of Clonmacnois] *challenged*

---

[18] NICHOLLS (ed.), Visitations of the dioceses, p. 146.

[19] Exchequer inquisition taken at the hill called Backe, 7th Nobember 1604, edited by
EGAN, The parish of Ballinasloe, pp. 304f.

[20] EGAN, The parish of Ballinasloe, p. 44n.

[21] SIMINGTON (ed.), Books of Survey, III, p. 128.

[22] Ibid., p. 132.

[23] Ibid., p. 131; EGAN, The parish of Ballinasloe, pp. 304f.

[24] SIMINGTON (ed.), Books of Survey, III, p. 131.

[25] Cal. Pap. Let. X, pp. 393-396.

more than he ought out of the lands of Ua Ceallaigh.[26] It seems the Ua Ceallaigh in question here was the Ua Ceallaigh bishop of Clonfert, who instigated the compilation of a register of the lands held by the bishop of Clonmacnois in his diocese of Clonfert. A member of the Ua Dubhagáin family was entrusted with the task of investigating the ancient records of the church of Clonmacnois and finding out about the extent of the church lands. Since he worked in the service of the bishop of Clonfert, the purpose of his researches and documentation would not have been to exemplify the greatness of the church of Clonmacnois, but to confine the territorial authority of the bishop of Clonmacnois in Connacht to a limited number of lands. It might be that the bishop in the end was not very pleased with the results of Ua Dubhagáin's research, since it proved too many lands to belong to the church of Clonmacnois. Ua Dubhagáin foreseeing this, wisely included in his compilation the passage about the agreement concerning his pay.

If this be true, it seems plausible that the episcopal rental of Clonfert was a kind of counter-declaration by the bishop of Clonfert, to the results of Ua Dubhagáin's research. Thus it could be explained that a considerable number of the lands, which were in possession of the bishop of Clonmacnois according to the Registry, appear in the rental list as paying rent to the bishop of Clonfert. The two documents would thus express rival claims to lands in the late fourteenth century. *Tuaimsruthra* (23), in possession of Clonmacnois according to the Registry, but paying rent to the bishop of Clonfert according to the rental, was still held by the bishop of Clonmacnois in the seventeenth century. This obviously confirms the suggestion that the bishop of Clonmacnois not only had actual possessions in Connacht, but also that he was able to defend them against the bishop of Clonfert.

However there are many cases where the opposite was true. The lands held by the bishop of Clonmacnois according to the Registry had come in the possession of other churches by the sixteenth century. Most prominent here was the bishop of Clonfert who held *Dunanoght* (1), *Dunmeadhain* (3), *Tuaim Catrighe* (6), *Grainsy* (8), *Kill Tormoir* (10), *Killorain* (11), *Kill Coirill* (13), *Killuir Beg* (15), possibly also *Killuir Mor* (14), and *Killithain* (17). *Killchuirin* (21) came partly into the possession of the bishop of Clonfert, the other part was held by the bishop of Tuam in the seventeenth cen-

---

[26] Registry, p. 456.

tury. Also there is the bishop of Elphin, who took over lands of Clonmacnois situated in his diocese. He held four quarters in *Killosaigelean* (18)
from at least the late sixteenth century onwards.[27] *Dysyort* (24) alias *Comyn
in Disert*, a townland in Dysert parish, was also in his possession in the year
1641, when the surveys were made.[28] At that time he also held *Killtuma*
(27), in the parish of Kiltoom.[29]

It appears therefore that those lands claimed as lands of St. Ciarán in the
name of Cairpre Crum (nos. 1-33) were, with the exception of *Tuaim
Sruthra* (23), no longer in possession of the bishop of Clonmacnois in the
sixteenth and seventeenth century.

7.2 The grant of *Ceallach mac Finachta*

In contrast, more than half of the lands claimed as donations by *Kellagh Mc
Finatacha Mc Oillille* have a continuous tradition as lands in possession of
Clonmacnois: *Coillin Molruany* (37) in Creagh parish, *Kill Killchuynne* (35)
alias Kilkenny, in Taghmaconnell parish, *Tuaim-taghar* (38) alias Ardnaglog in Moore parish, and *Killmeas* (34) in Rahara parish. Father Patrick
Egan, who examined the churchlands in this area in detail, pointed out that
practically the whole south-western half of the parish of Taghmaconnell was
churchland, and that the same applies to the parishes of Creagh and Moore,
south of Taghmaconnell. He assumes that the area was mainly controlled by
Clonmacnois in the early period, but was then transferred to the bishops, or
to the canons and canonesses of Aughrim, Clontuskert and Kilcreevanty in
the twelfth and thirteenth centuries.[30]

We are talking here about the lands situated between the river Suck and
the Shannon. They were conquered by the Uí Maine in the middle of the

---

[27] FREEMAN (ed.), Compossicion Booke, p. 169; SIMINGTON (ed.), Books of Survey, III, p.
280.

[28] SIMINGTON (ed.), Books of Survey, I, p. 107.

[29] Ibid., p. 98.

[30] P. K. EGAN, The Carmelite cell of Bealaneny, in: Galway Arch. Hist. Soc. Jn. 26
(1954/55), pp. 19-25, esp. 23.

eighth century.[31] Henceforward the Uí Maine were the immediate neighbours of St. Ciarán, west of the Shannon. The story about the donations of seven churches to Ciarán by Ceallach, alias Cathal, king of Uí Maine has its historical background in the early ninth century. The political setting of this period seems to provide the perfect constellation for a donation, since, as Professor Ó Corráin has pointed out, a land grant to the nearby church or monastery in a newly conquered territory was a characteristic practice in pre-Norman Ireland.[32] It seems therefore a reasonable assumption, that the seven donations by Ceallach mac Finachta, listed in the Registry, elaborate on a genuine grant, made by the king of Uí Maine to Clonmacnois in the first half of the ninth century. The lands formed part of the ecclesiastical estate henceforward. In the thirteenth century the bishop of Clonmacnois attempted to include these lands into his diocese. Around the same time the abbot's family had withdrawn to the lands west of the Shannon and claimed them as their possession. Despite the fact that they were eventually assigned to the bishop of Tuam, the bishop of Clonmacnois could maintain authority on other levels, and appears as one of the most important landowners in the area in the later middle ages.[33] This part of the Ua Ceallaigh section in the Registry might have formed part of the original *Red booke*, which Ua Dubhagáin used for his compilation.

7.3 The Ua Máelsechlainn donations

The Ua Máelsechlainn donations are situated in counties Offaly and Westmeath. They are distributed in the parishes of Clonmacnois (47, 48, 51), Kilmanaghan (54), Lemanaghan (45, 46), Tisaran (49,) and Gallen (50) in county Offaly. The parishes of Ballyloughloe, which in medieval times included Killcleagh as well as St. Mary's Athlone (42, 43, 53, 55, 59), Horseleap, or Ardnurcher parish (58), Kilcumreragh (41) and Ballymore (57) are the parishes in county Westmeath. Altogether the lands comprise an area

---

[31] AT (755); AFM 751; see above, p. 95.

[32] D. Ó CORRÁIN, Nationality and kingship in pre-Norman Ireland, in: T. W. MOODY (ed.), Nationality and the pursuit of national independence, Belfast 1978, pp. 1-36, here 25.

[33] See above, pp. 175-177.

reaching from the river Shannon in the west to Ardnurcher parish in the east, and from Gallen in the south to Ballymore in the north.

Some of the lands here have well established traditional links with St. Ciarán and his church. Lemanaghan, alias Tuaim n-Eirc was given to the saint by the ancestor of the Síl nÁedo Sláine, according to the Clonmacnois annals.[34] Lands in Athlone are claimed as Ciarán's possession in Mageoghagan's annals.[35] Archaeological finds, together with annalistic evidence, point to a connection between Clonmacnois and the neighbouring church of Gallen.[36] The hill Knockasta in Kilcumreragh parish is mentioned as the eastern boundary of a donation to Ciarán by Feradach mac Duach, king of western Mide.[37] Ballyloughloe parish contains the site of the church Íseal Chiaráin, where the brothers of Ciarán are said to have lived, and which seems to have been the residence of the Céili Dé at Clonmacnois. When the rights of the church were violated by the son of Conchobar Ua Máelsechlainn in the late eleventh century, *Magh n-úra* was granted to the Céili Dé in compensation. This was the name of the plain extending eastwards from Athlone in the direction of the modern town of Moate, at the border between the former parishes of Ballyloughloe and Kilcleagh. Another independent tradition confirms these lands as Ciarán's property. According to the tale of the hostel of Da Choga, St. Colum Cille scattered the clay (*úir*) of Ciarán in the plain, to banish the devils out of it - therefore, from the times of Colum Cille, it is called the plain of the clay, *Magh n-úra*.[38] Ardnurcher parish houses the graves and remains of Ciarán's father and his sisters.[39] Mag Eli,

---

[34] CS 646; AClon 642, p. 103; AFM 645. See above, pp. 114f.

[35] AClon, 1210, p. 224.

[36] T. D. KENDRICK, Gallen priory excavations 1934-5, in: JRSAI 69 (1939), pp. 1-20, here 9; DUMVILLE / GRABOWSKI, Chronicles and annals, 224-226.

[37] P. WALSH, The placenames of Westmeath, Dublin 1957, pp. 280-284; L. COX, Íseal Chiaráin, Appendix, p. 64f.; the grant is mentioned in the Book of Ballymote 61 and by Mac Firbis in the Book of Genealogies.

[38] WALSH, The placenames of Westmeath, pp. 5f., n.3.

[39] W STOKES (ed.), Félire Óengusso Céli Dé. The Martyrology of Oengus the Culdee, London 1905, reprint Dublin 1984, p. 203; STOKES (ed.), Lives of Saints, p. 119. After the Anglo-Norman invasion in the early thirteenth century the Clonmacnois lands in Ardnurcher were possibly donated to the Augustinian Canons in Greatconnell, founded as a dependency of the Welsh abbey Llanthony I by Meiler fitz Henry. According to the Song of Dermot and the Earl the cantred of Ardnurcher, as a part of Meath, was granted by Hugh de Lacy to

or Moyelly, roughly coextensive with Kilmanaghan parish, was the place where in the late eleventh century an abbot of Clonmacnois retired to. The territory formed part of the mensal land of the Uí Chatharnaigh (also nick-named na Sionnaigh, the Foxes) lords of Tethba.[40] They became most prominent in Clonmacnois in the eleventh century which was probably the time when the lands of Kilmanaghan came under St. Ciarán's authority.

The claimed Ua Máelsechlainn donations in the Registry cover the entire diocese of Clomacnois,[41] plus four parishes east of it, namely Ardnurcher, Kilcumreragh, Kilmanaghan and Ballymore (alias Lochseudi) which were part of the diocese of Meath in the later middle ages. According to the An-nals of Tigernach the diocese of Westmeath was annexed to the city of Clonmacnois, at the synod of Birr in the year 1174.[42] The territory in ques-tion here was possibly that represented by these parishes in county West-meath. They formed part of the diocese of Clonmacnois for a limited time only. It is generally assumed that Simon Rochfort, as the first Norman bishop of Meath, extended the territory of his diocese at the expense of Clonmacnois, as early as the late twelfth century.[43] The Registry here might supply a valuable source about the original diocesan boundaries, which would have included parts of Ballymore, as well as the parishes Kilcum-reragh, Ardnurcher and Kilmanaghan. Claims by the Anglo-Norman bishop of Meath would thus have reduced the diocese of Clonmacnois to the area in the immediate vicinity of the former ecclesiastical settlement, plus the lands of the medieval parish of Ballyloughloe, including Kilcleagh and the eastern half of Athlone parish. There is evidence that even this part of the diocese was at risk of being alienated from the bishop of Clonmacnois under the impact of Anglo-Norman church policy. All of the parish churches which constituted the diocese of Clonmacnois are said to have been granted by

---

Meiler fitz Henry (G. H. ORPEN [ed.], The Song of Dermot and the Earl, London 1892, pp. 228f.). In 1205 king John confirmed the possessions granted to Greatconnell by Meiler, amongst them lands in *Atornorohor* (Cal. Doc. Irel. I, p. 41, no. 273 [10. Sept. 1205]; DUGDALE, Monasticon Anglicanum, vol. VI, part 2, 1138). Most likely during this period the Welsh saint David was introduced and replaced St. Ciarán as patron of the parish.

[40] Cox, Historic Moyelly, pp. 238-241.

[41] Compare above, pp. 173-179.

[42] AT (1174).

[43] GWYNN / HADCOCK, p. 65; J. BRADY, Origin and growth of the diocese of Meath, in: IER 72 (1949), pp. 1-13, 166-176; GWYNN, The Irish church, p. 189.

their founder Richard Tuite, to the Cistercians of Abbeylara. It seems they could not take possession of their endowments, possibly due to the fact that, since a castle was built in Clonmacnois, the bishop there had Anglo-Norman support to defend his diocese.[44]

7.4 The Ua Conchobair donations

All of the presumed Ua Conchobair donations were known either as churchland in the later middle ages, or as early ecclesiastical sites. *Toberelly* (60) in Baslick parish was an early foundation, associated with Armagh in the old days, later becoming the site of a Franciscan cell.[45] *Tamhnagh* (61) in county Sligo was a church once under the authority of Armagh, but then assigned to Clonmacnois, according to the witness of Tirechán.[46] *Kilmurihy* (62) seems to have been situated in Baslick parish and housed Domincan friars in the later middle ages.[47] *Kilmacteige* (63) also in county Sligo is associated with St. Ciarán according to local tradition.[48] In Tulsk (64) Dominicans were settled in the later middle ages,[49] and *Killogealba* (65), probably Ogulla parish, might have been a monastic foundation of St. Brendan.[50]

Tawnagh and Kilmacteige fall out of the geographical centre of the majority of Ua Conchobair donations. They are situated rather far away in the north west in county Sligo; however links with Clonmacnois and these two churches are best documented in the sources. We know for certain, that al-

---

[44] See above, pp. 186-189.

[45] STOKES (ed.), Tripartite Life, p. 108; K. W. NICHOLLS (ed.), A list of monasteries in Connacht 1577, in: Galway Arch. Hist. Soc. Jn. 33 (1972/73), pp. 28-43, here 38.

[46] BIELER (ed.), The Patrician texts, pp. 142f., §25.2.

[47] NICHOLLS (ed.), A list of monasteries, p. 38, n.94.

[48] T. O'RORKE, History of Sligo town and country, reprod. Sligo 1986, vol. 2, pp. 152f.

[49] GWYNN / HADCOCK, pp. 230f.

[50] SIMINGTON (ed.), Books of Survey, I, pp. 76-79; FREEMAN (ed.), Compossicion Booke, pp. 153f.; the Compossicion Book of Connought does not mention Ogulla parish by name, but the bishop of Elphin appears as holder of land in *Cowrin mc Brenan*, in the barony Roscommon, which might stand for the former property of the monastery of St. Brenan in Ogulla? GWYNN / HADCOCK, p. 400.

ready in the late seventh century, Tawnagh belonged to the ecclesiastical jurisdiction of Clonmacnois. In Kilmacteige a well dedicated to St. Ciarán of Clonmacnois existed down to the nineteenth century and family names formerly associated with Clonmacnois are very frequent amongst its parish clergy in the later middle ages.[51]

The remaining four donations are located in the area around Tulsk, in the parishes of Ogulla and Baslick, all in the immediate vicinity of Carn Fraích, the traditional inauguration site of the Uí Chonchobair kings of Connacht since around the twelfth century.[52] It seems plausible that an original part of the claimed Ua Conchobair donations dates back to the early period, when Clonmacnois had ecclesiastical jurisdiction over considerable parts of Connacht. The lands situated around Tulsk, near Carn Fraích might have come into the possession of Clonmacnois some time after the late eleventh century, when the kings of Connacht became once more prominent as St. Ciarán's patrons and friends. The lands might have been granted to Clonmacnois by the kings of Connacht out of the royal mensal lands near their inauguration site.

7.5 The Ua Ruairc donations

The Uí Ruairc, lords of Conmaicne were the ruling family in Bréifne, a subkingdom in Connacht, between the tenth and the twelfth centuries. The lands claimed by the church of Clonmacnois in their territory are situated at the border between the counties of Roscommon and Leitrim, along the river Shannon, north of Lough Boderg. Cloone (67), Killenummery (68), Annaghduff (70) and Kiltoghert (72) have all a tradition as ecclesiastical sites from the early period. None of them is directly associated with St. Ciarán. There are, however, two of the early abbots of Clonmacnois who seem to have come from the territory of Bréifne.[53] There is also hagiographical evi-

---

[51] See above, p. 199.

[52] AConn 1225.5, 1228.4, 1310.7, 1315.7, 1407.9. DILLON (ed.), The inauguration of O'Conor, p. 186n.

[53] Abbot Ceallach mac Secnde (d.740) was of the Conmaicne; possibly abbot Snéidriagail (d.786) was of the Calraige Droma Cliab in north county Leitrim (see Appendix 1, A20, A30).

dence for links between Bréifne and Clonmacnois. In the Dublin Life of St. Maedóc, the founder saint of Drumlane and Rossinver, the two main ecclesiastical settlements of Bréifne, we are told that the saint once went to Clonmacnois to bind his allegiance and convenant with Ciarán.[54] It seems possible that this passage preserved a genuine tradition concerning the early affiliation of St. Maedóc's churches in Bréifne with Clonmacnois. The churches in Bréifne, belonging to Clonmacnois according to the Registry, could therefore well have been members of St. Ciarán's *paruchia* in the early period and formed an original part of the pre-reform church registry, the *Red booke*.

It is, however, difficult to trace the Uí Ruairc dynasty as benefactors of Clonmacnois in the sources.[55] Quite the opposite seems to have been the case, since throughout the eleventh century they appear as the lords of Conmaicne amongst the most notorious of the enemies of St. Ciarán.[56] The conflicts leading to their repeated raids on Clonmacnois seem to have resulted out of the political rivalries with the Uí Chonchobair kings of Connacht. Things changed when in the twelfth century, under king Tigernán Ua Ruairc they formed an alliance with Murchad Ua Máelsechlainn, the king of Mide. Tigernán married the daughter of his ally, and hence forward directed his political ambitions towards the declining kingdom of his father in law. Possibly in this context tentative approaches towards Clonmacnois were made. Ua Ruairc's wife Dearbhforgaill, Ua Máelsechlainn's daughter, sponsored the building of the church of the nuns in Clonmacnois in the year 1167.[57] Also there is the so-called Ua Ruairc's tower in Clonmacnois. It seems to have been originally associated with the Uí Chonchobair kings of Connacht, but later tradition assigned the building of the tower to Ua Ruairc.[58] Another curious tradition has it that one Fergal Ua Ruairc, chief of

---

54 PLUMMER (ed.), Bethada Náem nÉrenn, I, p. 251.

55 For the Uí Ruairc of Bréifne see K. W. NICHOLLS, Gaelic and Gaelicised Ireland in the middle ages, Dublin 1972, pp. 151-153; M. Ó DUÍGEANNÁIN, Notes on the history of the kingdom of Bréifne, in: JRSAI 65 (1935), pp. 113-140; K. SIMMS, The Ó Reillys and the kingdom of East Bréifne, in: Bréifne 5 (1979), pp. 305-319, esp. 305-307.

56 AT (1044); CS 1048 (recte 1050); AT (1065, 1095); CS 1111 (recte 1107).

57 AFM 1167.

58 The Round Tower was originally built, or finished in the early twelfth century by the then abbot of Clonmacnois together with Toirdelbach Ua Conchobair (CS 1120, AFM 1124).

Bréifne, was buried in Clonmacnois. A poem survives, lamenting him which is said to have been written by Erard Mac Coisse.[59] Twice the death of a poet of this name is recorded in the annals, once in an entry for the year 991, the second time in 1023.[60] The only Fergal Ua Ruairc who lived around that time had died in the year 966.[61] Since the poem mentions the battle of Clontarf the poet's grief would appear as a rather delayed lamentation over a fifty year old corpse. It therefore should possibly be understood as the poetic expression of later friendship between the descendants of Fergal Ua Ruairc and Clonmacnois, which strictly speaking one might have to call a forgery. The remaining problem would then be to date the period of friendship, which I would suggest was a time in the latter part of the twelfth century. The poem satirizes a certain Ua Máelchiaráin in Clonmacnois for his lack of hospitality. An ecclesiastical dynasty of this name was well known in Clonmacnois from the eleventh century onwards, they supplied a guest-master in the early twelfth century.[62] Of course there would be no need of, and no point in, such a satire if it made no sense to the contemporary listeners. Also there is evidence which points to the mid-twelfth century as a period of great literary activity patronized by Ua Ruairc,[63] the poem in question here might well be an outcome of this literary revival in Bréifne at the time. Towards the end of the twelfth century the Uí Ruairc came under increasing pressure from the Uí Raigillig, who then rose to power in Bréifne. The Uí Ruairc in consequence sought friendship with the Uí Chonchobair.

Only later tradition associated its building with Ua Ruairc (PETRIE, The ecclesiastical architecture of Ireland, pp. 391-393).

[59] Edited by J. O'DONOVAN (ed.), Elegy of Erard Mac Coise, chief Chronicler of the Gaels, pronounced over the Tomb of Fergal O'Ruairc, chief of Brefny, at Clonmacnois, in: Jn. Kilk. SE. Irel. Arch. Soc. 1 (1856-57), pp. 314-356. It has been suggested that the poem might be an eighteenth century forgery (see C. Ó LOCHLAINN, Poets on the battle of Clontarf, in: Éigse 3 [1942], pp. 211f., 216). Many thanks to Dr Katharine Simms, who enquired about the language of the poem for me, and confirmed the assumption that it might be a genuine medieval compilation.

[60] AT (990); AFM 1023.

[61] AU.

[62] For Ua Máelchiaráin see Appendix 1, AE7, G4.

[63] M. NÍ MHAONAIGH, Bréifne bias in Cogad Gáedel re Gallaib, in: Ériu 43 (1992), pp. 135-158, esp. 142-150, who suggests that one version of the Cogad was revised in the mid-twelfth century with an obvious Ua Ruairc-Bréifne bias.

As the allies of Cathal Crobderg they might have found admission amongst those who had the right of burial in Clonmacnois.

The lands mentioned as Uí Ruairc donations were situated in the territory of their vassals the Meic Ragnaill. They were lords of Muintir Eolais and, so the Registry claims, gave some additional lands in Killtoghert parish to St. Ciarán.[64] The territory of the Muintir Eolais comprised the south of county Leitrim. Ecclesiastical authority in the area was held, or claimed by St. Caillin, the founder saint of Fenagh. In the thirteenth or fourteenth century compilation, known as the Book of Fenagh, an impressive curse on those who fail to be buried in Fenagh is contained.[65] It seems to preserve a memory that Fenagh, at one stage the central burial place of the Conmaicne, was deserted for the sake of an apparently more attractive churchyard. Even though this might have concerned the neighbouring church of Cloone in the first place,[66] it seems plausible that the fame of St. Ciarán's church yard in Clonmacnois also spread in the territory of the Muinter Eolais and deprived St. Caillin of a substantial part of his income. Possibly this was the case in the tenth and early eleventh centuries, when propaganda for the salvation-bringing function of St. Ciarán's earth was much enforced. At that time the Muintir Eolais also supplied a famous *scriba* in Clonmacnois.[67]

7.6 The Mac Diarmada donations

The Meic Dhiarmada were a branch of the Síl Muiredaig of Connacht. They rose to power as the lords of Mag Luirg in the twelfth century and dominated the area around Boyle, comprising parts of the counties Roscommon north, Sligo and Mayo. The lands donated to St. Ciarán, Knockvicar (73), Killaraght (74) and Rahallon (75) are all situated in Mag Luirg. Knockvicar was the location of a Franciscan house in the later middle ages, while Kil-

---

[64] J. MEEHAN, Notes on the Mac Rannals of Leitrim and their country: Being introductory to a diary of James Reynolds, Lough Scur, county Leitrim, in: JRSAI 35 (1905), pp. 139-151.

[65] W. M. HENNESSY / D. H. KELLY (eds.), The Book of Fenagh, Dublin 1875, pp. 190-193; see also pp. 204f.

[66] Cloone seems to have been the graveyard for the Meic Ragnaill in the later middle ages, see e.g. AFM 1378.

[67] This was Odran Ua hEolais (AFM 994). See Appendix 1, S16 (d.995).

laraght is said to have been a Franciscan foundation. There is evidence for
early links between Clonmacnois and the peoples settled in the northern part
of Connacht, in the extended area of Mag Luirg. Amongst them were the
Gailenga, the Gregraige, the Luigne and the Dairtraige Coininnse, who from
the seventh to the ninth centuries supplied several abbots of Clonmacnois.[68]
Furthermore an accident which happened in the tenth century, testifies to the
fact that Clonmacnois exercised ecclesiastical authority in the territory
which later became Mac Diarmada's country. In the year 931, so we learn
from the Chronicon, the staff of Ciarán got lost in Lough Gara, and twelve
men drowned in the accident.[69] The precious relic certainly did not get lost
on a picnic of Clonmacnois clergy at Lough Gara, but would have been
brought to the Gregraige on a circuit, in order to collect the taxes and exercise supervision in the churches belonging to the *paruchia* of Ciarán in the
region. The Clonmacnois abbot at the time was Tipraide mac Ainnsine of
the Uí Briúin.[70] His family background is not further specified, but it is
possible that he was of the Uí Briúin in the north of Connacht, and therefore
intensified the ecclesiastical authority of Clonmacnois in his home country.
There is also evidence that the churches in the territory of the Gregraige
were at some stage under the ecclesiastical authority of Armagh. According
to a tradition, preserved in the Tripartite Life of St. Patrick, the saint was
once in the territory of the Gregraige of Lough Techet, i.e. Lough Gara, and
founded a number of churches, one of them being the convent of nuns in
Killaraght.[71] The Gregraige are portrayed as rather hostile to St. Patrick, and
are said to have thrown stones at him when he entered their territory from
the Uí Fiachrach over the river Moy.[72] It seems possible that this hostility

---

[68] Abbot Aedlug (d.652) was of the Gailenga of Corann, north of Lough Gara; Abbot
Cuiméne (d.665) was of the Cregraige of Loch Teched, i.e. Lough Gara; abbot Colmán
(d.683) was from Airtech, seemingly the *Crich Airtig near Lough Gara*. The same region
seems to have been the home of abbot Máeltuile Ua Cúana (d.877), who came from the
branch of the Luigne of Connacht, seated near Lough Gara; Abbot Martan (d.869) was of the
Dartraige, possible the Dartraige Coininnse. See Appendix 1, A8, A11, A12, A43, A40.
According to Tirechán the territory of the Gregraige in the late seventh century extended as
far east as Lough Key (see NICHOLLS, Some Patrician sites, p. 116).

[69] CS 930, AFM 930.

[70] Tipraide seems to have died shortly before the accident happened. See Appendix 1, A50.

[71] STOKES (ed.), Tripartite Life, p. 108.

[72] Ibid., p. 138.

originated from, or may be led to rival claims for ecclesiastical authority between Armagh and Clonmacnois.

The Registry's claim that the lands of the churches of Knockvicar, Killaraght and Rahallon once belonged to Clonmacnois could very well be founded on actual ecclesiastical authority which was exercised by the bishop of Clonmacnois in the northern parts of Connacht, around Lough Gara, in the early period.

7.7 The Mac Carthaigh donations

In a final section, the Registry names the claimed possessions of St. Ciarán in Munster. Mac Carthaigh is said to have given several churches in his kingdom to the church of Clonmacnois. Only three of them were readable in the copy used by the seventeenth-century scribe. However, evidence for links between Clonmacnois and Munster, and in particular the Mac Carthaigh family is very meagre indeed. Scattery island, Tuamgraney and Roscrea seem to have been the most southern boundaries of St. Ciarán's sphere of influence according to hagiographical evidence.[73] There is, however, a twelfth century church in Clonmacnois, known as Mac Carthaigh's church or *Temple Finghin*.[74] It might have originally taken its name from a saint named Fingen, to whom a church yard and a well in Clonmacnois was dedicated.[75] Later tradition associated the church with the Mac Carthaigh family, who in fact also had a special liking for the name Fingen. We suggested earlier that in the course of the compilation of the Registry in the thirteenth century under Cathal Crobderg, the allies of this king of Connacht found preferential treatment. Amongst them was one Fingen Mac Carthaigh, who fought in Cathal Crobderg's army in the course of the succession struggles for the kingship of Connacht.[76] He apparently in his youth was destined for an ecclesiastical career but had left the church to usurp the kingship of

---

[73] See above, pp. 87f.

[74] MACALISTER, Memorial slabs of Clonmacnois, pp. 145-150; PETRIE, The ecclesiastical architecture of Ireland, pp. 269-271; MANNING, Clonmacnoise, p. 30.

[75] CS 1013 (recte 1015) when the great oak of Fingen's churchyard was prostrated by a storm. For Fingen's well see AT (757, recte 758).

[76] ALCé 1202.

Desmond from his brother Domnall. For a brief period only, between the year 1206 and 1209 he could claim the title as king of Desmond.[77] It seems plausible that the donations in Munster, claimed in the name of the Mac Carthaigh family, went back to some hasty grants made by this claimant to the kingship, in the course of his alliance with the powerful king of Connacht in the early thirteenth century. The lands therefore might never have been under the ecclesiastical authority of Clonmacnois. They found admission in the Registry due to the very circumstances of the time of its thirteenth-century revision.

The same seems to apply to the Geraldine family, who are an exception as the only Anglo-Irish lords who appear in the Registry. They on their part might owe their status as benefactors of St. Ciarán to the circumstances of the late fourteenth century re-edition of the Registry. At that time the lord of Desmond acted as deputy to the king for Máel Sechnaill Ua Ceallaigh. It seems he was, like archbishop Muirchertach Ua Ceallaigh directly involved in the submission of the king of Uí Maine to Richard II. Part of their mission was to safeguard the lands of Ua Ceallaigh in Uí Maine against claims from the Butler lords of Ormond.[78] It seems plausible that for his merits the Geraldine family found mention in the Registry, and received the right to be buried in Clonmacnois, seemingly still an attractive reward in the later middle ages.

7.8 The abbatial lands

A further section of the Registry lists the livings belonging to the abbot of Clonmacnois. They consisted of half of the nun's land in Clonmacnois; five days in the nearby hill of Clonmacnois, possibly that on which the castle was built in the thirteenth century; half the income of the house of the dead, possibly Eglais beg, formerly the mortuary chapel of the monastery; half the tithes of Clonburren, the vicarage opposite Clonmacnois across the Shan-

---

[77] AI 1292; ALCé 1202; AI 1206; AI, ALCé 1209.

[78] E. CURTIS, Richard II in Ireland 1394-5, Oxford 1927, pp. 122f., 127f., for the letters to the king by Máelsechlainn Ua Ceallaigh and the archbishop. For Uí Maine as part of the Butler lordship for some time, since the late thirteenth century see C. A. EMPEY, The butler lordship in Ireland 1186-1515, Ph.D Thesis, Trinity College Dublin 1970, pp. 55-60; also ibid., Appendix II, p. xvi.

non; lands situated in Moore parish plus the lands of Ath Chiaráin, situated in Clonigormican parish, south of Tulsk (88-93). It seems very plausible indeed, that the abbatial lands in Clonmacnois should have been in the immediate surroundings of the ecclesiastical city. Moreover the list here finds confirmation through the lands named by Archdall as having been claimed by the Uí Mháeleoin, the former abbots of Clonmacnois, in the late thirteenth century. Like the present enumeration they comprised Clonburren as well as lands in Moore parish.[79]

There is also Ua Cillín (O Killyn) mentioned as the 'chiefe water cleark belonging to Cluain'. He secured his rights to two holdings in the parishes of Clonfert and Athlone (94-95).

Finally in what appears to be a seventeenth-century appendix to the Registry several families, the *O'Cobthy, O'Floinn, O'Hidersgoil, ... togither w[t]h O Tressey, O Cynnydhe and O'Cuaghan* are mentioned for having given alms to Clonmacnois.[80] These might simply have been families living in and around the late medieval parish of Clonmacnois, possibly still in the seventeenth century.

7.9 An attempt to reconstruct the extent of the lands under the authority of St. Ciarán

For the greater proportion of the lands listed in the Registry, there seems to be enough historical ground on which to base the assumption that they were, in the early period, genuinely part of the territory under the ecclesiastical jurisdiction of Clonmacnois. With the exception of the Cairpre Cruim proportion of the Ua Ceallaigh grant, the Mac Carthaigh and the Geraldine section, definite links between the respective benefactors and Clonmacnois can be established. On the basis of the evidence contained in the Registry we might therefore attempt to draw a picture of the extent of the lands in possession of the church of Clonmacnois prior to the church reform.

---

[79] ARCHDALL, Monasticon, p. 390. See above, pp. 175f.

[80] Registry, p. 459.

First of all there were the ecclesiastical lands very near Clonmacnois which seem to have formed part of the estate as agricultural acreage under cultivation. These were the fields in the vicinity of the church or monastery (*agellulís monasterio uicinís*) mentioned by Adamnán, when he talks about St. Colum Cille's visit to Clonmacnois.[81] These lands might have represented the *termon Ciaráin*, the lands belonging to the abbot, very near his church.[82] The whole area was possibly confined by the endpoints of the causeways mentioned repeatedly in the Registry as well as in the annals. There is the road from *Cluainlaigean to Cluain Finnlogh*, which is said to have been kept in repair by the Ua Máelseachlainn kings.[83] Also there was the causeway leading from Clunburren to the *Cruaidh of Failte* which still existed in O'Donovan's time, leading from the graveyard of the nunnery of Clonburren to Failtia townland in Moore parish. It is said to have been maintained by the Ua Ceallaigh lords of Uí Maine.[84] The road between *Cruan-na-Feadh to Iubhar Conaire, and from Iubhar to ye Logh* was to be maintained by Ua Ruairc.[85] This seems to have been a road leading west from Faltia, in Moore parish to *Iubhar Conaire*, the yew tree of Conor at the western borders of Moore parish.[86] The Registry might reflect a genuine tradition, concerning the maintenance of roadway, which is otherwise mentioned in the law tracts as a public obligation.[87] It can be very well under-

---

[81] ANDERSON / ANDERSON (eds.), Adomnán's Life of Columba, p. 24.

[82] CS 832, 833. Compare HUGHES, Introduction to A history of medieval Ireland, in: HUGHES, Church and society, chap. I, p. 20.

[83] Registry, p. 450.

[84] Registry, p. 457 n.3 and 4. Compare O'DONOVAN, Ordnance Survey Letters,co. Roscommon I, pp. 54-58, Letter from Ballinasloe, 18.6.1837.

[85] Registry, p. 452.

[86] Registry, p. 452 n.4; 459 n.3-5.

[87] Dr Colmán Etchingham pointed this out to me, refering to up to now unpublished work so that I take the liberty to quote from his letter on the subject: „ There are two references that I know of in the law-tracts to the public duty of keeping roadways clear; both are conveniently discussed in a major study of early Irish farming by Fergus Kelly, which will be published by next year and a typescript of which he very kindly gave me prior to publication. One reference is in a text which has not been translated and is printed in Binchy's *Corpus Iuris Hibernici* at p. 201, line 40f. This specifies that local farmers must clear the roads at the time of a public assembly (*óenach*) and also to facilitate lords travelling to exact due hospitality from their clients during the mid-winter 'guesting-season' (*aimser chóe*). This provision corresponds to one found in a second, short, text on roads, which Kelly edits and translates as

stood when we take into consideration the physical environment of Clonmacnois, which was basically situated in the middle of bogland. In fact,
recent ecxavations in the boglands around Clonmacnois brought to light a
number of wooden causeways, leading through the bogs, which could well
have represented the roads mentioned here.[88] We might deduce the approximate east-west extension of the ecclesiastical estate from these land-
marks, reaching from Clonfinlough in the east to the western borders of
Moore parish.

Apart from that there were streets within the 'city' of Clonmacnois,
which apparently were to be maintained by the respective abbots. There was
the heap of the three crosses, *Ulaidh na tri cross* as the central point from
where the roads led in the various directions. This is a little mount, to the
right hand side on the esker way, leading from Clonmacnois to the nuns
church in the east. There are three wooden crosses there today, which originally might have been stone crosses, each standing at the road leading east,
north and south from Clonmacnois which would have been in the west of
the junction.[89] In the year 1026 the road from the junction to the garden of
the abbess, presumably towards the nunnery was repaired by the abbot.[90]

---

an appendix to his book. A version of this text was incorporated in *Cormac's Glossary* of c.
AD 900 and is found in Kuno Meyer's edition (without translation) of the *Glossary*, p. 96 §
1082. This text contains an additional reference to the duty of local farmers whose land adjoins a road or open area adjacent to a king's stronghold (*dún*) to keep it clear. This is interesting because it relates to the best known reference to royal involvement with roadways
which is found not in the law-tracts, but in *Cogitosus' Life of Brigit* (§30 in Connolly's and
Picard's translation). Here a king ordains that the communities under his control construct a
roadway of rocks, branches and earth - partly over boggy terrain, which seems particularly
relevant to the context in which the Clonmacnoise causeways or *tóchair* may be supposed to
have been built."

[88] The excavations were carried out by Aenghus Maloney in Black Water Bog, and near
Clonfinlough, as well as in Clonfert Bog and Columba Bog on the west side of the river
Shannon. A report on the excavations will be published by Aenghus Maloney, who presented
his work in a paper, given at a conference in and on Clonmacnois, the 23rd of September
1994.

[89] Heather A. King suggested to me in a very helpfull discussion that this might have been
the original location of the three huge stone crosses now situated inside the walls of the
church yard, still known as the South Cross, the North Cross and the East Cross.

[90] The paved way from *Garrdha-in-bhainbh to hUlaiddh na ttri ccross* (explained by
Mageoghagan as the pavement from the garden of the nuns to the heap of stones where the
three crosses stand) was repaired by Bresal Conaillech in the year 1026 (AFM 1026; AClon
1026, p. 175).

Another road led from the junction to Cross Chomgall, and a third one to the western entrance of the settlement. Also there was a road from the *Cross of bishop Etchen* to *Irdom Chiarain*, the sacristy of Ciarán which might have been the ecclesiastical treasury. All these roads were repaired by the son of Conn na mBocht in the late eleventh century.[91]

Some of the lands in the city and its near surroundings are known by name. There is *Lios nabaidh*, the Abbot's fort, which seems to have been the name of an urban district within the settlement.[92] It has been suggested by Raighnall O'Floinn and others, that the house of the abbot was originally situated at the place where later the Anglo-Norman castle was built. It also seems possible that a bridge over the Shannon started off from here, since large stone and timber finds were made in the river, possibly the remains of a bridge. This might have been the brigde called *Cuirr Cluana*, which is mentioned in the Annals of Tigernach as having existed in the mid-twelfth century.[93] There was also the field of the milk cow (*Gardha na gamhnaighe*),[94] the fort of the gospel, *Lios-an-tsoiscela*,[95] the garden of Muiredach Ua Dubthaigh,[96] or the churchyard of St. Fingen.[97]

Other claimed lands were situated at a further remove from the monastic centre and seem to have originally belonged to churches which had come under the ecclesiastical overlordship of Clonmacnois. These churches in hagiographical language enjoyed the friendship of St. Ciarán, meaning they acknowledged him as their ecclesiastical overlord and paid their taxes. The

---

[91] AFM 1070.

[92] In 918 it is mentioned for the first time, as having been flooded by the Shannon (AFM 918). In the year 1135 it was plundered (AClon 1135, p. 194). According to Mageoghagan's annals fourty seven hoses at *Liseanabby* were plundered in the year 1205 (AClon 1205, p. 221).

[93] AT (1158); AFM 1158; AClon 1158, p. 204. R. O'Floinn made the suggestion, when giving a paper on 'Art and Patronage in Clonmacnois' at the conference, held the 23rd of September 1994. The suggestion was confirmed by Heather A. King.

[94] AFM 1150.

[95] AFM 1155; AClon 1153, p. 200, talks of *Lisan Tosgelty*.

[96] AClon 1135, p. 194.

[97] AFM 1013.

Registry specifies this relationship in the case of St. Ciarán's churches in south county Leitrim:

> whence it [recte in the MS: u] came that a comharb or corbe was sent from Cluain to Kill Tachuir .i. Dubsuileagh O'Conoil, who used to receaue the Bushop of Cluain's rents, and it was this, viz. Three Beeues and 3 hoggs at euery S' Martin out of Kill Tachuir, and two beeues and a hogg from euery one of the other six churches or chaples mentioned before in O'Ruairk's country, and the same O'Ruairk of his deuotion towards yᵉ church undertooke to repayre those churches and to keep them in reparation during his life uppon his owne chardges...

The taxes are set down in detail, they are payable once a year at St. Martin's day to the *comarba*, who would come as the bishop's deputy and collect the rent.[98]

Thus according to the evidence of the Registry, the land possessions of Clonmacnois further removed from the settlement itself, seem to have included holdings in Uí Maine, south county Roscommon, an area around Tulsk, in north county Roscommon, lands in the neighbourhood of Lough Gara, west of Boyle forming part of the counties Sligo and Mayo. Also there were lands in south county Leitrim, in the territory of Muintir Eolais, and finally the territory east of the Shannon, in counties Offaly and Westmeath, consisting of what later became the diocese of Clonmacnois, plus lands in Ardnurcher, Kilmanaghan and Kilcumreragh parish.

The focus of attention in the Registry is drawn to St. Ciarán's lands in Connacht, and the immediate vicinity to the east in counties Offaly and Westmeath. There might have been other parts to the original *Red booke*, which in the course of the two late medieval redactions of the document got lost. It seems, for example, plausible that the fourteenth-century scribe employed by an Ua Ceallaigh should omit the section concerning lands in a part of the country which was totally out of the sphere of interest of his patron. A similar Connacht bias might obviously have dominated the early thirteenth-century revision under the patronage of Cathal Ua Conchobair. Hagiographical material suggests that apart from the areas mentioned in the Registry, Ciarán had also authority over churches and their lands in county Louth, in the area around Devenish in county Fermanagh, in the territory around the churches of Fore, Roscrea, as well as on Scattery island and on the Aran islands.

---

[98] Registry, p. 452.

8 SUMMARY

The history of Clonmacnois was a history of change: everything began in the middle of the sixth century with a few houses erected at the shores of the Shannon, in the middle of one of the most boggy parts of Ireland, where a community of pious men had gathered to live their religious vocation. In the course of only two centuries the monastic settlement developed into a 'shinning and saintly city'. It had grown up under the secular patronage of the kings of Connacht, cherished friendship with the Uí Maine neighbours in the west and in the tenth century came under the influence of the Clann Colmain rulers in Mide. It had grown up despite ruptures, repeated caesurae imposed from outside like plaques, famine and armed attacks, which at times must have drastically diminished the number of inhabitants. A religious community was certainly a constant feature within the growing ecclesiastical establishment, although, already by the time of the eighth century most of the people in Clonmacnois would have been laymen, ecclesiastical tenants who lived with their families on the lands in and around Clonmacnois. The abbot governed the estate and administered the lands, but was no longer neccessarily a cleric. Very often, however, he was a member of a traditional Clonmacnois-dynasty, one of those families who over the centuries had managed to establish themselves in leading positions in the government of St. Ciarán's foundation.

The system lived by the dynamics between the secular and the spiritual dimensions which determined medieval life. The people in Clonmacnois, lay people as well as those who had taken vows, lived together under the idea of a common life in imitation and under the protection of St. Ciarán. The spiritual as well as the material needs of the individual members of the community were meat: those who worked in the service of St. Ciarán and his successors, could certainly count on an influential intercessor at the day of judgement. The community with its hierarchically structured organization gradually generated an ecclesiastical elite, which consolidated itself in the leadership of the estate. These families built their position upon a selfunderstanding as the heirs and the immediate executors of the founder saint. This structure of government turned into a decisive factor to guarantee stability, since it allowed for interaction with the outside world on equal terms with secular kings and lords, who in a comparable manner derived their status and power from royal ancestry. The patterns of leadership within the ecclesiastical settlement neatly fitted into the system of values on which social and political life in medieval Ireland relied.

This method of organizing community life functioned for over five centuries. It eventually collapsed in consequence of the changes brought about in the political and ecclesiastical landscape in Ireland in the course of the church reform and the Anglo-Norman invasion. Clonmacnois did not disappear, it came out of the transformations as the see of the bishop of one of the smallest dioceses in Ireland. For a start the descendants of the traditional ecclesiastical elite even took over episcopal dignity in the early years of the thirteenth century. Later in the fourteenth and fifteenth centuries many of the former 'Clonmacnois-family-names' can be traced in the administrative records, where they reappear amongst the local landowners on former monastic lands or amongst those running churches in the area. However, Clonmacnois had lost its position as a center of social, economic and cultural life within the medieval Irish church and society.

It remains to assess possible reasons. In the preceding chapters Clonmacnois has been described as an estate, from which power was exercised in terms of ecclesiastical overlordship. This seems to have meant in the first place money in return for friendship, probably including pastoral care, the provision with a priest as well as protection for the members of the *paruchia* of Clonmacnois. Evidence from the Registry of Clonmacnois, complemented by the study of the family background of the ecclesiastical officials, the literary statements concerning the respective benefactors of Clonmacnois plus the saga and hagiographical traditions about St. Ciarán, has been used to establish the approximate extent of the church lands. The taxes paid from these churches to their ecclesiastical overlord constituted the income of St. Ciarán's estate. The mechanisms of dependencies by which the many churches of St. Ciarán were bound to their overlord, were paralysed by the rearrangement of Irish diocesan structures in the course of the church reform. The individual churches came under the authority of the respective local bishop. Inis Cathaig (Scattery Island), for example, claimed itself episcopal status for a brief period, but later came under the jurisdiction of the bishops of Killaloe. The Clonmacnois-churches in the northern parts of Connacht, like Tawnagh, Killaraght or *Cellola Toch* became incorporated in the diocese of Achonry, Devenish and Inishmacsaint were eventually assigned to the authority of the bishopric of Clogher and St. Ciarán's lands in Uí Maine went to the bishop of Clonfert. The alienation of St. Ciarán's land was further enforced through the introduction of the new monastic orders in Ireland. We know that the nuns of Clonmacnois, who had adopted the Arrouaisian rule in the mid twelfth century were granted away to Clonard, the mother house of the Arrouaisian nuns in Ireland, by king Murchad Ua Máelsechlainn around the year 1144.[1] There is also evidence to support the assumption that Anglo-Norman nobles endowed their own monastic foundations in Ireland with lands formerly under the authority of St. Ciarán's successors. Richard Tuite seems to have donated parts of Clonmacnois' possessions in Ballyloughloe parish to the Cistercian house of Abbeylara in county Longford.[2] The Augustinian canons in Greatconell, county Kildare, might have received lands situated in Ardnurcher parish, which once used to belong to Clonmacnois.[3]

In short it seems that, at least in the case of Clonmacnois, the reorganization of the Irish church in the twelfth century brought about the gradual dissolution of the network of dependencies through which the bishop of Clonmacnois could claim ecclesiastical authority, and from which the successors of St. Ciarán drew their income. However, the urge for reform amongst the Irish from the late eleventh century, insinuated the already ongoing disintegration of the traditional system of values in Irish society, within which the ecclesiastical estate had once defined - and often redefined - its functional determination. Cogent influence from outside proposed new concepts of religious life, attracting those in search of a stricter observance. For Clonmacnois a situation arose, were the continuation of its very existance as an ecclesiastical centre was at stake. Its guiding principles, valid up to the twelfth century, its essential organizational structures as well as its traditional functions within Irish church and society, were endangered. In the course of time, all of these elements dissolved, and, in doing so, Clonmacnois itself passed from a living institution into the pages of history.

---

[1]   See above, p. 152.

[2]   See above, pp. 183-185.

[3]   See above, p. 225, n.39.

Appendix 1: Catalogue of the Members of the Community of Clonmacnois, Sixth to Thirteenth Centuries

Appendix 1.1 List of monastic officals

Abbots (A)[1]

A1. Ciarán mac in tsaír. Precise dates for the foundation of Clonmacnois or the death of Ciarán are not available. In the tenth century, at the time when the Clonmacnois chronicles were compiled or revised independently from the other annalistic compilations, it was apparently a well established fact that Ciarán, the founder saint of Clonmacnois died in the year in which Diarmait mac Cerbaill, the ultimate ancestor of the Southern Uí Néill kings of Mide, came to power.[2] The accession of Diarmait to the kingship is generally dated some time around the year 544, which would thus have been the year of Ciarán's death.[3] Ciarán is said to have been thirty-three years of age when he died and survived the foundation of the church of Clonmacnois for only a brief period (seven month or seven years?).[4] Tigernach and the Chronicon add that Ciarán was of the Latharna Molt, a branch of the Dál nAraide, a rul-

---

[1] For the abbots of the sixth to the eighth centuries see Ryan, The abbatial succession, pp. 490-507.

[2] AT (548); CS 544; AClon 547, p. 81; ACott 549; compare AU 549.1; AI 548. The same tradition, in a further elaborate version is preserved by St. Ciarán's Irish hagiographers, who claim that Ciarán help Diarmait mac Cerbaill to the kingship of Ireland (Stokes [ed.], Lives of Saints, pp. 130f.; AClon 569, p. 89).

[3] AU 544; Byrne, Irish Kings, pp. 90f.

[4] CS 544; Ryan uses the Irish Life of Ciarán to identify the year of Ciarán's death. There we are told that the saint died on a Saturday. The 9th of September, Ciarán's day of death, apparently fell on a Saturday in the year 545 (Ryan, The abbatial succession, pp. 491-493, §1). However Macalister, using the same way of argumentation came to the conclusion that 556 must have been the year in which the ninth of September was a Saturday (Macalister, Latin and Irish Lives, p. 159).

ing dynasty in Ulster.[5] According to the Dublin Life of Ciarán, however the Latharna were a people in Mide.[6] Mageoghagan, finally maintains that St. Ciarán's father was a Connacht-man.[7]

A2. A e n u [abb, AU; ab, AT; Ab, CS; second abott, AClon; abb, AI; abbas, ACott; abb, AFM] died in 570. Tigernach and the Chronicon add that he held the abbacy for twenty six year and was the son of Eógan of the Loígis Rete, a tribe in Leinster.[8]

A3. M a c N i s i [abb, AU; abadh, AT; Ab, CS; third abbot of Clonvicknoise, AClon; abb, AI; abbas, ACott; abb, AFM] died in 585. According to the Chronicon he was from Ulster.[9]

A4. A i l i t h e r [ab, AU; ab, AT; Abb, CS; abbot, AClon; abb, AI; abb, AFM] died in the year 599. Tigernach and the Chronicon add that he was of the Múscraige from Munster. During his abbacy Colum Cille came to visit Clonmacnois, whilst in Ireland for the foundation of Durrow.[10]

A5. T o - L u a t h e T a l l [abb, AU; abb, AT; Ab, CS; abbot, AClon; abb, AI] died in 614.[11] Tigernach has it that he was of the Corco Moga in Uí Maine.[12]

A6. C o l u m s o n o f B a i r d é n e [abb, AU; abbadh Cluana, AT; Abbad Cluana, CS; abbott, AClon; abb, AFM] died in the year 628. Tigernach adds a note concerning his origin of the Dál mBairdéne Ulaid, a people from Ulster settled in the area now represented by county Down.[13]

---

5   BANNERMAN, Studies in the History of Dalriada, pp. 1-8; BYRNE, Irish Kings, pp. 217, 109f.

6   PLUMMER (ed.), Vitae Sanctorum Hiberniae, I, p. 200.

7   AClon, p. 81.

8   AU 570.2; AT (569); CS 570; AClon 569, p. 89; AI 570; ACott 570; AFM 569; RYAN, The abbatial succession, p. 493, §2.

9   AU 585.1; AT (584); CS 584; AClon 587, p. 90; AI 587; ACott 585; AFM 589; his death is again recorded under the year 591; RYAN, The abbatial succession, pp. 493f., §3. *Ulaid* here is the territory now represented by the diocese of Down.

10   AU 599.1; AT(598); CS 599; AClon, 598, p. 97; AI 602; AFM 595; RYAN, The abbatial succession, p. 494, §4. Anderson /Anderson (eds.), Adomnán's Life of Columba, p. 24 §14a, compare above, p. 55.

11   AU 614.1; AT (613); CS 614; AI 615; AClon 617, p. 99; Mageoghagan makes two persons out of this abbot, one Lucaill whom he styles a brother of Ciarán, the other Folva who was abbot of Clonmacnois. RYAN, The abbatial succession, p. 494, §5.

12   This was a subject tribe of the Uí Maine, settled in county Galway, in the area situated between Mount Talbot, in the east and Kilkerrin parish to the west (O'DONOVAN [ed.], AFM II, p. 666, note n.; see also O'DONOVAN [ed.], The tribes and customs of Hy-Many, p. 84 note a.; BYRNE, Irish Kings, pp. 230, 234f.).

13   AU 628.4; AT (628); CS 628; AClon 627, p. 100; AFM 623; RYAN, The abbatial succession, p. 495, §6.

A7. C r ó n á n   m o c c u   L a e g d e [abbas, AU; ab, AT; Abb, CS; abbot, AClon; abb, AFM] died in 638. Tigernach has it that he was of the Corco Loígde.[14] This was a tribe at the south western coast of Munster, from which St. Ciarán of Saigir is said to have descended.[15] Abbot Crónán is sometimes thought to be identical with Crónán the founder saint of Tuamgraney, in county Clare, a church which in the tenth and eleventh century had close links with Clonmacnois.[16]

A8. A e d l u g   s o n   o f   C a m á n [abas, AU; ab, AT; Abbas, CS; abbot, AClon; abb, AI; abb, AFM] died in 652. According to Tigernach and the Chronicon he was of the Gailenga of Corann, settled in county Sligo, north of Lough Gara.[17]

A9. B a e t á n   m o c c u   C o r m a i c c [abb, AU; ab, AT; Abb, CS; abb, AFM] died in the year 664. The scribe of the Chronicon adds that he was of the Conmaicne Mara, who gave their name to Connemara in the very west of Connacht.[18] His origin is also given by the Four Masters but not in the Annals of Tigernach.

A10. C o l m á n   C a s [abb, AU; ab, AT; Ab, CS; abbott, AClon; abb, AFM] died in the year 665. Tigernach and the Chronicon give his origin of the Corco Moga of Uí Maine; his father's name Fulascach is added by Tigernach and the Chronicon.[19]

A11. C u i m é n e [abb, AU; ab, AT; Ab, CS; abbott, AClon; abb, AFM] died in 665, the same year as his predecessor, possibly of the plague in this year (*Buidhe Conaill*). According to Tigernach and the Chronicon Cuiméne was of the Gregraige of Loch Techet in Connacht, i.e from the area of Lough Gara in county Sligo.[20]

A12. C o l m á n [ab, AT; Abb, CS; abbott; ab, AFM] died in 683. He is the first abbot of Clonmacnois not listed in the Annals of Ulster. According to Tigernach and the Chronicon he was from Artech.[21] Mag nAirtig, south of Lough Gara, in the modern counties Roscommon and Sligo was, according to the Tripartite Life of Patrick, some time under the ecclesiastical jurisdiction of Armagh.[22]

---

[14] AU 638.2; AT (637); CS 637; AClon 637, p. 102; AI 640, where he is styled *abb Cille Dara*; AFM 637; RYAN, The abbatial succession, pp. 495f., §7.

[15] BYRNE, Irish Kings, pp. 170-173, 180f.

[16] GWYNN / HADCOCK, p. 46; for Tuamgraney see under A52.

[17] AU 652.1; AT (651); CS 649; AI 652; AFM 651; RYAN, The abbatial succession, p. 496, §8.

[18] AU 664.5; AT (660); CS 660; AFM 663; RYAN, The abbatial succession, pp. 496f., §9.

[19] AU 665.6; AT (664); CS 661; AClon 664, p. 107; AFM 664; RYAN, The abbatial succession, p. 497, §10; for the Corco Moga compare A5 .

[20] AU 665.6; AT (664); CS 661; AClon 664, p. 107; AFM 664; RYAN, The abbatial succession, p. 497, §11; BYRNE, Irish Kings, pp. 233-236.

[21] AT (679); CS 679; AClon 678, p. 109; AFM 681; RYAN, The abbatial succession, p. 497, §12.

[22] STOKES (ed.), Tripartite Life, p. 108; compare BYRNE, Irish Kings, pp. 234f. map.

A13. F o r c r o n [ab, AT; Ab, CS; abb, AFM] died in 686. Like his predecessor Forcron is not mentioned in the Annals of Ulster.[23]

A14. C r ó n á n B e c c [abb, AU; ab, AT; Ab, CS; abbot, AClon; abb, AFM] died in 694. Tigernach and the Chronicon add that he was of the Cuailgne. They were a branch of the Uí Méith, an Airgiallan tribe settled in what is now north county Louth, neighbours to the Mugdorna Maigen in county Monaghan.[24]

A15. O i s é n e, s o n o f G a l l u s t [ab, AU; ab, AT; Abbad, CS, abb, AFM] died in 706. According to a gloss in the Chronicon and the annals of Tigernach he was 'from Fremhain, in Calraige of Teptha'.[25] Ryan assumes that Fremhain was Dún Fremainne, west of Lough Owel, in the vicinity of Cró Inis, near Mullingar in modern county Westmeath, the ancestoral lands of the Clann Cholmáin dynasty.[26]

A16. F á i l b e B e c [abb, AU; espoc, ab, AT; Ab, CS; abb, AI; abb, AFM] latinized Failbeus Modicus, died in the year 713. Tigernach says he was a bishop and of the Gailenga Corann, settled in county Sligo north of Lough Gara. Abbot Aedlug came from the same branch (A8).[27]

A17. C u i n n l e s [abb, AU; abb, AT; abbot, AClon; abb, AI] died in the year 724. He was of the Sogan in Uí Maine, according to Tigernach. During his abbacy, in the year 723 Indrechtach mac Muiredaig, king of Connacht of the Uí Briúin is said to have died in Clonmacnois as a pilgrim.[28] The entries in the Chronicon Scotorum from the years 718 (recte 722) to 804 are lost.

A18. F l a n n S i n n a (a u i C o l l e) [ab, AU; ab, AT, abbot, AClon; abb, AFM], the grandson of Colla, died in the year 732.[29] Tigernach gives his name as 'Flaind Chualand', Flann of Cualu which associates the abbot with a territory south of Dublin in Leinster. How-

---

[23] AT (685); CS 682; AFM 684; RYAN, The abbatial succession, p. 497, §13.

[24] AU 694.1; AT (693); CS 690; AClon 689, p. 110; AFM 692; RYAN, The abbatial succession, p. 498, §14; BYRNE, Irish Kings, pp. 115, 118, in the early time they were vassals of the respective highking of the Uí Néill federation, in the first half of the eighth century (the reign of Áed Allán) they came under the domination of the Cenél nEógain.

[25] AU 706.1; AT (705); CS 702; AFM 704; RYAN, The abbatial succession, p. 498, §15.

[26] Donnchad Midi, king of Tara (d.797), ancestor of the kings of Mide, of the Clann Cholmáin is also called Donnchad Fremhann, in a poem added to his obituary by the Four Masters (AFM 792). BYRNE, Irish Kings, pp. 143n, 282.

[27] AU 713.2; AT (712); CS 709; AI 713; AFM 711; RYAN, The abbatial succession, pp. 498f., §16. He is the first abbot of Clonmacnois who is said to have been bishop as well; see also A49, A54, A55, A73.

[28] AU 724.4; AT (723); AI 724; AFM 720; RYAN, The abbatial succession, p. 499, §17. See AT (722) for king Indrechtach.

[29] AU 732.1, repeat the obituary in 733.9; AT (731); AClon 729, p. 114; AFM 726.

ever, Tigernach also states that Flann was of the Uí Chremthainn, an Airgiallan tribe settled quite a distance from Cualu, in the area of the modern counties Fermanagh and Monaghan.[30]

A19. C o n m a l (n e p o s L o c h e n i) [ab, AU; ab, AT; abbot, AClon; abb, AI; abb, AFM], the grandson of Lóchéne died in the year 737. The Four Masters state that he was of the Ciannachta Breg, a vassal state of the Southern Uí Néill settled on both sides of the river Boyne, in the area of what is now south county Louth.[31] The appearance of Ciannachta churchmen in offices in Clonmacnois has been interpreted as the result of links which existed between Clonmacnois and Inishkeen, the church of St. Daig mac Cairill.[32] The Ciannachta Breg, like the Uí Chremthainn of the Airgialla, were under pressure from the Cenél nEógain in particular during the reign of the highking Áed Allán (d.743).[33] This might have been an additional reason for the migration of churchmen from the north eastern parts of Ireland to the midlands.

A20. C e l l a c h s o n o f S e c n d e [ab, AU; ab, AT; abbot, AClon; abb, AFM] died in the year 740. According to Tigernach he was from the Conmaicne 'Buidemnaigh', very likely a branch of the Conmaicne in Connacht.[34]

A21. C o m á n [Pausatio Comani relegiosi, AU; Dormitatio Comáin releghiosí, AT; Coman the Religious Died, AClon; Comanus Rosíe uir sanctissimus in Christo quieuit, ACott; Comman ind Rois, + ba habb Cluana mic Nois esidhe, AFM] died in the year 747. He was abbot of Roscommon and Clonmacnois according to his obituary in the Annals of the Four Masters only. AU and AT give no information concerning the church which he belonged to. Tigernach adds that Comán was of the Sogan of Uí Maine.[35] In the year 744, the lex Ciaráni together with the lex Brendani was for the first time enforced in Connacht by King Fergus

---

[30] For Cualu see AU 819.1; the ale of Cualu was one of the symbols of power of the early kings of Leinster (see BYRNE, Irish Kings, p. 132, map, pp. 152f.; for the Uí Cremthainn see ibid., p. 115).

[31] AU 737.3; AT (736); AClon 734, p. 116; AI 737; AFM 732; RYAN, The abbatial succession, p. 500, §19; BYRNE, Irish Kings, pp. 68f., 89, 118.

[32] This has been suggested by Dr C. Etchingham in unpublished material on the paruchia of Armagh, which he kindly allowed me to read. Daig is sometimes referred to as bishop of the Ciannachta Breg (see HEIST [ed.], Vitae Sanctorum, p. 389, §1; see also §§4,7,16 for links betweeen St. Daig and St. Ciarán). Monastic officials from the Ciannachta Breg dominate in offices in Inishkeen during the ninth and tenth centuries.

[33] In the year 742 Conaing, son of Amalgaid, king of the Ciannachta was killed by Áed Allán (AU).

[34] AU 740.5; AT (739); AClon 737, p. 117; AFM 735; RYAN, The abbatial succession, p. 500, §20 thinks Conmaicne Buidemnaigh might be a mistake for Conmaicne Dúine Móir, who were settled in the area of the former barony of Dunmore in north county Galway. There were however other branches of the Conmaicne, settled in Mide, northern Tethba, and in south county Leitrim (see BYRNE, Irish Kings, p. 236).

[35] AU 747.12; AT (746); ACott 747; AFM 742 for Comman of Ross, styled abbot of Clonmacnois, AFM 746 for Comman the founder of Roscommon. The other alleged founder of Roscommon was the sixth century personality Comman, one of the disciples of Finnian; RYAN, The abbatial succession, p. 500, §20.a.

son of Cellach (d.751), which would support the idea that a Connacht men was abbot of Clonmacnois at the time.[36]

A22. L u c h r a i d [ab, AU; ab, AT; abbot, AClon; abb, AI; abb, AFM] died in the year 753, he was of the 'Corcelig' according to the Annals of Tigernach, which could be a contracted form of Corco Loígde, settled in the very south west of Munster, or Corco Roíde in West-meath.[37]

A23. C o r m a c [ab, AU; ab, AT; abbot, AClon; abb, AI; abb, AFM] died in 762. The annals of Tigernach give the Síl Cairpri as his family background, rendered by the Four Masters the Cenél Cairpre Chruim, who were the up and coming dynasty in Uí Maine at the time.[38] During the abbacy of Cormac, the battle of Móin Choise Blae was fought between the community of Clonmacnois and the community of Birr.[39]

A24. R ó n á n [ab, AU; ab, AT; abb, AFM] died in the year 764.[40] Tigernach says Rónán was of the Luaigne,[41] which might be a mistake for the Luigne, that at least is what the Four Masters thought.[42] They probably had the Luigne of Connacht in mind. Since from that area several Clonmacnois officials were recruited this seems quite a plausible assumption.[43] In the year of abbot Rónán's death the battle of Argaman between the community of Clonmacnois and that of Durrow took place. According to the Annals of Ulster a certain Bresal, son of Murchad with the community of Clonmacnois was the victor.[44] The Annals of Tigernach are lost for the following two hundred years from 766 to 973, so that for the fourty years between

---

[36] AU 744.9; see HUGHES, Church and society, chap. viii, pp. 103f. for the enactment of saint's laws in a territory, which was usually connected with the collection of a certain tax or tribute. Ciarán's law was promulgated in Connacht four times alltogether in the eighth and early ninth century, namely in the years 775 (AI); 788 (AU); 814 (AU).

[37] AU 753.3; AT (752); AI 753; AFM 748; RYAN, The abbatial succession, pp. 501f., §21; compare A7 for Corco Loígde.

[38] AU 762.3; AT (761); AI 762; AFM 757; RYAN, The abbatial succession, p. 502f., §22; Indrechtach mac Dlúthaig, of the Cenél Cairpre Chruim was king of Uí Maine from 750-755 (see KELLEHER, The Uí Maine in the annals, pp. 69ff.). However *Síl Cairpri* could also refer to the Cenél Cairpri, a branch of the Northern Uí Néill situated at the border to Connacht (see BYRNE, Irish Kings, pp. 248f.).

[39] AU 760.8; AT (759).

[40] AU 764.2; AT (963); AFM 759.

[41] *do Luaignib do* (AT [763]).

[42] *do Luighnibh do* (AFM 759). For the difference between the Luigne and the Luaigne see E. MACNEILL, Celtic Ireland, Dublin 1981, pp. 20, 57-58, 86; RYAN, The abbatial succession, p. 503, §23 assumes the Luigne here were those of Mide, in the counties Cavan and Navan; for the Luigne see also BYRNE, Irish Kings, pp. 67-69, 248f.

[43] S8 (d.857), S26 (d.1063). Their neighbours were the Gregraige and the Gailenga who likewise contributed to the provision of Clonmacnois officials.

[44] AU 764.6.

766 and 804, when the Chronicon takes up continuous recording again, we have no 'original' Clonmacnois chronicle.

A25. U a M i a n n a i g h [ab, sruithi Cluana M. Nois, AU], Miannach's grandson, abbot and senior of Clonmacnois died according to the Annals of Ulster in 768.[45] The title seems ambigious and maybe should be read as 'abbot of the seniors of Clonmacnois' (see Sen2).

A26. F o l a c h t a c h o f T e c h T u a [ab, AU; abb, AFM] died in the year 770. Tech Tua is Taghadoe, near Maynooth, in county Kildare. Kelleher thinks that Folachtach was of the Uí Chormaic Maenmaige, in Uí Maine and perhaps related with Fachtna, the abbot of Clonfert of who had died in the year 729.[46]

A27. F o r b a s a c h (n e p o s C e r n a i g h) [ab, AU; abb, AI; abb, AFM], a grandson or descendant of Cernach, died in the year 771. The Four Masters say that Forbasach was of the Uí Briúin in Connacht.[47] They rose to power in Connacht in the course of the eighth century, defeating their neighbouring tribes, the Uí Fiachrach (749), the Conmaicne (761) and the Uí Maine (770).[48] It is significant that during this period the Uí Briúin also provided the abbot of Clonmacnois for the first time (see also A34).

A28. C o l l b r a n n [ab, AU; Abbot, AClon; abb, AFM] died in 776.[49] In the last but one year of his abbacy the *lex Ciaráni* was again promoted in Connacht.[50]

A29. R e c h t n i a [ab, AU; abbott, AClon; abb, AI; abb, AFM] died in 784, the Four Masters say he belonged to the Cenél Cairpre Chruim (see A23).[51]

A30. S n é i d r i a g a i l [ab, AU; abbot, AClon; abb, AFM] died in 786, he was of the Calraige of 'Aelmhagh' according to the Four Masters, which O'Donovan thought to be identical with the Calraige an Chalad, in county Westmeath. Ryan suggests Calraige Droma Cliab, in north county Leitrim.[52] In the year of his death the Annals of Ulster report a horrible vision in Clonmacnois, which caused the whole of Ireland to do penance.[53]

---

[45] AU 768.3.

[46] AU 770.6; AFM 765; RYAN, The abbatial succession, p. 503, §24; KELLEHER, The Uí Maine in the annals, pp. 69, 71.

[47] AU 771.5; AI 771; AFM 766; RYAN, The abbatial succession, p. 504, §25. Links with the *mac Cernaig*, hereditary *oeconomi* in Armagh since the second half of the eighth century seem an attractive assumption, are however not possible since their eponymus ancestor *Cernach* died thirteen years after Forbasach in the year 784 (see Ó FIAICH, The church of Armagh, p. 78).

[48] BYRNE, Irish Kings, pp. 248-253.

[49] AU 776.4; AClon 769, p. 123; AFM 771; RYAN, The abbatial succession, p. 504, §26.

[50] AI 775; see above A21 (note) for St. Ciarán's law.

[51] AU 784.1; AClon 781, p. 126; AI 784, names him *Rechtabrat*; AFM 779; RYAN, The abbatial succession, p. 505, §27.

[52] AU 786.1; AClon 783, p. 126; AFM 781; RYAN, The abbatial succession, p. 505, §28.

[53] AU 786.3.

A31. M u r g a l [ab, AU; abb, AI; abb, AFM] died in 789, he was of the Uí Fiachrach, the most influential dynasty in Connacht before the Uí Briúin gained power in the course of the eighth century.[54] During Murgal's abbacy the *lex Ciaráni* was promulgated in Connacht for the third time.[55]

A32. S a e r b e r g [ab, AU; abbott, AClon; abb, AFM] died in the year 791.[56]

A33. I o s e p h (n e p o s C e r n a e) [ab, AU; abbott, AClon; abb, AI; abb, AFM], a grandson or descendant of Cerna, died in the year 794. The Four Masters say he belonged to the Ciannachta Breg, a branch subject to the Southern Uí Néill, settled in the territory of what is now south county Louth (see A19).[57]

A34. A n a i l e [ab, AU; abb, AFM] died in the year 799. He was of the Uí Briúin, according to the Four Masters.[58]

A35. F a i r c e l l a c h F o b a i r [ab*bas*, AU; Abb, CS; abb, AFM] died in 814.[59] He was of the Gailenga Mor according to the Chronicon, which resumes continuous reporting with the year 804. They were possibly a branch of the Gailenga of Connacht, seated at the river Moy, west of Lough Gara, neighbours of the Luigne and the Gregraige, who also supplied several officials in Clonmacnois.[60] In the year of Faircellach's death the *lex Ciaráni* was exalted in Connacht by Muirgius, son of Tomaltach, king of Connacht.[61] Again in the same year the annals record a joint campaign against the Uí Maine, by king Muirgius and Faircellach. It has been suggested that Faircellach here was the abbot of Clonmacnois, since he is the only person of this name mentioned in the annals at the time. The entry has been interpreted as an expression of hostility between Clonmacnois and the Uí Maine in the early ninth century.[62]

---

[54] AU 789.1; AI 789; AFM 784; RYAN, The abbatial succession, p. 505, §29; BYRNE, Irish Kings, pp. 231-233.

[55] AU 788.9. See above A21 (note).

[56] AU 791.1; AClon 787, p. 127; AFM 786; RYAN, The abbatial succession, p. 506, §30.

[57] AU 794.2; AClon 791, p. 127; AI 794; AFM 789; RYAN, The abbatial succession, p. 506, §31. There was Forbasach, another grandson of Cernach abbot of Clonmacnois, who died in 771. He was however of the Uí Briúin - so we have either a mistake by the Four Masters here or two different grandfathers with the same name. See A27 for Forbasach.

[58] AU 799.7; AFM 794; RYAN, The abbatial succession, p. 506, §32; compare A27 for the Uí Briúin.

[59] AU 814.7; CS 814; AFM 809.

[60] Gregraige: A11 (d.665), A43 (d.877). Luigne: ?A24 (d.764), S8 (d.857), S26 (d.1063).

[61] AU 814.11; see A21.

[62] AU 814.6; Kelleher suggested the campaign was performed in revenge of (a speculative) raid on the termon-lands of Clonmacnois by the Uí Maine (KELLEHER, The Uí Maine in the annals, p. 74). Byrne assumes a different connection. The bishop and airchinnech of the church of Aughrim (Echdruim) in Uí Maine was killed earlier in the year 814 (AU). Byrne speculates, that it was a dependent church of Clonmacnois, moreover that the Uí Maine had

Faircellach was from Fore, the church of St. Fechin, north of Lough Lene, in Westmeath. Several officials in Clonmacnois came from Fore during the ninth and early tenth century.[63]

A36. S u i b n e (m a c C u a n a c h) [ab, AU; Ab, CS; abb, AFM], the son of Cuanu, died in the year 816. The Chronicon adds that Suibne died only thirty days after the great fire, in which half of Clonmacnois was burned. There it is also stated that the abbot was from Connacht of the Uí Briúin Seola, the southern branch of the Uí Briúin seated in the former barony Clare in county Galway.[64]

A37. R ó n á n [ab, AU; Ab, CS; abbott, AClon; abb, AFM] resigned his abbacy in the year 823, but was back in office when he died in the year 844.[65] According to the Chronicon he was of the 'Laicchnibh Rois tethrach' possibly the Laigne of Ros Temrach settled in Navan.[66] It has been suggested, that Rónán resigned his office under pressure from the Uí Maine, since the Chronicon records the profanation of Clonmacnois by Cathal, son of Ailill, king of Uí Maine in the year of Rónán's resignation.[67] However, the entry reporting the violation of Clonmacnois by the king of Uí Maine appears to be a later insertion in the annals.[68] Moreover the attack was directed against the king of Munster, more precisely against his man in Clonmacnois, who was vice-abbot Flann. It seems more likely that the reason for abbot Rónán's resignation was linked to pressure from Munster, exercised increasingly during the reign of Feidlimid mac Crimthann. Eventually, after the king of Uí Maine had interferred in the conflicts on behalf of the community of Clonmacnois, Rónán resumed his office (see vA4, A38).

---

killed the airchinneach there, and that the secular and the ecclesiastical overlord together undertook a revenge campaign (BYRNE, Irish Kings, p. 252).

[63] GWYNN / HADCOCK, p. 36. Máel Mide, d.871 (vA9); Cormac, d.891 (vA11); Flann Fobair, d.922 (vA15); also possibly Cumuscach, d.835 (vA5). Mageoghagan tells the legend of St. Lorna, who after the death of the saint, carried St. Ciarán's bell to Fore, where it was kept henceforth (AClon 547, p. 83). A slab stone in Clonmacnois bears the inscription *or do fechtnach*. Petrie takes it that this was the grave stone of Fechtnach abbot of Fore, who died in the year 776 (AFM) (PETRIE, Christian inscriptions, I, p. 41, fig. 83). The slabstone inscriptions found and described by Petrie, which refer to members of the community will be cited henceforward, even though Macalister in a letter to R. Allen maintains that „Petrie's pictures are all wrong in each case" (British Library, MS Additional 37589, no. 370-388).

[64] AU 816.5; CS 816; AFM 811. See NICHOLLS, Some Patrician sites, p. 116 n.12.

[65] AU 823.6, reads *Ronan abbas Cluana M. Nois, reliquit principatum suum*; CS 823, 844; AClon 840, p. 139; AFM 842. Petrie found a cross in Clonmacnois with the inscription *Ronan*, which he dated to the ninth century (PETRIE, Christian inscriptions, I, p. 49, fig. 99).

[66] According to Hennesey, editor of the Chronicon Scotorum (CS, p. 144 n.1).

[67] Compare above, p. 100 n.39.

[68] According to the Chronicon the attack, in the course of which the vice abbot from Munster was drowned in the Shannon, happened in the year 823. The same source maintains that he was installed as vice-abbot in Clonmacnois in the year 827 (CS 827). The Four Masters report about the attack in an entry referring to the year 835 (AFM 834). Compare above, pp. 96-100.

A38. C é t a d a c h [ab, AU; Ab, CS; Abb, AI; abb, AFM] died in 850, he was of the Uí Chormaic Maenmaige in Uí Maine, and possibly got the abbot's chair with the support of Cathal, son of Ailill, king of Uí Maine.[69]

A39. C o n n m a c h [ab*bas*, AU; Ab, CS; abbot, AClon; abb, AI; abb, AFM] died in the year 868. The Chronicon give the *Cenél Echach Gall* as his origin, which should perhaps be read as *muintir Echar Gabul* or *Etar Gabul*, an unidentified monastic foundation in Leinster, attributed to St. Columba of Terryglass.[70]

A40. M a r t a n [ab, AU; Ab, CS; abb, AFM] died one year after his predecessor in 869.[71] The obituary in the Annals of Ulster reads *Martan abbas Cluana Moccu Nois + Daiminnsi, scriba, Niallán episcopus Slane dormierunt*, which looks like a joint obituary of three different people: Martan, the abbot, Daiminis, the scribe and Niallán the bishop. In the Chronicon *Daiminnsi*, alias Devenish forms part of Martan's title, so that he appears as abbot of Clonmacnois and Devenish at the same time. The scribe also adds that Martan was of the Dartraige of Devenish, near Lough Erne in Fermanagh.[72] A double abbacy in Clonmacnois and Devenish seem quite plausible since links between the two settlements are also attested otherwise.[73]

A41. F e r d o m n a c h [prin, AU; Princeps, CS; abb, AI; abb, AFM] died in 872. He is the first abbot of Clonmacnois, who bears the title *princeps* instead of *abbas*, according to AU

---

[69] AU 850.1; CS 850; AI 850; AFM 848 adds the following poem to his obit: *All have heard it, | both uncommon and common, | that an abbot at Cluain like Cedadach | will never again be seen*; O'DONOVAN (ed.), The tribes and customs of Hy-Many, pp. 37, 76, 77, 90, 91; KELLEHER, The Uí Maine in the annals, p. 77. See A37 for Cathal mac Ailella.

[70] AU 868.2; CS 868; AClon 866, p. 142; AI 868; AFM 866; according to O'Donovan they are identical with the Fine Gall, who descended from Eochaid, the father of Ailpin, who was King of Dublin in the days of St. Patrick and were seated at Dublin and in the east of the kingdom of Brega (O'DONOVAN [ed.], AFM I, p. 475, note b, p. 504, note z). For Echar Gabul see HEIST (ed.), Vitae Sanctorum, p. 228, §12; GLEESON / GWYNN, A history of the diocese of Killaloe, p. 37.

[71] AU 869.1; CS 869; AFM 867; there is some confusion in AU here, where *Daiminnsi* is (mis)taken as the name of a scribe.

[72] O'Donovan thinks this to be a mistake for *Dartraige Coininnsi*, which was the ancient name of the people settled in Dartry in county Monaghan (O'DONOVAN [ed.], AFM I, p. 510, note x).

[73] Máel Achaid, vice-abbot of Clonmacnois was also abbot of Devenish later in the ninth century (vA13). The houses are also linked according to evidence in the Life of Laisren (PLUMMER [ed.], Vita Sanctorum, II, p. 139, §32). There are three stones, referring to Martan or Marton, found in Clonmacnois. I suppose one of them must be the gravestone of abbot Martan here (PETRIE, Christian inscriptions, I, p. 26, fig. 40, *marthine*; p. 22, fig. 25, *martini*, and p. 50, fig. 103a, *or do martanan*).

and CS.[74] He was of the Mugdorna, an Airgiallan tribe settled near Louth, from which the Meic Cuinn na mBocht claimed descent.[75]

A42. E ó g a n   T o b a i r [abbas, AU; Ab, CS; abb, AI; abb, AFM] died in the year 877. He was of the Uí Chremthainn, of Airgialla,[76] who in the first half of the ninth century were competing with the Aithir and the Cenél nEógain for the abbacy of Armagh.[77] Possibly in consequence of this conflict Uí Chremthainn churchmen migrated to the midlands.

A43. M á e l   T u i l e   (n e p o s   C u a n a c h) [abbas, AU, Ab, CS, abb, AFM], grandson or descendant of Cuanu, died also in the year 877.[78] The entry in AU reports the death of the two abbots in a joint obituary, giving the impression that Eógan and Máel Tuile were abbots of Clonmacnois at the same time. In the Chronicon the two entries are recorded separately. Eógan is said to have died at the end of 876, and Máel Tuile in the beginning of 877. According to the Chronicon Máel Tuile was of the Luigne of Connacht, in a gloss is added *.i. do Grectraigib Arda*, Ryan assumes these were the Gregraige of Mag nAirtig, i.e. Artech south of Lough Gara. They were neighbours of the Luigne.[79]

A44. M á e l   P á t r a i c [Ab, CS; abb, AFM] died in 885, he is not mentioned in the Annals of Ulster. The Chronicon notes that he was of the Uí Maine.[80]

A45. M á e l   B r i g t e [ab, AU; Ab, CS; abb, AI; Abb, AFM] died in 892. In the Chronicon he is surnamed *na Gamnaidhe*, also we are told that he came from Gabar, further explained in

---

[74] AU 872.4; CS 872; AI 872; AFM 870. AU talks of the abbacy of Clonmacnois as *principatum* in the early ninth century already, at the occasion of the resignation of abbot Rónán (see A37 [AU 823]).

[75] BYRNE, Irish Kings, pp. 115f., 128; KELLEHER, The Tain and the annals, pp. 126f. For Ferdomnach's grave stone see PETRIE, Christian inscriptions, I, p. 30, fig. 51.

[76] AU 877.1; CS 876; AI 876; AFM 874. Flann Sinna, abbot of Clonmacnois in the first half of the eighth century was of the same origin (A18).

[77] Earlier in the century the Uí Chremthainn had been defeated by the Cenél n Eógain (battle of Leth Cam, 827) after which Airgialla became tributary to the the victors. The struggles for the abbacy of Armagh were connected with the struggle for the political supremacy between the Airthir, the Cenél nEógan and the Uí Cremthainn (see BYRNE, Irish Kings, pp. 116-118, 124f.; HUGHES, Church and society, chap. viii, p. 107; Ó FIAICH, The church of Armagh, pp. 78-83).

[78] AU 877.1; CS 877; AFM 874; the wording of the obituary in AU reads: *Eugan + Mael Tuile nepos Cuanach, duo abbates Cluana Moccu Nois in pace dormierunt*. There is a slab stone inscribed *Máeltuile* found by Petrie in Clonmacnois, which could refer either belong to this abbot, or the lector Máeltuile who died in 922 (S12) (PETRIE, Christian inscriptions, I, p. 32, fig. 56).

[79] BYRNE, Irish Kings, pp. 231f., 234f. map.

[80] CS 885; AFM 883; as a gloss in CS is added *oocig i. Lingaig*, which the editor corrects to *o tig inghine lingaig* signifying 'from the house of Lingach's daughter' (CS, p. 168 n.5). For Máel Pátraic's grave stone see PETRIE, Christian inscriptions, I, p. 34, fig. 61.

a gloss as *Ceall Ula dferaibh Umaill*.[81] The men of Umall according to Tirechán were settled near Croagh Patrick, in county Mayo near Westport. Máel Brigte was perhaps from Agh-agower?[82]

A46. B l a m a c [prin, AU; Princeps, CS; abb, AFM] died in the year 896. His father's name Tarcedach and his origin from Bregmaine is added in a gloss in the Chronicon.[83] Bregmaine, is the territory represented by the barony of Brawney in county Westmeath, at the eastern shores of Lough Ree, neighbouring the Cuircne. An anchorite of Bregmaine died in Clonmacnois in 1007 (An9).

A47. D e d i m u s was Blathmac's successor in the abbot's chair. He is known from the Chronicon only, according to which he was deposed in the year 901.[84] In the same year Máel Ruanaid the son of King Flann Sinna, was killed by the Luigne of Connacht. Perhaps the two events were related. Possibly Dedimus, like several of his predecessors, was of the Luigne or their allies. Abbot Dedimus was replaced in office by a certain Ioseph and became vice-abbot of Clonmacnois subsequently. He died in in the year 923 (see vA14).

A48. I o s e p h [ab, AU; Abb, CS; abb, AI; abbas, ACott; abb, AFM] succeeded to the abbot's chair after the (possibly forced) resignation of his predecessor Dedimus. He died in 904. His origin from Lough Conn (co. Mayo), of the Uí Fiachrach an Tuaisceirt is given in CS and ACott.[85]

A49. C o l m á n   s o n   o f   A i l i l l [prin*ceps* Cluana Iraird + Cluana M. No(is + scriba) + episcopus, AU; Princeps Cluana muc Nois et Cluana Iraird, CS; abbot of Clonvickenos and Clonard, a sage doctor, AClon; abb Clu[an]a Mac Nóis + Clu[an]a Iraird, AI; abb Cluana Ioraird, + Cluana mic Nóis, espucc + doctor egnaidh, AFM] died as head of Clonmacois and Clonard, a bishop and a scribe, in the year 926.[86] According to the Chronicon Colmán was of the Conaille Muirthemne, seated in what is now county Louth, a little north of the church of Louth. They were neighbours of the Mugdorna Maigen, from which the the Meic Cuinn na

---

[81]   AU 892.1; CS 892; AI 892; AFM 888; GWYNN / HADCOCK, p. 393.

[82]   BIELER, Patrician texts, pp. 152f., §38.4, where Patrick is said to have founded a church *in campo Humail* after he had stayed fourty days on Croagh Patrick (see also STOKES [ed.], Tripartite Life, p. 112). The name Máel Brigte appears twice on slab stones in Clonmacnois (PETRIE, Christian inscriptions, I, p. 39, fig. 81 and p. 42, fig. 84). GWYNN / HADCOCK, p. 28.

[83]   AU 896.1; CS 896; AFM 891. For Blathmac's grave stone see PETRIE, Christian inscriptions, I, p. 36, fig. 69.

[84]   CS 901.

[85]   AU 904.1; CS 904; AI 904; ACott 904; AFM 899. The Uí Fiachrach were a leading power in Connacht before the Uí Briúin began to dominate the kingship since the eighth century (see A31 and BYRNE, Irish Kings, pp. 84, 248f.).

[86]   AU 926.3; CS 925; CS 908; AClon 921, p. 148; AI 926; AFM 924 adds a quatrain to his obituary: *The tenth year, a just degree, | joy and sorrow reigned, | Colmán of Cluain | the joy of every tower died: | Albdann went beyond the sea.*

mBocht dynasty in Clonmacnois came.[87] The family of Colmán, surnamed *Conaillech* after their tribal origin, can be traced as an ecclesiastical dynasty down to the eleventh century.[88] Colmán's abbacy marks the heyday of Clonmacnois under the patronage of the Clann Cholmáin kings of Mide, during the reign of King Flann Sinna.[89] Close links between Clonard and Clonmacnois prevailed in this period, whereas the traditional links with Fore were no more cherished.[90] A stone church (*daimliag mór*) was built in Clonmacnois by King Flann and Abbot Colmán, in the year 909.[91] Probably around the same time the highcross known as the 'Cross of the Scriptures', standing in front of the main church, was built. In an inscription Abbot Çolmán is commemorated as the one who made the cross for King Flann. The inscription is accompanied by carvings, one of them showing two men holding a pole, which tradition interprets to be Ciarán and King Diarmait mac Cerbaill, the ultimate ancestor of the Clann Cholmáin, as co-founders of the church in Clonmacnois.[92] Finally during Colmán's abbacy, in the early tenth century, the 'Clonmacnois group of annals' starts to diverge con-

---

[87] KELLEHER, The Tain and the annals, 125f., suggests that the *Conaillech* of Clonmancois belonged to the Meic Cuinn na mBocht clann as well. See MURRAY, The Pictish kingdom.

[88] Members of the Conaillech family in Clonmacnois: Máel Tuile, son of Colmán, *fer léiginn*, died in 923 (son of the abbot? S12); Diarmait Conaillech *fer leiginn* (d.1000, S17); Bresal, *comarba Ciarain* (d.1030, A62); Ailill, son of Bresal, *sacart* (d.1044, P10). The father of Colmán might have been Ailill, son of Aengus, abbot of Old Kilcullen, east of Kildare (d.898 AFM). Many son of Ailill were active in ecclesiastical offices at the time and are listed in the annals: Áed, son of Ailill, died as abbot of Clonfert in 916 (AI, AFM 914); Máel Poil, son of Ailill, abbot of Inan, a bishop, anchorite and scribe died in the year 922 (AU 922.1; CS 921, AFM 920); finally there was Diarmait, son of Ailill, who succeeded his father as princeps of Old Killcullen. He died in old age in the year 937 (AU 937.1). It seems possible that the dynasty started the ecclesiastical career in Old Killcullen, and Colmán, son of Ailill became the founder of the Clonmacnois branch of the family.

[89] The story of Cairpre, a bishop of Clonmacnois, who is said to have been visited by the spirit of the father of King Flann (879-944), reflects on the friendship between the Clann Cholmáin kings of Mide and Clonmacnois (see B4).

[90] Compare BYRNE, The community of Clonard, p. 164. Flann Fobair (vA16) was expelled as vice abbot in Clonmacnois in 922. Only one more member of the community of Fore is mentioned in connection with Clonmacnois in the late tenth century (B16).

[91] CS 908; AFM 904, AClon 901, p. 144, calls the building the *church of the kings*.

[92] The inscription on the West face of the cross asks for a prayer for king Flann, son of Ma(elseachlainn), the king of Ireland. In an inscription on the East face the spectator is ask to pray for Colmán, who made the cross (for king Flann?) (compare above, p. 110 n. 76; Ó MURCHADA, Rubbings taken of the inscriptions, p. 50; see also PETRIE, Christian inscriptions, I, pp. 42-44, fig. 86-88; HENRY, Around an inscription: the Cross of the Scriptures at Clonmacnois, p. 44, who suggested that abbot Colmán himself might have been the architect of the stone church as well as the sculptor of the cross; MANNING, Clonmacnoise, pp. 36-39). The tombstone of Abbot Colmán, still visible in Clonmacnois in the mid-ninteenth century, has been described by PETRIE, Christian inscriptions, I, p. 51, fig. 104.

siderably from the Annals of Ulster. Independent chronicle keeping was begun in Clonmacnois.[93]

A50. Tipraide son of Ainséne [com, AU; Princeps, CS; Abb, AI; abb, AFM] died in 931. According to the Chronicon he was a Connacht man, of the Uí Briúin. The Annals of Ulster henceforward use the title *comarba Ciaráin* for the abbot of Clonmacnois; they add to Tipraide's obituary that he died after long suffering.[94]

A51. Ainmire Ua hAdlai [com, AU; Princeps, CS; abbott, AClon; abb, AFM] died in the year 948. He was of the Uí Mic Uais of Mide, according to the Chronicon. The Four Masters and Mageoghagan say he was abbot of Lackan in Mide as well.[95] The Uí mic Uais were an Airgiallan tribe, which became incorporated into the kingdom of Mide under the Southern Uí Néill. They were seated in what is now part of county Westmeath, west of the river Inny, between Lough Owel and Lough Sheelin. The church of Lackan was at the shores of Lough Derravaragh, in their territory.[96] Ainmire's next but one successor was of the same origin (A53).

A52. Ferdomnach Ua Maonaigh [com*arba*, AU; Abb, CS; abbot, AClon; abb, AFM] died the year 952. An interlined gloss in the Chronicon (in Mac Firbhisigh's autograph manuscript [Trinity College Dublin H.1.18]) states that Ferdomnach died in Glendalough and was of the Corco Moga, a subject tribe of the Uí Maine. According to the Four Masters Ferdomnach was abbot of Clonmacnois and Glendalough.[97] Rechtabra mac Maonaigh, (the abbot's father?) died as a priest of Clonmacnois in 948 (P4), one Muiredach Ua Maonaigh was abbot of Roscrea in the early eleventh century.[98] The family's surname, Ua Maonaigh, seems to derive from the *manaig*, the ecclesiastical tenants who lived around the church. It seems very plausible that these people should supply ecclesiastical officials in the church of

---

[93] MAC NIOCAILL, The medieval Irish annals, pp. 22f.; DUMVILLE / GRABOWSKI, Chronicles and annals, pp. 53-56.

[94] AU 931; CS 930; AI 931; AFM 929. A cross with a circular design bears the inscription *Annseni*. This is one of a group of crosses most characteristic for Clonmacnois with a circular expansion at the centre and semicircular expansions at the terminations usually filled with knotwork (MACALISTER, Memorial slabs of Clonmacnois, p. 25, no. 126; PETRIE, Christian inscriptions, I, fig 77, read the inscription as *ANNGENI*).

[95] AU 948.3; CS 947; AClon 943, p. 154; AFM 946.

[96] BYRNE, Irish Kings, pp. 89, 117, 120f.; O'DONOVAN (ed.), AFM I, p. 36 note r; GWYNN / HADCOCK, p. 396. In the early twelfth century the Uí Mic Uais of Mide appear as rivals to the Uí Mháelsechlainn kings of Mide (AFM 1106; P. WALSH, Uí Maccu Uais, in: Ériu 9 [1921-23], pp. 55-60).

[97] AU 952; CS 951; AClon 947, p. 156; AFM 950. MAC SHAMHRÁIN, Church and polity, pp. 138f., discusses the possibility that Ferdomnach's connection with Glendalough according to AFM might have resulted from a scribal mistake by the Four Masters. He comes however to the conclusion, that „the Four Masters do carry further entries linking the two foundations at points where lacunae occur in the other annals, which would suggest that they are relaying data from a lost Clonmacnois source...". For links between Glendalough and Clonmacnois compare also below B8.

[98] AI 1009.

their ecclesiastical overlord, and apparently even succeeded to assume leading positions in it.[99]

A53. C é i l e c h a i r   s o n   o f   R o b a r t a c h [com Ciarain + Finnian, AU; comorba Finnain ocus Ciarain, CS; abb Cluana M. Nóis + Cluana Iraird, AI; comharba Finnéin + Ciaráin, AFM] died in 954.[100] Céilechair like his last but one predecessor was of the Uí Mic Uais of Mide (A51). There might be a link with the Uí Robartaigh dynasty in Kells, their eponymous ancestor died the same year as Céilechair.[101] It was during Céilechair's abbacy that Congalach mac Máel Mithig, king of Mide of the Síl nÁedo Sláine granted perpetual freedom (soere) to the church of Clonard. Since Céilechair was head of Clonard and Clonmacnois at the same time, it is not unlikely that the privilege applied for both settlements.[102]

A54. C o r m a c   U a   C i l l í n [comorba Ciaráin ocus Comáin, ocus comarba Tuamagréne, ... Sapiens et senex, et Episcopus, CS; comharba Ciaráin, AFM] died in the year 966. The Chronicon also mentions him as the builder of the main church and a belltower in Tuamgraney.[103] The Uí Chillín were an ecclesiastical dynasty, active in Tuamgraney and Clonmacnois.[104] Several members of the family are commemorated on slab stone inscriptions in Clonmacnois.[105] The family belonged to the Uí Fiachrach Aidne, settled in the west of Connacht. The lord of the Uí Fiachrach Aidne had died in Clonmacnois, earlier in the tenth century.[106]

A55. T u a t h a l [com, AU; comarba Ciarain, ocus Episcop, CS; abb, AI; comharba Chiaráin, epscop + abb Cluana mic Nóis, AFM] died in the year 971, in consequence of a three days fast, according to the Chronicon.[107] His name was very frequent amongst the Uí

---

[99] DOHERTY, Some aspects of hagiography, pp. 315ff.; ETCHINGHAM, The early Irish church, pp. 105ff.

[100] AU 954.6; CS 953; AI 954; AFM 952.

[101] HERBERT, Iona, Kells, and Derry, pp. 82, 86, 91f., 99. Robartach (comarba, d.954), Ferdomnaig (comarba, d.1008), Robartach mac Ferdomnaig (comarba, d.1057), Domnall (comarba, d.1098) Máel Muire Ua Robartaigh (cenn in dísirt, ferlegind, d.1133), Ua Robartaigh, airchinnech of Louth (d.1081 AFM).

[102] AFM 949 (recte 951); HERBERT, Iona, Kells, and Derry, pp. 161f., 175.

[103] CS 964; AFM 964.

[104] Conall Ua Cillín was comarba Crónain, died in 1026 (AI, AFM 1026). Another Cormac Ua Cillín died as airchinnech of the guesthouse and vice-abbot of the Síl Muiredaig, in Clonmacnois in the year 1106 (CS 1102, see vA24).

[105] Petrie dates a stone with the inscription or do bran u caillen to the late ninth century (PETRIE, Christian inscriptions, I, p. 29, fig. 49). Another stone found in Clonmacnois bears the inscription or do ...Cillín icaneradin lecs [pray for Cillín, by whom this stone was made] (ibid., p. 72, fig. 165).

[106] Domnall, son of Lorcan, lord of Aidne died at Clonmacnois in 937 (AFM).

[107] AU 971.4; CS 969; AI 972.2; AFM 969. There are two slabstone inscriptions with the name Tuathal in Clonmacnois (PETRIE, Christian inscriptions, I, p. 23, fig 29; p. 25, fig. 35).

Muiredaig, the leading dynasty in Leinster.[108] Like bishop Dúnchad mac Suthainen (B8), abbot Tuathal therefore possibly belonged to the leading royal dynasty in Leinster, and had his ecclesiastical background in Glendalough.[109]

A56. D ú n c h a d   U a   B r a o í n [com*arba* Ciarain, optimus scriba + relegiosissimus, AU; comarba, CS; cowarb of St. Keyeran of Clonvickenois, a holy and Devoute anchorite, AClon; comarba Ciarain, ACott; abb Cluana mic nóis, sgnaidh + angcoire, AFM] died in pilgrimage in Armagh in the year 989. The exact date of his death, the 19th of January is interlined by a second scribe in AU. The Four Masters maintain that he was thirteen years in Armagh before his death and had intented to go back to Clonmacnois every year, but stayed in Armagh out of fear of the 'solicitation of the clergy' there. According to the same source he was the last saint who resucitated the dead in Ireland.[110] The Uí Braoín were an ecclesiastical dynasty in Connacht, based in Roscommon.[111] They were of the Síl Muiredaig, the branch of the Uí Briúin Ai of Connacht, from whom the Uí-Chonchobair kings of Connacht came.[112]

A57. M á e l   F i n n i a   U a   M a e n a i g h [com, AU; comarba , CS; comharba , AFM] died in the year 992. According to a gloss in the Chronicon he was the son of Spelan and of the Uí Beccon.[113] They formed a kingdom in the northern parts of Mide, situated north of Fore and tributary to the Southern Uí Néill.[114] The surname points to the abbot's descent from an ecclesiastical tenant (compare A52).

A58. U a   B e g u l á i n [Cumsgugadh .H. Begulain i cCluain muc Nois, CS] He was deposed, presumably as abbot, in the year 1002.[115] One Máel Pátraic Ua Begulain died as a

---

[108] Tuathal son of Augaire, who died as king of Leinster in 958 was the eponymous ancestor of the Uí Tuathal line (see MAC SHAMHRÁIN, The Uí Muiredaig, pp. 58f.).

[109] Links between Clonmacnois and Glendalough seem to be confirmed by annalistic evidence, since it has been observed by Mac Niocaill that central Leinster affairs are very prominent in AT, since the late ninth century (MAC NIOCAILL, The medieval Irish annals, p. 27).

[110] AU 989.1; CS 986; AClon 981, p. 160; ACott 989; AFM 974, 987 adds a poem in praise of Dúnchad by Eochaidh O'Flannagain: *The seat of Mach the treacherous, voluptuous, haughty | Is a psalm-singing house possessed by saints; | There came on within the walls of her fort | A being like Dúnchad O'Braein.*

[111] See AFM 1187; 1232, 1231, 1234 for other members of the family, also A67.

[112] BYRNE, Irish Kings, pp. 248-253, 234f. for map. See PINKMAN, Placenames of St. Mary's Parish, pp. 37f., for Ua Braoín, alias Ua Braeín or O'Breen as the chief family of Breagmuine, alias Brawney in county Westmeath, corresponding to the territory now represented by St. Mary's parish Athlone.

[113] AU 992.1; CS 990; AFM 991.

[114] BYRNE, Irish Kings, p. 89; O'DONOVAN (ed.), AFM II, p. 889, note t.; WALSH, Meath in the Book of Rights; RYAN, The abbatial succession, p. 508-521, here 515; a gravestone inscription in Clonmacnois asks for a prayer for Máelfinna (PETRIE, Christian inscriptions, I, p. 60, fig. 130).

[115] CS 1000.

priest in Clonmacnois in the year 1028.[116] Possibly this was one and the same person, who after his deposition turned to a life as a priest. The Uí Beguláin were a branch of the Uí Briúin Bréifne.[117]

A59. F l a n n c h a d   U a   R u a d á i n   [com, AU; comorba, CS; comharba, AFM] died a year after the deposition of Ua Beguláin in 1003.[118] He was from Uí Maine, of the Corco Moga, according to the Chronicon.[119]

A60. F l a i t h b e r t a c h   s o n   o f   D o m n a l l   [com Ciarain + Finnen, AU; comarba Ciaráin, ocus Finniain, CS; Comarba Cíarain, .i. Flaithbertach mcDomnaill, AI; comharba Ciaráin + Findein, AFM] died in the year 1014.[120] He was of the Clann Cholmáin and is commonly regarded to have been a brother of Máel Sechnaill Mór, son of Domnall, king of Mide at the time (980-1022).[121] Domnall, a son of king Máel Sechnaill, thus a nephew of abbot Flaithbertach, succeeded to the abbacy of Clonard in 1014.[122] The abbot's son Flann married Cantigern Ua Lachtnáin, the daughter of a lector from Clonmacnois (S23). Their two sons were kings of Mide in the late eleventh century.[123] The Annals of Clonmacnois have no entries for the years 1015-1021.

A61. M u i r e d a c h   s o n   o f   M u g r ó n   [com, AU; comarba, CS; comarba Ciarain, AI; comharba Ciaráin + Commáin, AFM] was Flaithbertach's successor in Clonmacnois. He died in 1025 according to the Four Masters he was abbot of Roscommon as well.[124] According to the Chronicon and the Four Masters he was of the *muintir Imligh fordeoraigh*, which might be Imbleach- Fiae, i.e. Emlagh in Meath,[125] or possibly another designation for 'Imbliuch Sescinn', near Lough Ennel, now in county Westmeath, a church under the authority of

---

[116] AFM 1028. The spelling of the name varies between *Ua Begulain* (CS) and *Ua Baoghalán* (AFM). The diphtong 'ao' changed to 'e' in the middle Irish period. Interchangeable use of the two was frequent at the time (T. F. O'RAHILLY, Irish Dialects Past and Present, Dublin 1932, pp. 31-34. Many thanks to Dr Damian MacManus from Trinity College Dublin for this reference and his advice).

[117] M. Ó DUÍGEANNÁIN (ed.), The Uí Briúin Bréifni Genealogies, in: JRSAI 64 (1934), pp. 90-137 and 213-256, here 213f.

[118] AU 1003.1; CS 1001; AFM 1002.

[119] For his grave stone see PETRIE, Christian inscriptions, I, p. 61, fig. 132: *or do flannchad.* ·

[120] AU 1014.9; CS 1012; AI 1014.3; AFM 1013; AU repeats this entry in 1015.8.

[121] BYRNE, The community of Clonard, p. 165.

[122] He died in 1019 (AU).

[123] WALSH, The Ua Máelsechlainn kings of Meath.

[124] CS 1023; AU 1025; AI 1025.4; AFM 1025. Another Muiredach son of Mugron died as scribe of Clonmacnois in 1076 (S29). A slab stone inscription in Clonmacnois reads *or do muredthach* (PETRIE, Christian inscriptions, I, pp. 75f., fig. 176).

[125] GWYNN / HADCOCK, p. 35.

Clonmacnois according to the Tripartite Life of Patrick.[126] An anchorite from *Imlech Fordeorach* had died in Clonmacnois in the year 751 (see An1); also there was an *airchinnech* of *Imlech Fia*, who according to the Four Masters died as a priest in Clonmacnois in the year 948 (see P4).

A62. B r e s a l   C o n a i l l e c h [com, AU; comarba, CS; comarba Ciarain, AI; comharba Ciaráin, AFM] died in the year 1030. He is praised in the annals for having paved the road leading from the garden of the abbess, to the *heap of the three crosses*, in Clonmacnois in the year 1026.[127] His soubriquet *Conaillech*, links him with the Conaille Muirthemne from Ulster, settled in what is now county Louth (see A49). Ailill son of Bresal, (the abbots son?) died as a resident priest of Clonmacnois in 1044 (P10).

A63. L o i n g s e c h   U a   F l a i t h é i n [com Ciarain + Cronain, AU; comarba Ciaráin ocus Cronain, CS; comarba Ciarain + Chronain, AI; comharba Ciaráin + Cronáin, AFM] died in 1042.[128] According to the Chronicon he was of the Cuircne - a subject tribe of the Southern Uí Néill, situtated in what is now county Westmeath.[129] The Uí Flaithéin were, like the Uí Chillín, an ecclesiastical dynasty wo had one foot in Tuamgraney the other in Clonmancois (see A54, A69).

A64. E c h t i g e r n   U a   h E g r á i n [com Ciarán + Coman, AU; comarba Ciarain Cluana muc Nois ocus Comáin, CS; comharba Ciaráin Cluana mic Nóis + Commáin, AFM], abbot of Clonmacnois and Roscommon, died in the year 1052. According to the Chronicon he died in pilgrimage in Clonard and was of the Sogan, in Uí Maine.[130]

A65. A i l i l l   U a   A i r e c h t a i g h [com, AU; comarba, CS; ard comharba, AFM] died in the year 1070. According ot the Chronicon he was of the Corco Roíde; the Four Masters maintain that, like his predecessor, Ailill died in pilgrimage in Clonard.[131] The Corco Roíde were a subject tribe of the Southern Uí Néill in Mide, seated in modern county Westmeath in the eastern neighbourhood of the Uí Mic Uais Mide and the Cuircni.[132]

A66. M á e l   C h i a r á i n   s o n   o f   C o n n   n a   m b o c h t [m. Cuinn cenn bocht Cluana M. Nois, AU; Maolciaráin mac Cuinn na mbocht, CS, Maolchiaráin, mac Cuinn na mbocht, comharba Ciaráin, AFM] died in 1079. The contemporary sources simply mention him as the

---

[126] STOKES (ed.), Tripartite Life, p. 78; see also the *Notulae*, where it is mentioned as a Patrician foundation (BIELER, The Patrician texts, p. 180, §19; ibid., p. 260 for identification).

[127] CS 1028, 1024; AClon 1026, p. 175; AU 1030; AI 1030.2; AFM 1030.

[128] CS 1040; AI 1042.6; AU 1042.2 (the surname *H. Flaithen* is interlined by a second hand); AFM 1042.

[129] BYRNE, Irish Kings, p. 89; Catasach Ua Garbain of the Cuircni died as lector of Clonmacnois in 1022 (S19).

[130] AU 1052.5; CS 1050; AFM 1052. For the Sogan see BYRNE, Irish Kings, pp. 230, 234f.; O'DONOVAN (ed.), The tribes and customs of Hy-Many, pp. 70-73, 159-165.

[131] AU 1070.9; CS 1067; AFM 1070.

[132] BYRNE, Irish Kings, pp. 69, 89 for map. The Uí Mic Uais of Mide were defeated by the Corco Roíde in 807 (AFM 807 note c). In post-Norman times the Uí Dalaigh, got control over the territory (AFM 1185 note n).

son of Conn na mBocht (see C1). Only the Four Masters style him *comarba Chiaráin*. They also state that in the year 1070 he paved two roads in the ecclesiastical settlement.[133]

A67. T i g e r n a c h U a B r a o í n [air*chinnech* Cluana M. Nois, AU; comarba Ciarain Cluana muc Nois, ocus Comain, CS; ardchomharba Chiaráin + Chomáin, AFM] died in the year 1088.[134] He was a member of an ecclesiastical dynasty in Clonmacnois who came from the Uí Briúin Aí of Connacht (see A56). Tigernach is sometimes, probably wrongly, assumed to have been the author of the so called 'Annals of Tigernach'.[135]

A68. A i l i l l U a N i a l l á n [com Ciarán + Crónán + M. Duach, AU; tanaise Abbad Cluana muc Nois, ocus comarba Crónán Tuama greine, et Mic Duach, CS; comarba Crónáin + Chiaráin, in t-escobb + in sruthsenóir, AI; tanaisi abbadh Cluana mic Nóis, Comhorba Crónáin Tuama Gréine, + comharba Colmáin Cille mic Duach, AFM] died in the year 1093. He was head of the churches of Clonmancois, Tuamgraney and Kilmacduagh. Like the Uí Chillín from Clonmacnois the family of Ailill was of the Uí Fiachrach Aidne (see A54).[136]

A69. M a c r a i t h U a F l a i t h é i n [comarba Ciarain ocus Cronain Tuama gréine, CS; comhorba Ciaráin + Crónáin Tuama Gréne, AFM] died in the year 1100. Four years before he died he went on pilgrimage to the territory of Magh Eli, the mensal lands of the Uí Chatharnaigh in the southern parts of Tethba, now represented by the parish of Kilmanaghan. He was plundered by the Muintir Tlamain, a subject tribe of the Uí Chatharnaigh in 1198, and apparently withdrew to Aghaboe, in what is now county Laois, where he died two years later.[137] Possibly he was forced to go on pilgrimage by ever increasing pressure from the family of Conn na mBocht, who supplied his successor in Clonmacnois. Macraith is the last abbot of Tuamgraney recorded in the annals.[138] The Uí Flaithéin were an ecclesiastical dynasty in Tuamgraney and Clonmacnois, belonging to the Cuircne (see A63).

A70. C o r m a c s o n o f C o n n n a m B o c h t [tanaiste abadh, AT; comarba, CS; tanaissi abbaidh Cluana mic Nóis, + fer sona, saidhbhir, AFM] died in 1103.[139] Cormac was the grandson of Conn na mbocht.[140] Ten years prior to his death, in 1093 he bought Íseal Chiaráin, an appurtenance of Clonmancois, situated in Ballyloughloe parish, from Ua

---

[133] AU 1079.1; CS 1076; AFM 1070, 1079. For a grave stone inscription with his name see PETRIE, Christian inscriptions, I, pp. 66f., fig. 149, pl. LXII, reads: *[or do ma] elchiarán.*

[134] AU 1088.3; CS 1084; AFM 1088.

[135] MACALISTER, The sources of the preface of the „Tigernach annals"; WALSH, Irish men of learning, pp. 219-225.

[136] AU 1093.2; CS 1089; AI 1093.14; AFM 1093. Not to be confused with Uí Nialláin, a branch of the Airthir, situated near Armagh, who supplied several equonimi in Armagh since the ninth century (Ó FIAICH, The church of Armagh, p. 82; BYRNE, Irish Kings, p. 118).

[137] CS 1092; CS 1096; AFM 1096; AFM 1100. COX, Historic Moyelly, pp. 238-241; for Aghaboe see GWYNN / HADCOCK, p. 28.

[138] GLEESON / GWYNN, A history of the diocese of Killaloe, p. 31.

[139] AT (1103); CS 1099; AFM 1103.

[140] Máel Finnén, son of Conn na mbocht was the father of Cormac (AFM 1056).

Flaithéin, then abbot of Clonmacnois and from Donmall son of Flann, king of Mide.[141] The church at Íseal Chiaráin appears to have been the residence of the Céili Dé in Clonmacnois, which apparently became the family residence of the Meic Cuinn na mBocht in the course of the eleventh century.

A71. F l a i t h b e r t a c h   U a   L o i n g s i g h [com Ciarain, CS; cowarb of St. Queran and venerable priest, AClon; comharba Ciaráin, + saccart mór, AFM] died in the year 1109.[142] He is commemorated in the Clonmacnois annals for having finished the roofing of the great church, which had been built by King Flann and Abbot Colmán Conaillech in the early tenth century (see A49). According to Mageoghagan Flaithbertach also finished the building of the tower end of the walls in Clonmacnois. All these works had been started under his predecessor in office, Cormac Mac Cuinn na mBocht (see B18).[143]

A72. G i l l a   C h r í s t   U a   M á e l e o i n [comarba Ciarain Cluana M. Nois sonus + sobarthu airchinnech chell nErenn, AU; Abb Cluana muc Nois, tobar ecna ocus deirce, cenn soma ocus saibriusa na hErenn, CS; ardchomarba Ciarain Cluana Muc Nois, cainell eneig + derci Lethe Cuinn, AI; abb comharba Ciaráin Cluana mic Nóis, tobar egna + désherce ordain + oireachais Leithe Chuinn, senn sonusa + saidhbhriosa Ereann, AFM] died in the year 1127.[144] During his abbacy further reparations were carried out in Clonmacnois. A church called the erdamh Chiarain was roofed in the year 1113. The renovations of the great belfry in Clonmacnois, begun during the reign of Abbot Cormac (A70), were finished by Abbot Gilla Chríst with the support of Toirdelbach Ua Conchobair, king of Connacht in the year 1124.[145] Also during his abbacy, the synod of Ráth Bresail, patronized by Muircertach Ua Briain, king of Munster was held in the year 1111. At the synod dioceses were created in Ireland, but Clonmacnois was not chosen as a bishopric. It seems that in response to this apparent injustice a local synod was held at Uisnech in the same year, where, under the lead of Murchad Ua Máelsechlainn and Abbot Gilla Chríst the arrangements of Ráth Bresail were revised and Clonmacnois was appointed as the diocesan centre the west of Meath.[146] The Ua Máeleoin family is sometimes said to have been a branch of the Uí Chonchobair, settled in Bregmaine, now Brawney, in county Westmeath.[147] The dynasty dominated Clonmacnois for the following century and remained acitve in the church in the area down to the later

---

[141] CS 1089; AClon 1087, p. 184, renders Íseal Chiaráin the hospital of St. Queran; AFM 1031 talks of Íseal Chiaráin as the house of Conn na mBocht. Liam Cox suggests, that Domnall, king of Mide might have had some rights to Íseal Chiaráin as as the grandson of Guaire Ua Lachtnáin, a scribe in Clonmacnois (S23) (COX, Íseal Chiaráin, pp. 6-14).

[142] CS 1105; AClon 1108, p. 189; AFM 1109.

[143] AClon 1100, p. 188; AFM 1104.

[144] AU 1127.9; CS 1123; AI 1127.9; AFM 1127. See PETRIE, Christian inscriptions, I, p. 69, fig. 154, and p. 70, fig. 160 or do Máel[eo]ain and Máeliohain eps.

[145] CS 1109; CS 1120.

[146] AU 1111.8; CS 1007; AFM 1111. MAC ERLEAN, The synod of Ráith Breasail.

[147] Royal Irish Academy MS 14. B 4: Notes relative to the O Malone family of Westmeath. In this case the Ua Maéleoin would appear as a close relative of the Ua Braoín (another ecclesiastical dynasty in Clonmacnois, who settled in Breagmuine). The territory corresponds to St. Mary's parish Athlone (see PINKMAN, Placenames of St. Mary's Parish, pp. 37f.).

middleages.[148] Gilla Chríst has sometimes, on doubious grounds been claimed to be the author of the Chronicon Scotorum.[149]

A73. D o m n a l l U a D u b t h a i g h [arch Bishopp of Connought and cowarb of St. Queran, AClon; Elefinensis episcopus, ocus comarba Ciarán Cluana mic Nóis, AI; Elfinensis episcopus + comarba Chiaran Cluana Mac Nóis, ACott; aird espucc Connacht, + comhorba Ciaráin, cenn eaccna + einigh an chóiccid, AFM] died in the year 1137, in Clonfert.[150] His family rose to power as an ecclesiastical dynasty in Connacht during the century of reform.[151] The Chronicon comes to an end in the year 1131 (recte 1135).[152]

A74. Á e d U a M á e l e o i n [comarba Ciarain Cluana Mc.Nois natus est, AU; cowarb of St. Queran of Clonvickenos, whoe for his great ritches , charity, and bountyfull hospitallity was called in generall the fountaine of all happiness of Leath Coyne, AClon; comharba Ciaráin Cluana mic Nóis, tobar sonusa + saidhresa Leithe Cuinn, AFM] died in the year 1153. He was born in 1098 according to the Annals of Ulster, which are missing for the years between 1134 to 1153.[153]

A75. T i g e r n a c h U a M á e l e o i n [comarba, AU; comurba, AT; comhorba, AFM] died in the year 1172. In the same year the death of Gilla Chríst, the son of the abbot, is recorded in the Annals of Ulster.[154]

A76. M á e l M o c h t a U a F i d a b r a (o r U a M á e l s e c h l a i n n) [abb, AU; ardab, AT; abb, AFM] died in the year 1173. The Annals of Ulster add Ua Máelsechlainn as alternative surname, which was accepted by the Four Masters.[155] According to the Chronicon one Máel Mochta, comarba Chiaráin was plundered by the Síl Anmchadha, and by Conchobar son of Mac Cochláin in the year 1145, in Clonfinlough, near Clonmacnois.[156]

---

[148] AConn 1461.16; AConn 1439.4.

[149] One of the manuscripts of the Chronicon (Royal Irish Academy MS 23. O. 8), has a prefixed title in which Gilla Chríst Ua Máeleoin is named as the author. The most reliable MS copy by an Dubhaltach Mac Fhirbhisigh (in Trinity College Dublin MS, no. 1292, formerly H. 1. 18) has however no title page, and gives no author. See HENNESSY (ed.), Chronicon Scotorum, p. xxxix.

[150] ALCé 1137; AClon 1136, pp. 194f.; AI 1137; ACott 1136; AFM 1136.

[151] Domnall died in 1136; Mauricius archiepiscopus Connachtie, died in 1150 (his garden in Clonmacnois is mentioned in AClon 1135, p. 194); Flannucan, episcopus Síl Muiredaig, died in 1168; Muirgius, primus abbas Buelli, died in 1174; Cadla, archiepiscopus Connachtie, died in 1201. See GWYNN / HADCOCK, pp. 98f.; GWYNN, The Irish church, pp. 231f.

[152] A supplement for the years 1141 to 1150 was added to the seventeenth century manuscript of the Chronicon by an unknown scribe (see HENNESSY [ed.], Chronicon Scotorum, p. xli).

[153] AClon 1153, p. 200; AFM 1153; AU 1098 (gloss in MS C).

[154] AU 1172; AFM 1172; AT (1172).

[155] AT (1173); AU 1173; AFM 1173.

[156] CS 1141; AFM 1141.

This might have been Maél Mochta Ua Fidabra, who held the abbacy in Clonmacnois for a time only, and was again appointed to the position in 1172, when the reformers with Anglo-Norman support eventually resumed strength in Clonmacnois. He must have been a fairly old man by then and survived his appointment to the abbacy for one year only. Another member of his family took over his office (A77) for the following eight years. They might have been related to the Ua Fidabra family in Armagh, who supplied an archbishop of the see in the early thirteenth century.[157]

A77. Máel Chiaráin Ua Fidabra [comarba ciarain, AFM] died in the year 1181.[158]

A78. Máel Muire Ua Máeleoin [abb, AU; abbott of Clonuicknose, a great and worthy house keeper, AClon; comforba Ciaráin Cluana mic Nois, ALCé; comarba, AConn; chomarba Chiaran Chluana Mac Nois, ACott; comarba, AFM] died in the year 1230. Mageoghagan styles him *a great and worthy house keeper* possibly in reminiscense of his ancestor and predecessor in office, Gilla Chríst, praised in his obituary as the *happiness and prosperity of the superiors of the churches of Ireland* (see A72).[159]

A79. Máel Chiaráin Ua Máeleóin [abott, AClon; ab, AConn; ab Chluana mic Nóis, ALCé; ab, AFM] died as the last abbot of Clonmacnois mentioned in the annals in the year 1263.[160]

A80. Tomás, abbot of Clonmacnois is mentioned by Archdall, when reporting about a conflict concerning lands, between the abbot and the bishop (Tomás Ua Cuinn) of Clonmacnois in the year 1268.[161]

[A81. Paule mc Teige, according to Mageoghagan died as *Cowarb or substitute of Clonvicknos* in the year 1384. According to the Annals of Connacht *Pol Mag Tethechan comurba Cluana* died in the year 1384.[162] Since the family was well established as an ecclesiastical dynasty in Cloone, it looks likely that Mageoghagan mistook *Cluana* here for Clonmacnois.[163]]

---

[157] Donatus Ua Fidabra was bishop of Clogher and since 1227 archbishop of Armagh (AConn 1237.3.) For his attempts to unite the diocese of Louth with Armagh see A. GWYNN, Armagh and Louth in the 12th and 13th centuries, in: Seanchas Ardmhacha 1, no. 1+2 (1954/55), pp. 1-11 and 17-37, here 32-34; see also SMITH, The Armagh-Clogher dispute, pp. 32-34.

[158] AFM 1181.

[159] AU 1230; AClon 1230, p. 233; ALCé 1230; AConn 1230.14; ACott 1230.

[160] ALCé 1263; AConn 1263.11; AClon 1263, p. 244; AFM 1263.

[161] ARCHDALL, Monasticon, pp. 390f.

[162] AClon 1384, p. 310; AConn 1384.8.

[163] Master Nichol Mac Teithechán of Cluain (i.e. Cluain Conmaicne in Leitrim) died in 1374 (AFM). Joseph Mac Teithechán bishop of the Conmaicne died in 1230 (AConn 1230.11).

[A82. N i a l l   O ' S h e r i d a n , is mentioned in a fourteenth century poem as late abbot of Clonmacnois.[164]]

[A83. C a h i r   M a c   C o c h l á i n   [airchinneach chluana mic nóis, AFM] died in 1539.[165]

Bishops (B)

B1. F á i l b e   B e c , abbot of Clonmacnois was also bishop, according to the Annals of Tigernach. He died in the year 713 (see A16).

B2. T u a d c a r   [Epscop Cluana muc Nois, CS] died in the year 889.[166]

B3. M á e l o d a r   [Epscop Cluana muc Nois, CS; epscop Cluana mic Nóis, AFM] died the following year, in 890.[167]

B4. C a i r p r e   C a m   [Epscop, CS; epscop, AFM] died in the year 904.[168] According to a note in the Chronicon the spirit of the father of king Flann, i.e. Máel Sechnaill, son of Máel Ruanaid appeared to bishop Cairpre. The story goes that Máel Sechnaill implored the bishop to make intercession for him, because he had failed to have a confessor during his life-time. No sooner had the poor soul got absolution than he pointed out to the bishop a treasure, which he once gained in a fight against the Norsemen.[169] Apart from this spiritual assistance for King Máel Sechnaill, bishop Cairpre was also involved in temporal affairs, acting as political negotiator on behalf of Flann Sinna, son of Máel Sechnaill, and king of Mide from 879 to 916. Cathal, the king of Connacht is said to have submitted to King Flann at the instigation of the clergy of Ciarán, under the leadership of Cairpre.[170] Close links between Clonmacnois and the king of Mide during the reign of Flann Sinna are also otherwise attested (see

---

[164] Mentioned by R. FLOWER, The Irish tradition, Oxford 1947, Dublin [2]1994, pp. 83f. The poem tells of the sorrow of Niall for his friend Murchad, who had in some way violated the solemnities of the Mass. Niall appears in a vision to one of the community of St. Ciarán and asks for intercession for the imperilled soul of Murchad.

[165] AFM 1539.

[166] CS 889. An inscription on a Clonmacnois slabstone reads *or ar tuathcharán*; Thuathcharán being the diminutive for Tuathchar or Tuadcar (PETRIE, Christian inscriptions, I, p. 45, fig. 91).

[167] CS 890; AFM 886.

[168] CS 904; AFM 899. Cairpre's gravestone, a cross bearing the inscription *or do corbriv crvm* is preserved in Clonmacnois. Macalister names a whole group of crosses in Clonmacnois the 'Coirpre Crom group'. They seem to be datable to the same period, the late ninth and early tenth century. Macalister assumes they are all cut by the same hand (see PETRIE, Christian inscriptions, I, p. 47, fig. 96; p. 49, fig. 98; MACALISTER, Memorial slabs of Clonmacnois, p. 45, no. 239; also pp. 98-100, for the artist who carved the crosses).

[169] For the tradition of the tale see above, p. 112 n.81.

[170] AFM 896; CS 899.

A49). The story about the *post-mortem* redemption of the king's father might therefore be a genuine literary product of the early tenth century.

B5. L o i n g s e c h [Epscop, CS; epscop, AFM] died in the year 920.[171]

B6. F e r d a l a c h [*episcopus*, AU; saccart, AFM] died in the year 922 (see also P2).[172]

B7. C o l m á n   s o n   o f   A i l i l l, *princeps* of Clonmacnois and Clonard is also styled *scriba et episcopus* in the Annals of Ulster. The letters preceding the title *episcopus* are completed by the editor as reading *scriba*, but possibly the original entry recorded the death of the abbot together with a second person who was a bishop (see A49).

B8. D ú n c h a d   m a c   S u t h a i n e i n [*episcopus*, AU; Epscop, CS; B. of Clonvickenos, AClon; espscop, AFM] died in 941.[173] The personal name of this bishop has strong Leinster connotations, and would appear to associate him with the Uí Dúnlainge. Moreover his father's name is highly unusual and only once recorded in the annals for a king of the Uí Muiredaig lineage of Uí Dúnlainge in the later ninth century.[174] A. Mac Shamhráin suggested therefore, that the bishop here was a son of the Leinster dynast of the Uí Dúnlainge, and attests to links between Glendalough and Clonmacnois.[175] In the year 952 an abbot of Clonmacnois died in Glendalough (A52). Also abbot Tuathal, wo died in 971 might have been from the Uí Dunlainge in Leinster (A55).

B9. Ó e n a c á n   s o n   o f   E c e r t a c h died in the y6ear 949. He was *airchinnech* of Eglais Beg in Clonmacnois and like his brother Dúnadach, a bishop as well (see AE3).[176]

B10. D ú n a d a c h   s o n   o f   E c e r t a c h [Epscop, CS; B. of Clonvickenos, AClon; espucc, AFM] died in the year 955.[177] Dúnadach was the father of Dúnchad (An8), and

---

[171] CS 918; AFM 918.

[172] AU 922.2; AFM 920.

[173] CS 941; AU 942.1; AClon 935, p. 152; AFM 940.

[174] The Four Masters mention *Suthenén mac Artúir* in an entry for the year 858 (AFM 856).

[175] For connections between Clonmacnois and Glendalough see above, pp. 61-63. See also MAC SHAMHRÁIN, Church and Polity, p. 139: „The increasing pressure to which Uí Dúnlainge was subjected in the early tenth century, ..., could well have prompted ecclesiastics from that kingdom to betake themselves to Clonmacnois, a foundation which had long retained a tradition of relative freedom from dynastic control." There was also Flann Ua Ceallaig, abbot of Glendalough who died in pilgrimage in Clonmacnois in the year 1030 (AU, AFM, ALCé, CS [1028]).

[176] CS 948; AFM 947; see AE3. See KELLEHER, The Tain and the annals, pp. 125-127, for the Meic Cuinn na mbocht.

[177] CS 954; AClon 950, p. 156; AFM 953; Mageoghagan adds here that Dúnadach was of the Uí Cheallaigh of Brega, whereas his brother Óenacán is said to have been of the Mugdorna Maigen according to the Four Masters (AFM 947); for the alternative ancestry of the Meic Cuinn na mBocht see KELLEHER, The Tain and the annals, pp. 125-127. A stone with the inscription *dunadach* is preserved in Clonmacnois (PETRIE, Christian inscriptions, I, p. 56, fig. 121).

great-grandfather of Conn na mBocht (C1). He and his brother Óenacán were tutored by Caínchomrac, bishop and *princeps* of Louth, who died in the year 903 (see AE3).[178]

B11. C o r m a c   U a   C i l l í n, *comarba* in Clonmacnois, Roscommon and Tuamgraney was also a bishop according to the Chronicon (see A54).

B12. T u a t h a l, *comarba* of Ciarán, was also a bishop (see A55).

B13. M a e n a c h   s o n   o f   M á e l   M i c h i l [Epscop, CS] died in 971, the same year as the abbot Tuathal.[179] There was a vice-abbot of Clonmacnois, called *mac Máel Mithil* (son of Máel Michil) in the late ninth century (vA12). His father's name might have become the family name of a dynasty in Clonmacnois in the tenth century.

B14. F l a n n   s o n   o f   M á e l   M i c h i l [ferleginn Cluana muc Nois, ocus Epscop, ocus aircinnech Cluana Deocra, CS; Lector of Clonvickenois, AClon; fear Leiginn Cluana mic Nois, epscop + airchindeach Cluana Deochra, AFM] died in the year 979.[180] As a bishop he was head of the monastic school in Clonmacnois and head of the church of Cloneogher in county Longford.[181] He came from the same family as his predecessor Maenach son of Máel Michil (B13, vA12).

B15. C o n a i n g   U a   C o s g r a i g h [sui Epscop, CS; sui epscop, AFM] died in the year 998.[182]

B16 M á e l   P ó i l [comarba Feichin, AU; Epscop Cluana muc Nois, et comarba Fechin, CS; epscop Cluana mic Nóis + comharba Fecheine, AFM] died in the year 1001.[183]

B17 C o n a i n g   s o n   o f   Ó e n a c á n [Epscop, CS; epscop, AFM] died in the year 1011.[184] Since according to the Chronicon he was of the Mugdorna Maigen, he was possibly another member of the Meic Cuinn na mBocht. His father's name Aodacain might be a variation of Oenagan, who was bishop and airchinnech of Eglais Beg in the mid tenth century (B9).

B18. F l a i t h b e r t a c h   s o n   o f   L o i n g s e c h [Epscop, CS; Lector and Bushopp, AClon; Mc Loingsich, fer legind Cluana M. Nois, quievit in Christo, AI; espuc + ferleighinn,

---

[178] AU 903; AFM 898.

[179] CS 969. A stone with the inscription *or ar maina...*, was found in Clonmacnois by PETRIE, Christian inscriptions, I, p. 30, fig. 50.

[180] CS 977; AClon 972, p. 158; AFM 977.

[181] GWYNN / HADCOCK, p. 32; MCNAMEE, Identification of certain placenames, pp. 16-20, identifies the church as situated in the vicinity of Ballynakill, in county Longford; P. GRAY, St. Ernan of Cluan Deochra, in: Ardagh and Clonmacnoise Ant. Soc. Jn. 2, no. 9 (1942), pp. 27-32. Compare J. P. FARRELL, Historical notes and stories of county Longford, Dublin 1886, reprint Longford 1979, pp. 66, 99, who locates Cluain Deochra, alias *Cloneogherie* somewhere near Clogher.

[182] CS 996; AFM 997.

[183] AU 1001; CS 999; AFM 1000.

[184] CS 1008; AFM 1009.

AFM] died in the year 1038.[185] There was Máel Choluim Ua Loingsigh, possibly a son of Flaithbertach, who was a scribe and priest in Kells, and died in Clonmacnois in the year 1061 (P12). Another member of the family was Flaithbertach Ua Loingsigh, abbot of Clonmacnois in the early twelfth century (A71).

B19. C o n n   n a   m B o c h t is sometimes wrongly assumed to have been a bishop (see C1).

B20. C é i l e c h a i r   (M u g d o r n a c h) [Epscop, CS; espoc, AT; bushopp; espug, AFM] died in the year 1067. The Four Masters call him *Mugdornach* and add that he was of the Uí Chellaigh of Brega.[186] This entry combines the two variant genealogies of the Meic Cuinn na mBocht, one claiming they were a branch of the Uí Chellaigh, a branch of the royal dynasty of the Síl nÁedo Sláine of Brega, the other stating that they were of the Mugdorna Maigen, a people in the immediate neighbourhood of Louth. Céilechair was most likely another son of Conn na mBocht.

B21. G i l l a   C h r í s t   U a   h E c h t i g e r n [Epscop, CS; espoc, AT; espucc, AFM] died in the year 1104. The Four Masters say he was *airchinnech* of Ardagh as well.[187]

B22. M u i r e d a c h   U a   M á e l d ú i n who died in 1106 was a bishop according to Magheoghagan. He was *secnab* according to the Four Masters which was the office traditionally held by the family (see vA21).[188]

B23. D o m n a l l   U a   D u b t h a i g h died in the year 1137. He was *comarba Ciarain* and bishop of Elphin (see A73).

B24. M u i r c h e r t a c h   U a   M á e l u i d i r [Episcopus Ua Maeludir Cluana Mac Nóis quieuit, ACott; espoc Cluana fearta, + cluana mic nois, AFM] died in the year 1186.[189] This man is said to have been present at the synod of Kells, but according to Ware he afterwards resigned the office.[190] His being bishop of Clonmacnois as well as Clonfert has been doubted.[191]

B25. C a t h a l   U a   M á e l e o i n [Cahall o'malone arch Bushop with the o'Neales and Connaught men; died the 8th of February, I mean the 8th of the Ides of February, he for his great riches, hapiness, learning, and many other good partes was held in great reverence, ended his life with a very happy and commendable end at Clonvicknose, AClon] died in the

---

[185] CS 1035; AI 1038; AClon 1038, p. 176; AFM 1038; see S22.

[186] CS 1064; AT (1067); AClon 1066, p. 179; AFM 1067. See KELLEHER, The Tain and the annals, p. 126.

[187] CS 1100; AT (1104); AFM 1104.

[188] AClon 1105, p. 189; AFM 1106.

[189] ACott 1186; AFM 1187. The Chronicon ends with the year 1131, or 1150, the Annals of Tigernach finish in 1178, and entries for the time between the year 1182 and 1200 are missing in the Annals of Clonmacnois: see AClonn, pp. 215f., where Mageoghagan complains about the *many leaves lost or Stolen out of the ould Irish Book which I Translate*.

[190] KEATING, Foras feasa ar Éirinn, vol. 3, pp. 314-316; WARE, De Praesulibus Hiberniae, p. 96, gives his name as *Moriertachus O-Melider*.

[191] GWYNN, The Irish church, p. 249.

year 1208.[192] The title seems rather pretentious and should probably be read 'high bishop with the Southern Uí Néill and with the Connachtmen'. Cathal's family held the abbacy in Clonmacnois in hereditary succession (see A73, A74, A75, A78, A79). Cathal was the first to assume episcopal honours, and possibly claimed episcopal authority in Mide and Connacht, by right of his family tradition as head of a church which held lands in both kigdoms, on both sides of the river Shannon.

B26. U a M u i r e c á n [episcopus, AU; bushopp, AClon; espic Cluana mic Nois, ALCé; epcsop, AFM] died in the year 1214.[193] His family was a royal dynasty in Tethba, and supplied several kings there in the eleventh century.[194] During that time many ecclesiastical dynasties from Tethba are found in Clonmacnois. The bishop's family apparently also cherished links with the Armagh associates Tynan and Antrim. Máel Muire Ua Muirecán was *airchinnech* of Tynan, a house associated with the Céili Dé in Armagh, he died in 1072.[195] Flann Ua Muirecán died as *airchinnech* of Antrim in the year 1096.[196] Ware mentions bishop Muirchertach as *Mureachus O-Murrechan, a learned man* and supposes that he was identical with *Muriertacum O-Murry*, whose name he says is preserved on a grave stone inscription in Clonmacnois.[197] The so-called Registry of Clonmacnois claims to have been composed in the name of *bishop Muirchertagh O'Muridhe*, possibly refering to this bishop here.[198]

B27. Á e d U a M á e l e o i n [epscob, AU; espuc Cluana, ALCé; epscop, AFM] drowned in the year 1220.[199]

B28. Á e d U a M á e l e o i n [bushopp pf Clonuicknos, AClon] died in the Cistercian house Kilbeggan in the year 1236.[200] A priest from Clonmacnois had chosen the same place for his retirement in 1196 (P16). Ua Finnén, bishop of Clonmacnois in the early fourteenth century was abbot of Kilbeggan before his appointment to the see of Clonmacnois.

---

[192] AClon 1206 (recte 1208).

[193] AU 1214; AClon 1213, p. 227; ALCé 1214; AFM 1213. In 1201 William de Burk plundered Clonfert and Clonmacnois, Mageoghagan talks of the *abbott* [abbey?] *of Malone and the bushop of Morican* (AClon 1201, p. 218).

[194] Ua Muirecán, alternatively spelt Ua Muirigán (AU 1072), Ua Muirecán (AU 1096), Ua Muirigén (CS 1091, CS 1097), also Ua Muirecáin (AFM 1066) and Ua Muireccein. For Ua Muirecean kings of Tethba see: Ua Muireccein, lord of Tethba (AFM 1038), Conaing (AFM 1066), Tadg (AFM 1066), Áedredan (AFM 1071), Domnall (AFM 1095, CS 1091), Cathal (AFM 1101, CS 1097).

[195] AU 1072; GWYNN / HADCOCK, p. 409.

[196] AU 1096, GWYNN / HADCOCK, p. 28.

[197] WARE, De Praesulibus Hiberniae, p. 97.

[198] Registry, pp. 459f.

[199] ALCé 1220; AU 1220; AFM 1219.

[200] AClon 1236, p. 235. Kilbeggan was found in the middle of the twelfth century by Mac Cochláin (GWYNN / HADCOCK, p. 137).

[B29. D a u i t m a c C e a l l a i g h, archbishop of Cashel who died in 1253 wrongly styled bishop of Clonmacnois in the Annals of Loch Cé.[201]]

Vice-Abbots, *equonimus*, *secnab*, *tánaisi* or *prior* (vA)

vA1. A i l m e d a i r [equonimus, AU; feirtighis, AFM] died in 797.[202] According to Ryan the *equonimus* was the office out of which the *secnab*, or vice-abbot developed.[203] The Four Masters add that Ailmedair was of the Síl Máel Ruanaid. This was another name for the Mac Diarmada family of Mag Luirg, who became an independent branch of the Ua Chonchobair dynasty of Connacht in the twelfth century; or the name might refer to the descendants of Máel Ruanaid, who lived in the early ninth century, and was the father of Máel Sechnaill, and grandfather of Flann Sinna, king of Mide of the Clann Cholmáin. In both cases the Four Masters' statement appears as an anachronism.

vA2. C ú C h i a r á i n [secnabb, AU; prioir, AFM] died in 809.[204]

vA3. C o n g a l a c h s o n o f I r g a l a c h [tanaisi Abbad, CS; prioir, AFM] died in the year 823.[205]

vA4. F l a n n s o n o f F l a i t h b e r t a c h [secnabad Muman, CS; prioir a Mumhain] was drowned in the Shannon by the king of Uí Maine, most likely in the year 834. He was a Munsterman, of the Uí Forga, a sept of the Múscraige Tíre, settled east of Lough Derg, in the northern parts of Munster little south of Birr.[206] The Chronicon reports with undisguised disaproval, that the vice-abbacy of Clonmacnois was given to a Munster man in the year 827.[207] This seems to have happened under pressure from Feidlimid, king of Munster. In this case his raids on Clonmacnois in the year 832 and 833 were probably the result of Clonmacnois's opposition to his man in such a high office in their church. Eventually the king of Uí

---

[201] ALCé 1253: *Dáuid mac ceallaig .h. Ghillaphadraic airdespuc C[luana mic Nois]*, *quievit*; AU 1253: *Dauid Mhag Ceallaig airdepscop Caissil quievit in pace*. See also AU 1263; AFM 1253. The abbreviation C. in ALCé has clearly to be read as Cashel, not as Clonmacnois. For a succession list of the bishops of Clonmacnois in the later middle ages see *A new history of Ireland*, vol.9: Maps, genealogies, lists, ed. Art Cosgrove, Oxford 1985, pp. 275-277. See also above, pp. 180-193.

[202] AU 797.2; AFM 792.

[203] RYAN, Irish monasticism, p. 273; see also p. 274, where Ryan suggest the *fer tighis* to be the early title for the guestmaster in Clonmacnois, it seem however obvious that it is the term used by the Four Masters for the equonimus of the original annals.

[204] AU 809.4; AFM 804.

[205] CS 823; AFM 821; CS 843 repeats this entry.

[206] BYRNE, Irish Kings, pp. 222, 172f., map.

[207] CS 827. The death of Flann is recorded in CS under the year 823, the entry seems misplaced here. AFM has the not concerning Flann's death for the year 834 (recte 835).

Maine interferred on behalf of St. Ciarán's community, killed the Munster vice-abbot and later installed a Uí Maine man as abbot in Clonmacnois.[208]

vA5. C u m u s c a c h   s o n   o f   A e n g u s   [secnap, AU; abbott of Clonickenois, AClon; prióir, AFM] died in the year 835.[209] One Ceallach son of Cumuscach, a learned and most talented young man, died as abbot of Fore in Mide in the year 868. Given the links between the two ecclesiastical settlements at the time, Ceallach might have been a son of the vice-abbot of Clonmacnois here.[210]

vA6. R u a i d r í   s o n   o f   D o n n c h a d   [secundus Abbas Cluana Iraird, tanaisi Abb Cluana muc Nois, CS; prior Cluana hIoraird + abb cheall noile archena, AFM] died in the year 838.[211] His parentage, together with the accumulation of ecclesiastical offices in his hand, suggests that he was the brother of Conchobar son of Donnchad, king of Tara of the Clann Cholmáin who had died in the year 833.[212] Since his obituary, unlike those of most other vice-abbots, is not recorded in the Annals of Ulster, it might be a later insertion, made when independent chronicles were kept in Clonmacnois. Ruaidrí, the son of Donnchad Midi, would have been an uncle of Máel Sechnaill, son of Máel Ruanaid, the father of Flann Sinna.[213] Possibly the reign of King Flann, in which Clonard and Clonmacnois were ruled by one head (see A49), was the time when the entry was inserted in the annals.

vA7. Á e d á n   [abbas Rois Cre, AU; prióir Cluana mic Nóis, + abb Rosa Cré, AFM] died in the year 839.[214]

vA8. Á e d a c á n   [tanaisi abbadh Cluana, + abb cheall niomdha, AFM] died in the year 867.[215] He is only known to the Four Masters.

vA9. M á e l   M i d e   s o n   o f   C u m u s c a c h   [secnap, AU; prioir, AFM] died in the year 871.[216] It is possible that he was the son of the vice-abbot Cumuscach son of Aengus (vA5), and thus a brother of Ceallach son of Cumuscach, the abbot of Fore. Given the possible connection with Fore, Máel Mide here might be 'Máel Meadha mall Fhabhrace' (Máel Mide, the

---

[208] See A37, also BYRNE, Irish Kings, pp. 220-223.

[209] AU 835.4; AClon 832, p. 136; AFM 834. There is the inscription *cumasa* on a gravestone in Clonmacnois (PETRIE, Christian inscriptions, I, p. 25, fig. 37).

[210] AU 868.1. For links between Clonmancois and Fore see A35.

[211] CS 838. The words *secundus abbas Cluana Iraird* in CS are written as an original gloss over the name of Ruaidrí (CS, p. 142 n.2.), see also AFM 837.

[212] AU 833; CS 832. King Conchobar was the father of Artrí, bishop of Armagh and seems to have supported him in the struggle against the rival abbot Eógan Mainistreach (see CS 827/832; also HERBERT, Iona, Kells and Derry, p. 72; BYRNE, Irish Kings, p. 282; BYRNE, The community of Clonard, pp. 170f.). For Ruaidrí's name in a gravestone inscription see PETRIE, Christian inscriptions, I, pp. 20f., fig. 20.

[213] BYRNE, Irish Kings, p. 282.

[214] AU 839.2; AFM 838.

[215] AFM 865.

[216] AU 871.9; AFM 869.

mild of Fore), mentioned in the poem by Enoch Ó Gillain, on the bodies interred at Clonmacnois.[217]

vA10. M a e n g a l [tanisi, AU; tanaisi, CS; prioir, AFM] died in the year 875.[218]

vA11. C o r m a c [prin*ceps* Fobair + tanisi ab*ad* Cluana M. Nois, AU; Princeps Fobair, ocus tanaisi Abbad Cluana muc Nois, CS; abb Fobhair, + tanaisi abbaidh Cluana mic Nóis, AFM] died in the year 891.[219] As head of Fore he was vice-abbot in Clonmacnois at the same time (for links between Clonmacnois and Fore see A35).

vA12. F e r g u s   s o n   o f   M á e l   M i c h i l [equonimus, AU; ferthighis, AFM] died in the year 894.[220] It seems his father's name became the surname of an ecclesiastical dynasty in the tenth century, when the family supplied two bishops of Clonmacnois (B13, B14).

vA13. M á e l   A c h a i d [tanu*si* Cl*uana* M. Nois, + prin*ceps* Daminis, AU; tanaisi Cluana muc Nois, et princeps Damainsi, CS; abb Cluana M. Nóis, AI; seacnabb, .i. prioir, Cluana mic Nóis, + abb Daimhinsi, AFM] was abbot of Devenish and vice-abbot of Clonmacois. He was killed in the year 896, by the Delbna Ethra in an act of revenge, because the son of the king of the Delbna had been slain by the community of Clonmacnois before.[221] Earlier in the century one Martan from Devenish was abbot of Clonmacois (A40).

vA14. D e d i m u s   U a   F o i r b t e n [tanaisi, CS; tanaised abbott, AClon] died as vice-abbot of Clonmacnois in the year 923.[222] It seems he was the same man who was deposed as abbot of Clonmacnois in the year 901 (see A47).

vA15. M á e l m u i c h e i r g e [feirthighis Cluana mic Nóis, AFM] died in the year 929 according to the Four Masters.[223] *Fer tighis* is the title used by the Four Masters for those officials styled *equonimus* in the annals of Ulster.[224]

vA16. F l a n n   F o b a i r [Dedmus .H. Foirbten, tanaisi Cluana muc Nois, quieuit; occus Flann Fobair uero anno uno interfuit et oem exprobrauerunt, CS] succeeded vice-abbot Dedimus for a year, but resigned apparently due to lack of support in the community.[225] He

---

[217] Edited by M. Stokes in Petrie, Christian inscriptions, I, p. 6, verse 13.

[218] CS 875; AU 875.1; AFM 873. An inscription reading *moen*, was completed by Petrie to Moengal (Petrie, Christian inscriptions, I, p. 45, fig. 92).

[219] CS 891; AU 891.4; AFM 887; see A35 for Fore.

[220] AU 894.3; AFM 889; Petrie, Christian inscriptions, I, pp. 35f., fig. 67 *fergus*.

[221] CS 896; AU 896.8; AI 896; AFM 891.

[222] CS 922; AClon 919, p. 147.

[223] AFM 927. A slab stone found by Petrie in Clonburren, in the neighbourhood of Clonmacnois, bears the inscription *or do Máel m[oich]eirg[e]* (Petrie, Christian inscriptions, I, p. 52, fig. 108).

[224] See vA1, vA12.

[225] CS 922. The MS reads *u° ano uno interfuit et oem expravert*. The abbreviation *oem* is probably a mistake for omnes. The meaning could be: 'And Flann Fobair came in between for one year and all reproached him'.

died happily and in old age as a bishop and an anchorite of Fore in the year 930.[226] Flann is the last of a series of vice-abbots of Clonmacnois who came from Fore.[227]

vA17. M u r c h a d   s o n   o f   R i a t a [Ab Ruis Comain, et tanaisi Cluana muc Nois, CS; abb Rossa Comain + prioir Cluana mic Nóis, AFM], abbot of Roscommon and vice-abbot in Clonmacnois died in the year 980.[228]

vA18. L o n g a r g   U a   M á e l d ú i n [secnab, CS] died in the year 1021.[229] His family held the vice abbacy in Clonmacnois in the eleventh and early twelfth century, over three generations and also provided a lector (vA21, vA23, S28). The Uí Máeldúin claim common ancestry with the Clann Cholmáin kings of Mide. Their ultimate ancestor Máel Dúin is said to have been a son of Diarmait mac Cerbaill, and a brother of Colmán Mór.[230]

vA19. D o n n g a l   s o n   o f   G o r m á n was *fer léiginn* in Clonmacnois and in Kells, the Chronicon Scotorum style him *tanaise Abbadh* (see S27).

vA20. C i n a o t h   U a   R u a d á i n [tanaisi Abbad, CS; tánaissi abbadh Cluana mic Nóis, senóir + cend athcomhairc, AFM] died in the year 1082.[231] Possibly he was killed in the raid on the Clonmacnois by Donnall son of Flann Ua Máelsechlainn in the year 1082.[232] The Ua Ruadáin family came from the Corco Moga in Uí Maine. Flannachad Ua Ruadáin was abbot of Clonmacnois in the early eleventh century (A59).

vA21. C o n c o b a r   s o n   o f   F o g a r t a c h   U a   M á e l d ú i n [secnab, AFM] died in the year 1089.[233]

vA22. A i l i l l   U a   N i a l l á n (d.1093) otherwise known as abbot of Clonmacnois is styled *tanaist abbot* in the Chronicon (see A68).

vA23. M u i r e d a c h   U a   M á e l d ú i n [bushop of Clonvickenos, AClon; secnab, AFM] died in 1106.[234]

---

[226] AU 930.2.

[227] See vA5 (d.835); vA9 (d.871); vA11 (d.891); vA12 (d.894).

[228] CS 978; AFM 979.

[229] CS 1019.

[230] From the genealogies in The Book of Lecan, fol. 178ᵛ; PENDER (ed.), The O'Clery Book of genealogies, p. 58, §764.

[231] CS 1078; AFM 1082.

[232] According to Mageoghagan (AClon 1080, p. 182): *Cwickney and others were slain by Donnell mc fflynn o'Melaghlin king of Meath on Loghry, and alsoe the houses in the church yard of the nunns of Clonvicknos together with their church was burnt.* The editor here suggests Cwickney to be a district in the former barony Kilkenny West, county Westmeath (AClon, p. 182 n.3). But the grammar of the sentence proposes a person rather than a territory; maybe *Cwickney* here stands for Cinaoth.

[233] AFM 1089; for the family see vA18.

[234] AClon 1105, p. 189; AFM 1106; see vA18 for the family.

vA24. C o r m a c   U a   C i l l í n [ard seacnab Sil Muiredaigh, ocus aircinnech tige aiged Cluana muc Nois, CS; Deane of the house of Clone, AClon; airchindech Tíghe aidheadh Cluana mic Nóis, AFM] died in the year 1106.[235] *Ard seacnab Sil Muiredaigh* seems to stand for the vice-abbot of Roscommon, the central church in the patrimonial lands of the Síl Muiredaig of Connacht. Possibly in his capacity as vice-abbot Cormac was responsible for St. Ciarán's churches in the territory of the Síl Muiredaig. In the battle of Corann, fought in the year 1087, Ruaidrí Ua Conchobair, king of Connacht defeated the Conmaicne under Art Ua Ruairc.[236] Cormac Ua Cillín participated in the fight, on the side of Ua Conchobair's army. According to the account of the battle in the Chronicon he carried the staff of St. Ciarán in front of the fighting Connachtmen, who, needless to say, were the victors.

vA25. G i l l a   a n   C o i m d e a d [Giolla an Coimdeadh mac Cuinn Dealbhnaigh, tanaisi Abbadh Cluana muc Nois, CS; Giolla an choimhdhedh, mac Mic Cuinn, tanaisi abbaidh Cluana mic Nóis, frí ré, AFM] died in the year 1128.[237] He might have been another member of the Meic Cuinn na mBocht. The Four Masters say he was vice-abbot for a time only, which should possibly be read as an indication that with the beginning of the Uí Mháeleoin rule the Meic Cuinn na mBocht were overthrown as a up to then leading dynasty in Clonmacnois (see A72). The original title of Gilla an Coimdead, might have been destorted by the seventeenth-century transcriber of the text. It seems possible that in the original Delbna was part of the vice-abbots title rather than of his name, like for example, *Gilla an Coimdead tanaisi Dealbnach*. If this be true it should be read in analogy to the title of Cormac Ua Cillín as 'vice-abbot of Clonmacnois, responsible for the churches in Delbna' (see vA24, vA26).

vA26. G i l l a   Í o s a   U a   B r a o í n [secnap ua maine senchaidhe sccribhighe, + fear dana, AFM] died in the year 1187.[238] No original Clonmacnois annals exists for this period. His connection with Clonmacnois is not explicitly stated by the Four Masters. Since Gilla Íosa came from one of the leading ecclesiastical dynasties in Clonmacnois the assumption that he was an official of the church of Clonmacnois seems justified (see A56, A67). His title *secnab Uí Maine* should possibly be understood in analogy to the title *senap Síl Muiredaig*, assigned to Cormac Ua Cillín (see vA24). Gilla Íosa Ua Braoín would thus have been vice-abbot in Clonmacnois responsible for St. Ciarán's churches in Uí Maine.

Priests (P)

P1. M á e l   B a r r f h i n n [sacardd, AU; sagart, CS; priest, AClon; saccart, AFM] died in the year 916.[239]

P2. F e r d a l a c h [ep*iscopus*, AU; saccart, AFM] died in the year 922 (see B6).[240]

---

[235] CS 1102; AFM 1106; AClon 1105, p. 189.

[236] AU 1087.6; AT(1087); CS 1083.

[237] CS 1124; AFM 1128.

[238] AFM 1187.

[239] AU 916.7; CS 915; AClon 910, p. 145; AFM 914.

P3. Guaire son of Máel Acain [sagart, CS; Priest, AClon; sacart, AFM] died in the year 944.[241]

P4. Rechtabra son of Maonach [primhsaccart Cluana mic Nois, airchinnech Imbleach Fia .i. Imleacha mBeccáin, AFM] died in the year 948.[242] The Four Masters explain *Imlech*, to be Imlech Fia', i.e. Emlagh in co. Meath (see A61). The abbot of Clonmacnois at the time was Ferdomnach Ua Maonaigh of the Corco Moga (A52) - the two were possibly related.

P5. Aengus son of Bran [saccart, + sruith senoir Cluana mic Nóis, AFM] died in the year 948.[243]

P6. Dubthach Ua Tadgáin [saccart, AFM; priest, AClon] died in the year 996.[244] His father's name was Dubhfinn according to the Four Masters. The Uí Tadgáin were the leading dynasty in Tethba, to which the Uí Chatharnaigh, the Foxes, belonged as well.[245] Adga Ua Tadgáin, son of Dubcenn, prince of Tethba had died in in Clonmacnois in the year 980. Dubthach was possibly a brother of this prince of Tethba.[246] Several of the slab stone inscriptions in Clonmacnois refer to the Uí Tadgáin.[247] The family also provided artists in the monastic community. The *cumdach* or shrine to contain the volume of the Stowe Missal, was made by a member of the family in Clonmacnois some time before the year 1052.[248]

---

[240] AU 922.2; AFM 920.

[241] CS 943; AClon 937, p. 154; AFM 942. Petrie reads the inscription *or do hu acan* on a stone in Clonmacnois as 'pray for Ua Acan', and suggests that Ua Acan became a family name, after Guaire's father Máel Acain (PETRIE, Christian inscriptions, I, p. 20, fig. 19). There is another stone with the inscription *or do guariu* (ibid., p. 55, fig. 117).

[242] AFM 948. GWYNN / HADCOCK, p. 35. The inscription *rechtar*, found on a slabstone in Clonmacnois might be a fragment of the name Reachtabhra (PETRIE, Christian inscriptions, I, p. 56, fig. 120).

[243] AFM 948.

[244] AClon 990, p. 163; AFM 996.

[245] See DOBBS, The territory and people of Tethba, vol. 71, pp. 101-110.

[246] AFM 979 (recte 980). *Duibhfind* might be a spelling mistake for 'Duibhcenn'.

[247] The most interesting one amongst them shows two inscriptions: The first reads *oroit do conaing* (or Cathail?) *mac conghail* and is obviously contemporary with the carvings on the stone and older than the second, which says: *oroit do dubcen mac thadggan* (PETRIE, Christian inscriptions, I, p. 48, fig. 98). There is Conaing son of Conghaile, king of Teathba who died in 822 (AU, AFM 821, CS 823). Other Uí Tadgáin inscriptions in Clonmacnois are: ...*ggán* (PETRIE, Christian inscriptions, I, p. 42, fig. 85) which is possibly the end syllable of Tadgán. One stone bears *or dó thadgan* (ibid., p. 48, fig. 97) as an inscription. There is also *tadgg*... (ibid., p. 50, fig. 103) and *or do th...gan* (ibid., p. 64, fig. 144).

[248] It bears the inscription *OR DO DUNCHAD HU TACCAIN DO MUINTIR CLUANA DO RIGNI* [pray for Dúnchad, descendant of Taccan of the family of Cluain, who made it.]. Dúnchad is not mentioned in the annals. See WARNER, The Stowe Missal, II, p. xlvi.

P7. C o n d m a c h   U a   T o m r a i r [sacart, + toiseach ceiliabhartha, AFM] died as chief singer and priest of Clonmacois in the year 1012.[249]

P8. F a c h t n a [ferleighind + sagart Cluana mic Nóis, airchinneach Fiondabhrach abhae, airchindeach indeidhnen, abb na nGaoidheal, AFM; lector and priest of Clonvickenos arch dean of Ffynnawragh, abbot of Hugh, archdean of Inenen, and abbot of all Ireland, AClon] died on his pilgrimage in Rome in the year 1024.[250] The accumulation of titles in the hand of this man seem suspicious, is however mentioned by Mageoghagan as well as the Four Masters. Fennor is a church a little south of Sláine, and Inan is situated about four miles north of Clonard, both in county Meath.[251] Links between Clonmacnois and Inan might have been cherished since the tenth century. One Máel Poil, son of Ailill appears as head of the church of Inan in the early tenth century.[252] He was possibly a bother of Colmán, son of Ailill, abbot of Clonmacois at the time (A49).

P9. M á e l   P á t r a i c   U a   B e g u l á i n [sagart, AFM] died in the year 1028. Abbot Ua Beguláin, who was deposed earlier in the century seems to have became a priest afterwards (see A58).

P10. A i l i l l   s o n   o f   B r e s a l [saccart foir Cluana mic Nóis, AFM], resident priest in Clonmacnois in the year 1044. Possibly he was the son of abbot Bresal Conaillech who had died in the year 1030 (A62).[253]

P11. M a c   S l u a g a d a i g h [uasal shagart, AFM] died in the year 1051. His name seems to belongs to the Uí Maine.[254]

P12. M á e l   C h o l u i m   U a   L o i n g s i g h [saoi + sagart Cluana mic Nóis, Ciaráin, ferleighind Cenannsa, eccnaidh derscaighth, AFM] died in the year 1061.[255] Donngal son of Gormán, another scribe from Kells was vice-abbot in Clonmacnois at the time (S27). Máel Choluim was possibly related to Flaithbertach mac Loingsigh, lector and bishop of Clonmacnois a generation earlier, who died in 1038 (see B18). The family supplied an abbot of Clonmacnois in the early twelfth century (A71).

P13. M á e l   C h i a r á i n ,   s o n   o f   C o r m a c   s o n   o f   C o n n   n a   m B o c h t [uasal shaccart tuir crabhaidhm + eccnae uasal chend Cluana mic Nois, AFM] died in the year 1134.[256] He was the son of abbot Cormac (A70), and the grandson of Conn na mbocht (C1). His brother Céilechair died the same year (see Sen10). According to the Four Masters both died in *Iomdhaidh Chiaráin* (*imleach Chiaráin*) the bed of Ciarán, which seems to have been

---

[249] AFM 1011.

[250] AClon 1024, p. 174; AFM 1024.

[251] GWYNN / HADCOCK, pp. 36f.

[252] ETCHINGHAM, Bishops in the early Irish church.

[253] AFM 1044.

[254] AFM 1051; see KELLEHER, The Uí Maine in the annals, p. 104.

[255] AFM 1061; see S24.

[256] AFM 1134.

the name of a chaple in Clonmacnois, possibly *Eglais Beg*, where St. Ciarán himself is said to have died.

P14. G a l l b r a t s o n o f D u a r i c U a T a d g á i n [sagart mor, AFM] died in the year 1168 (see P6 for his family).[257]

P15. C o n g a l a c h U a T o m a l t a i g h [ferleighind Cluana-mac Nois + uasalshaccart, AU; uasal shaccart, + airdfherleighinn Cluana mic Nóis + saoi segna na nGaoidheal, AFM], lector and a priest died in the year 1169.[258]

P16. U a C a t h a r n a i g h [...aigh hI Catarnaigh sacart mor Cluana mic Nois, ALCé] died as a novice in the Cistercian house of Kilbeggan in the year 1196. The Uí Chatharnaigh, surnamed *na Sionnaig*, the Foxes, were the leading dynasty in Tethba (see P6).[259]

Scribes, Lectors and Wise men (S)

S1. M a c C ú C h u m b a , the son of Cú Chumba [scriba, AU; sccribhneoir, AFM] died in 730.[260]

S2. D e d i m u s , grandson of Lígán [Mors Dedimi nepo*tis* Ligain sapientis Cluana, AU] died in the year 752.[261]

S3. G a l l b r a n U a L i n g á i n [scribhneoir, AFM] died in 773.[262]

S4. C o l g u U a D u i n a c h d a [ferleighind, AFM] died in the year 794. He is described as the one who composed the Scuaip-Crabhaid, the 'Bosom of Devotion'.[263]

S5. C o n n m a c h s o n o f M u i r m i d (n e p o s G u a i r e O i d n i) [scriba, AU; scribhneoir, AFM] died in the year 798.[264] According to the Annals of Ulster he was a descendant of Guaire Aidne, king of Connacht of the Uí Fiachrach Aidne. The Uí Chillín family in Clonmacnois came also of the Uí Fiachrach Aidne, who were seated in the south of Connacht at the border to Munster and provided several kings of Connacht prior to the eighth century when the Uí Briúin took the leading part in Connacht politics. King Guaire Aidne was a famous patron of the north-Munster churches such as Inis Celtra, Tuamgraney or Kilmacduagh. Links between these houses and Clonmacnois are attested to especially for the

---

[257] AFM 1168.

[258] AU 1169, see S32.

[259] ALCé 1196 the beginning of the name is unreadable in the MS.

[260] AU 730.5; AFM 724.

[261] AU 752.13.

[262] AFM 768.

[263] AFM 789, p. 396 note f, where O'Donovan cites Colgan.

[264] AU 798.3; AFM 793.

eleventh century. Two eighth century abbots of Tuamgraney appear to have been descendants of this king.[265]

S6. T u a t h a l   s o n   o f   D u - D u b t e a [scriba ocus doctor, AU; scribhneóir, egnaidh, + doctor, AFM] died in the year 814.[266] Eochu, a grandson of Tuathal(nepos Tuathail) died as an anchorite and bishop-abbot of Louth in the year 822.[267] It is possible that this man, as abbot of Louth was the grandson of a scribe of Clonmacnois.

S7. D u b i n s e [sgribhneóir, AFM] died in the year 819.[268]

S8. M á e l   A e n a   s o n   o f   O l b r a n d [fear leighinn, AFM] died in the year 857.[269] Like abbot Máel Tuile Ua Cuana, who died in 877, Máel Aena was of the Luigne of Connacht (see A43).

S9. L u c h a i r é n,   s o n   o f   E ó g a n [scribhnid, + angcoire, AFM] died in the year 865.[270] He is the first scribe, supplied by the Meic Cuinn na mBocht (see An5).

S10. S u i b n e   s o n   o f   M á e l   U m a i [ancorita + scriba optimus, AU; ancorita, CS; angcoire, + scribhnidh, AFM] died in the year 891.[271] The fame of Suibne's learnedness spread outside Ireland, he is mentioned as *Swifnch* in the Anglo-Saxon Chronicle. His tombstone with the inscription *suibine mac Máelaehumai* is described by Petrie.[272]

S11. S c a n n l a n   s o n   o f   G o r m á n [Scannal Roiss Cree + scriba Cluana m. Nois, AU; eccnaidh, scribhnidh toghaidhe, + abb Rossa Cre, AFM] died in the year 920.[273] He was scribe in Clonmacnois who came from Roscrea according to the Annals of Ulster.

S12. M á e l   T u i l e   s o n   o f   C o l m á n [ferleiginn, CS; ferleighint, AFM] died in the year 923.[274] He was the first *fer léiginn* of Clonmacnois.[275] It is possible that Máel Tuile

---

[265] Rechtabra Ua Guaire (AT 753, AFM 747) and Catnia Ua Guaire (AFM 789, recte 794); see BYRNE, Irish Kings, pp. 84, 242-246.

[266] AU 814.2; AFM 809. An inscription on a slab stone in Clonmacnois reads *or do thuathal* dated by Petrie to the ninth century (PETRIE, Christian inscriptions, I, p. 25, fig. 35).

[267] AU 822.9.

[268] AFM 814. A stone very similar to that of Tuathal, the scribe (S6) bears the inscription *Dubinse* (PETRIE, Christian inscriptions, I, p. 25, fig. 36).

[269] AFM 855. According to Petrie one of the stones in Clonmacnois with the inscription *Máeloena*, can be firmly dated to the ninth century and belongs to this scribe (PETRIE, Christian inscriptions, I, pp. 28f., fig. 48).

[270] AFM 863.

[271] CS 891; AU 891.8; AFM 887.

[272] PETRIE, Christian inscriptions, I, p. 39, fig. 82. The stone belongs to the 'Coirpre Crom group' of Clonmacnois slab stones, all showing great similarity in style and design (MACALISTER, Memorial slabs of Clonmacnois, p. 45, no. 237, see also under B4).

[273] AU 920.4; AFM 918.

[274] CS 922; AFM 921.

was the son of Colmán Conaillech, abbot of Clonmacnois at the time, and that he took over the leadership of the school in Clonmacnois with the support of his father the abbot (see A49).[276]

S13. D o n n g a l U a M á e l m i d h e [fer leighinn, AFM] died in the year 950.[277]

S14. F l a n n s o n o f M á e l M i c h i l was lector as well as bishop. He died in the year 979 (see B14).

S15. L o i n g s e c h s o n o f M á e l P á t r a i c [fearleighinn, AFM] died in the year 989.[278]

S16. O d r á n U a h E o l a i s [scribhnidh, AFM] died in the year 995.[279] As apparent from his family name he came from the Muintir Eolais in Bréifne, the territory now represented by south county Leitrim, later known as Mac Ragnaill's country.

S17. D i a r m a i t C o n a i l l e c h [Diarmaitt, .i. Conaillech, fer leighinn Cluana mic Nóis, AFM] died in the year 1000.[280] He was a member of the Conaillech Clan (see A49).

S18. D ú n c h a d s o n o f D ú n a d a c h [ferleighind Cluana mic Nóis, + a hangcoire iarsin, cend a riaghla, + a sencais, AFM] died in the year 1006.[281] He was of the Meic Cuinn na mBocht (see An8, C1).

S19. C a t a s a c h U a G a r b á i n [fer legind Cluana Macc Nóis, AI; ferleighinn, AFM] died in the year 1022. He was, like the Uí Flaithéin, from the Cuircne settled in the western parts of the kingdom of Mide (see A63).[282]

S20. F a c h t n a was a lector and a priest. He died in the year 1024 (see P8).

---

[275] The Four Masters applied the title *fer léiginn* to earlier scribes already (see above). The contemporary annals, however, use the title only from the early tenth century (see HUGHES, Church and society, chap. XI, pp. 247f.).

[276] A cross belonging to the 'Coirpre Crom group' of crosses in Clonmacnois was assigned to Máel Tuile by Macalister. The legible parts of the inscription read ...*TUI*... - since the date fits, this could well be part of the name Máeltuile (MACALISTER, Memorial slabs of Clonmacnois, p. 31, no. 156; see B4).

[277] AFM 948.

[278] AFM 988.

[279] AFM 994. A gravestone inscription in Clonmacnois reads *or do odrán háu eolais* (PETRIE, Christian inscriptions, I, p. 61, fig. 131; MACALISTER, Memorial slabs of Clonmacnois, p. 29, no. 145).

[280] AFM 999; see A49.

[281] AFM 1005.

[282] AI 1022.5; AFM 1022. Possibly related to Tuathal Ua Garbáin, who died as bishop of Old Kilcullen, in county Kildare in 1030 (AFM).

S21. A e n g u s   s o n   o f   F l a n n [fer legind Cluana, AI; fer leighind, AFM] died in the year 1034.[283] One Aengus Ua Flainn died as *comarba* of Brendan of Clonfert two years later in 1036.[284] He was possibly related with this *fer léiginn* of Clonmacnois.

S22. F l a i t h b e r t a c h   s o n   o f   L o i n g s e c h was lector in Clonmacnois and a bishop. He died in 1038 (see B18).

S23. G u a i r e   U a   L a c h t n á i n [fer legind Cluana M. Nois, AI; ferleighinn, AFM] died in the year 1054.[285] The Uí Lachtnáin were from Tethba (compare P6). The daughter of Guaire, Caintigern was the wife of Flann Ua Máelsechlainn, king of Mide (who himself was the son of an abbot of Clonard, see A60). The two sons of Cantigern, Murchad (d.1076) and Domnall (d.1094) became both future kings of Mide.[286] The Uí Lachtnáin produced many prominent ecclesiastics in the church of Connacht after the twelfth century reform.[287]

S24. M á e l   C h o l u i m   U a   L o i n g s i g h died as a priest in Clonmacnois in the year 1061, he was also known to have been *fer léiginn* in Kells (see P12).

S25. U a   M i a d a c h á i n [ferléighinn do mhuintir Cluana mic Nois, AFM] died in the year 1063.[288]

S26. C o n a i n g   U a   h E a g h r a [ferleighinn, AFM] died in the year 1063. His family was the ruling dynasty of the Luigne of Connacht, settled in what is now south counties Sligo

---

[283] AI 1034.6; AFM 1034.

[284] CS 1034; AFM 1036. Petrie assumes, that the slab stone in Clonmacnois with the inscription *or do angus*, was that of Aengus Ua Flainn comarba of Brenainn of Clonfert (PETRIE, Christian inscriptions, I, p. 39, fig. 79). Another member of the familiy held the abbacy of Clonfert later in the century (AI 1081).

[285] AI 1054.6; AFM 1054. There is a grave stone in Clonmacnois with the inscription *or do guariu* (PETRIE, Christian inscriptions, I, p. 55, fig. 117). Compare above, p. 278 n.241.

[286] DOBBS (ed.), The ban-shenchus, p. 190: *Caintigern ingen Guairi hUi Lachtnain d'airther Thefa (i. fear-leigind Cluana Meic Nois) mathair Da mac Flaind hUi Máel Eachlaind .i. Murchad + Domnall.* The second son Domnall was the king of Mide from whom Cormac grandson of Conn na mbocht bought Íseal Chiaráin in 1093 (see A70).

[287] Máel Maith Ua Lachtnáin, anchorite of Killaloe (d.1077.3 AI); Máel Muire Ua Lachtnáin, Archbishop of Tuaim and Magister in Canon Law (d.1249.14 AConn); Gilla Chríst Ua Lachtnáin, abbot of the Trinity in Tuam (d.1251.5 AConn); Lurint Ua Lachtnáin, Abbot of Assaroe, sometime abbot of Boyle and then abbot of Knockmoy and lastly Bishop of Kilmacduagh (d.1307.3 AConn).

[288] AFM 1063. Etru Ua Miadacháin died as bishop of Clonard in the year 1173 (AU, AFM); Tomás Ua Miadacháin succeeded to the bishopric of Luigne Connacht, i.e. Achonry in the year 1266 (AConn 1266.14).

and Mayo.[289] The church of Kilmacteige, according to the Registry an appurtenance of Clonmacnois, linked with St. Ciarán by local tradition was situated in their territory.[290]

S27. D o n n g a l   s o n   o f   G o r m á n [M. Gorman fer leiginn Cenannsa + sui ecna Erenn, AU; Donngal mac Gormáin, tanaisi Abbadh Cluana muc Nois, CS; Mc Gormain, fer legind Cluana M. Nois + Cenannsa, AI; ferlegind Cluana M. Nois + Cenannsa, AI; áird ferleighinn Leithe Chuinn, + tánaissi abbaidh Cluana mic Nóis, AFM] died in the year 1070. The Annals of Ulster know about a son of Gorman who was a scribe in Kells, the Annals of Innisfallen say he was scribe of Clonmacnois as well as Kells; the Chronicon finally talks about him as vice-abbot of Clonmacnois (compare vA18).[291]

S28. C o r m a c   U a   M á e l d ú i n [aird fherleighinn + sruith senóir Ereann, AFM] died in the year 1073.[292] His family provided three vice-abbots in Clonmacnois in the eleventh century (see vA18).

S29. M u i r e d a c h   s o n   o f   M u g r ó n [fer leginn, CS; ferleighinn, AFM] died in the year 1080.[293]

S30. M u i r c h e r t a c h   U a   C e a r n a i g h [airdfherleighind na nGaoidheal, AFM] died after a good life, in the year 1106 in Clonmacnois His origin of the Luigne of Connacht is also given in his obituary (see S26).[294]

S31. M á e l   M u i r e   o f   t h e   M e i c   C u i n n   n a   m B o c h t was killed in the church by plunderes in the year 1106.[295] No title is assigned to him in his obituary. He was the son of bishop Céilechair (B20) and grandson of Conn na mBocht (C1) and became famous as on one of the scribes of the Lebor na hUidre.[296]

S32. C o n g a l a c h   U a   T o m a l t a i g h was a lector as well as a priest in Clonmacnois (see P15).

---

[289] AFM 1063; Duarcán Ua hEgra, king of Luigne died in the year 1059 (AU). See BYRNE, The trembling Sod, p. 35.

[290] Registry, p. 451 n.7; O'RORKE, History of Sligo Town, II, pp. 152f.

[291] CS 1067; AI 1070.7; AU 1070.10; AFM 1070. For links between Kells an Clonmacnois see HERBERT, Iona, Kells, and Derry, p. 90 n.12.

[292] AFM 1073.

[293] CS 1076; AFM 1080.

[294] AFM 1106.

[295] AFM 1106. A grave stone inscription in Clonmacnois asks for a prayer for Máel Muire (PETRIE, Christian inscriptions, I, p. 68, fig. 152: *or do mailmaire*).

[296] See BEST / BERGIN (eds.), Lebor na hUidre, Introd., p. xiv; BEST, Notes on the script, p. 161.

Anchorites (An)

An1. A e l g a l [ancorita Cluana, AT; angcoire, Ó Imlioch Foirdeorach, + o Cluain mic Nóis, AFM] died in the year 756.[297] Links between Clonmacnois and *Imlech* are also otherwise attested (see A61).

An2. G o r m á n [Gorman co*mur*ba Mochta Lugbaidh .i. ath*air* Torbaig co*mur*ba Pat*r*aig, isse robai b*l*adain *for* us*ci* thib*r*at Fingen a C*luain* ma*i*c Nois, + adbath a n-ailithri i Cluai*n*, AT; Gorman do Mughdhornaibh, a quo nati sunt mic Cuinn; asse ro buí bliadhain *for* usce Tiprait Fingin; ocus in ailitri a ccluáin adbath, CS] abbot of Louth, the father of Torbach, abbot of Armagh, died in Clonmacnois in the year 758. The annnals of Tigernach state that prior to his death he lived for a year at the water of Fingen's well in Clonmacnois.[298] In the Chronicon his death-note, apparently a copy from Tigernach with additions, is inserted under the year 615. He was the ultimate ancestor of the Meic Cuinn na mBocht (see C1).[299]

An3. Á e d a c á n s o n o f T o r b a c h , s o n o f G o r m á n [Áedacán Lugmaigh dég in anailitre a cCluain muc Nois, CS; Aodhagan, mac Torbaigh, abb Lucchnaidh, décc ina ailethre hi cCluain mic Nóis. Eoghan, mac Áedhagáin, ro ansidhe hi cCluain mic Nóis, conadh uadha ro chiset Meic Cuinn na mbocht innte. AFM; Fiegann mcTorvie of Lough died in Pilgrimage in Clonn aforesaid, of whome issued the familye of Conn mboght & Muintyr Gorman, they are of the O'Kellys of Brey. AClon] abbot of Louth died on his pilgrimage in Clonmacnois in the year 835.[300]

An4. É o g a n s o n o f Á e d a c á n , s o n o f T o r b a c h [ancorita, CS; angcoire, AFM], died like his father, an anchorite in Clonmacnois, in the year 847.[301]

An5. L u c h a i r é n s o n o f É o g a n , s o n o f Á e d a c á n , s o n o f T o r b a c h [scribhnidh, + angcoire, AFM] died in the year 865.[302] He is the first scribe of Clonmacnois supplied by the Meic Cuinn na mBocht (see S9). His son Ecertach became *airchinnech* of Eglais Beg, presumably the mortuary chapel in Clonmanois (see AE1).

An6. S u i b n e s o n o f M á e l U m a i who died in the year 891, as a famous scribe of Clonmacnois was also an anchorite (see S10).

---

[297] AFM 751; AT (755).

[298] AT (757); CS 615.

[299] AU 808; AFM 807 (*Cinel Torbaigh, i.e. the Uí Cheallaigh Breagh*). Torbach is said to have been of the of the royal dynasty of the Uí Cheallaigh Brega, elsewhere (and more likely) the Meic Cuinn na mbocht claim descent from the Mudgorna Maigen seated near the church of Louth (see KELLEHER, The Tain and the annals, pp. 125-127).

[300] CS 835; AClon 832, p. 136; AFM 834.

[301] CS 847; AFM 845.

[302] AFM 863.

An7. F i n g e n [Quies Fíngen, anchara di Mumain, i Cluain Meic Nois, AI; Fingin, angcoire Cluana mic Nóis, AFM] an anchorite from Munster died in Clonmacnois in the year 900.[303]

An8. D ú n c h a d s o n o f D ú n a d a c h [ferleighind Cluana mic Nóis, + a hangcoire iarsin, cend a riaghla, + a sencais, AFM] a lector and ancorite, is praised as head of the rule and history of Clonmancois by the Four Masters (see S18). He died in the year 1006.[304] Dúnchad was of the Meic Cuinn na mBocht, the son of bishop Dúnadach (B10), and the grandfather of Conn na mBocht (C1).

An9. R o b a r t a c h U a h A i l g i u s [anchara i Cluain Macc Nois quieuit, AI; ancoire, AFM] died in the year 1007. The Four Masters add that he was of the Bregmaine (see A46).[305]

An10. M u i r e d a c h U l t a c h [anmchara Cluana mic Nóis, AFM; anchorite of Clonvick-enos, AClon] died in the year 1017.[306]

An11. J o s e p h s o n o f D ú n c h a d [anmcara, CS; anmchara, AFM] died in the year 1022. He was of the Meic Cuinn na mBocht, the son of Dúnchad, bishop and anchorite (An8), and father of Conn na mBocht (C1).[307]

An12. D u b s l á i n e [prímh anmchara na nGaoidheal, + saccart Aird brecain, décc hí cCluain mic Nóis, AFM] chief anchorite of the Irish and priest of Ardbraccan in Mide, died in the year 1024 in Clonmacnois.[308]

An13. D a i g h r e U a D u b h a t á i n [anmchara Cluana, AFM], an anchorite of Clon-macnois, died in pilgrimage in Glendalough in the year 1056.[309]

An14. C o n n n a m B o c h t, anchorite, head of the Céili Dé in Clonmacnois, died in the year 1060 (see C1).

An15. F o g a r t a c h F i o n n [anchorite and sage, AClon; eccnaidh + angcoiri, AFM] died in the year 1066. He was from Ulster according to he Four Masters. His name appears on a tombstone inscription in Clonmacnois.[310]

An16. F o t h u d U a h A i l l e [ard anmchara Cluana mic Nóis, + Leithi Cuinn, AFM] died in the year 1081.[311]

---

[303] AI 900; AFM 895.

[304] AFM 1005. For a poem refering to Dúnchad see RYAN, Clonmacnois, p. 17; compare S18.

[305] AI 1007.5; AFM 1006.

[306] AClon 1010; AFM 1017.

[307] CS 1022; AFM 1022.

[308] AFM 1024; GWYNN / HADCOCK, pp. 28f. for Ardbraccan.

[309] AFM 1056.

[310] AClon 1065, p. 179; AFM 1066; PETRIE, Christian inscriptions, I, p. 65, fig. 146: *fogarta*.

[311] AFM 1081.

Head of the Céili Dé, *cenn Chéile Dhé* or *cenn bocht* (C)

C1. C o n n   n a   m B o c h t [Conn na mbocht Cluana M.Nois, AU; Conn na mbocht Cluana muc Nois, CS; cend Celedh nché ocus ancoiri, Cluana mic Nóis, also: Conn na mbocht ordan + aireachus Cluana mic Nóis, AFM] died in the year 1060.[312] He became famous as the eponym of the Meic Cuinn na mBocht family in Clonmacnois. He is called Conn na mBocht, 'Conn of the Poor', and 'head of the Céile Dé in Clonmacnois' (for the title see C2). The Four Masters state that 'the reason he was called Conn na mBocht is because of the number of poor that he used to feed habitually, infact he must have enjoyed considerable wealth since he is praised by the Four Masters as 'the first to assemble a herd for the poor of Clonmacnois' and presented twenty cows of his own to it.[313] His family can be traced in the ecclesiastical settlement from the eighth century. They cherished a tradition as anchorites associated with the Céili Dé movement. Their appearance as heads of their community in Clonmacnois in the eleventh century seems the continuation of the anchorical family tradition. The Céili Dé community was seated in Íseal Chiaráin, an appurtenance of Clonmacnois in what is now Ballyloughloe parish, which in the later eleventh century became family possession of the Meic Cuinn na mBocht (see under Cormac of the Meic Cuinn na mBocht, A70). In the latter half of the eleventh century members of the family were involved in the writing of literature and contemporary chronicles in Clonmacnois. It seems that during this time the detailed pedigree of the family was included in the annals (see S18, S31).

C2. M á e l   C h i a r á i n   s o n   o f   C o n n   n a   m B o c h t [cenn bocht Cluana M. Nois, AU; Maolciaráin mac Cuinn na mbocht, CS; comharba Ciaráin, AFM] died in the year 1079.[314] The term *boicht* appears in the monastic context for the first time in the eleventh century and seems to refer to a a group of monastic dwellers who were either identical or closely associated with the Céili Dé. Brian Ó Cuív suggested that Conn and his son Máel Chiaráin were both head of the 'Poor' and the Céili Dé community of Clonmacnois.[315] The Chronicon simply refers to Máel Chiaráin as the son of Conn na mBocht.

---

[312] CS 1057; AU 1060.4; AFM 1031, 1059. He is sometimes assumed to have been bishop, resulting from a misinterpretation of an entry in the Chronicon Scotorum. There the obituary of Óenacán son of Ecertach reads: *Óenagan mac Egertaig, aircinnech Eglaisi bige, qui fuit germanus ataui Cuinn na mbocht, epscop Cluana muc Nois [quievit]* (CS 948). The title bishop belongs to Óenacán and not to Conn. The entry in AFM 1031 was often mistaken as an obit. A tombstone with the inscription *or do chunn* was still readable when Petrie visited Clonmacnois (PETRIE, Christian inscriptions, I, p. 65, fig. 147).

[313] AFM 807, AFM 1031. See Ó Cuív, Miscellanea 1, p. 107 for the translation here.

[314] CS 1076; AU 1079.1; AFM 1079.

[315] Ó Cuív, Miscellanea 1, p. 107, where he translates the title given to Conn by the Four Masters (*cend Celedh ndhé, + ancoiri Cluana mic Nóis*) as 'the person responsible for the Culdees and anchorites of Clonmacnoise'.

C3. U a r e i r g e   U a   N e c h t a i n [cenn Cele nDé Cluana muc Nois, CS; cend chéledh nde Cluana mic Nois, + a sruith shenóir, AFM] died in the year 1132. The family was from Uí Maine, of the Uí Fiachrach Finn of Maenmag.[316]

C4. M á e l   M ó r d a   s o n   o f   U a r e i r g e   U a   N e c h t a i n [cenn chelidh nDé Cluana, AT; sruith senóir déshearcach, sonus, + saidhbhres Cluana mic Nóis, cend a Chéled Dé, AFM] succeeded his father in office. He died in the year 1170, in the month of November.[317]

C5. U a r e i r g e   s o n   o f   M á e l   M ó r d a   s o n   o f   U a r e i r g e   U a   N e c h t a i n [uasal sruith do sruithibh cluana mic nóis, fer lán do dhesherc, + dá gach sóalchidh archena, + ceann cele ndé cluana, AFM] one of the noble sages of Clonmacnois, a man full of the love of God and of every virtue and head of the Céili Dé, succeeded his father and grandfather in office. He died, according to the Four Masters, the tenth of March in the year 1200.[318]

Seniors and Wise men (Sen)

Sen1. F o r g l a [sruithe Cluana mic Nóis, AFM] died in the year 768.[319]

Sen2. U a   M i a n n a i g h [ab*bas*, sruithi Cluana M. Nois, AU] also died in the year 768. His title in the Annals of Ulster is ambiguous, possibly he was abbot of the seniors (*abbas sruithe Cluana)* rather than abbot and senior in Clonmacnois (see A25).

Sen3. T u a t h g a l [abbas sruithe Cluana, AU], abbot of the elders of Cluain died in the year 811.[320].

Sen4. M á e l   G i r i c c [abb Tighe Sruithe Cluana mic Nóis, AFM] died in the year 929.[321]

Sen5. M á e l   C h o l u i m   U a   L o i n g s i g h died, a wise man and a priest, in the year 1061 (see P12).

Sen6. C o r m a c   U a   M á e l d ú i n was chief lector and learned senior of Clonmacnois. He died in the year 1073 (see S28).

Sen7. M á e l   M a r t a i n   s o n   o f   U a   C e r t a [sruith senóir Cluana mic Nóis, AFM] died in the year 1077.[322]

---

[316] CS 1128; AFM 1132; see KELLEHER, The Uí Maine in the annals, pp. 94f.

[317] AT (1170); AFM 1170.

[318] AFM 1200.

[319] AFM 763; the entry reads: *Forgla sruithe Cluana mic Nóis dég.* O'Donovan translates: „The most [part] of the religious seniors of Clonmacnois died" (AFM I, p. 366, note g).

[320] AU 811.5; AFM 806, O'Donovan translates „abbot of the religious seniors".

[321] AFM 927. A gravestone inscription reading *Máelcirigg* is preserved in Clonmacnois. According to Petrie it belonged to Máelisa O'Máelgiric, chiefpoet of Ireland who died in Clonmacnois in the year 1088 (ALCé) (PETRIE, Christian inscriptions, I, pp. 45f., fig. 93).

Sen8. M á e l   C h i a r á i n   U a   D o n n g h a s a   [sruith Shenóir Cluana mic Nóis, AFM] died in the year 1101.[323]

Sen9. M u i r c h e r t a c h   U a   C a t h a r n a i g h   [sruith tocchaidh do mhuintir Chluana mic Nóis, AFM] died in the year 1105.[324] The Uí Chatharnaigh, surnamed *na Sionnaig*, the Foxes, a branch of the Muintir Tadgáin, were the leading dynasty in Tethba since the eleventh century. *Muirchertach, the Cleric* is mentioned in the Tethba genealogies. He was the nephew of Muiredach mac Catharnaigh, king of Tethba in the mid eleventh century and had three sons, Becc, Fagartaig and Sittric.[325]

Sen10. C é i l e c h a i r   o f   t h e   M e i c   C u i n n   n a   m B o c h t   [sruith senóir Cluana mic Nois, CS; sruith shenóir, cenn comhairle, + tobar eccna, senchusa cend einigh + coimheda riaghla Cluana mic Nóis, AFM] was the son of Cormac son of Conn na mBocht, and died in the year 1134. The Four Masters style him *learned senior, head of the counsel and fountain of the wisdom and history, and head of the hospitality and keeping of the rule of Clonmacnois*. They also add a quatrain to his obituary and note that, like his brother Máel Chiaráin, he died in the 'bed of Ciarán', presumably another name for Eglais Beag (see P13).[326]

Sen11. M á e l   M u i r e   o f   t h e   M e i c   C u i n n   n a   m b o c h t   [primhshenóir Erean, AFM] died in the year 1180. Clonmacnois is not explicitly mentioned as his church.[327]

Head of the little church, *airchinnech Eglaisi Bige* (AE)

AE1. E c e r t a c h   [airchinnech eccailsi bicce, athair Aenacáin + Dunadhaigh, AFM] died in the year 898. He was of the Meic Cuinn na mBocht, son of Luchairén, the scribe (S9). He fathered two sons Óenácan and Dúnadach, both bishops.[328]

AE2. F i a c h r a   [Fiachra eccailsi bicce, AFM], Fiachra of Eglais beag, died in the year 923.[329]

---

[322] AFM 1077.

[323] AFM 1101. Two gravestones in Clonmacnois bear his name (see PETRIE, Christian inscriptions, I, p. 67, fig. 151; p. 66, fig. 149).

[324] AFM 1105.

[325] DOBBS (ed.), The genealogies of the Southern Uí Néill, pp. 9 ,11. Dobbs cites the genealogies from Trinity College Dublin MS H.2.7. p. 169f.

[326] CS 1130; AU has entries for the years 1132-1155; AFM 1134.

[327] AFM 1180.

[328] AFM 893.

[329] AFM 921. A Clonmacnois stone with the inscription *or do fiachraich* is mentioned by Petrie. The design on this stone is very peculiar; four heagons arranged in the form of a cross surrounded with a broad circular band and all the interstices filled in with rich ornaments of

AE3. Ó e n a c á n   s o n   o f   E c e r t a c h   [Aircinnech Egailsi bige, CS; aircindech Eccailsi bicce hi cCluain mic Nóis, epscop, + ógh iodhan, AFM] was the brother of bishop Dúnadach (B10). He died in the year 949.[330] The two brothers were apparently fostered in Louth, their tutor was Caínchomrac, bishop and princeps of Louth who had died in the year 903.[331] A gloss is added in the Chronicon noting that Óenacán was *germanus atavi* of Conn na mbocht.[332]

AE4. C a t h a s a c h   [airchindeach Eaccailsi bicce Cluana mic Nóis, AFM] died in the year 978.[333]

AE5. B r o e n   U a   h A e d h a   [airchindech eccailsi bicce, AFM] died in the year 987. The name belongs to the Múscraige in Munster.[334]

AE6. C a i r p r e   m a c   R o d a i g h e   [airchindech Eccailsi bicce, AFM], the son of Rodach, died in the year 1037.[335]

AE7. A i l i l l   U a   M á e l c h i a r á i n   [airchinneach Eccailsi bicce, AFM] died in the year 1060.[336] Compare below G4 for Ua Máelchiaráin.

AE8. 'H u g h   o ' K o n o y l e '[dean of the little church of Clonvickenos, AClon] was *airchinnech* of Eglais Beag according to Mageoghagan and died in the year 1092.[337] He seems to be the same person as Áed Ua Conghaile listed as *airchinnech* of the guesthouse in Clonmacnois by the Four Masters (see G3).

AE9. M á e l á n   U a   C u i n n   [airchinneach Eccailsi bicce, AFM] died in the year 1097. He might have been another member of the Meic Cuinn na mBocht.[338]

Guestmaster, *airchinnech tige oiged* (G)

G1. M a c   F i n n   [airchinnech tighe aoidhedh Cluana mic Nóis, AFM] died in the year 1031.[339]

---

interlaced bands, spirals and the diagonal form of a Greek fret (PETRIE, Christian inscriptions, I, p. 46, fig. 95).

[330] CS 948; AFM 947.

[331] AU 903.1; AFM 989.

[332] CS 948.

[333] AFM 977.

[334] AFM 986. Ua hAedha king of Múscraige died in 1010 (AI).

[335] AFM 1037.

[336] AFM 1060.

[337] AClon 1092, p. 185, compare AFM 1093.

[338] AFM 1097.

G2. Á e d   U a   C o n g h a i l e [airchinneach Taighe aidhedh Cluana mic Nóis, AFM] died in the year 1093.[340] The Uí Chonghaile were a family from Tethba.[341] They suplied guest-maters of Clonmacnois down to the second half of the twelfth century (see G6, G7). Possibly the Ua Conghaile family in Devenish in Fermanagh was originally from Clonmacnois.[342]

G3. C o r m a c   U a   C i l l í n [ard seacnab Sil Muiredaigh, ocus aircinnech tige aiged Cluana muc Nois, CS; Deane of the house of Clone, AClon; airchindech Tíghe aidheadh Cluana mic Nóis, AFM] died in 1106. He was vice-abbot of the Síl Muiredaig in Connacht as well as guestmaster (see vA24).

G4. C o n g a l a c h   M a c   G i l l a   C h i a r á i n [airchinneach Lis aeidheadh, AFM] died in the year 1116. Possibly the Four Masters' version of the name of Congalach's father should be read as a family name: Congalach the son of Ua Máelchiaráin.[343] This guestmaster might have been a son or greatson of Aillil Ua Máelchiaráin, who had died as head of Eglais Beg in the year 1060 (see AE7). One Ua Máelchiaráin is criticized for his lack of hospitality in a poem attributed to Erard Mac Coisse, in which the poet laments over the grave of one Fergal Ua Ruairc in Clonmacnois.[344] The peom seems to date from around the mid-twelfth century when the Uí Máelchiaráin were apparently still around in Clonmacnois.[345]

G5. C e i n n é i t t i g h   U a   C o n g h a i l e [airchinneach lis aoidheadh Cluana mic Nóis, AFM] died in the year 1128.[346]

G6. C é i l e c h a i r   U a   C o n g h a i l e [airchindeach tíghe aoidheadh Cluana mic Nóis, AFM] died in the year 1166.[347]

---

[339] AFM 1031. O'Donovan translates the „house of the guests" or „hospital of Clonmacnois" (AFM II, p. 822 note m).

[340] AFM 1093.

[341] Congal their ancestor is one of the sons of Tadgan, see DOBBS (ed.), The genealogies of the Southern Uí Néill, pp. 8f.: *Congal a quo hUi Congail*, one of the sons of Tadgan (according to Trinity College Dublin MS H 2.7. and Book of Ballymote, facs., p. 82); see P6 for other Tethba families in Clonmacnois.

[342] Fogartach Ua Conghaile was airchinnech of Devenish (d.985 AU); Aemann O Conghaile died in 1277 (AU) as airchinnech of Rossory, right in the neighbourhood of Devenish.

[343] AFM 1116.

[344] AFM 1060; J. O'DONOVAN (ed.), Elegy of Erard Mac Coise, chief chronicler of the Gaels, prounounced over the Tomb of Fergal O'Ruairc chief of Brefny at Clonmacnois, in: Jn. Kilk. SE. Irel. Arch. Soc. 1 (1956/57), pp. 341-356, here 348.

[345] See above, p. 233.

[346] AFM 1128. A fragment of an inscription in Clonmacnois reads ... *r ár cen*. Hennessy proposes the reading „or ár cendig" and ascribes it to this Cennedig Ua Conghaile (see PETRIE, Christian inscriptions, I, p. 27, fig. 44).

[347] AFM 1166.

Others (O)

O1. C o n d m a c h U a T o m r a i r was a priest and chief singer of Clonmacnois according to the Four Master. He died in the year 1012 (see P7).

O2. C e r n a c h [aistire Cluana mic Nóis, AFM] was *ostiarius* or porter in Clonmacnois. He died in the year 1028.[348]

O3. D u b i n s e [liachtaire Cluana mic Nóis, AFM] is mentioned as a bellringer of Clonmacnois. He died in the year 1032.[349]

O4. M á e l F i n n é n s o n o f C o n n n a m B o c h t [athair Chormaic, comharba Chiaráin, AFM] is commemorated by the Four Masters as the father of Cormac, *comarba Chiaráin* in the late eleventh century (see A70). Máel Finnén died in the year 1056.[350]

O5. A n o n y m o u s [rechtaire na mbocht, AFM; the steward of that familie, AClon] The superintendent of the Poor in Clonmacnois, was killed at Íseal Chiaráin in the year 1072, in the course of a fight between th community of the Céili Dé and the Poor there, and Murchad Ua Máelsechlainn, the son of the king of Mide. Since the Meic Cuinn na mBocht were the heads of the community, it seems likely that the *airchinnech* of the church was supplied by that family.[351]

O6. G i l l a C h r í s t s o n o f C o n n n a m B o c h t [maic cleirigh as ferr baoi in Erinn ina reimher ordán + oirechus Cluana mic Nóis, AFM], another son of Conn, died as the best ecclesiastical student in Ireland in his time in the year 1085.[352]

O7. M á e l Í o s a s o n o f C o n n n a m B o c h t [Mac Cuind na mBocht, AFM] died in the year 1103 without a title, he is just mentioned as the son of Conn.[353]

O8. G i l l a C h r í s t (U a M á e l e o i n), the son of the *comarba Chiaráin* died in 1172, the same year as his father Tigernach Ua Máeleoin (A75).[354]

---

[348] AFM 1028.

[349] AFM 1032.

[350] AFM 1056. Petrie mentions the inscription *or do Máelfinnia* on one of the Clonmacnois slab stones (PETRIE, Christian inscriptions, I, p. 66, fig. 148).

[351] AFM 1072; AClon 1069, p. 180.

[352] AFM 1085.

[353] AFM 1103.

[354] AU 1172.

Appendix 1.2: Tribes and families represented in offices in Clonmacnois.

(Questionmarks are put when evidence is ambiguous.)

Ulster

Ciannachta Breg (co. Louth): A19(d.737), A33(d.794).

Conaille Muirthemne (co. Louth): A49(d.926), ?S12(d.923), S17(d.1000), A62(d.1030), P10(d.1044).

Dál mBairdene Ulaid: A6(d.628).

Dartraige Daimhinsi (Dartraighe of Devenish, co. Fermanagh): A40(d.869).

Latharna Molt, a branch of the Dál nAraide: A1 (d.544?).

AIRGIALLA:

Mugdorna Maigen: A41(d.872).
   - *Meic Cuinn na mBocht*: An2(d.758), An3(d.835), An4(d.847), An5/S9(d.865), AE1(d.898), B9(d.949), AE3(d.949), B10(d.955), An8(d.1006), B17(d.1011), An11(d.1022), O4(d.1056), C1(d.1060), B20(d.1067), C2/A66(d.1079), ?AE9(d.1097), A70(d.1103), O5(d.1072), O6(d.1085), O7(d.1103), S31(1106), ?vA25(d.1128), P13(d.1134), Sen10(d.1134), Sen11(d.1180).

Uí Chremthainn: A18(d.732), A42(d.877).

Cuailgne (of the Uí Méith of Airgialla): A14(d.694).

Leinster

?Cenél Echach Gall: A39(d.868).

Loígis Rete: A2(d.570).

Uí Dunlainge of the Uí Muiredaig: B8(d.941), ?A55(d.971).

Connacht

Conmaicne

- *Conmaicne Mara*: A9(d.664).

- *?Conmaicne Dúine Móir (north co. Galway)*: A20(d.740).

Gailenga

- *Gailenga Mór*: A35(d.814).

- *Gailenga of Corann (co. Sligo)*: A8(d.652), A16(d.713).

Gregraige

- *of Airtech (or Lough Techet), south of Lough Gara*: A11(d.665), A12(d.683), A43(d.877).

Luigne (of Connacht): ?A24(d.764), S8(d.857), S26(d.1063).

Uí Briúin: A27(d.771), A34(d.799), A50(d.931).

- *Uí Briúin Seola*: A36(d.816).

- *Uí Briúin Aí*:
   - *Ua Braoín*: ?P5(d.948, mac Brain), A56(d.989), A67(d.1088).
   - *Ua Máeleoin*: A72(d.1127), A74(d.1153), A75(d.1172), O8(d.1172), B25(d.1208),
      B27(d.1220), A78(d.1230), B28(d.1236), A79(d.1263).
- *Uí Briúin Bréifne*: A58(d.1028).

- *?Síl Maelruanaid (MacDiarmaida)*: vA1(d.797).

Uí Fiachrach: A31(d.789).

- *Uí Fiachrach an Tuaisceirt (near Lough Conn, co. Mayo)*: A48(d.904).

- *Uí Fiachrach Aidne*: S5(d.798, nepos Guaire Aidne).
   - *Ua Cillín*: A54(d.966), vA24/G3(d.1106).
   - *Ua Niallán*: A68(d.1093).

Uí MAINE: A44(d.885), P11(d.1051).

Cenél Cairpre Chruim: ?A23(d.762), A29(d.784).

Corco Moga: A5(d.614), A10(d.665).
   - *Ua Ruadáin*: A59(d.1003), vA20(d.1082).
   - *Ua Maonaigh*: ?P4(d.948, mac Maonaigh), A52(d.952).
   - *Ua Nechtain*: C3(d.1132), C4(d.1170), C5(d.1200).

Uí Chormaic Maenmaige: ?A26(d.770), A38(d.850).

Sogan: A17(d.724), ?A21(d.747), A64(d.1052).

Munster

Corco Loígde: A7(d.638), ?A22(d.753, Corcelig).

Múscraige: A4(d.599).
   - *Ua hAedha*: AE5(d.987).
   - *Uí Forga (of the Múscraige Tíre)*: vA4(d.834?).

Mide

B r e g m a i n e (co. Westmeath): A46(d.896).
 - *Ua hAilgius*: An9(d.1007).

C o r c o   R o í d e (co. Westmeath): A65(d.1070), ?A22(d.753 *Corcelig*).

C l a n n   C h o l m á i n : vA6(d.838).
 - *Ua Máelsechlainn*: A60(d.1014).
 - *? Ua Fidabra, alias Ua Máelsechlainn*: A76(d.1173), A77(d.1181).
 - *Ua Máeldúin*: vA18(d.1021) S28/Sen6(d.1073), vA21(1089), vA23(d.1106).

C u i r c n e (co. Westmeath):
 - *Ua Flaithéin*: A63(d.1042), A69(d.1100).
 - *Ua Garbáin*: S19(d.1022).

D e l b n a : ?vA25(d.1128).

U í   M i c   U a i s   o f   M i d e : A53(d.954).
 - *Ua hAdlai*: A51(d.948).

U í   B e c c o n :
 - *Ua Maenaigh*: A57(d.992).

TETHBA:

- *Calraige of Tethba (Dún Fremainne, co. Westmeath)*: A15(d.706).

- *Calraige of 'Aelmhagh', i.e.Calraigh an Chalad, bar. Clonlonan, co. Westmeath, or Calraige Droma Cliab, in north co. Leitrim*: A30(d.786).

M u i n t i r   T a d g a i n : P6(d.996), P14(d.1168).
 - *Ua Catharnaigh*: sen9(d.1105), P16(d.1196).
 - *Ua Conghaile*: G2(d.1093), ?G4(d.1116), G5(d.1128), G6(d.1166).
 - *Ua Lachtnáin*: S23(d.1054).

Appendix 1.3: Churches from which ecclesiastical officials in Clonmacnois came.

(* indicates that the person died on pilgrimage in the church concerned.)

Aghaboe (church of St. Cainnech in co. Laois): *A69(d.1100).

Aghagower (co. Mayo): ?A45(d.892).

Ardagh: B21(d.1104).

Ardbraccan: An12(d.1024).

Armagh: *A56(d.989).

Clonard: vA6(d.838), A49(d.926), A53(d.954), A60(d.1014), *A64(d.1052),* A65(d.1070).

Cloneogher (co. Longford): B14(d.979).

Clonfert: ?A26(d.770), ?S21(d.1034), *A73/B23(d.1137), B24(d.1187).

Devenish: A40(d.869), vA13(d.896).

Echar Gabul (?Leinster): A39(d.868).

Elphin (bishopric): B23(d.1137).

Emlagh (Imlech Fia, in co. Meath, near Kells): P4(d.948).

Fennor (co. Meath): P8(d.1024).

Fore: A35(d.814), ?vA5(d.835), vA9(d.871), vA11(d.891), vA16(d.930).

Glendalough: B8(d.941), *A52(d.952), ?A55(d.971), *An13(d.1056).

Imlech-forderach (possibly another designation for 'Imbliuch Sescinn', at Lough Ennel, in co. Westmeath): An1(d.756), A61(d.1025).

Inan (or Indeidnen in the parish of Killyon, bar. Westmeath, co. Meath): P8(d.1024).

Inishkeen (co. Louth): A19(d.737), A33(d.794).

Íseal Chiaráin (in Ballyloughloe par., co. Westmeath): C1(d.1060), O6(d.1072), A70(d.1103).

Kells: P12(d.1061), S27(d.1070).

Kilbeggan: P16(d.1196), B28(d.1236).

Kilmacduagh (co. Galway): A68(d.1093).

Lackan in Mide (co. Westmeath): A51(d.948).

Louth: An2(d.758), ?S6(d.814), An3(d.835), AE3(d.949), B10(d.955).

Old Kilcullen (co. Kildare): ?S19(d.1022).

Roscommon: ?A21(d.747), A54(d.966), vA17(d.980), A61(d.1025), A64(d.1052), A67(d.1088).

Roscrea: vA7(d.839), S11(d.920).

Saighir (Seirkieran, co. Offaly, the church of St. Ciarán the Elder): ?A7(d.638).

Taghadoe (near Maynooth, co. Kildare): A26(d.770).

Tuamgraney: A54(d.966), A63(d.1042), A68(d.1093), A69(d.1100).

APPENDIX 2: THE LANDS OF CLONMACNOIS ACCORDING TO THE REGISTRY.

The Ua Ceallaigh donations (nos. 1-40)

1. *D u n a n o g h t* is Doonanought, now Donanaghta parish situated a little to the south-west of Clonfert, county Galway.[1] As a benefice belonging to the church of Clonfert it is listed in the report on the visitation of the diocese around the year 1565.[2]

2. *D u n   B e g l a i t t* is the townland Kilbegley, in Moore parish, in county Roscommon.[3] As *Kylbeglagh* the land appears amongst the possessions of Anthony Brabazon, according to a post mortem inquisition taken in 1604. He held it together with other lands in the area from the Bishop of Meath and Clonmacnois.[4] In the seventeenth century Kilbegley was still in possession of the Bishop of Meath and Clonmacnois.[5] O'Donovan mentions a tradition according to which the old church in Kilbegley belonged to the seven churches of Clonmancois.[6]

3. *D u n m e a d h a i n* seems, together with *Dunanought* and *Dun Beglaitt*, to form the *three Dunta, wch signifieth 3 houses, or els three stillocks or steep places of building* given to St. Ciarán by Cairpre Crum.[7] The place might be Kilmeadain, alias Kyllcomeddan, which like Kilbegley was amongst the lands in Connacht held by Anthony Brabazon in the late sixteenth century. He held it from the bishop of Clonfert.[8]

4. *S u i g h   K i e r a n*. The Registry says there Ciarán received from Cairpre Crum *three Townes in Suigh Kieran whithin the Suca from Belalobhar to Rath Catri*. The exact location is not clear.[9] Father Patrick Egan suggests Creagh parish as general location of Suigh Kieran, since the arrangement on the list of lands, places it between Kilbegeley in Moore parish (east

---

[1]   Registry, p. 454 n.1; SIMINGTON (ed.), Books of Survey, III, pp. 195f.

[2]   NICHOLLS (ed.), Visitations of the dioceses, p. 146. For maps and the modern designation of counties and parishes used in Appendix 2, see MITCHELL, A new genealogical atlas.

[3]   Registry, p. 454 n.2.

[4]   EGAN (ed.), Exchequer inquisition post mortem taken at Roscommon, p. 304.

[5]   SIMINGTON (ed.), Books of Survey, I, p. 62.

[6]   O'DONOVAN, Ordnance Survey Letters, co. Roscommon I, p. 49.

[7]   Registry, p. 453, 454 n.3.

[8]   According to: Exchequer inquisition taken at the hill called Backe, 7th Nobember 1604, edited by EGAN, The parish of Ballinasloe, pp. 304f.

[9]   O'Donovan identifies the place as „See Kieran" in barony Moycarnon. However, there is now no such place in the parishes Creagh and Moore (Registry, p. 454 esp. n.4).

of Creagh) and Tuaim Cathraigh, in Clontuskert parish on the other side of the river Suck (west of Creagh).[10]

5. *G o r t a c h a r n* is a townland in Clontuskert parish, county Galway.[11] It might be the same as *Gort an chuill* in Clonfert diocese claimed as bishop's land in the episcopal rental list from 1407, but in possession of Thomas *mc Cynnedigh*.[12] In 1641 the townland was in possession of several Ua Ceallaigh.[13]

6. *T u a i m   C a t r i g h e* is Tomcattry in Clontuskert parish, county Galway.[14] It is also known as *Kellysgrove*, there is still a children's burial ground in the townland, which probably belonged to Kilclooney parish in earlier times.[15] In 1641 the townland was in possession of the Ua Ceallaigh and the Ua Cobhtaig family.[16] There is however an earlier version, the Headford set of the Books of Survey and Distribution, where Tomcattry is marked as churchland occupied by *Edward Tully McKivas*, who was probably the son of Kyvas Tully, dean of Clonfert at the time.[17]

7. *C r o s   C o n a i l l* appears to be Cross Connell also in Clontuskert parish.[18]

8. *G r a i n s y* is Grainseach or Grange, a townland in the medieval parish Kilclooney, i.e the parts of the modern parish Ballinasloe, situated in county Galway.[19] The townland is mentioned as *Granshagh*, in the Book of Survey. Parts of it, together with other lands in Kilclooney parish were in possession of the Dean Tully, dean of Clonfert in the seventeenth century. The rest of Grange townland was held by several MacEoghans.[20] Edward, son of Kyvas

---

[10] EGAN, The parish of Ballinasloe, pp. 19f.

[11] Registry, p. 454 n.6. Also spelt Gortacarnan or Gortacarnaun (P. W. JOYCE, Irish Names of Places, Dublin 1869, III, p. 370).

[12] NICHOLLS, The episcopal rentals, p. 137.

[13] SIMINGTON (ed.), Books of Survey, III, p. 127; *Kelly, Donogh Mc Owen*, from Gortacharne in Clontuskert appears in the Transplantation report from 1654 (R. SIMINGTON [ed.], The Transplantation to Connaught, 1654-56, Dublin 1970, p. 96).

[14] Registry, p. 454 n.7.

[15] EGAN, The parish of Ballinasloe, p. 13.

[16] SIMINGTON (ed.), Books of Survey, III, p. 128. In the transplantation report from 1654 Daniel Oge Coffy, from Tumcattry - i.e. *Tuam-cattrim in par. Clontuskert*, appears (SIMINGTON [ed.], The Transplantation to Connaught, p. 95).

[17] EGAN, The parish of Ballinasloe, p. 44n. See further down, under Gransagh.

[18] SIMINGTON (ed.), Books of Survey, III, p. 127; SIMINGTON (ed.), The Transplantation to Connaught, p. 95.

[19] Registry, p. 454 n.9; Grange or Granshagh (ir.: Grainseach) was usually a place for grain, generally a monastic granary. The Irish word is borrowed from English (JOYCE, Irish Names of Places, III, p. 388; EGAN, The parish of Ballinasloe, p. 1).

[20] SIMINGTON (ed.), Books of Survey, III, p. 128 (for Mc Rogan read Mc Eagan); EGAN, The parish of Ballinasloe, p. 308.

Tully, the dean was proprietor of Tuaimcattry in Clontuskert parish.[21] [The MacTully, alias MacMaeltuile were possibly a former monastic dynasty in Clonmancois]. The ancient parish of Kilclooney, or Cill cluaine, is known as the place where St. Grellan, the patron saint of the Uí Maine found his church. A monastery in ruins in Kilclooney can be found on the Ordnance Survey Map. It is said to have been a dependency of Clontuskert.[22]

9. *K o y l l - b e l a t h a* was according to Egan the modern townland Kilmalaw in Kilgerrill parish, county Galway, at the western border of Kilcloony parish, north-west of Grange townland.[23] It seems possible that this was *Kilbegnata*, mentioned as a church in the diocese of Elphin in the early fourteenth century royal taxation list.[24] Today the whole of Kilgerrill parish belongs to the diocese of Clonfert.

10. *K i l l   T o r m o i r* is a townland in Kiltormer parish in county Galway.[25] According to the rental list of Clonfert from 1407 *Kiltormoyre* payed one mark as a yearly rent to the bishop of Clonfert.[26] It is listed as a benefice of the church of Clonfert in the report on the visitation of the diocese under Roland de Burgo.[27] In 1640 the townland Kiltormer was in possession of the O'Maddens.[28]

11. *K i l l o r a i n*, alias Cill Odrain, now Killoran, i.e. St. Oran's church is a townland in the parish of the same name in county Galway.[29] Killoran paid a yearly rent of half a mark to the bishop of Clonfert according to the repiscopal rental from 1407.[30] The lands were still held in feefarm from the bishop of Clonfert in the seventeenth century.[31] The vicarage of Kilorain in the middle of the sixteenth century was united to the monastery of Clontuskert in Uí Maine.[32]

---

[21] According to the Headfort set of the Books of Survey (EGAN, The parish of Ballinasloe, p. 44n).

[22] GWYNN / HADCOCK, p. 368.

[23] EGAN, The parish of Ballinasloe, p. 13.

[24] Cal. Doc. Irel. V, p. 224.

[25] Registry, p. 454 n.11.

[26] NICHOLLS (ed.), The episcopal rentals, p. 138.

[27] NICHOLLS (ed.), Visitations of the dioceses, p. 146.

[28] SIMINGTON (ed.), Books of Survey, III, p. 196; Kiltormer 1qr in bar. Longford is also named in: FREEMAN (ed.), Compossicion Booke, p. 72.

[29] Registry, p. 454 n.12. In 1641 this Killoran townland was in joined possession of *Walter Laurence fitz John fitz Walter, John Bryen fitz Christopher* (SIMINGTON [ed.], Books of Survey, III, p. 187).

[30] NICHOLLS (ed.), The episcopal rentals, p. 136.

[31] SIMINGTON (ed.), Books of Survey, III, p. 192.

[32] NICHOLLS (ed.), Visitations of the dioceses, p. 149.

12. *K i l l m o l o n o g* is Kilmalinoge, the name of a townland and parish in county Gal-way.[33] It was claimed as bishop's land in the time of Tomás Ua Ceallaig as bishop of Clon-fert.[34] Later in the century the vicarage was deserted. In the later sixteenth century *Willialmus Ó Cormacayn* was vicar of the church of *Kyllmolonoch*.[35] His family, active in various churches in the area, also held land in Kilmalinog parish in the sevententh century.[36] It seems the vicars family had got hold of the lands of the vicarage.

13. *K i l l   C o i r i l l*. The correct reading in the MS is Kill Goiril.[37] This seems to be Kil-gerrill the name of a townland and parish in county Galway.[38] In the seventeenth century the vicarage of *Kyllgarell* did belong to the Augustinian monks in Aughrim.[39] In 1640 the sur-veyors state about Kilgerrill townland that *this qur payes 4 li p Annu. to ye Bpp of Clonfert*.[40] ? [There is also Clonkeenkerrill, which formed part of the lands of the bishop of Clonfert, but since the time of bishop Muirchertach Ua Ceallaigh in possession of the bishop's family.[41]]

14. *K i l l u i r   M o r*. This is Killuremore, a townland in Killgerrill parish, county Galway.[42] As *Killownemon* the townland appears in the Books of Survey. Parts of it were in possession of Anthony Brabazon, the rest was held by several Ua Ceallaigh.[43]

15. *K i l l u i r   B e g*, like Killuir Mor in Kilgerrill parish. Appears as *Killowrebegg* in the Surveyors report and was also by Anthony Brabazon. According to the Exchequer inquisition taken in 1604 he held one quarter there from the bishop of Clonfert, *by what right the jurors know not*.[44]

---

[33]   Registry, p. 454 n.13.

[34]   NICHOLLS (ed.), The episcopal rentals, p. 138.

[35]   NICHOLLS (ed.), Visitations of the dioceses, p. 150.

[36]   NICHOLLS (ed.), Visitations of the dioceses, p. 150: *Thadeus, praebendarius de Kyll-cuayn, Eugenius, praebendarius de Drochte, Odo praebendarius de Benmore, Johannes vicar of Kyllmoconna, Mauritius vicar of Dunanought, Donatus vicar of Tyrkynesgrech*. In 1640 part of the quarter of Kilmolonog was held by *Erevan Mc Erevan O Corman*, together with *John Oge o Dolean, John Horne Mc Edmund, Garret mc Murrogh O Maddin* (SIMINGTON [ed.], Books of Survey, III, p. 180).

[37]   British Library, MS Additional 4796, fol. 39[r].

[38]   Registry, p. 455 n.1.

[39]   NICHOLLS (ed.), Visitations of the dioceses, p. 148.

[40]   SIMINGTON (ed.), Books of Survey, III, p. 132.

[41]   NICHOLLS (ed.), The episcopal rentals, p. 134n.

[42]   Registry, p. 455 n.2.

[43]   SIMINGTON (ed.), Books of Survey, III, p. 131.

[44]   Ibid.; EGAN, The parish of Ballinasloe, pp. 304f.

16. *K i l u p a i n*, is Killuppane, a townland in Ahascragh parish, county Galway.[45] An Ua Ceallaigh, the son of David son of Domnall Ua Ceallaigh (d.1295), was vicar of Ahascragh around the time when the Uí Ceallaig genealogies in the book of Uí Maine were compiled.[46]

17. *K i l l i t h a i n*, is Killyan or Killian, a townland giving name to a parish in county Galway,owned by several Ua Ceallaigh in 1641.[47] As *Kyllhillayn* this place is listed amongst the lands, the tithes of which belonged to the community of the church of Clonfert according to a papal letter from 1448.[48] The rectory of the vicarage of *Kylleayn* belonged to the nuns of Kilcreevanty in 1665.[49]

18. *K i l l o s a i g e l e a n* is Killosolan, a townland and parish in county Galway.[50] In 1585 four quarters in Killosolan belonged to the bishop of Elphin.[51] In 1641 the townland Killoso-lan was still in possession of the *Ld Bpp. Elphin*.[52] The Ua Dubhagáin supplied the rectors of Killosolan for most of the fifteenth century.[53]

19. *M a o l e a c h* is Moylough a townland and parish, south of Kilkerrin parish in county Galway.[54] There is also Mylech Sinna. Moylough at the Shannon, a vicarage belonging to the church of Clonfert.[55] However Moylough near Kilkerrin seems more plausible here since it fits better in the geographical arrangements of the lands listed.

20. *C l u n c u i l l* has been identified by O'Donovan as a townland in Kilkerrin parish in county Galway.[56]

---

[45]   Registry, p. 455 n.3; SIMINGTON (ed.), Books of Survey, III, p. 14.

[46]   He appears in the last generation, included in the Genealogy. See K. GRABOWSKI (ed.), The Uí Maine genealogies, in: K. GRABOWSKI, The interaction of Politics, Settlement and Church in Medieval Ireland: Uí Maine as a case study, Ph.D Thesis, Cambridge 1988, Appendix 1, pp. 546-655, here 650f.

[47]   Registry, p. 455 n.4; SIMINGTON (ed.), Books of Survey, III, pp. 258-260.

[48]   Cal. Pap. Let. X, pp. 393-396.

[49]   NICHOLLS (ed.), Visitations of the dioceses, p. 148.

[50]   Registry, p. 455 n.5.

[51]   FREEMAN (ed.), Compossicion Booke, p. 169. Indenture of Hy Many, in bar. Theacquin: *...also Toe [Teagh] nepallice consisting of 15 qrs, whereof belongeth to her Matie as in right of the friory of kilternepallice one qr. and to the Bishoppric of Elphin in killossallone 4 qrs, which is conveyed ouer to state of inheritance to the aforesaid Thomas Dillon of Curraghboy.*

[52]   SIMINGTON (ed.), Books of Survey, III, p. 280.

[53]   Cal. Pap. Let., VIII, pp. 201f.; VIII, p. 557; XII, p. 72.

[54]   Registry, p. 455 n.6; SIMINGTON (ed.), Books of Survey, III, pp. 268-272; 170 for Moy-lachmore tl.

[55]   NICHOLLS (ed.), Visitations of the dioceses, p. 146.

[56]   Registry, p. 455 n.7. The name does not appear in Kilkerrin parish (see SIMINGTON [ed.], Books of Survey, III, p. 174).

21. *Killchuirin* is Kilkerrin, a townland and parish in county Galway.[57] In the papal documents Kilkerrin appears as the rectory of *Kyllcaryn, alias Corkomaga* belonging to the diocese of Tuam.[58] The lands of *Corramore* were amongst the churchlands bought by Muirchertach Ua Ceallaigh sometime around the year 1407.[59] According to the Commpossion Booke of Connought 5 qr. in the parish belonged to the bishop of Clonfert in 1585.[60] A quarter in Kilkerrin townland is listed as belonging to the Bishop of Tuam in the Book of Survey (1641).[61]

22. *Dundomnaill in Maghfinn* is Dundonnell townland in Taghmaconnell parish in county Roscommon.[62] In the early fourteenth century the vicarage of *Theachinaconyll* is mentioned as a part of the diocese of Clonfert.[63] In 1407 one part of *Taghmcconayle* was belonging to the church of Clonfert, paying one mark rent to the bishop. The other part belonged to the church of Tuam.[64] The rectory of Taghmaconnel was, together with Creagh belonging to the monks in Kilcreevanty.[65] Magh Finn, or Moyfinn was a territory roughly corresponding to the parish of Taghmaconnell. The dean of Clonmacnois held a quarter in Moyfinn in 1585.[66] However Dundonnell townland was in possession of *Edmond mc Collo Keogh* in 1641.[67] The quarter of the dean of Clonmacnois in Moyfinn might therefore rather be Kilkenney in Taghmaconnell parish.[68]

23. *Tuaimsruthra* is the name of a townland in Creagh parish, county Roscommon.[69] The modern name is Ashford. The bishop of Clonfert received *ex terris de Tuaymsrura duae*

---

[57] Registry, p. 455 n.8.

[58] Cal. Pap. Let. IV, p. 426 (1413).

[59] NICHOLLS (ed.), The episcopal rentals, p. 139.

[60] FREEMAN (ed.), Compossicion Booke, p. 169: *...Corcomoe consisting of 24 qrs, whereof belongeth to the Bishoprick of Clonefert 5 qrs.*

[61] SIMINGTON (ed.), Books of Survey, III, p. 174.

[62] Registry, p. 455 n.9.

[63] Cal. Doc. Irel. V, p. 221.

[64] NICHOLLS (ed.), The episcopal rentals, p. 139.

[65] In 1565-67 the rectory of *Tymcconayll*, together with the vicarages of Creagh, Killalaghton and Killoran, was united to the monastery of Clontuskert in Uí Maine; Moyfinn, the rectory of which was also belonging to the monastery of Kilcreevanty, was held from the bishop of Clonfert for a yearly rent of one mark (NICHOLLS [ed.], Visitations of the dioceses, p. 149; see also Kilkenny in Taghmaconnel parish which must have been included here as well, no. 35).

[66] FREEMAN (ed.), Compossicion Booke, p. 168.

[67] SIMINGTON (ed.), Books of Survey, I, p. 105.

[68] See below, no. 35.

[69] O'Donovan thought this to be Tisara parish, south of Aghleague, bar. Athlone, Co Roscommon (Registry, p. 455 n.11).

marcae in 1407.[70] In the late sixteenth century, the *ruined castle of Tuam Srower and ...the quarter of the same name upon which the said castle is built* was held by Anthony Brabazon from the bishop of Meath and Clonmancois, according to a post mortem inquisition taken by the Exchequer in 1604.[71] One quarter in *Tuaimsrurra* in the dio. of Clonfert was leased *in perpetuum to Captaine Brabson of Ballynosloagh*, by the bishop of Clonfert in 1615.[72] The land was still in possession of the bishop of Clonfert in 1641.[73] Tuaim Sruthra has been identified by M. Connellan as Templereelan, St. Raoilean monastic foundation. He cites local tradition in the area of Ballinasloe, which connects Tuaim Sruthra with Clonmacnois, claiming that Ciarán at one stage contemplated to built his monastery in Tuaim Sruthra.[74]

24. *D y s y o r t* appears as *Disiort* in the manuscript and is corrected to Dysort by a second hand.[75] This is Dysart parish in county Roscommon.[76] The vicarage of *Disert*, forming part of the diocese of Elphin is mentioned in the royal taxation list of the churches of Ireland, dating from the early fourteenth century.[77] In 1641 the townland *Comyn in Disert*, was in possession of the Bishop of Elphin.[78] The two parishes of Dysart and Cam constituted the territory of Clann Uadach in the cantred of Tir Maine. Lands in the two parishes were granted to the Cistercians of St. Mary's abbey in Dublin by Ruaidrí Ua Conchobair, the brother of king Feidlimid.[79] It seems Richard de la Rochelle intended the foundation of a Cistercian abbey here, around the year 1270.[80]

25. *H a b a r t* could not be identified.

[70] NICHOLLS (ed.), The episcopal rentals, p. 139.

[71] Exchequer inquisition post mortem taken at Roscommon, 23 October, 1604 before John Crofton (Record Commissioners' Transcripts, Exchequer Inquisitions, Roscommon, P. R. O. I. 1a/48/87, p. 109), edited by EGAN, The parish of Ballinasloe, p. 304.

[72] EGAN (ed.), The royal visitation, p. 71.

[73] SIMINGTON (ed.), Books of Survey, I, p. 60.

[74] M. CONNELLAN, St. Raoilinn of Teampall Raoileann, in: Galway Arch. Hist. Soc. Jn. 20, no. 3+4 (1943), pp. 145-150; „Shorn of some silly accretions, the story goes, at one time it was contemplated building Clonmacnois' seven churches at Teampall Raoileann. Thwarted here, another attempt was made to build beside the ruins of St. Grellan's church in Kilclooney, two miles further west. The third attempt at Clonmacnois was successfull. The story has this much of a thread in it, that it shows the link between Clonmacnois and Tuaimsruthra was maintained in tradition even till now. ...“ (ibid., p. 149). See also EGAN, The parish of Ballinasloe, p. 27.

[75] British Library, MS Additional 4796, fol. 40^r.

[76] Registry, p. 455 n.12.

[77] Cal. Doc. Irel. V, p. 224.

[78] SIMINGTON (ed.), Books of Survey, I, p. 107.

[79] J. T. GILBERT, Chartularies of St. Mary's abbey, Dublin: with the Registry of its house at Dunbrody, and annals of Ireland, 2 vols. (RS), London 1884, II, pp. 5, 25.

[80] WALTON, The English in Connacht, p. 473; see also GWYNN / HADCOCK, p. 144.

26. *Tuaimgreiny* is Tuamgraney at the southern border of county Galway, belonging to county Clare. This was anciently the southern boundary of Hy Many.[81] Links with Clonmacnois are testified since the tenth century, the times of Cormac Ua Cillín, who was abbot of Clonmacnois, Roscommon and Tuamgraney.[82]

27. *Killtuma* is Kiltoom, a church giving name to a townland and parish in county Roscommon.[83] The townland Kiltoom in the parish was in possession of the bishop of Elphin in 1641.[84]

28. *Carnagh* is a townland in St. John's parish, county Roscommon.[85] There is *Cranagh als Killinecartan*,[86] and *Cranagh als Ballavaney*, listed amongst the townlands in the parish. The latter was in 1641 in possession of Loughlin mc Hugh Kelly.[87] It seems Carnagh townland was included in a royal grant of lands in Connacht to Richard de Exeter.[88]

29. *Cluain acha Leaga* according to O'Donovan is Cloonakilleg townland in Tisara parish county Roscommon.[89]

30. *Acha Obhair* is Aghagower or Gamehill, a townland in Fuerty parish in county Roscommon.[90] Fuerty, alias Fidhard is known as a cell founded by St. Patrick for Deacon Justus, who is said to have, in very old age, baptized St. Ciarán.[91] *Fidard* is mentioned as one of the churches in the diocese of Elphin in the early fourteenth century.[92] There is of course

---

[81] Registry, p. 455 n.14; SIMINGTON (ed.), Books of Survey, IV, pp. 7-12.

[82] He died in 966 (CS).

[83] Registry, p. 455 n.15.

[84] SIMINGTON (ed.), Books of Survey, I, p. 98.

[85] Registry, p. 455 n.16.

[86] SIMINGTON (ed.), Books of Survey, I, p. 114.

[87] Ibid.

[88] The royal confirmation of a grant of lands in Connacht to Richard de Exeter, dated the 20th of April 1301 includes the *villata of Lysmoirchethan and Kunathyth*, also spelt *Lysmorechethan and Cownach* in a second version of the document. Helen Walton has identified the placename *Kunathyth* or *Cownach* as Carnagh, the townland in St. John's parish in question here (Cal. Doc. Irel IV, nos. 802 + 806; WALTON, The English in Connacht, p. 479).

[89] Registry, p. 455 n.17.

[90] Registry, p. 455 n.18; SIMINGTON (ed.), Books of Survey, I, p. 128.

[91] According to Tirechán, see BIELER, The Patrician texts, p. 128, §7.2; pp. 146f., §28.1-3; STOKES (ed.), Tripartite Life, p. 104; GWYNN / HADCOCK, p. 385; for the ruins at Fuerty see Denis H. KELLY, Account of the inscribed stones at Fuerty, co. Roscommon, in: PRIA 8 (1861-64), pp. 455-458; H. S. CRAWFORD, A descriptive list of early cross slabs and pillars, in: JRSAI 43 (1913), pp. 151-169, 261-265, 326-334, here p. 160; O'DONOVAN, Ordnance Survey Letters, co. Roscommon I, pp. 100-105, Letter written in Roscommon, dated 29.6.1837.

[92] Cal. Doc. Irel. V, p. 224.

also *Achud Fobuir*, a Patrician foundation near Croagh Patrick, near Westport. This place would however fall out of the geographical arrangement of the other places mentioned here.[93]

31. *C r e a g h a*, Creagga in the original manuscript was according to O'Donovan Creggs parish in county Galway, in the former barony of Ballymoe. No parish of this name is known there today.[94]

32. *K i l l i a r a i n n* seems to be Killererin parish in county Galway, the northern parts of it forming part of the former barony of Dunmore.[95] The Compossicion Booke of Connought describes 4 qrs of land in Dunmore as belonging to the bishop of Clonmacnois: *The office of Ballymoe - also there is a quantitie of land in the Barrony of Dunmore, called the third of Walter Bermingham scept consisting of 70 qrs whereof belongeth to the Bishop of Clon mc Dnosy 4 qrs.*[96] The 4 qrs are not mentioned by name. However in the survey report from 1641 we find the townland *Caronkilleene* in Dunmore parish and barony, which was then in possession of *Ld Birmingham*.[97] Caronkilleene could well be the *carton of Killin*, the *quarter of Killin*, named after the Killin family of Clonmacnois. Is it possible that *Killiarainn* at some stage belonged to Dunmore parish ?

33. *R u a n* was according to O'Donovan in Creagh parish, near the river Suck.[98] No townland of this name, in Creagh parish is mentioned in the Book of Survey. There is Roan, a townland in Killallaghten parish, county Galway. In 1641 its proprietor was Laughlin Donnellan.[99] The rectory of the vicarage of Killallaghten belonged to the monastery of Clontuskert in 1565.[100]

Ceallach mac Fintach

34. *K i l l m e a s* seems to be Kilmass in Rahara parish, county Roscommon.[101] According to the Clonfert Rental list from 1407, a part of Raghara then belonged to the bishop of Clon-

93 See BIELER, The Patrician texts, pp. 150-153, §37.

94 Registry, p. 455 n.19; the manuscript itself reads *Creagga* (British Library, MS Additional 4796, fol. 40ʳ). See MITCHELL, A new genealogical atlas, pp. 55-57.

95 Registry, p. 455 n.20; SIMINGTON (ed.), Books of Survey, III, pp. 86-89; the parts of the parish Killerean, alias Killererin in the other baronies are not documented in the Books of Survey, see: bar. Dunmore (ibid., pp. 285-310), bar. Taiquin (ibid., pp. 173-176, 267-284), and bar. Bellamoe (SIMINGTON [ed.], Books of Survey, I, pp. 51-58). Compare MITCHELL, A new genealogical atlas, p. 56.

96 FREEMAN (ed.), Compossicion Booke, pp. 80f.

97 SIMINGTON (ed.), Books of Survey, III, p. 294.

98 Registry, p. 455 n.21.

99 SIMINGTON (ed.), Books of Survey, III, p. 123.

100 NICHOLLS (ed.), Visitations of the dioceses, p. 149.

101 Registry, p. 455 n.23.

macnois.[102] The townland was in possession of the bishop of Elphin in 1641.[103] According to Joyce Kilmass in Roscommon takes its name from *Coill-measa*, meaning wood of the nut-fruit (for feeding swine, &).[104]

35. *K i l l   K i l l c h u y n n e* is Kilkenny, in Taghmaconnell parish, county Roscommon.[105] It is described in the Book of Survey as *1 qr of profitable land, a Lough*, and was in posses-sion of Edward Brabazon in 1641.[106] Possibly he used to hold it also from the bishop of Meath and Clonmacnois, like Arnaglog and Cuillen in the near vicinity.[107] Taghmaconnel parish comprised more or less the territory known as Moyfinn in the later middleages. Kil-kenny might therefore be the quarter in Moyfinn held by the dean of Clonmacnois according to the Compossicion Booke of Connought.[108] The townland Kilkenny, in Taghmaconnell contains a site which is known locally to have been a church site and burial ground.[109]

36. *B e l a t h n a o n y* is the townland *Bellaneany* of which half a quarter was in Onagh parish and four quarters in Taghmaconnell (county Roscommon) according to the Survey in 1641.[110] Bealaneny is listed as a Franciscan house in the southwestern part of Taghmacon-nell by Ware.[111] There is also a tradition that Carmelites were settled in Bealaneny.[112]

37. *C o i l l i n   M o l r u a n y* is Culleenmulrony in Creagh parish, county Roscommon.[113] The modern name of the townland is *Cuillen* or *Killin*, there was a small convent of nuns. The church of St. Mary's Kyllin, with houses and other appurtenances was confirmed to the Arroasian nuns of Kilcreevanty in 1223 and again in 1400.[114] According to the surveyor's report from 1641 the lands in *Killinmulroney* contained good arable pasture and meadow, and

---

[102] NICHOLLS (ed.), The episcopal rentals, p. 139.

[103] SIMINGTON (ed.), Books of Survey, I, p. 116: *Killmas* in Raharrow'parish.

[104] JOYCE, Irish Names of Places, III, p. 424.

[105] Registry, p. 456 n.1.

[106] SIMINGTON (ed.), Books of Survey, I, p. 104.

[107] See below, nos. 37, 38.

[108] FREEMAN (ed.), Compossicion Booke, p. 168.

[109] EGAN, The Carmelite cell, p. 19.

[110] SIMINGTON (ed.), Books of Survey, I, p. 105; O'Donovan translates *Bellaneeny* as „vel atha an aonaaigh", „the mouth of the fair", but did not identify the place (Registry, p. 456 n.2).

[111] WARE, De Hibernia, p. 225. See GWYNN / HADCOCK, p. 287.

[112] EGAN, The Carmelite cell.

[113] Registry, p. 456 n.3.

[114] EGAN, The parish of Ballinasloe, p. 31. Compare St. Mary's Cloonoghil in Taghmacon-nell parish, which was also attached to the nunnery of Kilcreevanty (see EGAN, The Carmelite cell).

were held by the dean of Clonmacnois, who had leased it to Edward Brabazon.[115] Cuillen might be *Kyly*, which appears amongst the land held from the bishop of Meath and Clonmacnois by Anthony Brabazon in the late sixteenth century.[116]

38. *T u a i m - t a g h a r*. The rental list of the bishop of Clonfert from 1407 lists *Tuaim Yctair* as paying two marks rent to the bishop.[117] Father Egan suggests the modern townland *Ardnaglog* now in Moore parish, fromerly, in the seventeenth century in Creagh parish, as location of Tuaim-Taghar.[118] It is listed amongst the possessions of Anthony Brabazon in Roscommon, which he held from the bishop of Meath and Clonmacnois until his death in 1597.[119] Ardnaglog was the place to where Ciarán went, when hearing the news of Cairpre Crum's death. The legend has it that he went to Turlaig nDroma, where his clercy carried their bells around the dead body and rang them. From this incident the place took its later name Ard-na Cloc.[120]

39. *K i l l   l u a i n*. The vicarage of *Killuayn* appears in the report of a visitation of the diocese of Clonfert in 1565-67. The vicar then was Cornelius Ua Neachtain, it is also stated that the rectory of the vicarage belongs to the monastery of Aughrim, the first fruits go to two Ua Ceallaigh.[121]

40. *T e r m a n   b e l a f e a d h* might be Termon More and Termon Beg townlands in Kilkeevin parish, near Castlerea, county Roscommon.[122]

The Ua Máelsechlainn donations (nos. 41-60)

41. *K y l l e c r u y m e r y a c h r y*, now Kilcumreragh parish, otherwise Kill, also popularly called Rosemount, north-east of Moate, in county Westmeath.[123] There was an early Chris-

---

[115] SIMINGTON (ed.), Books of Survey, I, p. 60.

[116] EGAN (ed.), Exchequer inquisition post mortem taken at Roscommon, p. 304.

[117] NICHOLLS (ed.), The episcopal rentals, p. 139.

[118] EGAN, The parish of Ballinasloe, p. 14. O'Donovan gives no identification (Registry, p. 456 n.4); the Books of Survey do not list a townland of this name.

[119] EGAN, The parish of Ballinasloe, p. 304.

[120] MEYER (ed.), Wunderbare Geschichten, pp. 224-226; Registry, p. 453f. n.

[121] NICHOLLS (ed.), Visitations of the dioceses, p. 148.

[122] Suggested to me by Dr A. S. Mac Shamhráin.

[123] Registry, p. 449 n.39. I am much indebted to Liam Cox, who very kindly read through this appendix and who commented in detail in particular on the placenames in Offaly and Westmeath. Some of his comments will be cited in full length: „Much of the study such as it is that I've done on Clonmacnois goes back to the mid 1930s. You see I was born on the feast of Saint Ciaran 9 September 1908 almost 89 years ago, so if you come across some thing foolish or out of place please excuse it and know it is the result of old age or loss of memory or both. - There was an old tradition among the local people around Clonmacnois that in the

tian monastery here founded by St. Fiachra, called Cell-Cruimthir-Fiachrach, now Cill Chruimthir Fhiachrach.[124] An isolated branch of the O'Maelmhuaidh (O'Molloy) were settled in Kilcumreragh.[125] The townland Kilcumreragh in the parish according to the surveys in 1641 contained 230 acres of Glebeland, i.e churchland.[126] Knockasta, a hill is situated in the parish, which was also known as Connacosta or Cnoc Bhreacháin, is mentioned as one of the boundary marks of a piece of land granted to Ciarán by Feradach mac Duach, king of Uisneagh (d.582) once when Ciarán stayed in Íseal Chiaráin.[127] There is another story among the tales in the Aided Dhiarmada, according to which the hill was offered to Ciarán by Diarmait mac Cerbeill, the ancestor of the Southern Uí Néill. Ciarán however refused to take the land because the king had burned the house of one of his enemies there without the saint's permission.[128]

42. *Killcliathagh* is Kilcleagh parish, near Ballyloughloe in county Westmeath.[129] In the papal documents the vicarage of Kilcleagh, is often referred to as *Kyllomyleon*, which was the parish church, some 2 miles west of Kilcleagh. The vicarage was, with a brief intermission in the fifteenth century, united with the church of Ballyloughloe.[130] The name *Kyllo-*

---

calm of the evenings angels come and go between Heaven and the cemetery." (Letter to the author, dated the 25th of July 1997).

[124] GWYNN / HADCOCK, p. 390; the Uí Braoin of Cill Chruimthir Fiachrach are mentioned in Trinity College Dublin MS H. 2. 7., p. 176. See WALSH, The placenames of Westmeath, p. 19 n.1, pp. 280-284. Liam Cox commented: „It is interesting that the Uí Braoin at Cill Cruimthir Fhiachrach are mentioned here, as they were the Uí Braoin Breaghmaine usually associated with St. Mary's parish, Athlone. Evidently they were spread much further to the east in the early Christian centuries. There was Magh Breaghmaine in what is now co. Longford in the 14th, 15th and early 16th centuries and the Uí Braoin were around Durrow when Hugh de Lacy was murderer there c.1186." (Liam Cox, private correspondence).

[125] ALCé, AConn, Misc. Irish Ann., 1401, p. 163 for the Ua Maoilmuaidh at Kilcumreragh. „The O'Maelmhuaidh were otherwise settled in Feara Cell, a name now obsolete, refering to „that part of sw. county Offaly around the town of Kilcormac" (Liam Cox, private correspondence).

[126] LYONS (ed.), Book of Survey, co. Westmeath, p. 68.

[127] Compare above, p. 228 n.37.

[128] O'GRADY (ed.), Silva Gadelica, I, pp. 73f.

[129] Registry, p. 449 n.4. Liam Cox comments: „Kilcleagh, now popularly called Castledaly, adjoins the old parish of Ballyloughloe now Mount Temple. The latter parish was the patrimony of the Magawlys, called Calry. Kyllomyleon is/was ca. 2 miles w. of Kilcleagh and was at times the parish church. It is now written Killomenaghan, i.e. Cill Míanacháin from Míanach, son of Failbhe and brother of Manchán (see WALSH (ed), Genealogiae Regum et Sanctorum Hiberniae, p. 41). The same source (p. 116) gives Colman Cille Clettig so that the parish must have been dedicated to him. Manchán the brother of Míanacháin must be distinguished from Manchán of Lemanaghan. Míanacháin was he of Kilomenaghan in Killcleagh parish." (Liam Cox, private correspondence).

[130] In the papal documents Kilcleagh appears under a variety of different spellings and names, as Kyllonacon, alias Eyncolman, Killeomilenyn, Kyllomeliol, Killeliach, Killemil-

myleon seems very likely to derive from the Ua Máeleoin family from Clonmacnois who dominated the vicarage of Kilcleagh in the fifteenth century.[131] According to the seventeenth century surveys they were also the chief landholders in the parish.[132] The townland *Boggagh Malone* in Kilcleagh parish, also testifies to the presence of the family there.[133] The parish was dedicated to St. Manachan.[134] Five castles, Clonlonan, Farnagh, Kilbillaghan, Castletown and Newcastle were situated in Kilcleagh parish, they are all ascribed to the O'Melaghlins. A sixth castle there, Ballycahillroe is said to have belonged to the Mac Cochláins.[135]

43. *K i l b i l e a g h a n* is Kilbillaghan, a townland in Kilcleagh parish, the site of a castle built by Ua Máelsechlainn.[136] In 1641 the townland was in possession of *Murtagh and John Melaughlin*, in 1663 it was held in feefarm by *Edmond Malone*.[137]

44. *K i l l i m n i m h o g* could not be identified.

45. *C o i l l n a c u r r a n a g h* is Kilnagarnagh a townland right in the centre of Lemanaghan parish, in county Offaly, about seven miles east of the church of Clonmancois.[138] The rectory of *Killenecorenaghe* was belonging to the monastery of Granard at the time of the dissolution in 1540.[139]

46. *L y a h m a n a c h a n* is Lemanaghan parish in county Offaly.[140] A church was founded there in the mid seventh century by St. Manachán.[141] He was according to a popular tradition

---

chon, Keyneolman, Kyllomyleon. See MCNAMEE, Identification of certain placenames, pp. 15f.; COSTELLO (ed.), De Annatis Hiberniae, I, p. 148.

[131] Cal. Pap. Let. X, pp. 541f. (15. Jan. 1451-52); Cal. Pap. Let. XIII, p. 66 (1. March 1478); Cal. Pap. Let. XIV, p. 67 (29. Jan. 1484-85).

[132] Namely Edmond and Richard Malone, and Katherine Malone alias Pettit (LYONS [ed.], Book of Survey, co. Westmeath, pp. 121-125).

[133] Ordnance Survey of Irland, One inch to a mile, 1855-1900. (Phoenix Maps, Dublin 1989) sheet 108.

[134] WALSH, The placenames of Westmeath, pp. 11f.

[135] Ibid., p. 11. Liam Cox comments: „Ballycahillroe means the town of Red Charlie (Coghlan) but the Mac Cochláins were only there for a short time in the 16th century. There was a church there previously and glebeland." (Liam Cox, private correspondence).

[136] Registry, p. 449 n.5; WALSH, The placenames of Westmeath, p. 11.

[137] LYONS (ed.), Book of Survey, co. Westmeath, p. 122.

[138] Registry, p. 449 n.7; Ordnance Survey of Ireland, One inch to a mile, 1855-1900 (Phoenix Maps Dublin 1989) sheet 108.

[139] Fiants of Elizabeth, no. 1401, in: Appendix to the 13th Report of the Deputy Keeper, p. 209. This detailed list of possession of the former monastery dates from the year 1569; compare N. B. WHITE (ed.), Extents of Irish monastic possessions 1540-1541, Dublin 1943, p. 281.

[140] Registry, p. 449 n.8.

a brother of Ciarán of Clonmacnois, who lived however more than a century before his alleged brother.[142] Sometimes Welsh origin is attributed to St. Manchán, his church was a place of pilgrimage in the middleages.[143] St. Manchán is also mentioned as a fellow saint and friend of St. Patrick in the *Additamenta* to Tirechán's *collectanea*.[144] In the thirteenth century the monastery disappears from the records.[145] The shrine of St. Manchán survived his monastery and is now on display in Boher Church, Ballycumber, county Offaly.[146] The vicarage of Lemanaghan was a dependency of the Cistercian house in Granard in the later middle ages, down to the sixteenth century when the monastery was disolved.[147] According to the Clonmacnois annals Lemanaghan, alias Tuaim nEirc was granted to Clonmacnois in the middle of the seventh century by Diarmait son of Áed Sláine, the ancestor of the Síl nÁedo Sláine.[148]

47. *C l o i t h r e a n* is Cloghran townland in Clonmacnois parish.[149]

48. *C l u a i n - I m t h y n* is Cloniffeen townland also in Clonmacnois parish.[150] The name should possibly be read Cluain Afféin and might derive from Affén or Affinus of Glendalough, relecting on the *óentad* between the two settlements.[151]

---

[141] AFM 664. For a discussion of the various saints, called Manachán in the Irish hagiographical tradition see J. GRAVES, The church and shrine of St. Manchán, in: Jn. of the Royal Hist. and Arch. Association of Ireland 3 (1874), pp. 134-150, here 136f. Compare O'DONOVAN, Ordnance Survey Letters, King's county I, pp. 219-221, Letter from Lemanaghan, dated 18.1.1838, who resolves the confusion about the various saints by pointing out that „Archdall did not reckognize a priniting mistake in Colgan's Acta Sanctorvm".

[142] O'DONOVAN, Ordnance Survey Letters, co. Westmeath I, p. 63, Letter from Athlone, dated 9.9.1837 for St. Ciarán and St. Managhan.

[143] AClon 664, p. 107; WALSH, The placenames of Westmeath, p. 12 n.2.

[144] BIELER (ed.), The Patrician texts, p. 178, §15.2.

[145] AClon, 220 s.a.1205; ARCHDALL, Monasticon, p. 401.

[146] GRAVES, The church and shrine; H. S. CRAWFORD, A descriptive list of Irish shrines and reliquaries, in: JRSAI 53 (1923), pp. 14-93, 151-176, here 83-93; R. Ó FLOINN, Irish shrines & reliquaries of the middle ages, Dublin 1994, p. 16.

[147] Cal. Pap. Let. VI, p. 201 (18. Kal Sept. 1410); Fiants of Elizabeth no. 1401, in: 13th Report of the Deputy Keeper, p. 209.

[148] CS 646; AClon 642, p. 104; AFM 645. For Áed Sláine see O'BRIEN (ed.), Corpus Genealogiarum Hiberniae, p. 161 (144 b 44) brother of Colmán Mor, son of Conaill Cremthainn, ancestor of the Síl nÁedo Sláine.

[149] Registry, p. 449 n.9. For Clonmacnois parish see O'DONOVAN, Ordnance Survey Letters, King's county I, 166-197, Letter written in Banagher, 15.1.1838, who interviewed Mr. Patrick Molloy about the antiquities of the church. What is believed to have been St. Ciarán's crozier, was sold by some unnamed Irish family in England and bought by W. Frazer, who brought it back to Ireland (see W. FRAZER, On an Irish Crozier, with early metal crook, probably the missing „Crozier of St. Ciarán", in: PRIA 17 [1889-91], pp. 206-214; CRAWFORD, A descriptive list of Irish shrines and reliquaries, p. 169).

49. *Teagh-Sarain*, Saran's house now Tisaran parish in county Offaly.[152] According to the Registry Tisaran is situated in Kilbeg, where St. Saran built a church and paid tribute for it to Ciarán. He was also obliged to give shelter to those of the Uí Mháelsechlainn who went on pilgrimage to Clonmacnois.[153] It is difficult to trace St. Saran. The late-medieval Irish Life of St. Maedóc of Ferns tells the story how a certain Saran, who was *erenagh* of Temple-Shanbo (one of Maedóc's foundations) killed the king of Leinster. Maedóc, greatly concerned about the killing, not only resucitated the king but also made the arm of Saran falling off. The later repented and went away fom Leinster to built himself a church where he lived furtheron as a one-armed saint. There is however no hint about the location of his dwelling. Possibly Tisaran here was the house of this Saran from Leinster?[154] However, as Liam Cox pointed out to me, „the Genealogiae Regum et Sanctorum (ed. WALSH, p. 121) traces Saran of Tisaran to Cormac Cas mac Oilella, the common ancestor fo the Dál gCais and incidently of the Mac Cochlains of Dealbhna, the territory around Clonmacnois."[155]

50. *Killchamin*, St. Camin's church is Kilcamin townland in the parish of Gallen, or Ferbane, county Offaly.[156] There was an early monastery in Gallen, possibly a Welsh foundation.[157]

51. *Cluain Laigean Magharetighefinn*. Cluain Laigean has been identified as Clonlyon townland in Clonmacnois parish.[158] It seems it was situated in *Magharetighefinn*, the plain of the white house, the name is preserved as *Magheramore*, the great plain, the name of the lands, situated at the main road from Clonmacnois to the east.[159] According to the Registry the income from Clonlyon went towards the building of the road from Clonlyon to Clonfinlough, the name of a lake, and some hills in Clonmacnois parish, about one mile

---

[150] Registry, p. 449 n.10.

[151] S. Affén is mentioned in the Book of Lecan, fol. 373ᵛ. Thanks to Dr Alan MacShamhráin, who suggested this to me, and also commented very helpfully on other points concerning the identification of the place names.

[152] Registry, p. 449 n.11. The parish was dominated by the Uí Mháelsechlainn in the later middle ages (AFM 1541, 1542). See CRAWFORD, A descriptive list of early cross slabs and pillars, p. 265, for a description of the crosses in Tisaran.

[153] Registry, pp. 449f.

[154] Charles PLUMMER (ed.), Bethada Náem nÉrenn, I, pp. 231f., §§142-144.

[155] Liam Cox, private correspondence.

[156] Registry, p. 450 n.1.

[157] GWYNN / HADCOCK, p. 176; WARE, De Hibernia, p. 161; J. PINKMAN, The monastery of Gallen, Offaly, in: Ardagh and Clonmacnois Arch. Soc. Jn. 2, no. 10 (1945), pp. 48-51; W. W. HOWELLS, The early Christian Irish. The skeletons at Gallen priory, in: PRIA 46 (1940/41), pp. 103-220; KENDRICK, Gallen priory excavations 1934-35.

[158] Registry, p. 450 n.2 and 3.

[159] Ordnance Survey of Ireland, One inch to a mile 1855-1900 (Phoenix Maps, Dublin, 1989) sheet 108.

east of the monastic settlement.[160] This was a section of the 'great road', one of the main roads of Ireland leading from Dublin in the east to Kiltullagh, Clarinbridge in the west, dividing Leth Chuinn from Leth Mhogha.[161] It was maintained by the Uí Mháelsechlainn according to the claim in the Registry.

52. *Cluainard na cross* or *Ardnacross* was bestowed to Clonmacnois by Ua Máelmuaid.[162] One could assume, that this name was a mistaken version of *Ardnaglog* a townland in St. Mary's parish Athlone, where lands belonging to St. Ciarán are otherwise attested.[163] However, as Liam Cox pointed out to me, the Ua Máelmuaid never owned land near Athlone, and we should rather expect *Cluainard na cross* to be somewhere in Feara Ceall in sw. modern Offaly.

53. *Killcumynn*, together with the following six donations was given to the church by *Senimnyn McColmain*, as his share of the family lands. *Killcumyn* might be Kilcummin townland in Tisaran parish, county Offaly or, as Liam Cox suggests it was a townland in Kilcleagh parish, county Westmeath, where the *ClanColmain, alias O'Melaghlin* were seated.[164]

54. *Killmanachan* is Kilmanaghan parish east of Kilcleagh, north east of Lemanaghan. The greater part of Kilmanaghan parish is in modern county Offaly.[165] There was a castle, Moyelly, or Magh Eli in what used to be the mensal lands of the Uí Chatharnaigh, since the elventh century, who were very prominent in Clonmacnois at the time.[166] The patron saint of

---

[160] Ibid.; Registry, p. 450.

[161] Ó LOCHLAINN, Roadways in ancient Ireland, p. 471.

[162] Registry, p. 450 n.7 and 8.

[163] PINKMAN, Placenames of St. Mary's Parish, p. 39; AClon 1210, p. 224.

[164] See Ordnance Survey of Ireland, One inch to a mile 1855-1900 (Phoenix Maps, Dublin 1989) sheet 108 for Kilcummin in Tisaran parish. O'Donovan suggested Kilcomin parish, near Roscrea, where a monastery was founded by St. Cumin from Iona in the seventh century (Registry, p. 450 n.10; AU 669; GWYNN / HADCOCK, p. 389). I tend to follow Liam Cox who suggested: „Senimnyn Mc Colmain was, from his name, associated with the Clan Colmáin, the tribe name of the O'Melaghlins. The Annates in the 15th and 16th centuries refer to Kilcleagh parish as Clyncolman and Keyncolman obviously Clancolman hence, I believe Killcumynn was in or near the present townland of Boyannagh which was anciently called Boyannagh-colmanna. I had evidence of this location for Killcumynn, but I can't find it now." (Liam Cox, private correspondence).

[165] Registry, p. 450 n.11.

[166] AFM 1098. Cox, Historic Moyelly, pp. 238-241. „Moyelly was never a territory it was a castle belonging to Sionnach, otherwise the Fox, descended from the Ó Catharnaigh. Cloghatanny, i.e. Cloch an tSionaigh - the Rock of the Fox, was a Fox seat down to about 1780 in the same area. Kilmanaghan parish is now popularly called Tubber parish. The territorial name of the area was Muintir Tadgáin named from Tadgán, 9th century ancestor of the Uí Catharnaig, later the Sionacha or the Foxes." (Liam Cox, private correspondence).

the parish was St. Manachán, St. Ciarán's alleged brother.[167] The placename *Killmanachan* in the original manuscript of the *Registry of Clonmacnoise* is annotated in the handwriting of Ussher, as being situated in *Westmeath, out of the plantation*. This points to sometime around 1622, the year in which the surveys of the dioceses of Meath and Clonmacnois were taken under Ussher (then bishop of Meath), as the time when the transcript and translation of the Registry were made.[168]

55. *K i l l c h i* has been identified by O'Donovan as Killachonna townland in the parish of Ballyloughloe, county Westmeath. Liam Cox suggested to read *Killchi* as *coillte* and pointed to the woodlands in Clonlonan townland in Kilcleagh parish, county Westmeath as possible location of *Killchi*.[169]

56. *K i l l c h r o n a g h   w c h   i s   c a l l e d   T i g h - n a - c u a r t a*. The reading of the placename in the MS is unclear, the ink is spoilt by water.[170] It seems in O'Donovan's times the passage was still readable, he says that in a modern hand *Killbeacagh* was written over the original *Killchronagh*.[171] *Tigh na Cuarta* might be the 'house of the circuit', a place to stay for the abbot or bishop, whilst on tour in his paruchia.[172] However both places could not be identified.

57. *I n n e o i n* is Dungolman the name of a river and townland in Ballymore parish, county Westmeath.[173] Ballymore, alias Loughseudy was an important Anglo-Irish stronghold in Meath throughout the later middleages.[174]

58. *B e l l a   A t h a n u r c h o i r*. The correct spelling in the MS is Bellathanurchoir.[175] This is Ardnurcher, or Horseleap parish in county Westmeath.[176] There is a townland *Temple*

---

[167] O'DONOVAN, Ordnance Survey Letters, co. Westmeath I, pp. 60-64, Letter from Athlone, dated 9.9.1837, on Kilcleagh and Kilmanaghan. Compare above, nos. 42, 46.

[168] British Library, MS Additional 4796, fol. 36[r]; Thanks to Mr. O'Sullivan, who pointed this out to me. See above, chap. 6, for the date of compilation of the Registry.

[169] Registry, p. 450 n.12. Liam Cox doubts O'Donovan's identification: „I think it was O'Donovan himself who identified Killachonna as Cill Dachonna - Dachonna's church, but how he equated it with „Killchi" of the Registry I don't understand. „Killchí" looks like *coillte*, the Irish word for woods. But what woods?" (Liam Cox, private correspondence, compare below under Cluain lonan, nr.59).

[170] British Library, MS Additional 4796, fol. 38[v].

[171] Registry, p. 450 n.13 and 14.

[172] Dr S. Duffy pointed this out to me. For the definition of *cúairt* as the circuit undertaken by a poet or a churchmen see R. I. A. Dictionary.

[173] Registry, p. 450 n.15; LYONS (ed.), Book of Survey, co. Westmeath, p. 55. „Inneoin is the Irish word for anvil and at present the Dungolman river at Tang, co. Westmeath on its way to the river Shannon, is called Anvil river. The anvil is a particular hunk of rock in the river. Somebody made a fancy name for their residence from anvil when they called it Annville." (Liam Cox, private correspondence).

[174] WALSH, The placenames of Westmeath, pp. 330f., 334; AFM 1450, 1598.

McTyre in Ardnurcher parish, where there was an old abbey still in O'Donovan's time.[177] This seems to be the same place as *Tech meic in tsair*, where according to tradition Ciarán was brought up and where his father and three sisters were buried.[178] St. Ciarán as the patron saint of the parish was replaced in the post-Norman period by the Welsh Saint David.[179]

59. *C l u a i n   l o n a n* , is Clonlonan, a townland in Kilcleagh parish in county Westmeath.[180] The castle there was in possession of the Ua Máelsechlainn family.[181] The townland is listed as woodland in the Book of Surveys. In 1641 Upper Clunlunan wood was in possession of *Sir Luke Ffitz Gerald*, Lower Clunlunan wood was in possession of *Thomas Daly*.[182]

The Ua Conchobair donations (nos. 60-65)

60. *T o b a r   I l b e* , is Toberelva, or Toberelly a townland and a well in Baslick parish, county Roscommon.[183] Baslick, the church of bishop Sachell in Ciarraige, was according to

---

[175] British Library, MS Additional 4796, fol. 38ᵛ. For the various forms of the name Horseleap alias Ath an Urchair, see 'As Cartlann na Logainmneacha. Horseleap', Dinnseanchas 2 (1967), pp. 115-117, also vol. 3 (1968/69), p. 22.

[176] Registry, p. 450 n.16.

[177] LYONS (ed.), Book of Survey, co. Westmeath, p. 70; WALSH, The placenames of Westmeath, pp. 249-256; L. COX, Moate, co. Westmeath. A history of the town and district, Dublin 1981. „At Templemacateer in Ardnurcher parish according to the Ordnance Survey Field Name Book 41 was 'the site of an old abbey near a good farm house.' Bits of the old buildings were used as stables. Date 1837. There was a small church dedicated to St. Brigid in Ardnurcher townland in the 15th century. Her well is still there quite close to the main road at the village of Horseleap. The correct name is Baile árd an urchair - the *baile* or town of the height of the *urchar*, or cast or shot." (Liam Cox, private correspondence).

[178] STOKES (ed.), Félire Óengusso, p. 203; STOKES (ed.), Lives of Saints, p. 119, ll. 3999f.

[179] WALSH, The placenames of Westmeath, pp. 249-256; for Ardnurcher St. David's see for example Cal. Pap. Let. XII, p. 29.

[180] Registry, p. 450 n.17. Compare above no. 2, Kilcleagh parish.

[181] AFM 1553.

[182] LYONS (ed.), Book of Survey, co. Westmeath, p. 121. Liam Cox noted: „The castle here was Ó Melaghlin's chief one when this part of Westmeath became shireground about 1570. As a result Ó Melaghlin's territory became the barony of Clonlonan. The placename means the *cluain* or meadow land of Lonan, a man's name, possibly a saint. If Killchi under No.55 means woods as I suggest, Upper and Lower Clonlonan Woods could be the woods in question." (Liam Cox, private correspondence).

[183] Registry, p. 451 n.4; see also O'DONOVAN (ed.), AFM IV, p. 1090, note y.

Tirechán befriended with St. Patrick.[184] There were Franciscans of the third order established in Toberelly in the later middleages, the houses was deserted in the late sixteenth century.[185]

61. *T a m h n a g h*, seems to be identical with *Tamnuch* in the territory of Uí Ailella, identified as Tawnagh in county Sligo, some miles north of Lough Arrow near Riverstown. This was one of the churches in Connacht which were under the authority of Clonmancois as early as the seventh century, according to the witness of Tirechán.[186]

62. *K i l m u r i h y* was probably the townland Kilmurry in the parish of Baslick, county Roscommon, which once housed Dominican monks.[187]

63. *K i l m a c t e i g e* is Kilmacteige, a parish near the Ox mountains, half way, little south of the road between Ballina and Tobbercurry, county Sligo.[188] There was churchland, belonging to the bishopric of Achonry according to the Compossicion Booke of Connought.[189] Local tradition associates a well there, *Tubber Keeraun*, with St. Ciarán of Clonmacnois.[190]

64. *T u i l l s g e* is Tulsk, in county Roscommon, about eight miles north of the town of Roscommon, now in Ogulla parish, county Roscommon.[191] The *Old Castle 1 qr. & 1/2 Arable and Pasture* there, were part of Ogulla parish and in possession of the Earl of West-

---

[184] BIELER (ed.), Patrician texts, pp. 148f., §32.5; pp. 146f., §29.2. See also STOKES, Tripartite Life, p. 108.

[185] Archdall mentions the chappel as *Toberelly in Maghery*, identified by C. Mooney as the townland of Toberelvy in Baslick parish (see GWYNN / HADCOCK, p. 275); *The chappell of Tobbir oylise, waste and yet valued at 5s* is mentioned in NICHOLLS (ed.), A list of monasteries, pp. 28-43, here 38; see also ibid., n.93. In the seventeenth century Books of Survey *Tober Ilvy* is mentioned as *Crown land whereon standeth an old Chapell & a Well called St. Bridgets Well* (SIMINGTON [ed.], Books of Survey, I, p. 49).

[186] BIELER (ed.), The Patrician texts, pp. 142f., §25.2; see also NICHOLLS, Some Patrician sites, p. 114 n.5. Registry, p. 451 n.5. There is however also the townland *Tawnagh More*, in the parish of Kilmore, county Roscommon, which in the seventeenth century was claimed by the Earl of Westmeath (see SIMINGTON [ed.], Books of Survey, I, p. 30).

[187] The list of monasteries in Connacht, dating from 1577 mentions *The chappel of Kilmurry. Waste and yet valued at 5s* (see NICHOLLS [ed.], A list of monasteries, p. 38, n.94). There is also Kilmurry in Kiltullogh parish, in the former barony Ballintobber, county Roscommon (SIMINGTON [ed.], Books of Survey, I, p. 19); furthermore there is Killmurrie, in Tagh mac Walter parish in bar. Ballymoe, co. Galway, in possession of the bishop of Tuam in 1585 (FREEMAN [ed.], Compossicion Booke, p. 84). This was a Franciscan friary, otherwise known as Killowaine (see NICHOLLS [ed.], A list of monasteries, p. 38 n.65); see also GWYNN / HADCOCK, p. 279.

[188] Registry, p. 451 n.7.

[189] FREEMAN (ed.), Compossicion Booke, p. 122.

[190] O'RORKE, History of Sligo town, II, pp. 152f.

[191] Registry, p. 451 n.8; AFM IV, p. 793 note m.

meath in the seventeenth century.[192] A Domincan Priory was founded there in the early fifteenth century by an Ua Conchobair.[193]

65. *K i l l o g e a l b a* is Killogulla or Ogulla parish.[194] The bishop of Elphin was in possession of several lands in this parish of Ogulla in the seventeenth century.[195]

The Ua Ruairc donations (nos. 66-72)

66. *C l u a i n - c l a i r* appears to be Cloonclare in county Leitrim, where St. Patrick is said to have founded a church.[196]

67. *C l u a i n   l o c h u i l l* alias *Cluain leamhchoille*, the meadow of the elmwood seems to be Cloonlaughill, in the parish of Cloone, county Leitrim.[197] The church of Cloone, alias Cluain Conmaicne was an early foundation by St. Cruimthir Fraech. The erenagh's family in Cloone in the later middle ages were the Mac Tedhechain.[198]

68. *K i l l   I m o i r e* . „Kill Imoire may be Cill Iomaire, the church of contention or difficulty. Iomar also means a vat or font, especially for holy water. But where was it? Except that we'd expect it to be in Ó Rourke's territory of Breifne in modern counties Leitrim and Roscommon. Iomaire sometimes means a ridge or low hill and as such appears as Cill an iomaire, anglicised Killenummery, as the name of a parish in county Leitrim. It could be Kill

---

[192] SIMINGTON (ed.), Books of Survey, I, p. 79; Tilske according to index - Tidske according to text.

[193] Annals of Ireland from the Year 1443 to 1468, translated from the Irish by Duald Mac Firbis for Sir James Ware 1666, in: J. O'DONOVAN (ed.), Irish Archeological Society Miscellanea, vol. 1, Dublin 1846, pp. 198-302, here 220f.; FREEMAN (ed.), Compossicion Booke, pp. 153, 157; AClon p. 327 n.4; GWYNN / HADCOCK, pp. 230f.

[194] Registry, p. 451 n.9.

[195] SIMINGTON (ed.), Books of Survey, I, pp. 76-79; FREEMAN (ed.), Compossicion Booke, pp. 153f., where Ogulla parish is not mentioned by name, but the bishop of Elphin appears as holder of land in *Cowrin mc Brenan*, in the barony Roscommon, which seems to stand for the former property of the monastery of St. Brenan in Ogulla (GWYNN / HADCOCK, p. 400).

[196] Registry, p. 451 n.11; P. O'CONNELL, The diocese of Kilmore, Dublin 1937, pp. 130f.

[197] Registry, p. 451 n.12. There is also Cloonoghill, a convent of nuns in county Roscommon, little south west of Athlone, but this could hardly be claimed as an Ua Ruairc donation by Clonmacnois (see GWYNN / HADCOCK, p. 315).

[198] Muirgheas Ua Muireadhaigh, airchinnech Chluain Conmhaicne died on his pilgrimage (AFM 1101); Maigistir Niocól Mag Techeadain, *officel cluana do ecc* (AFM 1373); Iosep Mac Teithedan *espoc Conmaicne* (AConn 1230.11.); Pol Mag Teithechain *comurba Cluana* (AConn 1384.8). The comarba of Cluana, without a name is again mentioned in AConn 1471.17 and 1519.12. Compare GWYNN / HADCOCK, p. 32.

Imoire. Because Kill an Imoire means the church of the ridge. Local knowledge of the place could verify the identity or otherwise."[199]

69. *Kill McCoyril* now Killmackerrill, but where?[200]

70. *Eanagh Duibh* is Annaghduff in county Leitrim.[201] There was an early monastery possibly founded by Cummin, the seventh century abbot of Iona. A hospital, and the termon-lands of Annaduff are mentioned by Archdall as having existed in the sixteenth century.[202]

71. *Magh Anaile near Logh na Giall* could not be identified. Liam Cox suggested that Logh na Giall could stand for Logh Gill in county Sligo.[203]

72. *Kill Tachuir* is Kiltoghert, a parish at the Shannon in county Leitrim, near the town of Leitrim.[204] There was an abbey or a hospital there in the later middleages.[205] Kiltoghert was a stronghold of Ua Ruairc in the fifteenth century.[206]

The Mac Diarmada donations (nos. 73-75)

73. *Cnocauicarie*. This is Knockvicar at the river Boyle, near Lough Cé, now included in the parish of Kilmactranny.[207] There was a house of Franciscans of the Third Order here according to the list of monasteries in Connacht in 1577.[208]

74. *Killeathraght* is Kill Atrachta, now Killaraght, south west of Boyle, in county Sligo.[209] *Cella Adrochtae* was according to Tirechán founded by Patrick, Atrachta is said to

---

[199] Liam Cox, private correspondence.

[200] Registry, p. 451 n.14.

[201] Registry, p. 451 n.15.

[202] Cummin Fionn, abbot of Iona, died in 669 (AU); Archdall says that in 1559 a *Hospital, Termon-Irrenagh or Corbeship at Annaghyew* was endowed with 1/2 a tl. and 2 qrs of land (see GWYNN / HADCOCK, pp. 28, 346; J. J. MCNAMEE, History of the diocese of Ardagh, Dublin 1954, pp. 108f.

[203] Registry, p. 451 n.16. „*Giall* usually means a hostage, but could Logh na Giall be Logh Gill in county Sligo? Magh Anaile is the plain of Anaile, anglicised Annaly which was used to designate the lands of the O'Farrells in what is now county Longford. But the Mágh Anaile here was near Logh na Giall wherever that was." (Liam Cox, private correspondence).

[204] Registry, p. 451 n.17.

[205] GWYNN / HADCOCK, pp. 353, 366.

[206] AConn 1419.21; AConn 1442.3.

[207] Registry, p. 452 n.8; see AFM 1361; AFM 1595.

[208] In 1577 *The Chappell of Cnockenvicare [was found] in the occupation of Teig O Morane, priest and valued at p.a. 5s* (see NICHOLLS [ed.], A list of monasteries, p. 37 n.91; compare GWYNN / HADCOCK, p. 273).

have received her veil from St. Patrick. Here church was also in possession of patens and a chalice of St. Patrick.[210] The place was also called *Drummana*, or *Machari*. A convent of nuns still existed in Killaraght at the end of the sixteenth century.[211]

75. *R a t h   S a l a i n n* is Rahallon, which was a well known place also situated in in Magh Luirg in O'Donovan's time.[212]

The Mac Carthaigh donations (nos. 76-79)

76. *Kyllkyran   in   Desmond* would be the church of Ciarán in Desmond. According to O'Donovan this is Kilkerrin, about six miles from Clonakilty, in south county Cork.[213]

77. *Killcluain*, the church of Cluain or Clonmacnois could be Kilcloyne near Carrigtuohill, county Cork.[214]

78. *Killtorpain*. O'Donovan identified this place as Kilturpin, county Cork.[215] Temple Torpain was also the alternative name of Temple Dowling alias Temple Hurpan in Clonmacnois, according to the plan of Clonmancois in BL MS Add. 4784, f.20. Liam Cox confirmed the assumption that the two places were linked with the same Torpan.[216]

79. *Killa   Tleibhe*, was possibly Killatlevy, in county Limerick, near the borders of Kerry.[217] According to the seventeenth century transcriber of the Registry *the other fiue kills or cells cannot be reade....*[218]

---

[209] Registry, p. 452 n.9.

[210] BIELER (ed.), The Patrician texts, pp. 148f., §31.2; see also STOKES (ed.), Tripartite Life, p. 108.

[211] GWYNN / HADCOCK, p. 352; Benedict O Mochain archdeacon of Killaraght died in 1361 (ALCé 1361; AU 1361 where he is styled *erenagh*).

[212] Registry, p. 452 n.10.

[213] Registry, p. 457 n.9.

[214] Registry, p. 457 n.10.

[215] Registry, p. 457 n.11.

[216] Cox:"Westropp says IRSAI, 1907, p. 287, this was Temple Dowling. While there is no obvious connection between the two places Torpan may have been connected with the two. In a footnote Westropp says *ór do thorpain* appeared on a tombstone found in the old Franciscan churchyard in Athlone. This stone doesn' appear to be now available. There are modern tombstones of the Claffey families of Killogeenaghan in Temple Mac Labhthaigh, which with Temple Dowling, make up the double building known as Temple Torpain." (Liam Cox, private correspondence).

[217] Registry, p. 457 n.12.

[218] Registry, p. 457.

Donations by the Geraldines from Desmond (nos. 80-87)

80. *D u n   D o m n a l l   i n   C o n a l l a g h e* is now Dundonnell, an old church near the town of Kathkeale, giving name to a parish in bar. Lower Connelloe, co. Limerick.[219]

81. *A t h   D a r a* now Adare, in co. Limerick, the seat of the Earl of Dunraven, where the Geraldines erected three magnificent abbeys.[220]

82. *K i l l c l u a y n* is obiously Kilcloyne.[221]

83. *B r e g a i g*, now Bregogem parish in Bar. Orrery and Kilmore, co. Cork.[222]

84. *K i l l   D a r i r e*, now Kildorrery, parish in bar. Condons and Clangibbon, co. Cork.[223]

85. *K i l l c y u y l*. Killeagh (?) in bar. Imokilly, co. Cork.[224]

86. *K i l l   D r o c h a y l e*. Not known.[225]

87. *C r o o m a i g h*. Now the town of Croome, bar. Coshma, co. Limerick.[226]

The livings of the abbot of Clonmacnois (nos. 88-93)

88. *h a l f   o f   t h e   N u n n s   l a n d s*, seemingly land formerly attached to the nunnery, little east of the main monastic settlement of Clonmacnois. In the twelfth century the nuns church together with some lands were granted to the Arrouaisian nuns in Clonard, later to the convent in Kilcreevanty.

89. *T u l a g h a i t t*, was still known as the name of a hill at Clonmacnois in O'Donovan's time, possibly the hill where in the thirteenth century the castle was built upon.[227]

---

[219] Registry, p. 458 n.2.

[220] Registry, p. 458 n.4.

[221] Registry, p. 458 n.5. „Kill Cluayn is obviously Kilcloyne and so is Killcluain (no.77). The only meaning I can take of the two Kilcloynes is that there was only one which changed hands from the Mac Carthaighs to the Geraldines through war or otherwise. The Registry was apparently compiled from two documents at this point." (Liam Cox, private correspondence).

[222] Registry, p. 458 n.6.

[223] Registry, p. 458 n.7.

[224] Registry, p. 458 n.8.

[225] Registry, p. 458 n.9.

[226] O'Donovan has a lovely comment here: „This place originally belonged to the O'Donovans; but they were driven from thence shortly after the English invasion by the Fitzgeralds of Kildare, from which they took their motto of Crom-a-boo" (Registry, p. 458 n.10).

90. *Half the profitt of the house of the dead in Keaf Cass*, maybe the late medieval designation for Eglais beg, the monastic mortuary chapel.[228]

91. *Cluanburyin*, now Cloonburren where a convent of nuns used to be situated.[229] According to the Registry there was the causeway leading from Clonburren to Faltia in Moore parish. This road still existed in O'Donovan's time and a huge stone cross, known as the cross of Cairpre Crum stood in the middle of the road. According to tradition this was the place where Ciarán resucitated Cairpre Crum, king of Uí Maine.[230] The vicarage of Clonburren, together with Moycarnan, alias Moore belonged to the diocese of Tuam.[231]

92. *Ibhar-Conare* is defined as lying between *Druymglaisse* and *the mearing of Muigh Carnan*, *Druymglaisse* is Drumglass, in Moore parish,[232] the *mearing of Moycarnan*, the shores of the Shannon in Moore parish.

93. *Aithkyran in the Parish of Cluin Ó Cormacan*, seems to be Aith Kyran or Ahkeeran, in Clonigormican parish in county Roscommon, south of Tulsk.[233] The Ua Cormacan family appears as a dominant ecclesiastical family in Clonfert diocese, occupying many of the vicarages and rectories there.[234]

---

[227] Registry, p. 458 n.15.

[228] See above, pp. 41-43.

[229] Registry, p. 459 n.2.

[230] O'DONOVAN, Ordnance Survey Letters, co. Roscommon I, pp. 54-58, Letter from Ballinasloe, dated 18. 6. 1837.

[231] GWYNN / HADCOCK, p. 315. See above, pp. 173-179.

[232] Registry, p. 459 n.4.

[233] Registry, p. 459 n.6 and 7.

[234] See above Ua Ceallaigh donation, Kilmonologe, no. 12.

The livings of Ua Cillín (nos. 94-95)

94. *Cluain Leamchoill* could be Cloonloughill, in Cloone parish in south county Leitrim.[235] It seems also possible that it was near the nunnery Cloonoghil, little south west of Athlone.[236]

95. *Ferrann Ó Killyn in Cluain* must have been the lands of Ua Cillín in Clonmacnois.[237]

---

[235] This place is also claimed as a donation from Ua Ruairc, see above no. 67; Registry, p. 459 n.9.

[236] GWYNN / HADCOCK, p. 315.

[237] O'Donovan thought this to be Farranykenny in Clonfert parish, county Galway (Registry, p. 459 n.10.). Liam Cox: „I think this is a simple statement of fact. Ó Killyn was the local handyman, who looked after the water supply to the monastery, and the Registry says he built himself 'a Church house'. His name was Ó Cillín now represented by Killeen and Killion and common in the midlands. Fearann Ó Killyn in Cluain is Ó Cillín's land in Clonmacnois." (Liam Cox, private correspondence).

BIBLIOGRAPHY

Manuscripts

Royal Irish Academy, Dublin

MS Stowe D.ii.1.: The Book of Uí Maine.

MS 14 B 4: 'Notes relative to the Ó Malone family of Westmeath'.

Trinity College Dublin

MS 1292 (formerly H. 1. 18): The Annals of Tigernach.

MS 1298 (formerly H. 2. 7), fol. 14^r-15^v: The Uí Maine genealogies.

MS 1378 (formerly H. 5. 6), p. 150: Poem on the heros of Leth Cuinn by Conaing Buidhe Ua Máelchonaire (A reileag laoch leithe cuinn). See also MS 1291 (formerly H. 1. 17.).

British Library, London

MS Additional 4784, fol. 20^r: 'The plott of ye churches at Clonmcnoys'.

MS Additional 4787, fol. 276^r: 'A plan of Clonmacnois'.

MS Additional 4796, fol. 36^r- 43^v: 'The Registry of Clonmacnois'.

MS Additional 4814 fol. 3^r-7^v: 'A List of Franciscan Houses in Ireland'.

MS Additional 4817: 'The Annals of Clonmacnois as translated from the Irish by Conall Mageoghagan in 1627 written by Donall O'Sullivan in 1661'.

MS Additional 37571, fol. 548^r: 19th century photograph of the Cross of the Scriptures in Clonmacnois.

MS Additional 37575, nos. 46-64: Rubbings from the crosses at Clonmacnois, together with photographs nos. 114-117.

Primary Works

Account of the escheator, Pipe Roll X. Ed. I., in: Appendix to the 36th report of the deputy keeper, Dublin 1904, p. 61.

Account of the escheator. Pipe Roll a. r. XVIII Ed. I., in: Appendix to the 37th report of the deputy keeper, Dublin 1905, p. 40.

Adomnán's Life of Columba, ed. and transl. Alan Orr ANDERSON / Marjorie Ogilvie ANDERSON, Oxford 1991.

Annála Connacht: The Annals of Connacht (A.D. 1224-1544), ed. A. Martin FREEMAN, Dublin 1944, reprint 1983 [AC].

Annála rioghachta Éireann: annals of the kingdom of Ireland by the Four Masters, ed. John O'DONOVAN, 7 vols., Dublin 1851 [AFM].

The Annals in Cotton MS. Titus A. XXV, ed. A. Martin FREEMAN, in: Revue Celtique 41 (1924), pp. 301-330; 42 (1925), pp. 283-305; 43 (1926), pp. 358-384; 44 (1927), pp. 336-361.

The Annals of Clonmacnoise being Annals of Ireland from the earliest period to A.D. 1408, transl. into English A.D. 1627 by Conell Mageoghagan, ed. Denis MURPHY, Dublin 1896, reprint 1993 [AClon].

Annals of Ireland from the Year 1443 to 1468, translated from the Irish by Duald Mac Firbis for Sir James Ware 1666, in: John O'DONOVAN (ed.), Irish Archeological Society Miscellanea, Dublin 1846, pp. 198-302.

The Annals of Loch Cé: a chronicle of Irish affairs, 1014-1590, ed. William M. HENNESSY, 2 vols. (Rolls Series), London 1871 [ALCé].

The Annals of Tigernach, ed. and transl. Whitley STOKES, in: Revue Celtique 16 (1895), pp. 374-419; vol. 17 (1896), pp. 6-33, 119-263, 337-420; vol. 18 (1897), pp. 9-59, 150-197, 267-303, reprint in 2 vols., Felinfach 1993 [AT].

The Annals of Ulster (to A. D. 1131), ed. and transl. Seán MAC AIRT / Gearóid MAC NIOCAILL, Dublin 1983 [AU].

Annála Uladh. The Annals of Ulster, otherwise, Annala Senait, Annals of Senat; a chronicle of Irish affairs A.D. 431-1131: 1155-1541, ed. and transl. B. MAC CARTHY / William M. HENNESSY, 4 vols., Dublin 1887-1901 [AU].

De Annatis Hiberniae. A calendar of the first fruits' fees levied on papal appointments to benefices in Ireland A.D. 1400 to 1535, ed. M. A. COSTELLO, vol. 1: Ulster, Dundalk 1909.

ARCHDALL, Mervyn, Monasticon Hibernicum, Dublin/London 1786.

The ban-Shenchus, ed. Margaret C. DOBBS, in: Revue Celtique 47 (1930), pp. 282-339; vol. 48 (1931), pp. 163-234; vol. 49 (1932), pp. 437-489.

Die Benediktiner Regel, ed. G. HOLZHERR, Zürich/Einsiedeln 1976.

Betha Adamnáin: The Irish Life of Adamnán, ed. Máire HERBERT / Pádraig Ó RIAIN, London 1988.

Betha Colaim Chille: Life of Columcille compiled by Manus O'Donnell in 1532, ed. A. O'KELLEHER / G. SHOEPPERLE, Urbana 1918.

Betha Féchin Fabair. The Life of Féchin of Fore, ed. Whitley STOKES, in: Revue Celtique 12 (1891), pp. 318-353.

Bethada Náem nÉrenn. Lives of Irish Saints, ed. and transl. Charles PLUMMER, 2 vols., Oxford 1922, reprint 1968.

The Book of Fenagh, ed. William M. HENNESSY / Denis H. KELLY, Dublin 1875.

The Book of Lecan. Leabhar Mór Mhic Fhir Bhisigh Leacain. Facsimile edition, Irish Manuscript Commission, Dublin 1937.

The Book of Leinster formerly Lebar na Núachongbála, ed. R. I. BEST e. a., Dublin 1954.

Book of Survey and Distribution of co. Westmeath, ed. J. C. LYONS, Ladiston 1852.

Books of Survey and Distribution, ed. Robert SIMINGTON, vol. I: Roscommon, Dublin 1949; vol. II: Mayo, Dublin 1956; vol. III: Galway, Dublin 1962; vol. IV: Clare, Dublin 1967.

The Book of Uí Maine otherwise called „The Book of the O'Kellys", facsimile edition, ed. Robert Alexander Steward MACALISTER, Dublin 1942.

Calendar of documents relating to Ireland, ed. H. S. SWEETMAN, 5 vols., London 1875-1886 [Cal. Doc. Irel.].

Calendar of entries in the papal registers relating to Great Britain and Ireland: papal letters, ed. W. H. BLISS / J. A. TWEMLOW / M. HAREN / A. P. FULLER, London 1893ff. [Cal. Pap. Let.].

Calendar of patent rolls of the reign of Henry III preserved in the Public Record Office (1216-1266), ed. H. C. MAXWELL-LYTE, 5 vols., London 1901-1910 [Cal. Pat. Rolls Henry III].

A calendar of the reassembled register of John Bole, Archbishop of Armagh, 1457-1471, ed. Anthony LYNCH, in: Seanchas Ardmhacha 15 (1992), pp. 113-185. [See also National Library of Ireland, Dublin MS No. 2691, Canon Leslie Collection: Typescriptcopy of Bishop W. M. Reeves calendar of Primate Octavian, with an index by Rev. J. B. LESLIE, c. 1935; and Trinity College Dublin MS 557/9, Bishop Reeves' transcript of Primate Octavianus Register.]

Canastíc mac leghind, ticim ochluain chelbínd, ed. Rudolf THURNEYSEN, Mittelirische Verslehren, in: Whitley STOKES / Ernst WINDISCH (eds.), Irische Texte mit Übersetzung und Wörterbuch, Leipzig 1891, pp. 93f.

A Certificate of the State and Revennewes of the Bishoppricke of Meath and Clonemackenosh, ed. Charles R. ELRINGTON, The whole works of the Most Rev. James Ussher, vol. 1, London 1864, Appendix V, pp. liii-cxxv.

Chartularies of St. Mary's abbey Dublin, ed. John T. GILBERT, 2 vols. (Rolls Series), London 1884-86.

A chorographical description of West or H-Iar Connaught written A.D. 1684 by Roderic O'Flaherty, ed. James HARDIMAN, Dublin 1846.

Chronicon Scotorum. A chronicle of Irish affairs, from the earliest times to A.D. 1135, ed. and transl. William M. HENNESSY, London 1866 [CS].

COLGAN, John, Acta Sanctorvm Veteris et Maioris Scotiae sev Hiberniae Sanctorvm Insvlae, Louvain 1645, reprint with an introduction by Brendan JENNINGS, Dublin 1947.

The Compossicion Booke of Connought 1585, ed. A. Martin FREEMAN, Dublin 1936.

Corpus Genealogiarum Hiberniae, ed. M. A. O'BRIEN, Dublin 1962, revised by John V. KELLEHER, 1976.

DUGDALE, W., Monasticon Anglicanum, ed. J. CALEY / H. ELLIS, 6 vols., London 1817-1830.

Elegy of Erard Mac Coise, chief Chronicler of the Gaels, pronounced over the Tomb of Fergal O'Ruairc, chief of Brefny, at Clonmacnois, ed. John O'DONOVAN, in: Jn. Kilk. SE. Irel. Arch. Soc. 1 (1856-57), pp. 314-356.

The episcopal rentals of Clonfert and Kilmacduagh, ed. Kenneth W. NICHOLLS, in: Anal. Hib. 26 (1970), pp. 130-143.

Evangeliorum Quattuor Codex Durmachensis, ed. A. A. LUCE e. a., Olten-Lausanne 1960.

Exchequer inquisition post mortem taken at Roscommon, 23 October, 1604 before John Crofton (Record Commissioners' Transcripts, Exchequer Inquisitions, Roscommon, P. R. O. I. 1a/48/87, p. 109), ed. Patrick K. EGAN, The parish of Ballinasloe, Dublin/London 1960, p. 304.

Exchequer inquisition taken at the hill called Backe, 7 November, 1604, (Record Commissioners' Transcripts, Exchequer Inquisitions, Galway, P. R. O. I. 1a/48/86, p. 181), ed. Patrick K. EGAN, The parish of Ballinasloe, Dublin/London 1960, pp. 304f.

Expugnatio Hibernica: The conquest of Ireland by Giraldus Cambrensis, ed. A. B. SCOTT / F. X. MARTIN, Dublin 1978.

Extents of Irish monastic possessions 1540-1541, ed. Newport B. WHITE, Dublin 1943.

Félire Óengusso Céli Dé. The Martyrology of Aengus the Culdee, ed. Whitley STOKES, London 1905, reprint Dublin 1984.

Fiants of Elizabeth, in: Appendixes to the 11th-17th report of the deputy keeper, Dublin 1879-84.

Fled Bricrenn ocus Loinges mac nCuíl Dermait, ed. Ernst WINDISCH, in: Whitley STOKES / Ernst WINDISCH (eds.), Irische Texte, zweite Serie, 1. Heft, Leipzig 1884, pp. 164-216.

A fresh authority on the Synod of Kells, ed. Dean LAWLOR, in: PRIA 36 (1921), pp. 16-22.

Genealogiae Regum et Sanctorum Hiberniae, ed. Paul WALSH, Dublin 1918.

The genealogies of the Southern Uí Néill, ed. Margaret C. DOBBS, in: ZCP 20 (1936), pp. 1-30.

The genealogies, tribes and customs of Hy-Fiachrach, ed. John O'DONOVAN, Dublin 1844.

The great Chartulary of Glastonbury, ed. D. A. WATKIN, 3 vols., London 1947-52.

The inauguration of O'Conor, ed. Miles DILLON, in: John A. WATT / J. B. MORRALL / F. X. MARTIN (eds.), Medieval studies presented to Aubrey Gwynn, Dublin 1961, pp. 186-202.

Die Irische Kanonensammlung, ed. Herrmann WASSERSCHLEBEN, Leipzig ²1885.

Irish historical documents 1172-1922, ed. Edmund CURTIS / R. B. MCDOWELL, London 1943, reprint 1968.

KEATING, Geoffrey, Foras feasa ar Éirinn: The history of Ireland, ed. D. COMYN / P. S. DINEEN, 4 vols., London 1902-14.

The Latin and Irish Lives of Ciaran, ed. Robert Alexander Steward MACALISTER, London 1921.

Lebor na hUidre. Book of the Dun Cow, ed. R.I. BEST / Osborn BERGIN, Dublin 1929, reprint 1992.

Liber exemplorum ad usum praedicantium, ed. A. G. LITTLE, London 1966.

A list of monasteries in Connacht 1577, ed. Kenneth W. NICHOLLS, in: Galway Arch. Hist. Soc. Jn. 33 (1972/73), pp. 28-43.

Lives of Irish Saints, ed. PLUMMER, see: Bethada Náem nÉrenn.

Lives of Saints from the Book of Lismore, ed. Whitley STOKES, Oxford 1890.

LYNCH, John, De Praesulibus Hiberniae, ed. John Francis O'DOHERTY, 2 vols., Dublin 1944.

The Martyrology of Donegal. A calendar of the Saints of Ireland, transl. John O'DONOVAN, ed. James Henthorn TODD / William REEVES, Dublin 1864.

The Metrical Dindshenchas, ed. and transl. Edward J. GWYNN (Todd Lecture Series), Dublin 1903-1935, reprint in 5 vols., Dublin 1991.

Miscellaneous Irish Annals (A.D. 1114-1437), ed. and transl. Séamus Ó HINNSE, Dublin 1947.

The monastery of Tallaght, ed. Edward J. GWYNN / W. J. PURTON, in: PRIA 29 (1911), pp. 115-179.

Notes d'hagiographie Celtique. No. 17: Aní día fil manchine Chloinde Colmáin ocus Sil Aodha Sláine do Chlúain. Un miracle posthume de St. Ciarán de Clúain en faveur du roi Diarmait mac Cerrbéoil, ed. and transl. Paul GROSJEAN, in: Analecta Bollandiana 69 (1951), pp. 96-102.

The O'Clery Book of genealogies, ed. Seamus PENDER, in: Anal. Hib. 18 (1951), pp. 1-194.

Ordnance Survey, 6 inch maps, co. Westmeath, Dublin 1838.

The Patrician texts in the Book of Armagh, ed. and transl. Ludwig BIELER, Dublin 1979.

Le poème de Torna-Éices sur le cimetière de Croghan, ed. H. D'ARBOIS DE JUBAINVILLE, in: Revue Celtique 17 (1896), pp. 280-285.

A poem of prophecy on Ua Conchobair kings of Connacht, ed. Brian Ó CUÍV, in: Celtica 19 (1987), pp. 31-54.

Registrum Iohannis Mey: The register of John Mey, Archbishop of Armagh, 1443- 1456, ed. W. G. H. QUIGLEY / E. F. D. ROBERTS, Belfast 1972.

The Registry of Clonmacnoise; with notes and introductory remarks, ed. John O'DONOVAN, in: Jn. Kilk. SE. Irel. Arch. Soc. 1 (1856/57), pp. 444-460.

A reigleag laoch leithe cuinn, ed. from Trinity College Dublin MS no. 1291 (formerly MS H. 1. 17) by Margarete STOKES, in: George PETRIE, Christian inscriptions in the Irish language, ed. Margarete STOKES, Dublin 1872, vol. 1, pp. 79-81; see also a second edition from MS Rawl. B 512, by R. I. BEST, The graves of the kings at Clonmacnois, in: Ériu 2 (1905), pp. 163-171.

The royal visitation of Clonfert and Kilmacduagh 1615, ed. Patrick K. EGAN, in: Galway Arch. Hist. Soc. Jn. 35 (1976), pp. 67-76.

Silva Gadelica, ed. Standish Hayes O'GRADY, 2 vols., London 1892.

The Song of Dermot and the Earl: an old French poem from the Carew manuscript no. 596 in the archiepiscopal library at Lambeth Palace, ed. Goddard H. ORPEN, London 1892.

The Stowe Missal, ed. George F. WARNER, 2 vols., London 1906.

The synod of Ráith Breasail. Boundaries of the dioceses of Ireland [A.D. 1110 or 1118], ed. John MAC ERLEAN, in: Archivium Hibernicum 3 (1914), pp. 1-33.

Tairnic in sel-sa ac Síl Néill, ed. Brian Ó CUÍV, in: Ériu 34 (1985), pp. 157-174.

Topographical poems by Seaán Mór Ó Dubhagáin and Giolla-na-Naomh Ó hUidhrín, ed. James CARNEY, Dublin 1943.

The transplantation to Connaught, 1654-56, ed. Robert SIMINGTON, Dublin 1970.

The tribes and customs of Hy-Many, commonly called O'Kelly's Country, ed. and transl. John O'DONOVAN, Dublin 1843.

The Tripartite Life of Patrick, ed. Whitley STOKES, London 1887.

The Uí Briúin Bréifni genealogies, ed. Mícheál Ó DUÍGEANNÁIN, in: JRSAI 64 (1934), pp. 90-137 and 213-256.

The Uí Maine genealogies, ed. Kathryn GRABOWSKI, The interaction of politics, settlement and church in medieval Ireland: Uí Maine as a case study, Ph.D Thesis, Cambridge 1988, Appendix 1, pp. 546-655.

Visitations of the dioceses of Clonfert, Tuam and Kilmacduagh, c. 1565-67, ed. Kenneth W. NICHOLLS, in: Anal. Hib. 26 (1970), pp. 144-157.

Vitae Sanctorum Hiberniae ex codice olim Salmanticensi nunc Bruxellensi, ed. William W. HEIST (Subsidia Hagiographica 28), Brussels 1965.

Vitae Sanctorum Hiberniae, ed. Charles PLUMMER, 2 vols., Oxford 1910.

WARE, James, De Hibernia et Antiquitatibus ejus, London 1654.

WARE, James, De Praesulibus Hiberniae, London 1665.

The whole works of Sir James Ware concerning Ireland, vol. 2, part I: The antiquities of Ireland, ed. Walter HARRIS, Dublin 1745.

The whole works of the Most Rev. James Ussher D. D., Lord Archbishop of Armagh and Primate of All Ireland, with a life of the author and an account of his writings, ed. Charles R. ELRINGTON, 16 vols., London 1847-64.

Wunderbare Geschichten von Corpre Cromm mac Feradaig (Buch der Húi Maine, fo. 126 b 1), ed. Kuno MEYER, in: Archiv für Celtische Lexikographie 3 (1907), pp. 224-226.

Secondary Works

BANNERMAN, John, Studies in the history of Dalriada, Edinburgh/London 1974.

BEST, R. I., Notes on the script of Lebor na Huidre, in: Ériu 6 (1912), pp. 161-172.

BIGGER, Francis Joseph, The Franciscan friary of Kilconnell, co. Galway, in: Galway Arch. Hist. Soc. Jn. 1 (1901), pp. 145-167; vol. 2 (1902), pp. 3-20; vol. 3 (1903), pp. 11-15.

BINCHY, Daniel, Patrick and his biographers: ancient and modern, in: Studia Hibernica 2 (1962), pp. 7-173.

BLAKE, Martin, Knockmoy Abbey. The monastery of the „hill of victory". Notes on its history and some ancient charters relating to it, in: Galway Arch. Hist. Soc. Jn. 1 (1901), pp. 65-84.

BLOCH, Marc, Feudal society, transl. L. A. MANYON, Padstow 1961, reprint 1989.

BOYD, Katherine E., Tithes and parishes in medieval Italy, Ithaca/New York 1952.

BRADY, J., Origin and growth of the diocese of Meath, in: IER 72 (1949), pp. 1-13, 166-176.

BREATNACH, R. A., The Book of Uí Mhaine, in: Liam DE PAOR (ed.), Great Books of Ireland, Dublin 1967, pp. 77-89.

British Library catalogue of additions to the manuscripts 1756-1782, Additional manuscripts 4101-5017, London 1977.

BYRNE, Francis John, The rise of Uí Néill and the high-kingship of Ireland, Dublin 1969.

BYRNE, Francis John, Irish kings and high-kings, London 1973.

BYRNE, Paul, The community of Clonard, sixth to twelfth centuries, in: Peritia 4 (1985), pp. 157-173.

CARRIGAN, William, The history and antiquities of the diocese of Ossory, 4 vols., Dublin 1905.

CONNELLAN, M., St. Raoilinn of Teampall Raoileann, in: Galway Arch. Hist. Soc. Jn. 20 (1943), pp. 145-150.

CONNOLLY, Seán, Vita Prima Sanctae Brigitae. Background and historical value, in: JRSAI 119 (1989), pp. 5-49.

CONWAY, Colmcille, The lands of St. Mary's abbey Dublin, in: PRIA 62 (1962), pp. 21-25.

CONWAY, Colmcille, The story of Mellifont, Dublin 1958.

CORKERY, John, Cluan Chiaráin - The city of Ciarán, Longford 1979.

COTTON, Henry, Fasti Ecclesiae Hibernicae. The succession of the prelates and members of the cathedral bodies in Ireland, vol. 3: The province of Ulster, Dublin 1849.

COX, Liam, Historic Moyelly - Home of Colonel Richard Grace, in: Jn. of the Old Athlone Society 1 (1974/75), pp. 238-241.

COX, Liam, Íseal Chiaráin, the low place of St. Ciarán, where was it situated?, in: Jn. of the Old Athlone Soc. 1 (1969), pp. 6-14. [earlier published in: Ardagh and Clonmacnois Ant. Soc. Jn. 12 (1951), pp. 52-65].

COX, Liam, Moate. co. Westmeath. A history of the town and district, Dublin 1981.

CRAWFORD, Henry S., Athlone excursion. Descriptive particulars of places visited, in: JRSAI 37 (1907), pp. 318-348.

CRAWFORD, Henry S., A descriptive list of early cross slabs and pillars, in: JRSAI 43 (1913), pp. 151-169, 261-265, 326-334.

CRAWFORD, Henry S., A descriptive list of Irish shrines and reliquaries, in: JRSAI 53 (1923), pp. 14-93, 151-176.

CRAWFORD, Henry S., Bealin Cross, Twyford, county Westmeath, in: JRSAI 37 (1907), pp. 320-322.

CROKER, Thomas Crofton, Researches in the South of Ireland, London 1824.

CURTIS, Edmund, Richard II in Ireland 1394-5, Oxford 1927.

DALTON, John D., Ancient boundaries of Ardagh and Clonmacnoise dioceses, in: Ardagh and Clonmacnois Ant. Soc. Jn. 1 (1926), pp. 9-70; vol. 2 (1929), pp. 1-73.

DOBBS, Margaret C., The territory and people of Tethba, in: JRSAI 68 (1938), pp. 241-259; vol. 71 (1941/42), pp. 101-110.

DOHERTY, Charles, Clonmacnois, in: Lexikon des Mittelalters 4 (1989), pp. 2166-2169.

DOHERTY, Charles, The cult of St. Patrick and the politics of Armagh in the seventh century, in: Jean-Michel PICARD (ed.), Ireland and Northern France A.D. 600-850, Dublin 1991, pp. 53-94.

DOHERTY, Charles, The Irish hagiographer: resources, aims, results, in: Tom DUNNE (ed.), The writer as witness: literature as historical evidence, Cork 1987, pp. 10-22.

DOHERTY, Charles, The monastic town in early medieval Ireland, in: Anngret SIMMS / H. B. CLARKE (eds.), The comparative history of urban origins in non-roman Europe, Oxford 1985, vol. 1, 45-75.

DOHERTY, Charles, Some aspects of hagiography as a source for Irish economic history, in: Peritia 1 (1982), pp. 300-328.

DOYLE, Doirin, The story of Clonmacnois, Dublin 1970.

DUFFY, Seán, Ireland in the middle ages, Dublin 1997.

DUMVILLE, David / Kathryn GRABOWSKI, Chronicles and annals of mediaeval Ireland and Wales. The Clonmacnoise-group Texts, Woodbridge 1984.

DUMVILLE, David, Latin and Irish in the Annals of Ulster, A.D. 431-1050, in: Dorothy WHITELOCK / R. McKITTERICK / David DUMVILLE (eds.), Ireland in early medieval Europe. Studies in memory of Kathleen Hughes, Cambridge 1982, pp. 320-341.

DUMVILLE, David, Saint Patrick A.D. 493-1993, Woodbridge 1993.

EDWARDS, Nancy, The archaeology of early medieval Ireland, Philadelphia 1990.

EDWARDS, Nancy, The South Cross Clonmacnois, in: John HIGGITT (ed.), Early medieval sculpture in Britain and Ireland, Oxford 1986, pp. 23-48.

EGAN, Patrick K., The parish of Ballinasloe, Dublin/London 1960.

EGAN, Patrick K., The Carmelite cell of Bealaneny, in: Galway Arch. Hist. Soc. Jn. 26 (1954-55), pp. 19-25.

EMPEY, C. Adrian, The Butler lordship in Ireland 1186-1515, Ph.D Thesis, Trinity College Dublin 1970.

ETCHINGHAM, Colmán, Aspects of early Irish ecclesiastical organization, 2 vols., Ph.D Thesis, Trinity College Dublin 1992.

ETCHINGHAM, Colmán, Bishops in the early Irish church: a re-assessment, in: Studia Hibernica (forthcoming).

ETCHINGHAM, Colmán, The early Irish church: some observations on pastoral care and dues, in: Ériu 42 (1991), pp. 99-118.

ETCHINGHAM, Colmán, The implications of *paruchia*, in: Ériu 44 (1993), pp. 139-162.

FARRELL, James P., Historical notes and stories of county Longford, Dublin 1886, reprint Longford 1979.

FELTEN, Franz J., Äbte und Laienäbte im Frankenreich, Stuttgart 1980.

FLANAGAN, Marie Therese, Henry II and the kingdom of Uí Fáeláin, in: John BRADLEY (ed.), Settlement and society in medieval Ireland. Studies presented to F. X. Martin, Kilkenny 1988, pp. 229-239.

FLANAGAN, Marie Therese, St. Mary's Abbey, Louth, and the introduction of the Arrouaisian observance into Ireland, in: Clogher Record 10 (1979-81), pp. 223-234.

FLANAGAN, Marie Therese, Irish society, Anglo-Norman settlers, Angevin kingship. Interactions in Ireland in the late twelfth century, Oxford 1989.

FLICHE, Auguste, La réforme grégorienne, 3 vols., Louvain/Paris 1924, 1926, 1937, reprint Geneva 1978.

FLOOD, W. H. Grattan, The episcopal succession in Clonmacnois, in: IER 32, no. 4 (1912), pp. 76-82.

FLOWER, Robin, Catalogue of Irish manuscripts in the British Library, vol. 2, London 1926, reprint Dublin 1992.

FLOWER, Robin, The Irish tradition, Oxford 1947, Dublin [2]1994.

FRAZER, W., On an Irish Crozier, with early metal crook, probably the missing „Crozier of St. Ciarán", in: PRIA 17 (1889-91), pp. 206-214.

GALBRAITH, V. H., The East Anglian See and the Abbey of Bury St. Edmunds, in: English Historical Review 40 (1925), pp. 222-228.

GAMBLE, W., Clonmacnois, its history and achievements, Dublin 1950.

GIFF, William Lee M., The Story of Clonmacnois, Athlone 1957.

GLEESON, Dermot F. / Aubrey GWYNN, A history of the diocese of Killaloe, Dublin 1961.

GRABOWSKI, Kathryn, The interaction of politics, settlement and church in medieval Ireland: Uí Maine as a case study, Ph.D Thesis, Cambridge 1988.

GRAVES, James, The church and shrine of St. Manchán, in: Journal of the Royal Historical and Archaeological Association of Ireland 3 (1874), pp. 134-150.

GRAY, P., St. Ernan of Cluan Deochra, in: Ardagh and Clonmacnoise Ant. Soc. Jn. 2, no.9 (1942), pp. 27-32.

GWYNN, Aubrey / R. Neville HADCOCK, Medieval religious houses. Ireland. With an Appendix to early sites, London 1970, reprint Dublin 1988.

GWYNN, Aubrey, Armagh and Louth in the 12th and 13th centuries, in: Seanchas Ardmhacha 1, no. 1+2 (1954/55), pp. 1-11 and 17-37.

GWYNN, Aubrey, The first synod of Cashel, in: IER 66 (1945), pp. 81-92.

GWYNN, Aubrey, The medieval province of Armagh 1470-1545, Dundalk 1946.

GWYNN, Aubrey, Tomaltach Ua Conchobhair coarb of St. Patrick, in: Seanchas Ardmhacha 8 (1977), pp. 231-274.

GWYNN, Aubrey, The Irish church in the eleventh and twelfth centuries, ed. Gerard O'BRIEN, Dublin 1992.

HARBISON, Peter, The High Crosses of Ireland. An iconographical and photographic survey, 2 vols., Bonn 1992.

HARBISON, Peter, A lost crucifixion plaque of Clonmacnoise type found in county Mayo, in: Harman MURTAGH (ed.), Irish Midland Studies. Essays in commemoration of N. W. English, Athlone 1980, pp. 24-38.

HARBISON, Peter, The inscription on the Cross of the Scriptures at Clonmacnois, county Offaly, in: PRIA 79 (1979), pp. 177-188.

HENRY, Francoise, Around an inscription: the Cross of the Scriptures at Clonmacnois, in: JRSAI 110 (1980), pp. 36-46.

HENRY, Francoise, Studies in early Christian and medieval Irish art, vol. 3: Architecture and sculpture, London 1985.

HERBERT, Máire, Iona, Kells, and Derry. The history and hagiography of the monastic familia of Columba, Oxford 1988.

HICKS, Carola, A Clonmacnois workshop in stone, in: JRSAI 110 (1980), pp. 5-35.

HILL, Boyd H., Medieval monarchy in action, London 1972.

HIRSCH, H., Die Verfassung der Reformklöster des Investiturstreits, in: H. HIRSCH (ed.), Untersuchungen zur Verfassungsgeschichte des deutschen Reiches und der deutschen Kirche, Weimar 1913, pp. 26-65 [transl. Geoffrey BARRACLOUGH, Medieval Germany 911-1250. Essays by German Historians, Oxford 1967, vol. 2, pp. 131-173].

HOGAN, John, St. Ciarán, Patron of Ossory, Kilkenny 1887.

HOWELLS, W. W., The early Christian Irish: The skeletons at Gallen priory, in: PRIA 46 (1940/41), pp. 103-220.

HUGHES, Kathleen, The church in early Irish society, London 1966.

HUGHES, Kathleen, The church and the world in early Christian Ireland, in: Kathleen HUGHES, Church and society in Ireland A.D. 400-1200, ed. David DUMVILLE, London 1987, chap. VIII.

HUGHES, Kathleen, The distribution of Irish Scriptoria and centres of learning from 730 to 1111, in: Kathleen HUGHES, Church and society in Ireland A.D. 400-1200, ed. David DUMVILLE, London 1987, chap. XI.

HUGHES, Kathleen, Early Christian Ireland: Introduction to the sources, London 1972.

HUGHES, Kathleen, Sanctity and secularity in the early Irish Church, in: Kathleen HUGHES, Church and society in Ireland A.D. 400-1200, ed. David DUMVILLE, London 1987, chap. IX.

JACKSON, Kenneth, The motive of the threefold death in the story of Suibhne Geilt, in: John RYAN (ed.), Féil-scríbhinn Eóin Mhic Néill. Essays and studies presented to Professor Eoin MacNeill, Dublin 1940, pp. 535-550.

JENNINGS, Brendan, The abbey of Kilconnell, in: Galway Arch. Hist. Soc. Jn. 21 (1944/45), pp. 184-189.

JOYCE, P. W., Irish names of places, Dublin 1869.

KEARNEY, Patrick, The Cistercian Abbey at Abbeylara A.D. 1205-1540, in: Teathbha 1 (1969-1973), pp. 202-205.

KELLEHER, John V. , The Tain and the annals, in: Ériu 22 (1971), pp. 107-127.

KELLEHER, John V., The Uí Maine in the annals and Genealogies to 1225, in: Celtica 9 (1971), pp. 61-112.

KELLY, Denis H., Account of the inscribed stones at Fuerty, co. Roscommon, in: PRIA 8 (1861-64), pp. 455-458.

KENDRICK, T. D., Gallen priory excavations 1934-5, in: JRSAI 69 (1939), pp. 1-20.

KENNEY, James F., The sources for the early history of Ireland, vol. 1: Ecclesiastical, New York 1929.

KNOX, Hubert Thomas, Notes on the early history of the dioceses of Tuam, Killala and Achonry, Dublin 1904.

LANDAU, Peter, Ius Patronatus (Forschungen zur kirchlichen Rechtsgeschichte und zum Kirchenrecht 12), Cologne 1975.

LAUDAGE, Johannes, Gregorianische Reform und Investiturstreit, Darmstadt 1993.

MAC NIOCAILL, Gearóid, The medieval Irish annals, Dublin 1975.

MAC SHAMHRÁIN, Ailbhe S., Prosopographica Glindelachensis: The monastic church of Glendalough and its community. Sixth to thirteenth centuries, in: JRSAI 119 (1989), pp. 79-97.

MAC SHAMHRÁIN, Ailbhe S., The Uí Muiredaig and the abbacy of Glendalough in the eleventh to thirteenth centuries, in: Cambridge Medieval Celtic Studies 25 (1993), pp. 55-75.

MAC SHAMHRÁIN, Ailbhe S., The Unity of Cóemgen and Ciarán: a covenant between Glendalough and Clonmacnois in the 10th to 11th centuries, in: K. HANNIGAN / W. NOLAN (eds.), Wicklow: history and society, Dublin 1994, pp.139-150.

MAC SHAMHRÁIN, Ailbhe S., Church and Polity in Pre-Norman Ireland: The case of Glenda-lough, Maynooth 1996.

MACALISTER, Robert Alexander Steward, The memorial slabs of Clonmacnois, Dublin 1909.

MACALISTER, Robert Alexander Steward, The sources of the preface of the „Tigernach an-nals", in: IHS 4 (1944-50), pp. 38-57.

MANNING, Conleth, The earliest plans of Clonmacnoise, in: Archaeology Ireland 8, no. 1 (1994), pp. 18-20.

MANNING, Conleth, Clonmacnoise, Dublin 1994.

MCNAMEE, James Joseph, The chronology of the Life of St. Ciarán of Clonmacnois, in: Ardagh and Clonmacnois Ant. Soc. Jn. 2, no. 10 (1945), pp. 3-16.

MCNAMEE, James Joseph, Clonmacnois as a diocese, in: Ardagh and Clonmacnois Ant. Soc. Jn. 2, no. 10 (1945), pp. 27-36.

MCNAMEE, James Joseph, History of the diocese of Ardagh, Dublin 1954.

MCNAMEE, James Joseph, Identification of certain placenames, in: Ardagh and Clonmacnois Ant. Soc. Jn. 2, no. 8 (1942), pp. 3-27.

MCCONE, Kim, Clones and her neighbours in the early period: hints from some Airgialla saints' Lives, in: Clogher Record 11 (1984), pp. 305-325.

MCCONE, Kim, An introduction to early Irish saints' Lives, in: The Maynooth Review. Rei-viú Mhá Nuad 11 (1984), pp. 26-59.

MEEHAN, Joseph, Notes on the Mac Rannals of Leitrim and their country: Being introductory to a diary of James Reynolds, Lough Scur, county Leitrim, in: JRSAI 35 (1905), pp. 139-151.

MEYER, Kuno, Das Buch der Húi Maine (Stowe Collection, R. I. A.), in: Kuno MEYER, Neue Mitteilungen aus irischen Handschriften, in: Archiv für Celtische Lexikographie 2 (1904), pp. 136-146, here 138-146.

MITCHELL, Brian, A new genealogical atlas of Ireland, Baltimore [4]1994.

MOLLOY, Brendan, A guide to the ruins of Clonmacnois, Athlone 1957.

MONAHAN, John, Records relating to the diocese of Ardagh and Clonmacnoise, Dublin 1886 [see review in JRSAI 20 (1890), pp. 250f.].

MORAN, Patrick F., The see of Clonmacnois in the 16th century, in: IER 1 (1865), pp. 153-159.

MULCHRONE, Katherine, Book of Hy Many. R.I.A. MS no. D.ii.1 [no. 1225], in: Catalogue of Irish manuscripts in the Royal Irish Academy. Fasciculi XXVI-XXVII, Dublin 1942/43, pp. 3314-3356.

MURRAY, Laurence P., The Pictish kingdom of Conaille-Muirthemhne, in: John RYAN (ed.), Féil-scríbhinn Eóin Mhic Néill. Essays and studies presented to Professor Eoin MacNeill, Dublin 1940, pp. 445-453.

A new history of Ireland, vol. 2: Medieval Ireland 1169-1534, ed. Art COSGROVE, Oxford 1987 [NHI II].

Ní MAOL-CHRÓIN, Caitlín, Macalla as Cluain-mhac-Nóis A.d. 1050, in: Galvia 1 (1954), pp. 15-17.

Ní MHAONAIGH, Máire, Bréifne bias in Cogad Gáedel re Gallaib, in: Ériu 43 (1992), pp. 135-158.

NIC AONGUSA, Bairbre, The monastic hierarchy in twelfth century Ireland: the case of Kells, in: Ríocht na Midhe 8 (1990/1991), pp. 3-20.

NICHOLLS, Kenneth W., Gaelic and Gaelicised Ireland in the middle ages, Dublin 1972.

NICHOLLS, Kenneth W., The Mac-Coghlans, in: The Irish Genealogist 4, no. 4 (1983), pp. 445-460.

NICHOLLS, Kenneth W., Some Patrician sites of eastern Connacht, in: Dinnseanchas 5 (1972), pp. 114-118.

NICHOLLS, Kenneth W., Tobar Finnmhuighe - Slán Pádraig, in: Dinnseanchas 2 (1966/67), pp. 97f.

Ó CÍOBHÁIN, Breandán, Logainmneacha ó bharúntacht Mhaigh Fhearta. co. An Chlair - V. Inis Cathaigh, in: Dinnseanchas 4 (1970), pp. 113-125.

Ó CORRÁIN, Donncha, Ireland before the Normans, Dublin 1972.

Ó CORRÁIN, Donncha, Dál Cais - church and dynasty, in: Ériu 24 (1973), pp. 52-63.

Ó CORRÁIN, Donnchadh, Nationality and kingship in pre-Norman Ireland, in: T. W. MOODY (ed.), Nationality and the pursuit of national independence, Belfast 1978, pp. 1-36.

Ó CUÍV, Brian, Miscellanea 1. „Boicht" Chorcaige, in: Celtica 18 (1986), pp. 105-111.

Ó DUÍGEANNÁIN, Mícheál, Notes on the history of the kingdom of Bréifne, in: JRSAI 65 (1935), pp. 113-140.

Ó FIAICH, Tomás, The church of Armagh under lay control, in: Seanchas Ardmhacha 5 (1969), pp. 75-127.

Ó FLOINN, Raghnall, Irish shrines & reliquaries of the middle ages, Dublin 1994.

Ó LOCHLAINN, Colm, Poets on the battle of Clontarf, in: Éigse 3 (1942), pp. 211-216.

Ó LOCHLAINN, Colm, Roadways in ancient Ireland, in: John RYAN (ed.), Féil-scríbhinn Eóin Mhic Néill. Essays and studies presented to Professor Eoin MacNeill, Dublin 1940, pp. 465-474.

Ó MAOLEACHLAINN, Padraig L., Clonmacnois and the XII century Synods, in: Teathba 1 (1973), pp. 195-201.

Ó MURAÍLE, Nollaig, Leabhar Ua Maine alias Leabhar Ui Dhuibhagaín, in: Éigse 23 (1989), pp. 167-195.

Ó MURAÍLE, Nollaig, The background, life and writings of Dubhaltach Mac Fhirbhisigh, 2 vols., Ph.D Thesis, National University Ireland, Dublin 1991.

Ó MURCHADA, Dómnall, Rubbings taken of the inscriptions on the Cross of the Scriptures, Clonmacnois, in: JRSAI 110 (1980), p. 50.

O'CONNELL, Philip, The diocese of Kilmore, Dublin 1937.

O'CONOR, Frank, Kings, Lords and Commons, London 1961.

O'DONOVAN, John (e. a.), Ordnance survey letters, Dublin 1839, reproduced in typescript, Bray 1933 (now in the Royal Irish Academy).

O'DWYER, Peter, Célí Dé - Spiritual reform in Ireland 750-900, Dublin 1981.

O'GRADY, Standish Hayes, Catalogue of Irish manuscripts in the British Museum, vol. 1, London 1928.

O'RAHILLY, T. F. , Irish dialects past and present, Dublin 1932.

O'RORKE, T., History of Sligo town and country, 2 vols., reprod. Sligo 1986.

O'SULLIVAN, William, The Book of Uí Maine formerly the Book of Ó Dubhagáin: Scripts & structure, in: Éigse 23 (1989), pp. 151-166.

Ordnance survey of Irland, one inch to a mile, 1855-1900, Phoenix Maps, Dublin 1989.

ORPEN, Goddard H., Athlone Castle: its early history, with notes on some neighbouring castles, in: JRSAI 37 (1907), pp. 257-276.

ORPEN, Goddard H., Ireland under the Normans 1169-1333, 4 vols., Oxford 1911-20, reprint 1968.

OTWAY-RUTHVEN, A. J., The medieval church lands of county Dublin, in: John A. WATT / J. B. MORRALL / F. X. MARTIN (eds.), Medieval studies presented to Aubrey Gwynn, Dublin 1961, pp. 54-73.

OTWAY-RUTHVEN, A. J., The partition of the de Verdon lands in Ireland in 1332, in: PRIA 66 (1967/68), pp. 401-455.

OTWAY-RUTHVEN, A. J., A history of medieval Ireland. With an introduction by Kathleen Hughes, London 1968.

PETRIE, George, Christian inscriptions in the Irish language, ed. Margarete STOKES, 2 vols., Dublin 1872.

PETRIE, Georges, The ecclesiastical architecture of Ireland. An essay on the origin and uses of the Round Towers in Ireland, Dublin 1845, reprint Shannon 1970.

PINKMAN, John, Placenames of St. Mary's Parish, Athlone, in: Ardagh and Clonmacnois Ant. Soc. Jn. 2, no. 10 (1945), pp. 37-47.

PINKMAN, John, The monastery of Gallen, Offaly, in: Ardagh and Clonmacnois Ant. Soc. Jn. 2, no. 10 (1945), pp. 48-51.

PLUMMER, Charles, On two collections of Latin Lives of Irish saints in the Bodleian Library, Rawl. B 485 and Rawl. B 505, in: ZCP 5 (1905), pp. 429-454.

PLUMMER, Charles, Miscellanea Hagiographica Hibernica (Subsidia Hagiographica 15), Brussels 1925.

RADNER, Joan Newlon, The significance of the threefold death in Celtic tradition, in: Patrick K. FORD (ed.), Celtic folklore and Christianity. Studies in memory of William W. Heist, Los Angeles 1983, pp. 180-199.

RICHTER, Michael / Próinséas NíCHATÁIN (eds.), Irland und Europa. Die Kirche im Frühmittelalter. Ireland and Europe. The early church (Veröffentlichungen des Europa-Zentrums Tübingen - Kulturwissenschaftliche Reihe), Stuttgart 1984.

RYAN, John, The abbatial succession at Clonmacnois, in: John RYAN (ed.), Féil-scríbhinn Eóin Mhic Néill. Essays and studies presented to Professor Eoin MacNeill, Dublin 1940, pp. 490-507.

RYAN, John, Clonmacnois. A historical summary, Dublin 1973.

RYAN, John, Irish monasticism. Origins and early development, London/New York 1931.

RYAN, John, Toirdelbach Ó Conchubair (1088-1156), King of Connacht, King of Ireland co fresabra, Dublin 1966.

SANDERLIN, Sarah, The manuscripts of the Annals of Clonmacnois, in: PRIA 82 (1982), pp. 111-123.

SAYER, Jane, Monastic archdeacons, in: C. N. L. BROOKE (ed.), Church and government in the middle ages, Cambridge 1976, pp. 177-204.

SCHÄFERDIEK, Karl, Das Heilige in Laienhand, in: Henning SCHRÖER / Gerhard MÜLLER (eds.), Vom Amt des Laien in Kirche und Theologie. Festschrift für Gerhard Krause, Berlin 1982, pp. 122-140.

SCHMID, Karl, Adel und Reform in Schwaben, in: Joseph FLECKENSTEIN (ed.), Investiturstreit und Reichsverfassung, Sigmaringen 1973, pp. 295-320.

SHARPE, Richard, Some problems concerning the organization of the church in early medieval Ireland, in: Peritia 3 (1984), pp. 230-270.

SHARPE, Richard, Medieval Irish saints' Lives. An introduction to Vitae Sanctorum Hiberniae, Oxford 1991.

SIMMS, Katharine, The Ó Reillys and the kingdom of East Bréifne, in: Bréifne 5 (1979), pp. 305-319.

SIMMS, Katharine, The origins of the diocese of Clogher, in: Clogher Record 10 (1980), pp. 180-198.

SIMMS, Katharine, „Gabh umad a Fheidhlimidh" - a fifteenth-century inauguration ode?, in: Ériu 31 (1980), pp. 132-145.

SMITH, Brendan, The Armagh-Clogher dispute and the „Mellifont conspiracy": diocesan politics and monastic reform in early thirteenth century Ireland, in: Seanchas Ardmhacha 14 (1991), pp. 26-38.

STUTZ, Ulrich, Die Eigenkirche als Element des mittelalterlich- germanischen Kirchenrechts. Inauguralvorlesung, Basel 1894 [transl. Geoffrey BARRACLOUGH, The proprietary church as an element of medieval Germanic ecclesiastical law, in: Geoffrey BARRACLOUGH, Medieval Germany 911-1250. Essays by German Historians, Oxford 1967, vol. 2, pp. 35-70].

WALSH, Paul, The annals attributed to Tigernach, in: Paul WALSH (ed.), Irish men of learning, Dublin 1947, pp. 219-225.

WALSH, Paul, Meath in the Book of Rights, in: John RYAN (ed.), Féil-scríbhinn Eóin Mhic Néill. Essays and studies presented to Professor Eoin MacNeill, Dublin 1940, pp. 508-521.

WALSH, Paul, The placenames of Westmeath, Dublin 1957.

WALSH, Paul, The Ua Máelechlainn kings of Meath, in: IER 57 (1941), pp. 165-183.

WALTON, Helen, The English in Connacht, Ph.D Thesis, Trinity College Dublin 1980.

WATT, John A., The church and the two nations in medieval Ireland, Cambridge 1970.

WATT, John A., The church in medieval Ireland, Dublin 1972.

WESTROPP, Thomas Johnson, A description of the ancient buildings and crosses at Clonmacnois, King's county, in: JRSAI 37 (1907), pp. 277-306.

WOLLASCH, Joachim, Reform und Adel in Burgund, in: Joseph FLECKENSTEIN (ed.), Investiturstreit und Reichsverfassung, Sigmaringen 1973, pp. 277-294.

MAPS

Map 1. Tribes and Families represented in ecclesiastical offices in Clonmacnois

following the maps in BYRNE,
Irish kings and high-kings.
Compare Appendix 1.2.

342342342340

Map 2. Churches linked with Clonmacnois

according to hagiographical evidence and
the annals (compare above, chap. 1.3.
and Appendix 1.3. Questionmarks are
put behind those churches for
which identification is
uncertain).

1 Aghaboe

2 Aghagower

3 Ailech Mór ?

4 Aran

5 Ardagh

6 Ardbraccan

7 Armagh

8 Bangor

9 Birr

10 Caill hUallech ?

11 Cell Lothair in Brega ?

12 Cellola Toch

13 Cenn-eich ?

14 Clonard

15 Cloneogher

16 Clonfert

17 Devenish

18 Drumlane

19 Durrow

20 Echar Gabul ?

21 Elphin

22 Emlagh

23 Fennor

24 Fore

25 Gallen

26 Glendalough

27 Imlech Sescinn ?

28 Inan

29 Inis Ainghin

30 Inis Cathaig

31 Inismacsaint

32 Inishkeen.

33 Íseal Chiaráin

34 Kells

35 Killare

36 Kilbeggan

37 Kilmacduagh

38 Kilmore Mag Enir ?

39 Lackan

40 Lemanaghan

41 Louth

42 Old Kilcullen

43 Roscommon

44 Roscrea

45 Rossinver

46 Saighir

47 Taghadoe

48 Tawnagh

49 Tuamgraney

Maps 3. Parishes in which the lands of Clonmacnois were situated according to the Registry

(For the distribution of the parishes see Mitchell, *A new geographical atlas of Ireland*; numbers in brackets refer to Appendix 2.)

Map 3.1. Ua Ceallaigh donations

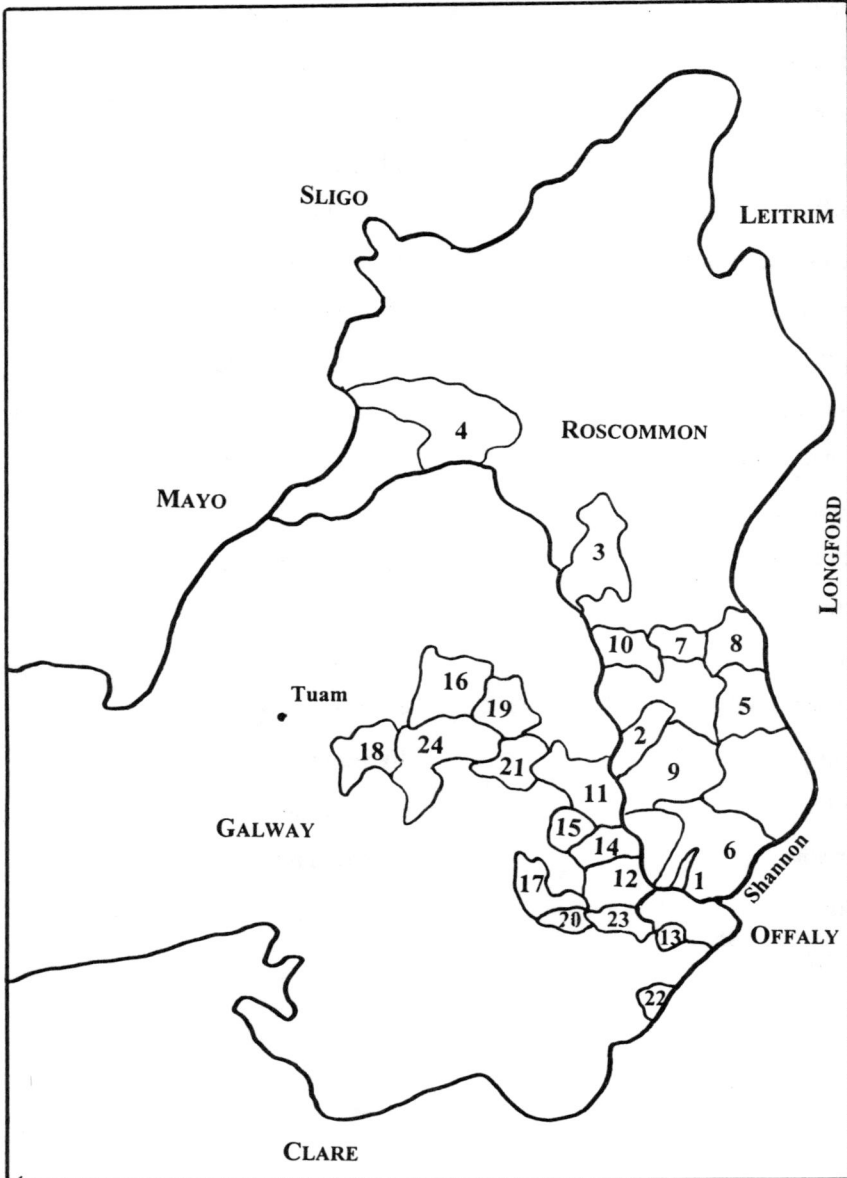

R O S C O M M O N

1 Creagh (*Suigh Kieran*, 4; *Tuaimsruthra* (23); *Coillin Molruany* (37).

2 Dysart - *Dysyort* (24).

3 Fuerty - *Acha Obhair* (30).

4 Kilkeevin - *Terman belafeadh* (40)?.

5 Kiltoom - *Killtuma* (27).

6 Moore - *Dun Beglaitt* (2); *Tuaim-taghar* (38).

7 Rahara - *Killmeas* (34).

8 St. John's parish - *Carnagh* (28).

9 Taghmaconnell - *Dundomnaill in Maghfinn* (22); *Kill Killchuynne* (35); *Belathnaony* (36).

10 Tisara - *Cluain acha Leaga* (29).

G A L W A Y

11 Ahascragh - *Kilupain* (16).

12 Clontuskert - *Gortacharn* (5); *Tuaim Catrighe* (6); *Cros Conaill* (7).

13 Donanaghta - *Dunanoght* (1).

14 Kilcloony - *Grainsy* (8).

15 Kilgerrill - *Koyll-belatha* (9); *Kill Coirill* (13); *Killuir Mor* (14); *Killuir Beg* (15).

16 Kilkerrin - *Cluncuill* (20); *Killchuirin* (21).

17 Killallaghten - *Ruan* (33)?.

18 Killererin - *Killiarainn* (32).

19 Killian - *Killithain* (17).

20 Killoran - *Killorain* (11).

21 Killosolan - *Killosaigelean* (18).

22 Kilmalinoge - *Killmolonog* (12).

23 Kiltormer - *Kill Tormoir* (10).

24 Moylough - *Maoleach* (19).

Map 3.2. Ua Máelsechlainn donations

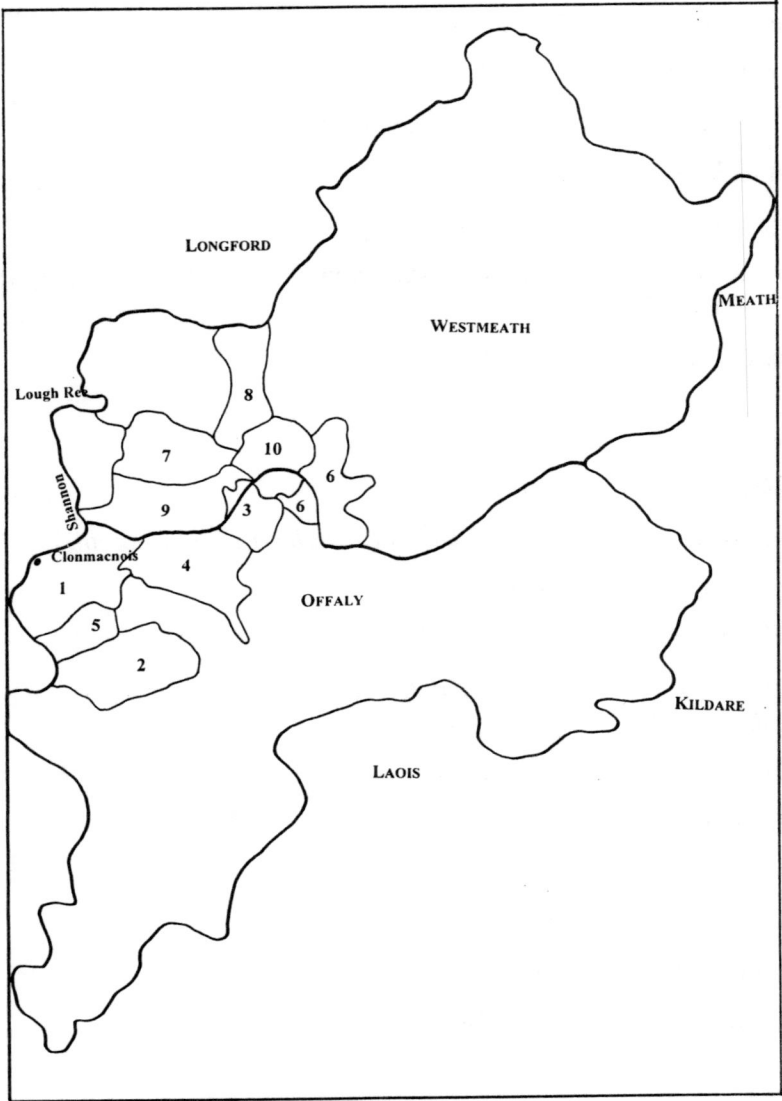

OFFALY

1 Clonmacnois - *Cloithrean* (47); *Cluain-Imthyn* (48);
  Cluain Laigean Magharetighefinn (51).

2 Gallen - *Killchamin* (50).

3 Kilmanaghan - *Killmanachan* (54).

4 Lemanaghan - *Coillnacurranagh* (45); *Lyahmanachan* (46).

5 Tisaran - *Teagh-Sarain* (49).

WESTMEATH

6 Ardnurcher or Horseleap - *Bella Athanurchoir* (58).

7 Ballyloughloe - *Killchi* (55).

8 Ballymore - *Inneoin* (57).

9 Kilcleagh - *Killcliathagh* (42); *Kilbileaghan* (43); *Cluain lonan* (49);
  Killcumynn (53).

10 Kilcumreragh - *Kyllecruymeryachry* (41).

11 St. Mary's Athlone - *Cluainard na cross* (52)?.

Map 3.3. Ua Conchobair, Ua Ruairc, Mac Diarmada donations

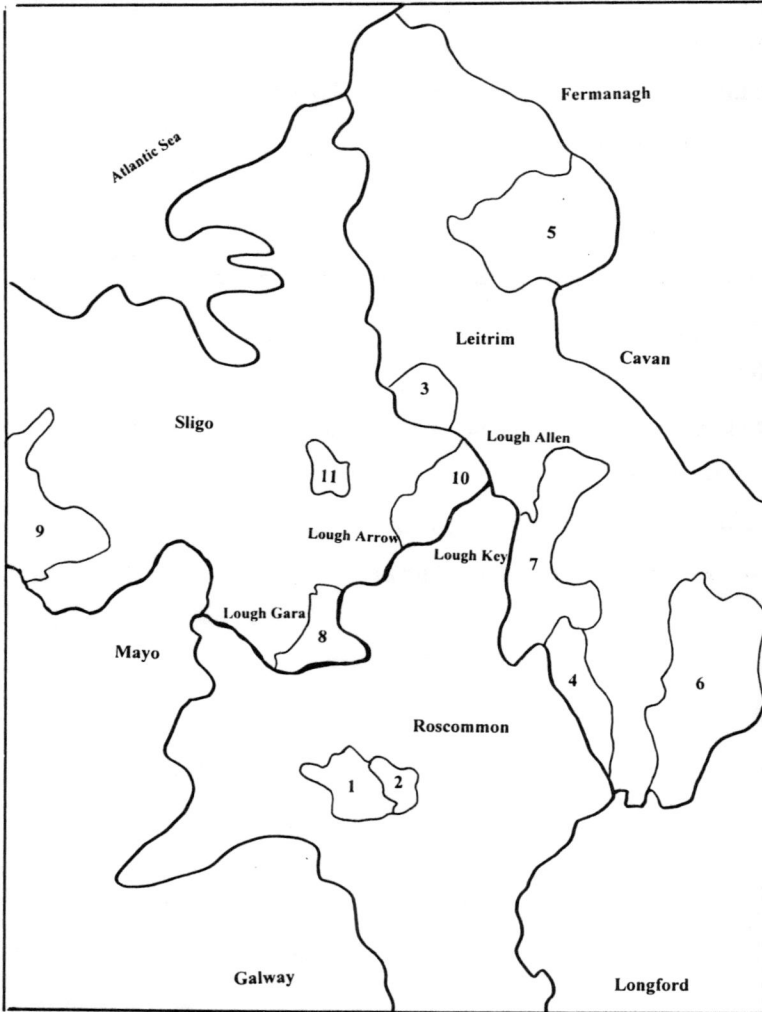

R OSCOMMON

1 Baslick - *Tobar Ilbe* (60); *Kilmurihy* (62).

2 Ogulla - *Tuillsge* (64); *Killogealba* (65).

L EITRIM

3 Killanummery - *Kill Imoire* (68).

4 Annaduff - *Eanagh Duibh* (70).

5 Cloonclare - *Cluain-clair* (66).

6 Cloone - *Cluain lochuill* (67).

7 Kiltoghert - *Kill Tachuir* (72).

S LIGO

8 Killaraght - *Killeathraght* (74).

9 Kilmacteige - *Kilmacteige* (63).

10 Kilmactranny - *Cnocauicarie* (73).

11 Tawnagh - *Tamhnagh* (61).

INDEX

relating to the list of monastic officials in Clonmacnois (Appendix 1)

Áed Ua Conghaile *G2*

Áed Ua Máeleoin I *A74*

Áed Ua Máeleoin II *B27*

Áed Ua Máeleoin III *B28*

Áedacán *vA8*

Áedacán son of Torbach, son of Gormán *An3*

Áedacán, Éogan son of *An4*

Áedacán, Luchairén son of Éogan, son of *An5*

Áedán *vA7*

Aedlug son of Camán *A8*

Aelgal *An1*

Aengus son of Bran *P5*

Aengus son of Flann *S21*

Aengus, Cumuscach son of *vA5*

Aenu *A2*

Ailill son of Bresal *P10*

Ailill Ua Airechtaigh *A65*

Ailill Ua Máelchiaráin *AE7*

Ailill Ua Niallán *A68, vA22*

Ailill, Colmán son of *A49, B7*

Ailither *A4*

Ailmedair *vA1*

Ainmire Ua hAdlai *A51*

Ainséne, Tipraide son of *A50*

Anaile *A34*

Anonymous *O5*

Baetán moccu Cormaicc *A9*

Bairdéne, Colum son of *A6*

Blamac *A46*

Bran, Aengus son of *P5*

Bresal Conaillech *A62*

Bresal, Ailill son of *P10*

Broen Ua hAedha *AE5*

Cahir Mac Cochláin *A83*

Cairpre Cam *B4*

Cairpre mac Rodaighe *AE6*

Camán, Aedlug son of *A8*

Catasach Ua Garbáin *S19*

Cathal Ua Máeleoin *B25*

Cathasach *AE4*

Ceallaigh, Dauit mac *B29*

Céilechair (Mugdornach) *B20*

Céilechair son of Conn na mBocht *Sen10*

Céilechair son of Robartach *A53*

Céilechair Ua Conghaile *G6*

Ceinnéittigh Ua Conghaile *G5*

Cellach son of Secnde *A20*

Cernach *O2*

Cernae, Ioseph nepos *A33*

Cernaigh, Forbasach nepos *A27*

Cétadach *A38*

Ciarán mac in tsaír *A1*

Cinaoth Ua Ruadáin *vA20*

Coimdead, Gilla an *vA25*

Colgu Ua Duinachda *S4*

Collbrann *A28*

Colmán *A12*

Colmán Cas *A10*

Colmán son of Ailill *A49, B7*

Colmán, Máel Tuile son of *S12*

Colum son of Bairdéne *A6*

Comán *A21*

Conaillech, Bresal *A62*

Conaillech, Diarmait *S17*

Conaing son of Óenacán *B17*

Conaing Ua Cosgraigh *B15*

Conaing Ua hEaghra *S26*

Concobar son of Fogartach Ua Máeldúin *vA21*

Condmach Ua Tomrair *P7*

Congalach Mac Gilla Chiaráin *G4*

Congalach son of Irgalach *vA3*

349

Index

Congalach Ua Tomaltaigh *P15, S32*

Conmal (nepos Locheni) *A19*

Conn na mBoch, Máel Finnén son of *O4*

Conn na mBocht *An14, B19, C1*

Conn na mBocht, Céilechair son of *Sen10*

Conn na mBocht, Cormac son of *A70*

Conn na mBocht, Gilla Chríst son of *O6*

Conn na mbocht, Máel Chiaráin son of *A66, C2*

Conn na mBocht, Máel Chiaráin, son of Cormac son of *P13*

Conn na mBocht, Máel Íosa son of *O7*

Conn na mbocht, Máel Muire son of *Sen11*

Connmach *A39*

Connmach son of Muirmid (nepos Guaire Oidni) *S5*

Connmach Ua Tomrair *O1*

Cormac *A23*

Cormac *vA11*

Cormac son of Conn na mBocht *A70*

Cormac Ua Cillín I *A54, B11*

Cormac Ua Cillín II *G3, vA24*

Cormac Ua Máeldúin *S28*

Crónán Becc *A14*

Crónán moccu Laegde *A7*

Cú Chiaráin *vA2*

Cú Chumba, son of *S1*

Cuanach, Máel Tuile nepos *A43*

Cuanach, Suibne mac *A36*

Cuiméne *A11*

Cuinnles *A17*

Cumuscach son of Aengus *vA5*

Cumuscach, Máel Mide son of *vA9*

Daighre Ua Dubhatáin *An13*

Dauit mac Ceallaigh *B29*

Dedimus *A47*

Dedimus Ua Foirbten *vA14*

Dedimus, grandson of Lígán *S2*

Diarmait Conaillech *S17*

Domnall Ua Dubthaigh *A73, B23*

Domnall, Flaithbertach son of *A60*

Donnchad, Ruaidrí son of *vA6*

Donngal son of Gormán *S27, vA19*

Donngal Ua Máelmidhe *S13*

Du-Dubtea, Tuathal son of *S6*

Dubinse *O3*

Dubinse *S7*

Dubsláine *An12*

Dubthach Ua Tadgáin *P6*

Dúnadach son of Ecertach *B10*

Dúnadach, Dúnchad son of *An8, S18*

Dúnchad mac Suthainein *B8*

Dúnchad son of Dúnadach *An8, S18*

Dúnchad Ua Braoín *A56*

Dúnchad, Joseph son of *An11*

Ecertach *AE1*

Ecertach, Óenacán son of *AE3, B9*

Echtigern Ua hEgráin *A64*

Éogan son of Áedacán, son of Torbach *An4*

Eógan Tobair *A42*

Éogan, Luchairén son of *An5, S9*

Fachtna *P8*

Fachtna *S20*

Fáilbe Bec *A16, B1*

Faircellach Fobair *A35*

Ferdalach *B6, P2*

Ferdomnach *A41*

Ferdomnach Ua Maonaigh *A52*

Fergus son of Máel Michil *vA12*

Fiachra *AE2*

Fingen *An7*

Flaithbertach son of Domnall *A60*

Flaithbertach son of Loingsech *B18, S22*

Flaithbertach Ua Loingsigh *A71*

Flaithbertach, Flann son of *vA4*

Flann Fobair *vA16*

Flann Sinna (aui Colle *A18*)

Flann son of Flaithbertach *vA4*

Flann son of Máel Michil *B14, S14*

Flann, Aengus son of *S21*

Flannchad Ua Ruadáin *A59*

Fobair, Faircellach *A35*

Fobair, Flann *vA16*

Fogartach Fionn *An15*

Folachtach of Tech Tua *A26*

Forbasach (nepos Cernaigh) *A27*

Forcron *A13*

Forgla *Sen1*

Fothud Ua hAille *An16*

Gallbran Ua Lingáin *S3*

Gallbrat son of Duaric Ua Tadgáin *P14*

Gallust, Oiséne son of *A15*

Gilla an Coimdead *vA25*

Gilla Chríst son of Conn na mBocht *O6*

Gilla Chríst Ua hEchtigern *B21*

Gilla Chríst Ua Máeleoin I *A72*

Gilla Chríst Ua Máeleoin II *O8*

Gilla Íosa Ua Braoín *vA26*

Gormán *An2*

Gormán, Áedacán son of Torbach, son of *An3*

Gormán, Donngal son of *S27, vA19*

Gormán, Scannlan son of *S11*

Guaire Oidni, Connmach son of Muirmid nepos *S5*

Guaire son of Máel Acain *P3*

Guaire Ua Lachtnáin *S23*

Hugh óKonoyle *AE8*

Ioseph *A48*

Ioseph (nepos Cernae) *A33*

Irgalach, Congalach son of *vA3*

Joseph son of Dúnchad *An11*

Lígán, Dedimus grandson of *S2*

Locheni, Conmal nepos *A19*

Loingsech *B5*

Loingsech son of Máel Pátraic *S15*

Loingsech Ua Flaithéin *A63*

Loingsech, Flaithbertach son of *B18, S22*

Longarg Ua Máeldúin *vA18*

Luchairén son of Éogan, son of Áedacán, son of Torbach *An5, S9*

Luchraid *A22*

Mac Cochláin, Cahir *A83*

Mac Cú Chumba *S1*

Mac Finn *G1*

Mac Nisi *A3*

Mac Sluagadaigh *P11*

Macraith Ua Flaithéin *A69*

Máel Acain, Guaire son of *P3*

Máel Achaid *vA13*

Máel Aena son of Olbrand *S8*

Máel Barrfhinn *P1*

Máel Brigte *A45*

Máel Chiaráin son of Conn na mbocht *A66, C2*

Máel Chiaráin Ua Donnghasa *Sen8*

Máel Chiaráin Ua Fidabra *A77*

Máel Chiaráin Ua Máeleoin *A79*

Máel Chiaráin, son of Cormac son of Conn na mBocht *P13*

Máel Choluim Ua Loingsigh *P12, S24, Sen5*

Máel Finnén son of Conn na mBoch *O4*

Máel Finnia Ua Maenaigh *A57*

Máel Giricc *Sen4*

Máel Íosa son of Conn na mBocht *O7*

Máel Martain son of Ua Certa *Sen7*

Máel Michil, Fergus son of *vA12*

Máel Michil, Flann son of *B14, S14*

Máel Michil, Maenach son of *B13*

Máel Mide son of Cumuscach *vA9*

Máel Mochta Ua Fidabra (or Ua Máelsechlainn) *A76*

Máel Mórda son of Uareirge Ua Nechtain *C4*

Máel Muire of the Meic Cuinn na mBocht I *S31*

Máel Muire of the Meic Cuinn na mbocht II *Sen11*

Máel Muire Ua Máeleoin *A78*

Máel Pátraic *A44*

Máel Pátraic Ua Beguláin *P9*

Máel Pátraic, Loingsech son of *S15*

Máel Póil *B16*

Máel Tuile (nepos Cuanach) *A43*

Máel Tuile son of Colmán *S12*

Máel Umai, Suibne son of *An6, S10*

Máelán Ua Cuinn *AE9*

Máelmuicheirge *vA15*

Máelodar *B3*

Maenach son of Máel Michil *B13*

Maengal *vA10*

Maonach, Rechtabra son of *P4*

Martan *A40*

mc Teige, Paule *A81*

Meic Cuinn na mBocht, Máel Muire I *S31*

Meic Cuinn na mBocht, Máel Muire II
   Sen11

Mugrón, Muiredach son of *A61*

Mugron, Muiredach son of *S29*

Muirchertach Ua Catharnaigh *Sen9*

Muirchertach Ua Cearnaigh *S30*

Muirchertach Ua Máeluidir *B24*

Muiredach son of Mugrón I *A61*

Muiredach son of Mugrón II *S29*

Muiredach Ua Máeldúin *B22, vA23*

Muiredach Ultach *An10*

Murchad son of Riata *vA17*

Murgal *A31*

Niall O'Sheridan *A82*

O'Sheridan, Niall *A82*

Odrán Ua hEolais *S16*

Óenacán son of Ecertach *AE3, B9*

Óenacán, Conaing son of *B17*

Oiséne, son of Gallust *A15*

óKonoyle, Hugh *AE8*

Olbrand, Máel Aena son of *S8*

Paule mc Teige *A81*

Rechtabra son of Maonach *P4*

Rechtnia *A29*

Riata, Murchad son of *vA17*

Robartach Ua hAilgius *An9*

Robartach, Céilechair son of *A53*

Rodaighe, Cairpre mac *AE6*

Rónán *A24*

Rónán *A37*

Ruaidrí son of Donnchad *vA6*

Saerberg *A32*

Scannlan son of Gormán *S11*

Secnde, Cellach son of *A20*

Sluagadaigh, mac *P11*

Snéidriagail *A30*

Suibne (mac Cuanach) *A36*

Suibne son of Máel Umai *An6, S10*

Suthainein, Dúnchad mac *B8*

Tigernach Ua Braoín *A67*

Tigernach Ua Máeleoin *A75*

Tipraide son of Ainséne *A50*

To-Lua the Tall *A5*

Tobair, Eógan *A42*

Tomás *A80*

Torbach, Áedacán son of *An3*

Torbach, Éogan son of Áedacán, son of *An4*

Torbach, Luchairén son of Éogan, son of
   Áedacán, son of *An5*

Tuadcar *B2*

Tuathal *A55*

Tuathal *B12*

Tuathal son of Du-Dubtea *S6*

Tuathgal *Sen3*

Ua Airechtaigh, Ailill *A65*

Ua Beguláin *A58*

Ua Beguláin, Máel Pátraic *P9*

Ua Braoín, Dúnchad *A56*

Ua Braoín, Gilla Íosa *vA26*

Ua Braoín, Tigernach *A67*

Ua Catharnaigh *P16*

Ua Catharnaigh, Muirchertach *Sen9*

Ua Cearnaigh, Muirchertach *S30*

Ua Certa, Máel Martain son of *Sen7*

Ua Cillín, Cormac I *A54, B11*

Ua Cillín, Cormac II *G3, vA24*

Ua Conghaile, Áed *G2*

Ua Conghaile, Céilechair *G6*

Ua Conghaile, Ceinnéittigh *G5*

Ua Cosgraigh, Conaing *B15*

Ua Cuinn, Máelán *AE9*

Ua Donnghasa Máel Chiaráin *Sen8*

Ua Dubhatáin, Daighre *An13*

Ua Dubthaigh, Domnall *A73, B23*

Ua Duinachda, Colgu *S4*

Ua Fidabra (or Ua Máelsechlainn), Máel
   Mochta *A76*

Ua Fidabra, Máel Chiaráin *A77*
Ua Flaithéin, Loingsech *A63*
Ua Flaithéin, Macraith *A69*
Ua Foirbten, Dedimus *vA14*
Ua Garbáin, Catasach *S19*
Ua hAdlai, Ainmire *A51*
Ua hAedha, Broen *AE5*
Ua hAilgius, Robartach *An9*
Ua hAille, Fothud *An16*
Ua hEaghra, Conaing *S26*
Ua hEchtigern, Gilla Chríst *B21*
Ua hEgráin, Echtigern *A64*
Ua hEolais, Odrán *S16*
Ua Lachtnáin, Guaire *S23*
Ua Lingáin, Gallbran *S3*
Ua Loingsigh, Flaithbertach *A71*
Ua Loingsigh, Máel Choluim *P12, S24, Sen5*
Ua Máelchiaráin, Congalach son of *G4*
Ua Máelchiaráin, Ailill *AE7*
Ua Máeldúin, Concobar son of Fogartach *vA21*
Ua Máeldúin, Cormac *S28, Sen6*
Ua Máeldúin, Longarg *vA18*
Ua Máeldúin, Muiredach *vA23, B22*
Ua Máeleoin, Áed I *A74*
Ua Máeleoin, Áed II *B27*
Ua Máeleoin, Áed III *B28*
Ua Máeleoin, Cathal *B25*
Ua Máeleoin, Gilla Chríst *A72*
Ua Máeleoin, Gilla Chríst *O8*
Ua Máeleoin, Máel Chiaráin *A79*
Ua Máeleoin, Máel Muire *A78*
Ua Máeleoin, Tigernach *A75*
Ua Máelmidhe, Donngal *S13*
Ua Máelsechlainn (or Ua Fidabra), Máel Mochta *A76*
Ua Máeluidir, Muirchertach *B24*
Ua Maenaigh, Máel Finnia *A57*
Ua Maonaigh, Ferdomnach *A52*
Ua Miadacháin *S25*
Ua Miannaigh *A25*

Ua Miannaigh *Sen2*
Ua Muirecán (no Christian name given) *B26*
Ua Nechtain, Máel Mórda son of Uareirge *C4*
Ua Nechtain, Uareirge *C3*
Ua Nechtain, Uareirge son of Máel Mórda son of Uareirge *C5*
Ua Niallán, Ailill *A68vA22*
Ua Ruadáin, Cinaoth *vA20*
Ua Ruadáin, Flannchad *A59*
Ua Tadgáin, Dubthach *P6*
Ua Tadgáin, Gallbrat son of Duaric *P14*
Ua Tomaltaigh, Congalach *P15, S32*
Ua Tomrair, Condmach *P7, O1*
Uareirge son of Máel Mórda son of Uareirge Ua Nechtain *C5*
Uareirge Ua Nechtain *C3*
Ultach, Muiredach *An10*

Vita regularis

Ordnungen und Deutungen religiosen Lebens
im Mittelalter

herausgegeben von Prof. Dr. Gert Melville
(Technische Universität Dresden)

Gert Melville (Hrsg.)
De ordine vitae
Zu Normvorstellungen, Organisationsformen und Schriftgebrauch im mittelalterlichen Ordenswesen
Der Band stellt Forschungsergebnisse von Mitarbeitern am Projekt L1 "Schriftlichkeit und Ordensorganisation" des Sonderforschungsbereichs 231 (Münster) vor. Ausgehend vom Sachverhalt einer hoch verdichteten pragmatischen Schriftlichkeit im Ordensleben des Hochmittelalters befassen sich die Beiträge mit rechtlichen Strukturen, mit Verwaltungspraktiken, mit dem klösterlichen Alltag und der Gestaltung von Außenbeziehungen vornehmlich bei den Cluniazensern, Cisterziensern und Prämonstratensern sowie ferner bei den Kartäusern, Lazariten und Dominikanern.
Bd. 1, 1996, 400 S., 68,80 DM, br., ISBN 3-8258-2586-8

Jörg Oberste
Visitation und Ordensorganisation
Formen sozialer Normierung, Kontrolle und Kommunikation bei Cisterziensern, Prämonstratensern und Cluniazensern (12. – frühes 14. Jahrhundert)
Zu Beginn des 12. Jahrhunderts erfanden die Mönche von Cîteaux das Organisationskonzept des modernen Ordens. Jährliche Generalkapitel, eine positivrechtliche Statutengesetzgebung, bürokratische Verwaltung und rationale Kontroll- und Kommunikationsmechanismen zeichneten dieses Konzept aus, das die institutionellen Strukturen der *vita religiosa* revolutionierte. Die umfassende Untersuchung des Visitationsverfahrens im Vergleich der drei größten klösterlichen Verbände der Zeit rückt die konkreten Verlaufsbedingungen und Probleme dieser Institutionalisierung in den Blickpunkt. Die Quellen zur Kontrollpraxis der Orden sind einzigartige Zeugnisse an der Schnittstelle zwischen religiösem Ideal und klösterlichem Alltag.
Bd. 2, 1996, 472 S., 68,80 DM, br., ISBN 3-8258-2587-6

Godula Süßmann
Konflikt und Konsens
Zu den Auseinandersetzungen zwischen cluniazensischen Klöstern und ihren rechtsabhängigen burgenses im Frankreich des 12. und 13. Jahrhunderts
Das hochmittelalterliche Frankreich war Schauplatz zum Teil gewalttätiger Konflikte zwischen cluniazensischen Klöstern und der von ihnen abhängigen Stadtbevölkerung, die danach strebte, die Rechtshoheit der Mönche abzuschütteln. In diesem Zuge entwickelten sowohl die betroffenen Städte als auch die Abteien und Priorate, die in zunehmendem Maße in den sich formierenden Cluniazenserorden eingebunden wurden, eigene Institutionen, deren Organisation und Selbstverständnis den Verlauf der Auseinandersetzungen wesentlich bestimmten. Anhand von zehn historischen Fallbeispielen zeichnet die vorliegende Untersuchung Ursachen, Verlauf und vor allem die institutionsgeschichtlichen Folgen der beschriebenen Konflikte nach.
Bd. 3, 1996, 400 S., 48,80 DM, br., ISBN 3-8258-2588-4

Kay Peter Jankrift
Leprose als Streiter Gottes
Institutionalisierung und Organisation des Ordens vom heiligen Lazarus zu Jerusalem von seinen Anfängen bis zum Jahre 1350
Im Mittelpunkt der Studie steht die organisatorische und institutionelle Entwicklung einer Leprosenbruderschaft außerhalb der Mauern Jerusalems zum Orden des Heiligen Lazarus. Vor dem Hintergrund einer Zeit, die als einzige Antwort auf die Schrecken der unheilbaren Lepra mit dem Entrechtung und Stigmatisierung einhergehenden Ausschluß des Erkrankten aus der Welt der Gesunden kannte, entwirft sie das Porträt einer außergewöhnlichen, von der historischen Forschung bislang weitgehend unbeachteten Gemeinschaft. Beschränkten sich die Lazariter anfangs auf die materielle und spirituelle Versorgung ihrer kranken Brüder, so ließen sie sie schon bald aktiv teilhaben an der bedeutendsten Mission der mittelalterlichen Christenheit: dem Kampf um das Heilige Land. Neben der Entfaltung des Ordens in den Kreuzfahrerstaaten, gilt die Untersuchung jedoch auch dem Schicksal der europäischen Lazariterhäuser. Die Ausbildung seiner hierarchischen Strukturen wird dabei ebenso analysiert wie seine normativen Texte, die mit denen anderer Ritterorden und den Statuten europäischer Leprosorien verglichen werden. Schließlich wendet sich die Studie unter Berücksichtigung der ökonomischen Ressourcen der Lazariter und der allgemeinen leprosenrechtlichen Entwicklung der Frage nach der militärischen und hospitalischen Bedeutung des Ordens zu.
Bd. 4, 1996, 272 S., 58,80 DM, br., ISBN 3-8258-2589-2

Clemens M. Kasper; Klaus Schreiner (Hrsg.)
Viva vox und ratio scripta
Mündliche und schriftliche Kommunikationsformen im Mönchtum des Mittelalters

Aus dem Inhalt: Lautes Lesen, fiktive Mündlichkeit, verschriftlichte Norm
Klaus SCHREINER
Einleitende Bemerkungen

LIT Verlag Münster – Hamburg – London

Bestellungen über: Dieckstr. 73 48145 Münster Tel.: 0251–23 50 91 Fax: 0251–23 19 72

ARNOLD ANGENENDT Religion zwischen Mündlichkeit und Schriftlichkeit
KARL SUSO FRANK Fiktive Mündlichkeit als Grundstruktur der monastischen Literatur
HUBERTUS LUTTERBACH Literalität und Mönchwerdung im frühen Mittelalter
FRANZ NEISKE Funktion und Praxis der Schriftlichkeit im klösterlichen Totengedenken
HERMANN HAUKE Der Stellenwert des nichtliturgischen Lesens
PETER OCHSENBEIN Privates Beten in mündlicher und schriftlicher Form
CLEMENS KASPER Text und Ton. Musik, Text und Sprache bei der Verschriftlichung des Chorals
JÜRGEN MIETHKE Verschriftlichte Mönchstheologie und Zensur
FLORENT CYGLER, GERT MELVILLE, JÖRG OBERSTE Aspekte zur Verbindung von Organisation und Schriftlichkeit im Ordenswesen
PIA SCHINDELE Reformweisungen von 1335 im Kloster Lichtenthal
Bd. 5, 1997, 320 S., 68,80 DM, br., ISBN 3-8258-2950-2

Burkhardt Tutsch
Studien zur Rezeptionsgeschichte der Consuetudines Ulrichs von Cluny
Bd. 6, Herbst 1997, 408 S., 79,80 DM, br., ISBN 3-8258-3200-7

Giles Constable; Gert Melville; Jörg Oberste (Hrsg.)
Die Cluniazenser in ihrem politisch-sozialen Umfeld
Bd. 7, 1998, 624 S., 79,80 DM, br., ISBN 3-8258-3441-7

Thomas Füser
Mönche im Konflikt
Zum Spannungsfeld von Norm, Devianz und Sanktionen bei den Cisterziensern und Cluniazensern (12. bis frühes 14. Jahrhundert)
Bd. 9, Herbst 1997, 500 S., 79,80 DM, br., ISBN 3-8258-3443-3

Münsteraner Einführungen: Studium der Geschichte

Peter Funke (Hrsg.)
Einführung in die Alte Geschichte
Bd. 1, 1998, ca. 300 S., ca. 34,80 DM, br., ISBN 3–8258–2247–8

Hans-Ulrich Thamer (Hrsg.)
Einführung in die neuere Geschichte
Bd. 3, 1998, ca. 300 S., ca. 34,80 DM, br., ISBN 3–8258–2248–6

Horst Gründer (Hrsg.)
Außereuropäische Geschichte
Grundwissen – Forschungsprobleme – Literatur
Bd. 5, 1998, 300 S., 34,80 DM, br., ISBN 3–8258–2250–8

Jahrbuch für historische Friedensforschung

herausgegeben von Gottfried Niedhart (Mannheim), Detlef Bald (München), Jost Dülffer (Köln), Andreas Gestrich (Stuttgart), Karl Holl (Bremen), Andreas Sywottek (Hamburg) und Wolfram Wette (Freiburg) in Verbindung mit dem Arbeitskreis historische Friedensforschung

Detlef Bald (Hrsg.)
Rüstungsbestimmte Geschichte und das Problem der Konversion in Deutschland im 20. Jahrhundert
Bd. 1, 1993, 210 S., 29,80 DM, br., ISBN 3–89473–263–6

Arnold Sywottek (Hrsg.)
Der Kalte Krieg – Vorspiel zum Frieden?
Bd. 2, 1994, 200 S., 29,80 DM, br., ISBN 3–89473–602–x

Jost Dülffer (Hrsg.)
Kriegsbereitschaft und Friedensordnung in Deutschland 1800 – 1814
Bd. 3, 1995, 220 S., 29,80 DM, br., ISBN 3–8258–2209–5

Andreas Gestrich (Hrsg.)
Gewalt im Krieg
Ausübung, Erfahrung und Verweigerung von Gewalt in Kriegen des 20. Jahrhunderts
Die Kriege der Neuzeit zeichnen sich durch eine zunehmende Grausamkeit aus. Die bei weitem größte Gruppe der Kriegsopfer sind inzwischen die Zivilisten – vor allem Kinder, Frauen und Alte. Die in diesem Band veröffentlichten Referate der Jahrestagung 1994 des AKHF untersuchen den Abbau von Gewalt- und Tötungshemmungen und fragen nach den verschieden Wurzeln der Brutalisierung des Krieges, insbesondere auch der Gewalt gegen Frauen. Erörtert werden aber auch die Bedingungen, unter denen Gewalterfahrung in Gewaltverweigerung umschlägt.
Bd. 4, 1996, 208 S., 34,80 DM, br., ISBN 3–8258–2359–8

LIT Verlag Münster – Hamburg – London
Bestellungen über: Dieckstr. 73 48145 Münster Tel.: 0251 – 23 50 91 Fax: 0251 – 23 19 72

Andreas Gestrich; Gottfried Niedhart;
Bernd Ulrich (Hrsg.)
Gewaltfreiheit
Pazifistische Konzepte im 19. und 20. Jahrhundert
Die Auseinandersetzungen zwischen einem radi-
kalen und einem pragmatischen Pazifismus, die
zur Zeit die Friedensbewegung beschäftigen, sind
nicht neu. Sie gehen auf die unterschiedlichen
Wurzeln der modernen organisierten Friedensbe-
wegung zurück. Der AKHF hat auf der Jahres-
tagung 1995 diese langfristigen Traditionen und
grundlegenden intellektuellen Probleme des Pazi-
fismus zum Thema gemacht. Daneben bietet der
Band anläßlich des zehnjährigen Bestehens des
Arbeitskreises verschiedenen Beiträge zu den Er-
gebnissen und zukünftigen Aufgaben historischer
Friedensforschung.
Bd. 5, 1996, 288 S., 48,80 DM, br.,
ISBN 3–8258–2877–8

Friedhelm Boll (Hrsg.)
Volksreligiosität und Kriegserleben
Nicht die religiöse Legitimation von Kriegen
durch Theologen und Kirchen steht im Vorder-
grund dieses Bandes, sondern die Bedeutung der
Religion und der religiösen Praxis für die Verar-
beitung der Kriegserlebnisse einfacher Soldaten
und breiterer Bevölkerungsschichten. Konstanz
und Wandel dieser bislang vernachlässigten Dimension einer Mentalitäts- und Sozialgeschichte
des Krieges werden anhand von Fallstudien zum
19. und 20. Jahrhundert untersucht.
Bd. 6, Herbst 1997, 200 S., 39,80 DM, br.,
ISBN 3–8258–3357–7

Imaginarium
Texte zur historisch-politischen Bildsprache
herausgegeben von Prof. Dr. Frank Kämpfer
(Historisches Seminar der Universität Münster)

Andreas Fleischer
"Feind hört mit!"
Propagandakampagnen des Zweiten Welt-
krieges im Vergleich
Bd. 2, 1994, 312 S., 68,80 DM, br., ISBN 3-8258-2023-8

Michaele Siebe
**Von der Revolution zum nationalen
Feindbild**
Frankreich und Deutschland in der
politischen Karikatur des 19. Jahrhunderts.
"Kladderadatsch" und "Charivari"
Bd. 3, 1995, 211 S., 68,80 DM, br., ISBN 3-8258-2230-3

Geschichte der Jugend
hrsg. von Arno Klönne (Universität Paderborn)

Bernhard Schneider
**Daten zur Geschichte der
Jugendbewegung**
Bd. 16, 1990, 200 S., 29,80 DM, br.,
ISBN 3–88660–446–2; 48,80 DM, gb., ISBN 3–88660–449–7

Dietmar Schenk
Die Freideutsche Jugend 1913 – 1919/20
Eine Jugendbewegung in Krieg, Revolution
und Krise
Bd. 17, 1991, 500 S., 68,80 DM, gb.,
ISBN 3–88660–574–4

Uwe Böseler
Katholische Jugend vor Hitlers Richtern
Der Dortmunder Prozeß von 1937. Mit
einem Nachwort von A. Klönne
Bd. 18, 1990, 248 S., 34,80 DM, br.,
ISBN 3–88660–682–1

Horst-Pierre Bothien
Die Jovy-Gruppe
Eine Lokalstudie über nonkonforme Jugend-
liche im "Dritten Reich"
Die Studie erzählt die Geschichte der sog. Jovy-
Gruppe, einer Gruppe von elf jungen Leuten aus
Bonn, die Ende der dreißiger Jahre in Konflikt
mit dem NS-Staat gerieten. Vor dem Hintergrund
ihrer zumeist katholischen Erziehung, beeinflußt
von der bündischen Kultur der Weimarer Republik
und angesichts einer zunehmend militärisch und
ideologisch ausgerichteten Hitlerjugend, suchen
die jungen Leute Mitte der dreißiger Jahren einen
"autonomen" Weg in ihrer Freizeitgestaltung. Es
entsteht nach Vorbild von Eberhard Köbels verbo-
tenen "deutschen jungenschaft vom 1. 11. (1929)"
eine eigene bündische Gruppenkultur. Als die
Gruppe auf Fahrten nach Frankreich Kontakte
zum Exilwiderstand um Karl O. Paetel findet, und
diese sich intensivieren, entstehen unter den älte-
ren Gruppenmitgliedern politische Diskussionen,
die zunehmend einen staatsoppositionellen Cha-
rakter tragen. Der Verhaftung durch die Gestapo
Ende 1939 folgen 1940 und 1941 Prozesse wegen
"bündischer Umtriebe" und "Vorbereitung zum
Hochverrat". Den Hauptangeklagten, Michael Jo-
vy, verurteilt der Volksgerichtshof zu sechs Jahren
Zuchthaus.
Die vorliegende Arbeit verwertet in der Darstel-
lung und Illustration der Geschichte und Kultur
der Gruppe neben zahlreichen Zeitzeugenin-
terviews und bisher unbekannten historischen
Quellen auch Privatfotografien der beteiligten
Personen.
Bd. 19, 1995, 250 S., 38,80 DM, br.,
ISBN 3-8258-2292-3

LIT Verlag Münster – Hamburg – London
Bestellungen über: Dieckstr. 73 48145 Münster Tel.: 0251 – 23 50 91 Fax: 0251 – 23 19 72

Jan Kurz
"Swinging Democracy"
Jugendprotest im 3. Reich
Verhielt sich der größte Teil der deutschen Jugend
im 3. Reich konform und paßte sich problemlos
in das System der NS-Jugendorganisationen ein,
so existierten daneben viele Gruppen von Jugendlichen, deren Verhalten ihre Nichtangepaßtheit,
ihren Protest und Widerstand zum bestehenden
System ausdrückte. Kirchliche und Bündische
Gruppen, "Edelweißpiraten" und "Navajos" waren Inseln einer kulturellen Eigenständigkeit und
Resistenz gegenüber dem Nationalsozialismus,
die sich in den Verhaltensmustern und Stilen der
Gruppen ausdrückten. Schillerndes Beispiel dafür
sind die "Swingjugendlichen", deren Auftreten
und Verbreitung in Deutschland und Europa nicht
nur aufgrund der Existenz des 3. Reichs erklärt
werden kann, sondern die vielmehr Protagonisten
und Repräsentanten einer völlig neuen Jugendkul-
tur sind. Von Seiten der NS-Organe gleichzeitig
gehaßt und gefürchtet, verfolgt und verboten, ist
die "Swingjugend" das Glied zwischen den Ju-
gendkulturen der Vorkriegszeit und jugendlichen
Subkulturen der Nachkriegszeit.
Bd. 21, 1996, 192 S., 34,80 DM, br.,
ISBN 3–8258–2608–2

Peter Schröder
**Die Leitbegriffe der deutschen
Jugendbewegung in der Weimarer
Republik**
Eine ideengeschichtliche Studie
Bd. 22, 1996, 128 S., 24,80 DM, gb.,
ISBN 3–8258–2827–1

Politik und Geschichte
herausgegeben von Prof. Dr. Helmut Bley,
Prof. Dr. Hans-Heinrich Nolte und
Prof. Dr. Adelheid von Saldern
(Historisches Seminar, Universität Hannover)

Adelheid von Saldern (Hrsg.)
**Mythen in Geschichte und
Geschichtsschreibung aus polnischer und
deutscher Sicht**
In Zusammenarbeit mit dem Historischen
Seminar der Universität Hannover
Keine Geschichte und keine Geschichtsschreibung
ohne Mythen und Legenden. Die Spannweite
ist groß. Mythen dienen der Legitimierung und
Identitätsbildung von Stämmen, Völkern und
Nationen, von Herrschern und politischen Sy-
stemen, von sozialen und politischen Gruppen
innerhalb einer Gesellschaft. Mythen reizen zur
Decodierung: das zeigen die hier veröffentlichten
Aufsätze. Es geht um die Analyse mythischer
Sinnstiftungen, um Legenden und Stereotypen aus
verschiedenen Epochen. Entstehung, Entwicklung

und Funktionen werden untersucht, ebenso die
Rolle der Historiker und Historikerinnen. Die mei-
sten Beispiele stammen aus der polnischen und
deutschen Geschichte; dabei spielt auch der My-
thos vom uralten Antagonismus zwischen Polen
und Deutschland eine Rolle.
Bd. 1, 1996, 272 S., 48,80 DM, br.,
ISBN 3–8258–2693–7

Hans-Heinrich Nolte (Hrsg.)
Deutsche Migrationen
Historiker und Politologen aus Chicago, Bonn
und Amsterdam sowie meist aus Hannover haben
untersucht, warum Juden im Spätmittelalter aus
Deutschland vertrieben wurden und niedersächsi-
sche Heuerlinge als Saisonarbeiter in der Frühen
Neuzeit nach Holland sowie westfälische Dienst-
mädchen nach Amsterdam gingen, was einfache
Russen von jenen deutschen Fachleuten hielten,
welche die Regierung des Zaren für viel Geld
in ihr Land einlud und weshalb die kaiserliche
Regierung im 19. Jahrhundert polnische Saisonarbeiter für die ostelbischen Güter nach Deutschland
holte. Es wird mit einzelnen Beispielen vorge-
führt, wie die Wirtschaft des "Dritten Reichs" von
Millionen Zwangsarbeitern abhängig war und wie
schnell solche Abhängigkeit der Wirtschaft von
der Arbeit von Ausländern sich nach dem Krieg
in der Bundesrepublik wieder einstellte – auch
wenn die Regierung sie mit dem Rotationsprinzip
gern als vorübergehend dargestellt hätte. Wie fan-
den sich aber jene Juden in Amerika zurecht, die
aus Deutschland in die USA vertrieben worden
waren? Und welche Traumata erleben türkische
Migranten heute in unserem Lande?
Wie hängen Sozialdisziplinierung und Fremden-
haß zusammen? Warum sind Frauen von den
Migrationen anders betroffen als Männer – ob
holländische Frauen deutscher Einwanderer im
18. Jahrhundert, jüdische Flüchtlingsfrauen in
New York oder türkische Frauen in Hannover und
Hamburg? Warum sind Städte und urbanisierte
Gesellschaften, von Riga im Mittelalter über Amsterdam in der Frühen Neuzeit bis zu Deutschland
in unserer Gegenwart auf Zuzug angewiesen?
Weshalb und zu welchem Ende brauchen wir
eigentlich den vielberedeten Multikulturalismus?
Und welche Bedeutung haben deutsche Migrationen im Weltsystem?
Ein spannender Sammelband, mit viel solide
recherchierter "Geschichte" und Antworten auf
Fragen, die uns auf den Nägeln brennen. Ein
Sammelband, in dem Roß und Reiter genannt
werden – wer holt wen ins Land, wer wirft wen
hinaus? Aber zugegeben auch ein Sammelband,
in dem auf einige Fragen, die formuliert werden,
(noch?) keine überzeugenden Antworten angebo-
ten werden können.
Bd. 2, 1996, 264 S., 48,80 DM, br.,
ISBN 3–8258–2724–0

LIT Verlag Münster – Hamburg – London
Bestellungen über: Dieckstr. 73 48145 Münster Tel.: 0251 – 23 50 91 Fax: 0251 – 23 19 72